The L/L Research
Channeling Archives

Transcripts of the Meditation Sessions

Volume 9
February 24, 1987 to October 30, 1988

Don
Elkins

Jim
McCarty

Carla L.
Rueckert

Copyright © 2009 L/L Research

All rights reserved. No part of this book may be reproduced or used in any form or by any means—graphic, electronic or mechanical, including photocopying or information storage and retrieval systems—without written permission from the copyright holder.

ISBN: 978-0-945007-83-8

Published by L/L Research
Box 5195
Louisville, Kentucky 40255-0195

E-mail: contact@llresearch.org
www.llresearch.org

About the cover photo: *This photograph of Jim McCarty and Carla L. Rueckert was taken during an L/L Research channeling session on August 4, 2009, in the living room of their Louisville, Kentucky home. Jim always holds hands with Carla when she channels, following the Ra group's advice on how she can avoid any possibility of astral travel.*

Dedication

These archive volumes are dedicated to Hal and Jo Price, who faithfully and lovingly hosted this group's weekly meditation meetings from 1962 to 1975,

to Walt Rogers, whose work with the research group Man, Consciousness and Understanding of Detroit offered the information needed to begin this ongoing channeling experiment,

and to the Confederation of Angels and Planets in the Service of the Infinite Creator, for sharing their love and wisdom with us so generously through the years.

Table of Contents

Introduction 7
Year 1987 9
    February 24, 1987 10
    March 1, 1987 14
    March 8, 1987 21
    March 15, 1987 26
    March 18, 1987 30
    March 25, 1987 34
    March 29, 1987 39
    April 5, 1987 45
    April 12, 1987 49
    April 15, 1987 53
    April 19, 1987 57
    April 22, 1987 62
    April 26, 1987 64
    May 3, 1987 69
    May 6, 1987 73
    May 10, 1987 76
    May 13, 1987 82
    May 17, 1987 86
    May 20, 1987 91
    June 21, 1987 95
    June 28, 1987 102
    July 12, 1987 108
    July 13, 1987 111
    July 14, 1987 114
    July 15, 1987 117
    July 17, 1987 123
    July 21, 1987 128
    July 26, 1987 130
    July 29, 1987 132
    August 2, 1987 135
    August 5, 1987 140
    August 12, 1987 143
    August 16, 1987 147
    August 23, 1987 151
    September 6, 1987 157
    September 10, 1987 162
    September 13, 1987 166

September 17, 1987	171
September 20, 1987	175
September 26, 1987	179
October 1, 1987	184
October 4, 1987	188
October 9, 1987	194
October 11, 1987	198
October 25, 1987	205
October 30, 1987	211
November 1, 1987	216
November 12, 1987	221
November 15, 1987	223
November 19, 1987	229
November 29, 1987	233
December 5, 1987	239
December 9, 1987	240
December 20, 1987	246
December 27, 1987	252
Year 1988	**256**
January 3, 1988	257
January 10, 1988	262
January 17, 1988	267
February 3, 1988	271
February 7, 1988	276
February 10, 1988	283
February 13, 1988	288
February 14, 1988	291
February 28, 1988	297
March 9, 1988	302
March 13, 1988	304
March 16, 1988	310
March 23, 1988	313
March 27, 1988	316
April 3, 1988	323
April 10, 1988	330
June 22, 1988	334
June 29, 1988	339
August 1, 1988	345
August 2, 1988	353
August 4, 1988	362
August 14, 1988	366
August 31, 1988	375

Table of Contents

September 4, 1988 376
September 18, 1988 379
October 9, 1988 383
October 17, 1988 388
October 30, 1988 391

Introduction

Welcome to this volume of the *L/L Research Channeling Archives*. This series of publications represents the collection of channeling sessions recorded by L/L Research during the period from the early seventies to the present day. The sessions are also available on the L/L Research website, www.llresearch.org.

Starting in the mid-1950s, Don Elkins, a professor of physics and engineering at Speed Scientific School, had begun researching the paranormal in general and UFOs in particular. Elkins was a pilot as well as a professor and he flew his small plane to meet with many of the UFO contactees of the period.

Hal Price had been a part of a UFO-contactee channeling circle in Detroit called "The Detroit Group." When Price was transferred from Detroit's Ford plant to its Louisville truck plant, mutual friends discovered that Price also was a UFO researcher and put the two men together. Hal introduced Elkins to material called *The Brown Notebook* which contained instructions on how to create a group and receive UFO contactee information. In January of 1962 they decided to put the instructions to use and began holding silent meditation meetings on Sunday nights just across the Ohio River in the southern Indiana home of Hal and his wife, Jo. This was the beginning of what was called the "Louisville Group."

I was an original member of that group, along with a dozen of Elkins' physics students. However, I did not learn to channel until 1974. Before that date, almost none of our weekly channeling sessions were recorded or transcribed. After I began improving as a channel, Elkins decided for the first time to record all the sessions and transcribe them.

During the first eighteen months or so of my studying channeling and producing material, we tended to reuse the tapes as soon as the transcriptions were finished. Since those were typewriter days, we had no record of the work that could be reopened and used again, as we do now with computers. And I used up the original and the carbon copy of my transcriptions putting together a manuscript, *Voices of the Gods*, which has not yet been published. It remains as almost the only record of Don Elkins' and my channeling of that period.

We learned from this experience to retain the original tapes of all of our sessions, and during the remainder of the seventies and through the eighties, our "Louisville Group" was prolific. The "Louisville Group" became "L/L Research" after Elkins and I published a book in 1976, *Secrets of the UFO*, using that publishing name. At first we met almost every night. In later years, we met gradually less often, and the number of sessions recorded by our group in a year accordingly went down. Eventually, the group began taking three months off from channeling during the summer. And after 2000, we began having channeling meditations only twice a month. The volume of sessions dropped to its present output of eighteen or so each year.

These sessions feature channeling from sources which call themselves members of the Confederation of Planets in the Service of the Infinite Creator. At first we enjoyed hearing from many different voices: Hatonn, Laitos, Oxal, L/Leema and Yadda being just a few of them. As I improved my tuning techniques, and became the sole senior channel in L/L Research, the number of contacts dwindled. When I began asking for "the highest and best contact which I can receive of Jesus the Christ's vibration of unconditional love in a conscious and stable manner," the entity offering its thoughts through our group was almost always Q'uo. This remains true as our group continues to channel on an ongoing basis.

The channelings are always about love and unity, enunciating "The Law of One" in one aspect or another. Seekers who are working with spiritual principles often find the material a good resource. We hope that you will as well. As time has gone on the questions have shifted somewhat, but in general the content of the channeling is metaphysical and focused on helping seekers find the love in the moment and the Creator in the love.

At first, I transcribed our channeling sessions. I got busier, as our little group became more widely known, and got hopelessly behind on transcribing. Two early transcribers who took that job off my hands were Kim

Howard and Judy Dunn, both of whom masterfully transcribed literally hundreds of sessions through the eighties and early nineties.

Then Ian Jaffray volunteered to create a web site for these transcriptions, and single-handedly unified the many different formats that the transcripts were in at that time and made them available online. This additional exposure prompted more volunteers to join the ranks of our transcribers, and now there are a dozen or so who help with this. Our thanks go out to all of these kind volunteers, early and late, who have made it possible for our webguy to make these archives available.

Around the turn of the millennium, I decided to commit to editing each session after it had been transcribed. So the later transcripts have fewer errata than the earlier ones, which are quite imperfect in places. One day, perhaps, those earlier sessions will be revisited and corrections will be made to the transcripts. It would be a large task, since there are well over 1500 channeling sessions as of this date, and counting. We apologize for the imperfections in those transcripts, and trust that you can ascertain the sense of them regardless of a mistake here and there.

Blessings, dear reader! Enjoy these "humble thoughts" from the Confederation of Planets. May they prove good companions to your spiritual seeking. ♣

For all of us at L/L Research,

Carla L. Rueckert

Louisville, Kentucky

July 16, 2009

Year 1987
February 24, 1987 to December 30, 1987

L/L Research

L/L Research is a subsidiary of Rock Creek Research & Development Laboratories, Inc.

P.O. Box 5195
Louisville, KY 40255-0195

www.llresearch.org

Rock Creek is a non-profit corporation dedicated to discovering and sharing information which may aid in the spiritual evolution of humankind.

ABOUT THE CONTENTS OF THIS TRANSCRIPT: This telepathic channeling has been taken from transcriptions of the weekly study and meditation meetings of the Rock Creek Research & Development Laboratories and L/L Research. It is offered in the hope that it may be useful to you. As the Confederation entities always make a point of saying, please use your discrimination and judgment in assessing this material. If something rings true to you, fine. If something does not resonate, please leave it behind, for neither we nor those of the Confederation would wish to be a stumbling block for any.

CAVEAT: This transcript is being published by L/L Research in a not yet final form. It has, however, been edited and any obvious errors have been corrected. When it is in a final form, this caveat will be removed.

© 2009 L/L Research

Intensive Meditation
February 24, 1987

(W channeling)

(Inaudible) wish to reassure them that she is responding well and to relax … We wish to allow her the opportunity to serve … without those feelings from … we are having some difficulty and wish to request that she refrain from analysis at this time. We would like to … define our source challenging. She is tuning much more … toward that which is essential. Request that she allow more greater contact and this is simply accomplished by removing her thought processes to allow more greater love through … channels. We would like to thank the one known as W for allowing us to use her as a vocal channel. At this time we will leave her in … the infinite Creator and transfer to the one known as Carla. I am Laitos.

(Carla channeling)

I am Laitos, and greet each again in love and light. Through this instrument as well we thank the one known as W, for the presence of mind necessary to initiate contact represents quite a substantial step forward in the process of learning to discern personalities within the universe of unseen personalities. The ones known as Jim and Carla were somewhat puzzled by our obvious presence yet their inability to hear our words, for the initiating of contact is not often done with this little previous experience. Thus, we are pleased with our disciple and thank the older instruments for not speaking what they did not hear and the new instrument for speaking what they did hear. With such simple honesty might all entities become magical!

The one known as W shall be offered our assistance not only in the training, which we of the Confederation of Planets in the Service of the Infinite Creator feel able to offer in the area of vocal channeling, but are also willing to put ourselves at this new instrument's disposal at the point at which this new instrument decides to explore some of the deeper motivations for the decision to learn this somewhat unusual gift and service. There shall be things which we are able to offer by our presence during this process, however, there is much work in thought which must [be] accomplished before this portion of our instruction may transpire.

Due to the necessity in contacting other contacts which may desire to speak, that the one contacting such entities must needs be single-pointed as a plane, and, in the sense which this instrument has read in spiritual literature, a warrior able passionately yet dispassionately to participate in the present moment with utmost appreciation and grace. Thus, this is a period in which the work of meditation shall be most valuable, for it is in the relaxation of the everyday personality that the more metaphysically alive portions of the subconscious mind and spirit complex may grow and reconfigure patterns and designs in order for an ever-improving subjective balance of personality.

Thus, we acknowledge to the one known as W that it is possible and perfectly acceptable that at the end of our tutorage and assistance this entity may well desire to be in relationship with a non-Confederation contact. We have the most cordial relationship with many of your so-called inner plane entities whose intentions towards incarnate individuals of your planetary influence are identical to our own, and thus we ask the instrument to channel what of our ideas and concepts it can by virtue of its own biases of mind, heart and spirit, knowing that there may well, if the entity experiences all appropriate stimulus, be more comfortable and more highly efficacious channeling [of] an entity which of its own self desires to speak through the one known as W.

We shall release this information, asking the entity to ponder it not because we are right or telling a great truth, but because were there no circumstances leading to a further eventuality of other channeling, yet still the practice of meditation and the careful seeking for the center of one's being are occupations which cannot fail to aid and improve the circumstance of any seeker.

Again, if this series of thoughts is not helpful, please leave it behind. We would at this time transfer to the one known as Jim for the purpose of answering any questions that those present may wish to ask. We now transfer. I am Laitos.

(Jim channeling)

I am Laitos, and greet you once again in love and light through this instrument. We are happy to be able to offer ourselves in the attempt to speak towards those concerns which you may have this evening. At this time may we ask if we may speak to a query?

W: In regard to the information which you just gave us, I would like some clarification in that to make sure I understand correctly what you just said, and by continuing to work with you through this weekly meditation group and by continuing on my own in terms of just meditation that I can learn to be an effective channel, and that if I so wish I could channel what entity feels most comfortable for me. Is this correct?

I am Laitos, and this is basically the thrust of our suggestion, for you are, as you are aware, able to engage in the service of vocal channeling with greater ease than most new instruments due to a preparation, shall we say, which has become more visible and usable within your incarnation at this time. We are aware that there is the possibility that the kind of contact which you have now begun to enjoy through our working with you is that which may continue in your future experience and that which also may be added unto as you discover further abilities to expand your service with entities which may or may not be members of the Confederation of Planets in Service to the One Creator.

There are many entities who are a part of what we find is called the inner planes of this particular planetary sphere who also seek to speak through instruments for the purpose of not only inspiring an instrument but of sharing information through an instrument with those who may seek in a fashion which is congruent with the entities making the contact. Thus, in whatever manner you choose to continue this service, we wish you to know that we appreciate the opportunity of working with you and we join you in expressing the desire to be of service to the one Creator and to those about you through this kind of service.

May we speak further, my sister?

W: *(Inaudible)* know that I appreciate your willingness to work with me. I'm curious about the entity that channels through *(inaudible)*, Brother Samuel, in that I was wondering what density he is in and in relation to what density the Confederation is?

I am Laitos, and to begin with the latter portion of the query first, those of the Confederation of Planets in the Service of the One Creator are composed of a variety of vibratory levels, including some of your own planetary sphere of late third density who have for a great portion of what you call time been able to appreciate a fourth-density vibration of love and understanding. Our membership includes the densities of love, of wisdom, and of unity, numbering four, five and six.

The opportunity for densities beyond the fourth to speak through instruments upon your planetary surface is greatly less than it is for those of the fourth density for it is towards this density of love and understanding which our planet—we correct this instrument—toward which those of your planetary sphere now move in their evolutionary process. Thus, it is these types of messages that are most often called for and able to be appreciated by the population of your planet.

The entity of which you speak is an entity which we find to be of a great desire to be of service to others, and beyond this point we feel that it is well to reserve comment, for to comment further in describing this entity's vibratory frequency could seem to be to judge, and we do not wish our words or comments to serve as any kind of stumbling block to any other seeker of truth. In the final analysis, shall we say, the source or origin of any particular contact is far, far less important than the content of the information which any contact may have to offer to any seeker. Thus, the seeker shall determine the information that is of most value to it.

May we speak further, my sister?

W: On that question *(inaudible)* very much appreciate the information *(inaudible)*.

I am Laitos, and we thank you as well, my sister. Is there another query?

W: To get back to the information which *(inaudible)* is there in terms of my meditations, are there any suggestions which would aid in developing communication or receptivity?

I am Laitos. At this point in your study of this particular service, my sister, we find that the ground work is well accomplished and the foundation is laid carefully. When a new instrument has been able to open itself to the contact which we offer to the degree that you have been able and to speak those concepts as clearly and freely as you have spoken them we can only add that the perseverance and the effort is the point most in need of focused attention. The daily meditative time which has been set aside is that time in which the desire not only to seek the truth, as you call it, to serve as an instrument through which portions of that truth may move in inspiration to others, is most helpful in the continuing deepening of such dedication. It is in these moments of communion with the one Creator that one may double and re-double the intensity of desire to seek and to share the truth. Take those times, then, and within the boundaries of your meditation seek to know more and more the heart of your own being and to continue the intensification of the desire to know and to be and to share greater and greater portions of truth.

May we speak further, my sister?

W: I've come to greater awareness of the lack of love for self with this awareness. I guess where I'm not quite sure and am inclined to ask, I have feeling that this has been what has been lacking in my conscious thoughts, what I have been in contact with on a subconscious level, that being my higher self and whatever other contacts have been made. Is this correct, and with this new awareness is this something that we can really *(inaudible)*.

I am Laitos, and we might comment by suggesting the perception which you have shared is in its own way relatively accurate, although there is another way of perceiving the lack of love for self which we would suggest at this time as a method, or portion of a method, for finding greater and greater love for, and by so loving the self becoming more and more able to love other selves about one which reflect to one the nature of self. And that perception is that the lack of love for self may be seen as a means of preparing the self for greater service. As one becomes aware of the lack of love and acceptance of the self, and turns to work upon that quality, one begins to build a stronger framework of the heart of self, and through the strengthening of the core perceptions of and feelings for the self, so is laid a firmer foundation for services that may then be offered to others.

Thus, one may see various imitations, obstacles and blockages not just as hindrances to one's progress, but means by which one's progress may be accelerated, for these areas are what you may call the food for growth, the catalyst, which, when processed, will allow the constant transformation of the inner being and its radiance into the entity and those about it.

Thus, a concentrated effort at working upon one's perception of self can allow one not only to achieve the broader point of view of the self by the self, but also allow one to then move the point of viewing further into the environment about one, and, indeed, to the smallest portion of the daily round of activities, until the creation about one begins to take on the feel and appearance of that which is sacred, unified and full of joy and perfect motion.

May we speak further, my sister?

W: Is it also that by experiencing certain challenges one in service to the other one is able to understand their situation *(inaudible)* service or help?

I am Laitos, and, indeed, we find this to be quite correct, for within your illusion, most of the purpose and means for fulfilling purpose for an incarnation is hidden from the seeker of truth, even from one who seeks most diligently and constantly. Those times of difficulty are the times during which the greatest growth is possible, for no muscle, be it physical, mental or spiritual, grows stronger through lack of use but only through greater and greater use. In the times of difficulty you are using all that you have of the spiritual, the mental, the emotional, and perhaps even the physical complexes in order to survive and to retain the balanced view. Thus, in truth, one may rejoice in difficulties, for at these times one is offered the opportunity to expand one's limited ability to perceive the Creator in all portions of the illusion and to be of service to those portions which seem unlovable and unacceptable.

May we speak further, my sister?

W: Is that where the concept of letting go comes in, allowing the Creator to guide as opposed to the self trying to manipulate?

I am Laitos, and we find that this is one fundamentally important portion of the opportunity for learning that presents itself in the times of difficulty. The entity suffering the difficulty will, by its very nature, respond in a fashion which is spontaneous, unrehearsed and perhaps even quite out of control as you would call it. Within these responses there lies the reflection of the limitations of the entity which are now presenting themselves for the opportunity of being stretched and expanded to the point where a greater view of the creation and of the self and the relationship between the self and the creation might be observed by the entity.

As the entity is looking upon its own experience and is in the middle of things, shall we say, it will find if the test be true and intensely enough experienced that there is a point beyond which the entity has little effect upon the movement of experience and the outcome of events. At this point the entity, perhaps in meditation, contemplation, or prayer will find it most helpful to surrender the smaller view of the conscious mind and its analysis of what to do and not to do to the greater self, which some call the higher self, and to those forces of light which guide and protect each entity within the third-density illusion.

In this way the entity is brought face to face with its own limitations and its need for inspiration and transformation of its point of view by surrendering the smaller point of view and belief system. The entity is making a path or channel through which aid may be offered by greater portions of the self, including the higher self and those guides and teachers which are drawn to an entity by the nature of its seeking. In this way the intuition may feed and nourish the conscious mind and aid in its expan …

(Tape ends.) ☙

Sunday Meditation
March 1, 1987

Group question: General question concerning the story in the Bible of Adam and Eve, whether it is an actual story of people that existed, or a symbolic story supposed to show us certain principles, etc.

(Carla channeling)

I am Q'uo. Greetings in the love and in the light of the one infinite Creator. It is a rare privilege and blessing to be called to this seeking group of pilgrims, and we are honored that we are guests at such a banquet of love.

The one who wishes to study the creation may fruitfully study what is popularly called the archetypical mind. Indeed, we know of no better name for this informational treasure house than the mind of the archetypes. It is archetypes, rather than individuals, which the stories of creation seek to illuminate, for creation of self-consciousness begins, subjectively, after creation. The consciousness [which is] conscious of creation is only that of the Creator, and within the illusions which all of us enjoy there is no direct road to clear perception.

It is necessary that expression be general, for the witness to creation is mute and lies within the infinite mystery of the potential intelligence of the uncreated and created Creator, whose mystery is whole and entire and has not and shall not be disturbed by the puny and petty ponderings of our kind. We are seekers, not finders, my friends.

And so within us lie the deepest hunches of what you may call your races. Upon some planets, all have the same archetypical mind. Some of the confusions about creation lie in the various stories of creation, generated by the archetypical minds of those from different planetary influences. There are many such upon your particular planet. It is well, in considering the archetypical mind, to work with a system which is found instinctively by you to be evocative of the rich fruit of suggestion and inference, for each image is designed to center one within a portion of deep knowledge about one's origin and definition, one's way of progression and hope for the future.

Let us look at the most well-known myth within this group of entities. In this story, the first man is made greater than all the animals and able to talk to the Creator. Now, my friends, there is rich food for thought in this image, and, indeed, one of your teachers makes fruitful use of the theme in what you call the parable of the prodigal son. Each of you has an Eden, a time of untrammeled and untroubled beauty, a golden time when the body, soul, mind and heart felt good, at home and well. The sun was happy and even the rain hardly noticeable. And yet somehow, somewhere, through the process of all the years of incarnation, as you call them, you have left the garden—and how alone you feel!

Yet, both in and out of the garden, there comes the second archetype—the helper. Each entity has within it the lonely warrior and the helper, the fount of all wisdom and solace. Your Logos has created a strongly biased sexual differentiation so that although each male and each female experience both needs, yet still to the male is given the striving for the freedom by nature; to the female, the centered feeling of untold riches of happiness, solace and peace.

Neither males nor females experience enough of freedom without an emotional bias, and neither males nor females experience most purely the joy of being of total service. Yet by the sexual choice of a chemical body at the beginning of incarnation each of you has chosen to experience the male archetype or the female archetype as regards that which is demanded by the culture. It is to be noted that only in highly cerebral cultures where education has been carried far does the idea of interchangeable roles surface, for it is not an idea which fits naturally with the genetic disposition of the third-density body which has been issued to each of you.

This is one small example of the archetypes which may be studied in the creation myth. Also of interest is the introduction, very early in the myth and with repeated emphases, of the eventual and inevitable fall, for repeatedly the archetypical male and female choose freely to disobey the Creator to whom they can talk. Each of you may feel a desire to speak directly to your Creator, but perhaps if the Creator's face were familiar the Creator might be taken for granted. Perhaps the Creator which is a mystery is the more understandable Creator and the more to be appreciated.

When the female archetype known as Eve met with the instrument which removed the couple from the garden, it was at the behest of a very important figure. It is to be noted that in the Tarot the serpent is the image of wisdom, and so it is intended in this creation myth which draws heavily upon the same cultural material. It is wisdom which can be the most effectively negative creation, for an over-abundance of love is more difficult to twist entirely. The habit of over-stimulation of the intellect is far more likely to end in a negative movement. Yet, does not all of your experiences as a race and as individuals depend almost completely upon the presence, the enthusiasm, and the action of the serpent in your lives, those seemingly negative forces which cause one to be experiencing life outside the garden, where each day has challenges and it is difficult to express or even feel faith and passion, hope and joy?

Yet is it not, when you look back upon those times that you see so often the greatest of progress made during those difficult times? What to praise and what to blame about the creation of the Father? It is difficult, nay, let us say impossible, to call any portion of the creation bad, for the debt of the pilgrim to the negative population upon your planet is great. You are experiencing life both in and out of the garden. Each portion of that story is a portion of a complex series of archetypes. The study of the archetypical mind is most helpful, yet we would not encourage you to study to the extent of mental and spiritual indigestion in order to feel that you are progressing along the spiritual path.

We would at this time make note that those things which are most important to learn, to grasp, and to make a part of the life are those things which are simple and devoid of the complexity of language and ratiocination, for you seek that which is found in silence and in eternity. You seek, therefore, in a foreign language and in an alien land, yet it is your native tongue and your native home. The language of the heart shall speak for you in the kingdom you now seek. We await you there and are with you there this moment. As your consciousness points and wills and meditates itself to be, so you shall be.

Be careful what you desire. Be assiduous in your meditations, and may you have our greatest thanks for asking us such an interesting question. It has been our pleasure to talk upon the subject and we hope that we have said a few things which may spark other questions or give you food for thought. Of course, we are fallible and prone to error, as is any seeker of mystery. If there is aught said that grates, please ignore our humble words and continue seeking, serene and confident in your own judgment.

We find that the there is a desire for one of our comrades to speak through the one known as Jim, and so at this time we shall leave the group, thanking it for the blessing it has given us in being able to share time and thought with you. We especially greet those whom we do not see each week, for to us all times are the same, and it is a great joy to see each soul with whom our vibrations have learned to dance in rhythm. We leave this instrument now, and each of you, in the love and in the light of the one infinite

Creator. We are those of Q'uo. Adonai, my friends. Adonai.

(Jim channeling)

I am Latwii, and we are most happy and honored to greet each in love and in light. It has been quite a period of your time since we have been able to speak through this instrument to this group and we are very happy that we have been called this evening and we offer ourselves at this time in the attempt to speak to those queries which you may offer to us. May we begin, my friends, with a query?

J: Would you explain the relationship between Q'uo and Latwii?

I am Latwii. I am not Q'uo. We may suggest that the relationship is that of fellow seekers. As those gathered in this domicile are each seekers of truth, sharing that seeking and sharing the path, so we share with those of Q'uo and with many others as well the seeking for truth in the vibrational frequency of wisdom or light. We are similar to those of Q'uo in that we are what you have learned to call a social memory complex, that is, a grouping of mind/body/spirit complexes which seeks as one being the nature of truth.

May we speak further, my brother?

J: I understand what you just said. Normally in our sessions, the question and answer session is also handled by the same entity that is channeled during the session. Can you explain [why] Latwii has decided to come through for this particular question and answer session?

I am Latwii, and we are happy to speak to that point, my brother. As we cast our thoughts back in your time, we find that there was a time during which we also spoke in the capacity of those of Q'uo in giving the opening message and followed that service with the honor of attempting to speak to queries. This service has largely of late been offered by those of Q'uo, for this group has in its progression of experience attracted to it this group of entities now known to you as Q'uo which is able to speak to the concerns of this group in a fashion which is more closely aligned with the group's seeking.

We have been called this evening to offer our services in the answering of queries by a member of your group which remembers us in, shall we say, our heyday when we spoke as the primary contact of this group, and we are honored to once again be invited to this group, for it has always been our joy to offer our services to this group, for this group has been able in most instances to grasp the ridiculous nature of our sense of humor when we have been able to express it through the rigid confines of this instrument's mind.

May we speak further, my brother?

J: No, thank you, that cleared that up. To get back to tonight's session, I would like to ask a question about the archetypical mind of … Let me regress just a minute. It was stated that wisdom, being the archetype of the serpent, was responsible basically for the ousting from the garden of Eden. Am I to understand from that our overindulgence in intellectual pursuits, rather than pursuits of the heart, does that lead to our ousting from the garden of Eden even today? Does that make sense?

I am Latwii, and we feel that we have the gist of your query in our grasp, and we shall respond with that supposition in mind. Please query further if we are mistaken.

The concepts, as we have listened to them being shared this evening, concerning the wisdom and the movement of the archetypical energies of the male and female principles out of the unity that was prevalent within the garden of Eden, as it is called, are a force; that is, wisdom, which allows for the gaining of experience by those portions of the Creator which comprise Its creation. This movement into experience is that which entities seem to experience from the state of grace, harmony and unity which is the nature of the garden of Eden in which all is provided without the need for seeking or striving or experiencing of any kind. Yet, it is the purpose of the creation to provide the Creator means by which It might know Itself in ways not available without the creation and without movement from the unity occurring within the creation by those who populate the creation.

Thus, those principles represented by Adam and Eve, the male and the female principles, present in each entity, are provided the necessity as well as the opportunity of gaining experience in order that the consciousness which they represent might become individualized to the extent that greater and greater experience is gained and greater and greater distortion, shall we say, or movement from unity results, thereby creating the need or the antithetical movement to again rejoin the unity of all creation, bringing with this movement back toward unity all experience that is gained in the movement from unity, thereby glorifying the Creator by the bringing of the harvest of experience home, shall we say.

The tendency of the quality of wisdom to individualize itself in consciousness is a tendency which can be intensified to the extent that an entity may so separate itself from all about it that it travels its journey of seeking upon the path that you might call the negative path, or that which separates self from all other self.

The compassion or love which the entities knew within the garden of Eden, and which seems removed from them as they journey from that garden, are forces which are most easily aligned with that quality that you might call the positive path or the radiant path. These qualities of wisdom and love are the representations of the nature of the Creator in creation, that any entity might choose as the path upon which it shall journey back into unity with all the creation and the one Creator.

May we speak further, my brother?

J: I think I understand most of what you said. Let me just ask one further question. Is mankind journeying back toward the garden of Eden, or away from the garden of Eden?

I am Latwii, and we assume that your query refers to the mankind that is the inhabitant of your third-density illusion, and if this be the case, we would suggest that your population within your vibratory frequency is that which is perfecting that quality of self-consciousness which is able to choose the path upon which it shall return to that condition of unity which is represented by the garden of Eden within your holy work.

Thus, the great journey that has been set upon in the creation has reached its culmination within beings such as yourselves who have succeeded in individualizing the consciousness to the extent that to most of your population it seems that each entity is quite separate, one from another, and that there is very little that connects beings in the creation, and that the creation itself, indeed, is that which is many things, each separate from the other.

Thus, at this time, those of your population of third density are beginning the process of making the choice which shall allow the return through much of what you call time and experience and the refining of those choices made within your illusion, back to the unity of all things and beings.

May we speak further, my brother?

J: No, thank you. That's all the questions I have tonight.

I am Latwii, and we thank you, my brother. Is there another query?

Carla: Yes, I guess I'd better ask S1's question. This is from S1. She sends her love and realizes that this is not precisely philosophical, and realizes that you do not infringe on free will, and anything you can say will be fine.

She says that in her sleep she's been going up against a glass wall, and when she wakes up, she's coming back through the wall, but she can't remember what she was doing on the other side. She wonders if she will ever be able to remember, and what the nature of the wall is?

I am Latwii, and we find that with this query we move quite close to the potential for infringing upon free will, and shall do our utmost to walk that line carefully. We may assure the one known as S1 that the process which she is now undergoing is one which is the normal outgrowth of her own inner seeking. The experience which she is able to remember will continue to expand in detail according to her ability to utilize in a conscious fashion the information which is contained therein. We may not speak as to the content or quality of this information, for this is that which is of necessity reserved for the exploration of this entity within her own experience in contemplation and meditation.

The protection that she has provided through ritualized intention is quite sufficient to give this entity the assurance of safe passage during her sleep and dream periods in which the passage through the wall occurs, and we commend this entity for its diligence in taking the time to provide itself with this quality of protection.

We can recommend to this entity that the focusing of the attention at the present time upon the feeling tones [that] are present when she is able to recall any portion of this experience is that which shall be helpful in tracing the path that now is only dimly lit, and which will, with time and intention of seeking, become more discernible to her subconscious and then conscious mind. The contemplation and meditation upon these feeling tones will prepare the conscious mind to accept more and more of that which is available to it through the subconscious mind from the experience that occurs beyond that wall of forgetting.

May we speak in any further fashion, my sister?

Carla: No, I'd just like to thank you for S1, and to tell you that I know she'll be very happy with the answer and really appreciates being able to contact you. And if she has another question, she can write me back and I'll ask you then. It's nice to hear you.

I am Latwii, and we thank you both, my sisters, for we take great joy in having the opportunity of speaking to each such seeker, and we are especially grateful that this instrument has provided us the opportunity to utilize its abilities at this time. We were about to make a somewhat less than serious comment about its abilities, but refrained at the last moment, for fear of causing too much giggling within a mind which needs a firm center at the moment.

Is there another query at this time?

J: Yes, I have a question. It harks back to the answer you just gave, one portion of it which is a small portion, but probably very important. I've always had a kind of thing about worrying about negative influences, when I meditate, entities that may be negatively inclined influencing me. I've always basically, and I know Carla and I have had discussions and she has chastised me lovingly a few times for my views on this, but I've never worried about negative entities influencing me or messing with me in any way. Sometimes, I used to think, well, maybe I'm just popping off, maybe I really do worry about it, or I'm afraid of it deep down. But I don't think I am, and I've never been one to back off from, if someone had something new they wanted to try, even something as silly as getting stoned and meditating real heavy or something. But, whatever, I mean, this would seem this would leave me open to a negative influence.

And my question, after all that is, you said that you appreciated that S1 protected herself against a negative influence on her journey. Can you, if— would a strong or a firm belief that you can't really be influenced by these negative entities be the same, sort of, and adequate protection against that? I don't really doubt they exist, but …

(Side one of tape ends.)

(Carla channeling)

I am Latwii, and we are again with this instrument. We may agree that the attitude of which you speak is of great assistance in providing the self with the armor of light that sings of radiance and service and of the sure step upon the path of seeking. This is a most helpful attitude for most entities who seek the nature of their reality. The more intensely one desires to be of service to those about one, the brighter does the light grow. This light is of a metaphysical nature, seen in these realms as a source of power, the power of radiance, the power of service.

There are those entities who travel a darker path who also notice a source of light and power and are attracted by this light so that they might continue upon their journey of gathering power for their own use, and will, if the light is powerful or bright enough, attempt to infringe upon that light in the attempt to gather it for their own use. This is a process which provides the natural balance, shall we say, within all life patterns, for the opportunity to taste of the positive polarity must be balanced with the opportunity to taste of the negative polarity. The entity who seeks within your illusion is one which faces choices at each step along the journey of seeking. That which is learned, then, creates within the entity the need for putting that which is learned into practice within the life pattern. Thus, the life must equal the learning.

If an entity has begun choosing in a purely positive fashion the path of radiance, and within its life pattern from time to time makes choices which do not reflect that which has been learned, and in fact become disharmonious and perhaps injurious to those about one, there is created within the life pattern an opening which may be accentuated by those of the negative persuasion, shall we say.

This is a natural process of testing that which has been learned, and may be used by the seeker of truth to reinvestigate and strengthen those qualities that have been found to be less than perfectly integrated into the life pattern. Just so, the qualities of the positive polarity may indeed be intensified by those of the positive path in the same fashion, so that one finds oneself usually in a manner which is not consciously noticed, traveling a path which has, shall we say, opportunities or tests which will allow the entity to demonstrate its ability to live that which has been learned, and to continue refining this ability until it is consciously moving itself along the evolutionary path in a fashion which perceives more than the outer nature of things.

Thus, there is no, shall we say, negative influence which is possible without the invitation or opening being created by the seeker. The attitude with which the seeker greets all such possibilities is the attitude which will increase or decrease the efficiency of the seeking.

At this point, we would ask if we might speak in any further fashion, for this is a field which is quite large in scope, and we do not wish to move too rapidly across it without asking for further queries.

J: I believe I basically understand what you've said so far. And that's sufficient. I sometimes wonder if I were really consciously tested in a real heavy manner, that is, if I did see a ghost, what would I do? Maybe I don't have … I wonder. I guess I question my conditions. Maybe I've got my light under a bushel basket and I haven't attracted anything for that reason. I'm not sure. But at any rate, I believe your answer is sufficient for me at this time. Thank you.

I am Latwii, and we thank you, my brother, and would only add that this process is one which is not usually noticeable within any seeker's life pattern, but is part of the great mystery of seeking, which each of us attempts to unravel as we continue in our journeys.

Is there a further query at this time?

S2: Latwii, this is not really a question—I'm hoping you can give me one of your confirmations. I saw several, what we erroneously call aliens, apparently working on R, and I wanted to know if you could confirm for me that that was indeed what was going on?

I am Latwii, and we choose at this point to speak in a fashion which shall not be overly specific and therefore risk the infringement upon free will. We scan your recent experience in order to discover the nature of this experience. It is possible for us to affirm that your vision is that which has seen the aiding of the one known as R in a fashion which is congruent with this entity's belief in the state of what you call health being a function of the attitude of mind and the attracting to the system of belief of those qualities of mind which have been lacking, shall we say, and which have provided the opportunity for the balance that will then set the stage, shall we say, for the regaining of that quality that you call health.

May we speak further, my sister?

S1: No, I think I'll have to read that one first. But, I wanted to ask you. Could you tell me why, whenever you show up, I get this really wonderful happy feeling? And I don't ever get it when anybody else shows up. And I was just wondering if you can tell me the reason for that?

I am Latwii, and as much as we would like to inform you as to the particular reason why you find our humble vibrations helpful and happy-making, we must refrain at this time, and are only able to give our gratitude in response, and we thank you for your happy reception of our vibrations. We look forward to all such opportunities of sharing, my sister.

Is there any further query?

Carla: I'd like to follow up on S2's. Is what you were saying was that S2's vision was a materialization very much like psychic surgery where it was a manifestation, an illusion, but a manifestation, symbolic of the inner healing that R and his higher self or some overshadowing helper or helpers, an inner healing that they were effecting, and that what S2 saw was a materialization which symbolized the inner process. Is that what you said, basically? I thought I caught that.

I am Latwii, and we find that you have nearly grasped the nature of that which we spoke. We would only add that the qualities which the one known as S2 has perceived are indeed representative of the inner work now ongoing with the one known as R, according to this entity's system of belief regards the concept of healing and health.

May we speak further, my sister?

Carla: So you're saying that the manifestation was for S2, but the inner healing process is ongoing and is for R?

I am Latwii, and this is correct. Is there another query at this time?

S2: I don't have a question, I just want to say, I think it's a heyday every time you show up.

Carla: Hey! With a call like that, he'll be back.

I am Latwii, and we have appreciated both the query and the shared silence. We rejoice at the opportunity of blending our vibrations with yours, and we hope that our humble words have had some assistance this evening to your seeking. We are, as you well know, quite fallible in our opinions and we do not wish any word to be overly weighted in your perception. Take those which do have meaning and leave those which do not. We shall leave this group at this time, rejoicing always in the love and in the light of the one infinite Creator. We are known to you as those of Latwii. Adonai, my friends. Adonai. ✣

L/L Research

L/L Research is a subsidiary of Rock Creek Research & Development Laboratories, Inc.

P.O. Box 5195
Louisville, KY 40255-0195

www.llresearch.org

Rock Creek is a non-profit corporation dedicated to discovering and sharing information which may aid in the spiritual evolution of humankind.

ABOUT THE CONTENTS OF THIS TRANSCRIPT: This telepathic channeling has been taken from transcriptions of the weekly study and meditation meetings of the Rock Creek Research & Development Laboratories and L/L Research. It is offered in the hope that it may be useful to you. As the Confederation entities always make a point of saying, please use your discrimination and judgment in assessing this material. If something rings true to you, fine. If something does not resonate, please leave it behind, for neither we nor those of the Confederation would wish to be a stumbling block for any.

CAVEAT: This transcript is being published by L/L Research in a not yet final form. It has, however, been edited and any obvious errors have been corrected. When it is in a final form, this caveat will be removed.

© 2009 L/L Research

Sunday Meditation
March 8, 1987

Group question: "L/Leema: For we wish to speak this evening of a kind of gem which is not found under the earth, the kind of star which is not found in heaven, a one-of-a-kind item which cannot be purchased. Indeed, we speak of the most beautiful and rare, indeed, unique, of all treasures—the treasure that knows it is a treasure—the self-conscious seeking entity."

(Carla channeling)

I am L/Leema, and I greet you in the love and the light of the infinite Creator. It is a blessing and a privilege to be speaking with you this evening, and our hearts are full with the joy of sharing this occasion with you. We wish especially to introduce ourselves to the one known as B. We find this entity quite sensitive to us, and we bless and greet this entity with appreciation and love, as we greet all whom we have had the privilege of meeting within this circle of seekers.

We find ourselves able to proceed in quite a leisurely manner, due to this instrument's recent training with the channeling, and would thank the instrument for continuing to work upon the clearing of the mind. It is not remarkable or amazing that the mind is so cluttered among your peoples or that so much unnecessary attention is placed upon unspontaneous creation of sense, for the spontaneously created meanings, symbols and manifestations are those which carry the most life and vigor; those long-pondered, becoming increasingly artificial in feeling. Thus, the most helpful channeling is usually done in a clear manner with the channel [not] analyzing. This is to be noted, for we could not speak this evening through this channel in the way which we shall were the instrument attempting to predict our paragraphs.

For we wish to speak this evening of a kind of gem which is not found under the earth, the kind of star which is not found in heaven, a one-of-a-kind item which cannot be purchased. Indeed, we speak of the most beautiful and rare, indeed, unique, of all treasures—the treasure that knows it is a treasure—the self-conscious seeking entity.

All things are treasures to the Creator, for all things are of the Creator, thus the Creator is in all things, yet there is one kind of created thing which is conscious of itself. The jewel-like quality of self-consciousness is not immediately apparent when viewing the crowded and cluttered lives of the jewels that live about you and the one which lives within your frame, thinking your thoughts. Indeed, although one can easily see the theory of humanity's divinity, it is designed to be quite impossible to perceive divinity in a steady state within most of the living jewels upon your sphere.

The crowding and cluttering of the mind has been placed there so that the self-conscious seeking entity will find itself to be alone. This is, of course, the deepest of the illusions of your planetary sphere, and it is the work not only of eyes, but of all senses of the physical vehicle. The senses of the physical vehicle are designed to convince one of an illusion, to see certain things and assume that unseen things are not real, to feel certain things, and assume that there is no other feeling, and so forth.

Thus, separation, the illusion of separation, is designed into the structure and function of your physical vehicle. Also designed into your physical vehicle are senses which allow you to see that which is unseen, remember that which has not happened, feel that which is impossible to feel, and so forth. However, in most of the entities among your peoples, these senses are not activated. You will find if you will gaze about the younger population of your planet, that more and more entities are being influenced heavily by the new vibrations of your increasingly strong fourth density and are beginning to be able to have access to the finer senses and the manifestations of ability in those senses. There is, therefore, much more connective work being done among your people's work in channeling, work in healing, and work in attempting to become more oriented towards living the life in a conscious manner.

Why have you worked so very diligently and carefully to place yourselves in solitude? This is a question to ponder again and again, for the treasures which come from the exploration of this series of thoughts makes always for a strong meditation.

We shall give some ideas which we have come to perceive upon the subject and offer them to you, knowing that you are aware, but wishing to remind you that we do not have an access to ultimate truths, and are sharing our humble opinion with you for your discrimination. We ask you to use this discrimination.

The greatest use of living in perceived solitude is the extreme artificial emphasis placed upon apparent relationships with other entities. For the third-density seeking entity, the importance in experience tends to lie in perceived relationships and the manifestation and continuation of those relationships, especially those which are the more intimate. If each entity were secure in knowing that all entities are truly one, and that all are children of the Father, the need to work upon perceived biases would be very much foreshortened, and there would not be the great activation placed by nature to improve, harmonize, equalize and coordinate two or more lives which are intertwined.

If two entities are quite sure that they are undeniably one, there is not the need to take the care with the words or actions, to take the thought with personal motivation and moral significance of whims, wants and desires. Further, being perceived by the self as a solitary entity makes it very difficult to assume a relationship with the perfect, the divine, the eternal and the invisible. Yet, within the mind is placed an ever-onward driving urge and instinctive desire to climb the upward-spiraling line of light to the Infinite.

Thus, you have arranged with creation to be incarnated into an environment in which that which you most desire to know is unknowable; that which is most deeply important to you is not to be had. You have placed yourself in an environment of perceived spiritual hunger. You have intended that this hunger will move you forward always, seeking the highest and the best of questions, gazing into the face of mystery without blinking at the shadows which hide all things. You have arranged to perceive yourself as known and the Creator as unknown, not to perceive yourself as unknown or the Creator as known. Most of all, you have hidden from yourselves the perception of yourself as divine, whole, graceful and godly. This is due to the fact that you cannot perceive with any outer sense any of the attributes of divinity.

Why has so much been hidden from you by yourself? Why has the Creator been moved afar off? Why have you armored yourself so thoroughly against a true and lasting understanding?

We may say glibly that you have done these things to prevent yourself from assuming intellectually based divinity, for as the third-density entity seeks love, it has not yet refined its grasp of compassion's great responsibility, a responsibility that equals the joy of actual perception of love.

Let us say that you are a gardener, and you plant and you sow, you till and harvest, and as you reap, you rejoice in the unconscious rhythm and sure deft bloom of each plant. Much, indeed, almost all of your work has been done by rote and without true understanding. Yet, by cooperating with the Father, you are able to perceive that which is deeper than the physical manifestation of bloom, for you have touched the earth, the plant, the beauty and the essence of each plant, touched the creation itself in its divinity. And as the creation, except for you, is not self-conscious, it laughs not at you, nor does it make fun. It feeds you with love, it touches you as you touch it, and it blesses you with all of its consciousness, for it does not believe itself to be alone.

There is, in the relationship with the Father, a dependency, a perceived dependency which angers, or at best, irritates most third-density entities, unable because of perceived solitude to see that you and the Father are one, that there is no difference in identity between yourself and the divine, but only a difference in the degree of blindness of all the inner senses which may be available to you, but open and viable to the Creator within. For if the Creator is far away, yet is the Father also near, far nearer than your breath or your bones, far more able to speak than your own limited self, equipped with a far wider and wiser grasp of actual priorities, advantages, disadvantages and right action.

Given the need to make an important decision, as indeed all moral decisions are, one would seek the advice of the wisest friends before deciding what should be done by the self. Yet, when one is faced with the need to seek the will of the Creator, the need is perceived as an enslaving and limiting one. Yet this perceived clash between personalities is an illusion. The choice—since each seeker is truly divine, in potentiation, and to a large degree in physical activation—the actual decision is whether to operate with most information removed from the process of decision, or to operate with as much information as possible, even though the conscious solitary self is usually not very aware of these facts in any conscious manner, after seeking guidance from the higher self, angelic entities, guides, what this instrument calls the Holy Spirit, or the Creator in whatever form you may understand it,

We ask you to experiment with breaking the chains of your solitude. It is a fool's work, and the world will tell you so, as will your own sense of perceived freedom. Yet, as each entity is a seamless portion of an infinite creation, is it not better, upon the pilgrim's path, to take each step with a feeling, a hope and intention of being one with the Father, whether the way be difficult or smooth? Yet, the greatest degree of freedom upon the path is not in the avoidance of the stones alone, but rather in some instinctive understanding which comes from a sense of where one is proceeding, whither one is going. For if the way is rough, yet it is known in some deep part of the unconscious soul that it is necessary to move this way to avoid deeper and rougher roads. If it is known that this is the way which must be gone to reach the end of the next adventure, to reach the next oasis of consciousness, then shall not all useless delay be stopped, and all energies be placed efficiently in the going?

Why were you born in a body which tells you you are alone? Where shall this question take you? We hope it takes you deep into mystery, deep into some attempt to grasp the relationship betwixt yourself and others and yourself and the divine within you, and most of all, yourself and the Father, for if you interpret the illusion through the eyes of the Father, you shall see a kingdom unavailable to those who see only with the eyes of the world. For all who are solitary, are sad, and see all of the darkness as if it should never lighten, all the despair as if it should never fade, all doubt as if it shall never stop, why do you feel solitary in such a crowded universe? Why do you feel lack and limitation when there is naught but love? Beings of light, we rejoice upon the path with you, and are most, most happy to be speaking with you.

It is not our forte, shall we say, to do the work which the one known as Q'uo does. Thus, it has been some time since we have been called to this group, and we are again most happy to be sharing with you. At this time, we would transfer to the one known as Jim, in order that any questions which any may have might be answered. We thank each, and offer ourselves as those who would join in meditation if mentally called. We do not wish to speak with any which are meditating alone, but only to be and to share the meditation vibrations in such a way that we may perhaps deepen the meditative state. We leave this instrument now, again with thanks, and move on to the one known as Jim. I am L/Leema.

(Jim channeling)

I am L/Leema, and we greet you again through this instrument in love and in light. It is our privilege at this time to offer ourselves in the attempt to answer those queries which each may find of value in the personal seeking. We remind each that we give but our fallible opinions, and do not wish to place any stumbling block in the path of another. May we begin with a query?

Carla: Well, if we are divine, how come we screw up all the time?

I am L/Leema, and, my sister, we look upon the query as that which is contained within a certain point of view which is the property of the illusion through which you move, for if you had but eyes to see beyond those veils which hide your own divinity, you would discover that those times of difficulty during which you seem to miss the mark and miss it yet again, are times in which you prepare within your being the opportunity and potential for enlarging your experience not only of yourself and your illusion, but your experience of a portion of the Creator, and by so doing provide the one Creator an opportunity to gain the knowledge of your experience in a manner not possible should you not be providing the avenues of exploration that your consciousness devises.

Within your illusion, you measure yourself and your activities and your thoughts, your responses, and every portion of your illusion that you can see and touch and about which you may contemplate, meditate and pray upon, for your illusion is one of seeming limitations, and within this illusion of limitations, the measurement of each portion is of great interest to those who inhabit your illusion, for it is the beginning effort to explore the creation about you, that has told you you have come a distance and experienced many things, and have yet a great distance to go, a distance which knows no apparent end. And as you measure yourself against your growing concept of that which is infinity, you will find that you constantly fall short of equaling even your small concept of infinity, and, even further, your concept of the illusion in which you exist and the accepted manner of moving through the illusion that is recognized in your own philosophical and religious constructs.

Thus, to take a portion of the whole, and to look upon it with the eyes which see only dimly and for the most part rest upon the exterior appearance of things, is to guarantee that the self, which you feel that you are, shall continually fall short of that self which you intuit that you truly are or can be. This falling short and the frustration which comes from it

are most valuable assets in the drawing forward of the self and the focusing of the attention so that there might be a progression of experience through which you come to know greater and greater portions of the creation and the Creator which lie all about you and within each portion of the creation.

May we speak further, my sister?

Carla: Only on the related point, because it was in the message. I didn't understand what the channeling meant when I got the part about the physical body being godlike in activation, mostly, or something like that. There was some aspect of the actual physical body that was divine. I just wonder what that might be?

I am L/Leema, and we feel that our response might be most direct if we suggest that the physical vehicle which provides the means of locomotion through this third-density illusion for each of its inhabitants is a conscious and intelligent portion of the same Creator that creates all experience within and beyond your illusion. Thus, the physical body is a being with a type of concept system which operates in what seems to be an independent fashion from the mind and spirit complexes, in that the physical vehicle is nourished by the constant application of direction, movement and the qualities of fertility, shall we say, that are associated with the root or base energy center, those related to the sexual reproduction, the nourishing of the vehicle through food intake, the rest and exercise, and the preservation of the integrity of the vehicle.

Thus, the physical vehicle in its own right perceives the illusion in which you find yourself at this time, and rejoices in the aliveness that propels it, and in the direction of the conscious mind which focuses this vitality. Thus, its divinity is pure in its beingness and its uninhibited expression of the life force which moves through it.

May we answer further, my sister?

Carla: Just so that I can understand you. What you're saying, then, is that, as instinctual animals, as second-density animals, the human animal as well as all other animals without self-consciousness, is divine. I know I've read a good deal about the strength of light and the strength of the Creator being in each cell of the body, so I can accept that okay. Is that what you're saying?

I am L/Leema, and this is the basic thrust of the information which we have attempted to share with you upon the topic of the divinity of your physical vehicles. The divinity of all creation is that which is represented in a dynamic fashion within the …

(Tape ends.) ❧

Sunday Meditation
March 15, 1987

Group question: How does consciousness group itself? Do we have conscious or spiritual families that we incarnate with? How do these groupings of consciousness express themselves? How do we discover them?

(Carla channeling)

I am Q'uo, and I greet you in the love and in the light of the one infinite Creator. We have greatly enjoyed sharing meditation with you and would speak with you this evening, as it has been our privilege to be called to you. We ask you, as always, to be aware of our fallibility and to realize that we are but fellow pilgrims, reaching a hand back to those a few steps behind us on the trail, and in no wise to be considered without error. We hope we may help, of course, and it is our privilege to be asked to do so.

We talk to you this evening about families, for you have asked what the nature of the spiritual family is and on what pattern we are, as entities, grouped throughout the planetary influence and throughout the infinite creation.

The concept of spiritual family is one which is difficult to address in a clear manner, because the perceived spiritual family or apparent spiritual family is by far more important to any entity within incarnation than the actual spiritual family in the absolute sense.

Therefore, as in many things pertaining to the greater understanding of things pertaining to incarnational experience, the best tools for working upon incarnational experience are forged within the experience, and pragmatism is found to be useful as a tool of thought.

The perceived spiritual family is all-important, for it is through what one is capable of perceiving as spiritually akin to one that one hopes to be able to enlarge one's understanding of the feelings and experiences which fill the cup of spiritual communion. The pilgrim hopes always to learn more and more about the spiritual nature of all things, and to redefine relationships along more freely flowing and spiritually encompassing lines.

However, it is the rare pilgrim in third density who is perceiving the absolute spiritual family. Indeed, all third-density entities begin with the harvest of second density, the spiritual family of one other entity, and the offspring of that entity. This spiritual family is the instinctual parent of relationships and the archetypical one of your physical vehicle, thus influencing much of the thinking within your species. It is to be greatly appreciated as the rich fount of catalyst it is.

In much of third density, the true spiritual family is greatly limited due to the perceived spiritual family's being the biological family. Because the long trail of incarnations forms patterns of association throughout thousands of your years, there began to grow in your species' present density experience the network of larger spiritual families, and, indeed, society as you know it today is a vast honeycomb of those whose memory, could they but see it, includes each other in vast and interlocking networks.

At this level of networking, the spiritual family is perceived through a feeling rather than through intellectual thought, and one experiences what this instrument would call the feeling of "birds of a feather flock together," the feeling of comfortable association with those whose thinking seems comfortably fitting with your own. This is a further substantial step in the perceived spiritual family.

One who perceives these networks of kinship has managed to begin the linking of all the species. Indeed, perhaps it has become obvious by now that we suggest that the spiritual family which may perhaps most come at the start and root of all other concerns for family, is the family of humankind which will attempt in fourth density upon this sphere to form a fourth-density positive social memory complex. Each connection made lovingly and freely, being manifested, draws closer to an entity the realizations of honest kinship which can only be felt by first extending kinship.

The leap of faith, as this instrument has it in her mind, is always necessary, for any transformation of thought is preceded by a desire to know, which precipitates the use of will at some point. Change is painful, and one who seeks to know his spiritual family shall endure the pain of each family member's miseries, for it is so that all who are conscious of the self suffer.

In suffering, much is learned. In dying, life is gained. In each resurrection, improvement is taking place. Yet, these things are not clear when one sees the hungry, the imprisoned, the sad, the fearful, and the alone. If a pilgrim wishes to know its true spiritual family, walk all the streets, deserts, jungles and battlefields of your sphere, and know that there is no spirit which breathes within physical manifestation that is not your own self—part of you, part of creation, part of the only heaven that is thinkable, the heavenly kingdom of wholeness and completeness, the one infinite jewel of existence,

There is one original Thought, one Creator, and one Creation. When you have become—and you will—a fourth-density social memory complex, you will begin to learn further lessons, lessons that if you only were clear enough, your bodies could teach you now, lessons of your true kinship in unity, not only with every atom of living energy in the infinite creation, but through thought with the one great original Thought, so that more and more consciousness becomes that of the Creator as well as the created.

Much is ahead, my children. There is truly nothing that is not one with you, and there is no consciousness that you do not share. Yet each within a family is unique and each within the family of your sphere is unique. Many are aware now that it is time to feel the family working more closely together, and you have called this networking. Think of it as reunion as well as work, for in the instinct to network, you may see the instinct that calls all to the family reunion.

Be aware that you did not enter this lifetime to enjoy the comfort of a family alone, but also to gain strength from it, that each may do its work with more love and more peace, that more hearts may be made merry, and more spirits at rest through the radiance of each light worker. In order to keep the self clear enough for what each came to do, we ask each to meditate on a daily basis, if for only a few minutes. That regular opening is all-important, that dependable silence life-giving.

We have enjoyed using this instrument and speaking with you, and we thank you for your energy and attention. We would at this time transfer to the one known as Jim. I am known to you as Q'uo.

(Jim channeling)

I am Q'uo, and greet each of you again in love and light. At this time it is our privilege to offer ourselves in the attempt to speak to any queries which those present may have for us. Again we remind each of our fallibility and our desire to serve by offering that which is our opinion and that which we have found useful upon our own journey of seeking. With that understanding, may we begin with a query?

Carla: Yes. What did you mean when you called me a yokel?

I am Q'uo, and, my sister, we were attempting to blend our vibrations with yours in a manner which loosened your own, and in this attempt we found this term to be helpful in describing the pure and simple manner of your being which allows us to speak through it, and we meant to imply that this was a happy country comfort, shall we say, that which could be said to be something of the yokel.

May we speak further, my sister?

Carla: No, I just wondered. It threw me. I must have challenged you ten times, I couldn't imagine why you said, "I have to go talk to the yokel." *(Giggles.)* Who were you talking to?

I am Q'uo, and we thank you for your query, which we find humorous as well, for we were speaking of your instrument in this case.

May we speak further, my sister?

Carla: No, thank you.

I am Q'uo, and we thank you, my sister. Is there another query?

G: What do we look like to you from your point of view? Could you describe us?

I am Q'uo, and, my brother, this query we feel is best answered by suggesting that we perceive you with more than the physical optical apparatus and to describe our perception of your vibration is best accomplished, we feel, by suggesting that that which is of importance in your journey of seeking, that which you are and that which you draw unto you, we perceive as a vibration, a note, if you will, that identifies a quality of being that vibrates in resonance with a greater or lesser portion of the environment or the creation about one. Thus, we see and feel and hear and sense your beingness.

May we speak further, my brother?

G: Well, nothing more specific than how you perceive my beingness?

I am Q'uo, and we perceive you, my brother, as one note among many.

May we speak further?

G: Do you like the note that you hear?

I am Q'uo, and we find great joy in perceiving this note that represents your beingness and take double joy, shall we say, in discovering it to be another part of our own being and of the one Creator as well.

May we speak further, my brother?

G: No, I enjoyed that. Thank you.

I am Q'uo, and we thank you, my brother. Is there another query?

G: I don't know if this is appropriate, but I was wondering if you had any insight into what lessons might be involved for me in having the seasonal sensitivities to pollen? This is for curiosity. I thought maybe there might be something interesting there for me to look at.

I am Q'uo, and may not speak in specifics in this instance, my brother, for, indeed, that which is of value in this query is that which has the greatest value when discovered through your own efforts, and we would not take that from you, but may speak in a general sense to suggest that if the experience of the allergy or any physical distortion leaves the impact of importance upon one's analytical and emotional sensing complexing, that that distortion then be looked upon as a symbol or direction indicator that may be pondered in meditation and in contemplation for any further image that may follow the original focus, and if the sense of value or importance continues, then the following of the images that present themselves to the conscious mind may then lead one to a less distorted image of the treasure which waits within.

May we speak further, my brother?

G: Yeah. It would be nice to have it rephrased in a little bit *(inaudible)* way. I was thinking about it this morning when I was walking on a path in the woods and I was smelling various smells and really enjoying the experience. And we stopped because I smelled a smell that smelled like honeysuckle. And so I went over and I found where the scent was coming from and I really enjoyed that. It was like finding a real neat discovery. And then we walked down the path a little way and I started sneezing. Could you maybe rephrase, using some of that, not specifically for me, but just using that kind of example or something so I can get it in my mind what you're saying a little more clearly?

I am Q'uo, and it was our desire to suggest that the enjoyment of the scent of the flower, as well as the response of the allergic reaction in this instance, if they can be said to have value or importance in one's spiritual journey, this experience will repeat itself in a fashion which is able to catch the attention, and the attention, then, over a period of time, will focus in contemplation, and, if able, in meditation, so that the sense of the value of the experience may be discovered in image which then points a direction with inspiration and enlarging of the point of viewing, so that the heart of what is available to one through such experience might be approached ever closer.

May we speak further, my brother?

G: No, I like what you said. *(Inaudible)*. Thank you.

I am Q'uo, and we thank you, my brother. Is there another query?

G: Do you like our music that we had this evening? *("The Green Cathedral," duet, a capella.)* Do you like New Age music? Do you have any preference between them?

I am Q'uo, and we find that the expressions known to your peoples as music each contain a delicate and unique portion of the one Creator which we experience more likened unto a symphony of sound and vibration, and each note of your experience excites that portion of our being which we share with you.

May we speak further, my brother?

G: I'll tell you, the way you're talking, I feel as though I limit myself tremendously, and yet you seem to take a tremendous pleasure and joy in so many aspects of how you perceive us and all of our world. It's really amazing.

I am Q'uo, and, indeed, we are in awe with you at the magnificence of each and all.

Is there another query at this time?

Carla: We thank you, Q'uo.

I am Q'uo, and it has been our great privilege to share our humble thoughts with this group this evening. We look forward, as you would put it, to all such events, and cannot thank each enough for allowing us this honor. We are known to you as those of Q'uo, and we leave each in the love and the light of the one infinite Creator. Adonai, my friends. Adonai.

Intensive Meditation
March 18, 1987

(Inaudible)

(Carla channeling)

I am known to you as Quanta. I do greet you in the love and in the light of the one infinite Creator and am sorry for the amount of time which it took our entity to examine, rehabilitate and use a thought form which was available to us. We were not ready for the challenge of this instrument for we were not completely familiar with the entity Jesus the Christ. However, we are of a vibration which is a blend of two worlds—the metaphysical planes exterior to your planet and the metaphysical planes interior to its sphere of influence.

The need for the teaching of somewhat different techniques indicates that there need be a meeting of the minds, shall we say, from an inner plane entity of green-ray energy known as Quanta and those of Laitos whose carrier energy greatly aids in the new instrument's facility in improving the channel.

We would start with the concept of the instrument as each element. It is well that the instrument be aware that each element has a rhythm, a dance and song, a pattern energy which is a signature cutting across and undergirding all manifestation. The one who works with natural energy is the one who perceives the dance, the song and the rhythm of each element. Sit upon the earth preferably in the shade, or within the cave to experience the meditation *(inaudible)*, the meditation of the body. Do you not know that no eagle which ever flew failed to have a need for the earth; some tiny piece of earth to sustain life, to nurture young?

Your physical nature speaks to you with nothing more than dust and nothing less than the Creator. Meditation of the body is the first meditation, and each time the feet caress the earth it is well to meditate briefly upon that brother, that sister, that mother and father, that child which shows off in all of its glory.

Let each footstep be a rich experience in the Creator, and know as you gaze into the earth of another's eyes, that you gaze also in to the Creator's, for relationships betwixt two immortal creations of the Father are not horizontal from earth to earth but upwards to the Creator, back down to the brother or sister, and heart to heart betwixt both the triangle of earth and the Great Father. It is well to make that triangle as tall and thin as possible until you see each child *(inaudible)* as a child of the Creator and each cave not only as earth but as infinite sky, infinite love, infinite light.

We appreciate this instrument's strictness in refusing the contact which was clearly perceived when we were unable to speak to the challenge and request that this instrument improve its discipline so that the process might be uninterrupted. We would at this time transfer, if we are able, to the one known as Jim. We are known to you as Quanta.

(Jim channeling)

I am Quanta, and greet you in the love and light of the one Creator. We thank this instrument for allowing our contact and for offering the challenge in the Christ Consciousness and service-to-others polarity, which we appreciate as well. We will take some time in adjusting our contact to this instrument for we are not as easily perceived by this instrument, but move with a lighter touch.

We would attempt at this time to utilize this instrument in its usual capacity of offering the vocal channel for the question and answer portion of your meeting. Thus we shall now ask if we might speak to any concern or query which those present may offer.

Carla: You are a combination of a social memory complex and a person from the inner planes, or a kind of person, a tribe?

I am known to you as Quanta. And we are what you would call a beginning complex of entities who have achieved the green ray vibration of compassion and understanding which allows our seeking to go forward as a unified conglomeration of mind, body and spirits and we have a contact and connection with this planetary sphere which is of a seed-like quality in that we now make it our home, though we are originally of another influence and have removed ourselves from that planetary influence of what you know as the third density in order to begin the new cycle of learning within this planetary influence and we serve as somewhat of the, shall we say, advance guard or servants that shall make this planet its home and we are thus newly—we search for the word—[confirmed] members of the Confederation of Planets which offers itself in service to the one Creator.

Does this speak to your query, my sister?

Carla: Well, to a certain extent. I'm trying to figure out what … So what you are is the … the small but growing … a fourth density memory complex … social memory complex of Earth, is what your saying, right?

I am Quanta, and this is correct, my sister.

Carla: The name is evocative of more that one giant step … One quanta is a quantum. Is there some purpose to naming yourself two jumps forward, which is what that kind of name connotes?

I am Quanta, and we have chosen a name which in your manner of speaking reflects the great leap in conscious awareness which those of our grouping have achieved together and thus many have taken the great leap of faith and moved their being to another level of perception which now offers its lessons that shall again inspire the stepping forward into the mystery of the one Creator.

May we speak further, my sister?

Carla: Well, I'll shut up in a minute … I'm just trying to figure out who you are and why you're here. What relationship do you have to any contact that wishes to work with my student on the inner planes? I had some perception while I was channeling that that was part of what was said. Am I incorrect?

I am Quanta. We have a connection with any upon your inner planes who have moved in their evolutionary journey upon a path which has this planetary sphere as its source and thus these entities who are of your planetary influence have occasionally offered themselves as contacts for third-density incarnate entities upon your planet through intermediaries that may make the transition more easily accomplished. That is necessary for those of the inner planes, as you may call them, in order to contact incarnate entities of the third density who have perhaps more difficulty in perceiving some contacts of this nature due both to the inexperience of the contact and the inexperience of the instrument. Thus, as we have both become members of the Confederation of Planets in the Service to the One Creator and inhabitants of this planetary sphere, we are in a unique position which allows us to serve in the capacity of intermediaries which may hopefully aid both the contact and the new instrument in the service which is possible through the vocal channeling.

May we speak further, my sister?

Carla: No, I'll let you go now. I think I understand what you're here for now. I'm glad you're going to help W and … You sound really interesting and I know we will be glad to listen to your opinions too. Nice to meet you and be talking to you soon. Thanks. That's all from me.

I am Quanta, and we greatly appreciate the warmth of the reception and the care in the discerning of the nature of our being and purpose, for we do not wish to impose our being or purpose upon any who does not wish such. Is there a further query to which we may speak?

Questioner: I'm confused.

(Group laughter.)

Carla: Well, you're not the only one.

Questioner: I don't understand what's going on or why … Quanta, perhaps you can simplify things for me?

I am Quanta, and we have a difficulty with this instrument for it has its own difficulty in perceiving our contact and it is somewhat reluctant to continue.

Carla: Let … hold onto the contact …

We do not mean to suggest that this instrument will not speak. It merely needs a moment. You are most helpful. We are merely those who seek to aid new instruments in contacting those sources of information which lie beyond the conscious threshold when these sources have offered themselves in a manner which may be of service to others, yet which may be aided by the help of those such as ourselves in making that contact known to new instruments.

May we speak further, my sister?

Questioner: So you serve others as an intermediary *(inaudible)*.

I am Quanta, and this is correct, my sister. May we speak further?

Questioner: *(Inaudible)*.

I am Quanta. May we ask if there might be a further query to which we may speak?

Carla: I would ask one more short one. You can merely confirm or tell me that I'm wrong. Is the reason that you cannot immediately answer the challenge of Jesus Christ that there is too much of Jesus who will come again to judge in my … in my concept of Jesus in my challenge and not enough of pure love? I've often thought that the Old Testament should perhaps be burned.

I am Quanta, and we found when faced with your challenge of our being and purpose that we needed to examine the nature of the challenge for there was contained within it the concept of the judgment of which you speak that somewhat distorted the pure emanation of the love of service to others which this entity's incarnation was the pattern that was offered for example. We were able to, shall we say, dismiss the more questionable portion of the characteristic of judgment and move to the heart of the nature of the challenge and determine from it that our vibratory nature was indeed in harmony with the challenge offered.

May we speak further, my sister?

Carla: No, thanks.

I am Quanta. May we speak to a further query?

Questioner: Would you *(inaudible)* evolve from the third density of another planet?

I am Quanta. This is correct, my sister. Is there another query?

Questioner: *(Inaudible)*.

I am Quanta. We seek to give this instrument that vibration of sound complex which you call name but find that to this instrument it is as foreign language which … which makes no sense to ear or tongue, thus we must apologize for the difficulty in the translation.

May we speak to another query, my sister?

Questioner: *(Inaudible)*. Did you just recently come to this planet in fourth density?

I am Quanta, and this is correct, my sister. We are quite new to this particular planetary influence and the ways of your peoples in the speaking and conceptualizing of thought and will be somewhat limited for a portion of your time and experience in our ability to speak in a manner which holds the greatest of sense for your manner of perceiving experience.

Carla: Tell me Quanta, did you come just to …

(Side one of tape ends.)

Carla: *(Inaudible)*. Did you come just to help W or did you have some things that you wanted to say in general?

I am Quanta, and we have found that this instrument has the necessity of attending to the mechanical device and we therefore paused for a moment in order to allow this instrument to complete its task. We have joined your group in order to provide those services which may facilitate the exercising of the new instrument known as W and in offering our services in whatever manner is most helpful according to the needs of any who should join this group and seek to become one who serves as a vocal instrument. We have our own journey of seeking and move upon it in harmonic resonance with this particular planetary influence and take our opportunity to serve in whatever manner may present itself and lie within our capabilities. We have somewhat less of a reach, shall we say, in the scope of our experience but may perhaps be able to utilize our newness to this planetary influence and its birthing fourth-density environment by serving as what we have described as intermediaries that are somewhat more recently familiar with the nature of the third-density experience and are also becoming informed as to the nature of the fourth-density experience in which you now find yourselves for the first time.

May we speak further, my sister?

Carla: No, thanks.

I am Quanta, and we appreciate your queries. May we speak to another?

Questioner: Are you the energy which Laitos mentioned in a previous meditation that was … that wished to realize me as their local channel?

I am Quanta, and am one of that naming and seek to introduce your instrument to yet others if the desire and progress upon this path of service continues to grow. May we speak further, my sister?

Questioner: No, thank you.

I am Quanta, and we thank you once again, my sister. Is there a final query?

Questioner: No, thank you.

I am Quanta, and we thank this group for allowing our presence and our thoughts to move through it. We would also thank this instrument for allowing our contact to continue at those times when it was somewhat in doubt, shall we say, as to the nature of our contact and the purpose for speaking to your group. We look forward to any future service which we might offer and share with this group and until that joyful time we shall bid each the fond farewell, leaving each in the love and in the light of the one infinite Creator of which we are all a portion. We are that portion known to you as Quanta. Adonai, my friends. ☥

Intensive Meditation
March 25, 1987

(Carla channeling)

I am Quanta, and I greet you in the love and in the light of the infinite Creator, of whom we are only all an infinite part. It is our privilege to be speaking with each of you this evening, and we greet each with love and with the desire to aid. We are aware that you would know more about us, and as we are still adjusting to this instrument and to the energies of this group, we shall chat a bit about ourselves in order to allow the group to continue tuning and to become more and more the infinite circle of one who seeks the truth.

We are several, in that we are a voice representing those of the Confederation whom you call Laitos, by whose wisdom you are being coached and aided vibrationally, and within the inner planes we represent also the potential for a contact with the instrument known as W. We ourselves are much as you are, with one single difference. We have made our choice, and we gaze now upon a task which makes the choice seem almost ridiculously easy, just as any refinement process becomes by degrees more and more painstaking.

The green-ray density, as this instrument calls fourth density, is a most congenial place in third-density terms, although you will undoubtedly be not particularly happy to know that the learnings which await us now seem as challenging as any ever did within any illusion. Yet, we, perhaps greatly more than you—or perhaps not—have a trust not often given to third-density entities in the relatively stable nature of the Creator and the Creator's representatives within any particular energy pattern or sphere of influence. As we attempt to learn our lessons, we hope to be able to serve, for in serving, we shall indeed learn all.

Do not mistake us for those who are wise. We are new to love and do not yet grasp the rudiments of wisdom. However, we believe that we are able to mesh energies and make them more compatible so that the transition, should contact and channel agree to work together, may be made with comfort and ease to the greater illumination of those who would be inspired, but without unnecessary difficulty to the instrument.

We thank each for settling down and firming up the energy patterns of this circle. We would like to, shall we say, interface to and exercise each channel. We ask each channel carefully, as always, to tune and challenge and just as carefully avoid the analysis messages while the message is ongoing. We would leave this instrument now and transfer to another. I am known to you as Quanta.

(Carla channeling)

I am Quanta, and am again with this instrument and greet each in love and light. We have found it necessary to pause, for the intention of our amalgamation was to transfer to the one known as Jim, which has *(inaudible)*. We apologize for this and we transfer to the one known as Jim. I am Quanta.

(Jim channeling)

I am Quanta, and greet each again in love and light. It is somewhat of a puzzle to this instrument as to why we have chosen to exercise it at this time. We have chosen to offer our contact to this instrument in order that it might also work upon its art, that of refining the abilities of the vocal instrument by the use of a technique which more approaches the word by word means of transmitting concepts. This is a new phase for this instrument, for it is one of those which functions as a rule by the clothing of concepts that are transmitted with words in order that that which is given in the contact is then mated with the ability of the instrument to utilize the choice of words in the chiseling of the message, shall we say. This is a function which we also enjoy offering to instruments which have the desire for continuing to improve the means of service which they have chosen.

At this time and before we attempt queries, we would attempt to make our contact known to the instrument known as W. If this new instrument will refrain from analysis of the thoughts which are sent and speak them as they are recognized, the process of transmitting our thoughts will be most easily accomplished. We shall transfer our contact at this time. I am Quanta.

(W channeling)

(W's channeling is lengthy but inaudible.)

(Carla channeling)

I am Quanta, and greet each again. We thank each instrument for working with our energies and for allowing us to blend them with your own. From our viewpoint we find it a creation of much beauty, the blending of vibrations betwixt entities, and especially betwixt the groups of entities, for there are many, many overtones and undertones to a unified group which create ever more varied and beautiful designs throughout the vast panorama of energy patterns in the infinite creation.

We would commend each upon the mechanics of channeling and request only that the reaction to the pauses between ideas and subjects not be a hasty one. To the relatively inexperienced channel, the pauses between thoughts and ideas may seem so very long that it may seem that the contact has been lost. However, each will find that we produce thoughts upon a subject in increments which are quite unpredictable, in such a way that if only the first train of thought is channeled, the basic message will be offered, or at least as large a portion of it as can be subsumed within one paragraph. The next train of thought shall be the second priority or the next most central thing which we wish to deal with, and so on, until the experienced channel sometimes has the patience to come to the end of all that we prepared to offer upon assessing the energy patterns of the group and of the individual channels.

The service of vocal channeling is aimed towards inspired speaking. It is designed not only to allow our voices to be heard, but to allow each instrument to make full use of its own instrument, full use of the tools offered by experience, education and any other asset which may be translated into spoken words which may aid those who seek the truth. It will not therefore be surprising that we hope more and more to sail off with each channel upon the voyages of thought rather than discourses only upon channeling itself.

There were those portions offered to each of those within the circle which were missed, and we include the instrument now speaking who misses perhaps not as much as it once did, but remains over-hasty due to lack of experience. Indeed, we might encourage each to be more and more conscious of the self as channel at all times, for there is a channeling process that operates within any conscious entity which desires the channeling process to be contained within the self, opening to the self all of the usually hidden resources of the deeper mind.

The same clearing and focusing of thought, the same tuning and the same challenging turned inward are tools which may aid a conscious speaking person to be, though conscious, yet also in an augmented state due to the process of deepening and [revering] the energy centers and the state of concentration.

We come now to some thoughts for the following few days. Picture with us if you will the great eagle which soars to the sky, and then picture the meditation of sky, for you who are earth-bound must use imagination as eagle's wings to mount up to the ethers which move forever towards the shining One. Gaze with eagles upon the white, white heaven which fades not away, but flows endlessly towards the illimitable white light. The clean, sharp river of good, which is the air, moves supporting the eagle, never combating, for the eagle meditates and does not struggle. The eagle soars and moves not one pinion, but only gazes and sees and acknowledges the white light, the white sky, the white river, and the white flood that moves from heaven in reflection to the beloved Earth, touching with white fingers all still things like the breath of the Mother, moves to touch all dead things with the life of the Father. Those two embrace all things in the Great Spirit. Hope then, and seek the feathers of the eagle and the eye to see the white sky.

Before we leave, we would say to the one known as N not to feel because there is not an entity which has already sought contact that these exercises are in vain. We hope we may be of service not only to those who wish to be vocal channels, but also those who wish to be in service to the infinite Creator in some capacity. We say to you straight that no matter what your service may be, the clear perception of it and wholesome unfolding of it rely heavily upon the process by which a channel becomes transparent before an acceptable inspired contact. We do not mean to make ourselves proud by calling our contact inspired, but only to express in a brief way that many, many inspirations may come from clearing the mind and seeking the will of the Father, for there is and has been and shall be agreement made betwixt each pilgrim and the Creator which it seeks, agreements to which you shall not often have conscious access, but agreements which come to one and feel appropriate. May these lessons bless each as we are blessed by your presence as we give them.

We would transfer now to the one known as Jim in order that any questions you may have … questions you may have may be entertained. We thank you and would leave this instrument. We are those of Quanta.

(Jim channeling)

I am Quanta, and we are honored to be able to offer ourselves at this time in the attempt to speak to those queries and matters of concern that may be with you. Without further delay then, may we ask if there is a query with which we may begin?

W: I have a query. I am under the impression that Quanta is a new fourth-density entity. Is that correct?

I am Quanta, and this is correct, for we who comprise the grouping that is known to you as Quanta have found this planetary sphere that is your home is to be ours as well at the dawning of your fourth-density experience, and we have the honor at this time in joining this planetary complex somewhat early as you may call it and serve in the manner that we now …

(Side one of tape ends.)

(Jim channeling)

I am Quanta, and am again with this instrument. Is there another query?

W: Yes. Do you service any other third-density *(inaudible)*?

I am Quanta. At this time we have the honor of speaking in the capacity that we now demonstrate with this group only with this particular group, though we offer ourselves to other groups by moving amongst those which call for our vibration and blending ours with theirs in a manner which allows the experience of love and compassion for an entity. Thus, we move in unseen patterns which may offer encouragement and inspiration that is offered by many such as we.

May we speak further, my sister?

W: I have another one. Is there some connection between the meditation which you suggested and what I would think about as relating to the *(inaudible)* this past week?

I am Quanta, and the relationship is that of balance, for the experience of the cave and the particular experience by which you came to ground yourself, or should we say to begin this grounding, must needs be balanced with the opening of the self through the concept of what you would call infinity which is represented by the air or the sky. In this manner you begin to build a foundation within your inner being which may eventually allow the expression of the vocal channeling in a stable manner through your instrument.

May we speak further my sister?

W: So what you're saying is [that] as you grow roots, you can also grow branches, right?

I am Quanta. This is correct. May we speak further?

W: *(Inaudible).*

I am Quanta, and we thank you, my sister. Is there another query at this time?

N: Yes, if you please. You spoke through the entity known as Carla and mentioned that I should not feel that I am trying in vain, so actually tonight I did not have a contact with you?

I am Quanta, and your contact with us was quite real, my sister, and we are quite pleased with your progress at recognizing our contact and verbalizing it. Your progress is to be commended. We were also desirous of assuring you that though the one known as W experiences our contact as an intermediate step, shall we say, in order that perhaps another contact which seeks to express itself through her instrument might do so, and such a contact has not [been] described for your own experiencing, that you would not feel that the learning of the vocal channeling was an expression that was in vain.

May we speak further, my sister?

N: So you're saying that because of your contacts with our group, either partially or mostly, it is to help W to be in touch and be able to recognize the contact of another entity which has been trying to come through her?

I am Quanta, and this is basically correct, my sister, though we also rejoice at the opportunity of working with each instrument within this group and allowing each instrument the opportunity to expand its abilities within the service of vocal channeling.

May we speak further, my sister?

N: No thank you, but I don't think that it is in vain, and I feel that I am almost glad that I'm further behind so that I can learn by example through other people. And I do appreciate being part of the group tonight. Thank you for your concern, and I do not feel so bad. Thank you.

I am Quanta, and we thank you, my sister, for allowing us the honor of working with you. Is there another query at this time?

W: Are you saying that you're sending us a lot more information than we're picking up and vocalizing?

I am Quanta, and this is correct and is a normal state of affairs for any new instrument, and indeed for many who are quite experienced in serving as vocal channels, for that which we have to offer may be seen to be offered with various levels of meaning and expression possible to the discerning inner ear. We may liken the message which we offer or which any contact may offer through an instrument to be likened unto one of your own beings, that is, composed of a foundation which may be seen as the skeleton, to have upon these bones flesh which fills in certain areas and brings a continuity to the being, which may further include the life blood and thinking mechanisms which enliven the being and give it a vitality that is quite easily recognized as being more than mere bone and flesh and blood.

New instruments and those still refining the art of vocal channeling must easily perceive the more general of the concepts and means by which they can be expressed. This is likened unto the bones of the skeleton, the basic fabric of the message. As an instrument becomes more practiced in its art, it is able to open itself so completely that more and more of what is available is able to be perceived by the instrument and expressed in a manner which gives more life and richness to the basic message that is being transmitted, for though we are limited by the very nature of words in contacts such as this, we can assure each that words may be used far more fully than most of your peoples realize in expressing those concepts which are able to be expressed and in pointing towards those that are quite beyond expression and capture by any word.

May we speak further, my sister?

W: Are there any suggestions about my challenging and my tuning?

I am Quanta, and at this stage of your experiencing of the vocal channeling we may recommend that practice upon that which you have devised is by far the most efficacious means by which to improve your art. As you choose that means by which you tune your instrument and the means by which you offer a challenge of the nature of any spirit or entity who wishes to speak through your instrument, you then intensify this technique by practicing it, [and] thus do you empower that which you have chosen by the repetition.

May we speak further, my sister?

W: No, thank you.

I am Quanta, and we thank you my sister. Is there another query?

Carla: Thank you. I enjoyed working with you.

I am Quanta, and we have greatly enjoyed this opportunity for exercising each instrument and blending our vibrations with yours in a manner which allows us to perceive a portion of your experience and to see the variety and richness with which the Creator expresses Its own being within the one creation. We look forward to each gathering with this group, and at this time would leave this group, rejoicing in the love and in the light of the one infinite Creator. We are known to you as Quanta. Adonai, my friends.

L/L Research

L/L Research is a subsidiary of Rock Creek Research & Development Laboratories, Inc.

P.O. Box 5195
Louisville, KY 40255-0195

www.llresearch.org

Rock Creek is a non-profit corporation dedicated to discovering and sharing information which may aid in the spiritual evolution of humankind.

ABOUT THE CONTENTS OF THIS TRANSCRIPT: This telepathic channeling has been taken from transcriptions of the weekly study and meditation meetings of the Rock Creek Research & Development Laboratories and L/L Research. It is offered in the hope that it may be useful to you. As the Confederation entities always make a point of saying, please use your discrimination and judgment in assessing this material. If something rings true to you, fine. If something does not resonate, please leave it behind, for neither we nor those of the Confederation would wish to be a stumbling block for any.

CAVEAT: This transcript is being published by L/L Research in a not yet final form. It has, however, been edited and any obvious errors have been corrected. When it is in a final form, this caveat will be removed.

© 2009 L/L Research

Sunday Meditation
March 29, 1987

Group question: The effect of Christianity upon the movement of the planet into fourth density; whether it's a helpful or hindering factor, or just how it works.

About relationships—how does one determine whether there is still love enough or reason enough to remain with a partner; what is the real binding force of a relationship?

(Carla channeling)

I am Q'uo. I greet you in the love and in the light of the one infinite Creator, the Creator whose love abides before, after and beyond all created things, and whose light forms all created things. I greet you, my friends, in the reality expressed in symbols of illusion. I speak to you as one who lives to those who walk in sleep, and in this mysterious way we explore together the mystery of love, light and reality, we who are creatures, never having seen all of reality, we who are finite, gazing at infinity.

And yet, we journey onward from realization to realization, ever finding the face of mystery to be that of love, reflected in the smile of those who show the Creator's love to us or speak the inspired word which comes through them to us. And we thank you that you have called us to speak with you this evening about the greatest single catalyst which involves those of third density in their seeking for spiritual evolution.

Relationships are the heart of your question, for the one query concerns when relationships betwixt two entities are helpful and when they are not, and the other query involves when Christianity is an helpful relationship for seekers to commit themselves to or not. Yet are not both queries concerning relationships?

And so we would speak upon the illness and health of relationships, not covering this deep subject, but perhaps provoking some further thought. If we are able to do this, we shall be extraordinarily gratified, for we are clumsy with your language and are grateful to vocal channels such as this one, that we may at least attempt to clothe our poor concepts with some semblance of grace.

It is written in your holy works that the master known as Jesus was once asked as to the purpose or the cause of a blind man's infirmity. The crowd wished to place blame upon one side or another of a relationship within a family. Was it the blind man's family's fault, or was it the fault of the blind man?

The teacher known to you as Jesus answered the query in a way which often has been misunderstood as an avoidance of the question. The master said, "For neither reason was this man blind, and blame belongs to none, but rather it was a design whereby the Creator would be glorified."

When two entities become mated, the landscape seems beautiful, prospects seem unlimited in the richness, value and joyfulness of experience to come, and all of life may seem as pleasant as the day which each in this group has experienced, the golden sun bringing ever more fullness to the celery green of young leaves, the cheerful forsythia and daffodil greeting the spring breeze, the spring of new grass and soft rain, the sound of bird calls and happy children at play.

When one forms an alliance with any religion, there is a mating betwixt an entity and the face of the Creator, the nature of the mystery, which the entity believes that that particular path shall best show to his or her. And so the individual's relationship with an individual or the individual's relationship with a societal entity which seeks the truth begins. An honeymoon ensues, wherein all that is good is shared freely without thought for the self, for one his been taken beyond the self in some realization of the Creator's face in the other individual or in the path which is offered by the spiritual organization.

It is easy to presume that relationships betwixt people and relationships betwixt people and organizations are different, and from detail to detail, this may indeed be so. But perhaps it is helpful to realize that in any relationship which a seeker has with anyone or anything, the fundamental dynamic in the relationship as concerns this entity is the entity itself. It is inevitable, just as fall and winter follow spring and summer, that two people shall finish their honeymoon and embark upon some challenge together—or apart. It is inevitable in any spiritual search within an orthodox religious path that the seeker shall find doubts so overwhelming that trouble clouds its relationship with the spiritual organization.

In both cases, the unfortunate actions which are catalyst for the seeker by an entity or an organization or entities within an organization shall be blamed for difficulty which is experienced by the seeker, and the attention is then turned outward in an attempt to find a way to repair, mend or replace the ailing relationship.

There are many options which the seeker may choose when attempting to assess right action within a painful set of circumstances which involve disillusionment at a relationship. Many of your peoples automatically choose to avoid pain, and by doing this they move into another arena, and inevitably seek other relationships with entities or organizations which will inevitably disillusion them once again, for it is the nature of the illusion in which you experience life at this time that all things shall pass, all successes shall fail, all days shall become night and all joy sorrow. It is equally inevitable that all sad things shall be made glad and all night end in dawn and sunlight.

Another option available to the seeker in a difficult relationship is doggedly to endure without analysis or thought, trusting that the night shall become day, the pain shall become gladness.

The third area of options is perhaps the more fruitful of the three we offer you for thought, and that is the withdrawal from decision-making and from the company of the relationship which has caused confusion for a period of personal, intimate and extremely private contemplation and meditation.

For you see, the conscious self of the seeker sees the relationship for the first time as it reacts to the catalyst which has been prepared before the incarnation by the self and all those parts of the higher self which become ultimately the complete expression of love of the one Creator. All good and all difficult things, alike, have been offered to you by yourself, not either to endure or to avoid, but to learn from, to study, to ponder, to reflect upon and, finally, to make choices on the basis of what has come to you in the process of seeking.

This cannot be done while the catalyst is present and you are busy reacting to the catalyst, thus gaining experience but not being free to evaluate experience. There is no time when meditation is not extraordinarily helpful, but when one wishes to know where the kingdom which you seek lies, where love lies, where right action lies in a difficult situation, it is well to go deep within in faith and trust that there is a sense of right action within you, given before time and space began, purified and clarified by dedication to seeking and continuation of meditation, so that the seeker becomes more and more profoundly aware of when the still, small voice, as this instrument would say, might cause the feeling of right action to surface.

The most difficult thing for the seeker who lives within the dream and gazes hopefully towards reality to do is to wait, to wait for clarity to come. Clarity can come from within, yet not from without.

Inspiration can cause one to think more deeply or with more faith, or perhaps have the will to work harder to evaluate experience, but no outside influence can truly aid spiritual choices, for only free will choices of the individual move one forward in spiritual evolution.

What you call church and what you call the mated relationship are equal partners in preparing the student of truth for more and more realization of where that truth might be and where it might not be. Personal and church related relationships equally are either helpful in preparing one for the fourth-density experience, or directly harmful in keeping one from being ready for the great challenge of more light, more love, a finer vision of reality, and a greater responsibility for manifesting it in the life experience.

Let us separate our subjects for a moment, for perhaps some of the differences cause the two who have these questions to be dissatisfied with this generalization.

The Christian's vision of Christianity is not one vision, any more than the Buddhist vision, the Shintoist vision, and so forth, is unified. Although each entity which calls itself Christian, for instance, believes because it has spoken a certain symbol it is a member of a great group, nevertheless, each individual is doing no more and no less than seeking the face of the great mystery of the infinite Creator, just as each non-church-going entity does or does not do. How many Christians there are who have no interest whatsoever in seeking the truth, but are responding to stimulus much in the same way that a second-density animal which moves with the pack follows the leader of the pack, and behaves as does his group. There are the most extravagant extremes, from what Christians call sainthood to what Christians call great evil, within that great body of entities called Christianity.

The one known as Jesus knew that the third-density experience was coming to an end, and hoped not only for a few to learn of forgiveness and redemption but for all to know the love and the light of the one infinite Creator. The creature which has grown up from this teacher's body of instruction bears almost no resemblance, and certainly no ideological resemblance, to the nature of the community of those who love each other, which the teacher known as Jesus the Christ wished to form.

Indeed, the one known as Jesus sought only to form a fourth-density experience at the ending of third density, and so is the spirit of those who wed or are mated in commitment intended to bring one more and more to the love that sacrifices all, to the caring which owns forgiveness and disowns any negative omission, wishing only happiness for the other self which has become the most loved self, the object upon which all virtue may be spent. In neither case can any two experiences be described together. Where then, in any situation of relationship, does the decision alight but with the entity who seeks the face of mystery for itself.

We ask those who ponder a choice to have infinite patience, if possible, and in order to have the patience to wait long enough for inner certainty, it may be necessary to seek solitude, time and space apart from that which puzzles and confuses one. There are no good or bad choices in terms of finding what Jesus the Christ called the Glory of God. There are many less efficient choices available to the entity which cannot wait long enough to receive that inner certainty, which shall be his or hers at some point when the waiting, the seeking, the praying for understanding has been fully accomplished.

If there is waiting and no hearing until one leaves the physical body, that too is acceptable, for the only element which polarizes an entity towards the love and the light of the infinite Creator in service to others is the simple and fastidious determination to await a knowledge of the higher will of the higher self, a knowledge of where and how glory and love shall enter the experience. Anything can be endured, if it be endured in certainty of the rightness of one's actions. Very little can be endured if the entity feels that enduring such is harmful for one's spirit.

The least helpful element of the mind, body and spirit during these times is the intellectual mind, for filled with reactions and emotions it cannot control, in situations too intense to easily and comfortably tolerate, the entity must seek avoidance, and that which must be done is usually done in such a way that much of the richness of the experience is jumbled, confused and lost.

Those who are Christian and those who are mated have a great deal in common, in that both the mated relationship and the spiritual mated relationship of the brothers and sisters of any religion expect and hope of each other that each will be a mirror to each, telling the truth, yet telling it with compassion, supporting while criticizing, constructing while changing.

When relationships are not such, it is time to await the consciousness within, for we can to the best of our limited knowledge assure you that wisdom comes to those who wait, in the watches of the night and in the noontime alike, for night and day alike have their lessons and realization shall come when least expected. May your ears be ready to hear and your eyes ready to see the harbingers of right action for you yourself, and may you never, never consider it the responsibility of another to have any part in the creation of a life lived towards spiritual evolution.

We feel in the silence about us the many thoughts of those who wonder why there cannot be said to be a preference, at least for harmony, betwixt peoples, and a looking forward together to the new age of understanding and love. May each experience such lovely pleasures and may each rejoice in those seasons when such occurs, yet when an individual's love seems to fail one, when one's religion or path seems to fail one, it is time to trust the desert experience of deprivation and want, pain and sadness, loss and disillusionment, not taking them as realities, but as illusion, just as the peaceful and contented times are illusions.

If each entity, whether seeking in relationship with another entity or with a societal religious group, could learn as intensively and carefully in each pleasant moment as it learns when faced with painful challenges, challenges would not have to be built into the life experience. But contentment and happiness seem to dull the powers of spiritual observation. Sharpen your ears, your eyes and your heart, my friends, in good times, and diminish painful experience. Yet when painful experience comes to you, seek to know in faith and will to remember that the desert experience shall give way once again to the experience of plenty and peace.

Therefore, seek during this period not to act in this way or in that, but to remain a listening, watchful, prayerful entity, open first to the voice of the Creator within, and only secondly to these things about one which demand the reaction, the emotion, the manifestation. Create your manifestations insofar as it comes naturally to you in any situation, and know well within yourself when you have not created, but have reacted.

You shall achieve the fourth-density level when your criticisms are only of yourself, your actions are taken because within you feel them to be so and right for you alone, and when the opinion of others is nothing more than interesting.

To sum, we may say that no outside element, including the most powerful group upon your planetary sphere, has power over you unless you as an entity react in a way you would not. Thus, seek always to know yourself more and more, to be yourself more and more, and to experience the glory of existence and consciousness with gratitude, only secondarily wondering what to do next, where to go next, and so forth. May your will, your faith, your love, and your attention be focused in the silence within, that when you act you shall know it to be right, and you shall be at peace regardless of church, family or friend.

We feel constrained to speak through this instrument in a special way, for there is a need for us to offer a special message and the message is as follows:

There are moments which may last for some time or may be transient, which many upon your planetary sphere which have studied the metaphysics, as this instrument [would] call it, would call initiation. There are some whose spirits have not completely married the earthly personality, and during these times of initiation, the experience of living seems extraordinarily difficult …

(Side one of tape ends.)

(Carla channeling)

We would at this time pause and retune, if the circle will be so kind, and then transfer to the one known as Jim. I am Q'uo

(Jim channeling)

I am Q'uo, and greet you in love and light through this instrument. It is our privilege at this time to offer ourselves in the capacity of speaking upon those queries which those present may find of aid in their own seeking. Again we remind each that we are but your fallible brothers and sisters, and do not wish that our words be overweighted. With that disclaimer, we should ask if we might begin with a query at this time?

Carla: Who was that last message directed to?

I am Q'uo, and we must respond by suggesting that that message was for those who have ears and need to hear it.

May we respond in any further fashion, my sister?

Carla: No, thank you.

I am Q'uo, and we thank you, my sister. Is there another query?

Carla: I have one more, since nobody else does, and it's still about that—I felt the presence of Latwii when that message was given, but not at any other time. Was Latwii moving along the same vibration as you, Q'uo? Or was that my imagination?

I am Q'uo. We find in this particular case, that we were joined by not only those of Latwii, but others as well that have found the honor of serving as the guide, in order that a message of potential importance might be delivered in a fashion which would be most easily understood by those to whom the message was directed. We were glad to have the assistance of these additional entities in transmitting this message, for we are not as able to discern the boundary which delineates free will from the area of one's experience that might more easily be influenced. Thus, it was helpful, we hope, that the message be delivered in this fashion.

May we speak further, my sister?

Carla: Yes, along the same lines. Wednesday, while Jim and I were teaching W and I was channeling Quanta, at a certain point in the channeling that I did at the last, which was most interesting to me as a channel, for I had no idea of the material, I sensed Laitos and Oxal and Hatonn in addition to Quanta, and I did not know but that there may even be others. It was a powerful kind of symphony, of various vibrations, all of which I could discern, but only Quanta was actually speaking. Was this the same thing? Was it oriented towards she who heard, or was it rather entities coming in aid of Quanta who is new to the job, aiding Quanta and making sure that Quanta was doing the work that it needed to do?

I am Q'uo, and we find that you have penetrated a significant portion of the experience which you felt in the previous channeling session. It is helpful for those such as we are to be aided in our service from time to time by others who have fields of specialty, shall we say, that complement our own and enhance that which we seek to share with your group. Those that you have recently come to know by the sound vibration, Quanta, are in need of such assistance in greater degree, for their experience with this group is quite new and there is much which these entities have yet to learn in regards the general phenomenon of the vocalized transmission of thought in general, and the needs of each individual who sits within the circle of seeking in particular.

Thus, those who have for a greater portion of, what you call, time served this group as, what you call, the telepathic contact, join at each gathering of this circle and offer assistance where needed in an effortless fashion which is made possible by the unified desire to be of service in this particular way.

Thus, you may expect in your future gatherings that this phenomenon shall repeat itself in order that the purpose of the sessions might be more fully realized.

May we speak further, my sister?

Carla: Q'uo, just in one other way. H was asking earlier about reincarnation and Christianity, and because I've fielded the question so often, I went ahead and spoke up. Do you wish to comment on this subject? I would greatly dislike misleading anyone in any way, and welcome any comment.

I am Q'uo, and we find that you have given somewhat of a synopsis of the topic that you have called reincarnation and its traces left within the holy work that you call the Bible. Within this work, there is but little remaining concerning the reincarnational aspect of third-density experience, for as you have correctly stated, there was a decision made in early days of the Christian faith, as it is called, that the work of the one known as Jesus the Christ was of such importance, and the time during which it might be implemented was of such short duration, that it would be, it was felt, most helpful to those who embraced this faith to be guided to the degree that their sight pushed no further than one earthly incarnation in order that the focus of attention would remain within the boundaries of birth and death in one incarnation. In this way, the elders of the Christian faith hoped that the efforts of the incarnation would be increased to the degree that a greater harvesting of souls would be possible.

There was much discussion and dissension at this time upon this topic, for it was felt by many that such deception was great disservice to the one known as Jesus the Christ, for this entity was one whose incarnation was based upon the light of truth and the power of love. Yet those elements within this governing body who wished to see this faith in the one known as Jesus continue in a fashion as pure and potent as possible held sway and were able to carry the votes necessary to delete those passages and portions of the Bible which referred in a direct fashion to the concept of reincarnation.

May we speak further, my sister?

Carla: That is all for me. I thank you very much.

H: I have a question maybe in the future. And that would be at some future date. And that would be, I just wondered in the last couple of weeks about a church in eastern Kentucky that has a very peculiar way that they worship, and I was just wondering if you could speak on that at some later date—this certain church that I'm aware of.

I am Q'uo, and we shall always be happy to speak in whatever fashion is possible for us, my brother, with the understanding that we must always observe the free will of each entity in each of our responses so that this free will retains intact. With that understanding, we are happy to speak upon whatever topic is chosen.

May we speak further, my brother?

H: Well, I think that's very nice. I don't think I'll get into that tonight—it's very lengthy. Thank you.

I am Q'uo, and we thank you, my brother. Is there another query?

(Pause)

I am Q'uo, and we are most grateful, my friends, for the opportunity of speaking our thoughts to this group and blending our vibrations with each. We are hopeful that our future experiences will continue to expand both our knowledge of your needs and our ability to be of service in regards to these needs, and provide some small amount of inspiration for those gathered, that they might be further inspired to move within the inner seeking that holds such great treasures for each. We shall take our leave of this group at this time. We are known to you as those of Q'uo, and we leave each in the infinite love and light of the one Creator. Adonai, my friends. Adonai. ✤

L/L Research

L/L Research is a subsidiary of Rock Creek Research & Development Laboratories, Inc.

P.O. Box 5195
Louisville, KY 40255-0195

www.llresearch.org

Rock Creek is a non-profit corporation dedicated to discovering and sharing information which may aid in the spiritual evolution of humankind.

ABOUT THE CONTENTS OF THIS TRANSCRIPT: This telepathic channeling has been taken from transcriptions of the weekly study and meditation meetings of the Rock Creek Research & Development Laboratories and L/L Research. It is offered in the hope that it may be useful to you. As the Confederation entities always make a point of saying, please use your discrimination and judgment in assessing this material. If something rings true to you, fine. If something does not resonate, please leave it behind, for neither we nor those of the Confederation would wish to be a stumbling block for any.

CAVEAT: This transcript is being published by L/L Research in a not yet final form. It has, however, been edited and any obvious errors have been corrected. When it is in a final form, this caveat will be removed.

© 2009 L/L Research

Sunday Meditation
April 5, 1987

Group question: *(From Carla.)* Concerning exceeding one's limitations in the hopes of maintaining a positive attitude under adverse circumstances. For her, it's physical health. How do you know that you've done all you can, without pushing too far and injuring yourself by the pushing, and how do you be sure that you've pushed far enough to maintain the positive point of view and enhance your chances of healing thereby?

(Carla channeling)

I am Q'uo, and I greet you in the love and in the light of the one infinite Creator. As dusk falls about your domicile, and your metaphysical circle becomes complete, many spirits range around this happy abode, rejoicing in the thanksgiving of friends who work in light for planetary healing. We all greet you and know that you greet us as you greet the sunshine, for we are truly intending help. Just as the sun shines on all, so do we, yet not all are equally able to absorb and thrive within the sun's hot rays. Just so, in the former case.

We move to the query this evening which has to do with limitations. If one has a frog in a lily pond, and encourages the frog to jump to another lily pad in the pond, the frog either will be able to make it, or will not be able to make it. There are limits beyond which a frog knows, in his small mind, that he cannot go. There is a safe distance, and then there is the border, that space which the human will, if you will, might address and achieve by giving an all-out effort. You will notice in the case of the frog, there is no moral impulse or communication of the kind typical of self-conscious entities, in order that he may speak with, reason with, or argue against what the Creator has ordained for him in the way of proximity of lily pads.

Each human has many, many resources available each time that it desires to know the precise limitation which it may accept in serenity and tranquility. As always, the answers lie first within, and then from empirical experience, for the true author of peace and love within each life is the life, is the peaceful and loving entity which is …

(Interruption from a cat. The group retunes.)

(Carla channeling)

I am Q'uo, and am again with the instrument. We apologize for the pause, but it was indeed necessary in order to avoid the loss of the contact. To continue.

The self-conscious entity within your density, unlike a frog, has many tools and resources at its disposal. The lily pads in the third-density existence are some physical and some nonphysical. The self-conscious entity manipulates the things about him which may be manipulated in order to please and comfort the self. However, many trials, troubles and challenges can be met with no rational or objective point of view. It is in these cases that discernment and judgment take their place beside prudence, all of these being subservient to and corollary of constant, daily, regular and disciplined communication from humankind to the Creator and from the Creator to humankind. Much of the individual identity of each person upon your planetary sphere resides yet within the Logos, the one great original Thought which is love.

Thus, when one says, "It is the Creator's will," one is not separating oneself from the Creator. One is rather acknowledging the relationship betwixt the shell of self which serves in an illusion and the core and heart of Self which resides in its true native land, a heavenly home not fitted out with harps and wings, but, rather, filled with light.

The queries which have to do with health often do not take into account the complex nature of energy blockages, thus, whether one presses hard on or accepts with grace a growing disability, it is one's offering of the self in thanksgiving and praise to the Creator which causes the life experience to become valuable. There are in each case reasons for and against doing too much for the physical, mental or emotional self to handle. Logic will not open this particular tin of sardines, shall we say. Packed neatly though they be, it is necessary for one to seek beyond the rational, in the land of mystery and hunch, wherein lies that greater portion of yourself which is the Creator, and has available to it far, far more of that which it is important for you, the seeker, to know than the conscious mind could ever produce.

Like a tree growing at the edge of a forest, a person who steps out a bit beyond that which others in the same condition do, is more noticed, for they are no longer of the forest, but dwell at the edge of the forest in pasture land. People, therefore, will view this particular tree as being different from the forest. In just such a way is an entity who is driven to produce visible fruits within the lifetime no longer a member of the crowd, but an individual. Yet, all trees are of the forest, whether in city streets or in the deepest jungle, the only difference being weather conditions which allow some to flourish in one place, and some another.

In just such a way, a seeker may feel that because it is in the limelight, so to speak, and entities within the forest of *(inaudible)* and dear ones are looking on in expectation, that all will be vigorous and well. This perception does harm to a balanced viewpoint having to do with the will of the Creator. And just as such a physically, mentally or emotionally ailing person …

(Pause)

We are sorry for the pause. We are attempting to regain contact. There is some pain.

I am Q'uo, and will cut this short, greeting each in love and light, for an end, and concluding our thought. Even though an ailing entity may be visible and an inspiration to many who enjoy the peaceful, serene health of foresthood, yet nevertheless, each tree is a part of the forest, and it does not aid in the development of the disciplines of the personality to regret any portion of that which occurs. It is appropriate, rather, to go always into meditation and to wait in hope, in faith and in an alertness to hear that great call which may seem like nothing so much as a small sound or movement, yet subjectively it is everything, for each question, time and light shall offer the answer.

We ask each to remember that twin values are sometimes antithetical. Prudence and bearing are two such. Let the courageous become more sensible, and let the overprudent go forth rejoicing in an abandon long denied.

We would now transfer to the one known as Jim in case there may be any questions. We leave you in love and light, and are known to you as those of Q'uo.

(Jim channeling)

I am Q'uo, and greet each again in love and light. We are pleased to have been able to utilize the instrument of the one known as Carla this evening, and thank her for offering herself with a whole heart and a firm determination to be of whatever service possible. The offering of the self in service was an illustration of the query which the instrument placed before us this evening, and the process by which it determined to serve is a process towards which it may turn in its future deliberations upon this topic.

At this time it is our privilege to offer ourselves for the answering of those queries which may yet remain this evening. Again we remind you that we are but fallible seekers and observers of the mystery of creation, and ask that you consider our words as those of brothers and sisters upon the same journey of seeking. Is there a query at this time?

Carla: I'd like to know if the time has passed—now that I really know that Don is dead and gone, I know there's not going to be a Ra contact—is it all right now for me to begin taking answers, you know, questions and answers? I don't want you to overstep free will, but I thought you might be able to tell me. I only wish to serve.

I am Q'uo, and we are aware of your query and your desire to serve, my sister. It is also our desire to be of service in our response, and for this reason we find some difficulty in speaking with the precision that is possible. We may, however, comment upon some general principles that may have application in this instance.

The difficulty in your serving as an instrument which offers itself in the channeling of the queries and responses to them in a session such as this session has been, in your previous experience, not recommended because of not specifically the contact that you enjoyed with those known as Ra, but the attention which that contact had drawn from entities of a more negative polarity whose desire was to gather that light unto themselves, and your own abilities, which for the most part in the area of vocal channeling meditation and the deeper levels of meditation that lead unto trance, were primarily unknown to your conscious mind, and, therefore, not under your conscious direction.

Therefore, the potential difficulty brought about by this combination of events was such that the format of the question and answer session was likely to trigger within subconscious areas of your own mind complex responses which would then move one's consciousness to the level whereby the process became automatic and out of the conscious control. Thus, the conscious ability to affect this process is that which is of primary concern in this regard, and takes precedence over the possibility of resuming the contact with those known as Ra.

May we speak further, my sister?

Carla: No. I'm just disappointed because Jim's had to do it for so long all by himself. Besides, I enjoyed channeling answers. I enjoy Latwii. Thank you.

I am Q'uo, and we thank you, my sister. Is there another query?

T: Yes, I have a question. It concerns my impending move to the country. I have a feeling that there is a reason below, under the surface, of why I'm moving to the country, other than just the apparent reason that I want to live in the woods, which is true. And I say, I know there's another reason, and I have an idea what it is, and why I'm doing it at this time. But I'm just wondering if you could comment and shed any light on the reason why I may be moving to the country now, apparently by myself, by myself to a great degree anyway. Can you help me on this?

I am Q'uo, and we find in this instance that there is a desire to know that which is known, which we find [is] the basic quality of the third-density experience, that each moves in a pattern or rhythm and seeks the melody which directs the feet, when, indeed, it is the movement in harmony with just this melody that represents the overall life pattern.

We look now at this particular situation, and may suggest that the thoughtful seeker which has remained faithful to its seeking will oftimes find the need to intensify this seeking in a manner which partakes more of purity both within and without the self. Thus, the surroundings of the natural environment of your planet are those which offer a nourishment to the thoughtful seeker which those things made of man are felt to omit. Thus, the natural environment calls to one which seeks the nature of its experience, its creation, and its movement through this creation. We find that this desire is one which is shared by many seekers such as yourself, but which must many times become manifest in a less direct fashion than is possible at this time for you, for your manifestation has an identity with the desire that will provide the purity that you seek.

May we speak further, my brother?

T: No, that's very good. Thank you very much.

I am Q'uo, and we thank you, my brother. Is there another query?

Carla: I have a small side question. I have been for the last six months or so thinking more about camping out on the ground. Now, a woman who has arthritis and an inability to *(inaudible)* sounds like a really bad risk for sleeping out, but I think, or at least I feel, that contact with the ground would really literally earth me more, and make me healthier and less scared. I wonder if you could comment on this concept?

I am Q'uo, and again we find a line beyond which we must not move in order that our response not infringe upon your own free will. We may suggest that the concept of grounding one's being within the third-density illusion by the exposing of the self to second-density environment is one which is sound. The means of implementing such in your case, my sister, is that which will take the careful consideration, for as you are aware, the damper environments for a prolonged period of your time are those which tend to aggravate the arthritic condition and the accompanying pain. If care is taken to provide the insulation of the arthritic joints, the experience of the grounding is one which, with the proper intention, may provide the enhancing of the grounding potential and the attitude of health as well.

May we speak further, my sister?

Carla: No, thank you, not right now. Oh, I just remembered what I wanted to ask. Does it have to be bare feet on earth, or sleeping bag, or can it be cot or an air mattress on the earth and shoes on the ground? Would that still ground me, or do I need to get naked in some way, just get on the earth? The reason I'm asking is because L was offering me his truck bed which has, of course, the mattress, but it has nothing in contact with the ground. That was the point.

I am Q'uo. The concept of the insulation of the arthritic joints from the cool and damp contact for a prolonged period is one which needs the careful compromise with the actual contact that is most efficient in providing the grounding effect. The insulation, as you may surmise, inhibits the grounding effect, yet allows the arthritic joints cohabitation with the second-density environment. Thus, it will be a product of your own creation which will allow you to determine your own limits and movement toward them. We apologize again for the abstract nature of our response, for the …

Carla: I'm sure it'll be very helpful for *(inaudible)*.

I am Q'uo, and again we thank you, my sister. Is there another query?

(Pause)

I am Q'uo, and we find that we have shared the extent of the queries which have found their fore in this evening, and for each we rejoice and offer our gratitude in return, for the concerns of the seeker are those which have the brilliance of intention and dedication to seeking which is a joy to behold and to share. We look forward to our presence with this group in your future gatherings, and we would at this time take our leave of this group, rejoicing in the love and in the light with each. We are known to you as those of Q'uo. Adonai, my friends. Adonai. ☙

L/L Research

L/L Research is a subsidiary of Rock Creek Research & Development Laboratories, Inc.

P.O. Box 5195
Louisville, KY 40255-0195

www.llresearch.org

Rock Creek is a non-profit corporation dedicated to discovering and sharing information which may aid in the spiritual evolution of humankind.

ABOUT THE CONTENTS OF THIS TRANSCRIPT: This telepathic channeling has been taken from transcriptions of the weekly study and meditation meetings of the Rock Creek Research & Development Laboratories and L/L Research. It is offered in the hope that it may be useful to you. As the Confederation entities always make a point of saying, please use your discrimination and judgment in assessing this material. If something rings true to you, fine. If something does not resonate, please leave it behind, for neither we nor those of the Confederation would wish to be a stumbling block for any.

CAVEAT: This transcript is being published by L/L Research in a not yet final form. It has, however, been edited and any obvious errors have been corrected. When it is in a final form, this caveat will be removed.

© 2009 L/L Research

Sunday Meditation
April 12, 1987

Group question: *(From L and A.)* As the harvest approaches, and the difficult times that come with this harvest occur, how can each person be of service to others and proceed along the personal evolutionary path?

(Carla channeling)

[I am Q'uo.] I greet you in the love and in the light of the one infinite Creator, and I greet each of you who are, in miniature, perfect creations of the perfect Creator. I greet you in mystery and illusion, in love and light, in seeking and in faith.

It is a great privilege to be with you this evening, and we would not wish to allow the opportunity to go by to greet the one known as L, and to offer our love and blessing within this entity's vibratory patterns. It is indeed a great pleasure to share meditation with each, and with the entity as a group. We ask that each word that we say be taken as what it is, the concepts of seekers upon a path, offered through an instrument, nothing more. These are our opinions; we are no ultimate source. We thank you for allowing us to be of service to you, and yet the greatest service that you may do for the Creator, for us, or for yourself is carefully to discriminate. Thus, if that which we say does not ring true, we ask that it be dropped from the mind, for we would not wish to be a stumbling block to any.

The question that you have asked this night is perhaps one of the central questions which faces what this instrument would call the pilgrim in his progress. We shall answer [this] question in two parts. Firstly we would address the concept of illusion and reality.

Each of you awakens and sleeps. The activity during the waking hours is considered reality, whereas the occurrences dimly remembered which occur within dreams is considered illusion, interesting perhaps, but not a true history of actual events within the inner being. Yet it is difficult from a metaphysical standpoint to decide which experience might be the richer, except by saying that one could not exist without the other, for both are the portions of a greater illusion which enfolds and encompasses you and the world about you.

Because the entire planetary sphere dwells within one local illusion which is regular in its habitual rules of physics, it is assumed that that which is perceived by some sense means constitutes reality. Within this model of the world, then, you allow yourself to be less real than the world about you, for although you are a part of the world, that which is without is greater than that which is within.

You, then, are the illusion, seeking to react appropriately to the various realities and circumstances of physical existence within third density upon your planetary sphere. The moods, the irritations, and all the frustrations of dealing with what is termed reality keep the pilgrim constantly off balance, constantly seeking the center point once again, constantly searching with one timid toe for the true fulcrum of beingness. We must admit that your illusion is difficult indeed to pierce. As one gazes upon the night sky, and upon all the things that have been discovered thus far by your peoples, and they are but a fraction, of course, of that which shall be discovered, it seems impossible that such a seemingly limitless and regular universe should be anything but reality.

Let us take you back to the third grade, as this instrument would call it, within the school. The world was small; there was a desk, crayons, a teacher, a few friends, home, entertainment and bedtime stories. The soul within was young and growing. You are that soul now—young and still growing. Growth does not lie in reacting to the circumstances about one, but rather in becoming more real than the illusion which you see all about you.

And why are you more real than any other part of an illusion which includes you? My children, there is such a thing as consciousness, because consciousness is that of the original Thought of love, the Logos which created all that there is. This Logos dwells within, and subjectively speaks to consciousness. Through consciousness it speaks to the illusion, but without the pilgrim's becoming aware of the need to remain unattached to the illusions of circumstance, it is very difficult to become an actor, a dramatist and a critic, rather than one in the audience which reacts, laughing and crying as the scenes pass, the actors play their parts, and the flat, painted scenery slides up and down.

The source of reality must lie within the self, because reality is subjective—as consciousness is subjective. You are the Creator, knowing Itself. You are also a pilgrim on the way to seeking the face of that Creator. Yet, where do you seek? Do you not seek within? Where is buried the life within you that is unaltered, the consciousness that is infinite, the spirit that is eternal, but within your own heart and mind?

Thus, the greatest service which a pilgrim can perform at any time is to be, that is, to be a conscious being, an actor, seeing circumstance as illusion, but illusion rich in spiritual possibility. It is one of the clichés, shall we say, of your culture, "There but for fortune, go I." There are needs which may be met, whether physical, emotional, mental or spiritual, in almost any situation, if the observer is patient enough and careful enough in precise observation. Certain things, such as starvation, are easier to spot. Far less easy to spot are those spiritual possibilities which arise from personal discomfort of one form or another.

Yet to live within an illusion is to experience discomfort. We might observe that many of your peoples react to circumstances in an inappropriate way. For example, this instrument has what she calls a canker sore on her tongue. It is sore, and we are aware of certain nerve endings which are activated when this instrument moves its vocal apparatus. Many of your peoples would avoid speaking because of the canker sore. We do not mean this literally, but as a parable. There is in almost any helpful spiritual activity, discomfort. It is the discernment of one who retains and maintains the consciousness of the love of the one infinite Creator that is able to adjudge correctly what possibilities lie spiritually within circumstances.

We would now move on to the second portion of the question.

We are aware that each is concerned, as well as hopeful, about the coming of a new age, the arrival of fourth density, and the beginning of a new spiritual climate of love and understanding. May we say that the probabilities are that in the last decade of third density within your planetary sphere there shall be some discomfort from one source or another. Yet the greatest discomfort of all shall be the agony of those who, not knowing where the source of being is, have not sought it, and, more, thirst for that which they know not but would have.

It is in those times that entities will remember the one who smiled and exhibited the lively grace of peace and joy. Simple lovingness is perhaps the greatest gift which man can give to man or God. It is appropriate for the beginning of fourth density that those entities which wish to be of help in the harvest allow the natural formation of communities and groups in order that the source of consciousness may be sought by a group which then encourages each other, thus beginning, just beginning, the establishment of group mind. It is not to be expected that in third-density physical vehicles entities will achieve other than momentarily the consciousness of total oneness.

However, the feelings which many among your peoples have of forming close alliances with a few and being in communication with many, these impulses are good. They speak to a reality which has its source in the perfect nature of the unfoldment of creation, which is ongoing. It may seem at times as if every entity was a seeker, and the world, which you know, is populated far too thickly with various believers in mutually contradictory things. Nevertheless, all of these entities are too few. We do not yet feel that there is a decisive strength of consciousness in a group sense. Thus, we encourage those who are drawn to groups to be aware of the possibilities and advantages of spiritual work together, for encouragement is very helpful to the faltering wayfarer. This is especially true because the single greatest source of centering, learning and transformation is that which is the hardest for your peoples, the stilling of the physical body, the mind, and the heart in order that the seeking will may open the door to the one infinite Creator in meditation. It is most important that this be done as regularly as possible.

Your monasteries are built for just such purpose, yet you will notice that they are walled, and do not permit the entrance of strangers for the most part, but rather live a self-contained life, praying and offering in service to the Creator. Some of you have been called to such a solitary and worshipful existence. However, it is well that each consider what he or she may feel encouraged within to attempt or accomplish, for not all who are, shall we say, spiritually oriented as most, would wish to manifest as such, but would rather instead manifest without the identity, the authority, and the respect that is given to those who are considered to be more devout. Many are called to be parents, homemakers, mechanics, factory workers and all the other careers, professions and jobs, all the ways to sustain life with your money and to enrich life with love. There is no circumstance which is better or best for the furthering of service to others at this time. You must listen, each to his own subjective consciousness, with discrimination and with care, but also, in the end, with trust and faith.

Thus, we say, in order to best work as harvesters in the valley of the shadow of death, it is best to behave, within limits, as you would if there were no valley, no shadow, and no death, for all these are illusions, and only beingness actually exists. You contain that beingness, your eyes, your mouth and your hands manifest it to others. Every look, smile, word and touch conveys to those about you that consciousness which lies within, and through all the illusion, within illusion, within illusion which passes for conversation amongst your peoples, the thread of consciousness sings its true song betwixt each two people.

And in the sensitive one, the one who is ready to be harvested, that shall be the gift that shall have infinite meaning, that shall be too dear for any price. Thus, meditate, find the center, and be who you are. The rest shall occur one moment at a time.

May you look upon all things spiritually, which is to say, without prejudice and with humor, for if consciousness delights in one thing, it is itself. May you enjoy and rejoice in your consciousness. May you throw open the door to gladness and creation. May you live in the present moment and be, before, during and after each thing that you do.

You will notice we said nothing whatsoever about survival. There is much material in this entity's mind upon that subject, and we find that it colors the question within the questioner's minds also. Thus, in closing, we would briefly address this.

We ask that you realize that there is no such thing as survival, for the entire incarnation is an illusion. You are at this moment deeply, deeply asleep, and attempting to sleep-walk, that in your somnambulation you may struggle in the darkness to see a chair for a chair, and not a bear, a mirror for a mirror, and not a flame.

May your hearts be light. We would leave this instrument in order that we may transfer to the one known as Jim. We thank each for sharing with us this energy. We are known to you as Q'uo.

(Jim channeling)

I am Q'uo, and greet each again in love and light through this instrument. We are honored at this time to have the opportunity to ask if there may be further queries to which we may respond. Is there a query at this time?

Carla: I have one that I didn't want to ask as a group question, but I've been wondering about because of M's objections to marriage. Is there something intrinsically negative in a marriage contract? And if so, is it possible to transform the energy into positive energy?

I am Q'uo, and we look upon this query as one which reflects the attitude of the culture in which you find yourselves pursuing your evolution. It is within the confines of the gathering of goods and affections and promises in which one who desires to enter a mated relationship will bring the conditioning which it has learned, and in the mated relationship will continue to pursue the gathering of obligations and collecting to the self of that which is considered valuable or desirable.

We find that within your culture there is the basic gathering instinct that has been somewhat distorted, so that the giving unto another freely and joyfully is not that which is naturally exercised. Thus, there is within many cultures of your planetary sphere the desire to better the self, with secondary concern for others. This basic desire is that which is worked upon by all who seek to move the self along the path of evolution, for it is the turning outward of the focus of the attention that allows an entity to widen the point of view to the degree necessary for embarking upon a service-to-others path in an harvestable fashion.

Thus, if it can be held uppermost within the mind that to give of the self in each situation which is shared with the mate, and others as well, this basic condition which focuses upon the self may become transmuted so that the radiance of the self becomes apparent.

May we speak further, my sister?

Carla: No, I'll study that when I get the transcript back, thank you. But I have another question on another topic. It was just a follow up to the channeling before. As I was listening to myself channel, I kept waiting for the part where it got to what the person did for his own personal spiritual evolvement. Everything that was said was about service to others and being and meditating so that you could be there so that you'd smile and people would remember and they would come to you when they were disturbed by signs of the end of the age. But you never said anything about how to move ahead in your personal evolvement. Did you mean to assume that if you were serving others, you would …

(Tape ends.) ♣

L/L Research

Intensive Meditation
April 15, 1987

(W channeling)

I am Quanta, and I greet you in the love and in the light of the infinite Creator. This channel was having difficulty in assessing whether this contact was viable or simply a so-called figment of her imagination. We wish to reassure her that this is not simply a figment of her imagination but that this is a real contact, and ask that she simply acknowledge and accept that which is coming through her at this time. It is good to be skeptical of events which occur in the process of channeling so that one is not taken by lesser or inappropriate information. We wish to reassure her that she has made a good contact this evening and we are pleased with her progress. We would like to address the issue of contact by means of vocal channeling.

There are numerous contacts available to those who seek to become vocal channels. We have worked only with this group at this time, and therefore it is inappropriate to consider or associate the one known as Quanta with any other form of vocal channeling. We would like to continue with the teachings which we have initiated with this group the last time we gathered, the time for joining together the inner plane entity and the vocal channel known as W, so that they may begin to associate if this is desired. At this time we will leave this entity and transfer to the one known as Jim. I am Quanta.

(Jim channeling)

I am Quanta. I greet each again in love and in light. We have chosen to take this opportunity to speak through this instrument and to offer ourselves in the capacity of responding to those queries which those present may provide for us while the one known as N becomes more comfortable with her physical vehicle *(N has been coughing.)* and is able to attempt our contact. Thus, if there are any queries at this time we would be happy to entertain them.

W: I'd like to ask, are you familiar with the term Wesak? And can you tell me—and can you give me some information on the Wesak moons which are occurring?

I am Quanta, and we must plead an ignorance in this regard, my sister, for we are not familiar with many of the customs and events of your peoples. This we seek to learn as we become more able to receive the information which is available in the experience of this planetary population.

May we speak to any other query, my sister?

Carla: I have a question. Then, what I would infer from that is that the group mind forms in a hierarchical fashion, first the upper or lighter or more shallow levels of the mind, which are the group mind, then the racial mind or archetypical mind, then the planetary mind, so that you're not yet in enough contact to get into an information—I guess you'd say—data base, since you're dealing with a biocomputer, the mind, the great mind that would have the information that W sought, is that correct? Could you comment on that if it is not correct, and correct my assumption about the way the group mind forms?

I am Quanta. We, in joining this planetary influence, are much as a traveler upon a journey in a distant and foreign land. We are familiar with the ways of consciousness and its association with itself in the manner that you have described as the hierarchy. We in our journey and visiting and joining of this planetary influence are attempting to correlate those general qualities of consciousness, and more specifically the third-density human consciousness, with the intricate and complex means by which this consciousness has expressed itself in the experience of the various cultures and nations, as you call them, in the history of this planetary influence.

Thus, we have, shall we say, access to a great store of records which provide an immense challenge to new students of this grouping of consciousness complexes. Thus, our study has to this point been that which has examined only the outline, shall we say, of this planet's history, emphasizing and concentrating upon the means by which various groupings of entities have sought the one Creator in the distortion known as love and compassion.

Where there has been a significant achievement, shall we say, that has been related to various points of your historical past we have in those cases studied somewhat more carefully. We are aware that this study is one which will take a significant portion of your time to accomplish, yet we undertake with great joy and anticipation of learning the story of many peoples and races which have joined upon your planetary sphere in the pursuit of polarity.

May we speak further, my sister?

Carla: Then, from what you say it sounds as if the archetypical or the group mind that you experience is not hierarchical, but merely a computer too difficult to use quickly. Is that correct? That it's all available to you at all the levels at once, but it is difficult to access any of it until you understand the computer, understand the group mind and its mechanical structure? Is that correct? I'm trying to get a picture of how the group mind forms in early fourth density, and you are a real godsend in that you're the only contact that we've had that's just beginning fourth density. Anything that you'd care to send would be interesting, I'm sure.

I am Quanta. The connection between individual experience and the larger groupings of mind complexes which eventually blend themselves into that great store of experience that many have called the Akashic record is one which is one-to-one, shall we say. Each entity which gathers experience that is significant in the personal evolution records this experience in its own conscious and subconscious mind complex. Each mind complex has access to greater and greater stores of information as the roots of the individual mind complex contain all that which has been gathered by the entity in all conscious experience and continues to move in an harmonic fashion with those of, you would say, "like mind" or in many cases the racial mind, in other cases the cultural mind, and in still other cases the unique groupings of mind that blend various factors, be they social and culture, philosophical or spiritual and religious, or racial or geographical.

Thus, there are many groupings of mind that serve as intermediary reservoirs of information and stand between the individual mind complex and the planetary mind or that which we have previously referred to as the Akashic record. This record or planetary mind is that store of information which shall be opened to all the population of the fourth density that is to reside upon this planetary sphere. Each entity then will look upon this planetary mind as its ancient heritage and that which is available to inform further thought and action as the various individual portions of the to-be social memory complex begin to seek further means by which the service of others may be accomplished.

May we speak further, my sister?

Carla: Is our Akashic record and social memory complex terms for the same referent?

I am Quanta. These terms have a close relationship in that the grouping of entities which shall comprise the fourth-density social memory complex of entities will have access to that Akashic record of experience which has been collected throughout the history of this planetary experience to date. Thus, the social memory complex is the grouping of entities that has as its heritage the Akashic record, not only of this planetary influence but of those planetary influences which shall also contribute a portion of the population of the fourth-density social memory complex.

May we speak further, my sister?

Carla: Only on another topic, and thank you for that. I hope that was not too long a digression—I was interested. Can you tell the name of—in this inner plane contact or any of the nature of this contact, what the contact is, what its desire is, and so forth, or does this have to—is it necessary for it to come through W alone, in terms of free will?

I am Quanta, and though it is not exclusively necessary that this information be transmitted through the one known as W, we are of the opinion that it would be best for the development of this new instrument if this information were discovered, shall we say, as a portion of the normal progression of a new instrument practicing its art, for we do not wish to overly prejudice the new instrument in this regard, but wish it to find its journey one of inner discovery and expression of that which awaits within.

May we speak further my sister?

Carla:. No, that's fine. Thank you.

I am Quanta, and we thank you, my sister. Is there another query?

W: To digress back to the first question. The information on the Wesaks which I was referring to was something I heard from another channel channeling an entity named Samuel, who referred to the Wesak moons as being a time when the new moon acts as a mirror, reflecting greater energy coming from the source to this planet. Is there still something which you as a new fourth-density entity aren't familiar with, or can you just say anything else about that to clarify it for me?

I am Quanta, and we are familiar with the concept of the alignment of planetary and celestial influences which provide windows of opportunity, shall we say, to entities seeking in a certain fashion at the opportune moment when the alignment of particular influences is favorable. It is as though the efforts of the student are increased by a lever, shall we say, so that at certain moments, if the student is alert and persevering in its seeking, it may at these moments experience a heightened—we search for a term within this instrument's mind—perception of the art which it seeks to master.

It is for the cautious and diligent student that such opportune moments may be investigated and utilized, for there is, indeed, the magnification of power, shall we say, that is available in such alignments, and with the increase in potential power for the student, it must be realized that the responsibility of the student to utilize its art in as pure a form as possible is also increased. With greater opportunity comes the balance of a greater responsibility to utilize the opportunity along the chosen path, be it the positive path of the service of others or the negative path of service to self.

May we speak further, my sister?

W: Not on that topic, thank you. You have previously given me some meditations—you've given the group some meditations. Are there any other recommendations you can give to facilitate my developing so that—in preparing me to meet whoever the entity is that wishes to use me as a vocal channel?

I am Quanta. We feel that we have given that which is of most benefit for the present time. It is the perseverance that is most helpful for the student of meditation and the student which seeks to utilize the clarified mental attitude achieved in meditation for the exercise of the vocal channeling art. Thus, we may only suggest at this time that the dedication to the regularized meditation be continued. This type of perseverance shall prove to be the greatest ally, we feel, for any instrument, be it new or more experienced.

May we speak further, my sister?

W: Yes. I meditate on a daily basis on a specific meditation given to me from the other entity that was channeled that I referred to. Is that sufficient, or would an additional specific meditation with the intent of connecting with this other entity be appropriate?

I am Quanta. We feel that for the present time the manner of meditation which is now your practice be continued and added unto only as the opportunity presents itself in a fashion which may be repeated faithfully, that is, if the desire and opportunity to manifest the desire is present for additional periods of meditation, that these be engaged in with no dedication to making a contact with any particular entity for the purpose of vocal channeling without the presence of the supporting group, the goal rather being more general, if additional periods of meditation are desired, in that the calming of the conscious mind be that which is focused upon.

May we speak further, my sister?

W: No, thank you.

At this time we feel it would be appropriate to attempt to close this meditation through the instrument known as N, if this entity will refrain from the analysis and speak those concepts which it finds moving through the mind. We shall now transfer this contact. I am Quanta.

(N channeling)

I am Quanta. I greet you in love and light. This instrument had that which we would attempt to *(inaudible)*. This instrument wonders if the *(inaudible)* old or new social memory complex and we don't have *(inaudible)* judged as *(inaudible)*. Although we are ever learning from the instruments which we are in contact with, therefore we are pleased and glad to be with this group as we learn from each entity and are pleased to be able to help each entity to learn and spread knowledge and *(inaudible)* to other seeking entities on this physical plane here.

We *(inaudible)* to leave this instrument with love and light. We are those known as Quanta.

(Side one of tape ends.)

(Carla channeling)

I Yadda. I greet in love and light of infinite Creator. I say, "How about Lao Tsu?" This instrument say, "Jesus Christ." "One Christ good as another," I say, so we come. We speak about skepticism. Hah! You want to know about skepticism. Open your eyes. What do you know? You know nothing. Look around. Look at tree. You see tree. What you know? You got root, bark, branches, bird's nest—and leaves! Hah! What you know about tree? Tell me how it grow there. Tell me how it began. Tell me anything about tree except name and wocation. *Lo*-cation. We gonna say it right!

Now, you look at any other thing, and tell me what you know. What is there not to be skeptical about? *Nothing!*

Now, let us take what we do not know. *Is everything!* Everything! What you gonna do? How you gonna think? You have to name names and pretend that you know things. But inside—what you gonna take?

Now, let me ask you another question. What you berieve—what you be*lie*ve. We getting good with our l's and our r's. What you believe is far more important than what you know—*because you don't know anything*. So, tell me what you believe in. What you say? How you declare yourself. We say one word—*love!* Hah! We said it right. This instrument think we crazy. This instrument not like to channel us because we mess up her face. Heh, heh, heh *(giggle)*.

Now you know you not know, but you do not know what you believe, do you? Huh-uh. No. Why you wasting time on knowing things when you cannot know anything? We leave this instrument in love and light of infinite Creator. We know what we believe. We believe in love—for it created us and all that there is. What do you have to say that about? We can never ask a more basic metaphysical question. Adonai, my friends. We are those known to you as Yadda.

L/L Research

L/L Research is a subsidiary of Rock Creek Research & Development Laboratories, Inc.

P.O. Box 5195
Louisville, KY 40255-0195

www.llresearch.org

Rock Creek is a non-profit corporation dedicated to discovering and sharing information which may aid in the spiritual evolution of humankind.

ABOUT THE CONTENTS OF THIS TRANSCRIPT: This telepathic channeling has been taken from transcriptions of the weekly study and meditation meetings of the Rock Creek Research & Development Laboratories and L/L Research. It is offered in the hope that it may be useful to you. As the Confederation entities always make a point of saying, please use your discrimination and judgment in assessing this material. If something rings true to you, fine. If something does not resonate, please leave it behind, for neither we nor those of the Confederation would wish to be a stumbling block for any.

CAVEAT: This transcript is being published by L/L Research in a not yet final form. It has, however, been edited and any obvious errors have been corrected. When it is in a final form, this caveat will be removed.

© 2009 L/L Research

Sunday Meditation
April 19, 1987

Group question: Concerning the attitude and action to take toward and in response to the world being too much with one, the regular daily routine and maybe a few added difficulties seeming to bring a heavier burden to the shoulders. How does one respond? How does one look at it, and what is the most effective attitude to view such?

(Carla channeling)

I am Hatonn, and I greet you in the love and in the light of our infinite Creator. It is a great pleasure and blessing for us to be sharing this meditation with you, and we would, if we might, pause before we begin to speak to the subject at hand, that we might revel and thoroughly enjoy the circle of oneness which the seekers present have created, and which we are now privileged to be a part of. We would then pause. We are Hatonn.

(Pause)

I am Hatonn, and once again I greet you in the love and the light of our infinite Creator. We offer you what you upon your planetary sphere call the Easter greeting, and because your question is concerning the life of the busy, mundane activity, and how to deal with it in order to be more clear and peaceful within the busyness, we ask you to come with us in mind to a grave which is very vivid in this instrument's mind, as it has been contemplating this grave for three days, so involved is it in its Christian activities.

It is the tomb of Jesus, the man of Nazareth, a carpenter by trade and an itinerant teacher by chosen profession. Come to the cold, gray dawn of a desert morning. Three women, all of whom love the newly killed Jesus, come to the tomb seeking the beloved body of a family member, or in the case of Mary Magdalene, a dear friend and teacher. It is not possible for there to have been a change within the grave, for the body that is so loved to have disappeared, but it has been stolen or taken. Mary, the mother of Christ, is frantic. Mary Magdalene weeps. Their focus is upon a tomb and not upon that which is there no more.

When you within your third-density experience become too close to those things which you are seeking which you love and which you wish to care for, your focus shifts into a gazing upon not the heart of soul, not the living spirit, not the breathing fire of that which you care for, but the dead and life-deadening house, tomb or structure within which that which you care for lives. To be even more specific, and at the same time, more universal, each which dwells within a physical vehicle dwells within a walking tomb, the tomb of chemical life, a life which grows up and dies away, in a cosmic sense, almost too quickly to be noticed, each of you being but a breath upon the wind, and then dust.

Yet there is great life, great beauty, and great joy in that which is alive within each builded structure of man and man's thinking. This instrument plans for the great occasion, figuring entertainment and food, glasses and cutlery, losing sight of the magic of metaphysical significance which the great event harbors, nurtures and cherishes, if it can be seen with a proper focus. Each may gaze within at the concerns of the day, and see which is the living, breathing source of joy and excitement and which the whited sepulcher, the open grave.

We are not among those who recommend extremes of asceticism in order to flagellate and deny oneself earthly joy, for in there, in the most mundane thing, [is] that living atom of the consciousness of love which cannot be overvalued, for its value is infinite. In every step that is taken by any entity, in every thought, in every word spoken, there is the living fire of creation which moves, as upon the face of many waters, creating in each entity a newness of life and love and strength, and this shall occur for each, whether or not any cooperates. This process is inevitable. It can be retarded, but it cannot be stopped. You cannot do yourselves ultimate harm, no matter how confused, how sad, how despised or how miserable you may feel.

However, it may aid those who wish to part at last from the clutch upon the inner rock of the tomb to realize that the tomb is not the risen source of joy, for that which is alive goes before one, drawing one onward, just as the master known to you as Jesus was not be found anywhere near a tomb, but rather had walked on into another portion of the country.

We do not know whether this may aid you or not, but it is the way we see your discomfort at this time. It is a matter of placing the attention upon achievements made in tomb building, rather than the joyous and free expression of love for everything that exists. One may gaze, for instance, upon an old house, and see all that needs to be done. The house has become a tomb. Or may gaze upon the same identical edifice and ask that edifice, "House, which has borne my love, my grief, and my passion, tell me, what would you have me do for you this day?" You may even ask that angel within, that spirit of life, "What shall the day bring?" Thus is the day blessed with the same seeming routine that once cursed, narrowed and limited the mind. There is no occasion, circumstance or possession which cannot become a tomb, nor is there any of those things which is not at heart a source of life, a wellspring of joy, and a fountain of peace.

We gaze upon the minds of each, and we find that we have not discussed the one circumstance that blocks and entombs all which are present, and that is the mystery of illness and death.

Each within the domicile which breathes the breath of life, breathes also, in only slight anticipation, the musty odor of the tomb. Do you then identify yourself with the tomb? We do not think so. Where, then, is your identity, if it does not lie in breath and heartbeat? Your identity lies within consciousness. That which is given you shall never be taken away, for you have been and will be. You are a precious and unique portion of the creation of the Father. So are all those about you. Perhaps you see one who is ill mentally, perhaps one is ill emotionally, perhaps another has physical ailments, and you sympathize at the pain which living causes and wonder where the source of joy in life could possibly be for those who must suffer.

My friends, within your bodies, you have been dying since you first drew breath. It is a common cliché within this instrument's mind that there is no cell within you which was yours seven years previous to this night. Eventually, in a twinkling of an eye, this incarnation shall be past. What then shall you find as your source of joy and peace? It shall not be the body shell, nor yet the mind with all of its adornments and embellishments, nor even yet the emotions, though noble they be at times. It is rather that within you which seeks the face of the mystery of the Logos, the one original Thought of Creation, that shall love and live and serve as you do now, for an infinite length of time.

You think of yourself without your tomb—that is how you remove the busyness from the mind. Put in perspective that which lasts and that which does not, and encourage one another in love, for your consciousnesses are made of that creative and glorious substance.

We would at this time leave you, for there is another which wishes to work with the instrument known as Jim. We cannot tell you how much we have enjoyed this chat with you. It has been some time since we have been called to this group. We are, as this instrument would say, those who take questions of a very general nature, and we are sometimes considered introductory. It is a pleasure to work with the consciousnesses of this group, and perhaps you shall agree that no basic question is so basic that it can be answered once and for all. We feel this group is very special, and we love each and thank you once again for allowing us to share our thoughts with you. Please remember, as always, that our thoughts are merely opinion, and not to be read as the gospel truth. We are those of Hatonn. We greet and leave each in the love and in the light of the infinite Creator. Adonai. Adonai vasu borragus.

(Jim channeling)

I am Latwii, and we greet you, my friends, in the love and light of the infinite Creator. We are overjoyed to be able to utilize this instrument and to speak to this group, for as it has been with those of Hatonn, also it has been a great portion of your time since we have had the opportunity of speaking to this group, and we greatly rejoice at this opportunity, and thank each for allowing us this privilege at this time. We are always happy to entertain those queries which each may offer to us, and at this time we would ask if we might begin with a query?

Carla: You're S's favorite channel. If you would, could you offer any comments that you might want to pass on to S at this time? Anything that might be helpful that you would like to say to the one known as S in Denver?

I am Latwii, and we are happy that we have our, shall we say, following of those who appreciate our message and perhaps even our poor humor. We cherish each who opens the mind and the heart to what words and experiences we might have to offer. We can only echo the words of our brothers and sisters of Hatonn when we speak to any of your group, and especially to the one known as S at this time, for as each seeker finds itself securely placed within the illusion, and finds this illusion becoming more and more with the considerations and feelings of the seeker, and at times becoming overpowering, we can only suggest the stepping back in the mind, and in meditation, to look upon that which is the life and that which has gone before and taught well the student of life, so that the student might take a larger and longer view at that which is its present moment and which is the doorway to its future moments, looking at all portions of the incarnation as one pattern of experience that will allow the gaining of those attributes which are most desired by the seeker.

The illusion is that which teaches. It is an illusion, for it seems to be quite other than that which it is, yet well does it instruct in the ways of service and the ways of dedication, in the ways of perseverance, and in the ways of accepting and loving those qualities of self and other self which seem unacceptable. By throwing the self into the experiences of confusion, frustration, difficulty, disharmony and disease, the seeker of truth might test its ability to find the perfect reflection of self within each moment, in order that it might, piece by piece, experience by experience, construct the complete picture of the self, the creation, and the Creator as one being.

May we speak further, my sister?

Carla: No. I thank you for that message, and I know that S will appreciate it. Thank you.

I am Latwii, and we thank you, my sister. Is there another query?

Carla: Well, I had one on my own hook. I was trying to listen to the channeling while I was channeling, which is always dangerous, in that you don't get it, but it just … I was asking myself, was the message to stop doing the things which were not lasting, or to change the mind so that in doing the same things, you thought you were doing a different thing? Is that a clear enough question?

I am Latwii, and we believe that we grasp the heart of your query, my sister. If we have understood that which our brothers and sisters of Hatonn have shared with your group this evening, one may look at any portion of the life experience in either of two fundamental ways. One may see that which remains to be done and which pulls one onward. One may see that as the incomplete nature of experience, of self, and of the illusion, as there is always that which may be refined, may be added, and may be completed.

Or one may look upon any life experience or any portion of the self as that which is whole within itself, complete and perfect, existing as a unique expression of that which it is, a portion of the Creator, a companion to the seeker of truth.

When one looks upon a situation or entity in the latter manner, one feels the peaceful contentment of that which is complete, and needs no further attention or action. It is well to nourish the self, especially within the meditative states, from time to time with this overview of one's experience within an incarnation,

And yet, it is also well that one continue upon the journey, for within the incarnation and within this illusion the opportunity is constantly presented to take that which is and vary it or add unto it a manner which is unique to oneself, rich, intense and varied according to one's free will choices. Thus is there progress within the evolving consciousness that allows the widening of the perspective. Thus, both points of viewing are helpful, each in its own time and in a balanced manner.

If either is dwelt upon to the exclusion of the other, there will be either the constant worry that things are never done, or the opposite contentment that moves not into new and richer experience.

May we speak further, my sister?

Carla: No, thank you.

I am Latwii, and we thank you, my sister. Is there another query?

T: Yeah, I've got a question, and I hesitate to ask it, but I think I'm going to go ahead and do it. First off, I wouldn't even ask this were I not in the presence of two of my very best friends. If there were other people present, I wouldn't even ask the question. I feel like I'm belaboring a point, but maybe it's only because it's been on my mind so much, so maybe I'm not belaboring it with other people. I said earlier, talking with Carla and Jim, that I'm having a lot of problems, and I have, but I think I know the root cause of most of my problems. And that quite simply is that I'm lonely. And I'm looking for someone, obviously, and Jim and Carla know this, and I've made reference to this before. And I guess my question is, maybe I'm trying too hard. Maybe I should let it go, because maybe my idea is to try to learn to be more complete within myself before I actually find someone else.

But the real reason for my asking is, one time before I found myself basically in this situation, and at that time I did what I consider forcing the issue. I got very down, I got very emotional about it, and it wasn't very long—in other words, I got to the, as they say when it looks the darkest, that's when the answer comes or some help comes. Okay, I let myself get into that kind of a frame of mind before, and I had gotten very dark, and lo and behold, it wasn't long and I met a lady with whom I had a very long and beneficial relationship. It wasn't the one I was looking for, but it was close.

So my question after all that dancing around it is, is it good to try to force this? Because I had the feeling I could do it again, but I may wind up with someone again that is not that person, the person that I really want. Or should I just let it go? Because it is, quite frankly, bothering me an awful lot. And at times I seem to be able to handle it, and other times it gets the best of me. If you can make anything out of all I've said, I'd appreciate any comments.

I am Latwii, and we thank you for your query, my brother, and shall attempt to speak upon this interesting subject.

The burden of free will for each seeker within your illusion is heavier for those who seek consciously. The further one travels upon the path of self-knowledge, the greater one feels the awareness that one is conscious, that one has feelings and that there is that great mystery and unknown which is called your future that lies before one and which will be formed by one's own choices. It is difficult, we understand, for any seeker of truth to look upon any portion of the life experience as being indeed but a portion, as being that which shall at a certain time become transformed and be another experience. It is as though one were attempting your physical exercise, attempting to push the limits of the physical vehicle further, and in this pushing, one reaches the point at which it seems there can be no further repetition of the exercise without failure and collapse.

Just so are many experiences of the mental, emotional and spiritual nature as well. Each entity decides for itself, either before the incarnation or during the incarnation, that it wishes to undertake to learn certain lessons that may be manifested in such and such a fashion. The means of the manifestation may frequently be secondary to the lesson itself, and as the lesson is carried out within the incarnational experience, it is oftentimes felt by the seeker that no more can this experience continue without fatigue and failure and the desire to escape this particular set of circumstances.

We counsel for all such entities in this situation the lightness of touch and breadth of viewing which you may call the sense of perspective or humor that will allow one to experience the seeming retrograde moments of experience without undue distress, for it is true for each seeker that many are the steps of the path and many are the pieces of the puzzle, and each shall eventually fall into place as each is meant to fall.

The question then is, how shall the seeker prepare the self in the attitude, to witness and experience each placing of the foot upon the path and each piece of the puzzle in its place? It is, as you have noted, frequently possible to push the envelope, shall we say, and attempt to force a certain set of circumstances to take root within the life pattern. Oftentimes much may be learned by such forcing. This may be in addition to that which was first intended and may in some cases merely delay the original intention. However, those choices which have been made by your own will previous to the incarnation carry a weight which shall eventually be felt in the manner which is desired.

We can only add at this time that when one considers the difficulty of the present moment, it is well to look to that which has become placed within the perspective of the past, as experience gained, which at a certain point in the past was itself a difficulty unresolved. If one may look at …

(Tape ends.) ❧

Intensive Meditation
April 22, 1987

Group question: "Laitos: We would speak concerning the excellence of meditation."

(Carla channeling)

I am Laitos. I greet you in the love and the light of the infinite Creator. We thank you for calling us to your meditation and for allowing us to work with the new instrument known as N.

We would like to speak through this instrument for awhile while we work with the one known as N to achieve the best contact of which we are capable at this time. Each time that the instrument practices and exercises its channel the pathway of interlocking vibratory complexes is made clearer and more strong. Thus, we continually adjust the contact as we are able, just as each instrument learns more and more to tune itself to the highest and best that it may receive in a stable manner.

We would speak concerning the excellence of meditation. The concept of meditation we are able to discern easily has a great deal of attractiveness to each present, yet each wishes that it were more wholehearted in the meditations which it has, and in the case of the one known as N even the attempt to meditate has not always been taken. If only for five minutes in any day, it is well to meditate that much, rather than go through an entire day without acknowledging the Source of one's energy and love and centering oneself within that clarified and purified energy which is the energy of the greater Self, the energy of the Creator, the energy of creation.

We are aware that for many it is most easy to worship that great Source of all that there is within the setting of the environment of the Creator, that is, the natural world—forest, stream and meadow. To marry meditation and solitary sojourning with nature is an excellent way to allow the inner self which is in contact with the higher self to be fed from the streams of living water, as this instrument would call them, which are a profoundly accurate description of the love which created all that there is.

We cannot urge enough that meditation be done on a daily basis. We do not suggest judging the excellence of the individual meditations or even attaching great importance to the time therein spent. When the desire is ripe within one, that attention will be there, and that progress will be made. However, without the disciplines of the daily meditations, if only for a few minutes, the preliminary work needed in order that the season of each pilgrim's own transformation may well pass unnoticed, lost in the hurry and scurry of daily activity.

Spiritual seasons are very definite, and the soul which is in its blooming season on a continual basis is a rare one indeed. It is natural within your density for there to be relatively few moments in the incarnation of which advantage may be taken, in which an opportunity for great transformation is born. It is to the one who watches and waits daily that that time will not come and go unnoticed and unheeded, much less unused.

This instrument is experiencing self-doubt, and we request that the instrument refrain from analysis. This is a small group and we are responding to those vibrations which are within the group. May we say for the instruction of this instrument that it is the desire for knowledge which calls us to the group, and it is this knowledge which is being called for by the one known as N, and to a lesser extent by each. It is not for us to judge, but only to inform. We have great love for each within this group and we thank each for the opportunity to share these thoughts.

Now we would move onward, my friends, and as the one known as N would say, "Get on with it." We hope that each is satisfied that we took the extra time for this particular message in the appropriate manner, and we thank this instrument for continuing the channeling, although it had some difficulty with analysis due to its own opinion of this information. We pause that the group may retune. We are Laitos.

(Pause)

(Carla channeling)

I am Laitos, and we rejoin this instrument with thanks for the retuning, especially on the part of this instrument. The practice of channeling is a very specialized form of a general practice which we would also call channeling, for is not each a channel in every thought, idea, emotion and speech which it makes? Is each entity not always a channel, either for love and light or for some darker force of separation? There are some, indeed, which do not wish to be channels at all, but rather to deaden the senses. And to those we say, sleep and be comfortable, for there is an infinite amount of time. But to those present who wish indeed to progress, we say, "We rejoice with you, and would speak with you about love." For the face of the Creator may be seen in many, many shapes. In your springtime the face of the Creator is seen in violet and snowdrop, in daffodil and hyacinth, in fruit tree blooming and lilac. Yet other ways there are too of seeing the love of the infinite Creator.

We would transfer this contact at this time to the one known as N. We ask the instrument not to analyze, but simply to speak the thoughts that are given. We are those of Laitos. We transfer at this time.

(N channeling)

I am Laitos. We greet you in love and light. This instrument has reached the point where she feels our communication as one from friends and …

(The rest of N's channeling was not transcribed.) ❧

Sunday Meditation
April 26, 1987

Group question: Patience.

(Carla channeling)

I am Latwii, and I greet each of you in the love and the light of the one infinite Creator. May we offer a special greeting, blessing and our love to the one known as K. It is most precious to us to be able to greet this entity, and, indeed, precious it is to greet each of you. We are enthralled with the energies of the night creatures of your woodlands, and of the portions of your metaphysical planes as well which awaken for the night watches just as those of the day are quieting and stilling their energies until the dawn comes again. The hushed peace of your abode is most enjoyable and all the homely sounds of domestic machinery most pleasant to the ear. We thank you for calling us to your meditation this evening. It is always a pleasure and all too rare for us to share our humble thoughts with you.

This evening we would speak upon a kind of love which is called among your peoples, patience, for there are those in your extended group, though this instrument knows it not, who greatly desire to hear words upon this subject, and we would request that this topic be sent to the one known as S, although we cannot promise to offer any inspiration, but can only hope that our thoughts may have some help in them.

As one walks upon the road and sees oneself upon a pilgrimage of a spiritual nature, patience seems part of the plan, and each step begins and ends in a perfect pattern at first. The thrill of spiritual life and spiritually-oriented thinking fills the mind and the heart and inspires each and every day. There is, however, something about the spiritual path that is not often given as the best feature [of] such a path, and that is the steep and stony nature of it, the points at which it disappears, seemingly, in a swale of mud and tarn grasses, encroached upon by the persistent and annoying heartbeat of the earthly life.

Soon enough, the spiritual path is difficult to see, and the heart and mind that was so filled with peace becomes impatient. First it may become impatient with the earthly and mundane concerns which keep it from spiritual things. Some of those things may be shorn away that the spirit may thrive, and yet if the mundane concerns are important upon the surface of the life, the lack of them may truly disrupt the spiritual life as well, more than the concerns do. And so the spiritual seeker is back at what this instrument would call square one.

Then, perhaps, the seeker becomes impatient with the self and thinks, "If only I were a more evolved and realized being, I would not be impatient and out of sorts, I would move on, buoyed by faith, and keep one foot in front of the other in a steady rhythm until my path found me again. But alas, I am not so wise or so patient."

The spiritual seeker which criticizes the self is one at war with the self, and it is never recommended by us that the errors which one makes be considered any longer than is necessary to note the mistakes, to correct the missteps which can be corrected, and then to move on.

Now, my friends, at whom shall the seeker be irritated and impatient? It cannot choose those mirrors of the self about it, for it has discovered that all mundane concerns beside one are just that— things to be taken as seriously as necessary in order to live the life most conducive to seeking. The self cannot be angry at the self forever, for no progress is made by one at war with the self. Is the self then to be impatient with the Creator for creating such an imperfect universe? This is the choice which most often takes the longest to work through.

Let us look now with patient eyes at a thoroughly bemusing creation, the creation of the Father and the co-creation of humankind.

Patience is an infinite part of that infinite thought which created all that there is, for the infinite intelligence which is love cannot experience impatience. All times are the present time; all places are the present place; all things are one thing. The universe is a singular thought, and the eye of intelligent infinity sees unity in infinity. It is the co-creators of creation, those who are self-conscious and own the gift of consciousness, which create a distortion of unity, a distortion of infinity, and a distortion of endlessness, another term, perhaps, for patience.

For true patience is not that which waits, but rather that which bides endlessly. Love creates you, each of you, and thus you are manifested unto the world of illusion, equipped with a clumsy, yet very lovely, physical vehicle, equipped with a multitude of ideas, thoughts, dreams, hopes, all the many gifts that consciousness gives. And because of what you desire and what you fear, each of you co-creates the universe in which you live. Almost without exception, that universe is not a universe of endlessness, not a universe of unity, not one of a consciousness of infinity, for the illusion is with you, and so it must be in order that experience be gained.

"Why," the pilgrim may ask, "must I be kept from my spiritual seeking by so many distractions of the mundane kind?"

It is our opinion, my friends, that each mundane step which you take is a step along the most spiritual path of which you are capable at that moment. The experience which is gained may be uncomfortable, yet it is the experience which the deeper portion of your being has resonated to, has attracted, has drawn unto the self and now rejoices at experiencing.

The secret of patience is the knowledge that it is a portion of love hidden within the deep beingness of mind, that portion of the mind which lies below the sensors, below thought, below idea, creating in a powerful and creative way each experience which manifests itself through you and to you. Thus, patience is a resource, part of the glory within which each spirit contains.

There is an inner opening to infinity, and patience is the doorkeeper. Difficult experiences of the mundane type, whether they be relationships or situations, are designed to place the pilgrim in the perfect place for the experience it needs to overcome deep biases which are unbalanced in the personality. To be impatient with the world because it has made you sad or angry or defeated is to be impatient with yourself, and by this time the seeker has already decided that if the self is unworthy, that is certainly too bad, for the self is here and the self must seek to be the best and the highest that it can be.

Each self is perfect in some way at some level. This is acknowledged at some point by the seeker. The paradox betwixt the perfect and the blatantly imperfect self is accepted that it does not matter that there is a paradox, but that one must still seek and not be at war with the self.

Thus, we ask each to meditate when impatience with the world becomes that which keeps the consciousness from its joy, for it is in the manifestation at least of peace, serenity and patience that sunshine will spring from your eyes regardless of the external weather. It is then that you shall become a blessing to all whom you see.

We are sorry and sympathetic when we gaze at the suffering of good and true-hearted pilgrims within your third-density illusion. We find you to be very brave, carrying on in faith when there is no evidence to prove the assumption of the goodness of the

Creator. Yet, we must share with you, my friends, that your journey is truly a journey where patience shall be a great tool, resource and ally.

Each of you seeks for that moment when unity with the infinite source of all things is experienced and a sure knowledge of the universe as it really is is finally revealed. Be patient, my friend, be patient.

We have been most blessed to be able to use this instrument. We are attempting to keep our sense of humor to a manageable quota so that we do not remove ourselves from the possibility of offering honest comment, however, we must tell you that our hearts are full of glee and merriment at being with you, and we almost dance as we speak through this instrument, for we are most excited to be able to speak. We would at this time transfer to the instrument known as Jim. We leave this instrument. We are those of Latwii.

(Jim channeling)

I am Latwii, and greet each again in love and light. It is our honor at this time to ask if there might be any queries to which we may speak? Therefore, may we begin with a query?

Carla: I recently had a book go off to the printers called *The Channeling Handbook*. I was wondering if you had any comments on the subject of channeling, since I don't believe I have asked you? Just comments about how to help those who are interested in channeling or those who are channeling to be more clear about what they are doing.

I am Latwii, and we look upon the work which you have done upon this topic and give thanksgiving that you have chosen to share that which you have learned in a free and open manner with those who have interest in this area, for as you have noted previously, there are many of your people at this time who find a fascination with the service of the vocal channel, as is the tendency of those who seek in this manner for the first time. The means of seeking is often with little regard for the service and its responsibilities, shall we say.

We see ourselves as channels, as each who offers a service to another is indeed a channel for the one Creator to the one Creator, and we feel this to be of a sacred nature, for it is the radiating of light that is the fabric of your illusion, and indeed of all creation, and is the sharing of the body, shall we say, of the one Creator as a kind of communion with those who

thirst and hunger for that metaphysical nourishment that may be offered by those who have moved somewhat further along the path of seeking. We welcome all attempts by new instruments and those who would be new instruments to speak those words of inspiration and perhaps some few words of instruction to others who might benefit from such speaking, and we would hope that each entity who partakes in this service might do so with diligence, with thanksgiving, and with a dedication not to the results of such service, but to the offering of such service with every fiber of the being and ounce of purity that is possible.

Thus, a work such as the book which you have collected that is the product of your own seeking and service is that which offers a means by which others who wish to travel the same path might do so with the greatest of efficacy, having the trail, shall we say, opened somewhat more fully by the efforts of those who have gone before. Thus, we extend our thanksgiving and appreciation for each such effort.

May we speak further, my sister?

Carla: No, thank you. I'll ponder those words.

I am Latwii, and we thank you, my sister. Is there another query?

Carla: Was there anything that was not channeled satisfactorily for S that might be better channeled through the one known as Jim?

I am Latwii, and we are happy with the manner in which we were able to speak through your instrument, my sister, and find there is no need for adding to that which has been laid out, shall we say. May we speak further?

Carla: So what you're saying, basically, is that patience is infinity, or a sense of infinity, rather than patience being the ability to wait for long periods of time for some result. Is that right? Patience is sort of being in the present moment? I mean, I never thought of patience as being the same thing as being in the present moment, but it seems like that would be the only way it could be timeless.

I am Latwii, and it is our perception that one helpful way of defining or looking upon that term which we have called patience is that of so fully accepting the present experience in any present moment that one is full of that experience and has little concern for any which may have come before or which may follow it, that the moment is indeed sufficient unto itself, as each moment is a portion of the one Creator, which contains in it the doorway to the fully experienced presence of the one Creator. Thus, to give the proper respect, shall we say, to each moment is to have a kind of love for the Creator that we have called patience. To abide with and to find fullness within any moment is to glorify that portion of the Creator that has revealed unto the seeker for that portion of experience.

May we speak further, my sister?

Carla: Well, just a little further. I think I'm coming to the end of my questions. I think about S's situation, and I know that she's got a situation that's been going on for a long time, and promises to go on for as long as she's alive, unless she herself changes it, where there are things about the situation in which she's not appreciated and not understood, and it's just part of what she experiences every day. And what you're saying is that as she experiences each of those moments, that there's something within that's more to be experienced than the relationship itself. Does it transform the relationship, or do you just get out of the relationship and experience the creation? I guess that's why I'm kind of confused. If I were S, that's what I'd ask, I think.

I am Latwii, and it is our intention to express the possibility that for any seeker in any moment, if the seeker and the moment can be seen as whole and perfect unto that moment, then the doorway of perception is thrown wide open and the experience of the seeker is that of completion, for it is the limiting ways in which entities form their perceptions and expectations that squeeze the moments and limit the ability of the seeker to experience that which is always before one.

We do not mean to criticize overly the tendency of your peoples to see with narrow vision and to exclude that which lies beyond the boundaries of perception for most upon your planet, for, indeed, it is the narrowing of the vision and the point of view that allows the work of refining and balancing distortions to proceed in a manner which is intense, pure, rich and varied. But we might suggest that there is within each moment the possibility for removing the boundaries which have been placed for certain purposes and to allow the fullness of the Creator to move through that moment for the seeker, and to feed the seeker in a manner which you

may see as being of a spiritual or metaphysical nature, to give the seeker that which shall, through its future experience, nourish it and propel it in a manner which shall accentuate its ability to learn those specific and well-focused lessons that it has chosen before the incarnation to learn.

We both applaud the focus and ask that the seeker consider the possibility of expanding that focus in order that a greater portion of experience might be made available as a source of sustenance to those who have long sought within narrow boundaries to learn those carefully chosen lessons.

May we speak further, my sister?

Carla: I notice that you did not encourage meditation in this talk. Is that because this particular discussion had to do with something that the analytical mind needs to be at work upon rather than the intuitive, or what?

I am Latwii. We may always encourage the meditation without any hesitation, for it is in the meditative state that one may most easily discover the sufficiency of the moment of which we have been speaking. However, the concept of patience is one which most properly finds its focus within the daily round of activities and the workings of the conscious mind. If it may be kept in the front, shall we say, of the conscious mind that the focus is one which has a purpose, but one which may from time to time become somewhat tedious, and may, through a change of focus, be relieved in a manner which nourishes the spirit, then we feel that the most appropriate application of the concept of patience is that which finds its working within the conscious or intellectual faculties, the mind.

May we speak further, my sister?

Carla: Not to me, thank you, I'm finally through. I think it's a most challenging concept. Thank you.

I am Latwii, and we thank you, my sister. Is there another query at this time?

(Pause)

I am Latwii, and as we have reached the end of the queries for this evening, we again wish to extend our great gratitude to each for inviting our presence. We have been some time, as you would measure it, in our speaking to this group, and we are happy that there has been the call for our presence this evening. We remind each that we do not wish our words to be given too much weight, shall we say, and ask that each take those which have meaning, and leave those which do not for the present have the meaning in the personal journey of seeking. We are known to you as those of Latwii, and we leave each in the love and in the light of the one infinite Creator. Adonai, my friends. Adonai vasu borragus. ✢

Sunday Meditation
May 3, 1987

Group question: Along the lines of when does one realize when the conscious attempts to affect one's progress or evolution, a relationship with another, has gone far enough in the way of trying to control it? And when does one begin to surrender to the flow or the rightness of the moment or simply be that which one has been seeking?

(Carla channeling)

I am Q'uo. I greet you in the love and the light of the one infinite Creator. We nearly swoon with the light, as we perceive the springtime freshness through this instrument's senses. The third-density physical vehicle is, indeed, one which affords an enormous amount of various sensations to occur simultaneously and the vernal shower is a most heady experience for us.

We join your meditation at your call and thank you with deep appreciation for the privilege of speaking with you upon the subject which has been requested, that being the choice between control and lack of control, desire and lack of desire. We hope that each realizes that our thoughts are not infallible. If anything which we say seems to present any stumbling block, please forget our words immediately, for we wish only to aid, not confuse the seeker who seeks after a mystery greater than words and beyond all telling.

Many is the time that you upon your planet have gazed upon the cycle of the seasons and have observed the ritualistic rhythm of cadenced seasons passing, the bloom that springs to life on time, and the leaf that withers in its autumnal turn. To the tree, the decision of whether to control or to release control is not in any significant degree a meaningful question, for nearly all trees, being of second density, have that relationship with the Father which precludes thought, thought being necessary only to offer one information upon which to base choices.

Thus, the tree seems wildly to gyrate from fullness, through dying, to stark skeletal nudity, and then once again to new life when warm weather coaxes buds from the dead leave's stumps. Each season brings its own reality which suggests to the eye and ear of the seeker that this reality shall go on forever—this is the way things are. So one thinks in the heat of summer or in the cold of winter. So one is led to think by the slowness of one's dance through the river of time. Things last forever, and then they are gone. This is the way in which time is perceived. This is the way in which change is perceived.

You who ask these questions are not second-density creatures, but those with a consciousness which offers a co-creatorship to each. Each of you is, with the Creator, the co-creator of its own experience and destiny, and unlike those of second density, each of you seeks such information in order to make many, many choices.

There is an enormous storehouse of information which cannot ever be known in the proper sense of that word. It cannot be scientifically or objectively known. Yet this source of information is extremely helpful in the making of decisions. It is a source of information used extensively and almost to the exclusion of any other source by those in beginning fourth density. It is that portion of the mind found in the subconscious, according to your terminology, and described in various ways by those among your people who understand the great well of knowledge which intuition may offer. The intuitive faculties, the heart, this instrument would say the gut, the stomach of the mind, that which feels rather than thinks, is, when shallow and prurient feelings are removed from the mix, an extremely useful and helpful faculty for the making of choices.

The third-density person, then, is caught betwixt the utter creatureliness of second density, in which thought, for the most part, is simply impossible in any self-conscious sense, and the fastidious and conscious use of the intuition which informs those of fourth density, having lost the veil which lies between conscious and subconscious minds. A third-density entity seeks—or decides not to seek—very much in the dark.

Now that we have nicely described and delineated the predicament of third-density humankind, perhaps we can say a few helpful things about the rhythmical use of intuition.

The basic job description, shall we say, of the third-density seeker is to observe and, if possible, to draw conclusions, to act upon those conclusions, to record in the mind and heart the results of the actions from those conclusions in such a way that gradually certain biases shall be built up within the heart and mind that shall last. So it is in every season of the life, and human seasons do not follow the year only, but many, many cycles, seasons and times that are unique to it, to it alone. Thus, the world may be experiencing summer, but you on the other hand may be experiencing the deepest winter or the first blush of spring.

Thus, a modest and diffident, yet absolute, independence from any other source of feeling needs to be a portion of that identity which is yours, not to defend to the death, for that is unnecessary, but to respect and to make other people aware of, if that becomes necessary. The observation of the self begins with the simple observing of the feeling tones so that one may discover what season one is in, what time of day. Is this a morning for you? Is this the dark of the night? There are many, many seasons and times, and the subjective time which you experience is the stuff of your universe.

You then examine what is happening, hour by hour, minute by minute, and certainly day by day. Observation of this kind at first bewilders and then, after a few months of care, one can begin to see a pattern, an ebb and flow, one begins to see the true signs of seasons and of seasons' change when that does occur. The basic responsibility of third-density humankind is to observe this process and gradually to become aware enough of the preferred reactions to the various spontaneous seasons that one may illuminate and elucidate and then soften the blow of the difficult wintry times and then that one may celebrate and share those seasons which are prosperous, blooming and bursting with fruit.

There is always a balance in spiritual excellence, not a leaning in one direction to the exclusion of another, but the balancing of the polar opposites which are both excellence, but which apart from each other do not create or sustain the consciousness of love. We could say to you, "Allow the flow of events to control you always," and be giving excellent advice, and just as well could we say, "Use more discipline and meditate more during each day." Both of these things are true in their season, and when the urge comes upon you to meditate more, to use more discipline and so forth, we suggest that by all means you follow your own intuition.

Yet, if more than one circumstance seems to be echoing to you, saying to you or indicating to you that there is too much discipline and control in the life, listen to that intuition.

The basic question here is a question of the trust which you have in the Creator and in yourself as a part of the Creator, which knows more than any outside source, including us, what is needed at the present moment. If you are ever to see life in third density as a unified and meaningful experience, you will see it as a creation of ultimate subtlety and yet startling simplicity in which, borne upon the water of the spirit, the frail barks of humankind sail about, some with rudders, some without, in search of many grails, many islands, many native homes. Some wish to go away from everything; some wish to go to the heart of everything. And to each, his or her own journey.

We use as an example the one known as T, who reports the "coincidence" of the numbers of entities who are sick in the same way, all known to him in a short period of time. This is a cluster of events which alerts the intuitive self which lies mostly within the subconscious that a message is coming through. What is that message? We would not learn for that student by teaching, but may say simply that when an entity is holding on to a consciousness of lack, a consciousness of "I wish I could have done more," then just that long will the opportunity to feel that feeling be made available.

Every thought is in one form or another a desire. It is almost impossible not to desire. Thus, attempt first to observe clearly the thought patterns, the seasons of the life, and the harbingers of change, so that you may celebrate when the season is at its height and ameliorate any uncomfortable circumstance when the day is short and the winter night of the soul is long.

We are through with that question, and would only pause now to say how very much we have enjoyed the vibrations of the group. It is truly a blessing for us to be here and we [in] return bless each of you and thank you through this instrument. We would now transfer. I am Q'uo.

(Jim channeling)

I am Q'uo, and we greet you again through this instrument in love and in light. At this time it is our privilege to offer ourselves in answering of further queries which those present may offer to us. We thank you for each, and we seek to speak that which has been our harvest of experiencing. Is there a query at this time to which we may speak?

Carla: I guess my only question is that the wisest man I ever knew, Don Elkins, always said that happiness was not an objective, and that basically if something felt good it was bad for you, and if something felt bad it was good for you, and you should never react to anything, but just be the creator of your own actions which is, I would say, widely at variance with what you're describing. I like your idea better. Could you address the possible problem, say, with the "Hundred-and-Eighty Degree Rule," as Don always called it?

I am Q'uo, and we speak to this query in order to offer the possibility for consideration that there is great difference between what one may become aware of through the intuitional faculties and what one may think with the intellectual is an appropriate course of action. It is possible for one to become aware of the speaking of the intuition, the small voice that speaks in stillness within the heart of being, through the exercise of meditation which has been primed, shall we say, with the intense contemplative and intellectual analyzing of possibilities. This priming or opening of a path through the intuition, when accomplished, will in its season of appropriate time allow the communication from the deeper levels of the mind to the conscious mind. This response is that which seeks to fulfill the desires of the seeker of truth in a manner which is appropriate for the seeker according to the plan that it has laid out for itself prior to the incarnational experience.

It is oftentimes the case that the seeker will hesitate upon first becoming aware of the speaking of the intuition, and will doubt that which has been given, and will, indeed, [attempt] to construct in a mental fashion an appropriate, in its own mind, permutation of this speaking of intuition, and satisfy itself that it is following the dictates of the deeper self in so doing. We hasten to add that in the greater picture of one's incarnational patterns, those movements of mind, body and spirit which seem at some point to be inappropriate or incorrect, are in the larger sense often quite valuable in the overall fulfilling of the preincarnative plan. However, we realize that those present wish for the ability to, shall we say, zero in on the heart of the process and make each step count as much as possible.

Thus, although we might agree that when one thinks upon a certain path and desires it through the thinking, that it is oftentimes necessary for the action which results from such thinking to continue to be refined until the heart of the matter is obtained, and is oftentimes obtained in a fashion that is distinctly different than the thoughts of the seeker, the pure and undiluted feeling direction of the intuition is that which needs the acquiescence and obedience of the seeker in order that that still, small voice may be heard ever more clearly and ever more frequently within the life of the seeker of truth, for it is that which speaks from the heart of the being, and offers a clue as to the means whereby the seeker in its thoughts and actions may strike closer to that heart.

May we speak further, my sister?

Carla: Just a couple of little things. I believe that were I to ask how to get to the heart, how to get to the still, small voice, the intuitive mind, I would be given a discussion of meditation. Is this correct?

I am Q'uo, and it has been said that if one seeks, that one shall find, and if one knocks upon the door, the door shall be opened. In meditation it is truly the case that within such hallowed inner ground one may seek and knock and ask in a manner which is more purified than the daily waking consciousness, yet also within this daily waking consciousness may one chant as a silent mantra the desire to seek, to know and to have the inner doors opened.

May we speak further, my sister?

Carla: But is that not a beseeching, a dunning of the Creator along the lines of T wondering whether it were acceptable to control, control, control and try to get, say a new girlfriend in the life? You're saying, control, control, control and desire the fruits of meditation, right? I'm having trouble with the paradox.

I am Q'uo, and we would agree that the line is quite fine which separates that desire which has a certain outcome from that desire which seeks only that which is appropriate. We recommend that desire be harnessed in a fashion which provides the seeker with the opportunity to offer the self completely and without hesitation to that which is appropriate rather than designating that which the seeker feels might be appropriate or helpful. Thus, the desire does not have a goal or idol, shall we say fashioned, of the mind of man.

May we speak further, my sister?

Carla: No, that pretty well says it all. Thank you.

I am Q'uo, and we thank you, my sister. Is there another query?

(Pause)

I am Q'uo, and again we rejoice at the sounds of the springtime shower that are evident to us through this instrument's ears, for we see and feel those sensations available to us through such instruments as the further examples of the all-compassionate nature of the one Creator which gives in all seasons those qualities of sustenance that will enliven and nourish the spark of consciousness that resides in each portion of the creation, that each spark may in its season grow, ripen, bloom and bear fruit, and provide to those portions of the creation about it the beauty and interrelationship that weaves a pattern of unity, binding all creatures and creations in one Thought of love.

We have greatly enjoyed beyond all possible expression through words the opportunity of joining this group this evening, of sharing our humble words with those who seek the nature of the life that each lives and offers as glorification to the one Creator. We look forward to joining this group in its future gatherings. For the nonce, we shall take our leave of this instrument and this group. We are known to you as those of Q'uo. We leave you in the love and in the light of the one infinite Creator. Adonai, my friends. Adonai.

(Unknown channeling)

I am Nona. I *(inaudible)*. *(Intoning)* Omm …

(Tape ends.) ☙

L/L Research

Intensive Meditation
May 6, 1987

(N channeling)

(N's channeling was not transcribed.)

(Carla channeling)

I am Laitos. We greet you once again in the love and in the light of the infinite Creator. We will speak but briefly through this instrument, but wished to use it as it is a bit more experienced in using the word by word method which we prefer to use for this transmission.

We continue to be pleased with the gradual adjustment of the contact with the new instrument known as N. The stage is now set for a movement in channeling which mimics the same movement within the spiritual life of any seeker. When a seeker is new, it assumes that all information, realization and knowledge impinge upon the self as it is experiencing itself consciously. This is a mixture of the present moment with heavy overlays with thoughts of the future and disturbed thoughts about portions of the past. Seldom is the consciousness of the seeker a clear mirror of what is actually occurring at any given present moment.

So it is with the channeling. Although we have thoughts which seek and hope to inspire to offer, yet first must we make sure of the mechanical portions that insure a comfortable and stable contact. There is much training which must be done, and it is largely specific. There comes a time when the new channel is no longer new and it realizes that the technique is basically learned. And now it is time to open the self to new thoughts and to the potential, subjectively speaking, for disaster, for how can one speak thoughts which one has not yet thought? Thus, it is that there is a crisis anew, and the fear of being a fool keeps the magic at bay.

Again, we urge the new instrument who faces now the graduation to take heart and to analyze before and after each occurrence, but to refrain from analysis during. We have thoughts to give from the first thought to the last, which any instrument may channel from the Confederation of Planets in the Service of the Infinite Creator. Those thoughts will ring with what we believe to be the truth, and that is that all of creation is one thing—one great Thought which thinks itself out in infinite portions. The unity of all creation is not something that is unusual or new as a thought, but it is all we have to offer. We hope and trust that our humble gifts may find favor with those who channel them and those who listen as well.

We thank the one known as N for listening to our lecture—we are afraid that we do give them from time to time. It seemed to be a good idea, for we find in the one known as N's thought processes a very clear train of thought which tends towards logic, thus, we thought it would be a simplifying thing if the instrument [were] to know what comes next, and be perhaps ready not to analyze and not to be afraid when an idea comes which is not linked directly to the progress of the self in channeling. This shall occur soon if the instrument continues as it is now in these sessions. We would now transfer to the one known as Jim. I am of Laitos.

(Jim channeling)

I am Laitos, and we greet each again in love and light through this instrument. At this time it is our privilege to open this session of seeking to queries which those present may have to provide us. We wish to remind each that we offer but our opinions and do not wish to offer authority. Is there a query to which we might speak?

N: Yes, Laitos. I feel that in channeling one is trying to become closer to their inner self. I heard a phrase the other day, "breaking down the barriers," referring to taking a mind-altering substance such as LSD or acid or mushroom, and I guess my question is, do they have any helpful purpose to breaking down the barriers and finding out more about oneself or the world?

I am Laitos, and we consider the possibilities of this query for the infringement upon free will, and may speak in a general sense concerning the use of the substances which have the capacity to, as you have stated, break down those mental constructions that hold the mind/body/spirit complex upon a certain course within certain distinct boundaries for the purpose of its gaining of experience.

It is quite true that there are various substances, including those which you have mentioned, that may be utilized in the expanding of the point of view and the gathering of the fruits of that expansion for use in personal evolution. We find that for those of your population that utilize such substances that the effect is that which is most usually random in nature, for the barriers, as you have described them, which continue to hold the focus of the mind and the experience within certain distinct boundaries is a function which is difficult to affect or control, shall we say, by most of your peoples, and the circumstance of the ingestion of such substances, as in regards to the current mental attitude and the environment, are those faculties which in a general and uncontrolled sense lay the groundwork for the experience, and oftentimes the groundwork is not solid enough or well enough constructed to support the increased energies that are available upon such occasions and the experiences thus are randomly generated and vary greatly in their effectiveness and ability to increase the seeking of the student.

There is great care necessary in utilizing such substances. This care is that of the magical nature which utilizes ritual in the dedication and consecration of such an experience to a specific purpose related to the student's personal pattern of evolution. And in such cases there is always the possibility that the student will not be adequately prepared in its normal rhythm of evolution to adjust its perceptions to the increased influx of energy available.

Thus, it is not our recommendation that such substances be utilized, for the barriers, indeed, will be altered in a significant fashion, and the increased opportunity for learning which is presented the student must be, in our opinion, balanced with the increased opportunity for utilizing such an experience in a metaphysical manner that is adequate to the opportunity offered.

The student of the mystery of creation has in its life pattern a rhythm, a song, if you will, which is unique to each student. There are times during which the pace or movement or dance of the melody shall be quickened, and there are likewise times when it shall be slowed. And there shall be opportunities for the variation and acceleration on new experiential levels for each seeker. These present themselves as a function of the student's utilization of catalyst efficiently within its daily round of activities. When the student is properly prepared, then, by its own progress in the efficient utilization of catalyst, the increased opportunities are then presented to the student. To seek to jump ahead, shall we say, and gather for the self the opportunity for an acceleration of the process of learning is a risk, shall we say, which, we have attempted to explain, may provide those opportunities, but in a fashion which is randomly generated and which must be properly prepared for by the student. The student which is able to utilize such substances in a magically or metaphysically appropriate fashion is rare, yet such students exist.

May we speak further, my sister?

N: No thank you.

I am Laitos, and we thank you, my sister.

(Tape ends.)

Sunday Meditation
May 10, 1987

Group question: The question, of a general nature, is what lesson is to be learned when goals seem unattainable after a great deal of effort has been expended?

(Happy Birthday, Jim McCarty!)

(Carla channeling)

I am Q'uo. I greet you in the love and in the light of the one infinite Creator. It is a great blessing to us to be asked to share this meditation with you, and we would pause with you for a few moments of silent meditation so that we may truly become one with you and flow in harmony and in rhythm with your thoughts and your needs at this time. We shall pause. We are Q'uo.

(Pause)

We are again with this instrument. We are Q'uo, and again we greet you in the love and the light of the One Who Is All. Your query is concerned with what your peoples call ambition, an ambition to succeed, an ambition to fulfill the potential. It is based upon an interesting supposition among your people, namely that something smaller than the life experience of the life itself is that which is called the work.

The difficulty in recognizing one's true work seems to stem from that distorted value which your peoples place upon that tool of power which your peoples call the money. It is assumed that that which is done in exchange for money is that which is the work, and it is assumed that, therefore, even when one is not receiving money for something, one may still be in a training period for some time, but after a certain time it is assumed that the work itself shall begin. Such is the distortion which money has created by its distortion among your peoples.

It is our opinion—and we stress that it is opinion only and is not an irreducible truth—that the only work which may be called "The Work" of any entity is that work done in consciousness during an incarnational period which has a net result as judged by the self after the incarnation of polarizing the entity more and more strongly towards service to the Creator and to others. Thus, life is the work, and work is the life.

This may rearrange the thinking upon the query of this evening, which is, "What is the possible reason for such extended effort and then no expected outcome?"

The emphasis upon the outcome is that which has been distorted by your money system. If it is seen that one's own life is a gift which is going to be created by the self by life's end within this density, then it may be seen that whether one had an expected or an unexpected outcome for training, that the actual work lay not in results, but in attitudes and biases which have been gained during the training, and that this process would go on regardless of the outer circumstances changing by apparent success or apparent failure.

Let us back up a bit and speak in a deeper way, as you know we are fond of doing, my children. You know that each of you is a perfection unique and amazing to the Creator, just as the Creator is unique and amazing, mysterious and wonderful to each of you. You know that as you gaze upon each other, you gaze upon the face of great mystery. And yet, somehow each entity manages to stop the ears and blind the eyes of the miracle of each moment in order that it may function in what is seemingly the here and now of a hustle-bustle life experience.

How blessed it feels to kick off the shoes of the workaday world, to tuck a metaphorical piece of grass between the teeth and gaze into the metaphorical open sky for daydreaming. How very, very good it feels to unwind and relax, to let one's mind drift. My children, it is not only pleasant—it is life itself to that entity which dwells within, which is learning the true lessons and doing the true work of the incarnation.

We are speaking here of meditation and of those states of mind associated with meditation which may seem to be a waste of time to the civilized mind. We find this word in the instrument's vocabulary has many connotations, and we wish them all to be recognized, for civilization is also an artificiality, and all of those notions and belief systems which arise from the cultural medium which you enjoy can be a deadening and numbing influence upon those who are not aware that at some point it is necessary to remove oneself from the grip of civilization in order that the creature which dwells within in illimitable light might move about, breathe the fresh air of unconstructed thought, and go deeper and deeper into that portion of mind which is nourished by light and love and contemplation and which gives as fruit of this kindness from the conscious mind a harvest to the conscious mind of health and right knowledge. The aid which meditation may yield to an entity is equal to that entity's desire for that aid.

There is no desire which is not fulfilled, and when one feels that one has worked for a long period of time and yet the goal has not been accomplished, it is often interesting to go back and reexamine the deep desires of the heart and mind. It may be that there is a far, far deeper desire for the deeper learning which is brought about when one has a long-standing and seeming failure. This consciousness of clay feet and imperfection causes a kind of unhappy tension which is called suffering, and this suffering creates a frame of mind in which the deeper senses become more and more sensitive and begin to make choices.

We question each who has an unfilled dream whether in the suffering which has gone into disappointment there has not been a great deal learned which could never have been learned in the face of continued contentment and happiness.

The strength of desire is the measure of the result of desire, for the universe is completely rhythmical and responds to that which is asked. There is a spontaneous simultaneity about existence, and in that still point, as one of your poets has called it, it is truly there the dance is. When one finally rests in meditation after great suffering and hoping and seeking, one may finally get a glimpse of what has been learned by the deep self.

To those to whom that glimpse has been given, no suffering ever seems so hard again, for those are the ones fortunate enough to grasp the deep reality, which is that in terms of the deeper desire of the heart they have not been unsuccessful at all, but instead successful beyond their dreams.

You see, my children, the movement in development of personality is from the surface of things, deeper and deeper into them, until finally the seeking and the sought become one; one thing, so that you are not meditating, but finally you are the meditation, and this meditation is your perfect poem, your arrangement of your consciousness, and you know in an instant that this consciousness is the gift which you shall give to the Creator, and so no longer can you feel unsuccessful.

We are aware that the moments when one accepts the self as the Creator must be few and far between for those of you who dwell in third density, for it is the function of your physical illusion to fool you quite efficiently. If you do not suffer in some way, if you are not made uncomfortable by circumstance, shall you seek at all? We found in our studies that our third-density experience was not as vivid as the experience which you have upon your planet. This is due to the fact that our Logos, as we find this instrument to use the word, did not choose quite so vivid an archetypical expression of the one infinite Creator.

You, in the planetary sphere you enjoy, have an especially excellent illusion. How then are you to embrace yourself and the consciousness within you in the midst of an illusion which delivers to your consciousness a distorted and incomplete report of the self? Again, we suggest meditation, that in the still moments of meditation, you might come upon yourself, and, not looking directly, still recognize that self as both self and a greater Self. And in the greater Self's persona, perhaps you shall catch a glimpse of the glory that lies within you.

The development of faith and will is in large part a development of the will to seek and the faith to keep on seeking. A persistent, sustained seeking throughout an incarnation, regardless of any results that appear within the incarnation, is in our opinion the very best gift which can be created by you. You are creating a life, and you shall not be done in that great career until your last breath has left the physical vehicle and you yourself move from space/time into the time/space of metaphysical life, that greater life which you hunger for while caught within the clumsy prison of the physical vehicle. You shall be light and free. You shall be full of light and full of freedom. Yet, here and now, within the prison of the earthly body, is your great chance to be faithful to your own consciousness.

So seek, my children, seek always, and know that while it is well to move according to the tides of circumstance, it is far more deeply helpful to have an inner life which is completely independent of outer circumstance, a life in which meditation and contemplation are both that which is desired and among the fruits of that desire. If you are not enjoying your meditations, may we suggest that you vary the conditions under which these meditations occur. And do not refrain from meditating because of a difficult patch, for in any difficulty, yet to remain faithful to the seeking is a very helpful thing for one who wishes to polarize more and more towards service to the Creator and others. The development of that will which under the velvet offers the strength is much recommended.

We find that there are queries within the group this evening, and we would like to answer as many of them as we may. We would at this time transfer this contact to the one known as Jim, We are those of Q'uo. We thank this instrument and would now transfer.

(Jim channeling)

I am Q'uo, and greet each again in love and light through this instrument. It is our privilege at this time to offer ourselves in the attempt to respond to those queries which those present may have for us. We remind each that we offer but our opinions and wish to appear not as an authority, but as brothers and sisters who seek as you seek on the same journey of seeking. May we begin, then, with a query?

Questioner: Yes, I have a question. Recently I read some literature concerning crystals and their properties and their value, and I've also read things in the past that said the opposite of what I have recently read. One is positive and the other one is negative. Could you comment on the use of crystals to a person who is seeking what value they have maybe in helping a person to polarize their—I guess, their direction of seeking? Anything you could say about crystals would be appreciated.

I am Q'uo, and we find that there is much that can be said upon this topic, and it is our desire to speak in those areas which might be of most use in this instance. Any aid of the nature of the crystal that an entity employs in its journey of seeking may be valuable in that seeking according to the desire and purity of desire for polarization that the entity contains within its heart of being as it utilizes the crystal or any other gadget, shall we say, for it is the crystallization of the self or the personality of the self which is the process of evolution for each seeker.

As the seeker is able to regularize the thoughts, desires, actions and words that proceed from its being, and to focus these energies in a manner that partakes of service to others toward a positive polarity, the entity is making of itself, and more specifically the energy centers or chakras of the metaphysical self, a kind of crystal that accepts the white light of the one Creator and refracts it in a balanced fashion so that each energy center lends its distinctive coloration of vibration and yields again the white light.

If an entity wishes to accelerate the process of evolution, the process of utilizing catalyst in the daily round of activities, and gleaning from that catalyst the bias in consciousness towards service, then the entity may seek to share that quality of polarization with others by means of the healing that is possible in the use of the crystal. This healing is a process which is first used upon the self as the entity gathers the experience of its journey and allows the fruit of this experience to move through its being, to enter into the crystal and resonate in harmony with it and become amplified by this harmonic resonance and move to an other self that is in need of the kind of balancing of energy centers which your peoples term healing.

As the crystal is utilized for the enhancing, the balancing, or the healing of the energy centers of self or other self, it must, however, be understood that there is the attendant responsibility to utilize the increased energy patterns or intensified patterns in a manner congruent with the chosen polarity, for, indeed, the enhanced experience carries the responsibility to be utilized in a manner that is as pure an offering of love to the one Creator as the seeker is able to make.

May we speak further, my brother?

Questioner: No, thank you. That was very good.

I am Q'uo, and we thank you, my brother. Is there another query?

Carla: So what you're saying about the lesson of working hard for a goal and the goal not being accomplished is—you're saying that it is if that trying has crystallized or regularized that person's metaphysical personality, then the real goal of creating a better crystallized personality is being done, and therefore the real goal is being accomplished, and it just looks like the goal is not being accomplished. Is that right?

I am Q'uo, and we find that you have in general summarized that which we have attempted to offer this evening in response to the query offered us …

Carla: But sometimes people succeed wildly, or at least adequately. I mean, not everyone has goals that they haven't achieved. So, are the people who are actually seemingly successful less so?

I am Q'uo, and we have not yet finished the response, and would at this time attempt to cover the additional information that you have requested. It is our observation that the peoples of your planet have so succeeded in placing about the mind complex those veils which shield it from far-seeing and becoming aware of the deeper patterns of experience that are realized in each incarnation and the work done in each incarnation, that the efforts of any one seeker in the metaphysical sense are largely unknown to that seeker, for what you seek within your illusion is the quality known as love or compassion and the expression of that compassion or attitude of compassion within the consciousness in such a focused fashion that one polarizes the being so that it is more and more able to accept increased love and light energy from the one Creator, and proceed therefore upon the path of evolution.

The polarization prepares the personality that it might be able to accept the increased energy of vibration in a stable manner without disintegration. The ability to discern the precise manner by which this process is accomplished is a lesson which lies beyond that which you now attempt to learn, and is described by many as that known as wisdom. Those of your peoples within third density who seek the lessons of love do well to gain even a small portion of that lesson, and do not yet reach the quality or lesson of wisdom which allows the clear perception of the white light in its movement throughout all of creation.

Thus, the qualities which you seek to nurture within your being, those of will and faith to persevere in the seeking of love, are those qualities which discipline the personality in a fashion which allows further seeking and further progress upon the journey of seeking. The process is largely unseen, and not dependent upon the outcome for particular effort or group of efforts within an incarnation that are designed by the seeker as its attempt to polarize in consciousness.

The attempt and the intention are those qualities which further enhance the will and faith and thus the polarization of the being, and it is these qualities that one works upon when one seeks to survive the moments and long periods of disillusionment, confusion, frustration and the various trials that test the entity's dedication to service and to seeking. And these moments of difficulty are seldom appreciated amongst your peoples as being those times during which the greater work is accomplished.

(Side one of tape ends.)

(Jim channeling)

I am Q'uo, and am again with this instrument. We shall continue.

It is often those times of the seeming accomplishment of a goal which one has long sought that seekers look to as a sign of work well done. However, we would suggest that there is little possibility of entities within your illusion ever being able to see with eyes clear enough to know when work has truly been accomplished, and it is those times of difficulty in general which are most valuable to the seeker of truth. Truly, there is no means by which one cannot serve and seek to be of more service, yet it is far better to continue the effort of seeking with great perseverance and without the necessity of counting the return that is most valuable to the seeker within your illusion, for the fruits of your seeking are metaphysical in nature and escape, for the most part, detection by those within your illusion.

May we speak further, my sister?

Carla: I'd like to take the opportunity to ask one more question, with apologies to everyone else for the hogging the questions, because I have a stake in this myself. *(Name)* is not the only one who keeps thinking that surely there is an outcome that has not been achieved, and I'm learning a lot tonight too. Two years ago I lost a very, very dear friend, my beloved companion Don Elkins, and it was very sad the way it happened. My mind has been full of the sadness of it ever since. And even as I come up to such a joyous occasion as my wedding, and even as I'm involved in very, very happy preparations, yet still the sad parts haunt me. And it's as though I were Don, thinking Don's thoughts during the time that he was suffering, and so I still suffer. Even though I'm sure he himself has gone on, yet I still suffer with him in those last days and minutes of his life when he really felt alone and there was nothing I could do about it.

And I just wonder, is there an intrinsic value to this suffering that I go through? I know that a lot of the work that I've done in the last year is the result of some of the deepest suffering that I went through in which I discovered a lot about my own personality and how to be a powerful personality. Should I just rejoice in this continued suffering, and assume that there is an intrinsic value in it? Is there an intrinsic value to suffering? Or being unfulfilled—let's make it more general.

I am Q'uo, and again, my sister, we remind you that the true nature of your experience is that which is hidden for the most part from your ability to sense or perceive. Indeed, there is value in suffering. Have you not produced a fruit from the suffering? Can this not nourish others? In the larger sense, the Creator is able through your suffering to be glorified as the suffering is borne with a joyous heart, for it is the expression, then, of the discovery of love where one would not expect to find such.

It is not often or expected that each seeker will find even a small measure of love in a conscious fashion within any portion of the life experience which is devoted to suffering. Yet, it is true that within each such moment exists the one Creator, whole and perfect, full of joy and balanced in love and light. As the seeker who suffers discovers more of that joy in the moments of suffering, thus does the seeker remove yet another veil that covers the greater view from inner and outer eyes.

May we speak further, my sister?

Carla: No, Q'uo. I thank you.

I am Q'uo, and we thank you, my sister. Is there another query?

Questioner: Q'uo, concerning the crystal, does the crystal have any value to—does it have any extra special value unto itself, if it is just left where it is or if it is just, not utilized, just as a crystal? What value over and above anything else does a crystal have?

I am Q'uo, and we see that there are many ways in which we may respond to this query. We see the query focuses primarily upon value determined by use, or in a more general sense, the value of the thing in itself. Indeed, the creation known as a crystal has value, as does any portion of the one Creation, and has more particular value as a regularized portion of light which may in an harmonic fashion intensify the movement of light. Thus, the crystal is that which offers a passageway for light of a metaphysical nature to move and to offer itself in service to other portions of the one creation by enhancing the beingness of the vicinity in which the crystal resides. This quality is like unto the faucet which in your domiciles offers the nourishment to those in thirst and need of refreshment.

May we speak further, my sister?

Questioner: Thank you. That did answer it.

I am Q'uo, and we thank you, my sister. Is there another query?

Carla: We'd just like to thank you very much for being here tonight.

I am Q'uo, and we find that for the moment we have exhausted those queries which have been presented to us with joy and sincerity, and we thank each for these gifts of your love. We have enjoyed this opportunity to share with you our journey of seeking, and we look forward, as you would say, to those times within your future gatherings that we may so join this group again. We are known to you as those of Q'uo, and we leave each at this time in the love and in the light of the one infinite Creator. Adonai, my friends. Adonai.

(Carla channeling)

I am Nona. I greet you in the love and in the light of the infinite Creator. We have been called to this group this evening to offer our healing sounds and we thank this group for requesting healing. We are not much used to words, and so will take leave [of] you except for our song. We are those of Nona.

(Carla channels a healing melody from Nona.)

Intensive Meditation
May 13, 1987

(Carla channeling)

I am Quanta. I greet this company in the love and in the light of the infinite Creator. It is my privilege to have been called to this group, and we are most thankful for this honor. We would speak briefly through this instrument and attempt to continue through all the instruments, for we wish to exercise the new channel known as W in a more creative fashion during this working, if the instrument is in agreement. The philosophical thoughts which we wish to impart are indeed general, yet we hope they are helpful. It is our desire to express through each channel's words some thoughts concerning meditation and the balance that love may bring to the hurly-burly of day-to-day activity. We offer you then a meditation of [all this.]

Across the infinite expanse of interstellar space lies strewn the Creator's field of celestial flowers—the seeds of consciousness. Each sun, held in perfect stasis while constantly moving by the dynamics of all of the fields which surround it, which are part of it, which it has created. Each sun which contains planets in turn washes the balance of those beings which dwell upon the surface of the planet, for many inhabited planets there are. And within each planet those flames, flickering with consciousness, which are called humankind upon your planet, create in their turn an infinity of small and large thoughts, thrown off and rotating as planets about the sun.

Thus, the entity whose mind is in balance is sustained and sustaining just as is your sun; held in place and holding in place by its planets—the thoughts, the children of its love. And when the mind is not in balance, then do the thoughts become confused and go awry, for the Creator's hand is not in the midst of them, that creator being your own consciousness. When that which has been created achieves ascendancy over the Creator, then are things truly out of balance. How blessed it is, then, to seek the balance of love and light in daily meditations, for meditation is a wellspring of balance, light and love.

We would at this time transfer this contact to the one known as W, requesting that this instrument merely say what comes into the mind, word by word and phrase by phrase, fearing not, for that which is sufficient shall be given. We commend the instrument on challenging and tuning. We are pleased. We would now transfer. We are known to you as Quanta.

(Long pause.)

(W channeling)

I am Quanta, and I greet you in the love and in the light of the infinite Creator. This instrument is having some difficulty—correction—we were having some difficulty in adjusting to this instrument's *(inaudible)* in establishing contact with the one known as W. We are now readjusting and making a stronger, more established contact so that there will be less difficulty in utilizing this instrument.

We would like to continue with the story and establish the desire, teach. The Earth is a sphere which has the purpose of radiating energy into the galaxy. The sun also in its turn radiates to the Earth. There is a symbiotic *(inaudible)* relationship established between the two planets without which neither one would exist. This relationship [is] also established from the balance of the outer and inner roles which one must maintain [with regard] this planet, for it can either be outer or inner, but the combination of the two such that harmony is achieved between the outer and inner meditation is a way of establishing better harmony between outer and inner by giving to that [end role] which needs to be more firmly established, by quietly sitting and meditating upon all of the ways one becomes more attuned to the inner sanctuary of the spirit, not just the occupation with the physical.

So it is indeed an important daily practice to meditate and find that inner sanctuary and establish a workable relationship with the environment around which we are surrounded. Similar to the Earth and the sun, your outer and inner roles need a balance and communication in order to coexist. If one or the other were to dominate, the balance is disrupted *(inaudible)*.

At this time we would like to further establish contact with the one known as W [with aid in developing] a *(long pause)* another entity. We are pleased with the progress and wish to commend the improvement in the vocal channeling. We have begun quite satisfactorily, and soon we wish to aid in establishing contact through *(inaudible)*. It is quite an honor to be allowed to realize *(inaudible)* for the purpose of vocal channeling. We wish to thank you all once again for allowing us to do so.

As we adjust the contact, we are having some difficulty in maintaining with this contact as we adjust to her energy levels. At this time we would like to transfer to the one known as Jim, but we continue to adjust this instrument. We are known to you as the one that is known as Quanta. We will now transfer to the one known as Jim.

(Jim channeling)

I am Quanta, and we greet you again through this instrument. It is our desire at this time to allow the one known as W to enhance her recognition of the deepened state of meditation and to enhance her ability to receive a discernible contact while in this state so that there might in future experiences become possible the contact from others who wait to speak through this new instrument. When the basic and more mechanical aspects of the vocal channeling process have been mastered to a sufficient degree, it is then that the new instrument may find itself in the position of needing to refine means by which contact is recognized and transmitted, for the new instrument begins to make a progress which then is less mechanical and more inner or metaphysical in nature, this refining having to do with the careful alignment of the inner sensing which will become the most vital tool for the new instrument as it begins another stage of its work.

At this time we feel that we have taken the one known as W as deeply as is comfortable to this new instrument, and have allowed her to begin to open to a greater extent the deeper doors of perception that she will utilize in a continuing fashion as she improves and perseveres with the vocal channeling process. Thus, we shall at this time open this gathering to any queries which those present may feel appropriate in asking.

W: Can you answer questions regarding crystals?

I am Quanta, and we have had experience of a general nature with the crystal and would be happy to share that which is ours to share.

W: Is there a reason why I'm drawn to crystals? Could you explain that?

I am Quanta, and we find in this instance that the query points not so much in the direction of the crystal as it does in the direction of the personal inclinations which are part of your own pattern of experience that draws not only from this incarnation but from others which have the use of the crystal form much imbedded within their patterns.

May we speak further, my sister?

W: In regards to crystals themselves, what are the properties of the amethyst?

I am Quanta, and we look at the crystal which you have called the amethyst and see that the character of this crystal is one which is useful in a general sense for the soothing, calming or pacifying of a basic attitude of the mind complex, for the crystal is one which works as more of the broadband transmitter of the calming qualities of light and tends to balance the mental faculties which have been much overused, shall we say.

May we speak further, my sister?

W: What is the significance of the double terminated quartz?

I am Quanta, and we again may speak in a general fashion with the qualification given that each particular crystal may be used in a variety of fashions by any seeker and may be used in an even greater variety of fashions by various seekers. There are certain functions which each crystal more easily fulfills than would another, and as we look at the quartz crystal which has the double terminix, as you have called it, we see the general quality of enhancing the meditative state when placed in a certain ratio position by the seeker, this varying from the placement directly above the crown chakra to the position of being held in the palm of the hand which rests upon the lap. The use in this instance being to allow a clearer movement of intelligent energy through the entire system of energy centers or chakras, first focusing upon the ingress of intelligent energy, then upon its outflow.

May we speak further, my sister?

W: No, thank you.

I am Quanta, and we thank you, my sister. Are there any further queries at this time?

Carla: Will it be possible for W to work with the contact which desires to speak with her within a challenging situation in which I am challenging in the name of Christ?

I am Quanta, and we find this quite acceptable, my sister.

Carla: Thank you.

I am Quanta, and we thank you, my sister. Is there a further query?

Carla: Then the presence that I sensed right before W began having trouble catching the contact, that it was a negative entity which was not the contact—is that correct? Because I challenged him until he went away.

I am Quanta, and again this is correct, my sister.

Carla: Thank you.

I am Quanta, and again we thank you. Is there a further query?

Carla: Not from me, thank you.

W: I'm experiencing a deeper sense of a meditation than I have since we've been working, and I'm curious about that, and I'm wondering if the entity which chooses to channel through me is also present?

I am Quanta, and the deepened state of meditation is that which has been achieved through a combination of your desire to serve in this fashion and our desire to aid in your service. The entity which awaits the possibility of speaking through your instrument is not at this time in the appropriate configuration, shall we say, to utilize your instrument, but instead observes from a position that allows it to experience some of your contact circuitry, shall we say, which is a way of describing the configuration of mind and beliefs and desires which arrange the deeper mind in such and such a fashion that makes it unique. Thus, this entity begins to familiarize itself with this configuration as you travel deeper into your own subconscious mind.

May we speak further, my sister?

W: On a slightly different tack. I've yet to feel comfort—connected to my guides and my higher self. Are they present, and what would facilitate establishment of a better contact?

I am Quanta, and we might suggest that the contact of which you speak is one which is not normally a comfortable or easily established and proven state for the third-density illusion. Such contact is that which has its season, shall we say, according to need and opportunity. The conscious efforts of the seeker to establish a mystery-filled contact are often the primary obstacles in the accomplishment of this contact. We might suggest the calm and peaceful relaxation into the knowledge that such contact is always available and need not demonstrate itself in any fashion which is consciously perceivable.

May we speak further, my sister?

W: No, thank you.

I am Quanta, and again we thank you, my sister. Is there a further query at this time?

(Pause)

I am Quanta, and we wish to thank each for allowing us to join your meditation and to speak our humble words through each instrument. We feel that there has been progress made by each this evening, and we look to your future gatherings for the opportunity to enhance that which has begun. At this time we shall release our use of this instrument and take our leave of this group. We are your brothers and sisters of Quanta. We leave you in the love and in the light of the one infinite Creator. Adonai, my friends. Adonai. ☥

Sunday Meditation
May 17, 1987

Group question: From J, having to do with the nature of electricity. We use electricity, but nobody really knows what it is, the engineers or the scientists, and J was wondering if there might be a better description, perhaps even in metaphysical terms, as to the nature of electricity, what it is and how it really works.

(Carla channeling)

I am Q'uo. I greet you in the love and in the light of the one infinite Creator. We rejoice at the joining of our vibrations and thank you for calling us to your meeting this evening. You wish to know something about electricity. Indeed, many among your peoples would wish to understand this power and force in order that it might be exploited, yet all have firsthand experience of the nature of electricity, for that which is called electricity is one manifestation of the love of the one infinite Creator. One might perhaps think of it as electrical desire.

We find it difficult to speak forthrightly through this instrument, for the concepts which we place within the instrument's head have no objective referent within her experience. However, we do wish and feel we are able to say through this instrument that there is no electricity that is free of the bias which is the companion of electricity, that being magnetic effect, for, in truth, electricity is a part of the way the Creator has drawn forth the created universe from that which was not articulate at the beginning of this creation.

The experience which most among your peoples enjoy in its appropriate time which is electrical in nature is the experience of your physical orgasm. That creative act is that which not only puts forth material which may become viable for a physical vehicle, but also puts it forth in a biased manner so that there is an electrical combination as well as a physical merging of the male and female cells. Thus, each infant has at the very beginning of its life that which is known as electricity to thank for the viability of the physical vehicle.

The galvanizing effect of your electricity is well known among your peoples, yet perhaps there has been within the mind and spirit the experience of the galvanizing electrical effect of some entity's concepts and words, some entity's deeds which provoke one to an electrical feeling of excitement, reverence or awe.

Metaphysically speaking, that which is creative is that which has electricity. That which is creative is that which shapes. That which is creative is that which empowers.

There is an alignment of love in such a way that love is bonded in passion to light, thus causing sense to form of that which was before made of no consciousness. The secret of electricity lies in its generative and creative possibilities, and, indeed, although this instrument is not aware of any information of this kind, we believe we can impress upon this instrument that there is a large body of material and research done by scientists for many of your years upon the fascinating effects of love aligning light, that is, electricity, and its effects upon living organisms.

In your future it is possible that the increased understanding of electricity and magnetism as being love and light shall bring about a culture in which electricity may be used in simple and subtle ways to aid in the prevention of the development of diseases which are in some way egregious in the balance of one or another polarity. Electricity then will be measured in terms of its shaping ability—that is, its electromagnetic ability and its field effect instead of merely in terms of the force of charge or the amount of it.

However, it is not necessary for those who seek to uncover the face of mystery to wait for the scientific acumen to reach that which is intuitively known already among many of your peoples. It is quite possible to work with the meditative time in such a way as to include within the meditation a fairly intensive period of tuning the mind and spirit more and more keenly upon one galvanizing image. Meditation upon this image with fixed intensity will bring about a heightened and changed mental attitude. It is a difficult practice and one which sometimes may be slow in producing results, however, it is quite rewarding for those who seek the inner electricity which some have called ritual magic.

The steady visualization of an electrifying image in order to evoke its wondrous energies is the purpose of many positively oriented magical rituals. The steady visualization may be of any object, however we suggest that the visualization object be an object which is, indeed, electrifying and exciting, evocative of all that is best and highest in the life experience thus far. The meditation is held in visualization of one image until the mind becomes fatigued. This shall occur at first very quickly, but the student will find that practice does increase the concentrated power and thus the metaphysical electrical effect of the …

(Pause)

I am Q'uo, and I greet you once again in love and light. We are sorry, but this instrument was feeling out of its depth, and we lost contact with it as it was analyzing. You see, there is no such thing as too much experience. To finish the sentence of the image.

(Pause)

We are attempting merely to reestablish the contact, and thank you for your patience. We are sorry that we do not have an instrument with a larger vocabulary, however, we have found that in some ways those with no preconceived ideas of the nature of a thing often make clearer channels to the extent of their vocabulary than those who feel they understand a phenomenon and merely wish to improve that understanding.

Perhaps what we would like to offer before we leave this instrument is the encouragement to view the self as a person possessed of the fire and brilliance of electricity, for each seeker has a consciousness, and that consciousness is of love, love unmanifest and unpolarized and love electrified by desire. Each entity is incredibly powerful, making and remaking the creation each and every day of the life experience. Whatever this day has been, it is what you have made it. Whatever this night brings to you is brought to you as a favor to yourself by yourself. All is desire and the fulfillment of desire, and the more that that desire is carefully considered and single-heartedly placed, the more that the life experience will be heartfelt, single-minded, glad and productive.

When a seeker views the self as one which is acted upon by circumstance, one then sees the self lying down before the electricity of experience and having that experience burned into self. We suggest that the human desire has the strongest and highest electricity, metaphysically speaking, which is available upon the planet Earth in the third density at this time. Thus, the will, the heart, and the soul of humankind is far more powerful than any problem, any disease, or any natural phenomenon. Exceptions will be made in natural phenomena by appeal to a higher electricity, a higher creativity, a higher understanding of love.

May your meditations be full of the Creator which is love, and as you muse and contemplate upon the great mystery of the one great original Thought which is the Creator, may you become more and more imbued with the sense that electrically and creatively you shall happen to your environment and to those circumstances which greet you. Let *you* be the actor which decides what part to play, not one which hurriedly makes entrances and exits without ever quite learning the lines. See yourself as powerful in love and light.

We thank you for allowing us to work with this instrument with this query, and would at this time transfer to the other instrument in order that any questions which you may have may be answered. We would at this time transfer. We are those of Q'uo.

(Jim channeling)

I am Q'uo, and greet each again through this instrument in love and in light. We would at this time like to open this gathering to any further queries which those present may have to offer for our opinions and thoughts. May we speak to any query at this time?

J: Yes. From tonight's session I understood that in order to increase our own personal electricity and magnetism, we can meditate upon a single image, and that image should be electrifying and evocative in nature. My question is, what would be—once this is done to the point where one does increase his electricity—what is the manifestation of that? What does the individual experience?

I am Q'uo, and we are aware of your query, my brother. The focus of the desire upon an ideal or image which has emotional value and spiritual potential, shall we say, for the seeker is effective within the seeker's experience. When the focus has been as sharply drawn as is possible for the seeker to accomplish with the combination of inner images and intensified desire along the chosen path, the manifestation of such a focus of intentions is what you may call the vitality of the life experience. Some have given it the name *élan vital* or the joy of living which the greater influx of directed love, prana or energy has provided to the seeker as a result of the seeker's forming a channel or circuit for this influx of love and its creative power.

Thus, each moment is seen with new eyes and felt with new sensation, and the vitality of creation is made more available to the seeker who has been able to focus its being in a manner which resonates in harmony with those potentials within each succeeding energy center or chakra of each seeker.

May we speak further, my brother?

J: The process of the raising of the kundalini from the base chakra to the crown, is this an electrical process?

I am Q'uo, and though we find that it would be incorrect to describe this process as merely an electrical process, it is a process that contains the qualities of the movement of energy in a fashion which is similar to the movement of electricity through various circuits.

The south or magnetic pole of the seeker at the base of the spine and soles of the feet draws into the auric field of the seeker the catalyst or unprocessed experience which the seeker shall work upon according to its unique configuration of energy center blockages and clear circuit pathways. Thus, each seeker will perceive the daily round of activities in a manner which is congruent with this configuration of energy centers and will find its focus of attention drawn to the level or frequency of vibration that is appropriate for its current learning.

As succeeding energy centers or circuit areas within the energy centers of the seeker are opened and balanced to a minimal degree through a great portion of time and experience, the prana or love of the Creator will move further and further up the, as you have called it, path of the kundalini until there is the mating with the guiding light or Polaris of the self, where the seeker is already at one with the creation, so that an experience of conscious unity with the creation becomes available to the seeker. This completing of the circuit of the series of energy centers has been described by many of your peoples using various terminology, the enlightenment, the contact with intelligent infinity, the nirvana, as some call it,

Thus, the seeker may be seen as a configuration of circuits or series of lessons and balances to achieve, with each day offering further opportunity to move the flow of love further along the inner pathways that will eventually culminate in the bringing into harmonic resonance each portion of the seeker's being.

May we speak further, my brother?

J: Would it be possible to expedite this process of the raising of the kundalini by the use of electrodes at, let's say, the base and the crown chakras with a small amount of current induced between those two poles? I'll leave my question at that.

I am Q'uo, and though the physical vehicle may be enhanced in its ability to transmit various forms of electrical current, we find that any specific technique of a mechanical nature which lacks the metaphysical principle of the processing of catalyst as the primary means by which the mind, body and spirit are prepared in unison for the increased flow of prana or love energy is a technique which invites some degree of imbalance within the entity's total being and is that which would therefore be less than efficacious in the overall progress of the entity's mind, body and spirit complexes.

May we speak further, my brother?

J: The Atlanteans, we know, used crystals in many ways, and I wonder if they had the same understanding or use of, or let me say, the technology that we possess today of electricity, or was their technology more based on the use of crystals and galvanic materials?

I am Q'uo, and as we distill and translate the capabilities of this civilization of which you speak, we find that there was much of the present technological abilities with the addition of various others which were also utilized in a fashion which was distorted toward the manipulation of things, peoples and events for specific purposes rather than the utilization of the available technologies for the enhancement of the evolutionary goals of each citizen. Therefore, the direction of technological advance and movement within this society was that which turned toward the negative pole more than was able to be sustained in a manifested sense by this culture and those about it which eventually resulted in the down-sinking of this culture as a result of the separation of entities culminating in the condition that you call war.

May we speak further, my brother?

J: No, thank you. That's all the questions I have.

I am Q'uo, and we thank you, my brother. Is there another query at this time?

H: Yeah. Did Edgar Cayce use electricity in any of his healing processes?

I am Q'uo, and as we attempt to scan the contributions of this particular entity, we find that the allusions to the use of the quality which you call electricity is most general in some locations within this body of work and does not partake of the specifically applied use of the power of the electrical current.

May we speak further, my brother?

H: Not on that. I don't think there's anything else. Thank you.

I am Q'uo, and we thank you, my brother. Is there another query?

Carla: I have two short questions. First of all, is there a unified field theory that can be discovered in third density, or is it going to have to wait to fourth density? Is it this metaphysical aspect that's causing us all to be unable to figure it out?

I am Q'uo, and we find that the conceptualizations which are necessary to grasp the nature of the various forces which are considered primary within your illusion are conceptualizations which must be the result of removing various portions of the veil of mystery which is so great a portion of your fabric of illusion. There are many who have discovered significant portions of the concepts that will yield the eventual unification of the various theories of the source and motivational power of energy. However, this final goal is that which draws many within your illusion forward in their seeking, and the mere seeking is that which is most helpful in the resolving of the mysteries of your very being.

May we speak further, my sister?

Carla: No, thank you, I appreciate that. The other question is just, I suspect that you'd rather deal with this as a general question, but I didn't know for sure. And I wondered, is it correct that you would prefer to treat as a general question advice on someone about to be married. I wouldn't mind hearing what you have to say on the subject.

I am Q'uo, and we find that it is possible to speak in any fashion which is desired …

(Side one of tape ends.)

(Jim channeling)

I am Q'uo, and am again with this instrument, and greet each in love and in light. We would ask, my sister, if you wish us to speak briefly upon this topic or would wish to have the topic as a general query at another time?

Carla: If you are willing to treat it as a general query, I would prefer that. Actually, I'd prefer to hear it at length, this is—you know. So we'll wait until next week on it. Thank you.

I am Q'uo, and we thank you, my sister. Is there another query?

(Pause)

I am Q'uo, and we are most grateful to have had offered to us those concerns in your journey of seeking which you have so joyfully shared with us this evening. We cannot express in words the gratitude that we feel for being allowed to share our humble thoughts with you upon those topics which are of concern in your thinking and in your being. We look forward to each such gathering with this group, and would at this time take our leave of this instrument and this group. We are known to you as those of Q'uo, and we leave each in the love and in the light of the one infinite Creator. Adonai, my friends. Adonai.

L/L Research

Intensive Meditation
May 20, 1987

(W channeling)

I am Quanta, and I greet you in the love and the light of the one infinite Creator. We are pleased to be with you once again. It is an honor for us to share with you …

(Very softly spoken. The rest of the beginning portion is inaudible.)

We would like to begin this *(inaudible)* with a story.

There was a time when the earth was dark and *(inaudible)* to the light of the universe. This light *(inaudible)* desert of *(inaudible)*. There appeared a spark which *(inaudible)*. For the spark. Chose this planet to serve as a beacon to the universe, to speak of love, to shine for a beacon of love in the cosmos. *(inaudible)* wished that the planet …

(The rest of the story is inaudible.)

We are pleased with the progress of the one known as W. She has successfully responded to the challenge of initiating *(inaudible)*. We would like to thank her for her willingness to refrain from analysis and attempt to connect *(inaudible)* with the concepts which we have put forth. We would now transfer to the one known as Carla. I am Quanta. We leave in the love and the light.

(Carla channeling)

I am now with this instrument. I am Quanta and greet you through this instrument in the love and light of the One Who Is All. And so you sit in meditation in 1987, attempting to ponder the mystery of the truth, attempting to see through thick darkness the outlines of eternity and to grasp the nature of the Love that created all that there is. And as we seek and grope in the darkness of our thoughts and of mundane concerns and of the world in general, we perhaps feel as though we have come not to the epitome of creation, but to its beginnings. And, indeed, that we feel that as much as do you, for though we are just a bit further along the road than are you, still we feel like rough diamonds indeed.

And yet, that image of diamonds is one we would ask you to hold before you, for that spark, that light, that fire which has brought forth shape, substance, form and particularity brings forth now each of you. And each of you then must needs attempt to become gemlike and crystalline that you may trap light, increase it, divert it, and become reflective illuminations of gathered light, that the sparks may keep shining out of each entity's eyes, so that those who are still truly in the darkness of earth and mundane affairs may see that there is joy and peace bubbling forth from the face and personality of those who seek the light and the love of the one Creator. You are part of the spark of the divine. You are the

Creator to those whom you meet and greet and speak with. Thus, encourage yourself to seek light, to dwell in light and to commune with light, for the story of creation continues with you.

We would pause at this time while maintaining some contact with each member of this group in order that the one known as W may, if both contact and instrument agree, experience some conditioning from an entity which has wished to use the one known as W. This is a delicate matter and we appreciate the patience if those present. We shall now pause. We ask the one known as W to remember those things which have been discussed concerning challenging and, above all, tuning. Perhaps as the weeks have gone by, the one known as W has found more and more surely that nature of the self which aids so much in the tuning. We are those of Quanta.

(Long pause.)

I am Quanta, and am again with this instrument. We are pleased that there has been some contact. We did not wish it to go on for too long a period at first, for it is beyond our ability to nourish the contact until it is more seated within both the contact and the instrument. There is a certain amount of delicacy to this since there is a crossing of dimension. We therefore greatly thank the one known as W and would now transfer to the one known as Jim. I am Quanta.

(Jim channeling)

I am Quanta, and greet each again through this instrument in love and in light. At this time we would offer ourselves in the attempt to speak to those queries which those present may have for us, reminding each that we offer but that which is our experience and our opinion. May we begin with a query?

Carla: What dimension is crossed by the contact in attempting to contact W? Is it third or fourth density, since it's using Quanta and then back to third—is that it?

I am Quanta, and the density that must be traversed is that of the fourth density which attempts to speak to one within the third density using an intermediary, shall we say, which is ourselves, that may facilitate a crossing for both the contact and the instrument.

May we speak further, my sister?

Carla: So the contact is fourth density?

I am Quanta, and this is correct, my sister.

Carla: Thank you.

I am Quanta, and we thank you, my sister. Is there another query?

Carla: Is it fourth density and on this planet or fourth density from elsewhere?

I am Quanta. The entity of which we speak is of the fourth density with this particular planetary sphere as its home planet, for it has for a significant portion of your time and experience been a resident of the inner planes of this particular planetary sphere, having achieved the graduation previously as a result of the incarnations spent fruitfully pursuing polarity upon this planet.

May we speak further, my sister?

Carla: Well, I would like to make a guess that it's one of the Brotherhood of the Seven Rays, the group that the contact known as Ra said that one hundred and fifty of them achieved harvestability in the second major cycle of this master cycle, but decided not to go on, but rather to stay here and help others. Is it that group that is attempting to contact W?

I am Quanta, and this is basically correct, my sister, though there is much which must remain somewhat hidden at this point and left to the discoveries of the one known as W in the adjusting of the vibrations to accommodate this contact.

Carla: Yes. Well, sufficient unto the day are the revelations thereof. Thank you very much. That's interesting.

I am Quanta, and we thank you once again, my sister. Is there another query?

W: I have a question I'm not sure you can answer or not. I have the impression—I've been working lately as a waitress—that I'm there for another reason than for just making a living. Is this part of the work which I am here to do or is this part of, is this sort of like a master plan sort of thing to be in contact with other people and awakening them to other possibilities? Can you give me any information on that?

I am Quanta, and we may speak by suggesting that there are no portions of any conscious seeker's life experience which are not significant portions of the incarnational plan. Much is hidden from the conscious eye and all the senses of the seeker, even for those activities which are well worn within the seeker's experience, for the eye of third density does not penetrate far past the surface of things on a frequent basis, but dwells in that realm where shape and shadow move and intermingle with seeming randomness. Yet, each experience and encounter contains the seeds of that garden which has been planned carefully aforetimes, and who can say when any seed shall be nourished sufficiently to take root and produce the fruit that was desired?

Thus, my sister, we might suggest that you look at each moment within your incarnational experience as that which is precious and sacred and designed to provide you the perfect opportunity for your own growth and your service to others.

May we speak further, my sister?

W: No, thank you.

I am Quanta, and we thank you, my sister. Is there another query?

W: We're going to be having a break in our meditations for a short period of time. Is there anything in particular other than the daily meditations which might facilitate the establishment of connection with this other entity I'm attempting to channel?

I am Quanta, and we can only suggest that the daily meditations be pursued with the regularity and desire for service that you have thus far demonstrated. It is the perseverance and regularity of perseverance which prepares each seeker to become regularized and crystallized enough to transmit those higher frequencies of love and compassion which each has incarnated to do. Thus, the seeming mundane nature of setting aside a few moments each day dedicated to seeking and serving are most helpful in this regard.

May we speak further, my sister?

W: I have another query. I have been getting in touch with a lot of feelings around *(inaudible)*, through illuminating them. As I do that I am more capable of experiencing love for myself and for others, and I have at times experienced what I would consider a lack of compassion towards, and I'm wondering if that is a true observation on my part or if it's because I'm so used to old patterns that I do not recognize compassion in the new patterns. Can you respond to that in any way?

I am Quanta. You may find as you pursue the uncovering of those feelings which have long been covered that there spring up further feelings which may also require the attention that you have given to the first feelings. Thus, if any feeling has not yet found its fruit of love, compassion and acceptance for any other entity or experience, you may consider pursuing that feeling with the same technique of magnification until the feeling draws unto itself its opposite balance, and within this balance of feelings then may be birthed the compassion which equals the acceptance that each portion of the one Creator has as its birthright. This technique is best accomplished, we find, within your contemplative or meditative states as the focus is much more finely tuned in this state of awareness.

May we speak further, my sister?

W: I'm not sure I fully understand the technique which you suggest I use in meditation. Could you be a little bit more specific and clarify it for me?

I am Quanta, and we have some difficulty with this instrument for we draw some from the instrument's experience and it is somewhat doubtful that this is helpful. However, we shall continue.

The feelings of which you speak that are difficult yet for you might be taken with you into the meditative state and enhanced until they become large, large enough to draw to them their opposite. Within this balance may then lie acceptance of oneself for allowing the Creator to experience Itself through one's feelings, thoughts and actions.

May we speak further my sister?

W: I have another question. During a discussion we had earlier this evening, we were talking about channeling and were questioning whether the person's channeling could result in, like, a divergence from the spiritual path as opposed to—in other words getting too involved in the channeling and therefore not continuing on their own spiritual path and become too dependent on channeling. Not that I'm too concerned about it at this point, but it's a good point raised and I'm wondering in what ways my pursuance of channeling will either distract or enhance along the spiritual path?

I am Quanta, and this cannot be said, my sister, for it is a function of your free will. We are aware that many give great weight to the words that are spoken by those unseen and who utilize instruments such as those gathered this evening. When one allows any portion of the path of seeking to take on proportions that are larger than one's own discrimination, then it might be suggested that other avenues of investigation be pursued in order to balance that which has been overemphasized. Any seeker may take any portion of the one creation and follow it to the Source of All That Is. The seeker who travels the trail most efficiently is one who moves with the lightest of touches and does not feel overattached to any portion of the creation, seeing it all as a portion of the puzzle, giving each portion its due and moving further onward.

May we speak further, my sister?

W: No. Thank you very much.

I am Quanta, and we thank you, my sister. Is there another query at this time?

W: I have no further queries.

Carla: Nor have I, but thank you very much.

I am Quanta, and we thank each as well, for by this opportunity of speaking through each instrument, we are able to learn the needs of yet another portion of the Creator, and move in a pattern of service that would not be possible if we had not been invited to join this circle of seeking. We look forward to each gathering with the hope of continuing our own learning and service. At this time we shall take our leave of this instrument and this group. We are known to you as those of Quanta. We leave each in the love and the light of the infinite Creator. Adonai, my friends. Adonai. ☙

L/L Research

L/L Research is a subsidiary of Rock Creek Research & Development Laboratories, Inc.

P.O. Box 5195
Louisville, KY 40255-0195

www.llresearch.org

Rock Creek is a non-profit corporation dedicated to discovering and sharing information which may aid in the spiritual evolution of humankind.

ABOUT THE CONTENTS OF THIS TRANSCRIPT: This telepathic channeling has been taken from transcriptions of the weekly study and meditation meetings of the Rock Creek Research & Development Laboratories and L/L Research. It is offered in the hope that it may be useful to you. As the Confederation entities always make a point of saying, please use your discrimination and judgment in assessing this material. If something rings true to you, fine. If something does not resonate, please leave it behind, for neither we nor those of the Confederation would wish to be a stumbling block for any.

CAVEAT: This transcript is being published by L/L Research in a not yet final form. It has, however, been edited and any obvious errors have been corrected. When it is in a final form, this caveat will be removed.

© 2009 L/L RESEARCH

Sunday Meditation
June 21, 1987

Group question: On why the question of death and suicide is becoming more prevalent in people's thoughts, not just considering other people's death and suicides, but thinking of their own.

(Carla channeling)

I am Q'uo. I greet you in the love and in the light of the one infinite Creator of whom we are all a part. I greet you furthermore in stone and sky and fence and street and city. I greet you in the many details of creation, from the smallest to the greatest. I greet you in the riches of consciousness and of each others' consciousnesses. It is a great privilege to be called to your meeting for the purpose of talking about why many find thoughts of death and suicide to have happened into their minds in the last few years.

We find that there are two parts to answering this query. One portion is more basic than the other, and it is with that that we will start.

We have used the terms "the way of that which is" to describe the path of the positive polarity and "the path of that which is not" to describe the path of negative polarity. Both paths reach the same Creator. The mind is what is usually considered to the exclusion of any other asset or dynamic of an individual, and yet the body with its complex working arrangements and provisions for various contingencies of survival, constitutes another way of expressing and manifesting the path of that which is and the path of that which is not.

The body is by definition both positive and negative in polarization. Like the path of that which is, it grows, expands and develops. Following the path of that which is not, it seemingly dies. In general, then, you would say that there is a natural progression within the mind complex as the physical vehicle partakes less and less of growth and more and more of gradual self-destruction, that the mind complex would begin receiving as echoes from the body complex thoughts pertaining to the logical end of various minor frailties which begin to be experienced as a living entity increases in age.

As the body complex grows more and more to embrace the path of that which is not—that is, as the body participates more and more in that grand illusion of death and separation—so the mind is affected. Furthermore, as the body ages, so does the mind, and events begin to batter some mind complexes with their intensity. This grows more frequent as body and mind become more tired, worn and the feeling of inadequacy towards the physical situation or the emotional situation deepens.

We find that there is, however, at this time a second dynamic which has accelerated the process of what you would call aging. As mind and body housed together enter with the Earth itself new areas of space and new vibratory patterns of subatomic particles, the conditions upon your sphere are naturally changing, so that the mind is made more powerful than previously to affect the body. Year by year, as we understand your time demarcations, the body becomes less and less able to distinguish between the thoughts in the mind complex and the thoughts, if you may call it that, of the body complex itself. Thus, woes and travails, that would perhaps not come into physical manifestation but would merely be dealt with as situations, are now taking their toll in illness, both emotional or mental and physical.

It is thought patterns that have always been part of the vocabulary of humankind, but year by year these thoughts become more powerful. Thus, more than ever before, we find it is good to stress the precious nature of positive affirmation. When the mind despairs, grieves, feels anger or has resentment, it causes the mind complex a certain amount of difficulty. More than that, as you have experienced with new diseases, it can cause physical illness and death.

In the fourth density you will find that these thoughts are, indeed, of that nature, that is, that that which is thought occurs. Each entity has the power at all times to think into reality a desired result. Indeed, the most general of affirmations having to do with the faith that all will work out well is more medicine than any prescription which can be offered by any druggist. That precious state of mind in which one is at peace and feels full of the life and spirit of the Creator …

(Pause)

We are Q'uo and we apologize for this pause. We shall continue.

The positively oriented frame of mind is to be prized more and more, for it is the most efficient tool for protecting your third-density physical vehicles and insuring a continuing good association between mind, spirit and body. The intensity of events and feelings not only has been increasing, but will continue to increase, until at some point—we would not wish to guess how many decades from now—it will no longer be possible for the third-density physical vehicle to dwell upon planet Earth.

However, it will be unnoticeable to those who live and die in third density, for those now being born among your societal groups have a dual activated body. You will find these new entities far more full of energy than one would think possible. It is an energy to which third-density physical vehicles alone cannot associate very well. It does not give each of you more pep and vigor unless the attempt is made on a regular basis to evolve the frame of mind into that frame of mind which avoids negative thought. This frame of mind, of course, is best pursued in meditation.

Look at that which is your consciousness with a cold eye, in the abstract, and you shall see at the heart a gem, invisible except by faith, and surrounding it the rough shape of the unhewn, unfaceted stone. The crystal qualities are there, but they lie waiting for the skilled hand of the artisan to chip and facet until the heart of the stone has been revealed in all of its polished splendor.

Each of you has some control over this process of crystallization of the personality. It takes a great deal of dedication to correct lifelong habits of negative assertion, and we are aware that although many may see this information and nod, very few will be those that will actually attempt a continuously positive mindset. Moreover, we find that among your peoples the distractions of your culture have become the dumping ground for negatively oriented thought patterns, and that often the ceaseless voice of the media speaks to those who have the choice between distraction and negative imprinting and coming face to face with the intense reality of the moment and forging for the first time a truly positive mindset.

The desire to trust is in everyone. The belief in the possibility of crystallization of the personality, of betterment of the personality, of mastery of the self lies within everyone. The discipline which will bring about a continuous effort towards seeking the positive viewpoint in each and every situation is very difficult to maintain.

Yet we say to you that these things are but trifles of the moment. Much of what you attempt will be attempted in such a way that failure is inevitable for reasons that you cannot see within third-density experience. Yet that which has occurred within the mind will live and will be your new personality as once again you gather yourself together for further experience along the road we all travel, the infinite road to the face of the Creator.

Failure, my children, is completely irrelevant to the value of your attempt. You see, each of you will be claimed by death, or so it will seem. The reason for this is that illusions are just that—illusions. They are created and they have their moment and then they pass. That which is at your center, at your core, is a portion of the infinite love, the great original Thought which has never come into manifestation and is not manifested within you, but lies rather as the dynamo, the reality that fires and underlies all experience. It has sent out into the creation, for a marvelous merry-go-round of infinite proportions, your spirit in exploration.

And so you explore and report and gather your strength and again explore. And so do we all. The fire that lies within you can never be touched, can never be altered, but can only be eventually found because you have honed the personality until it is brilliant and clear and the properties of the crystal are yours. Then may you carry light as the Creator is Light. You do this now, but in a distorted manner. You ponder now, you suffer now. May we hope that you also heed that side of you which is most in touch with the light and love within, so that you may see the impermanence of all that seems to die.

We find that we have tired the instrument somewhat. It has been some time since this instrument has channeled. We are disappointed, for we had more to give her. However, we feel that it is best left to another time. We would at this time transfer this contact to the one known as Jim. I am Q'uo.

(Jim channeling)

I am Q'uo, and greet each again in love and light. At this time we would offer ourselves in the capacity of attempting to respond to queries which those present may find have risen in the mind. As always, we remind each that we give but our opinion and wish that to be understood in order that we may speak freely without overweighing any consideration. May we ask if there is a query with which we may begin?

J: Yes, I have a question. It goes along the lines of the words that were just delivered. I've heard a lot of different things about the thought of the person [that] "takes their own life." Some people seem to think that you hardly have a right to do that, and that you build up an awful lot of extra lessons, if you will, that you have to learn, as karma as some people want to call it, crime and punishment, however you want to view it. But I've heard other schools of thought that say that a person, since they are in charge of their own life and responsible for it, and a portion of the Creator, if you determine that that's the end of it, you've done all you can here, you are justified, or you've had the right to go ahead and get out of this life.

Like I say, I've heard that both ways, and I tend to sort of lean toward the last one, but then again my gut feeling, my emotions, would sort of make me afraid to do something like that for fear that I would have to come back and learn a lot of things over again. Can you comment? And is the answer to that maybe just dependent upon the person's belief system, maybe it's that sort of thing?

I am Q'uo, and to answer in a general fashion is misleading, for each entity is one which pursues a course of learning which has been determined by that entity's higher self to be appropriate, each course being pursued within the confines of what you call an incarnation, where the scope or reach of view and experience is limited by birth and death and the veil which separates the conscious and unconscious minds. Thus, it is not so much the act itself within any one incarnation which carries the potential of building a momentum or bias which needs to be balanced at some point within another incarnation that is of importance, but the biasing or building of momentum itself, no matter what the action is which builds this momentum.

For each entity within each incarnation seeks to pursue an exploration of the creation of the one Creator in a fashion which in a cumulative sense throughout all incarnations shall build as a structure of the soul, a foundation and framework which is balanced in nature, in order that the further evolutionary process may be constructed upon firm ground and partake of a symmetrical strength that reflects the wholeness and balance of creation. Thus does each individualized portion of the Creator reflect the wholeness and balance of the one Creator. The entity within any incarnation is the one Creator with the full rights and responsibilities, shall we say, that one may ascribe to such a portion of All That Is.

It may be, however, that when one leaves the boundaries of the incarnational experience, that the increased ability to view that which has come before and that which shall proceed from the incarnation will present to the entity a picture which will convince it that certain actions and thoughts within the incarnation are in need of further balancing experience or that which you call the karma. Thus, it may not be said with definite surety that any one action or even a series of actions or thoughts will guarantee that there will be the building of the momentum or karma that must be balanced within a future incarnation, for it may well be that such actions or thoughts are themselves the balance to previous ones which now in a completed sense will allow the entity to pursue further lessons in other areas.

May we speak further, my brother?

J: No, thank you. Thank you very much.

I am Q'uo, and we thank you, my brother. Is there another query?

Carla: Maybe I didn't understand you correctly. You said it depends upon the circumstance a little bit whether taking your own life would be balanced or imbalanced. And it just seems to me that any time you took your own life it would be a definite embracing of the path of that which is not, and therefore it would be an unbalanced act. You're saying, then, that there are balanced suicides, are you not?

I am Q'uo, and we mean to leave the room for the possibilities that in some cases this is so. However, in the general run of the third-density incarnational experience, your assumption concerning the nature of the taking of one's own life is correct in that it is a partaking in that separation of self from the incarnation which reflects the path of that which is not, and this path in its final form pulls that which is and there must eventually be the balanced point of view which the building of the karmic momentum will necessitate within a future, as you would call it, incarnational experience.

May we speak further, my sister?

Carla: Well, it comes to me that perhaps Jesus the Christ was one example when he turned towards Jerusalem of a man who basically committed suicide—he knew he was in trouble when he went there, I mean, he was telling people he was going to die and be raised in three days before he ever went there. And he knew all that was going to happen and it still happened to him, but he thought that he could save other people by it. Is that the kind of suicide that would perhaps qualify for being in balance?

I am Q'uo, and this is correct, my sister, for the taking of one's life or the laying down of one's life for the benefit of others is an action which partakes of that path which is and that path reflects the desire to give of the self in a manner which is of service to others, even if the giving requires that all which one has be given. Thus, one finds within your culture many instances in which the life is given for others and the giving may take a great portion of the incarnation, such as the sacrifices which many of the parents, as you call them, make for the offspring over a great portion of the incarnational experience. Or the giving may be of a moment's inspiration, such as when one of the young soldiers, as you call them, throws itself in harm's way in order that a comrade may survive.

May we speak further, my sister?

Carla: Then, this would presumably extend to psychic danger? If someone threw himself on a psychic grenade it would balance suicide more, wouldn't it?

I am Q'uo, and this is correct, my sister. Though of far, far less occurrence, it is that which is indeed possible.

May we speak further, my sister?

Carla: No, thank you.

I am Q'uo, and we thank you, my sister.

C: Yes. Change the subject a little bit. Once the connection has been made between two people, whereby each can experience, each one is able to pick up on another's problems or virtue, things of that nature, take on part of that to themselves rather than the other, fully experience it, such as one feels an emotional or physical pain and the other is able to absorb part of that. Once a connection like that has been made, does it ever break, short of death?

I am Q'uo, and this type of bonding between entities, my brother, is one which is of strength and soul significance, shall we say, and reflects the garnering of a great amount of experience, usually within a number of incarnations, though it is possible to build such connections within a single incarnation. These connections, when in place and functioning, are those pathways of communion which allow entities to share the conscious experience of the creation in a fashion which not even the process that you call death can separate. This type of connection, however, may be enhanced or reduced in its effect by the attention which is given it once it has been established. However …

(Side one of tape ends.)

(Jim channeling)

I am Q'uo, and am again with this instrument. May we speak further, my brother?

C: How does it work if one doesn't consciously seem to share the experience, yet it still occurs?

I am Q'uo. In this instance, my brother, we find the situation analogous to the piano which has been allowed to go out of tune. The melody is still recognizable, yet there is much of clarity which has been lost.

May we speak further, my brother?

C: I'm not sure I understand what you meant.

I am Q'uo. If one has neglected the conscious exercise of the pathway of communion that enables the consciousness of another to be shared with greater and greater clarity of perception and accuracy of perception, this accuracy and clarity will become somewhat muddied and unclear so that the finer nature of the emotions shared is lost and the more obvious or gross nature of the emotions is that which is communicated over the pathways which have been neglected, shall we say.

May we speak further, my brother?

C: No thank you.

I am Q'uo, and we thank you, my brother. Is there another query?

Carla: I have another query, but I'm still thinking about what you and C just went through, trying to see if I could work on that a little bit, because I thought that was interesting material you gave. I took it that C was saying, "At one time there was communion, and then at some point one stopped wishing communion. Can it be dissolved?" And basically you said, "It doesn't get dissolved—it just goes out of tune." Is that a correct perception of what you said? So, basically what you're saying is, "By avoiding the harmonizing, or your desire not to communicate, deadens you, not the other person." Is that what you're saying?

I am Q'uo, and this is basically correct, yet it must be remembered that if such pathways are unused by the conscious neglect of either party, each will feel the deadening effect.

May we speak further, my sister?

Carla: No, not on that. I would like to ask a question about an experience that I had at the beginning of meditation. I was sitting with my hand in the other instrument's hand and the other hand on the other side of my body and my feet touching at the ankles. And I got a heat buildup to the point where I couldn't believe it—I was really steaming hot. For me that's extremely unusual, especially in my feet. It got so uncomfortable, that just out of impulse I shifted my weight and I moved my feet apart and it felt like a breeze was blowing over me again, which is the way I usually feel when I'm sitting under a fan—which I am. What happened? Where was the heat coming from and why did it go away when I moved my heels apart?

I am Q'uo, and we find that there has been in this particular meditative gathering the influx of energies from our contact which has accentuated a difficulty with the heat-sensing portions of feet, specifically, that have been in recent times more sensitive than usual due to certain effects of the medications which you have been ingesting.

May we speak further, my sister?

Carla: That's interesting. How did I change the situation by moving my feet? It was definitely that movement that changed things.

I am Q'uo, and this gross physical realignment of the feet was analogous to opening a circuit so that the energy in this case manifesting physically as heat was no longer able to move freely and was thus drained away as an open circuit is wont to do.

May we speak further, my sister?

Carla: Not on that subject, thank you.

I am Q'uo, and we thank you. my sister. Is there another query at this time?

J: I don't have a query, but I do have a comment, because I felt the exact same thing. I was sitting over here burning up for about ten or fifteen minutes. And I believe I took my socks and shoes off and that helped a lot. I was grossly *(inaudible)*, so it was the same thing.

I am Q'uo, and we shall comment upon your comment. We find that this particular group is one which has for some period of your time enjoyed a harmonic communion which allows an easy blending of the seeking energies, and this greatly enhances our ability to make contact with this group. And with this enhanced contact, each within the group may feel some physical manifestation, the heat being the most easily and commonly perceived manifestation of the harmonic blending of energies made possible by this particular group configuration. We apologize for any discomfort which our contact may cause and appreciate the comments which alert us to these discomforts.

Is there any further query at this time?

Carla: Well, I've been pondering over in my mind—I'm afraid when I channel I don't really get everything. But it seems to me from what I've got out of the message, that we can help each other, not by throwing ourselves on physical grenades or even psychic grenades—that's for heroes—but help each other by being there. In other words, it seems like sympathy, given out to another person, from some of the things that were said, is truly helpful if the other person catches enthusiasm from it or finds a more positive attitude from it.

It also seems that natural healers, people that can make contact with the harmonics of other people's bodies and minds and souls, have got a real problem. How do they defend themselves from having a life-term relationship with everybody that they meet? How do they avoid the responsibility for what they know about people? Those were two other things that I pondered from the session. If you care to comment, I'd be grateful.

I am Q'uo, and, indeed, it is so, and has been designed in this fashion that each within your illusion has the ability to be of service to those about it in the most basic fashion of simply sharing whatever experience is of concern to another. If there is an experience which is difficult, in that disease or fear of any kind is brought into the conscious mind, the sharing of this concern with another is that which begins the healing process, in that the energies expressing themselves as difficulty have an easier movement through the being when they are freely discussed and shared with another. Thus, the entity with the difficulty is assured at the most basic of levels that it is acceptable to another and that another cares for it and is willing to share with it on the difficulty.

One who seeks to become that called the healer and which on a regular basis places itself in this relationship to another suffering the difficulty, the one serving as healer must, after a portion of experience in this field of service, develop the ability to give of itself to another in a fashion which does not retain the residue, shall we say, of the difficulties being healed. This manner or technique or shielding the self is one which must be constructed by the self in a manner which is congruent with the healer's concept of the healing, the disease, and the part each plays within the greater picture of the incarnation in particular and the creation in general. Thus, the protection, shall we say, must be that which reflects the healer's philosophy of life, as you may call it.

May we speak further, my sister?

Carla: Yes. It seems to me, then, that you're describing two kinds of healing where you could call one of them active, where the healer is sympathetic and sharing and takes on pain in order to ease pain, and impersonal or passive healing, where the healer is nothing more than a catalyst, and actually takes no part whatsoever in the healing. I gather the latter perception from conversations that Don Elkins had with Ra, and the former kind of definition of healing from what we've been talking about here. They seem to be two different types of healing altogether. Would you care to comment?

I am Q'uo, and this description is one which we would suggest describes one process, that of learning to become the healer.

Carla: I see. So the thing to learn is how to get out of the way and not take on pain in order to ease pain, but simply be there. Take in nothing, give out nothing, but be there and act as catalyst. That must be a powerful lesson to learn.

I am Q'uo, and, indeed, my sister, it is one that does partake of that quality known as power and the discipline which is necessary to seek it. Each entity within your illusion may serve as the simplest form of healer by sharing another's difficulties. As one refines the desire and the practice, becoming a healer, one is able to move further along the line of learning this art, so that it is indeed without will and a passive conduit through which the energies of the

Creator may move in the most appropriate fashion for the one to be healed.

May we speak further, my sister?

Carla: Yes. And is that why the first person a healer must heal in the traditional mystical literature is the self, because until one can have the self understood and grasped, one can't get it out of the way?

I am Q'uo, and this is correct, my sister. May we speak further?

Carla: No, thank you very much, it was very interesting.

C: The situation where you're not consciously seeking to heal someone, but your subconscious continues, what best can you do as far as not going to the point where you're damning yourself, taking along others?

I am Q'uo, and it is difficult, my brother, to speak in a specific fashion with the information that is given. However, there is one particular means by which such an entity may at once seek to aid another and yet refrain from absorbing the difficulties of the other. And the means by which this may be accomplished is composed of the heartfelt desire being generated for the well-being of the other, and this desire being given to the other without condition, while at the same time, shall we say, the condition of the other within the mind of the one seeking to heal being seen as whole and perfect and being given over to the greater forces of the higher self for the appropriate action, shall we say. Thus, to give without condition and to see the one which is in need, it would seem, of the healing, as receiving that which is needed and appropriate from those forces of light which surround and inform each entity within each portion of the incarnation.

May we speak further, my brother?

C: I'm only just speaking from personal experience that I'm in a form of almost gun-shy of trying to help heal, but it seems like it still occurs though. It seems that without seeking to do it, others who have sought me out to do it, and I'm not at the time thinking that, yes, I'll take this on, and want to share, but it occurs anyway, *(inaudible)* thoughts where it almost feels like it's damaging to me, just going through the mood changes and physical depression that goes along with it. I know that I want to help, but it seems like at the same I'm doing it involuntarily also.

I am Q'uo, and in this instance, my brother, we may suggest the reflective meditation in which one seeks the deepest level of one's desires that one can find in order that the mind and the heart may join hands in one unified direction in order that the self does not fight against the self.

May we speak further, my brother?

C: No, thank you.

I am Q'uo, and we thank you, my brother. Is there another query?

Carla: Thank you, Q'uo. It was very interesting tonight.

I am Q'uo, and we are full of gratitude for each in this group as well, for we have learned much during this evening of seeking which we rejoice in the learning and in the sharing. We remind each that our words are but opinion and we wish each to be considered as possibilities. We shall take our leave of this group at this time, rejoicing in the love and in the light of the one infinite Creator. We are those of Q'uo. Adonai, my friends. Adonai vasu borragus. ✣

L/L Research

L/L Research is a subsidiary of Rock Creek Research & Development Laboratories, Inc.

P.O. Box 5195
Louisville, KY 40255-0195

www.llresearch.org

Rock Creek is a non-profit corporation dedicated to discovering and sharing information which may aid in the spiritual evolution of humankind.

ABOUT THE CONTENTS OF THIS TRANSCRIPT: This telepathic channeling has been taken from transcriptions of the weekly study and meditation meetings of the Rock Creek Research & Development Laboratories and L/L Research. It is offered in the hope that it may be useful to you. As the Confederation entities always make a point of saying, please use your discrimination and judgment in assessing this material. If something rings true to you, fine. If something does not resonate, please leave it behind, for neither we nor those of the Confederation would wish to be a stumbling block for any.

CAVEAT: This transcript is being published by L/L Research in a not yet final form. It has, however, been edited and any obvious errors have been corrected. When it is in a final form, this caveat will be removed.

© 2009 L/L Research

Sunday Meditation
June 28, 1987

Group question: "Q'uo: You have asked about the metaphysical meaning and implications of covenants, for that is what your marriage is, a covenant, a promise made by two people to each other for a specified span of time and with specified conditions."

(Carla channeling)

I am Q'uo, and I greet you in the love and in the light of the one infinite Creator. I greet you in the love that ties together all that there is, that matches that that cannot be matched, that reconciles those things which cannot be reconciled, and I greet you in light, the light of all manifestation, of all spiritual knowledge, and of all being. I greet you in the one great original Thought of the infinite Creator, for it is in that spirit that we come and that you call us. How grateful we are to be asked to share in your meditation and to blend our vibratory patterns with your own. And how charming the sounds of your domicile and the surrounding neighborhood sound to us as we are able to use this instrument's senses to hear as you hear. It is a very special treat.

You have asked about the metaphysical meaning and implications of covenants, for that is what your marriage is, a covenant, a promise made by two people to each other for a specified span of time and with specified conditions.

What is the function of a covenant? Why do seekers find a universal necessity for finding promises and believing in them? A promise may perhaps be compared to a journey. One who has no clear goal makes an aimless trip and learns many interesting things and grows from the experience. There is grace and beauty to all that happens, yet perhaps the traveler at the end of the journey is disappointed, without being able to put his finger upon the source of the disappointment. Had the seeker who wished to go on a journey thought quietly, he might have set for himself conditions and goals that would give the journey structure and a summit, a place which, having been reached, would serve as a marvelous foundation from which to look back and gather information upon the implications of the journey.

Your peoples have been able to create many, many varieties of acceptable mating procedures. The largest and most common solution to the question of how to handle your people's attractions for each other has been called marriage, and as a social garment it wears well and does the job which the culture requires of it, providing for the care of children and the peaceable life of all people.

Looked at from this point of view, there is no spiritual benefit to be gained from a marriage ceremony, and many of those who enter into marriage certainly do not have the desire to seek out the metaphysical implications of the mated relationship which has been blessed by your orthodox religion. It is merely a commonplace of life, that which is to be done when two people feel that they have fallen in love. Indeed, many of those who wander to your planet find themselves virtually unable to understand or grasp why their brothers and sisters indulge in such a foolish practice.

Yet, there is a great potential for the partners in the marriage ceremony, the potential of the travelers who decide upon their destination and some of the conditions of the journey before they begin, thus shaping perceived experience along the biases of a metaphysically rich life.

The first area to be studied with care and prepared for carefully is the marriage service itself, for there the covenant is made. There spiritual principles are evoked to come to life in the relationship and in the spiritual children of that relationship—the man and the woman which have agreed to work for transformation through marriage. The language of your western culture's marriage ceremonies, though general, is quite adequate to show the covenant as being spiritual, mental and physical.

The promises have to do with honoring, cherishing, serving and loving under any conditions whatsoever. Thus, metaphysically speaking, the marriage ceremony is among the most stringent possible promises or covenants, and requires the greatest degree of which the seeker is capable of loyalty, patience and sacrifice, for those who prepare for the ceremony as they think upon those promises know that difficulties will ensue at an unpredicted time or place with an unpredictable extremity.

Yet, past experience teaches that experience is always variable and that the changes come without warning. Only those entities which believe that they may have a creative effect upon their environment can honestly promise such a covenant, for in the natural run of things, the seeker stumbles often and may, indeed, fail to keep the promises of that long-ago ceremony. And so one prepares for the promise by visualizing and accepting the better and the worse, the balance of all things which shall come after the promise is given.

The second area or arena of importance is that which is immediately lost sight of by those seekers which have entered into the covenant of marriage, and that is the life experience whose shape is too large for the mind within the incarnational experience to picture or fathom. Yet, it is well for the metaphysically oriented seeker to bring into the mind each day the remembrance of the shape of the covenant, the life experience. That which occurs in a day or a week or a month or a year has a far different aspect when looked upon as a part of one unified experience which ends with physical death than it would have if looked upon immediately or in the context of the present moment. Certainly the experience at the end of the covenant, when one of the two marches towards new life and the death of the physical body, is transformed by remembering that this experience, even if it be years long, is only a small part of the entire experience of the promise.

Let us return to the simile of the journey, for we feel that the question asks not only what the implications are in marriage, but what the implications may be for those who do not wish to marry, but who wish to do spiritual work together.

Let us say that upon the one hand those who wish to do spiritual work together, but not physical or mental work together, are wiser to maintain the relationship of companions which are upon the road together and wish to help each other. It is a relationship which concentrates upon the present moment. The uses of memory and of looking towards the future are somewhat limited in such a spiritually oriented relationship. Just as the spiritual side of a lover's relationship is fragmented and often lost, the journey taken by those who are spiritually agreed to journey together may be very rich and satisfying. Very productive work may be accomplished. Each may serve as mirror to the other, each aiding the spiritual journey of the other, and deep friendship may ensue, that friendship which eliminates time and space.

The seekers which wish to do spiritual work together, emotional work together, mental work and physical work together, all at once, take for themselves an added burden and an added hope— the hope of fulfilling the covenant. If each of you is a crystalline being attempting to hone, clarify and sharpen that crystal which lies within, so too a relationship which has been stated clearly, spiritually and angelically is a crystal also, and throughout the life experience each of the two in the married pair may do all those things which are given to those who agree to seek together, yet there is also the responsibility for physical, mental and emotional loving, cherishing and honoring. The conditions are more clear, the responsibilities are greater and the end result is a crystalline structure that may become part of the higher self of both in the marriage, not only within the life experience, but in the cosmic or eternal portion of the self, until such time as personhood is no longer. Those who have created the jewel of a promise fulfilled create a light source that, like all other light sources of love in the creation, are available whatever the time, whatever the space.

It is difficult for us to give to this instrument our words, for the nature in truth of metaphysical marriage contains a third party. This is not a thought which this instrument finds easy to channel, however, in any metaphysical covenant there is a third party which overshadows both entities. You may call that being the Creator in whatever face you see. Perhaps we would do best to call it living love. Those who do not marry and seek together, seek alone for the face of love. Those who seek through the covenant of marriage incorporate that which they seek into their seeking. This gives to those who grasp and understand the metaphysical meaning of marriage a gracefulness and a tenderness that would not come naturally otherwise.

There are other covenants that are most valuable. The covenant between parent and child, between friend and friend, between brother and sister, are all beautiful and spiritually useful. Yet, perhaps, it is in the completeness of the covenant of marriage that its great strength lies, for in no other covenant do two people give to another body, emotion, mind and spirit. Two together then seek instead of one and one.

This instrument is surprised that we are still with it. We shall pause for a moment if you will pardon us.

(Pause)

We are again with this instrument. Sometimes this instrument forgets that she does not need to know about the subject about which we speak. We shall continue briefly through this instrument.

We speak now of the concept of failure in relationships. The promise of marriage is often ended with the equivalent of a statement of withdrawal or divorce. What happens then to the covenant in metaphysical terms? It is still valuable. It is valuable inasmuch as and insofar as the seeker was sincere in claiming the metaphysical promise for itself. It is the nature of illusion to entrap, deceive and thwart one, and often it does occur that promises are broken, marriages end. Yet, metaphysically, the strength of the promise, the strength of the will to serve in abiding by the promise do much to strengthen and balance and regularize one's inner seeking.

There is, of course, no way for one, who goes to the place of the promise and makes it, to know for sure that he will be able to keep it, for within the illusion that you experience, various forces may be brought to bear which may break apart your foundation, and shaken from the roots that you have put down, you simply drift away, and in your confusion you wonder if there was any use to all that you experienced. We assure you that there is a great deal of use to all the attempts that have been made to keep the promises that you have made. Each day, each hour, if a failure seems to have occurred, it is well to remember that the failure is within the illusion, but the promise is eternal, not a promise to be kept eternally, returning to one mate over and over again throughout the endless cycle of time, but rather a light which is eternal made by two which have become one metaphysically, which have sought together to mastery.

We urge those who contemplate marriage or who are engaged in keeping the promise of the covenant of marriage to center the self in meditation daily, and before the meditation is through, remember and bless that promise, for it is a vehicle which may carry two to unity beyond themselves with the face of the Creator.

We are so happy to have been able to speak upon this subject. We would like to speak upon any other subjects which you may wish to ask about, and for that purpose we would wish to use the instrument known as Jim. If this instrument would be accepting of our contact, we would at this time transfer. I am known to you as Q'uo.

(Jim channeling)

I am Q'uo, and greet each again in love and light. At this time it is our honor to offer ourselves in the attempt to speak to those queries which may be upon the minds. We remind each that our words are but the fruits of our own seeking and are our opinions, and we do not wish any to take our opinions as the absolute truth, but that gift which brothers and sisters in seeking give to those who follow upon the same path for their consideration in the further journeying upon that path. Is there a question at this time with which we may begin?

T: Yes, I have a question. If two people set out on a relationship, and it seems in the beginning that the relationship has a very high probability of either failure or at least a whole lot of very hard times associated with it, but that there's one or two good things that could come from it, is it usually advisable to go ahead and set out on that relationship, that marriage, or that whatever, whatever the relationship is, knowing full well that there's going to be a lot of really negative things to come from it? I guess what I'm saying is, is it worth it for the good that comes out of it, to create some additional negativity or some additional problem?

I am Q'uo, and am aware of your query, my brother. We would begin by suggesting that even to the eye in what seems to be an obvious and clear manner, much is hidden within your illusion, for within your experience there is the shielding, shall we say, of the conscious knowing so that much experience is gained in groping through what you might call a metaphysical darkness. You live and move and have your being in mystery, and you seek portions of that mystery with every thought and action that proceeds from your being. With each thought and action that sums into experience, you are able to piece together more and more of the picture of the creation about you and your place within it. As you move into those relationships which are of primary and profound significance within this journey of seeking, there is much which the conscious mind will assume and presume to know. Yet, if decisions are made only in regards to what may be known in the mental sense of the conscious mind, then much will be missing that can serve as resource …

(Side one of tape ends.)

(Jim channeling)

I am Q'uo, and am again with this instrument. We shall continue.

The subconscious mind, then, through the faculty of intuition may offer much to one who seeks—the manner by which it shall continue its journey and with whom it shall journey and in what manner the journey shall be accomplished. We cannot tell you, my brother, or any particular entity, whether what seems to be the truth is that which should be heeded, for, indeed, even the most difficult of situations oftimes presents the greatest of opportunities for learning in the metaphysical sense, even though within the boundaries and definitions of your illusion the relationship and the experiences within it have proven most difficult. It cannot be known before or during such experience what treasures are, indeed, gathered in the metaphysical sense. The entire incarnation then partakes of mystery which shall become clear to the far-seeing eye only after the doors of what you call the physical death have been passed through and the veil dropped which shields the conscious mind from the subconscious mind and the greater portion of the experience about one.

May we speak further, my brother?

T: No, I believe that pretty such sums it up, even though a lot people have gotten themselves into some hard situations by following their heart rather than what their logical mind told them. I understand what you're saying. Thank you very much.

I am Q'uo, and we thank you, my brother. Is there another query?

G: Yes. I have one to ask you. What the value is of using crystals and sound on the spiritual path?

I am Q'uo, and we find that the objects of which you speak and the qualities of vibration which are embodied within the sound vibratory complexes may be used to enhance the finer portions of the spiritual journey in order that the inner eye may perceive with greater clarity the countryside, shall we say, through which the seeker travels. The use of the crystalline structure is that which enhances the seeker's ability to perceive the finer and more subtle energies that ever surround one, and enhance the ability to utilize these energies for the continued advancing upon the spiritual path.

The use of any such device or technique is that which is empowered by the desire and intention of the seeker, thus, the usefulness of any such technique or device is in direct proportion to the purity and intensity of the desire to seek knowledge in order to serve others that the seeker of truth emanates from its very being and by which it empowers all that it does and all that it is.

May we speak further, my sister?

G: Yes, please.

I am Q'uo, and we mean by our query to ask if there is any further question which you might have for us upon this subject.

Carla: Well, I would ask—I was thinking—you kind of implied that a crystal by itself doesn't have an intrinsic power, that it's the empowerment by intention, by the use of the will in seeking, in, I guess you'd say, magnetizing the crystal that gives it its usefulness. Is that correct? I think of crystals really as being independently powerful, being able to focus and reflect light in different vibratory ways and people using that intrinsic power, but you're suggesting that the true power of the crystal is extrinsic, in other words that it's put into the crystal by the person's relationship with the crystal. Is that true?

I am Q'uo, and we meant by our suggestion that the desire of the one utilizing such a device as the crystal was that which gave direction and therefore power to accomplish the work in consciousness which the crystal has as its contribution to such a seeker. The crystal structure itself is as you assume, that is, its power exists without a desire from another being to form it, yet such desire and purpose of intention then can direct the movement of energy rather than allow that energy to become diffused by the non-use in a conscious fashion of this energy.

May we speak in any further fashion, my sister?

Carla: No, just a personal question about crystals. I seem to be sensitive to most crystals except diamonds. Diamonds are fine—they don't bother me, I can wear them, I enjoy them. But if I try to put a crystal around my neck or near me, I'm uncomfortable after awhile, and I don't know why, but I just want to move it a certain distance from me. They don't bother me on other people, no matter how close the people are, but they bother me in connection with me. Could you comment on that? I've never understood why that's so. I'm sure I'm not the only person that has that reaction.

I am Q'uo, and we find that your query is one which we may answer in a certain sense without stepping over the boundary of your own free will. Your sensitivity is that which has increased in nature as you have proceeded through your incarnational experience. The crystal form, as we have previously spoken, is that which funnels various energies, and in many cases magnifies these energies in a fashion which oftimes may not be in harmonic resonance with your own inner sensitivities which have become finely tuned and are easily upset, shall we say. Thus, it is well for your own comfort for you to either be careful that the crystals within your range of sensitivity be tuned to your own vibratory nature or removed to a distance which is outside of your range of sensitivity.

May we speak further, my sister?

Carla: No, thank you.

I am Q'uo, and we thank you, my sister. Is there another query?

Carla: I've always had the notion about marriage or any relationship that it doesn't end. It seems to end, but, in actuality, if you don't shut the person away or kill the person off in your mind I guess you'd say, that the relationship has perfect validity. It's just that the person isn't around. And I wonder if this is true?

I am Q'uo, and as one might expect within a universe of infinite possibility, there is infinite probability that entities which have engaged in the mated relationship for a period of your time and then found reason to end that relationship yet continue in what may be either the conscious or subconscious fashion to share experience and offer a portion of the self to the other even when the relationship has in the physical sense been terminated. In many cases this pathway which each has forged to the other becomes somewhat dusty and falls into disuse, yet from time to time is utilized for the gathering and sharing of experience upon the metaphysical levels of experience.

May we speak in any further fashion, my sister?

Carla: Well, let me clarify my first question, because I didn't mean that relationships that have stopped continue. What I meant was that it has always seemed unlikely to me that love would just go away. It seems that if you have an experience of love with another person, that the experience may end, but that the love remains. As long as it remains in memory, it remains truly. The reason that this is important to me is that I have had more than one relationship in my life, and it's comforting to think of the light and love that those relationships created as having a life independent of the failure of the relationship for one reason or another, the ending of it.

I am Q'uo, and, indeed, my sister, all that remains from any experience within your illusion and all that is ever recorded within the nature of the soul is love. Whatever experience of love one is able to create and to share within any relationship or experience within your illusion is remembered and is gathered as the true harvest of the incarnation. All else is but the means to this end.

May we speak further, my sister?

Carla: No, thank you.

I am Q'uo, and again we thank you, my sister. Is there another query at this time?

(Pause)

I am Q'uo, and we find that we have for the moment exhausted those queries which you have so graciously offered to us this evening. We thank each for allowing our presence and for presenting to us the gifts of your queries and your comments, for as we speak upon your concerns, we speak upon those topics which are a portion of our own being and seeking, and by sharing with you that of our experience, our experience becomes refined and enriched with your own journey of seeking. At this time we shall take our leave of this instrument and this group, rejoicing in the love and in the light which each has brought to this seeking. We are those of Q'uo, and we leave each in that love and in that love of the one infinite Creator. Adonai, my friends. Adonai vasu borragus. ✦

L/L Research

L/L Research is a subsidiary of Rock Creek Research & Development Laboratories, Inc.

P.O. Box 5195
Louisville, KY 40255-0195

www.llresearch.org

Rock Creek is a non-profit corporation dedicated to discovering and sharing information which may aid in the spiritual evolution of humankind.

ABOUT THE CONTENTS OF THIS TRANSCRIPT: This telepathic channeling has been taken from transcriptions of the weekly study and meditation meetings of the Rock Creek Research & Development Laboratories and L/L Research. It is offered in the hope that it may be useful to you. As the Confederation entities always make a point of saying, please use your discrimination and judgment in assessing this material. If something rings true to you, fine. If something does not resonate, please leave it behind, for neither we nor those of the Confederation would wish to be a stumbling block for any.

CAVEAT: This transcript is being published by L/L Research in a not yet final form. It has, however, been edited and any obvious errors have been corrected. When it is in a final form, this caveat will be removed.

© 2009 L/L Research

Sunday Meditation
July 12, 1987

Group question: "Q'uo: We would focus this evening upon an aspect of love and compassion which is very difficult to manifest while under the influence of the third-density distortions of mind, body and spirit. We speak of forgiveness."

(Carla channeling)

I Yadda. I greet you in love and in light of infinite Creator. We not have very much to say, only wish to welcome newcomer to group and oldcomers also. We with your group very often, for we find that this group make many joke, and this is sign of some advancement among your peoples. So many on your spiritual path that cannot make a joke, that cannot laugh. This make the journey heavy and mud cake the feet of the poor pilgrim along the way and cannot go very far. Make yourself merry, my friends, be full of joy. Let it bubble forth, and you will find wisdom beneath the laughter. We go now, we only wish to say hehwoe—hel-lo. That better! Hah? We goin' speak this language soon. We go in love and in light of infinite One Who Is All in All. Farewell, my friends. I Yadda.

(Carla channeling)

We are those of Q'uo, and we greet you in the love and in the light of the one infinite Creator. It is a great benefit to us that you have asked us to share this meditation with you and to share what thoughts we might have with this circle of light, this band of seekers whom we join this day.

We thank you for the great privilege of such intimate sharing of heartfelt desires, and we assure you that we also have that goal of every seeker—to know the face of mystery, to be with the Creator in an illumined fashion. How far we are all from that great and all-consuming goal—the Creator's face, the articulated Logos. What a dear and precious mystery. That mystery is all wrapped up with love, a love that has been called compassion by those who seek to deepen the meaning of that word love, that word which has been so abused, misused and trivialized by common usage.

Indeed, the one who challenges in the name of Jesus Christ challenges in the name of love itself, and all challengings which are superlative and honestly felt, whatever the words of challenge, that challenge is the challenge of love, that compassion against which nothing may stand. What is the nature of compassion? How does compassion touch each as each seeks along the path and finds the road rocky or smooth, steep or plain.

We would focus this evening upon an aspect of love and compassion which is very difficult to manifest while under the influence of the third-density distortions of mind, body and spirit. We speak of forgiveness.

What occurs when forgiveness is withheld? You may see the separation immediately. The one who does not forgive is separated from the one who is not forgiven, and then the one who is not forgiven may choose not to forgive that, and there is further separation. Indeed, before a patching up and recombining of the energies of two who are thus separate can be achieved, four forgivenesses must take place. Each must forgive the other, and each must forgive the self.

If one were to visualize the pattern and tapestry of a lifetime, one would see those portions of time and space when forgiveness was withheld from the self or from another as being places where the thread, the warp and woof of the tapestry of life, was coated with black, sticky substance, which stiffens and makes ugly the tapestry of existence.

Now, it is sure that no one wishes not to forgive. There seems to be no question in the mind of anyone who is seeking along the path of positive polarity in the third density that it is very desirable to forgive and to accept forgiveness, yet there may be nothing harder in the catalog of human weakness, shall we say, or distortion, than the unbalanced feeling of helplessness when one realizes one is quite incapable of altering the consciousness which is not forgiving. Hardness of heart among those who seek is very often totally unmeant and undesired. It is the nature of the third-density illusion of your planetary sphere that within the illusion you will be taken beyond your limits and fail according to the conscious methods of judging among your peoples. This is perhaps the most common source of the lack of forgiveness among your peoples—the difficulty of forgiving the self for having seemingly failed. Also, and almost as common, there are those dynamic tensions betwixt members of the same family which involuntarily renew themselves and prohibit forgiveness.

The chief roadblock stopping one from forgiving is the instinct for self-preservation. One who forgives is changed—something dies and something is born. Yet that which is born cannot begin to be born until whatever it was that was not forgiven has been done away with by true forgiveness. To hold the self or another in unforgiveness is [to] hold in a pristine and clear condition a relationship or a self-concept.

When forgiveness takes place, there is a little death, and sometimes not so very small a death indeed, for sometimes that which is to be forgiven has been held in a hard heart for a long time. It is natural to fear death, yet the road to joy, or shall we say, the way to perceive joy along the road we all travel is to rush towards whatever oblivion must be embraced in order to forgive, for the creation that springs forth from the heart to one who has truly forgiven is a beautiful and fresh manifestation.

It is very difficult to create appropriate atmosphere for forgiveness using the conscious mind. The conscious mind is a kind of business man, ordering things, prioritizing them, and moving them about. It is within the province of that great subconscious mind which is so important to the seeker that the seeds of forgiveness are sown, are nourished, and grow. Thus, the attempts to forgive by consciously stating, "I wish to forgive," are likely to be failures, although the attempt is metaphysically important, and is a part of the soul's history. It is more effective by far to await meditative time before doing work in the consciousness of forgiveness.

If you wish to speed the process of forgiveness, may we suggest that you take the object which has not been forgiven by you and hold that object within the heart and mind, enveloped and encircled in light, light infinite and light illimitable, hoping and praying for every good for that which you cannot forgive. Thus, you are engaging a deeper portion of yourself to begin opening doors, so that that which is unforgivable to the conscious mind slowly becomes that which must be forgiven. It cannot be forced; it cannot be taught. And when someone attempts to persuade the seeker into forgiveness, and does so on its own energy, then as soon as the intermediary removes itself, the hardness of heart returns.

Please remember at all times when you see hardheartedness in others or yourself, that you are powerful to serve as messengers of love, peace and joy. You may encourage, exhort, commune and just be with one who is having difficulty, and by your mirroring forgiveness and love to the one you wish to aid, you are connecting your subconscious and your companion's subconscious in great echoes of compassion. Sometimes no word need to be said for this comforting effect to take place. Never doubt your value to one another, for you are the Creator. You are love, each to the other. May you dwell in a world where forgiveness is actively sought and joy is nourished by all conversation.

My friends, it seems while you are in the midst of the third-density illusion that the stream of your life experience moves slowly and endlessly. Yet, we urge you to make some attempt to realize how very fleeting birdsong, brook's rill and the wind in the trees are, how very short is your time to gain experience upon your beautiful planetary sphere. May you find zest and joy in your inward walk. May your eyes behold the creation of your brothers and sisters of air, earth, wind, fire and all the creatures of those densities. May you love life as you experience it, and may you find comfort in each other.

It has been a great privilege to speak with you. We feel particular love for each of you, and would send you our blessings through this instrument. We wish you to know that at any time that you are meditating and you wish us to be with you in that meditation, you have merely to mentally request our presence. We do not speak in a lone meditation, but many find our vibrations to cause meditative states to become achieved more easily and held for longer periods of time. We also find great benefit from sharing in your vibration. We would transfer at this time, with thanks to this instrument. We are Q'uo.

(Jim channeling)

I am Q'uo, and greet each again in love and light. At this time it is our honor to attempt to speak to those queries which may be placed before us. Before so doing, we would remind each that we speak according to our experience and our opinion, and do not wish our words to be taken as anything other than that. May we begin with a query, my friends?

(Pause)

I am Q'uo, and we find that we have in our opening message spoken to much which was upon the mind of one or two, and which for this evening will suffice for the answering of queries. We thank each, as always, for inviting our presence and for allowing us to speak our humble words to each here and to each heart. We join with this group in the seeking of the love and light of the one Creator through all experience, and we rejoice that we have traveled this distance with this group this evening. We shall be with you in your future gatherings, and shall be happy once again to share that which is ours to share. At this time we shall take our leave of this group, leaving each, as always, in the love and in the light of the one infinite Creator. We are known to you as those of Q'uo. Adonai, my friends. Adonai vasu borragus. ✥

L/L Research

Intensive Meditation
July 13, 1987

(Carla channeling)

I am Hatonn, and I greet each of you in the love and the light of the infinite Creator. It is a privilege and a blessing to have been called to this meditation, and we greet each within the group with joy, for to know the Creator in each unique system of vibratory fields that weaves the essence and jewel of each of you is an enormous thrill and privilege. It has been to us that the call was given this evening, for although we are not those which in the majority of cases work with the new channels, we find that to the one known as R our sent message lies within the range of configurations of reception which should make for the most comfortable and lucid feeling of contact.

We would say a few words about the practice of vocal channeling. First of all, we feel it is important to stress that channeling is not alien to the condition of humankind, but is inherent in the nature of mind, body and spirit which is called personality, for the spirit dwells within mind and body and expresses itself and receives nourishment in such distorted or clear fashion as the body chooses to channel to it and accept from it. All of the life experience is, in essence, a channeling of some force, either within or without the self into each action of the self.

Thus, it is the nature of humankind to be receptive, as a channel is receptive, and then to be a broadcaster, so that those who may find aid in your words may have access to them. Needless to say, the varieties of channeling are endless. There are those souls who channel such healing into the pie or roast that each bite that is taken at the dinner table fills not only the stomach but the heart with the love of the one who channeled perfect love into food.

The vocal channeling is one way of being of service—that is all. It may be that the new channel, once having discovered channeling, may feel that its gift does not lie properly within channeling. This is acceptable to us, for we feel that the experience of moving energy from the subconscious through the conscious with the intention of being of service is a discipline which will inform and improve whatever form of service is undertaken in whatever subsequently. We are always extraordinarily appreciative of those who wish to channel our words. They are humble words and in large part our opinion only. We have been wrong in the past and shall be wrong in the future, for though we are many steps ahead of you upon the path of seeking, yet still we are finite and prone to error.

Most of all, we send you our love and wish for each the joy that service to others brings back to the self. You shall be surprised by the love that is mirrored back to you from time to time, simply because you have a wish to be of service. This wish is the legacy of the kingdom within, that kingdom which is often called heaven. Yet, does it not lie within, my friends?

And do you not bring to channeling the very essence of that which is to be channeled? For are you not in God and the Creator in you? Thus, fear not the experience of channeling, nor be concerned what you shall say.

We shall be taking time in the next few sessions to attempt to correct any discomfort which may be felt by any of the channels, especially those who are new. May we ask that if there is a discomfort in [the] neck or any other portion of the physical vehicle, that you mentally request that we adjust the contact. We attempt to be aware of comfort in the channel, but must confess that we are not perfect by any means at correcting an uncomfortable position or influence about the electrical field of the body and consequent muscle reaction. Please realize that we wish for the channel to be comfortable and to not simply live through an uncomfortable experience. A mental request is usually quite enough. Repeat that request mentally as many times as necessary to adjust the contact, and if the contact is not comfortable after [a] small length of time, we urge the channel to relinquish the contact and we shall continue to work to adjust comfort while other channeling is going on. You see, my friends, there are advantages to being a social memory complex—we can do many more than one thing at one time.

We ask the new channels to relax, become aware of the soft susurration of the rain upon the thirsty land, of the delicate breeze which moves within the domicile which is filled with the pearly-evening glow of the quiet countryside. Be sure that your physical vehicle is quite comfortable so that there may be the focus upon the brow chakra and the crown chakra, for you see, we are moving through the violet-ray chakra of the crown into the indigo ray chakra of the brow, and when we have been able to journey, welcomed, through these ports of entry, we may then activate the blue-ray energy center and communicate our humble thoughts.

As we work, may we ask that when the name is heard or felt within the mind, that it simply be repeated, that is, what phrase that is heard needs to repeated word for word. The reason that this is necessary is that the mechanism is such that it is like a game of pitch and catch. First one concept cluster, ranging from one word to quite a few, is thrown or tossed at the channel. The channel catches it with the metaphorical hand of consciousness and then throws it on just as it was received, leaving the catching hand empty for the next concept to occur. When this realization of concept occurs, then simply repeat that which has been heard, refraining from analyzing the message, evaluating it, doubting its reality or any other thought which will move one from that point of concentration which is focused entirely upon catching the concepts that flow one at a time from the subconscious.

We would now like to work with the instrument known as K. We have become most affectionate towards this seeker and can only thank this seeker that those of the Confederation have been most generously called and are able thus to accompany this entity. We greet the one known as K, and would like to exercise her channel, if she would relax, refrain from analyzing and speak that which occurs within. We shall transfer at this time. I am Hatonn.

(K channeling)

I am Hatonn, and I greet you once again in love and light through this instrument. We find this instrument is experiencing some surprise, adjusting to once again speaking the thoughts which are *(inaudible)* as she has been accustomed the last few months to … *(The rest of this channeling was not transcribed.)*

(Carla channeling)

I am Hatonn. We are making some contact with the new instrument known as R, but there is a good deal of adjusting to do, and we would request that the instrument remain calm and comfortable and wait our greeting. We will send only the words, "I am Hatonn," and will attempt to continue to adjust, sending that few words until the instrument is aware of that concept moving through the veil of consciousness. Again we ask the new instrument to relax, refrain from analysis and to repeat what occurs within the mind. We thank this new instrument for embarking upon this path and hope that we may make ourselves known at this time. We are those of Hatonn, and will now transfer to the one known as R.

(R channeling)

I am Hatonn. *(The rest of this channeling was not transcribed.)*

(Carla channeling)

I am Hatonn. We rejoice at the ease of contact with this instrument, and apologize for causing slight discomfort. We shall, each time we work with the new instrument, attempt to ameliorate the effect of contact. For the most part these effects do not continue for long unless it is requested by the instrument.

You form a ring, my friends, as you sit about the room of your domicile. The domicile forms a ring about you, and the yard about the domicile and the town about the yard, and the continent, then [the] world in which you have lived. Then that great round, the galaxy, and the timeless, convoluted roundness of the creation itself. And each of you wishes to serve the roundness of the galaxy and of all creation. And the roundness of one circle sitting in light wishing to be of aid to fellow seekers is equally powerful. We know you will seek to be stewards of the power which is yours for good or for ill, and we rejoice greatly in the light and the love …

(Side one of tape ends.)

(Carla channeling)

… which you who dwell in mystery yet achieve through faith in the light and through the will to know and to give love. We would wish at this time to transfer to the one known as Jim. We are known to you as Hatonn.

(Jim channeling)

I am Hatonn, and we greet each again in love and light. At this time we would open this gathering to the queries which may have the value in the asking. May we begin with the first query?

Carla: Are you able to bring into mind the golden beings which were around Jim and me at our wedding, and if you are, could you comment on the possibilities in general of accompaniments from the inner planes and/or the outer planes at such metaphysically potent rituals?

I am Hatonn. Each seeker, according to the path which it travels, gathers to it those friends and teachers from the metaphysical realms which are ever present in the life experience. There are moments within the incarnational pattern which offer themselves to rejoicing and celebration and to the further gathering of those friends, both seen and unseen, which lend their very being to the ceremonies and rituals that signify the further enhancing of the potential for serving the Creator and for rejoicing in the creation of the Father. Thus, within your own pattern of experience, you have also called unto yourselves those presences which respond in joy at the call, and lend the brilliance of their being to your joyous celebration.

May we speak in any other fashion, my sister?

Carla: No, thank you.

I am Hatonn, and we thank you, my sister. Is there another query?

(Pause)

I am Hatonn. We find that the experience which has been shared this evening has been sufficient for the moment to instruct and to prepare for further instruction those present, and we thank each again for inviting our presence and for allowing us to move within your life experience and to become part of that greater desire to be of service to others who seek also the nature of the mystery within which we all move and the heart of which we [are] known as both source and destination of our being. At this time we shall bid each a fond adieu, and leave each in the name of the love and the light of the one infinite Creator. We are known to you as those of Hatonn. Adonai, my friends. Adonai. ☥

Intensive Meditation
July 14, 1987

(W channeling)

I am Quanta. *(The rest of this channeling was not transcribed.)*

(Carla channeling)

I am Hatonn, and I greet this company in the love and in the light of the infinite Creator. We would wish that you be aware that there are several presences from the Confederation of Planets in the Service of the Infinite Creator joining your meditation this evening, those energies which are Oxal, Laitos, Latwii and Quanta. These brothers and sisters wish to aid each in the deepening of the meditative state. The one known as W will be experiencing the companionship of Quanta as further work is done in that new instrument's indigo-ray plan of progress.

We would wish to turn the attention to the blessedness of the intention to serve. When entities discover within themselves the desire to serve, they cast about for a satisfactory path of service and frequently become embroiled in the mechanics of producing the chosen service. In that seeking forth the perfect service, life and joy are stripped from the endeavor. This is not to say that it is not valuable to continually improve and refine one's ability to serve, one's perspicacity and tact in service. However, the analytical mind often takes over the faculty of evaluation from the proper means of evaluation, that is, the deeper self, and in that surface evaluation of the attempt to be of service, many imperfections are found and thus the seeker becomes disappointed in the self and in the service. This adversely affects future attempts at service as entities become disillusioned with their own abilities.

My friends, each has in general a path which shall include opportunities for service and opportunities for the gaining of experience. To some a gift such as the vocal channeling may be given, just as to some the ability to produce music from a complicated instrument such as the piano or the guitar. If the seekers which are within this domicile at this time were to compare their attempts at vocal channeling with the mature vocal channeling of one who has started with the gift of far memory of previous concept communication, it is likely that there would be some disappointment. However, in discovering vocal channeling, the seeker is discovering a portion of his or her own birthright. Vocal channeling is a way of linking three levels of being: the deep mind, the conscious mind, and the mind of the Logos.

We are messengers of this Logos, imperfect and often befuddled, yet we come to you as those who may have some small portion of wisdom to offer from our experience. We speak not to your conscious mind, but to your deep mind in concepts. This conversation betwixt the deep mind and the cosmos is going on all the time. Almost no one in the physical vehicle of third density is aware of this communication, however, when the channeling occurs, pathways are being made deeper and clearer each time the channeling is practiced for the greater and greater facility of the conscious mind to have access into the deep mind and thus have access to the collected wisdom of the cosmos. Indeed, both we and you are in essence an entire and complete Creator, an unlimited creation and the most powerful force in that creation.

We say this because we wish each of you to grasp the fact that it is not necessarily one's path to be of service through vocal channeling, but it is always useful to have experienced the overshadowing of the self by a personality which is external to the self. Let these experiences flow naturally and evaluate in relaxation at other times the degree of attraction which channeling itself actually holds for you, keeping in mind that the work that you are doing is most helpful both to yourself and to others who you may serve as you become more and more aware of the wisdom and glory which lies within and to which you do indeed have access.

We would like to transfer at this time to the one known as K, if she will relax and allow our words to flow freely without the analysis. We shall transfer now. We are those of Hatonn.

(K channeling)

I am Hatonn, and greet you once again in love and light through this instrument. We reiterate our pleasure at being with this group this evening, for it is always a privilege to serve in this manner with you and through you. We are also most pleased to be called to offer whatever aid we may to those new channels, and in exercising them we find great benefit to ourselves as well. We ask that you remain conscious of your desire to serve for it is … *(The rest of this channeling was not transcribed.)*

(Jim channeling)

I am Hatonn, and greet each again. We appreciate the opportunity to utilize each new instrument this evening, and we hope that each will bear with this sufficiently as we move about the circle and attempt to exercise each new instrument in turn. The process that each goes through is much the same, though each entity will find that there are various strengths and weaknesses that may be noticed within the Earth's instruments, and thus each may learn from each in a manner which would not be possible without each new instrument seeking together a means by which to be of service through vocal channeling.

At this time we would attempt to make our contact known to the one known as R. If this new instrument would relax the mind and body, and after feeling our presence and offering the appropriate challenge, then simply speak those words which she becomes aware of in her own mind, she will find that the process will begin to move much more smoothly forward. At this time we would transfer this contact to the one known as R. I am Hatonn.

(R channeling)

I am Hatonn. I am speaking through a new instrument and the tuning is not yet fine. The instrument has some physical discomfort that causes the problem that speaking to through is not the contact but it might be that as the discomfiture eases and the practice is greater this will be easier for the instrument. This can be a comforting knowledge and as the veil of pain is overcome, it will become easier for us to make a contact, for the instrument has desire and is most willing and apt. Due to the discomfort we will withdraw. I am Hatonn.

(Carla channeling)

I am Hatonn, and am now with this instrument, and renew our greeting in love and light. We thank the one known as R for continuing through discomfort. We have been attempting with the help of the one known as Oxal, which energy is quite suited to the one known as R, to adjust our ingress into this entity's web of vibratory nexus, and have been aware that the entire torso as well as neck was causing difficulty.

We encourage the tuning, the challenging, and the reprimanding of all contacts. You who serve as channels have a responsibility in this fertile and crowded metaphysical universe to choose the contact that is the highest and best that you may stably choose. Thus, the challenging is something we do not at all begrudge, but rather encourage, for we wish each channel to feel that it has control of the conversation which proceeds during the channeling process. It is also important to complain mentally and to nag ceaselessly if the physical vehicle is uncomfortable for one reason or another. Each instrument is wired differently, in this instrument's terminology, possessing various locations for ingress, and thus when we first begin working with a new instrument, we move in with a standard adjustment. Like most standard things, it seldom fits anyone but is, shall we say, close enough for a beginning. We ask each instrument to take responsibility for controlling the contact, refusing it if [it] seems less than what it should be and certainly refusing to accept discomfort. There is no need for this to occur as long as we are not working in the trance state. Work in the trance state requires a physical toll for the production of words. Conscious channeling, which is actually done in a light trance, does not require this cost and the instrument should not accept discomfort but should persevere mentally until comfort is established.

At this time we would like to continue working through the instrument known as N, whom we greet in love. If the instrument will relax, we shall attempt to pass its challenge. We transfer now. We are Hatonn.

(N channeling)

I am Hatonn. We are pleased that the entities in this group are from such willingness to become channels and therefore … *(The rest of this channeling was not transcribed.)*

(Side one of tape ends.)

(N channeling)

We are happy to be of service to this group. I am Hatonn, and I leave you in love and in light.

(Carla channeling)

I am Hatonn, and I greet you one final time, as always, in love and light, as love and light are all that there is. We have rejoiced in your company, and feel that each has made good progress this evening. We leave you in that same love and that same light, glorying with you in your birthright, rejoicing with you that your Creator lies closer to you than your heart or your breath so that we all are in the Creator and are all thus the Creator to each other.

It is often said by those of us in the Confederation of Planets in the Service of the Infinite Creator that the seeds of creatorship dwell within each. When the seeds of the rose are planted, that which comes forth is a rose. If the seeds of the Creator are planted within you, my friends, shall your bloom and flower not be the Creator? We are those known to you as Hatonn. Adonai.

L/L Research

L/L Research is a subsidiary of Rock Creek Research & Development Laboratories, Inc.

P.O. Box 5195
Louisville, KY 40255-0195

www.llresearch.org

Rock Creek is a non-profit corporation dedicated to discovering and sharing information which may aid in the spiritual evolution of humankind.

ABOUT THE CONTENTS OF THIS TRANSCRIPT: This telepathic channeling has been taken from transcriptions of the weekly study and meditation meetings of the Rock Creek Research & Development Laboratories and L/L Research. It is offered in the hope that it may be useful to you. As the Confederation entities always make a point of saying, please use your discrimination and judgment in assessing this material. If something rings true to you, fine. If something does not resonate, please leave it behind, for neither we nor those of the Confederation would wish to be a stumbling block for any.

CAVEAT: This transcript is being published by L/L Research in a not yet final form. It has, however, been edited and any obvious errors have been corrected. When it is in a final form, this caveat will be removed.

© 2009 L/L Research

Intensive Meditation
July 15, 1987

(Carla channeling)

I am Hatonn, and I greet you in the love and light of the infinite Creator. We are most grateful for having been called to your group by your desire, and to be able to share in your beautiful meditation, to serve as much as we can and to learn as we always do when we work with groups such as yours. As always, we find the contact with one of your peoples to be exhilarating. The quiet sounds of the evening as nature stirs about your dwelling place, the gentle hum of the fan which cools each seeker—your atmosphere and company are indeed delightful, and we thank you again.

This evening we would like to attempt a teaching technique for new instruments which has been found to be useful in the past. We would like to tell a story in many parts. We will start with this instrument and move according to that name given in each piece of channeled material. You see, my friends, there comes a time when the new channel must shake itself loose from the dependence upon known subject matter by the telling of a story in small segments, each instrument giving only a small part of the story. The mind of the channel may be at rest, for it knows not how the story comes out, it being a story never told before.

We ask that each channel remember carefully the tuning and be conscious also that those who are not channeling at the time, but are in the circle, may be of great aid to the one channeling at the moment by offering such visualizations of light and healing, energy and power and compassion as will aid that instrument in the regularizing of the energies which it is receiving. A newer channel usually has more difficulty retaining a steady vibratory level. This is why we ask that you continue tuning whenever you become conscious that you are not totally involved in the meditation. A simple phrase that is of meaning to you will suffice. We find this instrument to be just as nervous as the rest of you, as she has no more idea than any what we may be about to tell.

It is in just such a way that the seeker receives realization. The seeker cannot know what he seeks, for that which is named is not worth seeking. And when it comes, it is a surprise, and yet that which must be, and must be just as it is. We shall begin.

There was once a shipbuilder in an ancient land. His father and his grandfather before him had worked upon the beautiful ships with their high prows that sailed from the north land. The young shipbuilder had keen eyes, and he watched the ships come and go and listened to tales of conquest and riches. Yet, he did not fancy himself a pirate and continued working upon the land.

Intensive Meditation, July 15, 1987

We shall transfer to the one known as Jim. For this particular exercise we shall eliminate the giving of our name at each transfer. We transfer now.

(Jim channeling)

The young man in his work often thought of what must lie beyond the reaches of his port city in the far sea. Many tales did he hear, and yet he was for the most part content to remain and do his small portion of work building the great ships that moved upon the waters out of sight and circled the globe. Yet within his heart there was the beginning of the desire to know more than what was available to him within the confines of his work, his home, his friends, and his city. He pondered more and more what might be available to him in the way of adventure and learning and experience if he should leave his home and friends. And thus he considered this possibility with some fear and some excitement.

We shall transfer to the one known as K.

(K channeling)

One day, as the young man was working about his accustomed tasks in the shipyard, he saw a strange ship appear over the horizon and come into the port. It was tall and had red sails, and the people were at first afraid, for they feared an attack. And being a warlike nation themselves, the took up their arms and stood ready to defend themselves. But when the ship landed, they could see that there was no danger to fear, for the men aboard the ship carried no weapons. It was a merchant ship, the cargo of goods the like of which many, indeed most, had not seen before, for it carried fine cloth and spices from far different lands—we correct this instrument—far distant lands to which the ships of the north had not yet ventured. The merchants on the ship were interested in trade and in discovering new lands and new markets for their trade. And as the young shipbuilder watched and listened, he knew that his opportunity had come to see distant parts of the world without having to be a pirate. And so when the foreign ship sailed again, he sailed with them as part of their crew, and set forth into the world to discover what he might.

We transfer now to the one known as R.

(Carla channeling)

We are those of Hatonn, and we are now with this instrument. We find that we are experiencing difficulty in the communication, and perhaps have worked this new instrument too hard. Therefore, we shall move back to the one known as R later. We would at this time transfer to the one known as N.

(N channeling)

The young man [was] on this trip on this ship far [from] land, farther than he had been away before. He would look over [towards] the land and he could see the deep blue of the ocean, but he could not see any land. He was thrilled with the newness, but the journey was long there on the ocean. Many, many days, and some of the crew had gotten ill, he himself had been sick, and was able to overcome the sickness, but because of the long and tedious journey had wondered if the lands which they were headed to would not contain more of the same. Although there many things which he could not anticipate, he looked to the sky in the evenings and early mornings and saw beauty which he had never seen on land before, in the sky.

We wish to continue the story through the instrument known as K.

(K channeling)

As the boy gazed upon the stars in the heavens, he wondered at the vastness of the universe and wondered if there was wisdom in the heavens. He wondered at the significance of his small, small self in that boat upon that ocean. And he dreamed of many lands and many peoples of many [paths].

And he realized after much concentration that the only understanding he would have of the world, of the sky, of the stars and the universe, was to seek out wisdom which he knew was contained within himself. And only there would he find the answers to his small questions. With that knowledge, he reached a new perspective of the world and of his life, and it gave him great joy and meaning to all that he looked upon, for he realized that he was but one small cell in the infinite vastness of the universe, yet within that small cell was contained all the knowledge and the wisdom that he sought around him.

One day the ship came within sight of new land, and as it approached, he realized that he would leave the ocean at this shore and once again work upon the land. He was glad that his ocean voyage would soon be coming to an end, and realized that he had gained far more than any pirate could have ever plundered from any ship or any shore. On that voyage upon that ocean he had gained a knowledge of the self that no gold could ever pay for, that had no price and that was priceless only to himself.

He looked forward to once again working in a shipyard where he might build ships that would send other men upon the vast ocean, hopefully to gain the knowledge which he himself had secured.

We would like at this time to transfer to the one known as D.

(Carla channeling)

I am Hatonn, and am again with this instrument. To the one known as D we would apologize for startling him with our importunate transfer. We had found that this instrument has a natural affinity for our contact. Put in other words, it would mean that were we of your form, and sat in the room among you, it is to D that we would probably most be drawn to speak. We thank the one known as D for giving a Herculean effort, and assure this effort that we will work with him at a slower pace. It was worth a try, as this instrument would say.

To conclude our story.

Many were interested in the strange-looking, exotic blonde and blue-eyed man of the sea who had come to live in their far different clime. When asked why he had come, he would only reply, "To look at the stars." His inquirers would look up, and ask the keen-eyed sailor, "What is special about these stars?" He would smile and say, "When one has keen eyes, one thirsts for something which to see."

My friends, it is not important under which stars you dwell, but vastly important that your gaze upward be keen and persistent. Many times in any incarnation there will be the need for the dark night and the lack of humankind's banishing of the night, for only in the deepest darkness can one truly see at their very best those starry dominions which are symbols of light and love.

Find the deep sea within yourself in the waters of meditation, in the strong ship of your builded soul. Take the tiller and take responsibility for your seeking. Never apologize, however, for dwelling upon the land, for that which you do in the midst of your fellow human beings is that which builds the ship that carries your soul upon the stretches of the inner deep.

Before we take questions, we would like to exercise the new instrument. While we are exercising the one known as R, we would ask that the one known as D relax and allow us to begin making a good, comfortable contact. If discomfort ensues in any way, we ask that the one known as D declare his discomfort and request that it be removed. We are sorry that we are somewhat clumsy when first entering into the energy level of the new instrument, but each instrument is a bit different, and our first few attempts do need some adjustment.

We would now say a few words through the one known as R, asking that this instrument would relax, and once the challenging has been done, refrain from analysis, for material may be analyzed at any time after it has been recorded, yet in the recording it is best that the analytical mind be removed from the process. I am Hatonn. We now transfer to the one known as R.

(Carla channeling)

I am Hatonn. We are continuing to make adjustments with the one known as R, and will attempt again to transmit a simple message to this instrument. We ask this instrument not to be concerned at the small difficulty of the present moment, for we were one of those which first contacted this instrument, and this instrument was not nearly as apt a student as the one known as R. We feel that we have made better contact at this time, and would again wish to greet each through the one known as R. We transfer now. I am Hatonn.

(R channeling)

I am Hatonn. I greet you … in light and love …
(The rest of this channeling was not transcribed.)

(Carla channeling)

I am Hatonn, and am again with this instrument. We are most pleased with each of the new channels, and before we take questions, we would appreciate your patience as we allow the one known as D to become more and more used to our vibration. We would like to identify ourselves through this instrument, if the instrument would relax, and when our greeting comes into the conscious mind, simply repeat it. That which we send is concept, and is sent below the level of the conscious mind. Thus, our sendings to instruments move into the conscious mind, concepts in search of words, feeling exactly like one's own thoughts …

(Side one of tape ends.)

(Carla channeling)

… process. It is never intended by those of the Confederation that work with you now that we initiate a trance communication.

We intend for a portion of that which is said by us to be drawn from the experiences, the reading, and the vocabulary, in other words, the resources of the instrument. We have a very simple message, yet because of the richness of your languages and the infinity of uniqueness among peoples, we find that the portion which is added to the basic concept material by each instrument creates an excellence which we by ourselves could not achieve. That is the great advantage of concept communication in a conscious manner. However, we will not attempt to send concepts yet to the one known as D, but will be satisfied if this instrument can hear and repeat our greeting. We now transfer to the one known as D. I am Hatonn.

(D channeling)

I am Hatonn, and I greet each of you in the love and light of the infinite Creator.

(Carla channeling)

I am Hatonn, and am again with this instrument. We are so pleased and grateful to each of the new instruments for attempting to learn this service, this bridge of words through which concepts far deeper than any words can convey move. We know that each of you desires to be excellent, and we feel that each of you is excellent. We urge each to realize within themselves those gifts which they already have, those things which benefit others.

To be of service to others is an elusive and baffling goal, and yet we find the hearts of each true and the desire of each to serve. May your sacrifices of time and caring in all that you do be a channeling of love and light, and may the channeling itself, for those of you who find it a helpful thing to continue, be a source through you of that great spreading light which more and more is being lit up with great lights among your peoples. More and more of you upon your sphere are becoming lights, channels of love, and, as for us, we love each of you and bless you for all that you have given us.

We would like to transfer now to the one known as Jim. We thank this instrument and each of you for asking us to be here and for working with us. We are known to you as Hatonn and will now transfer.

(Jim channeling)

I am Hatonn, and it is our privilege at this time to offer ourselves in the attempt to speak to any query which those present might offer to us. We would state that we offer opinion and the fruits of our own seeking, whatever value they may be to any seeker, but we do not wish any to take our words as absolute. With that understanding, may we ask if there is a query to which we may speak?

K: Last night you mentioned several members of the Confederation that were here with us during our meditation, and you also mentioned a couple of them specifically that seemed to have a particular affinity for particular ones of us. I'm curious as to what the connection is between various members of the Confederation and various ones of us, what the nature of that is? I assume it has something to do with vibratory patterns, but I don't really know much about it. Could you comment on that for me?

I am Hatonn, and, my sister, each seeker within this circle works the puzzle of existence within a creation that is mysterious. Each seeker seeks in a fashion which is appropriate for that seeker and which asks the queries that reflect the nature of that seeker's being. Each seeker, then, is as the one who has discovered new land and wishes to settle upon it and expand its ability to understand and survive within the new land, and as it gains the basic skills of this simple survival, begins to refine them so that there is a certain grace and even elegance to the means of surviving, prospering and bearing a fruit of experience that may be shared with others. Thus, each seeker vibrates or resonates in a certain frequency that calls unto itself that which is just beyond the ability to understand.

This range is somewhat different for each seeker, and thus the response to each seeker is somewhat different from those who are members of what you have come to know as the Confederation of Planets in the Service of the Infinite Creator. In some cases the difference is marked enough that different members of our Confederation make answer to the call for assistance in the seeking by each seeker.

In a general fashion, the nature of such calls may be seen to fall within three major categories, each with many, many subdivisions, shall we say. There is that seeking that is of love and for compassion and understanding and the attempt to accept more and more of the creation as a portion of the self. There is that seeking which partakes of that known as wisdom or light which reveals unto the inner and outer eyes of the seeker more and more of the nature of the creation which Love has formed. And there is that seeking which partakes of the balancing of these two of love and of wisdom into a force or source which may be seen as unity or power, and which partakes of the blending of love with wisdom by wisdom. Thus, a seeker may throughout an incarnation move into each of these three general categories of seeking, and by the nature and intensity of the seeking call unto itself the assistance of those unseen teachers, guides and friends which vibrate in harmony with the nature of the seeker.

May we speak in any further fashion, my sister?

K: No, that's very helpful. Thank you.

I am Hatonn, and we thank you, my sister. Is there another query?

Carla: I would welcome any suggestions that you could give on the teaching of channeling, anything that I might be able to learn as a teacher.

I am Hatonn, and, my sister, we are very happy to be able to move within the boundaries described by the desire of each seeker within this circle this evening, and can only reinforce the means by which our contact is recognized, prepared for, challenged and spoken, as these means have been utilized in your past, as you would call it. The channeling of the desire to be of service to others is that which we see as being of the greatest importance for each who would seek to become that known as a vocal channel or instrument.

Thus, your role as one who serves as teacher is to share that which is yours to share, the experience which you have gained over the many years during which you have served as a vocal instrument, and to share that experience in the manner which makes the most, shall we say, sense to you, for it is your own fruits of seeking that provide the greatest nourishment to those who wish to learn from it. If you were but one which parroted that which we or others gave you, there would be no vitality within that which you share, and the impact, shall we say, upon the student would be but short-lived.

Thus, my sister, we take much of your time and use many of your words to suggest to you that you may do that which you do and know that it is that which is most appropriate and efficient for you, as one who would teach this service to others, insofar as [it] can be taught.

May we speak further, my sister?

Carla: No. I get the gist of it. Thank you. I was afraid that I was on my own there.

I am Hatonn, and we thank you, my sister. Is there another query?

Carla: Is the instrument tired?

I am Hatonn, and we find this instrument to be in relatively good shape, shall we say, and able to offer itself as instrument for another few queries.

R: I have a question. On August 16 and 17 of this year the Mayan calendar ends, and people are organizing what's known as the Harmonic Convergence. And I was just wondering what you would care to say in regards to that or what it meant or anything you might want to comment on.

I am Hatonn. There are cycles within the pattern of experience of all seekers and all groupings of seekers, and, indeed, within the planetary and solar system influences in which you find yourselves at this time. These cycles provide opportunities that may be seen as wider or narrower portions of the road upon which each moves in the evolutionary pattern of existence. The period of time that now approaches in your near future of which you speak is a portion of a greater cycle, and as the gateway, shall we say, to this increased vibratory pattern offers to each conscious seeker the opportunity to intensify the desire to know the self and to be of service through that self-expression to those about it in a fashion which may be likened to the magnification of possibility. Thus, the desire which resides deep within the heart of each seeker, much like the seed in the fertile soil, will have the opportunity to become nourished with the living waters and to take root more firmly within the being, that it might produce more abundant fruit within the manifesting work, shall we say.

May we speak in any further fashion, my sister?

R: No, thank you.

D: Could I ask you to expand somewhat on the same subject. What is the significance of this occurring at this particular time as opposed to another point in history?

I am Hatonn. If you could see your portion of the, as you call it, galaxy, and more specifically the solar system in which you now exist, it would look somewhat like a three-dimensional face of a clock. There is the movement of planet and solar system and galaxy itself through what you know of as time and space, that has, just as the face of the clock, portions of time and space that, when reached, offer increased opportunities to utilize the intelligent energy of the one Creator in whatever fashion and direction the individual and group desires of such conscious beings have determined. Thus, it is the desire of each seeker that determines the ability to utilize the increased vibratory energies, and it is this same desire to know the self and to serve others with this knowledge that may make an efficient use of these increased opportunities for knowing and for serving.

May we speak further, my brother?

D: Thank you, no.

I am Hatonn, and we thank you, my brother. Is there another query at this time?

D: In establishing a connection with me a while ago, I wonder if you became aware of a degree of fear which stands in my way of opening up. And, if so, can you give me any suggestions about the source of that fear and how to minimize its effect?

I am Hatonn, and, my brother, we have found within your beingness the general desire not to become that known as foolish, which each new instrument may be expected to contain in greater or lesser degree, for the process of serving as a vocal instrument is that which requires a certain gullibility in that one speaks the beginning of a thought, the ending of which is unknown. Thus, to step upon such seemingly shaky ground is that which any new instrument may show a certain fear for.

We may suggest to you as a new instrument, and to each new instrument, that one cultivate the desire to step upon such ground and to risk becoming foolish, for, indeed, it is a foolish endeavor to speak words that are not heard from entities that are not seen to those who may not understand a message which begins and ends in mystery. And yet, so each desires as a means of service to others to penetrate the difficulties, the confusions and the mysterious nature of being itself, in order to find a surer center to the self and a firmer framework for the mind to make its expression of the quality or character of being in order that experience may be gained, knowledge may be acquired, and service may be rendered to others.

Thus, my brother, we encourage you to become foolish and to step upon the shaky ground, for, indeed, with each step the ground grows in firmness and the feet find support and a path is fashioned which may lead one to the desire to serve and the means by which to serve. The faith to follow this path, the faith that such leads to a destination, that offers inspiration and encouragement to the self and to others, and the will to persevere beyond difficulty are those qualities which serve each seeker and each new instrument well; the faith and the will to continue to move into that which is unknown and to begin to know that which is unknown as another portion of the self.

May we speak in any further fashion, my brother?

D: That was very eloquent. Thank you very much.

I am Hatonn, and we thank you once again, my brother. Is there a final query at this time?

(Pause)

I am Hatonn, and it has been our great honor to have shared this meditation with each of you this evening. We cannot express the joy that grows within our being at each opportunity to join with you in your seeking. We look forward, as you would say, to your future gatherings, and we encourage once again each new instrument in the traveling of the path of the vocal instrument. We treasure each new instrument as another unique opportunity to share that which we have gained in our own seeking with others of your own *(inaudible)* that might seek such an information as an aid in their journeys. And so each of us aids the other as a portion of the one Creator comes to know itself as the one Creator. We are known to you as those of Hatonn. We leave you at this time in the love and in the light of the one infinite Creator. Adonai, my friends. Adonai vasu borragus. ☥

Intensive Meditation
July 17, 1987

(W channeling)

[I am Quanta,] and I greet you in the love and the light of the infinite Creator. We would like to welcome you all to this meditation this evening. We are pleased that you have gathered once again to practice the art of vocal channeling. We would like to let you know that we are here to aid and assist in whatever way possible in order to facilitate your vocal channeling. We are pleased with the progress that each of you has made these past few evenings, as you know it. We would like to thank the one known as Carla and the one known as Jim for aiding and guiding these new instruments. We would like to commend you on a job well done. We wish at this time to leave this instrument and allow for further tuning to the entity which wishes to make contact with her. You need only to request our assistance, and we will be there to aid and guide in whatever way we may be of service to you. We are known to you as Quanta, and we leave you once again in the love and the light of the one infinite Creator.

(Carla channeling)

I am Hatonn. I greet each in the love and the light of the one infinite Creator. We have enjoyed the becoming one with your vibrations. We were attempting to initiate contact through the one known as K, however the natural reserve of this new instrument was causing the instrument a considerable amount of distraction. We however did make good contact with the instrument and do appreciate the effort that this instrument makes. This being said, we would once again like to contact the one known as K. We are those of Hatonn.

(K channeling)

I am Hatonn. I greet you once again, my friends, in love and light through this instrument. It is as always a privilege to share with you in your endeavors as you seek to serve by being vocal channels … *(The rest of this channeling was not transcribed.)*

(R channeling)

I am Hatonn. … *(The rest of this channeling was not transcribed.)*

(Carla channeling)

I am Hatonn, and am now with this instrument. We are aware that the one known as D is having continuing difficulty due to the tendency to analyze, coupled with some fatigue. We are delighted in the progress that we have made, and are aware that the instrument is already often able to perceive the contact, and have been pleased with those practice times. We feel that at this time we [will] allow this instrument to rest and will be with this instrument upon mental request. We will not be channeling, but will greet the new instrument. In this way practice in contact can be made.

Please, we ask the one known as D, and, indeed, all new channels, to when practicing tune your instrument and be careful with the challenges to all spirits, just as though it were a group meeting, for you need to be far more fastidious when working alone than when supported by the group energy which is phenomenally greater than the energy of one alone. We are most pleased with the subjective rise in each individual amount of trust in the benign nature of our contact and the benign nature of channeling itself.

Channeling is actually a fourth-density commonplace, as each entity is aware that within it lies the glory of the Creator. It naturally makes the choice to channel that energy. Those of you in third density can often not see with the physical eyes the seeds of wonder and godhead in ourselves and each other. Yet, that resource, pure and undistorted, lies full-blown within each consciousness' heart. As you learn to channel the best that we have to offer you, and we offer it in all humility as our opinion only, realize that we are only attempting to aid you in learning to channel your own divinity, that impersonal, caring and life-affirming portion of the self, which with great compassion and justice gazes upon a fruitful and beautiful creation.

We would end our musings for this evening through the one known as W before we ask for questions. We are those of Hatonn. We transfer now.

(W channeling)

I am Hatonn, and I greet you once again … *(The rest of this channeling was not transcribed.)*

(Side one of tape ends.)

(Carla channeling)

… to express itself through her. We are known to you as those of Hatonn.

(W channeling)

We are here, and we are pleased that the one [known as] W has been able to allow us to speak using her as a vocal channel. We were so happy to have the opportunity to speak with you this evening. We are still in the process of making adjustments with further tuning to ease in the contact in communication with this entity. We have been waiting long, and yet not so long, to begin working with this vocal channel. We would like to thank once again all of you for being patient and allowing us to make ourselves known to you at this time. We are honored to be here with you this evening and we will leave now, as those of the Confederation of Planets would say, in the love and the light of the one infinite Creator.

(Carla channeling)

I am Hatonn, and I greet [you] once again in the love and the light. At this time we will transfer to the one known as Jim so that queries may be entertained. We are known to you as Hatonn.

(Jim channeling)

I am Hatonn, and greet each again in love and light. At this time we have the privilege of asking if we might attempt to speak to any query which those present may have for us. Is there a query with which we may begin?

Carla: Yeah, I'd like to ask one. I've always had a prejudice against people working by themselves when they were new channels, but I was never able to say it was because it didn't work; it does work by yourself. And from what you said, I'm wondering if my prejudice doesn't have its basis in the fact that one is more protected with a couple of people around, especially experienced people. Comment?

I am Hatonn, and it is also our recommendation, my sister, that new instruments practice the art of vocal channeling only in the company of those who seek in like manner information of an inspirational nature from sources such as our own. It is further recommended, as you have also been accustomed to recommend, that the new instrument, for the greater portion of its initial practice, place itself within a group that contains a more experienced instrument, in order that the finer points of the channeling process might be noted and used as teaching devices.

It is easy for a new instrument to be able to make the contact and to vocalize the contact, yet, as you are aware, there are many considerations that each new instrument needs to be aware of that are most easily noted by a more experienced instrument.

May we speak further, my sister?

Carla: No, thank you.

I am Hatonn, and we thank you, my sister. Is there another query?

W: This evening I felt a lot of different intensities of energy working with me, and I was just wondering if that is further adjustments or whatever to this new entity which I've started channeling?

I am Hatonn, and this is correct, my sister. May we speak in any further fashion?

W: Not right now, thank you.

I am Hatonn, and we thank you, my sister. Is there another query?

W: In the practicing by oneself by just mentally receiving the contact, can you comment more about process?

I am Hatonn, and it is our recommendation to the new instrument, and, indeed, any instrument which wishes to experience our contact or the contact of any of our other brothers or sisters within the Confederation of Planets in the Service of the One Creator, that the contact be made only in the form which would allow recognition of the contact and the deepening of the meditative state. We do not recommend even the reception of mental images or words from unseen contacts while in solitary meditation, for it is easy for the new instrument to believe that it has recognized a contact sufficiently enough to speak the words and impressions that are received, and in many cases this would be a workable situation for a certain period of time. Yet after this period of time, which is variable for each entity, there is the likelihood that there would be the infringement upon the contact by other unseen entities who may have less than helpful desires as their motivation for attempting to confuse the original contact with their own. It is far less easy for such an infringement to occur when an instrument places itself within a circle that includes at least three as the minimum number. Three entities, then, blending their seeking for knowledge and the ability to utilize it in a service to others as a kind of protective device that ensures a cleansed working place and the conditions necessary for the working to proceed in a stable manner.

May we speak further my sister?

W: So, as I understand it, the request is made for contact. Is the request made of a specific entity such as yourself or whoever might be available from the Confederation, or how should that proceed?

I am Hatonn. We would recommend that contact be requested from those entities with whom one is familiar through previous work. In your particular case this would include the ones known as Laitos and our own social memory complex. It is our recommendation that additional contacts be experienced within a group which includes the more experienced instrument in order that a kind of cross-referencing may be utilized to verify that a certain contact is who it says it is.

May we speak further, my sister?

W: No, thank you.

I am Hatonn, and again we thank you, my sister.

Questioner: Yeah. In daily meditation I attempt to make connection at times, to seek guidance of my own higher self. How am I then to determine whether that information which I believe I've made is indeed my higher self, and not, as you speak, of other entities? In other words, how do I differentiate between the part of me that I call on in my meditation from other entities that are out there?

I am Hatonn. We might suggest that the proper respect and personalized ritual be accorded to this type of seeking for guidance and information in that the meditative state would be utilized as the general arena or place in which such work might be accomplished, and this place of working then would be prepared in the mental sense by the intensity and purity of desire to seek knowledge in order to grow and to be of service to others.

This purification of the inner desire may be accomplished in any fashion which has meaning to you. The visualization of white light surrounding and protecting your inner place of working is one manner that might be utilized in a variety of fashions as the light is formed in various meaningful symbols by your own conscious application of attention. The repeating of words written either by yourself or others which are of an inspirational nature and which direct your desire in a certain fashion which expresses your nature and your desire to learn and serve may also be utilized.

The principle which is of fundamental importance in this instance is some regularized manner of preparing the place within your meditative state to which you shall repair only for the seeking of a contact with a greater portion of your being, whether it be your higher self or other portions of your mental complex that may contain useful information for the direction of your journey of seeking. This ritual then repeated each time that you desire such contact will suffice to provide a cleansed and protected place of working as you undertake this type of seeking.

May we speak further, my sister?

(Inaudible)

W: When you refer to other mental complexes, is that what some would refer to as their guides?

I am Hatonn. It is possible that such additional entities may also be contacted within this type of situation. However, in our previous statement we were referring to other portions of your own mind complex which lie beneath the conscious level or awareness which may also be tapped for useful information as regards certain avenues of seeking and endeavor.

May we speak further, my sister?

W: So, basically it's the way in which you approach the meditation and the desire to contact certain portions of yourself that protect or direct that which you receive? Is that it?

I am Hatonn, and this is basically correct. The attitude with which one attempts such a type of meditation and the regularized manner of focusing that attitude through the general principle of the ritual are the qualities which are most important, in our opinion, in this type of seeking.

May we speak further my sister?

W: No, thank you. That was very helpful.

I am Hatonn. We thank you once again, my sister. Is there another query at this time?

W: I have another question. Can you give me any information on the nature of the entity working with me in terms of its purpose of contacting me and utilizing me as a vocal channel?

I am Hatonn. This entity, as all entities of a positive nature, seeks to utilize yet another means through which to be of service to the one Creator by sharing that which is their fruit of seeking the experience that has been gathered through the evolutionary process. It is the case with positive entities that after the choice has been made to seek in the positive or radiant service-to-others sense, that after a very short time upon this path, it becomes apparent that further progress upon this path is achieved not through personal gain of knowledge only, but more especially through the sharing of this knowledge and experience with others in a fashion which furthers the potential for growth in other selves. Thus, the opportunity to utilize a vocal instrument is one which is greatly cherished by entities who seek to be of service to others.

May we speak further, my sister?

W: Not right now, thank you.

I am Hatonn, and again we thank you, my sister. Is there another query at this time?

D: I have a number of questions, but once I get started I *(inaudible)*. Well, I would like to ask for comment—this may not be of interest to anyone—on the process of attempting to channel during the last year, on the style and approach, which is a lot different from this in the setting in which it has been done, the manner in which it has been done. Are there inherently difficult things, or dangers, or opportunities to be misguided as we have been practicing channeling?

I am Hatonn, and we are not completely aware of the conditions of which you speak, for we operate through an instrument which may transmit the information which it is given and which provides us with our primary contact with your group. We, with some reluctance or difficulty, could attempt to scan the mental complex of an entity such at yourself and determine certain qualities, but find that in such a scanning of the mental complex, the opportunity to infringe upon the free will of another is somewhat increased, and we would prefer that the queries which are addressed to our group would be specific in their formation so that the information which is requested of us might be drawn, then, from the query which is stated in as complete a fashion as possible.

At this time we would ask if we may speak in a more specific fashion as the final query of the evening, for there is the fatigue that many in the circle feel and which makes the maintenance of a steady contact somewhat difficult for this instrument which is also somewhat fatigued. May we speak to a final query?

D: Very briefly. Do disciplines, such things as diet, play a major role in opening as a channel for some? And if so, how can you determine, from a neophyte's status, something that would be helpful to oneself?

I am Hatonn, and the utilization of the diet would be helpful if the dietary plan were to be seen as a symbol for a greater purpose, the cleansing of the, not only, body but mind and spirit complexes as well, for example. Or perhaps the bringing into balance of the physical complex with those of the mental and spiritual as well. The diet in itself, beyond the point of a reasonably healthy maintenance of the physical vehicle, is not necessarily a useful means of aiding a new instrument in serving as such, but may become so if used as the means towards a greater end.

May we speak further on that topic, my brother?

D: Can you verify that last phrase, "used as a means to a greater end"?

I am Hatonn. By this statement we were attempting to describe how the use of a certain dietary plan might be seen as a symbol by the new instrument that would allow it to achieve more than the healthier physical vehicle, and would serve as somewhat as a lever, shall we say, in springing the instrument's mental, physical or spiritual complexes or combinations or combinations thereof into a more balanced alignment that would then become that configuration that would be most helpful in the learning of the art of becoming the vocal channel.

May we speak further, my brother?

D: You certainly have a way with words. Thank you.

I am Hatonn, and we thank you, my brother. We apologize for the necessity of bringing this gathering to a close when there are further queries which await the asking. We enjoy each query greatly and treasure each as an opportunity to share our opinion upon points of interest to all in the seeking of inspiration and a wider point of view. However, this evening we find that each in the group has expended a great deal of attention and energy in maintaining the focus upon the tuning and the desire to serve as the vocal instrument, and this focus has caused some discomfort to a number in this group. And therefore we shall at this time take our leave of this instrument and this group, thanking each for inviting our presence, and, as always, we leave each in the love and in the love and in the light of the one infinite Creator. We are known to you as those of Hatonn. Adonai, my brothers and sisters. Adonai vasu borragus.

Intensive Meditation
July 21, 1987

(K channeling)

[I am Quanta,] and I greet you in the love and the light of the infinite Creator. We are honored once again to be a part of this gathering. We are pleased to see your continued efforts in the art of vocal channeling and wish to assist in whatever manner we can. We would like to recommend that the one known as W begin to relax and deepen her meditative state so that further conditioning can occur. We are aware that she has begun to make contact with that entity which wishes to use her as a vocal channel, and we are pleased with the progress she has made to this point. We would recommend that she continue to meditate on a daily basis to help further the connection which she is establishing. We would like at this time to transfer to the one known as Carla in order to allow a stronger connection to be made. I am Quanta.

(Carla channeling)

I am Quanta, and greet you through this instrument. We would like to say a few words about contact with those which are not of the Confederation of Planets in the Service of the Infinite One, for there are ways in which interplane contact is like contact with the Confederation and there are ways in which it differs. The challenging and tuning mechanisms of the instrument remain of the same importance, regardless of the nature of the contact, regardless of whether the instrument is conscious or in trance, regardless of whether the contact is inner plane or outer plane.

We strongly suggest that entities not agree to accept the contact which does not declare a name. Few among the Confederation have retained names in the sense that you know them, yet in order that we may speak with those who have names, in order that there be trust and recognition and companionship, we have taken those vibratory characteristics that are most ourselves and molded sound vibration complexes to create the most accurate name we could. It is not well to accept an unnamed contact, for that which does not have a name may indeed evade challenge.

There is a great variety of strengths and powers of personality among those dwelling in the inner planes of your planetary energy web. We say this not because the entity which attempts to call you is negative—this is not so—but rather because in the instrument's present situation, it would be surprising if the new instrument were not greeted by more than one entity, the extraneous contact being of a less than desirable nature.

It is impossible to place the same standards of information upon inner plane masters and outer plane servants, for those within the higher planes of the Earth's system are often agreeably pleased with themselves for achieving such a high level of understanding. This is because such entities often have put off the day when, for the first time, they move on into fourth density. Thus inner plane channeling can become most uninspiring due to the instrument's encouragement of self-aggrandizing material, and [if it] is willing to channel such material.

We ask the instrument to remain faithful to that which may be more difficult to achieve than some contacts, in order that when that contact is established, it may offer much to those who may wish to ask questions of it. Be aware that only through practice does the inner ear become keen. Know, too, that inner plane masters, having by definition had at least one incarnation upon your Earth plane, have the right, and to various degrees the ability, to offer personal material, that is, material concerning someone who wishes to know about previous lifetimes or the efficacy of future actions. It is in the instrument's hands to direct the contact in the most helpful fashion, that is to say, not as we see a helpfulness nor as anyone else sees helpfulness, but in the one known as W's mind, in that way of seeing helpfulness, visualized clearly, shall the one known as W attempt to encourage the contact.

We would at this time leave this instrument in the love and the light of the one infinite Creator. I am Quanta.

(Long pause.)

Carla: In the name of divine love and the service, I ask the entity who wishes to speak through W to clothe itself in the name and make that name known to the one known as W. May that name be acceptable and right [for her]. I thank you, spirit, and leave you in love.

(W channeling)

(The transcription is approximate because of the quality of the recording.)

I am *(sounds like)* Christine, and I have met with your challenge for the name. We feel that names are but labels which do not [clearly] represent that which we are, however it has been necessary to continue at this time. However, this is merely a *(inaudible)* version *(inaudible)* and that which we own. We find at this time that the name Christine will best serve our needs. However, there are those of us who feel this name *(inaudible)* that which we are and make further modification or expansion as we further establish a working contact with this entity.

We recognize the efforts on the part of the one known as Quanta in preparing and establishing the connection which we have been able to develop with the one known as W. We are most honored and pleased to have the opportunity to work with this instrument, and we recognize the efforts of the one known as Jim and the one known as Carla in aiding this instrument in her endeavors to establish contact. We are happy now that we can begin working on greater portions of the carrier which has been established now that this entity has begun vocally channeling that known to you as Christine. We are preparing for further contact with other portions of our complex, and shall expand the answers, for we wish to proceed as rapidly as possible in attaining and refining that which we have begun.

In order to further establish this contact we request that the entity known as W *(inaudible)* the [inclinations] toward the more healthful lifestyle, such as practicing the art of yoga meditation and internal cleansing which she has begun to feel directed toward. We wish not to require or demand such procedures, but merely to suggest that through these practices the connections which she has begun to establish and the strengthening.

We are most pleased with the progress she has made over the past year and recognize that much has accrued and there has been great change within her. We are aware of the difficulties which this entity is having as we further condition and establish contact. Therefore, we will end this vocal channeling at this time. Again, we are most pleased with the progress which she has made and wish to send to *(inaudible)* that we are one in the love and light of the one true God we all serve. I am Christine [and now we leave you].

(Tape ends.)

L/L Research

Sunday Meditation
July 26, 1987

Group question: What is depression and how do you deal with it?

(Carla channeling)

I am Q'uo. I greet you in the love and in the light of the one infinite Creator. I come to you from farther away than usual this evening, for we are engaged in some light work of a planet in the star system—we have difficulty transmitting the name to this instrument—Regulus. Yet, still we maintain connection with this instrument as it is our privilege indeed to have any opportunity to address this light group.

Your question about depression and what to do about it is a difficult one for us to answer, in that what we would do about depression would be very different from what the people of your planets consider the practical and efficacious approach. However, we will share our views with you and thank you for the privilege of doing so.

It has been written in your holy work known as the Bible that the master known as Jesus is a vine and his students branches thereof. If you consider yourself as a cosmic citizen, you and all other consciousness in the universe are rooted in one vine, that is, the life-giving vine of love. We use that word, although it is inadequate to express the mystery of the Creator, because as ill-used as that word is among your peoples, it nevertheless evokes knowledge of the most extreme of human emotions. Pure living love, stemming directly from the Uncreated in perfect order, in perfect love, is a force of unimaginable magnitude, a force which has propelled into being all consciousness, and a force which wishes to assist each portion of consciousness in its full circle through experience and back to the Source of love, that which is uncreated, that which is always the same, the one great original Thought.

Depression is one of many human experiences, as you would call them, in which a branch of the vine is damaged by the cutting off of the supply of food from the root. The invisible strangling of love can come about because of many circumstances. In its worst cases, one may observe in its results those personalities which do not have an emotional bias against murder, theft and so forth. When one looks for the invisible garrote that has so strangled love within such an entity, one cannot see it, although earnest scholars equate the loss of life-giving emotion with lack of love or even lack of a home in the murderer's early years.

With the emotional experience of depression, we may see a person which is experiencing a strangulation, to a certain extent a loss of love from the root, and when the person looks to see what the source of this strangulation of love might be, again it is invisible, for it has taken place within the mind itself.

If this material concerning what depression is is not satisfactory, we gladly invite your queries after we have concluded the opening discussion.

Now, it is not merely an illusion to say that you are experiencing depression. Indeed, we feel that overemphasis on all being an illusion is perhaps detrimental to the balanced progress of a seeker.

It is well to attempt to gaze at and consider the self and all of its vagaries. The one who attempts to change depression by denying negative feelings is perhaps on the right track, however, that person has little chance of creating an easement of the strangulation of love simply by speaking it so, for in depression, that which ties the cord too tightly around the vine, that which holds back the supply of love, is a desire to hold in the mind circumstances which seem unacceptable. This desire, whether quite conscious or relatively unconscious in nature, has a very adverse affect upon the supply of the life-giving energy of love which is falling constantly into each of the portions of the Creator's consciousness.

Thus, large portions of the subconscious mind begin to be distracted from processing the catalyst of the present in terms of the present, and begin to process catalyst in terms of an unacceptable portion in the memory of the one who is depressed. It is as if there were a drag upon an engine, so that the engine had to work harder and harder to produce the same amount of work. Or perhaps even better as an analogy, it is as if in a depressed person the unacceptable thing creates a blockage in the fuel line so that the engine of the mind is ultimately unable to function.

Since the entity who is depressed can blame only itself, a disassociation almost inevitably begins within the mind of the depressed person, which then adds to the inertia that is dragging down or to the block in the fuel line that is keeping fuel from the engine of consciousness. It is as if there were two consciousnesses, one healthy and free and thriving, which exists in our dreams and at the core of all illusion, and that consciousness which has come to a standstill, getting, instead of love, a fueling supply of fear and anxiety.

Because the rupture lies within the self, it is most efficacious for the depressed entity to call upon two general archetypes. First, it is well to call upon the archetype which you have in essence conjured up in the process of self-strangulation, that is, your consciousness has made the self its own scapegoat. Some there are in your illusion which go through a lifetime of incarnation never blaming themselves for anything. These entities move in a sleepy existence and do not trouble their hearts or their digestions with a conscience. We speak to those who are sensitive and creative enough to pay attention to their consciousnesses to ask themselves questions and to seek in whatever way they can.

After gazing at the scapegoat and considering how little you truly wish to make yourself such an archetype, it may then be efficacious for the one who is depressed to consider the archetype of the unfed consciousness. We have spoken a great many words about consciousness in the opportunities we have had to communicate with this group. You know that to us it is a synonym for your words "spirit" or "soul." You know that consciousness is almost never seen without some distortion. Depression is merely a very disturbing distortion.

We say to you that depression is impossible in a consciousness that is new. If an entity gazes about itself at any point in the lifetime experience, it will see some things which are pleasing and some things which are not. The consciousness which has been your source of life sees the creation with eyes of love, for it is love, and in this love all things are as they should be.

Contradistinctive to undistorted love is the operation of free will which moves within each particle of consciousness in such a way as to make choices possible. Thus, the new consciousness, by the operation of free will, would turn each moment, like a stone, to see each facet of beauty, unity and love, or perhaps to marvel at those balances which are particularly unusual in those about it. This new consciousness is that which the depressed entity may acquire not only through meditation, but also through remembering at each moment when it is first noticed that the experience of depression is becoming active.

There is another portion as well to new consciousness, and that is its insatiable curiosity. Let the curiosity of the unfed consciousness sink into every thought process that has been stultified by the distortion of depression. Curiosity is that which can unblock …

(Tape ends.)

Intensive Meditation
July 29, 1987

(Jim channeling)

I am Quanta, and greet each in the love and in the light of the one infinite Creator. We are pleased to be able to make contact with this instrument, and thank each for opening each instrument to our use. The one known as N and the one known as W have been aware of our contact, but due to the period of time which has elapsed since our last gathering, these new instruments have felt somewhat hesitant in the beginning of the contact, and this is understandable, my friends, for the skill that is being gained in this type of service is that which responds most effectively to the periodic exercise of the instrument in order that the confidence of each new instrument might be increased with each exercising.

We are pleased that the new instruments have maintained their dedication to this service over the period of time which has elapsed since we were privileged to speak through each new instrument. This dedication and perseverance is the primary quality which any new instrument may utilize as the foundation stone of the structure of its service to others. Without the dedication to continue and the will to persevere, no talent, no matter how great or varied or inspiring, can continue to burn as a beacon to others. Even the most rudimentary and basic of vocal channeling skills can be added unto on a continuous basis by the one which burns with the desire to hone this skill that it might be of service to others. We commend each instrument for maintaining that dedication, and we look forward, as you might say, to working with each as each gathering brings new opportunities for expansion of these skills.

At this time we would like to exercise the instrument known as N in order that it might refresh its own abilities and add to that confidence which is building within the inner being. At this time we would transfer this contact to the one known as N in order that we might speak a few words through this instrument. I am Quanta.

(N channeling)

(The initial channeling was not transcribed.) We would like to transfer to the one known as W, *(inaudible)* and thank this instrument. We are those of Quanta.

(W channeling)

(The initial channeling was not transcribed.) At this time we would like to transfer to the one known as Jim. We are known to you as Quanta.

(Jim channeling)

I am Quanta, and greet each again in love and light through this instrument. At this time it is our privilege to offer ourselves in the attempt to speak to those queries which may be upon the minds this evening. Again we would like to remind each that we offer but our opinion which we do not wish to have any confuse with absolute truth. Please take that which we offer as opinion and as that which we have gained in our own seeking. May we begin with a query at this time?

W: How does one seek absolute truth?

I am Quanta, and, my sister, there is that which we call the one Creator which appears to us and to our teachers to be the one absolute Source of all that is, and each conscious being at some point within the experience of consciousness decides to seek that known as the Source or the Truth and to seek it in terms that can be comprehended and can be utilized as means by which the individual consciousness might move over greater and greater vistas and views and points of viewing that which is the creation, that which is the self, and that which is the journey of the self through the creation. This is a natural function of the conscious mind. However, we have discovered that for each portion of what seems to be truth that we gather unto ourselves in order to complete more of the puzzle of our existence, the greater grows the mystery of the nature of the one Creator from which all comes.

Thus, we find ourselves situated within a paradox. We seek to know as do all seekers of truth, and we gather pieces of that truth, and we move forward upon the journey of evolution and our steps seem sure and our experience serves us well, yet oftentimes we find that as we continue our journeys, that which was true at one time most often gives way to a greater truth that seems in comparison to be far surer and more reliable than any previous piece of knowledge we may have gathered.

Thus, our advice and that which we have to offer to each seeker is to gather all possible sources of information, to consider them in meditation and in comtemplation and in prayerful attention, and then to be moved by that which resonates with the inner being and to realize that the movement which shall be the fruit of such considerations is a movement into mystery which, as far as we can see, is infinite in nature.

However, that which is of the greatest truth for each seeker of truth seems to reside within the being of that seeker, and comes forth as that which is felt and then that which is known, as it begins to resonate with that which is sought and that which is attracted by the seeking to the seeker. Thus, the desire of the seeker draws from many sources that which is most appropriate for that time within the seeker's experience and draws from within the seeker that which is already there and which ripens at the appropriate time according to the seeking that is expressed.

May we speak further, my sister?

W: Not on that question, thank you.

I am Quanta. We thank you, my sister. Is there another query?

W: Yeah, I have another a question. Over the past few months I have become almost totally freed from any kind of [grounding] attachments, such as animals, and only remain to have one animal, which is my horse. And I'm wondering if there isn't some reason why this is my *(inaudible)* and also whether or not it would be appropriate for me to find a new home for my horse [that at this time is loved], and I would just like your opinion on that.

I am Quanta, and to take the last query first, we do not feel it appropriate to guide to the point of specificity in such matters which are properly located within the realm of personal choice. However, upon the first part of the query, we might suggest that which is already supposed by the questioner, and that is to say that the seasons of the soul as it seeks its source are various and have the manifestations that are seen in the outer world and which often perplex the seeker. It may be that in a certain season that various opportunities pertaining to a single theme are presented to the seeker in any of many fields of interest and activity such as the nature of the home environment, the system of support within your culture known as the working or the job description, the nature of friendships and relationships with those close to one and the attitude given by the seeker to various possessions. The points or possibilities of each theme offer to the seeker the opportunity to evaluate that which is essential upon the journey at a particular point upon that journey.

There is what you may call the testing, oftentimes referred to as initiation of one kind or another. The attitude that is the means by which the seeker views and accepts the manifestations of the various seasons of the soul's seeking is that which is of most importance in each testing, for if it can be discovered within the point of view of the seeker that each situation has a metaphysical implication that revolves about the concept of love and acceptance of that which is, then the seeker is more able to take advantage of the more specific lessons that orbit the primary concept of love that may be found in each cycle or season.

Thus, the testing is accomplished by the fires of experience touching the incarnation in a manner which concentrates the attention so that the greatest possible attitude of acceptance and peace then colors the mind.

May we speak further, my sister?

W: No, thank you. I appreciate that answer.

I am Quanta, and again we thank you, my sister. Is there another query?

W: I have one more. I'm just wondering how we're doing, [because] we're getting closer to contacting whoever's going to contact us.

I am Quanta, and though the future, as you would call it, cannot be seen with the perfectly clear eye, for it is yet to be a function of ever-changing free choice, we can suggest that this group has moved in its progress to the point that very fine tuning is all that is required in order that the next opportunities to serve in this manner might be experienced.

May we speak further, my sister?

W: No, thank you.

N: I have a question. I was just wondering if you could tell if the entities which we're in touch with, some or all of are likely to be in touch if I was, perhaps, to move to another land?

I am Quanta, and as we scan your recent memories and ascertain the destination of which you speak, we may suggest that the answer to this query resides within your own desire and ability and accumulation of confidence, for it is possible for your exercise of the vocal channeling service to continue as a function of your own desire and free will choice no matter the land to which you move or the time which elapses between your departure and arrival, for if you are able to place yourself within a circle of seekers which desires this service, you shall find yourself as the seed which takes root in fertile ground and grows according to the nourishment given by your own desire and the desire expressed by those within your new circle of seeking.

May we speak further, my sister?

N: No, thank you.

I am Quanta, and we thank you, my sister. Is there another query at this time?

W: Yeah, I have one more. In regards to attuning, which you just mentioned, is it just a continued tuning, or can you give me any more information about what type of tuning is necessary?

I am Quanta. The tuning of which we speak is primarily that ability to recognize a contact that is being made with your instrument and to successfully challenge and receive confirmation from that contact in a manner which assures you of its nature and allows you then to open your channel that you may speak its words. This evening, for example, due to the time which had elapsed and the slight eroding of the confidence, this ability to discern contact from our group was somewhat diminished. More practice and the gathering of confidence shall allow this type of discernment to again be polished to the point that the ability to discern not only our contact, but contact from other sources, is enhanced.

May we speak further, my sister?

W: No, thank you.

I am Quanta, and we thank you, my sister. Is there another query?

(Pause)

I am Quanta, and we feel that we have, for the moment, exhausted those queries which we appreciate each offering to us. We look forward, shall we say, to the future gatherings of this group and feel that the foundation has been well laid for the service which has been undertaken. We hope that we shall be able to continue this progress with each new instrument and are confident in that possibility. At this time we shall take our leave of this instrument and this group, thanking each for allowing our presence this evening. We are known to you as those of Quanta. We leave each in the love and in the light of the one infinite Creator. Adonai, my friends. Adonai. ☥

L/L Research

L/L Research is a subsidiary of Rock Creek Research & Development Laboratories, Inc.

P.O. Box 5195
Louisville, KY 40255-0195

www.llresearch.org

Rock Creek is a non-profit corporation dedicated to discovering and sharing information which may aid in the spiritual evolution of humankind.

ABOUT THE CONTENTS OF THIS TRANSCRIPT: This telepathic channeling has been taken from transcriptions of the weekly study and meditation meetings of the Rock Creek Research & Development Laboratories and L/L Research. It is offered in the hope that it may be useful to you. As the Confederation entities always make a point of saying, please use your discrimination and judgment in assessing this material. If something rings true to you, fine. If something does not resonate, please leave it behind, for neither we nor those of the Confederation would wish to be a stumbling block for any.

CAVEAT: This transcript is being published by L/L Research in a not yet final form. It has, however, been edited and any obvious errors have been corrected. When it is in a final form, this caveat will be removed.

© 2009 L/L Research

Sunday Meditation
August 2, 1987

(Carla channeling)

I am Q'uo. I greet you in the love and in the light of the one infinite Creator. We bless each and thank you for inviting us to dwell with you in your meditation this evening. The instrument has instructed us to speak loudly in order that our words may be heard over your fans and we shall attempt to effect this.

Your question this evening has to do with the so-called harmonic convergence taking place within the energy web of your planetary sphere in third density upon your dating of August 16 and 17. These days are very near.

We would begin by saying that there is a continuing daily need for the planetary seeking of harmony. The recognition of special occasions is appropriate and efficacious to a certain extent, but it is the faithful seeker which marks each day as a day of harmony which shall create as a gift to the Creator the fuller fruit and the more universal spirit.

Imagine, to use an example more familiar to this instrument, that each day was celebrated as a birthday. We are not speaking of the gifts that come in ribbon and paper, but of that special holiday feeling that comes with having your day be your very own special Earth day. Is not each day your very own special day? Thus, we would perhaps in our professorial manner dampen the spirits of those who wish to celebrate two days especially. However, it is well to recognize and cooperate with those moments of opportunity which are given by circumstance.

These dates of which you ask are such an occasion. There are various levels of cosmic energy instreaming into the planetary vortex of energy which surrounds your Earth's sphere. An unusually high degree of transparency exists during that upcoming period, making that spirit which is Love within more easily apprehended and shared. Each seeker will find opportunities during these hours to offer the great intention of coming into balance more and more with the planet itself in its physical form and in its spiritual form.

And those who are, like yourself, willing and hoping to be a part of that critical mass of humankind in its seeking for a higher consciousness will be able to do work more easily during this period to bring your intentions into balance and to offer your service to the Creator, to live in a more and more harmonious fashion using the energies which have been put into the planetary energy web from the cosmos.

The effect upon entities will be various, for each entity which seeks, seeks upon its own path, having its own assets and able to offer its own gifts. There are some whose gift is with the practical, and to those entities the world will call and perhaps will be heard, for there are the hungry to feed, brothers to be embraced and a damaged planet to redeem. There are those whose skills and love lie largely in dreaming, hoping and loving, and we encourage entities which are of this nature to take their dreams, hopes and love with the utmost of seriousness that they may offer themselves [as] channels of light in a dark world, for sending love is perhaps the most powerful action of a seeker.

The deeper importance of the so-called harmonic convergence is archetypal. We may suggest to each that a silent meditation be carefully planned and immaculately executed, a meditation which asks no questions and seeks no answers, a meditation which is rich in nothingness, in darkness, in stillness of thought, for archetypal days are with you more and more. This work has nothing to do with any mental processes of the conscious mind, and it is perhaps one of the more exacting types of meditation. Yet, as your planet moves into new energy vortices, the archetypes of mind, body and spirit will be affected. It is far better to encourage the process of archetypal change, that is, not changes within the archetype, but changes in how much of archetypal images might be made available to the conscious mind through seeking.

For many of your years a large portion of the peoples of your planet have dwelt within a system of archetypes which leaves almost entirely out of powerful place the archetype which this instrument would call the High Priestess. As each of you moves in consciousness towards that fourth-density barrier, the other side of which the veil of forgetting shall be lifted from the conscious mind, that veil gradually shall become more transparent. However, the upcoming time of August 16 and 17 is a time powerful in possibility for the declared intention-making of each seeker.

We might suggest furthermore that those seekers which wish to make use of this time create for themselves some form of purification or cleansing for a short period prior to the meditation of which we have spoken. When we spoke of purification, we found this instrument's mind beginning busily to analyze what we meant and considering sadly the food that she was going to miss. We would like to indicate that we do not necessarily suggest such physical cleansing as fasting, for there are many ways mentally to remind the self repeatedly during a purification period of one's desire. If one's desire is strong and persistent, then shall the occasion be used to the fullest.

We hope that your celebration of this harmonic convergence shall be merry and gay, for you will find that when one has surrendered to the utter silence within and sought nothingness, one's surrender creates a joyful sense of freedom. And one then begins to dance within the mind and within the life.

The concept of balance is perhaps the most important concept which we feel in our opinion is to be focused upon at this time—the balance between the celebration and the nothingness, for both of these things are the self. Both of these things are the universe. Both of these things are a portion of what we may say about the Creator, for as you gaze at your consciousness and watch that balance roll back and forth within your own mind and life, so you see the Creator in endless balancing. We do not say that the Creator is celebration, nor do we say that the Creator is nothingness. We say that the Creator is beyond both and beyond any understanding or word. We reluctantly use the word love to describe the Creator—it is the closest word which your language has. May you dwell in this love until you know yourself to be a channel for that love.

May you learn to trust more and more your ability to be harmonious, may you let go more and more of those sharp edges, those bad habits of thought which take the power from your loving and the truth from your words, for each has the behavior, born of pain and sorrow. These pains, these sorrows, held to the breast, create strife evermore. Held instead to the light of love and accepted, it is then possible to have them let go so that pain and sorrow become transformed into compassion, the strong compassion that shares the deep awareness of the oneness of sorrow in all peoples, and beyond that the ultimate rhapsody of oneness in living love.

A time of dedication draws near, and this, my children, is at a time when those who wish to form light upon this planet grow in light until a nearly critical mass of spiritual consciousness is being achieved at some moments within your experience at this time. More and more entities are coming into harmony and beginning to create what this instrument would call a social memory complex, of the beginning of fourth density upon your planet.

We thank you for listening to our words. We trust that you understand that we are only your brothers and sisters, and would not wish to be a stumbling block to you in your spiritual seeking. Therefore, we ask that those things which we have said which do not aid in seeking be discarded without a second thought. We would at this time transfer this contact, with thanks to this instrument. I am Q'uo.

(Jim channeling)

I am Q'uo, and greet each again in love and light through this instrument. At this time it is our honor to open this gathering to the queries which those present may have for us. We wish to serve those present in a manner which speaks more directly to the nature of the personal journey, therefore we take this opportunity to offer ourselves in this capacity. May we begin with a query?

Carla: Is this inpouring of cosmic energy … does it have anything to do with the kind of energy that comes from crystals? I think of the planets and the stars, and they all revolve and they're all changing, as kind of big crystals that are sending certain energies our way. Is this at all accurate?

I am Q'uo, and this is, indeed, my sister, a most perceptive way in which to look upon the event which has been called the harmonic convergence, for just as each energy center within a mind/body/spirit complex adds unto the whole of the entity according to its crystalline nature, so does your planet serve as that of a crystal that is a portion of an ever-enlarging relationship of planetary spheres, solar systems, and galactic clusters of these systems of revolving planetary spheres.

Thus, as each moves as likened to the cells within a great body of being, the relationship of each to the other and to the entirety constantly moves and changes so that those energies which have set each in motion are facilitated in their movement through those planetary spheres. The entirety may be seen as similar to the face of a clock which has three dimensions and in the case of your planetary sphere is moving into a fourth dimension. The dimensions of being for each planet then affect the ability of the influx of intelligent energy or love to move in a fashion which enhances the ease of movement and the intensity of movement.

Thus, as the alignment of various planetary spheres becomes more in harmony, or in what might be seen as favorable conjunctions, the intelligent energy of the one Creator then is made more apparent to those who dwell upon the planetary spheres which have achieved the completion of certain cyclical experiences. Thus, your planetary sphere at this time moves into an area of time and space which is the representation of the completion of one phase of being and the beginning of another. These relationships may be seen as likened unto the facets of a crystal which have certain relationships to the entire crystal, and which because of these relationships allow the passage not only of light, but also of finer energies through them in a manner which tends to enhance the quality of those light and finer energies so that they become more focused and available for the doing of what you may call work in consciousness.

May we speak further, my sister?

Carla: Well, just a clarification. When you said dimension, is that the same as density? You said we were going into a fourth dimension.

I am Q'uo and this is correct, my sister.

May we speak further?

Carla: Not on that, thank you.

I am Q'uo, and we thank you, my sister. Is there another query?

Carla: If you could make any comments, I'd appreciate it, about the Mayan calendar. Certainly a persuasive case can be made for intelligence other than earthly intelligence giving that to the Mayans as a gift. Could you comment at all on that?

I am Q'uo, and as we look at those energies which have been experienced as those of the race known to you as Mayan, we see that this grouping of entities shares with many others of your planet's historical experience a contact with those from elsewhere which was in response to a call of these peoples that sought clues to the mysteries of the creation and of their own being and place within the creation. It was these peoples' tendency or predilection to think or see their environment in relationships or ratios, so that the mathematical means of describing the nature of the planetary spheres within their night sky was decided upon as the most efficient manner by which to express a portion of the relationship that these peoples and their planetary sphere shared with the civilizations of planets beyond this sphere of which these entities were quite aware and for which they generated great curiosity.

May we speak further, my sister?

Carla: I've always been curious about why the calendar stopped.

I am Q'uo, and we find in this query the movement into an area which must of necessity remain somewhat shrouded in mystery so as to preserve the integrity of free will within your population. There was for the Mayan culture the great span of what you know of as time that remained between the initial stages of this culture, its beginning to grasp the nature of its relationship to the creation as an whole, and the completion of that which was called the great cycle by these entities. During this span of time, these entities sought to gain not only an understanding of the larger environment in which they lived, but of a manner by which this understanding could be applied to their personal existence. The ending of their manner of marking a revolution of this planet about its solar system is similar to the practice that became popular within your Christian tradition of seeing the …

(Side one of tape ends.)

I am Q'uo, and am again with this instrument. Is there another query?

Carla: Well, I just have one more, and then I'll stop. It said in the message to have a special meditation on nothingness. I've been dissatisfied with my channeling for as long as … with my meditating—well, my channeling too. I've been dissatisfied with my meditating for as long as I can remember, ever since I started meditating. I've never been able to get the music out of my head. I just don't have silent meditations. Do you have any suggestions?

I am Q'uo, and, my sister, that which we have to offer as suggestion may seem worn out by this time within your experience of meditation. However, we find there is no greater manner by which a meditation might be enhanced than by persevering with the desire and the intention to meditate with a full and open heart and with a mind which seeks a focus upon the one Creator above all else. And though this goal might seldom be realized, yet and nevertheless to desire to achieve the perfect meditation as the greatest gift to the Creator is that which we feel is the finest fruit that one might produce with the discipline of meditation.

May we speak further, my sister?

Carla: No, thank you.

I am Q'uo. Is there another query?

Carla: I do have one more question, but if you think the instrument might be too tired, just save it 'til next time. And the question has to do with the teaching that we've been doing. I've been concerned over sending folks who have learned to channel back into environments where they do not have a support group, and all they're really able to do is make contact and feel the contact. They really can't in any safety as totally inexperienced channels do the work on their own. In the context of someone who has learned to challenge and has learned to tune, but who wants to work alone, is automatic handwriting or typewriting a psychically well guarded affair? Does it take place within the self? Could I suggest to someone who wanted an outlet for the channeling, now that they'd learned it, to do that alone, or would that too need a support group to be safe?

I am Q'uo. We look upon this topic as one which not only moves close to the possibility of infringing upon your own free will, but also that which is of significant importance to those who study the art of becoming the vocal instrument, and thus we speak as specifically as possible without infringement.

The practice of the, as you have called it, automatic handwriting is one which differs somewhat from the vocal channeling process in that the concepts and words which move through the one serving as instrument must be filtered more completely through the unconscious mind in a manner which renders the concepts more a part of the instrument's being rather than having concepts more of an external or alien nature moving through the upper reaches of the subconscious mind, and for the most part having their effect within the conscious mind as is the case in the conscious channeling, a technique which is being utilized this evening within this group.

Thus, the process of automatic handwriting is one which, though somewhat more easily accomplished in a stable manner by a single entity, is one which also through its very mechanics of being accomplished alters to a significant degree the information which is transmitted. The entity who practices the automatic handwriting, then, is one who would benefit most from this practice if its desire is that of reaching deeper levels of its own being, and in this reaching accomplishes the construction of a channel, if you will, which not only will allow the automatic handwriting to occur, but which will provide a more easily traversed pathway for the experience of the contact with entities who may wish to utilize the instrument as a vocal channel at another time at which there would then be gathered about the instrument a supporting group which would provide the necessary protection while the process was ongoing for the instrument and also provide the focusing function that any support group provides as each within the circle gathers with the intention of seeking information that might be of service to others in their journey of seeking.

May we speak further, my sister?

Carla: Just to sum up then. You're saying that automatic handwriting puts one in touch with portions of the deeper self because it is a solitary act. You're also saying that I need to do some meditating on ways to protect the person so that he doesn't get outside of his own consciousness. And I induce from what you've said that if a person did automatic handwriting with a support group, that the automatic handwriting then would not have that personal bias, and it would be possible to have an impersonal principle or entity channeled just as if one were vocally channeling. Are those three items correct?

I am Q'uo, and the first we find to be correct. The second is not that which we have suggested, in that we were not describing a means by which the entity would be protected …

Carla: No, that's what I said; you left it to me.

… within the process of the automatic handwriting. The third is, to our best understanding, also incorrect in that with the support group present, the vocal channeling and not the automatic handwriting would be the practice recommended, provided the entities within the support group were of a like mind, shall we say, and were desirous of supporting an instrument which was making a contact with sources external to itself for the purpose of gathering information that would be useful in serving others' journey of seeking.

May we speak further, my sister?

Carla: No, thank you, I'm through.

I am Q'uo, and we thank you once again, my sister. Is there another query?

(Pause)

I am Q'uo, and we thank each for allowing us to speak our humble words this evening. We enjoy the opportunity to offer that which has been the fruit of our experience to those who seek this type of nourishment. We remind each that we offer but our opinion and we do not wish to provide the stumbling block for any. Thus, take those words which have meaning in your own journey and leave those which do not. At this time we shall take our leave of this group, rejoicing at the opportunity to blend our vibrations with yours. We are those of Q'uo, and we leave each in the love and in the light of the one infinite Creator. Adonai, my friends. Adonai vasu borragus. ✦

Intensive Meditation
August 5, 1987

(Carla channeling)

I am Hatonn. I greet you in the love and the light of the infinite Creator. We are full of gratitude that you have called us to your meeting this evening, for it is such a great pleasure for us to drink in your vibrations and the vibratory beauty that surrounds you.

We have been listening to your conversation, and would like to say a few words concerning the operation of the process of initiating contact. This instrument was correct in stating that it is helpful for the new instrument to start the process before the process is completely matured. In other words, it is well that instruments who are learning to perceive by concept communication begin somewhere, and attempt continually to manifest whatever words seem to come forth.

However, this instrument did not quite have the reasons in line with our opinion, as this instrument felt that it was helpful to channel portions of self. From our point of view, as those who are sending to a receiver, we find it helpful that the receiver be turned on. It is as simple as that. When the receiver is on, that is, when the instrument is availing itself of whatever communication it can, be it garbled or not, we are able to assess and calibrate that particular receiver's needs so that we may enter into the energy web of the biochemical body of the instrument with as little discomfort as possible and emit our communication concept by concept within the upper reaches of the subconscious mind. This is the way we begin with a new instrument. One may think that one is availing oneself of contact and turning one's instrument on by simple intent. However, until a new instrument has had some experience in what happens when the instrument is on, it is quite impossible for a new instrument who is not actually channeling to know whether or not the receiver is actually working.

Now, some ability in channeling of a kind is part of almost every new instrument's experience. The experience occurs betwixt two entities in a relationship which, for some reason, is well tuned, so that the two instruments are able to receive fragments of communication by concept from each other. Needless to say, since the new instrument is certainly not adept at sending information or receiving it, these experiences are often had, but seldom complete.

Thus, each new instrument has some experience in concept communication. This is what we offer. We offer, in the conscious channeling program, concepts which must then be clothed with vocabulary. The simplicity of the process works against new students, for your peoples, when attempting creativity, tend to multiply concepts with detail rather than honing constellations of concepts into simpler and simpler terms. As the new instrument becomes more experienced, we are able to offer longer and more detailed series of concepts, and thus that which we ask the instrument to unlearn at the beginning of the process—that is, the multiplication of detail—is then relearned with one notable exception and difference—that is, that the governor which the conscious mind is has been damped down by the instrument so that external thoughts—that is, thoughts external to the communication—are allowed to flow away from the instrument, thus keeping the concentration of the instrument upon the most simple thing—that is, listening within.

Channeling becomes, then, one way to experience an improved meditation, for when the channel is busy listening for the next concept, the mind is stayed upon that point, becoming one large receiver. When we ask instruments to cease analyzing and relax, we are asking basically that the inner ear be turned on and that a continuing attention be paid to it. This is, in brief, a satisfactory definition of meditation, for when the conscious mind is turned down and the inner ear listens, then it is that the Creator speaks in whatever way is creative at that time and place.

What a new instrument is engaged in is creativity. A channel produces out of nothing a something which, it is hoped, will be beautiful, inspiring or useful, or perhaps all of those. Creating beauty, creating the feelings associated with divine love, is one great purpose of the existence of all consciousness, and the vocal channeling is one way of achieving the creative act which expresses the trust and love that each feels for that great love which is the Creator.

We therefore ask the instrument to relax. We shall attempt to create some movement in the facial and throat area as an indication that we are present, as the instrument has requested. We would like to speak our greeting at this time through the one known as D. We would at this time transfer. I am Hatonn.

(Long pause.)

(Carla channeling)

I am Hatonn. I am again with this instrument. My friends, we have about stretched this instrument's jaws off, but are having somewhat more difficulty in moving the mandible of the one known as D. We shall again attempt to contact the one known as D. I am Hatonn.

(Long pause.)

(Carla channeling)

I am Laitos, and I greet you also in love and light. We have the privilege of coming among you so that, by experiencing various contacts, the one known as D may begin to have some subjective intimation of the reality of our presence. We are at this time attempting to seek ingress into the new instrument's web of electromagnetic energy. We are those which often teach new instruments within this group. It was thought by us that the one known as Hatonn, being closer to the vibration to the one known as D in resonance and harmonics, would be the better choice to initiate contact. However, we can see that the very compatibility of this contact mitigates against the instrument's demand—which it does not wish to make but is making in spite of itself—for proof.

It may be obvious by now that there is no proof. We are sorry for the disappointment of those who wish proof, but we are heart and soul, as this instrument would say, of the belief that any sort of objective proof of our presence or the proof of our statements is an infringement upon the free will of those who at this time in your density are making their choice to create, as co-creators with the Father, or to destroy, as co-creators with the darker energy.

We of Laitos like to encourage people to meditate. Indeed, ours has always been considered by this instrument to be somewhat of a simple contact—Johnny-One-Note we have been called by this instrument. She is embarrassed that we see this, yet it is true. Five seconds or five minutes is enough time to move into contact with that Being which is the Source of all beings, and within which each being has its being.

Let us now transfer to the one known as D, that the new instrument may experience our energy and perhaps find those slight differences which do exist between contact and contact. We transfer now. I am Laitos.

(Pause)

(Carla channeling)

I am Laitos, and am once again with this instrument.

We would suggest at this time a technique that has never been used with this group before, yet we feel that it is perhaps time—if we may use that term—to bring it out. We would ask that the circle come out of meditation, be seated upon the floor, and create, with or without thought, in as rapid a manner as one voice may come after another, a series of statements which imitate the channeled message. We ask the instruments to do this without thought, if possible; with thought, if necessary; but above all, with no pause between sentences except insofar as it is necessary to hear the previous sentence. We suggest that this be done for a period of approximately ten minutes, using two minutes and then resting, then another two minutes and then resting, and so forth. We suggest the use of one of your timers.

This instrument is questioning this process, for it is making up a channeling, which the instrument feels is taboo. However, in our opinion, the necessity with the one known as D is in overcoming the reluctance to speak. The force of this technique may be assessed after the ten minutes of practice have been completed.

My brothers, please do not think that we wish you to create your own channeling. Yet we have, with other groups, used this technique, and it has aided some who were armored against encroachment upon the inner planes. We may say to the one known as D that there is a strong guard upon the entrance to the world of the creation that lies within this instrument. The guard is there for a reason, yet the instrument wishes it to be removed for this one opportunity. Thusly, the work lies ahead. We wish each the luck and the enjoyment of this technique, and we thank you for having the desire to serve the infinite Creator. We, too, wish to serve.

We shall speak with this group again. For now, however, we shall leave you. We are those known to you as Laitos. We leave you in love and light. ✿

Intensive Meditation
August 12, 1987

(Carla channeling)

I am Laitos. I greet you in the love and the light of the infinite Creator, Whose kingdom interpenetrates the mundane world, Whose truth penetrates all illusion. We thank you for calling us to your group this evening. It is a great privilege to be with you and to experience in your in-breathing and out-breathing the unique experience of third density.

We would like to speak our greeting to the one known as D, if he would avail himself of our contact and refrain from analyzing, but simply speak the words which come into the mind. We would now transfer to the one known as D. I am Laitos.

(D channeling)

I am Laitos. I greet you all in the in the name of the Creator … *(The rest of this channeling was not transcribed.)*

(Carla channeling)

I am Laitos. We are once again with this channel. *(Inaudible).* We are most pleased to have made such an auspicious beginning with the one known as D. We feel most *(inaudible)* for this new instrument, for this instrument has been *(inaudible)* in its persistency to be of service to others through the vocal channeling. We find this new instrument's mind to be rich in [experience complex] and with the questions, about which other constellations or concepts which have been gained with the reading and studying, a most rich mind out of which we may make new combinations of thoughts and ideas so that that same story may be told ever in new ways. We find the instrument known as D to be questioning the validity of its messages, due to its familiarity with the material which was channeled. We would not ask the inexperienced channel to transmit *(inaudible)*. But first we wish to make *(inaudible)*. Then we wait while the experience is *(inaudible)*. If the instrument analyzes its own material … *(The rest of this channeling was not transcribed.)*

(Jim channeling)

I am Laitos, and greet each again in love and light through this instrument. It is our privilege at this time to offer ourselves in the attempt to answer queries which may be offered to us. We again hope that each will remember that our words are but our opinion. We share them freely and hope they will be some small service. Is there a query with which we may begin?

D: I was speaking earlier about a couple of questions that I had, the first concerning the state in which I was last week and whether it was my own spontaneous drowsiness, the result of fatigue and sleepiness, or whether it was the result of some contact or influence from outside of my own mind and whether it was useful in the contact at that particular time or only to be avoided. Can you help me understand that?

I am Laitos, and the level of fatigue which you experienced at our previous working was not a product of the working itself, but of your normal round of activities. That was somewhat expanded and the body's response therefore was to approach the levels that you associated with the beginning of the sleep process. We might suggest that the most efficacious of level of consciousness for this particular kind of transmission of thought concept is that in which the mind is alert and the body as relaxed as is comfortably possible. The mind needs a kind of flexible perception that is at once sharp or acute and yet pliable, so that the one serving as instrument might become aware of thoughts and while speaking these thoughts be able to allow further thought [to] enter the mind complex.

May we speak further, my brother?

D: No, thank you, not on that. I'm left wondering somewhat by this channeling a few minutes ago [about] a number of questions, and yet I know it can be over-analyzed, and feel that perhaps its better not to beat it to death. But any further comments that you would volunteer, though I know that's not your usual approach, I'd appreciate.

I am Laitos, and as we mentioned previously, we are most happy with the progress which you have shown this evening. It is what we would call a major breakthrough in your particular experience as a new instrument. The beginning of the contact is that which is oftentimes the greatest hurdle for any instrument, for it is the first thought of the new instrument that it is making up the progress and manufacturing the speaking that occurs. We encourage each new instrument to simply allow the process to begin, to partake as one who does not give over-concern to the process while it is ongoing, and only afterward seek to understand the mechanics, shall we say.

Thus, in the experience of this evening your channeling was of a degree which we find quite acceptable in the ratio of our contact and the utilization of concepts familiar to your own experience. We make the simple suggestion to continue with this process and keep those thoughts which you become aware of as the contact is transferred to your instrument. Each session we shall attempt to seek either in a lengthier fashion or in a fashion which is qualitatively different in some manner or use a combination of these techniques by which the new instrument may be exercised and confidence gained.

May we speak further my brother?

D: At a certain point I felt a *(inaudible)* that seemed to draw back to cut myself off and feel the need for feedback at that point. I guess I felt like I was wandering down a path and I wasn't sure I was wandering by myself, but I seemed to reach a point where I was unwilling to go further. Was I perceiving only my own concern, or was it my interpretation of your own completion of the message?

I am Laitos, and we found within the channeled experience that there was a momentary digression which was, however, accompanied by our contact, and the digression, which is a normal portion of the training of a new instrument, was then utilized by us for the continued energizing of the channel contact. Your perception, therefore, was partially correct, but we may assure you that such digressions are to be utilized by both the instrument and the contact as the new instrument gains in confidence. Therefore, we suggest the putting away of the worry and the simple continuing of the contact and the challenging process.

May we speak further, my brother?

D: No, thank you.

(The sound of many sirens is heard.)

Carla: I'd like to ask a question—and it's not "What's on fire?" I gave R about an hour and a half of advice today. Would have given her more, except the tape ran out …

(Side one of tape ends.)

Carla: … and there was something that I was, after I gave the advice, questioning my own tact and good sense in giving it. R's channel gives her very jargonish language— "The unfoldment of the evolvement of the beautifulment of humanment"— you know, that kind of thing, with some "indeeds" in there. And I feel that she's heard this kind of fakey language from channels that are famous right now, like Mafu, that used the device. Also, she uses the device of the second person singular intimate, "thee, thou and thine," although almost never getting it right. So I suggested to her that she learn the declension of thee and thou and thy and thine and how to use them, and give some thought to asking her contact to use "unfolding" instead of "unfoldment" when, for words like that which are just made-up words, that are not true words in the sense of being in the dictionary. I even saw "initiationment" at one point, really jargon.

After I wrapped the tape up, I suddenly realized that what I might be doing was interfering with her ability to channel at all, by interfering with the language. She has a strong contact; she's a natural medium; she's got a good channel, but I don't want to give her a stumbling block. What I did was I advised her to ask her contact to clean up the language. Is that good advice, or should I write and retract it?

I am Laitos, and, my sister, that we find that in this query we must be aware of the line across which is an infringement of your own free will if we should step too far in our response. The attempt to be of service empowered by the desire to serve is that which is of the moment the finest offering which one can make. When this attempt is made and given with a full and whole heart, then one has done the best that one can do. This is to be applauded in any entity and any effort. We know that your doubts are also grounded in the desire to be of the most service possible. However, we do not wish to guide your thoughts or actions to the point of making the decision for you as to the full nature of your response to the one known as R. Therefore, we may only suggest that the response which finds the blend of the honesty and truthfulness of wisdom with the nurturing of compassion be that which forms the parameters of your final response to this entity.

May we speak further, my sister?

Carla: Let me ask the question in a different way. I feel you can give me information of which I would like to know, regardless of what I do about R. When you are working with an instrument such as I, or D or Jim, if I requested the "thee" and "thou" in the transmission, would you then offer such? Or would you find it difficult to have any limits put on your transmission?

I am Laitos. It is the duty of any instrument, new or experienced, to hone itself in those basic tools which aid in the functioning of the instrument such as the ability to utilize the language which is unfamiliar to the instrument. It is well for an instrument to prepare itself for a means of communication which will allow that communication to proceed in the most understandable and efficient manner. Thus, if it would be the desire of an instrument to effect a certain type of phraseology, it would be necessary, then, for that instrument to not only request that such be utilized by its contact, but that it familiarize itself with the correct usage.

The requests of this nature by instruments are few and are frequently acceptable to the contact as long as the requests are not of a nature which tends to focus more upon the contact or the instrument rather than the message.

May we speak further, my sister?

Carla: No, thank you, Laitos, that was very good. I feel that I know more now, and I really appreciate that.

I am Laitos, and we thank you, my sister. Is there another query?

D: I wonder if you would feel that there is any specific homework task that I could work on between now and the next time that I am here with you that would be helpful to firming the contact or trying to facilitate the channeling?

In addition to the regularized periods of meditation, the exercise which was given at our last working is that which we feel might yet be of assistance in maintaining the growing flexibility of your newly developing instrument.

May we speak further, my brother?

D: *(Inaudible).*

I am Laitos, and we thank you once again. Is there another query?

Carla: I'd like to ask a question about challenging. It seems to me when one challenges, when a request is made that the entity be of God, that is not sufficient to challenge a negative entity, since negative and positive entities are equally of God. It seems to me that there would have to be a specific or service-to-others orientation stated in the challenging statement. Is this accurate?

I am Laitos, and this is correct, my sister. May we speak further?

Carla: *(Inaudible).*

I am Laitos, and again we thank you, my sister. Is there another query?

D: I'm somewhat puzzled by that idea of challenging, and I've gotten some explanation of it from Carla, but I feel—my intuition tells me that one's own alignment is generally sufficient, that one intuitively or unconsciously accepts or rejects the incoming energy. Maybe that's easy for me to say because I've never experienced, to my knowledge, a negative entity's attempted contact. But I just seem to feel no interest in that aspect of the challenging. Can you make any comments about that attitude and whether it's erroneous or dangerous?

I am Laitos. For most who engage in the phenomena, as you may call it, of the vocal channeling, the experience is one which is of a shallow nature and can be expected to play its course, shall we say, after a certain amount of the experience has been shared, and there is little of the development of the metaphysical power, shall we say, that would as a beacon attract the attention of entities of a negative polarization who would then desire to gain the use of that power for themselves, or barring that, to put that beacon of light out. Thus, for most entities the channeling process is not one which provides the avenue for the beaming or expressing of great metaphysical power.

However, for any entity who is desirous in the extreme to be of service to others by means of serving as a vocal instrument and who wishes to serve as such in as pure a manner as possible, it is most centrally necessary to proceed with a certain degree of caution, for this avenue of service is one which offers the potential of gaining metaphysical power and using this power for the service to others. Therefore, it is necessary for each instrument to master the ability to tune its inner desire in such a fashion that it places this desire at the highest point within its being that it can stably maintain, and thereby open a pathway which will serve as the connecting channel to entities of an unseen nature which the instrument hopes will, in conjunction with the instrument, transmit concepts which may be formulated into those principles which aid in the evolutionary process, thereby enabling the power to affect changes in consciousness for those who utilize these principles in a persistent and conscious fashion.

The challenging of unseen spirits is quite necessary, for as populated as your illusion is, we may assure you that those illusions beyond your own are at least as equally populated, and there are many who stand ready to speak through instruments, and instruments need a means by which to be assured that the entity speaking through them is one of the highest positive polarity possible in order to gain information that is as sound and useable as possible, or else the value of the information is small.

Thus, it is our recommendation that each instrument determine for itself its own desire to serve as an instrument, and if its determination is that it wishes to do so in as pure a fashion as it might, then it shall gather about itself those qualities which it feels are its essence and utilize these qualities in a fashion that may be formed into that which is called the challenge of the spirit, so that the contact which is made may know who you are and what your desire is in a clear fashion, for this is your first communication with it.

It, as all contacts, has this clear knowledge of itself and speaks as an entity full of that essence of itself. Thus, the instrument must needs determine the highest and best contact that it might sustain in a stable fashion by means of this technique of the challenge of the spirit.

May we speak further, my brother?

D: When you said, "gather about yourself the qualities," by that you mean hold in mind such things as service to principles of love and to keep those—well, I don't know how to ask the question, but your words put a picture in my mind which I guess for the moment I will trust this as good, and perhaps if there is a question it will come later. Thank you very much, that was very helpful.

I am Laitos, and again we thank you, my brother. As this instrument is experiencing some degree of discomfort, we will suggest the ending of this session at this time.

Carla and D: Thank you.

And we thank each for allowing our presence and for allowing us to work with each. We appreciate the opportunity to offer our service, humble though it is. We feel a great joy at each gathering of this group. We are known to you as those of Laitos, and we leave each in the love and in the light of the one infinite Creator. Adonai, my friends. Adonai. ✤

L/L Research

L/L Research is a subsidiary of Rock Creek Research & Development Laboratories, Inc.

P.O. Box 5195
Louisville, KY 40255-0195

www.llresearch.org

Rock Creek is a non-profit corporation dedicated to discovering and sharing information which may aid in the spiritual evolution of humankind.

ABOUT THE CONTENTS OF THIS TRANSCRIPT: This telepathic channeling has been taken from transcriptions of the weekly study and meditation meetings of the Rock Creek Research & Development Laboratories and L/L Research. It is offered in the hope that it may be useful to you. As the Confederation entities always make a point of saying, please use your discrimination and judgment in assessing this material. If something rings true to you, fine. If something does not resonate, please leave it behind, for neither we nor those of the Confederation would wish to be a stumbling block for any.

CAVEAT: This transcript is being published by L/L Research in a not yet final form. It has, however, been edited and any obvious errors have been corrected. When it is in a final form, this caveat will be removed.

© 2009 L/L Research

Sunday Meditation
August 16, 1987

(Carla channeling)

I am Q'uo. I greet each of you in love and in light, in the love and the light of our infinite Creator. It gives us great pleasure to have been called to your meeting, and we rejoice to be with you to experience these quiet moments of meditation and companionship and to experience through this instrument's senses the peaceful drowsy sounds of a summer evening. This instrument has requested that we speak loudly and we shall attempt to do so without removing this instrument's vocal cords completely from service. We are also happy at what this instrument terms potluck, for this indeed gives us the occasion to speak of those things which have not been asked, yet which may perhaps be on the mind.

We would speak with you about being and doing, two verbs that seem simple and yet are not. We, as you, are students of that great mystery which hides the face of the Creator from all of us. We, as you, seek more and more to know and to be with the Source of all that there is, the Love which created all that there is, the Light which sustains all that there is. We find great love and harmony in being and great love and harmony in doing, and yet the tension between those two poles of behavior and consciousness is felt by many seekers, and, indeed, can be a stumbling block, for one desires, in doing spiritual work as in any other work, to be occupied, to have accomplished something, to have gotten somewhere. Yet is consciousness ever and always at the base a being, not an activity.

As each of you came to the circle this evening that portion of yourself which *is* underlay but probably did not totally influence that which was being done by each, for the cares and concerns of each day are many and it seems that the less important a detail is the more time it takes to accomplish it, so that as you sat down perhaps your thoughts were scattered, pleasantly or not, but scattered, and the consciousness lay as your foundation, largely unnoticed in the flurry of activity. Then each began to merge more and more into a harmony of seeking, into a consciousness that was felt by the self and shared about the circle. This group consciousness is powerful and acts just as a search light shining in metaphysical energy which, with many other groups such as your own, forms a pattern of light sources upon your planet at this time.

Now, this energy is the energy of beingness. It is your own and no one else's. Each consciousness source in the creation is unique. Thus, it is valid always for the seeker to be attempting through all that which it does to more and more carefully choose the path of seeking, choose the way of service, and choose the source of experience so that at the end of all experience there shall be a consciousness which is more and more full of love, more and more able to channel that great original Thought which created all, that Logos which is love.

We do not wish to speak too long to this group, for this instrument has mentally told us that an hour and a half is definitely too long. Therefore, we will content ourselves with offering a thought upon doing and a thought upon being.

My children, you live within an illusion. Your physicists will tell you this. All that looks solid is not; all that looks still is moving. Your senses participate in an illusion, thus all your doing is exercise within an illusion. This system of illusion was created in order that you may play and work and do all manner of activity until you have decided upon a certain choice, that choice very simply being service to others or service to self. The nature of the illusion is imperfection, thus each thing that is done within the illusion participates in imperfection. Good deeds don't turn out right; relationships go awry; a word quickly said is long regretted. There are an infinite number of ways to make mistakes in behavior according to your own opinion of yourself.

We ask you to avoid the emotion of discouragement. Perhaps the best way to avoid that is to give encouragement to others. Thus, we suggest that you love each other and serve each other. It is an antidote for the blues, for it balances that which within you felt unbalanced. It is only our opinion, but we believe that good intentions, a true desire to do well, is far more important than how things actually come out in the illusion. So be of good cheer. We do not ask you to be silly and funny in the face of tragedy, but try to keep the light touch, for when one embarks upon the path of spiritual seeking and attempts to accelerate the pace of one's seeking, experiences can become intense and discouragement is easy to come by.

Now a word about being. There is a place within the mind and within the heart of each of you which the holy work called the Bible describes as the inner room, that place where you are at last alone with the self and with the Creator. Here in this meeting between yourself and the Creator lies the ground and essence of your being. Here, indeed, lies the entire universe, for each of you is a seed of the divine spark which some call Christ Consciousness. And that portion within you in the innermost space of your heart and mind is a hologram of all that there is, so that you contain universes and all that you see

dwells within you also. At that level you never learn but only remember what you already knew and recognize it once again.

We encourage and recommend the daily practice of meditation, the tabernacling in the inner room of the silent consciousness, for that consciousness touched into often enough may more and more begin to shine through that which you do that you may become radiant, a more and more pure channel for the love of the infinite Creator. If you find it difficult to find time to do this each day, we still suggest it would be worth the effort to create a short time for touching into this consciousness. Indeed, it may be done momentarily when the clock strikes or the siren sounds at noon. Remember who you are and what you seek, and open the door to that inner room and just for a moment close it behind you and say to that great mystery which lies in darkness all round the heart, "Here am I."

The teachings of the spirit dwell in mystery and their riches are hidden in the darkness of the metaphysical universe. Yet, paradoxically, the illumination which is found in these searchings is very bright indeed. We greet you each upon the path. We are all companions. We thank you for your company and for all that you teach us, and hope that our humble thoughts may prove useful in some way to you. Please know that if any thought is not acceptable, we urge you to discard it at once, for we are those perhaps a bit further down the path than you. We have more experience, yet that has only taught us how much more there is to learn of the infinite Creator. We are companions in a great mystery, my children. May your seeking give you joy and may your path be full of light.

We would like to transfer this contact to the one known as Jim at this time. We are those of Q'uo.

(Jim channeling)

I am Q'uo, and greet each again in love and light through this instrument. It is our privilege at this time to open this gathering to any queries which might be yet upon the mind. Again, that which we offer is but our opinion. We share it with a whole heart but with no desire to direct your steps in any way that you would not choose. Is there a query with which we might begin?

H: Yes, I have one. Would it be appropriate or would it be selfish to ask what the signs might be on changes to come on this new earth that we're in now? Is that a selfish question?

I am Q'uo, and am aware of your query, my brother, and we find it is one which is much upon the minds of those who look into what you would call your future and the changing of the age, as it has been called. We find that though this curiosity is most common, that however the signs which many describe that are to usher in, shall we say, this new age and experience are often given in a manner which generates much of fear and confusion among your peoples, for many see as signs those things that are catastrophic upon your illusion at this time. And here we speak of the geophysical changes, and those of powers and principalities that shall [rise] and fall and have their day. And yet we would say to you that though much of this may indeed be true, the signs that should alert each seeker to the change in experience are those which are borne within the geography of one's interior mind and being.

It cannot be said with certainty that such and such exterior events will occur at a certain time within your illusion, and yet each seeker shall in its own time experience the shifting of perceptions and desires that shall signal to it that there is a transformation within that beckons most assuredly and which will offer to each a wider point from which to view the self and the illusion and the journey through the illusion.

Thus, we would say to you, my brother, that when you look outside the self and see the environment and populations of your planetary sphere changing in many various ways, that you utilize these illusory changes within your illusion as those guideposts which shall alert your inner self to that which awaits the inward eye and the renewed desire to be of service to those about you.

May we speak in any further fashion, my brother?

H: No, that's enough. Thank you.

I am Q'uo, and we thank you, my brother. Is there another query?

Questioner: Yes, I have one. How would you thus suggest that we find our spiritual path? And our service to others?

I am Q'uo, and for such a choice, my sister, we can only recommend that that which you do is fueled by that which you desire. As you desire to know that which is a means of seeking that is your own, you can only gather that which is about you as your own experience, whether it is the interaction of self with other selves, the peace of meditation, the intellectual stimulation of a book, a program, any source of such information, then take all this into your inner room and sift it through to find what speaks to you, and as more and more speaks in a clearer and clearer fashion, then seek more of that.

And when you have found much that speaks to you, and arranged it in your thinking and in your experience as a process which is lived, then you begin to find the clues here and there within your own experience that will suggest to you the next step to take upon this journey which has no beginning, and has, in your way of looking, no end. And at some point, you will begin to feel the beingness, your own essence, awakened and quickened to the harmonic resonance of that which you have found as helpful information, and you will begin to direct in a more conscious fashion this seeking and move the focus from outside the self to within the self so that you begin to call upon those inner resources which you have gathered in many experiences before this one. And you will then begin to express in your own way the blend of that which is within and that which you have learned in outer experience. And thus shall you build that pathway through the infinite creation that shall be your journey and your service in glorification to the one Creator.

May we speak in any further fashion, my sister?

Questioner: No, thank you.

I am Q'uo, and we are grateful for your query, my sister. Is there another query at this time?

Carla: Just one, which I don't think I've ever asked, but maybe this is the time. It has always seemed to me that some of the most strongly positive people that I've ever met were women who were full time mothers. And they just seem like beacons of light to me. Is it possible that for them the spiritual path is doing exactly that? Staying home and raising kids, nothing glamorous—just that?

I am Q'uo, and many are the ways, my sister, in which love may be produced and shared. There are as many as there are seekers thirsty for this love, and each chooses a manner in which to contact the living love, that power which sets all which is created into motion, and then to share this love with others. The way of which you speak is one which is full of this potential.

May we speak further, my sister?

Carla: No, thanks.

I am Q'uo, and we thank you my sister. Is there another query?

(Pause)

I am Q'uo, and as it appears that we have for the nonce exhausted those queries within this circle of seeking, we shall take this opportunity to once again thank each for inviting our presence within your circle this evening. It is a great honor to join in such unified desire and we look forward, as you would say, to each such gathering. We are known to you as those of Q'uo. At this time we shall leave each in the love and in the light of the one infinite Creator. Adonai, my friends. Adonai. ☙

Sunday Meditation
August 23, 1987

Group question: What do those of Q'uo learn as they interact with the people of this planet through answering calls and attempting to channel information of one sort or another?

(Carla channeling)

I am Q'uo. I greet each of you in the love and in the light of the one infinite Creator. We bless and offer love to each of you as well as our gratitude for requesting our presence within your meditation this evening.

The pause before beginning our discussion was somewhat prolonged due to this instrument's perception of two contacts. The second contact was, in our opinion, a very close match to our own, and we are pleased and grateful for the instrument's competence in the challenging of spirits, for it is not our wish to enter into struggle in order to speak, for those of the [positive] polarity come as they are called and do not call themselves to entities such as you. We give this information in order to confirm for the instrument the dynamics of the situation. As we understand it, this entity is attempting to understand the safeguards necessary in the practice of vocal channeling.

The question that is before us is why we say that we gain more from our contacts with you than you gain from us. You are wondering how you can be of service to us, as you are supposedly the students and we the teachers. To give you a thorough answer is beyond the scope of this evening, however we shall attempt to articulate some of what we find valuable and lovely and full of learning about entities within the third-density who sit in circles such as yours, seeking the light and aware of the darkness.

We were as you, that is, within a third-density illusion with dense chemical bodies which required daily fuel and numerous other items to attend to, merely to extract comfort from the raw given ambient temperature and so forth which third density entities experience as their planetary home, their dwelling and so forth.

We, as you, gradually became aware over many lifetimes that what was occurring was not what it seemed, that is, that our perceptions of what was occurring was not complete, and we began by choice a free will and persistent investigation into the nature of ourselves, our creation and the mystery which lay behind and beyond the selfhood of the self and the beingness of the creation. We, as you, were engaged in a search to know the face of the Creator, that blank and mysterious face that is glimpsed once in many lifetimes from the corner of the eye or seen for an endless moment in brilliant light, and then forgotten, for no incarnate soul can bear such knowledge.

We seek the unknowable, as you. Yet, gone are the days for us when the peculiar fascinations and glory of a chemical body befuddled our senses and limited sensuality to the sensuality of the physical. Gone are the days when the great choices betwixt service to others and service to self were hidden in veils upon veils of mystery, illusion, deception and bias. Those days are gone when we could look at confusion and see order; those days are gone when we could look upon order and see chaos. An unimaginable amount of time, millions of years in fact, have passed since we dwelt before the choice, gazing at the choice, hoping and wishing and praying to see love and choose love, to see separation and shun it.

Our choice is now made, and we have walked many steps in a path that is straight and narrow—the path of the present moment. Much refining has been done of our grasp of service to others. Much refining, therefore, has been done in our understanding of the nature of that mystery which is the Creator of all that there is.

We spend now our personal time in an intense and protracted seeking for the consciousness of total unity, for we are of your fifth density, which is the density of wisdom, and we feel at this time that the lessons of the sixth density call to us, so that we attempt to balance the wisdom and the compassion in our apprehension of each moment which occurs.

That is why the path of seeking is straight and narrow. The path of seeking consists in one present moment and then another. Not the present moment with burdens of the past, not the present moment with digressions about possibilities which have not yet been explored. Each footstep, as you may call it, upon the path of seeking is a step into the enormous depth, power and richness of the present moment, and to this realization we are committed. This is one of the reasons we have much to gain from gazing at the life patterns of each of you and seeing the enormous vitality and love of fun and of the present moment of which each of you is capable.

We find it incredibly moving that entities which labor as if underwater, hampered by a clumsy physical vehicle, can still look past the shimmering surface of the passing of time and see not the tick-tocks of the river of time, float not upon the canoe of shallow thought, but with such encumbrances still dive deeply into the moment and gather treasures of love from it.

We find your peoples to be endlessly creative, creativity being nothing more than an aesthetic awareness of the nature of time, that is, the plunging into that which seems to be real in a moment, whether it be a vase of flowers, a reclining nude, a mountain, a seascape or anything else which inspires the artist and the artistic eye. Realize that time is not a river, but that each present moment is plangent and brilliant and full to overflowing with a deeply moving kinetic upsurge of deeper meaning and endless connotations which inform the soul that seeks of the nature of the Creator.

It is not remarkable for us to visualize and experience the gifts of time, the gift that is of the present moment, for as far lighter beings than yourselves we enjoy vision and sense which is able to record more nearly the incredible energy and creative movement which is the love within each moment. When we find each of you seeking and trusting and finding that creative and active principle in the present moment, we are touched, and in our hearts there arises a great compassion. It is the spontaneous outpouring of love which is the highest service of which we are aware. We are able to do this on an impersonal basis of course, and, indeed, there are planetary entities which devote themselves to this very task, that is, of being a beacon of radiant love which is broadcast throughout the creation.

Perhaps you feel that we look at you as infants or children, and in a way this so; we feel the nurturing care for you that a mother or father would, for we see your vulnerability and have an instinct to care for you. Yet our overriding feeling for your peoples is one of admiration, for that through which you now go is by far the most challenging illusion which you will face, the most difficult density to penetrate and find the love within.

We would say one or two words more about time before we move on. We encourage those present, indeed, all those which have a feeling for that which is aesthetic, to ponder deeply the nature of perception, for if perception is of the present moment, then one may see in a vase of flowers far more than one who sees viewing the vase of flowers as that which moves upon the river of time. For to the seeing eye and the understanding heart, those flowers and all those things which echo from them—scent, beauty, death, birth, growth, love of light—all of these things adumbrate and echo, and perception becomes capacious and generous, and then that which may be brought back from an instant's perception may take much time upon your river of time to execute. Yet, not every perception needs to be executed and manifested. The greatest perceptions of time, the greatest fruits gained from sinking into the moment of time are those gifts of opened ears, opened eyes, opened hearts, and opened lives.

Another way in which you serve us is very simply that you call for us. We are those who await the asking, those who have dedicated a portion of a long incarnation to working with those who wish to accelerate the speed with which they may spiritually evolve. If no one calls us, then we stand idle, sending our love to those who have not asked for it and who often reject it unconsciously. Thus, our love surrounds your planet and your peoples, but without those who ask our help we are those who knock upon a door which no one will open, missionaries, if you will, in a tribe which needs no strange idols. Or to perhaps make a more true analogy, peace corps volunteers who attempt to dig wells to make clean water, yet find their shovels vanished.

There is little we can do for your planet, although we are enormously ready to aid without the request of those who wish the aid. And what aid we have to offer is little enough, yet who knows what may make the difference for someone who seeks. The right word at the right time is enormously powerful, and we are hopeful always of so reading the hearts and minds of those who seek within this circle that we may perhaps touch some frayed leaf of regret or pain, some smudged blossom that was plucked too quickly or not watered enough, so that we may help you bloom and find yourselves. Along those same lines, we gain a great deal from the attempt to be of service. It is in our opinion the most challenging task available to a seeker of truth.

Service among your peoples is often service from the standpoint of the one who serves. For instance, service was given by the one known as Andrew Carnegie when this entity endowed many libraries. When entities come into those libraries, they may see the beauty of the structures which were built in honor of knowledge, and they may learn from the knowledge within the books housed within that structure. On the other hand, the one known as Andrew could not serve those who did not wish to read books. So often when one attempts to serve another, it is the equivalent of building the library for the one who does not read books.

"Well, then," we seem to be saying, "to serve another, you see what that entity desires and give it to him." This is a far purer attempt to serve, yet those who wish to be served seldom have the discrimination to know what truly would be of service to themselves, and so they ask for the cotton candy, the cookie, the cake, the pie, and do not ask for the discipline of the bran, the cabbage, the cauliflower. One must then hearken to those deep inward biases which you as well as we have built up through incarnation after incarnation after incarnation, those biases especially concerning the nature of true spiritual service.

Any one of these three types of service—service seen by the seeker of service, service seen by the giver of service, and service which appeals to a higher definition of service—are ways we may use to attempt to serve you. Yet, only as we speak and share with this instrument the effort of creating a service, and then as we see the effects which our words may have, only then do we know if we have been on target or if once again we have been biased in our service and thus created a stumbling block, however infinitesimal it may be.

Lastly, we say that we gain more from you than you from us, because both you and we seek the Creator, and we gaze upon thee, you cannot gaze upon us. It is as if we were telephoning a message, yet we can see your thoughts dance, your aura's light and your feelings move like great waters. You cannot see us. Thus, we see in you the Creator in a way which is kept from you by the limitations of your organs of perception. What beautiful jewel-like beings you are, my children, and how deeply grateful we are to be working with you, to be learning from you, and to be sharing meditation.

This by no means concludes all that we might say upon this subject, yet it is this instrument's wish that we refrain from speaking too long, in order that the hearing and thinking and meditating that you all do during this period of time not give way before we are through to the discomfort of having sat in one position too long. You see, we had not considered that, for we do not have to rest our vehicles. We have much to learn from you about service, for you see, that very consideration should have been easy for us to see, yet with all of our thinking and learning, still we forgot until this instrument spoke.

We will be gentle beings before we lose our identity once more in the Source, and so will each of you. The way to that gentility of being lies in seeking the present moment, seeing the present moment, diving deeply into the present moment, and at the dark heart of the depths of that moment's waters, communicating suddenly and irretrievably with the blinding light of the face of the Creator. Seek and know that this is possible.

We would at this time transfer this contact, with thanks to this instrument. We are those of Q'uo.

(Jim channeling)

I am Q'uo, and greet each again in love and light. At this time it is our honor to offer ourselves to the queries which each may have for us and in this way again be able to [ascertain] more about the nature of the Creator and the means by which It expresses Itself through your being. Is there a query at this time with which we may begin?

Carla: Well, I have a question that's really off the subject, but J wrote this week to inquire whether you were of the same vibration or the same basic entity as Djwhal Khul, I don't know how you say that, and although it was my impression from when I first challenged you the first time that you spoke, that you were, indeed, of that vibration but did not want to include the inner plane vibrations in that, I was unwilling to say that until I had had it from you. Is this correct? Or can you tell me?

I am Q'uo, and we are of a very similar vibration to those that you know of as Djwhal Khul. However, the studies which we have pursued have dealt far more emphatically, shall we say, with the beginning of the blending of wisdom with the compassion which we were privileged to gain in our previous experiences within the fourth density illusion. Therefore, we attempt to temper that which we offer of wisdom with that you would know as compassion.

May we speak further, my sister?

Carla: No thank you.

I am Q'uo, and we thank you, my sister. Is there another query?

Carla: Is there physical or mental sickness in the fifth density? And if so, how does it manifest in a social memory complex?

I am Q'uo, and you have asked a query which may be answered in many ways …

(Side one of tape ends.)

(Jim channeling)

I am Q'uo, and am again with this instrument. To continue. Not all within the fifth-density experience choose to continue the evolutionary process within the social memory complex. Therefore, the imbalances that you would see as a disease are not always expressed in the societal complex. But, in general, we might suggest that such disease takes more the form of a desire or yearning to be of service in a certain way which is yet unfulfilled. Thus, that which is not in balance in the way of service and learning calls unto us in a manner which you might see as a vacuum which seeks to be filled. This empty place, then, within our being is represented by a manner of serving which is possible to render but which lies unused, and in its appropriate time makes itself known and is then fulfilled.

May we speak further, my sister?

Carla: No, thank you.

I am Q'uo, and again we thank you, my sister. Is there another query?

Carla: From your point of view, what was the planetary result of all of the light groups' various and sundry efforts all over the planet to create a raising of human consciousness of harmony during the recent so-called harmonic convergence? And what happened, if anything, other than that—what happened to the planet or what happened to the energies coming into the planet?

I am Q'uo, and if you can picture in your mind the gathering of many at one of your sacred sites, perhaps one of your churches as we find occurred many times this day, and imagine each participant singing the same sacred song of joy, each in his own tongue and way, you may begin to understand the nature of such celebrations and observations by groups of your peoples, for it is in such gatherings that the model, shall we say, for a consensus of consciousness is begun.

Thus, as the eyes, the minds, and the hearts of great numbers of your peoples begin to focus upon one issue or another, there is the movement towards this kind of consensus of consciousness which marks the beginning of the, as we find it has been called in this group, social memory complex, that is the means by which evolution of mind, body and spirit continues within the fourth-density illusion.

As the focus of the attention is moved higher and higher up the racial and planetary energy centers which correlate to those within each entity's vehicle, the nature of the concern of the focus then is raised in vibratory frequency so that concern for the self moves to concern for another, to concern for other groups that are known to the self, for concern for groups yet unknown in a personal sense, to a concern for the providing for the welfare of all, and so forth, so that the focus of attention is likened unto a progression up a scale of notes, with the scale corresponding to the expanding perceptions and ability of the population so focusing to express itself in a manner more and more approaching that of unconditional love or compassion.

May we speak further, my sister?

Carla: Then you're suggesting that the continuing mass prayer days like the Prayer for Peace Day at the New Year and this day—and I suppose the big rock concerts for "USA for Africa" and like that—are all sort of practice runs at our becoming a fourth-density social memory complex. Is that correct?

I am Q'uo, and this is correct, my sister, and may serve [for] some further comment, as we might suggest that all efforts which blend great numbers of your peoples offer this same opportunity for the exercising of the mass consciousness of this planetary sphere.

May we speak further, my sister?

Carla: Then the Pan American games and the Olympics would have some of that same characteristic except, of course, for the competitiveness between countries. Is that right?

I am Q'uo, and this is indeed correct. As each grouping of entities is able to see beyond the self to its own group, and then perhaps to other groupings of those with whom the competition is shared, the boundaries of perception, then, are expanded to include that which was previously excluded. Therefore, such opportunities are excellent training devices for the expanding of the boundaries of perception.

May we speak further, my sister?

Carla: Then great tragedies, like the plane crash, and I guess more than that, the shuttle, when it exploded—I know the whole world just felt wretched for the seven who were lost. Those are also unifying spiritual experiences, aren't they?

I am Q'uo, and again this is correct, my sister. The entity which is the planetary consciousness then has many portions which begin to recognize the nature of their own being through such foci of attention, whether it be of great joy or sadness.

May we speak further, my sister?

Carla: And then people who are artists and their work is heard or seen all over the world, anybody from Picasso to Elvis Presley, people that are just tops in their field, you know, and everybody in Russia and America and Japan, you know, everybody knows them equally, their value isn't only in what they produce, but in that they have a world that can all talk about one thing. They bring people closer to a social memory complex, don't they?

I am Q'uo, and this is quite correct, my sister.

Carla: Hmm. Then technology is indeed our friend because so many more things can be seen by the whole world now by satellite—yes?

I am Q'uo, and it is quite true that the technological advances which have marked these last decades of your experience offer what might be seen as a training aid for the mass consciousness of the planet itself and its population.

May we speak further, my sister?

Carla: Viewing all this, I guess I'm tempted to say, "What can we do?" since there's no ambition in me to alert the entire planet at one time of anything. Should I just get my perspective back down to scale, and not worry about attempting to serve in aiding the social memory complex?

I am Q'uo. We do not wish to speak to the point that we direct one's action, for the free will of each is paramount in the progression both of the individual and the mass minds. Each entity moves in its own sphere of influence, shall we say, according to those preincarnated programs which have been joined with many others in order that various lessons and services might be pursued within the incarnation that would aid many in the growth of mind, body and spirit.

Thus, as each moves in that pattern of being and experience, one becomes aware that there is a vast and infinite interconnection between all things, and the actions and thoughts of one affect many, and eventually the mind of the planetary population is brought to the point that the resources of all become available to each in his or her own manner of perceiving so that each entity is able to draw upon this vast library of information to further the individual expression that has been chosen as its unique manner of expression and pattern of lessons and services that will be offered during the incarnation.

May we speak further, my sister?

Carla: No, my teacher, that's all for tonight, thank you.

I am Q'uo, and once again we thank you, my sister. Is there another query?

(Pause)

I am Q'uo, and again we thank each for inviting our presence. We enjoy greatly the opportunity to blend our vibrations with yours and to share our humble opinions as the fruit of our own seeking upon that same path which each of your peoples also treads. We rejoice at the sharing of this journey, and look forward to each such gathering that we might so share again. We are known to you as those of Q'uo. At this time we shall take our leave of this group, leaving each in the love and in the light of the one infinite Creator. Adonai, my friends. Adonai. ✤

Sunday Meditation
September 6, 1987

(Carla channeling)

I am Q'uo. I greet each of you in the love and the light of the one infinite Creator. It is truly meat and drink to us to share consciousness with you as you sit in the circle of honest seeking, together unified by desire and by love. How fortunate we are to have been called to share this experience with you and to share a few thoughts. We would especially like to welcome the one known as H, who is new to us, but not by any means new to this light group or to the persistent seeking of the love and the light of the one infinite Creator. We love and bless each of you and ask that as we offer opinion, you take what is useful and leave the rest behind.

This evening we find within the group questions upon the mind, questions of time and purpose, money and suffering, questions of how best to pursue the road of learning, of seeking that point of view which may yield contact with love itself, with that fuller consciousness that embraces, accepts and grasps the unity of all things.

Time seems to be inexorable in its demands upon the seeker's time. Busy time upon busy time seems to flow within your experience, and there seems to be no respite from the chores and the details to be seen to which constitute the mundane day-to-day living experience. Were it not necessary to house and clothe and feed the physical vehicle which manifests for you within this illusion, time would be your plaything, utterly free. Yet that which is utterly free is often discounted.

Yet there is a way of gazing upon the day-to-day experience which can create a double perception within the self, that most complex of entities. The time in its mundane river-like existence of earthly things moves on inexorably, rhythmically, cyclically and sweeps all of immediacy before it. Yet there is another kind of time. It is the time of the timeless moment, a moving vertically upward and downward upon the moment to feel the echoes of love, meaning and manifestation in one moment that removes from time its horizontal inexorability, its forced progress, and makes for the seeker opportunities of timelessness.

One may seek through meditation to still the inexorable march of moments and minutes and minutes into hours, hours into days, and days into years, for within meditation vertical time, or time/space, is available. Time itself may be stopped within the consciousness of the deep mind, and in that moment of timelessness, that within you which is real beholds the mystery—face-to-face. What matters it if the face of mystery is dark and the mystery only deepens as one spends more and more time in communion with the absolute?

The practice of timelessness begins, after many repetitions of visits to this point of view, to unfold for the seeker an unlimited point of view, a point of view that sees the mundane limitations and necessities of the everyday life, yet dwells as a native son or daughter in that kingdom where love abides without the mask of illusion.

Time is a difficult subject upon which to speak, yet those within the circle seek knowledge of how better to use their time, of how better to dwell with ultimate reality, even within the illusions of third-density life. Therefore, we tackle the subject. Perhaps the crux of pondering upon time lies in one's conclusion about the absolute. It is a principle by which we live that there is an absolute and unchangeable reality which undergirds and holds together all creations, all of the infinity of illusions and all consciousness. It is our opinion that we came or were created from the very stuff of reality—absolute, infinite, unchanging, unpotentiated, passive and final reality. This reality has seemed to us to bear a certain character: that character is love.

The reality which indwells each created consciousness is of a nature which is infinitely creative, infinitely free, which retains in its original and undifferentiated form that quality of love which cannot be given or shared in words, but only caught as a shadow, a hint, an insinuation by inspired turn of phrase or sudden realization within the seeker's deep heart or mind. It is our opinion that it is possible and profitable for seekers of the truth about the nature of creation to seek persistently, comfortably and with the light touch that mysterious reality which undergirds all the myriad of illusions of which your Earth plane is but one.

The challenge which you face within third-density illusion is the challenge of one whose eyes are covered, whose ears are stopped, whose mouth is without speech. By persistent and loving seeking, by the desire to know and to feel the love of the infinite Creator, the seeker may experience timelessness and the strength of the ultimate reality of perfect love. Yet what fruit can the seeker produce as a result of this contact? For he has seen things which he could not see, he has heard that which no ear has heard, he has spoken in communion with love which is always and always creative. And so you find entity upon entity attempting each in its own to describe the undescribable, to move into horizontal time the vertical timelessness of the awareness of the infinite Creator.

We urge each of you to value those moments of inspired verticality when you may seize one precious moment and gaze up and down and all about you, knowing that at that moment, by desire you stand upon holy ground. And you may hear and see and feel infinity and be overwhelmed by the joy of that one moment. What may that moment be—the call of a bird, the striking of a clock, the red light in traffic, the moment with a fellow seeker when a glance is exchanged and mutual gifts given.

Within the everyday life there is no moment which does not contain the possibility of this union with timelessness, and the more you hunger for that which is real, the more motivated you may be to take with rejoicing those moments which are yours, gifts from the hullabaloo of a busy life, and in that one moment, by will and faith, see and acknowledge the contact of the small self and that great Self which is love, love undivided, love coherent, love creative, love unending.

My children, may we say each of you has gifts to give to each other, gifts to give to humankind. There are those things which you before your incarnations have planned to do in the service of the one infinite Creator. Please know that the very first of those things which each seeking soul hopes to do while in the manifestation of human consciousness is to become a channel for love, that others trapped in the mire of earthly time may have their despair turned to hope by seeing and sensing what they cannot explain: that light within your eyes which speaks of a happy and sweet union with infinite love. The light from the eye of one who has spent time in the presence of that mysterious and unknowable Creator can be startling, but always is that which is a channel for renewal of hope and faith in others.

It is a paradox, yet it is true that when you seek to advance in knowledge of the one infinite Creator, the progress of that seeking is marked not so much by one's own realizations, but by the degree of generosity with which those moments of companionship with the divine source have been shared in the life experience with others. Think over your experiences of this day. Were there times when a realization of love could have been shared by a smile, a touch, an understanding ear, a caring heart, that were missed? "Lay up for yourselves," it is said in one of your holy works, "treasures in heaven where moth and rust do not corrupt nor thieves break in and steal."

You, my children, dwell in two realities—the apparent reality of time and the immanent and overshadowing reality of timeless infinity, an infinity made of love. How we with our free wills have distorted that love, yet in each moment there is the same complete possibility for intimate contact with infinite love. We urge you, then, not only to meditate within each day, but to choose moments within the most busy of your hours wherein you sink into the verticality of timelessness for one instant and see that each entity and thing which you behold is beautiful, perfect and lovely.

With this point of view, the knotty and insoluble problems of one day or another may be seen again and again in timeless moments as configurations of energy wherein there is a challenge to learn a lesson about love. Sometimes the lesson seems simple, sometimes heart-rendingly difficult, yet with the point of view available to you of timelessness, you may see at the very least the inner reality of infinite love within troublesome entities with whom you are in relationship and within situations which seem troublesome. This means not that you can become a happy person with no problems, for it is not for this that you chose to come into incarnation at this time, but rather it is that you may begin to feel the deep celestial rhythms of a cosmic point of view which sees patterns extending from incarnation to incarnation and from creation to creation. The generosity of the infinite Creator we feel to be overwhelming in offering with each lesson that is to be learned about love that cleft in the rock, that safe hiding place where one may dwell with the Infinite and fly with the wings of immortality. This you may do in but an instant. This you may do because your deeper nature is already timeless.

My children, we ask you to love one another, for it is in the practice of offering love to others, to situations, and to life itself that you yourself become aware of the incredible sea of love in which the universe swims. It is those who keep the love inside that never experience infinite love in its fullness. Thus, you may be the bringer of a sense of wonder and love and peace to another, and though you wish only to be one who serves and gives love, it is then that you shall receive in overflowing measure the reflection of your service, for love returns and becomes a marvelous infinitely complex circle or net of shared energy.

Each of you has the opportunity to form the bond of infinite love with all portions of the illusion you experience, that which you call the natural world—the world of unseen things, wind, thunder, intelligence without bodies. And you, having taken on the physical chemical body of illusion, move into worlds and can reach into the Earthly world as a light bringer, a love giver and a love sharer.

We would at this time transfer this contact to the one known as Jim. We thank this instrument and each. We now transfer. We are those known to you as Q'uo.

(Jim channeling)

I am Q'uo, and greet each again in love and light through this instrument. At this time it is our privilege to offer ourself in the attempt to speak to those queries which those present may offer to us. Is there a query with which we may begin?

Carla: I have a question that's been on my mind for awhile, and it has to do with channeling. I have a student who got channeled information eighteen months ago that he was to be a very important channel within six months. This man I have taught now for about a month, and can honestly describe him as a person who has no natural ability, no native gift for channeling, and therefore it seems to me that he has suffered rather cruelly, because he's really taken it to heart that he hasn't been able to channel. I do have him channeling a bit now, but he is unsure of his gift, and it's certainly going to be a hard pull for him just to be the kind of channel I am, much less a very important channel, although he is capable of that, of doing as well as I can do.

I realize that entities which have dwelled on Earth have the right to give advice and prophecy, but it seems to me that it is and can be very destructive. I wonder if you could comment on what I call inner plane channeling, channeling from people who have at one time been alive. Is there anything that I might write to people who ask me about this …

(Side one of tape ends.)

Carla: … advice that I could give that would help curb this kind of damage done to someone who believes simply because it was channeled, and then knocks himself out with guilt, simply because he has not been able to do what the channel said he could?

I am Q'uo, and am again with this instrument. As we look at the query upon its surface, we find that there is some portion to which we may respond without infringing upon the free will of various entities involved within the situation described. Those who seek to serve as instruments for information that may have value in the evolution of another offer themselves in various manners in order that this desire might be fulfilled. Because the art of serving as a vocal instrument is not that which is plain to all who seek to serve in this manner, the efforts of many are somewhat short of what is possible for these entities. Thus, the contacts are in many instances somewhat commingled with the personal biases and inclinations of the instrument. This is possible in any kind of contact and often confuses much of the information which is transmitted with personal opinion.

It must also be recognized that any contact which attempts to look into that which you call the future of another entity, sees many possibilities which may be described with more or less precision, but which cannot be determined to be inexorable. And when such information is given that such and such an event will occur in such a fashion upon such a date or within a certain span of your time and experience, there is a greater possibility that liberty has been taken with the interpretation of what has been seen upon what you would call the inner planes, for the free will of each entity is always in motion and is that primary factor which determines the shape and time that events shall manifest within.

Thus, it is our suggestion to each entity which looks to this kind of inspiration for information and guidance that that which is looked for be of a more general nature that may be applied as a principle, shall we say, within the life experience rather than be described in a certain and limiting fashion which offers only a portion or glimpse of that blending of energies which shall eventually be experienced by any entity; that a certain kind of channeling, in this instance, the channeling of what you have described as inner plane entities who have previously walked as third-density beings within your illusion, may fall prey to this difficulty. For many who have served valiantly and frequently within your third-density physical illusion seek, after moving to the finer planes of your third-density illusion, to offer themselves as sources of inspiration and guidance for those who yet remain within the boundaries of physical illusion, and in this offering of themselves as servants, give that which is theirs to give. Yet it must be remembered that each such entity yet works within its own boundaries of limitation, though these boundaries may indeed be more spacious that those which you now enjoy. The words of those who cannot be seen by the outer eye must be weighed as carefully as the words of any which ring upon the ear, within the mind, and in the heart.

There is much that is learned by the process of what we find you call the trial and error method. Discrimination is that which is hard-won, my sister, and in this process much of tolerance can be achieved as those lessons requiring finer and finer discrimination are encountered. Thus, we would not wish to warn all away from this or that source, this or that kind of contact, for each has much to teach which may not be apparent upon the surface of things, and oftentimes that which is learned is not that which was attempted, but proves to be far more valuable.

May we speak in any further fashion, my sister?

Carla: Yes. The same fellow was told that he had guides. I am capable, because I've been through Silva mind training, of putting him in contact with his guides, yet I'm reluctant to offer him something which he may find unsatisfactory later on, as he himself has expressed a feeling of dependence upon the guides in the same way that he has expressed dependence upon what the channel told him to do. In other words, the request for guides is also a request to give up discrimination and do whatever he feels the guides direct.

Consequently, I find the ethical question to be, "Should I do this?" knowing that it's very possible that this perfectly good technique for seeking the deeper opinions of the deeper self—knowing that he may well put himself in bondage to what he considers the guides have to say. If you can't comment on that specific question, you're welcome to comment in general on how to be of service to people that want guides.

I am Q'uo, and with this very concern for most mystery in our thinking, we wish to offer that which enhances your own ability to exercise your free will in order that your steps be taken in full responsibility, and the benefit from such journeying might then truly accrue to your total beingness. That which you offer another is offered most efficiently when given with a whole heart and in the joy of serving another portion of the Creator in a manner which rings of truth to your own sensibilities. Thus, we would not wish to speak in a definitive manner so that a rule, shall we say, would be laid out which would be seen as being inflexible.

However, we again turn your query back upon your own ability to discriminate, for much you have offered in the query which may be placed within its answer. This, my sister, is our way of suggesting that you know that which is most appropriate as a means for your sharing. And that choice may not be fully clear to your conscious mind, but may be discovered by further searching within. We do not wish to seem to ignore that which you ask, but wish instead to reaffirm your own ability to respond to your query in the fashion which is most appropriate for you.

May we speak in any further fashion, my sister?

Carla: Yes, Q'uo, just one more question. Jim and I have been increasingly pleased with your contact and find it to be a clear one, and perhaps one which we should be taking with a more careful point of view, and had conceived the idea of either having additional sessions to Sunday, or simply on Sunday evenings, pursuing a line of questioning from one Sunday to the next, or if we wanted to leave Sunday spontaneous so that whoever came in could affect the meeting and have that meeting be more for them. Do you have any comments on our thoughts about setting up a continuing group where we ask carefully thought-out lines of questioning which extend over more than just one session at a time. Is this something that you would see as an additional service? Is this something that is compatible with your desire to serve?

I am Q'uo, and we are happy to serve in whatever manner we are asked that does not infringe upon another's free will.

May we speak in any further fashion, my sister?

Carla: No, thank you, that's all.

I am Q'uo, and we thank you once again, my sister. Is there another query at this time?

(Pause)

I am Q'uo, and we thank each for allowing us to speak that which is our opinion and the fruits of our own seeking. We again remind each that we wish not to influence overly much with our humble offering, and we hope that we have been of some small service this evening. At this time we find that we have offered that which has been asked, and in the comfort and joy of this knowledge, we shall take our leave of this group, rejoicing in the love and in the light of the one infinite Creator. We are known to you as those of Q'uo. Adonai, my friends. Adonai. ☙

Intensive Meditation
September 10, 1987

(Carla channeling)

I am Hatonn. I greet each of you in love and light. It has been interesting to note the progress of the group operation, which so rapidly moved from the busy matters of the day when light was visualized. We appreciate the degree of focus and concentration which each brings to the persistent seeking with faith, trust and truth.

We would tell the one known as D the basics of our nature. We are those of the density of love, and as a planetary group offer our contact to those which may have some use for it.

This evening it is our desire to work with the basic visualization in the inner self by which the vocal channeling is transmitted. In order to offer a disciplined experience of this, we would like to tell a story in round-robin fashion, speaking only a short while through each instrument and continuing 'round and 'round until the story is done. This is excellent practice for the channel as the story is not long *(inaudible)* yet in the end it will be seen to have flown easily in meaning and texture.

We would speak of a young teacher—a teacher who wished greatly to offer his services to the children whom the loved. We shall call this young man "Jamie." Jamie enjoyed children of all ages, yet he found no employment as a teacher for he did not have the background and education which the authorities of school districts demand. Jamie had been very ill throughout childhood and had never been able to attend classes, nor to receive degrees. Jamie could not move about with great ease. In fact, for all but four hours of each day, this entity was told that he must rest quietly.

We would now transfer to the one known as Jim. I am Hatonn.

(Jim channeling)

And thus under these conditions Jamie found it necessary to begin a process of educating himself so that he might obtain the kind of knowledge that he so treasured in the acquiring and in the passing on to others. His process of educating himself was one in which he partook not only of that which was offered through books—of which he had many; he was eager to seek more—but also through the conversations with those more learned than he. And in this manner, [he] began to gather about him resources which fed his desire to know and which illumined those portions of his mind which were awaiting the investigation of his eager curiosity. It was also in this manner that he first began to impart his knowledge to others who were drawn to him by the same eagerness, desire and curiosity which drew knowledge to him. Many of those were younger than Jamie and came, both upon a regular and an irregular basis, to Jamie's home where he was able to set aside the short period of each day for the more formal portions of his teaching to others.

We shall transfer now to the one known as D.

(D channeling)

As Jamie stood before those who had gathered around him one evening, he was asked …

(Carla channeling)

Miss Judy asked Jamie, "What is the purpose of life?" Jamie said, "That is an interesting question, although it has little to do with that which we were discussing." Said the student, "I have watched you, you are so greatly *(inaudible)* with literature and art, music and poetry, and I find all these things fascinating. Yet they do not raise questions which puzzle me as much as this one."

Jamie lay down his books which he had spent so long studying and attempted to reflect on the purpose of life. "Perhaps life is a struggle," he said, speaking to himself. How much he struggled through his hours of rest, chafing with impatience until he could once again rise up and be with people out-of-doors.

We shall now transfer to the one known as Jim. I am Hatonn.

(Jim channeling)

Jamie pondered long upon this question for it was one which he had considered frequently before and the answer, as before, was that which was slow in coming, for he could see many possibilities. There were considerations of service, of struggle, of adventurous moving into the unknown, of completing a larger plan of mysterious and unknown nature, and perhaps even the possibility of random chance moving places and people and ideas.

However, to the student who first queried him on this topic, Jamie could only reply that the wonder of it all was far greater than his ability to express in words what little he was able to glean [in a] coherent manner which could even begin to show a basic or simple description of such an immense possibility. Thus, he continued to seek the knowledge of various portions of human study that had been pursued by others before him and to impart this knowledge to those with whom he shared the relationship of teacher and student.

We shall transfer at this time.

(D channeling)

Years went by as Jamie's studies continued in response on the subject of life, matured in the light of his own increasing experience and inspection. The students came and went, coming to know him as not only knowledge[able] but as kind, compassionate and patient—that is, wise—and in the eyes of more sensitive and [poetic].

Jamie came through these years of attention to him, questioning life—the meaning of life, and his meditations on the meaning of his own life. It seemed that his life had become *(inaudible)* as an answer to that question. He had lived through many years of enforced physical inactivity, transformed to deep meditation during which he had patterns of his own misfortunes and gifts to make sense of.

We will transfer now.

(Carla channeling)

It is generally *(inaudible)* in a service-filled life he pondered his struggle and his service *(inaudible)*. He was also self-critical, pondering why his limitation had been so great. He began to *(inaudible)* into that divine discomfort. An angel of light who spoke in clear vision [said], "Turn and look *(inaudible)* at the limitless number of hours you have had to seek deeply within." And so Jamie pondered. Again the angel came and asked, "What is the purpose of your life?" Jamie said, "I can guess; it is to be of service." "Perhaps that is a important part of it," said the angel, and left to let Jamie ponder again.

After many sleepless nights Jamie became aware of something *(inaudible)*, something that felt quite dangerous. His inward eye seemed to open and as he gazed about his darkened room, he saw the wild whirling of his bedclothes and a strenuous heaving of the *(inaudible)*. He saw the light whirling and swirling in infinitely various patterns *(inaudible)*. He saw his own skin leap and rejoice, for he had asked and had been given the vision of the purpose of life.

Again the angel came and saw Jamie. "Tell me now, what is the purpose?" And Jamie smiled, "The purpose is *joy!*" he said. "Joy in life and sharing." "That is good," said the angel, "but that is only half of the job."

We shall now transfer. I am Hatonn.

(Jim channeling)

Again Jamie considered the question of the purpose of his life, for he had felt that the experience and joy and the liveness of the creation about him and within him and the service to others that he might render, comprised all that one might hope for as a purpose for any existence. And yet the angel had left him to ponder what further purpose there might be in not only experiencing and sharing joy but also pursuing that which was beyond joy and service to others.

This caused some discomfort within the very soul of Jamie for the joy that he had known in that brief but powerful vision seemed, in itself, far more than he could comprehend. And to look for that which was beyond such joy seemed a task far too great for him to hope to complete. Long and often did he consider further purpose within his own life, wherein again passed many sleepless nights.

And after yet another sleepless night, and just before the dawn was about to break upon another busy day—for he had continued his studies and teaching—the angel appeared once again to ask if Jamie had discovered further purpose to his life. And Jamie replied that he had thought of every possibility but could only return to his confusion and that which he had already discovered by his experience. And the angel said to Jamie, "That is a good beginning, for within such confusion and desire you will begin to find a greater expression, purpose. Continue to look within your confusion, and within your desire, and you shall find a nourishment there. And that shall reveal to you what now is hidden."

Now we shall transfer.

(D channeling)

Jamie's nights continued to be restless. He pondered the worth of his own efforts to fulfill the meaning of life, and he thought his efforts to understand that and gain a suitable understanding of the depth which men shall not seem to attempt *(inaudible)*. He saw his life as his best effort to fulfill his concepts and service, struggle and joy. But he enjoyed each step of his realization. Then, too, the path of his insights, though valid and rightly guided, were incomplete. He began to wonder if he could ever come to a true understanding in his life of its meaning. At this point he began to wonder if, in the truest sense, life had meaning. What could ever be summed up or put in human words?

He looked back at his life as a continual process, continual progress along a path that is soul-searching and self-knowing, and felt again the joy that the search had brought him. He thought back to his early manhood when he first had been directed along this search by a questioning student and he realized his own gratitude to himself for not having attempted then and there to answer that question or fail to recognize its depth. A search for the answer to that question had shaped his life and contributed much, he realized then, to its meaning.

After all that, for all those years of attention, concentration and meditation on this question, he knew that it had not brought him even now the complete answer. He knew that the meaning of life was even more than the search for its meaning and the discovery of its meaning in real terms than he could ever explain to another. He realized that with the asking of that question his life had been set on a course of *(inaudible)* nor did he wish it to. He knew at this point he had only once seen an infinitely long path. For a while the same joys and frustrations, his troubles and dead-ends that he had dealt with for years *(inaudible)*.

We will transfer now to the one known as Carla.

(Carla channeling)

He drew near he was *(inaudible)* at the end of his life except the mystery of *(inaudible)*, his trouble and his joy. Speaking out loud in great emotion, Jamie prayed for the first time in his long life. "Oh, God up there, if there is a God, I do not understand the purpose of this life or the capacity for all things, as in my vision, to be joyful." Suddenly he felt an immense peace and feeling of connection betwixt himself and the mystery he had acknowledged. In that peace he gave up the struggle and saw only *(inaudible)* that is love of beauty and saw only the mystery.

"Well," he said, out loud to no one seen, "I do not understand but I feel You listened to me and I know now that I should listen more carefully to You". Suddenly he saw the many, many hours of enforced idleness as being a great adventure and he saw his struggle disappear.

We pray—we who used to aid in the ways of love—that each seeker may seek the peace in the struggle and the mystery in joyful service. We pray that the listening heart may come to know that it is not a common purpose of life's beginnings that the creation grows in rejoicing, but rather it is the deepest consciousness of spiritual beings. May each dare to plunge deeper and deeper into our love which is the source of itself. We pray that each may sink like a star into the peace of the deep part wherein those depths are standard.

We thank this group for its desire to improve in the practice of vocal channeling. We know that much is upon the mind which may attempt to distract each from the chosen service and we appreciate that discipline which is the product of the holding discomfort and impatience which *(inaudible)* to move along the path of serial realizations, never continue to rest upon the laurels.

We would at this time transfer to the one known as Jim.

(Jim channeling)

I am Hatonn, and at this time we would offer ourselves in the capacity of attempting to speak to any queries which those present may have for us. May we begin with a query?

(Transcript ends.)

L/L Research

L/L Research is a subsidiary of Rock Creek Research & Development Laboratories, Inc.

P.O. Box 5195
Louisville, KY 40255-0195

www.llresearch.org

Rock Creek is a non-profit corporation dedicated to discovering and sharing information which may aid in the spiritual evolution of humankind.

ABOUT THE CONTENTS OF THIS TRANSCRIPT: This telepathic channeling has been taken from transcriptions of the weekly study and meditation meetings of the Rock Creek Research & Development Laboratories and L/L Research. It is offered in the hope that it may be useful to you. As the Confederation entities always make a point of saying, please use your discrimination and judgment in assessing this material. If something rings true to you, fine. If something does not resonate, please leave it behind, for neither we nor those of the Confederation would wish to be a stumbling block for any.

CAVEAT: This transcript is being published by L/L Research in a not yet final form. It has, however, been edited and any obvious errors have been corrected. When it is in a final form, this caveat will be removed.

© 2009 L/L Research

Sunday Meditation
September 13, 1987

Group question: Concerns the concept of Christianity and the usual concept that people hold, at least the common one, that if you simply believe in the name of Jesus that you will be saved, without having to do or live a certain kind of life that might be exemplified by the eleventh commandment, "Love one another." Is it possible to get information that would resolve between "living the life" versus "simply believing"?

Also, as an aside to that, regarding the representations of the various religions and their various prophets—Mohammed, Jesus, Confucius, Lao Tsu and so forth, is each religion and master approximately the same? Each for a certain group of people?

(Carla channeling)

I am Q'uo. May I greet you in the love and the light of the one infinite Creator. We thank you, as always, for the great opportunity of joining in your meditation and sharing your energy. We thank this instrument for seeking to be of service and we thank each listening ear, for without you our service could not be offered. Indeed, we thank all upon your beautiful planet who, despite so much evidence to the contrary within the illusion which you call life, persist in believing that there is a truth somewhere beyond all the paradoxes which confound science and philosophy alike.

We, too, seek the truth by faith alone and not by word or concept. Yet it is with the clumsy tools of words and thoughts that we must address each question that you ask. We apologize for the inadequacy of language and the poverty of conceptualization, yet it has ever been so, that truth and inspiration, beauty and glory lie betwixt the words and the lines of sentences and paragraphs so that the inspiration is the product of far more than the sum of the words used to present it. And so may we join you in going forth to attempt to gaze at the truth within, the mystery which surrounds every question that has import in the seeker's life.

You wish to know how it is that the one known as Jesus the Christ could be the only son of God, as the Christians believe.

It is more than understandable that spiritual seekers would hope for a savior. However, the one known as Jesus the Christ saw himself as a shadow, a being whose every hope and true identity lay in the reflection of the Creator and Father that overshadowed him.

It has often been thrown in the faces of non-Christian people that Jesus' words, "I am the way, the truth and the life; no one comes to the Father except by me," make it virtually impossible to achieve eternity without being in turn overshadowed by the one known as Jesus the Christ.

It is interesting to note that in the tradition of Judaism, in which the master known as Jesus spent his childhood as a very good student, the most secret name of the Father was an unpronounced consonantal word meaning "I Am That I Am," or "I Am The One That Is." That great I Am is, indeed, the Father and all else. Consciousness is of the Father and the Father indwells all consciousness.

Thus, consciousness, that original undistorted Consciousness which is Love, is indeed the Way; it is indeed the Truth; it is indeed Life itself—and eternal Life at that.

I Am. I Am. This is the mantra, if you will, of creation. And it was intended by the one known as Jesus, not that he be seen over against the Father, but instead it was intended by the master known as Jesus that he be seen as a messenger, as a servant, as the shadow of the One who sent him.

"He who sees me, sees not me, but the Father," he said. "I do nothing but that which is done by the Father," he said. And he said then too, "All these things you shall do, and greater also."

We realize that all these things are written down that we have quoted, that they have been there for scholars to see, for priests to teach, for your many years. Yet, because the concept of a channeled life is foreign to those who wish to preserve that which you call the ego, it has not been seen that the master known as Jesus was transparent and became, though human, a living channel through which could flow undistorted the powerful and perfecting love of the one infinite Creator.

You have asked how it can be that one human, no matter how divine, could die for the sins of the whole world, and have wondered whether it can be true that there is no need to live the life of discipline, but only to believe in the sacrifice of Jesus the Christ, made for all humanity.

My friends, we are picking and choosing our words here, for this instrument has refused three times the beginnings of paragraphs. We find this somewhat amusing, yet we realize also that you cannot listen to us for hours at a time. We shall therefore attempt to speak to this enormous subject with a terseness which does not usually characterize our presentation. If there are questions after we have spoken, we trust that you may continue until you are satisfied, if not at this session, then at another.

The master known as Jesus was a man, living a channeled or inspired and very impersonal life, yet containing and expressing emotion and affection. The master known as Jesus saw a pattern emerge during the short time of his actual ministry. It was the pattern of a warlike people, his own people, the Jews, who wished to become again a great kingdom as it had been at one time. It was felt by this teacher that as had his friend John the Baptist gone, so would he.

He wished for his people a realization. He wished them to realize and truly know that their identity, their nationhood, and their kingdom was eternity itself. He wished them to lay down those weapons which make kingdoms of Earth and pick up instead those tools of peace and love which might create the growing and life-giving knowledge of a greater life, a greater kingdom than this Earthly one. Thirdly, this entity wished by his death to be remembered as one who intended to die of love for those who killed him.

He wished to be remembered as one who loved. He wished to be a symbol of that greater kingdom which was the true kingdom of his people and all people. His instructions about bread and wine were that these be taken in remembrance, that when this food was taken, it would be food not of this Earth, not filling the hunger of this illusory plane, but, rather, he hoped that it might be seen as the true manna which is infinite and which feeds an infinite hunger—the thirst for truth and right action.

Above all, he did not intend that any who wished to be a disciple rest back upon his laurels and think again and again in gratitude upon the savior while continuing a life which was uninformed by those principles which the one known as Jesus taught. Indeed, the master known as Jesus had a stark vision of the nature of this illusion you experience. He saw the type of consciousness which you share, with all of its distortions and limitations, as producing a situation in which martyrdom was the nature of the life experience. The brevity of life within the physical body was a melancholy fact to him. The master wished therefore to imbue the suffering, the martyrdom of brief lives with a deep and abiding sense of the value and worth of the sacrifice of living a life.

His instructions to his disciples included these words, "If you wish to follow me, take up your cross and follow." This entity also said, "Be ye whole or perfect as the Father is whole or perfect." The discipleship hoped for, that is, the discipleship which Jesus the Christ hoped to inspire, was a discipleship of sacrifice, the sacrifice of attachment to treasure, the sacrifice of the overwhelming attachment which most entities feel to doubt, despair, darkness of mind and disconsolation.

This entity believed wholeheartedly with every fiber of its being that the kingdom which he called Heaven was within and all about all of us. He saw the kingdom of Heaven in seeds, in fields, in the leaven of a loaf and in the heart of any human being. He hoped by rising again to give hope to those whom he knew and loved. He hoped that those whom he had left behind would share the excitement of eternity. Many others have seen souls who have left the Earth world, have spoken to them, have touched them, and have known that life is, indeed, an infinite process. The one known as Jesus the Christ also wished to leave this remembrance behind—and this he did.

You ask whether the one known as Jesus, the one known as Mohammed, the one known as the Buddha, and the one known as Lao Tsu had approximately equal roles in inspiring the peoples among whom they lived. Insofar as each entity lived a life overshadowed completely by the Father, this is to some extent correct.

It is our bias that the life of the one known as Jesus the Christ is perhaps the most artistic realization of the nature of undistorted love indwelling in the third-density illusion. It is felt by us that the teachings of the ones known as the Buddha [Siddhartha] and Lao Tsu were those teachings which might well appeal more to those entities who are attempting to learn the lessons of wisdom. It has always been the nature of consciousness that it is eager, as eager as a horse at the beginning of a race, as eager as a lover at the onset of a tryst, for more knowledge and more experience of the one infinite Creator. The wisdom teachings are most eloquent, yet there is the lack of communication caused by the one known as Siddhartha's lack of desire to communicate faith and love to those which are to a great extent still unawakened to wisdom.

The third density is the density wherein one attempts to learn the lessons of love, therefore it is our feeling, which is only an opinion, that the wisdom teachings are perhaps not as generally useful to awakening souls, but rather are helpful at a point at which the heart has been opened to compassion, for wisdom without the grounding of compassion can be a cold and indifferent thing, and the Father of all things, though perhaps characterized as unbiased, is certainly not cold or indifferent, for the Creator dwells in all consciousness, and consciousness which is alive has a nature which is anything but indifferent, anything but cold, has a nature which grows and rejoices and spirals ever into a greater and greater sense of well-being and stability and infinite grace. The teachings of the one known as Mohammed we find as incomplete, shall we say, as those teachings of a similar nature within what is known as your Old Testament.

As a final note, and we hope we have not spoken at too great a length, may we urge each to disregard our discussion at any point which does not seem correct to each and to remember that the truth—and we do believe that there is a truth, though we do not know what it is—lies inside each one of you and each one of us and all that there is in an articulate, enormously simple configuration, so that that which one hears is accepted as true not because of authority from the outside, but because the heart and mind within say, "Yes, I remember. That is the truth." There is an inner wisdom, an inner compassion, an inner spark of love and light that is not like the Creator, it is not from the Creator—it *is* the Creator, so that the Father is in all things and all things are in the Father.

May we say that this instrument is somewhat chauvinistic, and we do apologize, for we do not mean to infer that in our opinion the Creator has gender, for it does not have polarity but is therefore Father and Mother, Creator and Nurturer. That Creator which you will know most within your life, you may perhaps gain from studies of inspired lives such as the master known as Jesus, that when you experience the love that that master encouraged each to seek, that love is experienced as nurturing, supporting, enabling and inflaming the life, the words, the heart, and the mind of each seeker. The one known as Jesus hoped to encourage each soul upon the journey home. May you love each other and encourage each other in the path towards that home—that is what the one known as Jesus would hope for.

We leave this instrument now and transfer to the one known as Jim. We leave this instrument in love and light. We are known to you as Q'uo.

(Side one of tape ends.)

(Jim channeling)

I am Q'uo, and greet each again in love and light through this instrument. We are privileged at this time to offer ourselves in the attempt to speak to those queries which may yet remain upon the minds. Again, we remind each that we offer that which is the fruit of our own seeking and if it does not have that taste of truth to your own way of experience, then we ask that you disregard that which is not fitting. May we speak to a query at this time?

Carla: I was surprised that you rated the various world leaders of religions. It would seem that by inference you were saying that Jesus was a better leader or a more articulate leader than the others, and yet two thirds of the world's people, I believe it is, are either Shinto, Taoist or Buddhist, and doing just fine. Could you comment?

I am Q'uo, and as we spoke concerning the nature of the teachings of those great masters which have walked upon your planet, we spoke concerning the essence of that message which each offered. Each was well aware that there were those to whom the messages would ring with a tone of clarity and those to whom their messages would not resound in such harmony, for there are many upon your planet who are from origins quite different each from the other. Yours is a population which is quite divergent in both the source or origin and the nature of the path which each group travels as the third density is utilized as a class, shall we say, that studies a certain expression of consciousness.

This illusion in which you find yourselves is one in which the lessons of love and compassion are those which are of paramount importance, for they are the very fabric of your learning and your experience. However, there are many who have needs that move into realms of what may be called light or wisdom, and it is to these entities that many masters and teachers have offered their inspiration and guidance and example. We have the bias, as we mentioned, towards the teachings of the one known as Jesus, for in our estimation these are the most simplified and clarified that have been presented to the general population of your planet.

The simplicity and clarity are quite effective and necessary, in our opinion, characteristics in aiding a population which is, if we may again enter our opinion, confused, and in the degree of need as we find your population in general is, therefore we remain in the opinion that this body of teaching that has remained from the teacher known as Jesus the Christ is that which is most easily apprehended by a population which has difficulty in apprehending truths that transcend the material illusion.

May we speak further, my sister?

Carla: Well I just have so many questions. By associating the Old Testament and the Koran teachings together, you sparked something in my mind that is from earlier research which suggested that the Jewish people were a genetically improved brand of the species that was tinkered with by an entity called Jehovah, to make them more wise, more intelligent, more physically able and so forth, so that they would be better able to seek the truth.

The teachings of Mohammed—it happens to be the same area of the world exactly, it's the same people, just different tribes, basically—I was wondering if these two teachings shared what I might call a Jehovahist influence? In other words, was Mohammed also the prophet of the One God who was being relayed through the distortions of the one known as Jehovah?

I am Q'uo, and we may suggest in this regard that the similarity between these two great teachings is due primarily to the fact that each culture was in the time of its flourishing existing under conditions which were somewhat hostile in regards not only to the other cultures which surrounded them, but in regards to the very physical environment in which they sought to make their homes and to grow as cultures.

Thus, the, as you may call it, racial perspective was such that the struggle for growth and survival was viewed as one which was difficult, even harsh, and at times foreboding. Therefore, the call for illumination and inspiration which these cultures sent forth by their very being was answered in a manner which presented to these people information and inspiration which was seen or filtered in such a manner that the information was filled with injunctions and conditions that required a physical and mental and even spiritual struggle to be undertaken with some degree of that which you would call fear to motivate the effort.

Thus, the information which came to these entities in response to their call was colored, shall we say, by their response to their experience as a culture.

May we speak further, my sister?

Carla: I'll leave that one alone and read it. I didn't really get what I wanted out of the answer, but on the other hand, I didn't understand it fully. I'm only going to permit myself one more question, and if the answer would be considerably long—I suppose that would be over five minutes—I would request that you simply say so, and I'll save this question for another session.

I listened to my own channeling as best I could. Matter of fact I almost lost the channel a couple of times because I was very interested in what was being said, and I didn't feel, I didn't catch it if you did it, when you addressed the question of, "Is Jesus the only Son of God?" I wonder if you could comment on this, or if you wish to make this a separate session?

I am Q'uo, and we spent but little time upon this subject, for, indeed, it is one which covers a great amount of territory, as you may say. We attempted to give a small amount of information in this regard when we gave information concerning the one known as Jesus being overshadowed by the Father in respect to the manifestation of love which this entity saw as being the Father, and when this entity spoke unto its disciples saying that if they would follow this entity that they then should take up their cross and follow, and that they, the disciples, would do greater things as well, as would all who followed the one known as Jesus in this manner.

Thus, this entity was presenting a model or pattern by which any other entity might attain to the similar state of consciousness, that of being overshadowed by the love of the Father. We would welcome the opportunity to utilize a further session in order that more attention might be given to this interesting topic.

May we speak further, my sister?

Carla: "Firmly," she said, "just one more." I think I know the answer to this already, but it doesn't hurt to ask. L/L Research was thinking of either on Sunday nights working with previously drawn-up questions so that we might do more impeccable research, or having a series of closed sessions with certain people repeating each time. Would you be able to comment in any way on the good points and bad points of more carefully controlling the questions, and also whether you feel that you would be interested in working with us in this manner?

I am Q'uo, and we are honored to serve in any manner in which we are asked. As long as we might avoid the infringement of free will, we honor each request for inspiration and information, and we do not wish to put any limits upon the manner in which we offer ourselves in this regard. Therefore, we are at your service, as we see you are aware.

May we speak further, my sister?

Carla: No, that is indeed all. Thank you.

I am Q'uo, and we thank you, my sister. Is there another query?

(Pause)

I am Q'uo, and at this time we find that we have completed those queries which have been so generously offered to us. We thank each once again for allowing our presence. We are overjoyed at each opportunity to join your group, and we look forward to those times in your future when we shall again be offered the opportunity to do so.

At this time we shall take our leave of this instrument and this group, as always leaving each in the love and in the light of the one infinite Creator. We are known to you as those of Q'uo. Adonai, my friends. Adonai.

(Carla channeling)

I am Nona, and I greet you in the love and in the light of the infinite One. We feel the desire for the healing tones that are our service to you, and we come through this instrument. We have trouble speaking the words, so we will let our sounds be our language. We leave you in love and in light. We are Nona.

(Carla channels a healing melody from Nona.)

Intensive Meditation
September 17, 1987

(Carla channeling)

I am Latwii. I greet you in the love and the light of the one infinite Creator. We teach first this instrument and then turn to the main teaching. This instrument became concerned because no one wished to speak through her. "Who comes in the name of Christ?" she said. And Q'uo answered. "Do you wish me to speak now?" she said. "No," said Q'uo. This was repeated with our own vibration and with that of Hatonn. We wish to say to the instrument known as Carla that silence is often an effective form of communication. We spent some time attempting to originate a contact through the one known as Jim. However, we found that this was not possible, so we begin.

We begin by thanking each of you for the great privilege of allowing us to work, especially with the new channel, but, indeed, with each in this room.

We wish to speak about that which is so often removed from the point of view of spiritual seekers, and that is the sense of humor, the sense of proportion, and the light touch. It would seem that when a seeker tackles the great questions of truth and life and being, every effort must be focused and there is no time for frivolity. Yet, the greatest lessons are those learned by balanced souls, and usually the balance [of] an incarnated soul is the product of a generous sprinkling of the small vices, excesses and overages of your Earth *(inaudible)*. This makes each seeker aware of its own imperfection, and allows the seeker to see the cosmic humor of living in physical vehicles made of clay. We would translate—we correct this instrument—we would transfer this contact to another instrument. We are Latwii.

(Jim channeling)

I am Latwii, and we shall continue. The great attention that is of necessity, it would seem, directed toward the maintenance of the physical vehicle is that which seems to take a disproportionate amount of one's time, and the efforts planning for the sustenance and comfort of the physical vehicle then becomes an activity of the mind as well. The mind is focused for a great portion of each day with those matters which concern the survival of the entity which seems to be made primarily of body and mind, and these efforts are those primary expenditures of energy for each entity within your illusion.

There comes a time, however, when each entity begins to ponder, in those moments of rest and silence, just what more there might be within the daily round of activities and the overall plan of the life than the continual maintenance of survival and expenditures of these kinds of energy. It is then that the seeker becomes aware that there is that which is not material, and frequently does not carry a certain name, and yet forms a kind of yearning within to know more of the nature of the life, the nature of the creation in which the creature finds itself, and the source of all that occurs about one and within one.

And thus the yearning to know what is loosely called the Truth begins to inform the activity of the seeker, so that as it focuses upon the survival of the physical vehicle and the directing of the mental energies, it also has within a secret and safe portion of its being, the room for seeking greater truths and more nourishing perceptions of reality and the self.

We shall transfer at this time.

(Carla channeling)

I am Latwii, and I am with this instrument. We enjoy this communication very much, yet we find that the one known as D has constricted his channel because of the fear of misperceiving our words and speaking others. We encourage the new instrument to take the risk of misperception, for there is the difficulty of the rehearsal. It is distasteful, perhaps, to sight-read and to spend the long hours in moving slowly through passages. The concert at the end of that time seems far away, and the hours of practice do not seem to be so rewarding. Yet, when the concert finally comes, the student is ready.

In this analogy we mean to imply that the one known as D can make the mistaken notes, the errors in fingering, and all of the mistakes which would mar a perfect performance, for the entity is a student, only just begun upon a quite long course of study, a study in which learning takes place for many lifetimes, as quickly as the student acknowledges the need for further skill. Thus, we ask the instrument known as D to relax and allow thoughts to flow from within, questioning not once the tuning and challenging has been done, but merely accepting the gifts of the conceptual subconscious. We move through the conceptual subconscious, and our thoughts are indeed your thoughts; there is no perceptible difference in your or any instrument's ways of realizing experience.

We would again transfer to the one known as D, and wish this new instrument beginner's luck. We are Latwii.

(D channeling)

I am Latwii. The instrument has been somewhat intimidated by what it perceives as the quality of our initial teaching, and feared—and felt a lack of ability to bring through teachings of similar perceived quality. Such perfectionism is admirable in its own way, but serves at this point to erect an insurmountable barrier. This instrument can allow itself to be free of judgments and comparisons. We can help it to establish a new pattern of expectation based on spontaneity and eventually on confidence that what appears accurately reflects our message.

Let us talk to express an experience which is creating this confusion. When a concept is initially picked up, it is relatively easy for us to direct the working out of its expression. It is *(inaudible)* experienced as that caused by a break in the path, in the train of thought. But after completion of the expression of that concept, while the instrument probes its own mind, looking about in some confusion as to which direction to turn now, it is at this point that the rational mind has an opportunity to erect new blocks of doubt and analysis. These moments are as hurdles, which will become easier to clear with practice.

Doubts can originate at other times in this process, and the mind can indulge itself in an infinite regress of questioning.

(Carla channeling)

I am Latwii, and am again with this instrument. We are most grateful for the opportunity to exercise the new instrument, and may we say how satisfied we are at those concepts which we were able to transmit. They may well be helpful for the instrument, and indeed we hope so. Yet, more helpful than anything that we can say is that answering "amen" from that inner room within which holds all the knowledge and understanding of the Creation, that great storeroom which speaks not to the mind but to the heart, and resonates when the mind hears the heart's truth.

We shall not preach much more. We wish only to finish the thought we began with this evening, for we find that humor—and, my friends, we are made of humor—is not overly valued among your peoples, and we should encourage its value. Using the terminology which we find this instrument uses and which is also that taught to us by our teachers, we would gaze at the usage and helpfulness of humor, regardless of which energy center it resonates within.

Humor which lays bare the awkwardness of the human body in sexual terms, the differences betwixt sexual beings and all of those things having to do with the sexual drive, are those images of red ray, which are painful for the mind/body/spirit complex to assimilate, especially during that part of your incarnation where you go through puberty.

There are strong needs for orange-ray humor, humor about relationships, humor about living intimately with people who are imperfect. Within your density, this ray may be considered a pressure-cooker with no vent, and humor is indeed a blessing.

We find you have your racial jokes, your ethnic jokes, your religious jokes, jokes at which what this entity would call civilized people do not actually wish to laugh, yet they do, and they must, because work in yellow ray has not yet been completed by the majority of your peoples, and these bits of humor are a marvelous safety valve, a marvelous way of sharing and thus defusing the poison of prejudice.

The humor of the heart chakra is perhaps the greatest blessing of all, for it sees the human comedy in balance, in all its foolishness and all its beauty.

The blue ray sense of humor is not shared by as many among your peoples as all the other forms. It is what this instrument would call the punning, the playing with words to make them dance and live and create new combinations of thought.

The humor of indigo ray is silent, explosive, peaceful and spontaneous, yet that humor is also a sardonic humor, a humor in balance, and most often a humor without words.

All of these portions of laughter and joy in its various distortions are healers, healers of the broken rhythms of imperfectly perceived lives. We say imperfectly perceived, yet we hope that you understand that in the end each perception is perfect. It is only that the seeker's path moves on, and habits of mind which limit the viewpoint often need to be shed, yet humor abides, and perfection abides, and in every change and combination of events still are you who you are, *(inaudible)*.

Do you not find this humorous that one can be imperfect and yet perfect? That one can be in a body of dust and clay, and yet live forever? What a marvelous maker are we who are the Creator. Rejoice in the endless humor of an infinite universe.

We would close through the one known as Jim. It has truly been a pleasure using this instrument, and we thank it. We are those known to you as Latwii, and we transfer now.

(Jim channeling)

I am Latwii, and before we extend our closing through this instrument, we would ask if our assessment of the evening has been correct and that there seem to be few queries. Before we leave, however, we would ask if there might be a query to which we could speak?

D: Well, I'm always able to provide questions. My real question is sort of a meta-question, a question about questions, and whether it's counterproductive to analyze my experience at this point or whether it could be productive and there are things to be learned by questioning and trying to understand intellectually. I know there are some phenomena that are better simply experienced, at least temporarily, and not impeded with questions. How do you see this process at this stage in relation to my usual attempts to understand things intellectually?

I am Latwii, and we are again with this instrument. We find that your demonstration of ability at this time is that of the neophyte, and is that which is progressing as best as one could hope for the beginning instrument. Each instrument will find a certain level of questioning and analyzing in regard to its own progress of aid. In your particular instance, you are aware that your tendency to intellectualize the process is that which can both be of aid and be of somewhat of a hindrance, for the remaining within the intellectual mind which needs the rational for each movement and the explanation for each result is that which can both block and hinder the transfer of thought from mind to mind when this process is not totally explainable in terms that may be understood.

Therefore, we cannot give you a clear indication of whether it would be in your best interests to question and question further. We must leave this decision in your capable hands, for you are at this time working with the knowledge that the questioning has two edges, shall we say. We are happy to speak to any concern which you may have, and we open ourselves to that possibility at this time.

D: Is there anything to be gained from specific feedback? I mean, I could ask you about almost every thought that entered my mind in the process of vocalizing—verbalizing the message. I mean, I would be capable of accepting that kind of feedback—whether this is coming through clearly or being overly colored by my own mind. Is there any value in that sort of questioning—in moderation, of course—or is that more likely to lead to impediments?

We feel that the questioning to this degree would be somewhat deleterious to your progress, for you are, as we stated before, progressing according to the general pattern of a new instrument, which is to say that in such a situation the percentage of thought transference from the contact through the instrument in ratio to the instrument's own thoughts that are fed into the transmission is usually weighted in favor of the instrument's providing thoughts which the contact will then attempt to turn, slowly but steadily, toward the theme or message that is being transmitted.

Therefore, in your contact with our vibration this evening, we found that the most efficient way of making our presence known and of transmitting our thoughts through your instrument was to activate some thoughts within your own conscious and subconscious minds that might be helpful in your understanding of the process of channeling, and also in partaking of this process by speaking those thoughts, which we then were able to infuse with a greater and greater portion of our desired contact.

Thus, it must be understood that in the initial stages, much of the new instrument's contact will be that which has been activated by the entity speaking through the instrument. That will then be blended and bent toward—shall we say—the information that awaits transfer.

May we speak further, my brother?

D: No. That was extremely clear. Thank you very much. No more questions.

Carla: None from me.

I am Latwii, and we see that we have convinced you that there are few queries this evening. We are also a transparent manipulator, but are very happy to be manipulated in turn, for we find that in your culture it is that turnabout is fair play, and we wish to be more than fair with each, for we are most happy to be able to speak our humble words through each instrument, and we hope that each this evening has found our assistance to be helpful.

We look forward to those times during which we may be able to join this group. We are old as a contact with this group, but have been little used of late, for there are others within the Confederation of Planets in Service to the One Infinite Creator who have found the ability and honor of speaking to and through this group to be that which is of greater necessity and efficacy than is our own desire to speak through this group. We cherish each moment shared with those within this circle of seekers, and at this time would bid each a fond adieu, and would leave each in the love and the light of the one infinite Creator. We are those of Latwii. Adonai, my friends. Adonai.

L/L Research

Sunday Meditation
September 20, 1987

Group question: Each of us has memories of childhood experiences with family and friends which have formed a part of our personality. Some are happy and helpful; others seem to be problems or hangups needing therapy. How much of such early childhood programming is designed to help us grow along a certain path? What kind may actually harm us? And is any by chance?

(Carla channeling)

I am Q'uo. I greet this circle in the love and in the light of the one infinite Creator, and express my deep gratitude at being invited into your midst. You are, for us, very special people and we bless and love each. We hope we may be of service by sharing some few thoughts about childhood [discipline], about that period in the young life of the incarnate soul when it is small and the world is large.

We would first, in order to have a reference point, gaze at the spirit which has not yet entered manifestation in incarnation. That spirit is an unique one, as are all individuals. It has the harvest of many lifetimes collected within its complex vibratory pattern, and because it is not within third-density manifestation, the spirit is aware of itself and its relationship to other entities and to the Creator of all things, for these relationships are as apparent as is light to the physical eye.

This entity in a discarnate state is, therefore, a solidified distortion of the one original Thought of the infinite Creator; that is, each unit of consciousness, each spirit, is a clear distortion of love, for indeed, love must be materially distorted as light to bring anything into manifestation at all. And once light has been distorted in such and such a manner and consciousness resides within, so shall consciousness work with and thus distort the one original Thought.

This discarnate spirit has an opinion arrived at after long and careful thought, and aid from those who help on what needs to be done, what needs to be changed, what needs to be reemphasized. In other words, what work needs to be done to rearrange the distortion of that one original Thought which is the essence of the self, in order that the self may be less distorted and thus may be a clearer channel for love itself.

Let us pause before we plunge into incarnation in our thoughts and gaze at the immensity of the creation and the infinite bits of consciousness which are distorting love, creating ever-anew ways of expressing the Creator, ways of expressing Love. Each bit of consciousness, at some point in its evolution, begins making its own choices about what it needs to learn next, and so you see the process taking place over an infinite span of time, whereby consciousness, having become distorted by coming into manifestation, works with each distortion slowly, patiently and lovingly for the most part until, one step following another, that state of consciousness which is known to your peoples as the Kingdom of Heaven is again achieved by experience and grace.

When the spirit is born into incarnation, it has set up the larger patterns which it wishes to concentrate work upon during the incarnation. Most often these choices include the choice of parents and all that that implies, the choice of geographical location and condition of existence. Those who feel pangs of heavy sorrow for a starving child may surely do so to their own benefit, yet it must also be pointed out that it is very likely that this entity is doing valuable work in consciousness through the experiencing of this seemingly negative incarnation.

This entity who has been brought into manifestation has agreements with mother, with father, and with others within the incarnation, and each of these agreements will to some extent be realized depending upon the ability of this spirit to remember, and by intuition to trust those feelings of familiarity when the significant persons are met.

Now let us focus in upon this young entity whom we shall call John. John has chosen a father who must work very hard to make a living. This entity has powerful prejudices, formed because of the pressures under which he works, prejudices against race and against some religions. Agreement has also been made with his mother, a woman who clings to father and to son, a woman who controls by being in suffering of some kind, by being the victim of many pains, aches and ailments.

John then gains from his childhood the prejudices of the father and the guilt of the mother's son who could never completely please or satisfy. John is now an adult, and as he gazes back upon his childhood, he can see that among the many good things he gained from childhood, he still must count racial prejudice and instinctive guilt towards women as those influences which have hindered him in his expression of love.

Perhaps by now you may see the sense of what we say to you, and that is that those influences picked up during childhood, and of course later on also, cannot hurt from the outside in, though they can indeed hurt if they are taken up and used from the inside out. These same good things from childhood also cannot help, cannot be good things, if John himself does not as a mature entity originate these things from within himself.

The illusion which your world is is very efficient, is very believable, and can be very opaque, and it would be easy to blame John's problems upon mother's influence and father's influence, yet we say to you that the mother and the father exist, insofar as this question goes, only as quite distorted images within the creation, the metaphysical creation which John is in the process of building and revising within the inner universe of John's own mind and heart.

We are not saying that there is not what you would call an objective reality. The mystery which we all seek is indeed that absolute reality, and we affirm that we have the bias that it does exist. However, in terms of the growth of consciousness, each entity's actual perceived universe is totally subjective. The only entity which has ultimate control is the creator of that universe, the self. Thus, John's mother and John's father are just that—characters in a play which is all about John.

Each entity is utterly responsible for itself. The influences of early, late and middle childhood, all influences whatever, let us say, are designed as catalyst, chosen by the self before incarnation, and encountered while the mind dwells within an illusion which keeps the entire mind from knowing how the greater mind hoped that the lesser mind would react. However, you will find that you and those who helped you before your incarnation used a fairly heavy hand with the hints that point the seeking self to do the work along the lines that were intense before incarnation. Again and again throughout an incarnation, John will find, and you will find, that there is a return and again a return to a particular theme of learning about love and service, something that is difficult, something with which you grapple, and each time that you face it, you understand just a bit more, and you recognize the bones beneath the flesh of catalyst, so that you can say, "Aha, I know this anatomy. I have healed the break in these bones before." And thus, little by little, you work with that lesson which you have given yourself to learn, healing more and more the distortion that you have wished to heal, and turning more and more to a clearer, more lucid perception of the great thought of love, which is the life of all creation.

You wish to know if any significant details of the life come to one by chance. There is an element of chance that cannot be denied, a rogue element, indeed, in every equation of manifestation and metaphysics. The rogue element is a part of consciousness itself, and, indeed, is that distortion without which manifestation would be impossible. We speak here of free will. It is possible that a headstrong entity might, indeed, push so very hard that a life pattern is seriously disturbed, and chance must buffet that individual until it has somehow found appropriate footing once again.

It is always dangerous to desire without understanding the responsibilities of that desire, for that which you desire, you shall get. This is nothing more than simple metaphysical arithmetic. If any entity finds itself lost, regardless of material status or position, then is the time not to push further, but to sit and allow the self to recollect the intended path. It is difficult, but not impossible to move significantly off of a life path. Once off the life path, there will be the need for an honest surrender to that will which was yours as you come into incarnation. This is not a surrender to an outside, impersonal and unfriendly Creator, but rather a surrender in trust to yourself and those helpers with whom you have worked.

We shall linger only to comment that the pain of dealing with the so-called hangups given one as a child causes within us a sorrow, a fellow feeling, for we remember the process through which you now go. As you think and look back upon your hangups and all of those things learned by the bumps and bruises of life in incarnation, remember that your incarnation is a miniature of a process through which all of creation must go, for the period of birth, existence and death is repeated again and again infinitely, from microbes to galaxies, and in the end all of creation shall move back into the limitless of infinite intelligence, and once more there will be that great pause wherein nothing is manifest and all consciousness dims.

We would like to move on at this time, and would transfer to the one known as Jim. I am Q'uo.

(Jim channeling)

I am Q'uo, and greet each again in love and light. At this time it is our honor to offer ourselves in any further queries which those present may find the value in asking. Again we remind each that our words are but opinions and we do not wish overemphasis to be given them. Please take those which have value to you and leave those which do not. Is there a query at this time with which we may begin?

Carla: Well, it just seems to be that there is so much that is unpredictable about society, that chance must come into the equation more than just a little bit. Do you want to speak any further about chance and learning?

I am Q'uo, and when we spoke concerning the random element within any incarnation, we were suggesting that there are within each entity's incarnational pattern the general categories of types of experience and hoped-for responses to these experiences which the entity will find occurring in a pattern within the incarnation. This is not to say that each individual experience was seen beforehand, shall we say, and dutifully logged within the program for the upcoming incarnation. Rather it is to say that the entity which moves through the incarnation shall find various outer stimuli, we shall call them, presented at various times during the incarnation, and there is for each kind of stimulus an hoped-for response which will either balance an existing distortion or create a new bias in the consciousness of the seeker.

Thus, it is not the particular experience that is precisely planned, but is rather the potential for a certain response or attitude of response which is indeed planned in the sense that the predisposition for such response is carefully fitted into the incarnation. Thus, the pattern of an incarnation is not so much dependent for its success upon certain outer stimuli as it is upon the entity's response to the various stimuli that it finds within its incarnation. Thus, much which seems to be random is easily utilized by the predisposition to see general categories of stimuli in a certain fashion that is preincarnatively programmed.

May we speak further, my sister?

Carla: Yes. You spoke several times of helpers. I really couldn't get any other word than that—it was a difficult concept for my instrument to carry. I'd like you to try to clarify through Jim if you could. Who are the helpers? Is it one or more, or is it a euphemism for all impersonal principles beside the self?

I am Q'uo, and am aware of your query, my sister. The term "helpers," or alternately the term "guides," and occasionally the term "teachers," are means by which a description may be given of entities of an unseen nature, unseen to your third-density eyes, which attempt to guide and in some instances protect the third density in whose service they have bound themselves by preincarnative choice, that is, the preincarnative choice of the entity living the incarnation.

Such helpers or guides may be of various origin, but are most usually for each third-density entity also of that planetary origin, and have for a certain period of what you may call time or experience chosen to remain in a discarnate form in order that they may serve another entity as that which you call the guide or helper and in some cases the teacher. This is a service which also teaches these entities, for all experience offers the opportunity to learn and to use that learning for the teaching of others as well as the self.

In most cases entities within the third-density illusion have the triad of helpers, one being of the male principle, another of the female principle and a third which may be seen as androgynous, in order that these elements within the third-density entity's nature may find a balanced expression.

Many third-density entities have through many lifetimes gathered within their auric field other helpers, shall we say, which are drawn to an entity according to the entity's unique nature of seeking in a particular fashion which is shared by others who, because of this shared quality, gather together at certain intervals of experience to serve one who has manifested this seeking in a third-density incarnation.

Each entity, of course, is always accompanied by a greater portion of the self which you find you call the higher self. For each third-density entity there is this greater part of the self which oversees each incarnation, and in most cases makes itself known more clearly during the experience between the incarnations when the previous incarnation is reviewed and the incarnation to follow is determined. Thus, each third-density entity has a great company of souls that surround it …

(Side one of tape ends.)

(Transcript ends.)

L/L Research

Sunday Meditation
September 26, 1987

Group question: Concerning the nature of the energies that are now pouring more into our reality and people's lives and how they're affecting people, causing more tension, stress, strain and confusion in relationships at home, at work, and so forth.

(Carla channeling)

I am Q'uo. Joyfully do I greet each of you in the love and in the light of the one infinite Creator. It is a great blessing for us to share with you the consolation of meditation and the precious and fruitful gift of silence together. We offer our greeting to each and our love, and especially do we welcome those known as C and J who are new to our acquaintance in this group. How grateful we are that you seek our humble opinion upon the question of what is occurring to cause so many entities upon your planet's sphere at this time a seemingly never-ending array of stress and difficulty.

Let us first gaze at a great pattern, a pattern of creation in which the Creator not only creates but continues to create in a certain rhythm, so that vast galactic cycles are begun and time begins to have sway. The cycles continue from galaxy to constellation to solar system to planet to individual, for you, just as each planet and star, are a part of the Creator and a part of every whit of energy that has begun and is continuing and shall begin in the future within the universe. You, then, holder of the name of creator and co-creator with the one original Creator bear within your frail physical bodies the seed of every rhythm and cycle within creation.

To bring the scale back down to the question, we ask you to gaze at the remarkable unique cosmic entity that has seeded itself within that physical shell that you wear. This physical shell is subject to the pressures and energies of many different cycles of creation. Thus, when we begin to speak about difficulties which are peculiar to your time and place upon this planet within this incarnation within this space and time nexus, we must talk about not one but several influences.

The greatest in scale of these influences is the pressure of creation to gain and persevere in movement. The restless free will, which is the cornerstone of all manifested creation, is of such a nature that it expresses itself within the third-density personality such as your own by gazing at whatever catalyst comes its way with an eye towards movement of some kind.

This restless free will is further influenced in a benign way by the nature of third-density existence. That nature may be expressed by one word: choice. This is that level of being within which each of you shall ultimately make your choice of paths toward the one infinite Creator. Each of you will choose now or eventually to serve the Creator by serving others or to serve the Creator by serving the self. The almost ludicrous over-dramatization, which catalyst often seems to offer one, stems from the rather obvious and definitely dramatic choice which each entity must needs make. These influences would be the same for any third-density planetary environment.

This particular planet offers another rhythm or cycle which influences entities at this particular time. Much has been said about the coming of a new age of harmony, love and understanding. The so-called golden age has already had its birthing, and thus there are more and more entities upon your planetary sphere which are nascent fourth-density beings, incarnated in dual third-density and fourth-density bodies, those who have come as pioneers to attempt to express fourth-density understanding within the environment you now experience.

Thus, each of you may well feel the challenge and immediacy of making your choice, for time grows near when there shall no longer be incarnational opportunities in third density for your planet, for soon it shall be vibrating in fourth density.

Now let us bring the scale down as small and as infinite as each entity's heart and mind. The third density is a density wherein people are attempting to learn lessons connected not only with experiences with others, but also with groups of others. Thus, as each of you incarnates again and again, you come closer and closer to making the choice, and therefore you are more and more biased in your thinking.

This is also true of those who are tending toward a decision to seek the Creator by following the service-to-self path. When entities which wish to serve the Creator by serving the self achieve what you would call political power, they come to be effective instruments of the failed attempts to control others, which is termed warfare. Failed, we say, because power and freedom lie in a place which no one and no power can shake or remove. The greatest of altercations can end only in the freeing of the individual who has been brutalized through the gates of physical death.

Now we wish to address that level from which we feel, in our opinion, that so very much confusion and stress arise from. It is interesting for us to note that among your peoples, and by this we mean those which dwell within your culture which this instrument would call American or Western, great store is set upon information. We find that within what seems to us to be an eyeblink of time you have gained information potential from your telephone, your wireless radio, your television, your computer and all those systems which employ the gadgets which mankind has created as co-creators.

We ask you to ponder the implications of the explosion of information. Consider what a life experience would be like dwelling within an environment in which communication was exceedingly slow, in which demands could not possibly be met immediately because they could not be stated without climbing upon the back of one of your animals or riding in a carriage pulled by one of your animals or walking a small or large distance in order to do your business. That which was desired would be shaped, enjoyed, planned for, but without the anxiety for instant gratification. The television which offers instant events in word and picture also offers information concerning travel, cosmetics, aids to alleviate pain—in other words your advertising—bringing you the opportunity to desire many, many things and to expect those desires to be met very quickly.

This is the nature of your outer environment. It is one which is dictated by the will of a people who do not wish yet to awaken. By and large this people is not expected to move on to fourth density. Many, many upon your planet shall once again don the third density garment of body and move through another cycle upon another planet. There is all the time in the world, or shall we say, the creation. No single spirit is ever lost. There is always movement. In some entities it may be rather slow compared to those who, with a ready will and great desire, keep their minds and their hearts upon that choice of service to others.

When this question was first expressed, we believe the questioner spoke of relationships that failed, employment that failed, that it seemed that people had great difficulties, more so than in the past. Perhaps you may see that a goodly portion of this stress is based upon the raised expectations which have been brought before the eye of the seeking soul by all of the means of communication, by all of the information concerning that which is possible to achieve. Expectations are raised higher and higher, and free will insists that each expectation be followed to some conclusion.

When we say to you that each of you designed your incarnation with a careful eye to placing before yourself certain obstacles and disappointments, we are perhaps telling you nothing new. However, to those who expect that all things shall be calm and peaceful at all times, we can only remind each that none of you came into incarnation to go on leave, or as this instrument would say, to take R and R. There is within you, remember, the Creator, much blurred, much distorted in expression, but true seed of that one great original Thought. Yes, my children, as you grow, as that seed within you sprouts and flourishes more and more, what you shall grow into is the Creator, nothing more, nothing less. This is your nature. But how to find, how to rediscover that lost wholeness which each of you instinctively knows is there?

Let us look, for instance, in answer to this question at a relationship which may have become muddied and confused. The purpose, spiritually speaking, of relationships is for each of the partners to express to the other partner as would a mirror the reflection of what that partner has given to you. When another communicates with you, especially in response to something you have said or done, that entity is serving as your teacher. It is to be hoped always that that entity will serve as a clear and honest teacher, giving you accurate information about what you are showing by what you say or do.

When an entity keeps reflecting to you again and again a less than positive, happy face, a less than peaceful tenor, then many who have not yet awakened to spiritual reality say that their relationship is no longer good, that their relationship has suffered, that they are not meant for each other—and this may be true, but not, not, my children, ever because there is a seeming disharmony between two mirrors reflecting each other. The great gift of this relationship, then, is its very disharmony as well as the harmony that is so easy to love and enjoy.

The trick of the mind which puts a seeking spirit back upon the spiritual track is to stop the process of reaction to seeming disharmony long enough to ask what the source is that created that reflection that seems so painful to you, and then to turn from disharmony by acknowledging that your partner's reflection must indeed be true at some level. This then clears the way for you and your partner—you and your mirror—to come together in mind and heart, and seek together the distortion that lies behind the disharmony. Each of you may help the self and the other merely by being honest and open and acknowledging each situation as being spiritually meaningful and worth the untangling.

At the back of every argument there lies a wonderful challenge. This is so too of difficulties within the workplace, and, indeed, of any difficulties whatever. If you within yourself have committed yourself to the wakeful vigil of conscious seeking, then perhaps you shall be more eager than some to mine every disagreement as if it were productive of gold—for indeed there is no situation, no challenge, no difficulty that is not filled with grace, the grace that is available to a heart which seeks in faith that there is a reason, perhaps a mysterious one, but one which tends toward your good. One may gaze then upon war, argumentation and conflict upon any level and see people like yourself who have not yet made their peace with the system by which entities within incarnation upon your planet gain in spiritual strength and compassion.

Each of you has a central general lesson which you have set for yourself. Each of you has gifts, gifts which are the product of incarnations and incarnations of development, which express themselves most usually in smiles and laughter and the ability to share joy and cheer with others. May each of you have that faith which it takes to deal with all the cycles which bring about stress, from the petty raised expectations of your television to the increased vibratory disharmonies which mark the end of a dualistic age, to that great slow heartbeat of creation which is the movement of the ceaseless free will of the one infinite Creator.

At this time we would leave this instrument and transfer this contact, with gratitude, to the one known as Jim. I am Q'uo.

(Jim channeling)

I am Q'uo, and greet each again in love and light through this instrument. At this time it is our honor and privilege to open this gathering to any further queries which those present may find the value in the asking. We would again remind each that we give but that which is our opinion and fruit of seeking and wish each to take only those words offered that find meaning, forgetting those that do not. Is there a query at this time?

Carla: Okay, I have a question. I read an opinion by a woman that was called only Peace Pilgrim, not too long ago, and she suggested that the reason that people didn't get along so well anymore, or they didn't get along for very long and kept splitting up, was that so many people were old souls and they had a bunch of different lessons to learn from different people, and that it shouldn't be held against anybody, that people should be encouraged to leave what people call bad marriages because that was just the natural rhythm of things. And that seemed like a very lovely answer, although it hasn't matched my experience. And from your answer it seemed like you were suggesting that you'd almost be glad if there were some conflict between you and your partner because that would mean that you're doing work. You don't mean to carry that to the extent of suggesting that you look for challenging situations, or do you?

I am Q'uo, and to speak to the latter portion of the query first, we would not suggest to any seeker that difficulty beyond that which normally arises in any life pattern be sought, for if one has the frame of mind of looking for that which is difficult, it might become the experience of such an entity that difficulty without resolution would become the pattern of the life experience. Rather we offer the suggestion that each incident …

(Side one of tape ends.)

(Jim channeling)

I am Q'uo, and am again with this instrument. Is there a further query, my sister?

Carla: Yes, just one more along the same line. You were talking about heightened expectations and what springs to my mind first, I guess, is romantic love. I've often read it—although I've seldom heard it said in my lifetime—that romantic love is a very foolish and immature thing, and that arranged marriages were the better way of mating because then the two partners understood the nature of their relationship and were not disheartened when difficult times came, since they were not expecting to be blissfully happy always. What do you think of romantic love?

I am Q'uo. The terms "romantic love" are a description of one aspect of the love and compassion which exists as a natural force between all portions of the creation. Each entity develops with its being an image or perception that corresponds to any or many aspects of love which are perceived by any who seek in this direction. The means of perceiving through the mental images of a culture and an individual experience distorts that which is seen and sought in a fashion which corresponds to that which has been learned and experienced. Each will adapt any learned image to the personal experience, and thus both offer the opportunity for the expansion of the point of view and the containment of the point of view within new and understandable boundaries.

The romantic aspect of love which is provided in your culture of instant communication is that which offers a kind of continual infatuation, that force which draws the naive male and female together as the iron filing to the magnet. This is a necessary portion of the mating process, for it offers the first feeling of pleasure and purpose that will begin the interaction that may ripen over time and experience into that learning which the entity has placed for itself before the incarnation. However, the expectation that this beginning attraction will continue untarnished and untested throughout the duration of the relationship is often most unrealistic and provides yet further catalyst for growth within the relationship.

May we respond further, my sister?

Carla: No. As a born romantic, I thank you for showing that it's a necessary and good part of things. I'm very satisfied with that. I appreciate that. Thank you.

I am Q'uo, and we thank you, my sister. Is there another query?

(Pause)

I am Q'uo, and we feel that for this evening we have exhausted those queries which we take great pleasure in entertaining and responding to. We would at this time like to thank each for offering to us the opportunity to speak and to blend our vibrations with yours. It is a great honor to join such a company of seekers. We look forward to each such opportunity and at this time would take our leave of this instrument and this group, leaving each in the love and in the light of the one infinite Creator. We are known to you as those of Q'uo. Adonai, my friends. Adonai.

Sunday Meditation, September 26, 1987

(Carla channeling)

I Yadda. I greet you in love and light of infinite One. We have to say we come in name of Christ again. Why not once Zoroaster? Huh? We wish that this instrument would stop being so provincial, but we come in name of Christ—of course.

So. We want to be a part of this team show, you know. We going to say a few words to you about this subject of the evening. We want to know why you people are so interested in one thing and do another? This puzzle us. Say you love the clothes. Why it not make you happy to go try on all your clothes? Why, you could spend hours that way. Hmm? Or, if you want to be peaceful, why you not be peaceful? You all the time talking and arguing as if that was what you wanted to do. The strife and confusion leave the one who does not want strife and confusion. So, drop away and forget what you have decided is not important, and then you will have a merry life, a merry life!

I Yadda. We want you to have a life of joy. We want for us to have a life of joy and we have one. Oh, we enjoy ourselves. Now you too, desire more clearly and visualize your peace and your love, and this love will be all around you. Be merry. We leave you in love and light of the infinite Creator. We are Yadda. Adonai. ✣

Intensive Meditation
October 1, 1987

(Unknown channeling)

I am Hatonn, and I greet you in the love and light of the infinite Creator. We have spent some time dwelling in thought with each in the circle, conditioning each, making those contacts, those reference points within each of your feelings that would make it more comfortable for us to use each for instruments. We find that each has a great deal upon their mind, many concerns, and yet we find because of deeper truths which each is seeking, the difficulties of the day have caused undo confusion, and we find this to be most appropriate for those who are seekers upon the path. For there are many in the fad and fashion who speak of deeper truths, yet there are few whose devotion and faith in those deeper truths are such that the search itself creates its own peace. Each of you creates your own peace, each of you creates your own understanding. Each of you uncovers and recognized your own wisdom. Each of you, by being careful, have self-prepared that self for the overshadowing of the one great religion so that love and compassion flow through you.

We would speak on, and I would transfer this contact to the one known as Jim. We leave this instrument for now. We are the ones of Hatonn.

(Jim channeling)

I am Hatonn. We shall continue through this instrument. As you move in your daily round of activities, it is the design of each incarnation to partake more and more intimately and consciously of this love and compassion. However, the process is unique for each entity, and one cannot necessarily from any one experience extrapolate the degree of success, shall we say, of another's entity's expression and experience of love and compassion. Each entity has fashioned that which may be called a channel of his incarnation, and more than this, of its entire, what you may call, soul history which has then achieved as a result of many forages, shall we say, into the third-density of illusion which you now inhabit.

Thus, each incarnation is entered by a unique entity, lived by such and exited by the same. Thus, each seeker of truth is indeed a channel for the connection of each with the one great original Thought is near enough at hand that all further refinements of this one great Thought may be seen as the creation of a channel through which moves the great power of love and [which] forms through light a certain field or configuration of energy or love that becomes the soul experience which partakes of the incarnations.

Thus, the work we do this evening as you study the art of serving as a local channel is further and specific refining of this funneling, forming or channeling process which all creation joins with you in. The perfecting, the study of the vocal channel then becomes the consciously chosen focus for the expression of various facets of this great creation which renews and creates itself again and again, moment by moment. Each entity steps into the stream of experience and is not only enriched by the living waters of love and light but by the interaction of its own field of experience, and enriches that which it touches by its own being.

At this time we shall transfer this contact to the one known as D. I am Hatonn.

(The group sings "Listen to My Heart.")

(Jim channeling

I am Hatonn, and I am again with this instrument. We are aware of the challenge which the one known as D and the one known as N [face], for we have spoken through experienced channels, and now wish to speak through inexperienced channels. We would like to express our deep appreciation for difficulty that this has as an illusion to the one known as D. We [would like] to assure this instrument that there is no competition betwixt those who receive our contact, for each has something unique and eternally special to offer.

When we move to inexperienced instruments we expect a large percentage of what we give to a more experienced [instrument] to be unavailable to that new instrument because that new instrument cuts off the train of thought by the question [of] the one the analysis is about. This is acceptable to us, and indeed acceptable were that to be all we were ever able to express, merely the most simple of thoughts, yet would we be extremely pleased, for, you see, it is our nature to be extremely simple. This is a sincere reflection upon our part of our understanding of the nature of creation. That is that the creation is extraordinarily simple, and being of one substance or energy or self or one intelligence.

We have to correct this instrument and an extremely simple message to offer that message were it to be offered nakedly, unclothed with poetry, for circular concept might still, if heeded, tune this planetary population in *(inaudible)* and kindly preparation. Congratulations, Mr. *(inaudible)*.

We would again move to the one known as D, with the request that the instrument simply repeat that which comes to him. We say this also to the one known as N, that is, refrain from the analysis, refrain from the hesitation, speak foolishly and promptly that which comes up through the subconscious into the mind when a contact has been made. Picture yourself as one working in an exercise knowing that one may become somewhat better through that exercise. That also one may continue becoming better through any conceivable number of such exercises.

The process of achieving clear reception telepathic vibration is an infinite one for those which dwell within the physical form. Even [as]the self that you are you do not express fully. How could you express a telepathic contact fully? Let this be the exercise, the work out, and the dedication at all times, this energy, this love, this hope, this service to the one infinite Creator.

Again we shall transfer to the one as D and thanks. I am Hatonn.

(D channeling)

I am Hatonn. We find that, as in the past, this instrument speaks most fluidly on the least analysis acknowledge that it states and progresses from that acknowledgment who uses that acknowledge as a truth process of origination. We are comfortable allowing the gratitude and encouragement when a new channel is able to find *(inaudible)*, to speak in the process of organization, this one hurdle overcomes with us which leads to the next, which is nothing more than permitting us to guide the speech which has been established. Thus, we ease him to a process expressing ourselves through a new channel in such a way that it is second guess and analysis is accepted in the first instance which is virtually avoided thereafter.

The growth and the process of the coming channel which is manifest in the setting aside all factional processes and question the analogy in spiritual growth within anyone who comes in closer contact with the inner planes. It is analogy. In fact this can be a time to one's attitude toward life and one can become more spiritual through the practice of channeling and learns to trust impulse and to trust nature of love. The fabric of life is only and is made to control the thought and speech during channeling is given up on one's analogy and the flow of totality of one's life as life offers his abilities as a channel and stops listening to others and practices.

Once again to the entire pattern of life …

(Side one of tape ends.)

Intensive Meditation, October 1, 1987

(D channeling)

We have begun to establish a surer contact with this instrument. And share its help this *(inaudible)* establish more easily emotionally in the future, and now we take our leave of this instrument and transfer to the one known as N. We are Hatonn.

(N channeling)

I am *(inaudible)*. I greet you with love *(inaudible)*. We feel most glad to be with this instrument and we feel that through contact with or loss of there is more acceptance to accept with us *(inaudible)*. We would like to answer this instrument's questions although we feel that to handle these transmissions with us each in transfer to a form *(inaudible)* instrument. We found also *(inaudible)* a feeling that although a person on this Earth is surrounded by nonproductive thoughts of others and a person can use that to return their own positive thinking not always a person will come to negative difference. We would like to leave this instrument and answer questions that are always a way of learning. We leave this instrument. We are those in Hatonn.

(Jim channeling)

Hi. I am Hatonn, and greet each again in love and light through this instrument. At this time we would open this meeting to those queries for those that are present might find the value in asking. Again, we might remind each that we give that which is our opinion and though we give it in joy we do not place great weight upon it, for we wish each to take that which has value to the personal journey and leave that which does not. Is there a query to which we may speak?

Questioner: Yes, Hatonn, I have a couple questions. Do you come to join with us to seek, help us in our search to become better people? Do you in turn, when you are with an entity, do you get anything out of our relationship? Do you learn from us?

I am Hatonn. Indeed, my sister, that which we learn is great though not often easy to express in your words for we see from a vantage point that you are not privy to at this time, for in the region which you inhabit you pursue those lessons that you have set for yourself. There are many veils and hindrances, shall we say, to clear seeing. It is as though you climb a great mountain that has many ridges and valleys, trees, streams and outcroppings of stone and earth that restrict the vision of the climber so that the summit of the great mountain is not seen. And the experiences through which it passes, the beliefs that it holds in its mind form for them the foliage, the trees, the outcropping, and the very structure of the mountain itself.

When we join in your meditations with you and become aware of those pieces of information for which you seek and for all we become aware of many different ways of perceiving the creation of unity and the means by which a unified creation may be utilized to pursue various lessons which seek to join that which seem separate within an entity's so balances once again can restore and the vision becomes clarified upon point after point and piece after piece of the great puzzle of your existence. We see and we learn how entities such as yourself can valiantly struggle when inner and outer circumstances become chaotic and frequently seem to present little else but challenges for *(inaudible)*.

We see, in short, how each entity may wander through what seems a metaphysical darkness and yet with delight and hope and faith and those qualities of compassion and mercy and love continue to search for greater light and greater love and greater experience amidst the darkness. We learn of courage, of endurance, of faith, of a variety of perceptions that provide endless possibility of learning, of growth and of service. Yes, my sister, we learn a great deal, far, far more than can be described through your words, and we hope that we may offer even a tiny fraction to you of that which we learn.

May we speak further, my sister?

Questioner: No, thank you, Hatonn.

I am Hatonn, and we thank you, my sister. Is there another query?

D: As usual, I'm interested in feedback. At about midpoint in my channeling tonight, about where the train of thought shifted, I felt a sort of expansive feeling in my mind. It was almost overwhelming in a subtle sort of way, if you can be overwhelmed. I wonder if you were aware of that process going on in my mind at that time and if it had to do with the direction between our energies? Can you shed any light on it at all?

I am Hatonn, and this subtle overwhelming, as you called it, is the product of two qualities which you were able to demonstrate in the reception of our contract. The first was the resolve on your part to begin the channeling process when it was offered for the second time with as little hesitation on your part as possible so that you could initiate a new process. The second feature of this contact upon your part was the ability to maintain the contact and continue receiving thoughts in a steady stream long enough to be able to feel a certain confidence and comfort with the contact.

This confidence, then, combined with your resolve to speak without analysis enabled our contact to mesh more firmly and completely with your own present vibratory being, thus revealing of expansiveness and facility was our contact becoming synchronized with your own receptiveness.

May we speak further, my brother?

D: Is—was this, in a sense—is this a sensation that I would expect to feel in general when a contact is established and confirmed in the future? Is this something I can accept as a kind of signal, this happening when we are coming together in a good way?

I am Hatonn, and this is probable, my brother. There may be new sensations that you as a new instrument may experience as further example and confirmation that the contact is progressing in a satisfactory manner.

May we speak further, my brother?

D: This was a sensation which was a natural outgrowth of our contact rather than a sensation used intentionally by you. Is that correct?

I am Hatonn, and that is correct, my brother. The experience we share with you during our contact is an unique one, which is both your nature and ours and the present moment that we share.

May we speak further?

D: No, thank you.

I am Hatonn, and we thank you, my brother. Is there another query?

(Pause)

I am Hatonn, and it appears as we have spoken to those concerns of the evening, we shall take this opportunity to thank each for allowing our presence. We feel there has been great progress made this evening and we would like to say to the one known as N that the regaining of their former facility in the channeling shall be possible with her perseverance and we commend her for it, again seeking this means of service and for offering herself as a vocal instrument. At this time we will take leave of this instrument and this group.

We are known to you as those of Hatonn. We leave each in the love and the light in the infinite Creator, my friends. ✤

Sunday Meditation
October 4, 1987

Group question: Why is it so difficult to radiate in love and light to those nearest and dearest to us, our mates for example, rather than being as easy as to those we don't know as well?

(Carla channeling)

I am Latwii. I greet you in the love and in the light of one infinite Creator and in gratitude do those of us who call ourselves Latwii send blessings and love to each, yet most especially to the one known as B whom we have not sat with in this circle for some time. Please know that we travel, even to Nova Scotia, and are with the one known as B at her request. It is indeed a delight to be with this group. We have great delight in sharing your meditation and are even hopeful of taking a flyer at the question posed this evening. We hope you will pardon us our adjustments and non-meaningful comments as we adjust ourselves to this instrument whom we have not used for some of your time. We would tell jokes, except it would disturb this instrument's concentration; for our sober delivery we do apologize. We like to put a little more color in our meetings, but this instrument has grown sober minded of late, we fear. We feel we have good contact now.

You state that love and light seems far more easily given to any besides the immediate family, the mate, the loved ones. And you wonder why this is so and what can be done to bring the situation to balance. We would like to take a long look, a look from another vantage point, at this same situation in hopes that we may be of some service. As always, we could be wrong, for we are only pilgrims, as you. Therefore, we pray that you will use your discrimination to recognize what is true for you and pass the rest.

The entity which is in incarnation within third density upon your planet's surface at this time is an entity of a certain kind. This is an entity which is, within the heart, and the heart of hearts, one with the Creator and co-creator of the entire universe. Around this seed of love, love being the nature of deity, there grows a large amount of material, thoughts, biases, motives, opinions, understandings, experiences, mind, heart, emotions, the body and the demands of the body. And where the field of force of a unit of consciousness seemingly stops, there starts the vibrations of all else which are perceived by the incarnate being as those things which are other than the self and which in some way may need a reaction from the self. This is your incarnate situation.

Perhaps you have thought about why you are in incarnation at this particular time under these particular circumstances. When the circumstances are difficult, that concern, that query, that, "Why me? Why now? Why this?" becomes a threnody of unspent tears, restrained grief, quiet sorrow. And it is all too easy to see things from within the body which is within the other and far, so very far, from the light whence all sense they have come and for which each pilgrim yearns.

Yet, let us examine this stance and see if we really think this is the situation. It is the opinion of Latwii that the situation is other. It is our understanding that the one infinite Creator and all those helping forces, which you call by name such as guardian angel, higher self, spirit guides, and teachers, have conspired with you in your heart of hearts, e'er incarnation ever began, gazing at the plan of the one infinite Creator for harmonizing all things, balancing all things, offering the maximum opportunity for service, for learning, for growth.

It is our understanding that out of this creative collaboration of the personal self, the impersonal self, and that great non-personal self, which is the Christed deity of love, have offered an incarnational plan which is without reference to what might have been or what should have been, the precise plan for maximizing the opportunities of the incarnation for learning, for growth, and for service. Thusly, when the question is asked, "Why this? Why now? Why me?" the question by itself, by its very nature, blocks the flow of the harmonious unfoldment of the self's plan which is the Creator's plan as it concerns your precious, much adored and eternal self.

With this said, it may be seen that, in our opinion, the correct question to ask in the circumstance of seeming disharmony is along the lines of a love letter to the self:

Dearly beloved, sweet confused Self," you should say to yourself. "It must be so that this circumstance is blessed, for there is nothing in all creation that is not blessed. Therefore, Creator/Creation, show me, speak to me, let me know where is the love, where the learning, and where the service in this situation which I know beyond all appearance to be good.

Signed, Your puzzled surface mind

Let us suggest that the surface self—by which we mean the entire conscious thinking self of which you are aware—is a hostage sent out into a seemingly chaotic sea of experiences which are grounded in the love and the light of the one infinite Creator. Upon your planet you have the trading of money and the buying of land and ownership seems to be reality. In truth, one has only to gaze upon your beautiful planet from the vantage point of orbit about it to see that it is the Creator's planet, every square inch. Your life also is not owned by you. You are rather a tenant, one who rents temporarily the honeyed spark of Earth life, the sharp sting of experience, for pleasure or for woe.

Now, how does a lease-holder operate when the landlord is seemingly absent? Often, because there is no ownership, the premises are not fixed up or repaired, the grounds are not beautified, and the rented place has the look of transience, not the look of loving care. Yet, what if that property were owned by your Father, who gives freely, loves dearly and asks only that as you rent the property, you love it, cherish it, beautify it, harmonize it, so that it welcomes all in comfort. Such is your choice in the living of the tenanted life in a temporary physical vehicle.

Know and remember that the circumstances that you have are the house of your experience at this time. Treasure your Father's house and know it to be good and bring it increase by planted seed which takes faith, in brightly covered pillows and cushions of thought and deed, to beautify even more the Creator's wonderful gift. Know that your stewardship of this life which you count from the first breath to the last of your physical body is the stewardship of a spark of infinite creation, a consciousness that is the consciousness of love itself, and honor that which you are.

Those who hear these words may perhaps also take comfort in the following thought, and that is that some of you have chosen not only to experience within the incarnation to learn to grow and to serve, but also to maintain the high places within the consciousness, the watchtowers of love, which beam forth as light sources to the planet upon which you now enjoy incarnation, to the entities upon it, to the Earth itself and to those energetic vibratory levels within the Earth's atmospheres which are in dire need of that great watch, faithfully held.

Those of you to whom these words express a recognizable duty and honor may know that whether you seem to be a businessman, a homemaker, a queen or a shepherd, there is that inner citadel, at the top of which is a watchtower, and the only lamp that is lit is the lamp lit by the deepest heart as it gazes in worship and adoration from light into light, knowing light, accepting light, blessing light and allowing the crystal of the heart of hearts to turn the self into the metaphysical lamp upon the hillside, the city upon the hill, not for the notice or understanding or thanks of mankind, but for the doing of it alone, for the keeping of the watch. In many cases this, the keeping of a faithful watch, is the primary mission or task set for the self before the incarnation.

There are many wanderers which will recognize themselves in these words, wanderers who have come to a confused and baffling plane and are saturated in the intricacies of incarnation, yet who still, again and again, in thought stray to the watchtower.

If it calls you, go, not only in meditation. Allow the watchtower to call you again and again, for moments, for minutes, hours, for the incarnation, until your desire to serve as conduit for light and love on the totally unspoken vibratory planes is satisfied.

One more thought as we leave you through this instrument. The entities which have come within the care of those who find these relationships difficult are entities that you may have chosen to learn from by suffering, coming to understand the expectations and attachments which lead to suffering and moving thence more and more towards a balancing of "the way of a man with a maid," as this instrument would quote.

It is rare, in these latter days of your cycle, that any two mated entities are together for the first time. Often the two are together, one to challenge the other and the other to challenge the first, for those things which are the most difficult within physical incarnation are indeed the expressing of a clear love energy to the entity closest to one. This has nothing to do in general as a principle with the relative pleasantness or unpleasantness of the personality with whom you are involved. It has to do rather with the dailiness of experience and that great tendency of the personal self to form attachments to the outcome of one's behavior. It is, if not easy, certainly easier to love the stranger, the acquaintance, or the friend whom one sees only socially, to share with that person all love and all light, than it is to express that full-fruited, open-hearted song of joy to one who has not fulfilled your expectations.

Now, my friends, we ask you to examine your human personalities. There is within them a strong instinct for justice, for rightness, for fairness, for absolute values. These desires, these hopes are excellent. The difficulty lies in attempting to apply them in service to self, for it is service to self to wish that others might behave toward you in a certain manner, might give you certain portions of the time, the money, the caring, the touching. How difficult it is to set one's mate completely free and to stand only and eternally as friend and partner within the life experience. How very difficult that challenge feels. We do not negate it for you and tell you it is a small thing. It is one of the greater lessons of third density to cease in the expectation of any outcome for any action which you may choose to do in your desire to be of service.

Think of yourself, then, as a spiritual being, as the Creator Itself, one which does not need others except so that it may be of service to the Creator by means of service to them. Experience the joy in a mated relationship of knowing that that entity which is your mate will mirror to you those very things about the self that are out of balance so that the self may work upon them. There is a harmony within the universe which is absolute. All that you experience and all that you see and all that of what you hear is a portion of an harmonious development of creation which in every fiber praises, expresses and manifests that great original Thought of love.

If you are weary, move in thought to the citadel which has windows to heaven, and gaze beyond the stars at the profound and tumultuous joy which is crystallized in every star, in every piece of the infinite creation, in every piece of consciousness, and know that you are in the process of shaping and faceting and crystallizing your own expression of the infinite Creator so that your consciousness more and more has a heartbeat of joy and peace. And if that joy and peace flees before the footstep of the dearly beloved mated, one with which one does not agree, acknowledge the disagreement, smile at the thought of remaining upon the surface, and move away from the here and now of illusion into the far deeper, timeless present of infinite love.

Five seconds within the citadel of that consciousness may indeed create that mind even upon the surface of things which may see the true harmony that is the plan of the infinite Creator, a plan which incorporates free will at every turn, a plan where the essential and unmovable lessons are there in emotional and mental structure awaiting the clothing of circumstance, so that if you face a circumstance and are not able to see love within it, you may rest secure and peaceful in the realization that that same circumstance shall come to you again and it shall be a time of testing. And each time, it matters not whether you win or lose the game of consciousness-raising; it matters greatly whether you purely, deeply, lovingly intend so to create love.

Those about you may not understand your point of view. It is not necessary …

(Side one of tape ends.)

(Carla channeling)

… it is not necessary that any understand you. Let it be your hope, rather, to gaze upon the situation with the faith and truth in the Creator's plan, in your own plan, and with firm intention to offer to the situation your love, your understanding, for you shall not receive love and you shall not receive understanding by seeking it, but only by attempting to give it.

We shall be with you in the citadel of the waiting, trusting, loving consciousness. We shall be with you, as part of you is in the citadel, and the other doing the ironing, the dishes, the blueprint, the lesson plan, the design, the painting or whatever occupies the life. Those who serve most effectively are quite simply those who remain persistently and doggedly and joyfully aware that there is rightness, appropriateness and wonderful opportunity in your situation right now.

You certainly do not know all about why the situation is helpful. This is far better learned in meditation, and may we say that we see meditation as a time of moving up into the citadel and then moving away from the window into the inner room, into the darkness, into the silence, into that which seems nothing, that you may trust and allow the silence and the darkness to teach you, to fill you, to repair you, to nurse, cherish and comfort you. Then you may in mind climb down the tower steps, step out onto your tenanted life experience, gaze at the troublesome mate, the difficult situation, with faith and love anew and know that you are an ambassador, an ambassador of love and light.

May each of you treat his or her mate as a friend, expecting nothing, offering all and knowing when that balanced all is sufficient, so that you do not become the martyr, but rather do all things in joy, without reference to any other, but acting as a sovereign, a king or queen of the great kingdom of your consciousness. Thus, you shall be a bad tenant no more, but rather exercise great stewardship in your days and nights, moving into whatever streets, whatever alleys, whatever situations your harmonious unfolding plan offers you, yet remaining more and more within the citadel where a portion of you keeps faithful watch for all of humankind.

If you knew the tears of joy that we feel as we gaze upon those who keep that lonely watch, lost to true knowledge of what they are doing, going only on faith and trust, you would perhaps feel comforted, for you are never alone in the citadel that gazes upon the Creator.

We have been most grateful to have used this instrument which is somewhat fatigued. We hope that we have not spoken overlong. We were attempting to be very brief and snappy but perhaps the question was too good for us to answer in any briefer way. We appreciate the great concern each of you has for the living of a love-filled life. We leave this instrument at this time and we transfer to the one known as Jim. I am Latwii.

(Jim channeling)

I am Latwii, and greet each again in love and light through this instrument. At this time we are honored to offer ourselves in the attempt to speak to any further queries which those present may offer to us. Again, we offer that which is our opinion, and wish it to be known that it is no more than that. Is there a query with which we may begin?

Questioner: My mother is very ill. I would like very much to be part of a healing. Can you shed some light on her illness?

I am Latwii, and that which we may share in this instance is perhaps far less than you had hoped, for we desire not to tread upon the life path of another to the degree that we may alter the steps taken in any fashion. But we find that there are some general qualities of this life experience which we may share.

The entity is one which has for a great portion of its incarnation given in a selfless manner to those that are close to it, and has felt the love in return for this service. That it would give in such a manner was a portion of the choices made previous to the incarnation, as each entity sets about the blueprint, shall we say, for the incarnation prior to its beginning. The difficulty which is now apparent within the physical incarnation is that which provides a symbolic representation of further ramifications and refinements of the balance to the giving, that is, in some degree and in some sense, to receive.

The exact nature of this process is that which must remain, from our paint of view, yet hidden, for the untangling of each knot of experience offers to those who work the puzzle a certain inspiration and strength of being and doing that is, shall we say, nutritious to the soul, however mistaken or ignored by the conscious mind. The overall movement in this physical difficulty is one which is toward the light of illuminating the life pattern in a sense which would not be possible without this experience.

May we speak further, my sister?

Questioner: No, thank you.

I am Latwii, and we thank you, my sister. Is there another query?

Carla: I didn't really hear all of the foregoing because I was channeling it, but I didn't hear anything in the channeling which really gave me an instant handle on, say I'm a wife and I'm working very hard and my husband isn't making any money right now, and he comes home and he criticizes my housework. This is manifestly unfair because I'm totally overworked, but he does it anyway. How exactly do you stop yourself from reacting to the unfairness? What can you use to keep yourself from entering into a transaction at that point?

I am Latwii, and it is not that we suggest one block the normal and spontaneous response to any situation, for it is most necessary that each entity not only express that which, shall we say, bubbles forth in a spontaneous fashion from within the depths of the being as a response to any situation, but that there be an attempt made following such a response to remove the small conscious self from the world of mundane things and place the consciousness within that location we have termed the citadel, that the greater view might be taken of the experience just past. By such retreat, one may begin to appreciate a greater purpose within the life pattern for the transaction which has occurred and might take, then, this appreciation into further communication with the other self in the light of the greater view and with the dedication to love and the granting of perfect freedom to the other self, that the wounds that may have been created might now be healed.

It is not that difficulties should be avoided, but that they might be utilized as catalyst for further growth and service and inspiration to others.

May we speak further, my sister?

Carla: Yeah, I'm still not satisfied. I got a clear impression towards the end, there was a sentence something about treat your mate as a friend. Now what you do with a friend, we basically know, is you comfort them when they're discouraged or down and we pat them on the back when they're great and we hope for the best for them and like that. That's friendship. But when somebody's coming at you in a confrontational manner, it's hard to react to that person as a friend, because usually friends don't do that to you, at least not without good reason, you know, not that unjustifiably—although I admit that there are some friends … But I'm trying to figure out how you can do that, how you can make your spouse or your mate or your lover your friend, and really make that primary. I think that was what you were trying to say, wasn't it?

I am Latwii, and, indeed, my sister, this was a significant portion of that which we intended to convey, for if two spirits who have joined in the third-density illusion to learn and to serve in a certain fashion can begin to recall together within the illusion a greater and greater portion of the plan, shall we say, for the incarnations, then the difficulties that arise within the daily round of activities might at some point within their resolution be seen from the wider perspective of those mates of the soul who travel the same journey together and who, though convinced from time to time within the small moments of the life that such a thing must occur in this or that manner, realize more fully that each is there to serve the other and the one Creator in all and that the small, dedicated decisions that are used to pilot the daily round of activities might be released, and each might seek and praise the one Creator within the experiences that provide catalyst and growing difficulties for those who are unable to appreciate the opportunity within difficulty.

May we speak further, my sister?

Carla: So, basically you're saying at some point the instinctive reaction will be, "Look at this person, this person is not in harmony with his plan, therefore he's run afoul of certain immutable laws and he's in trouble. I feel for this person, I'm sympathetic to this person, I want to console this person." This is the transformation that you're suggesting might come out of more time spent in the citadel. Is this correct?

I am Latwii. Not only is this correct, but there is the further implication that as one becomes more completely involved in the mutual attempt to utilize catalyst fully, that one will not only develop a compassion for the other, but one will begin to see the self within the other and will begin the more intensive work upon the self and the point of view that is bounded by the conscious beliefs that there might be work done upon the self in a fashion which alters the point of view to the extent that where others may see difficulty, one begins to see an opportunity to serve and to learn before any other feature of the situation is noticed.

May we speak further, my sister?

Carla: No, that really spoke to the heart of my query. Thank you.

I am Latwii, and we thank you once again, my sister. Is there another query?

Carla: If everybody's through, I'll just be frivolous, because I love to know. What color are you in these days? Are you still doing your scientific work?

I am Latwii, and we have shown this instrument a variety of colors, for we are experimenting, shall we say, with the blending of various subtle, what you could call, plum, with the apple green and tangerine, in order that the subtler energies that produce these vibratory oscillations that are perceived as colors might be available for study of their correlations within your planetary population, as it seeks to move from the individualized self that corresponds to the orange or tangerine and begins its movement into the all-compassionate love of the heart or green-ray energy center, and through further catalyst and processing of such begins the transformation that affects the Buddhic body or that which is of the violet ray. We study the color emanations, for within these vibrations there is contained much information of a nature that cannot be discerned by the outward eye. It is within our own citadel that we study in this manner.

May we speak further, my sister?

Carla: Those colors are the colors of Ariel, the west archangel. I was just wondering if this principle of earth and harvest and fullness is aiding you from the Earth plane in this study?

I am Latwii, and, indeed, it is the harvest, as you have called it, and the energies that are now a portion of this season upon your planetary sphere which we study intensively now in these realms of which we have spoken.

Carla: Yes, thank you.

I am Latwii, and we thank you, my sister. Is there another query?

(Pause)

I am Latwii. We have enjoyed greatly, my friends, the opportunity to join your meditation. It has been a great portion of your time since we have had this great privilege. We rejoice at such opportunity to be with you and to step upon the same journey with you. At this time we hope that we have not worn out your ears. We are so happy to have had the chance to speak, we fear we may have gone a bit far. "Too many words," it may be said, but we hope that our joy at being with you has made this endurable for you. We shall take our leave at this time, thanking each again for inviting our presence, leaving each, as always, in the love and in the light of the one infinite Creator. We are known to you as those of Latwii. Adonai, my friends. Adonai vasu borragus. ❧

Intensive Meditation
October 9, 1987

(Carla channeling)

We are known to you as Hatonn, and we greet you in the love and the light of the infinite Creator. What a privilege it is to speak with you and to be called to your meditation. We greatly enjoy merging our vibrations with your own in the silent seeking *(inaudible)*.

We are pleased that these new instruments have been persistent in the practice of vocal channeling. The excellence which the more experienced channel may seem to have is only that excellence relative to the first beginnings. Indeed, the discipline of a life which involves the service of channeling is a rigorous one, not necessarily materially, but in the sense of the entity requiring of itself the discipline in constancy of attention and acceptance of the need to persist continually in moving in life experience ever closer to that personality which the instrument uses to stand before all external personalities which are unseen. We encourage you in the unending process of growing to know the self, appreciate the self, and discipline the self in appropriate ways to enhance the manifestation of the service which you have chosen. These words, indeed, apply not only to those who serve through channeling, but to all who seek to serve in whatever manner.

We are greatly encouraged to view so many new instruments developing well or poorly in so many portions of your Earth plane. May we say we appreciate those such as this instrument and the one known as Jim, who attempt to nurture entities which are in the process of learning the discipline of the self, the freeing of the spirit, and the art and gift of vocal channeling. Such companions upon the way are indeed most helpful to those attempting a new skill. We find the energy moving much better now. We indeed hope that these remarks have been helpful, but more than that we wish to improve the tuning of the group, for the energy is quite low for this group, and it is gaining more and more as you and we sit in meditation and approach that inner sanctum of the self, move through the inner door, and rest once again in the infinite darkness of inner space

We shall transfer at this time to the one known as D.

(D channeling)

I am Hatonn, and I greet you once again. We gave this instrument somewhat of a shock, hoping to take advantage of the mental state which would somewhat have enabled the sidestepping of the usual analytic tendencies. When the mind is drifting in a state which is known to you as hypnogogic, it is a relatively simple feat to direct the stream of thought. To use this state with facility might be thought of as the worthy initial goal or step along the path to vocal channeling. Becoming the passive observer of this state has other practical advantages in the growth and development of sensitivity to inner processes. Unfortunately, like the electron which quantum physicists disturb by observing it, to make use of this state and to report on it as in the act of channeling, is disturbing to the state itself until sufficient practice enables one to attain a *(inaudible)* processes.

(Carla channeling)

I am Hatonn, and we move to this instrument and greet you again in the love and the light. To continue. It is indeed a challenge to the new instrument to remain tuned, open, and accepting of concept, yet discriminating in the choice of those thoughts' clothes which are words. Perhaps it may aid each instrument to consider that at each and every moment, an entity is making some use of the deeper level of consciousness. The powers of concentration lie not within the rational mind, but within the more instinctive, *(inaudible)* or intuitive mind, thus achieving a state of concentration which approaches sleep yet is awake and remaining there while using the other side of the mind to choose those daughters of thought with which you shall clothe our concept.

It is a frame of mind which has the pointed lesson within it, for is not all of manifestation within your illusion benefited and enriched by the most relaxed and most focused point of view, the very point of view which instruments attempt to attain? One great fallacy of channeling theory is that the message is apart and other from and than the message. Yet, we say to you, the channel, the message, and the creator of that link 'twixt teacher and student partake of one self, one mind, one heart. We move certainly from a point external to your incarnate self to find our place nestled as a part of your enlarged self. This involves the laying down of the barriers which keeps self from self. We cannot come without invitation. Once asked and once there, we are an extension of your self, and both of us are an extension of the Creator, a cooperative instrument to share helpful thoughts with those who may find them of use.

We ask that you begin more and more as entities and as instruments to trust the self, to relax within the self, so that there is within the heart a growing atmosphere of who the self really is. We ask you to feel good about yourselves. Simple words, but difficult in their application. As each uses the tools of meditation and contemplation, converse with those of like mind, and the communication of self with nature, each will find more and more that the state of mind which is conducive to the practice of vocal channeling is approached by the self in more and more life experience, which means that upon a personal level, the deep mind and all of the riches which it has to offer shall be in a position to be channeled from the self to the self, those deeper thoughts and intuitions coming forth into manifestation and greatly informing the process of ratiocination.

For most, this focused, peaceful, receptive state of mind is one learned through experience. Though some are naturally gifted, most must practice to achieve that state of mind wherein deeper desires and sources of information may *(inaudible)* and make themselves known. And what shall come out of such discipline? Not only the vocal channeling, though this is indeed, if this be your application, most greatly appreciated by us in levels *(inaudible)*. Yet more than all this, when we hope that these disciplines of knowing the self's identity, of declaring the self confidently, and that of surrendering to the will and the love of the Creator, will be those which you may use in the life's experience. The self-consciousness of humankind is a great stumbling block, a block thrown up by the *(inaudible)* self to prevent change, yet each of you wishes to change, and we are most happy at your desire to serve.

We will at this time transfer to the one known as N. I am Hatonn.

(N channeling)

I am Hatonn, and I greet you once again. We ask that the instrument occasionally receives *(inaudible)* physical change *(inaudible)* to make a change while the instrument is just that *(inaudible)* required such as *(inaudible)* occasionally happens. We are pleased with the perseverance of this group, and feel that, because of its *(inaudible)* and informality, proceedings—the procedures are advancing quite nicely. We are again pleased to join this group and happy that the entities *(inaudible)* are giving their time to teach their *(inaudible)* brothers.

We take leave of this instrument at this time. We leave you in love and light. I am Hatonn.

(Jim channeling)

I am Hatonn, and we teach once again through this instrument. At this time, we shall ask if we may serve in a further fashion by attempting to respond to any queries those present may have to offer us. Is there a query with which we may begin?

N: Yes. I may ask—you had said earlier tonight that this group was one of low energy. Did you mean at this point, at this session, or *(inaudible)* this group is perhaps with more low energy than others?

I am Hatonn. Our reference to the level of energy of this group was directed toward this particular evening, for each of those present has a marked degree of physical and/or mental weariness, which is not characteristic of this group, for each *(inaudible)* in the more normal configuration of energy complexes is quite well supplied with the necessary energy levels, and we made that comment to assure each that we can work with this group when it is experiencing less than normal energies, and that we were aware that each was experiencing some degree of fatigue.

May we speak further, my sister?

N: No, thank you.

I am Hatonn. We thank you, my sister. Is there another query?

D: Well, one of the most valuable, the priceless thing about this experience, opportunity, that I have here is the immediate feedback you are able to give me on my own experience. Tonight I felt like I was really carrying the ball on my own, that I did not feel a contact. I felt that I was generating most of what I was saying. Was that the case tonight more than usual? Could you comment on the—I guess what you refer to as the proportion factor tonight?

I am Hatonn. At the outset of our contact through your instrument, we were pleased that we were able to make the contact quickly and, as you may say, cleanly, in that there was an easy initiation of the transfer of our thought through your instrument. The contact for the most part was of the majority of our transmission. However, as the ending …

(Side one of tape ends.)

(Jim channeling)

I am Hatonn, and am with this instrument once again. The physical sensation of the shock was an attempt upon our part to alert you in a fashion which would be easily apparent that the contact was impending. We are not always successful with this technique, for we are not well trained in the adjustment of our contact to new instruments, and we were hopeful that we could provide a physical reassurance that the contact was being made without causing undue discomfort.

D: Well, I wasn't sure if I generated that myself, because I was expecting you to transfer to Jim, and besides, it's reassuring to have that kind of feedback about the sensation.

I have another question, unrelated. N, do you have anything to ask while I formulate this, or Carla?

Carla: No, I don't have any questions tonight.

N: I can't think of anything right now.

D: You spoke earlier, and I don't remember the exact context—it's gotten away from me—about what I have been thinking of as fears of the ego, the self-consciousness or embarrassment, and something which to a higher level might be a fear of ridicule or loss of self-esteem. I've been thinking just in the last week or two of the origin of that kind of ego-based fear as opposed to fears which might be more based in our instincts and wondering what the connection between them is. I've had a sort of a theory through much of my life that most of our fears that lead to neurotic behavior have roots in the fear of death, and our other fears are just transformations of that basic fear, but I do not see a connection between that type of fear and these other ego fears. Would you have anything to contribute to that subject in response to this very poorly asked question?

I am Hatonn. Within your third-density illusion, the process of the individualization of a portion of consciousness which you call your self has reached its zenith in that there is no doubt to any of your peoples that each exists as an entity unto itself. The process of this individualization of consciousness has evolved through the state of the second density, plant and animal alike, as you know them—in which the preservation of the self through the mechanism that you know as fight or flight is the foremost concern of the entity. This almost universal drive for survival, then, carries forth into the third density, and is diversified or refined by the conscious description of the self to the self in terms that are learned as a part of the socializational and educational processes which each of your entities undergoes in some fashion.

Thus, each third-density entity thinks of itself as being this and that, not this and not that, in the various areas of study and learning, until each entity has compiled a foundation sense of self with variations for each entity in certain areas. Thus, the entity begins to think of itself in a manner that has certain boundaries. When these boundaries are challenged or threatened by any other self, whether it be the physical challenge or the mental and emotional challenge of ridicule, questioning, and the like, the conscious self begins to gather its defenses when the alarm of fear of losing a certain portion of the self is *(inaudible)*.

May we speak further, my brother?

D: So you might say they're sort of similar and synchronous effects, but one doesn't derive from the other. They have a common root. Is that correct?

I am Hatonn. The first is more of the unconscious mind and the second—that of the conscious description of the self to the self—is of the conscious construction of the entity. However, since this construction takes place of the entire period of the incarnation, the feeling of selfness thus constructed is quite strong and in various areas way be liable to the threat of intrusion or dissolution, depending on the nature and strength of the perceived threat.

May we speak further, my brother?

D: No, not at this time. I would like to study what you said. This has been a major issue in my life, and I may like to ask you about it later. Thank you very much.

I am Hatonn, and we thank you, my brother. Is there another query?

D: I have nothing else.

I am Hatonn, and we thank each for presenting the queries that are of importance in the personal seeking, for we learn much about each within your illusion when we observe such queries, and are grateful for the opportunity of offering our humble opinions in each area of concern. We again commend each in this group for the continued pursuing of the practice of serving as a vocal instrument, and we look forward to each gathering as an opportunity to refine not only each instrument's abilities, but as an opportunity also to refine our abilities to work with each instrument in a fashion which allows the greatest development of the potential for service that exists in each entity.

We shall at this time take our leave of this group, thanking each again for inviting our presence. We are known to you as those of Hatonn. We leave each in the love and the light of the one infinite Creator. Adonai, my friends, Adonai. ☙

Sunday Meditation
October 11, 1987

Group question: (Continued from last week.) Why is it so difficult to radiate in love and light to those nearest and dearest to us, our mates for example, rather than being as easy as to those we don't know as well?

(Carla channeling)

I am Latwii, and I greet you, my brothers and sisters, in the love and in the light of the one infinite Creator. It is our great privilege to join this circle of light to feel the oneness of honest seeking and caring to know. We are fellow pilgrims who have perhaps walked a few more steps than you upon this path of service and love, and we most thankfully hope that we are able to share some thoughts with you which may bear fruit. Please know that our thoughts are our opinions only and may unbeknownst to us be blemished in some way by inaccuracy or bias. Therefore, please listen to what we have to say with your discrimination, knowing the truth by recognition and not by authority, for, my friends, as you have said yourselves, the truth is already within you; you have only forgotten it.

May we say we were most pleased that this instrument realized that there was that material which we would wish to share upon the topic of difficult relationships and situations. We were unable to condense our thoughts enough to satisfy this instrument who requested us to bring our discourse to an end, however, we are so pleased to have an opportunity to share with you further thoughts upon this interesting subject. For you see, my children, when one encounters difficulties, one experiences what is universally known as negative emotions, and within the framework of what we may call the surface thinking among your peoples, it is evaluated as a situation to be ended, avoided, ignored or changed. It is in the interest of one who seeks a deeper truth to move beyond that which satisfies some, the quick answer, the hasty action, the removal of pain. There are other points of view, there are other possible realities which may be discussed and considered.

We would speak with you this evening upon the central theme of trust. Yet, we must build a framework for our discussion by moving to first principles, for trust is a trust of something or someone, and thus we cannot speak of trust without establishing that in which we are suggesting the seeker may trust in order to ameliorate difficult situations and relationships.

Each of you is a portion, or may we say perhaps more clearly, a miniature replica of the Creator, that one great original Thought of love, love which dwells in the most part uncreated, unmoved, unbiased and singular. That part which has never come into manifestation, that part being the greater part, is unconscious of its consciousness. Through the action of free will, that great original Thought which has thought the creation, that Logos which we often call love, is at the very core of each of you in an undistorted and true verity. Surrounding this core in energetic vibratory patterns are the biases which you as an entity have accumulated through experience and evaluation of that experience.

As you have been through many, many lifetimes, you have also evaluated many, many experiences. And each lifetime of experience gives you its harvest of biases. These biases or distortions of the great original Thought often seem unlovely, for many there are who have the biases of prejudice, meanness of thought, selfishness, anger and all those ways of being and doing which seem not at all to reflect the Creator that is love.

The creation has in the infinity of time a beginning and an end, just as each of you as a creature has a beginning and an end. The creatural dies; the Creator is eternal. Thus, the scale of bias and learning and seeking moves on not only from lifetime to lifetime, or from beginning to end of creation, but you who have been in one creation shall be the seeds of those who learn in the next. Thus, all activity within the creation upon whatever scale of activity is part of an infinite process wherein love's great desire to learn of the self is more and more satisfied. For that which is eternal within you records everything which you have learned.

The goal of one who incarnates into third density, designed before your incarnation, is to attempt to sow experience and evaluate the experiences of the lifetime that your self, your beingness, your consciousness becomes more and more as you would have your gift to the Creator to be. For ultimately, at the end of an intentionally lived life, is the giving of the life as a gift to that Creator whence you sprung and whither you are bound once again to lose yourself.

Very well, then, the way in which one sees life is all-important to the interpretation one makes of it, and that is where trust becomes most, most helpful. The truth which we ask you to trust, if indeed your heart vibrates in tune with this thought, is the truth that as eternal beings we have one purpose more primary than any other, for before circumstance came to be, our consciousness came to be. And that which is most important, therefore, is an investigation into the nature of our consciousness, the nature of that force which created us and the nature of our relationship with that force or principle of creation.

Therefore, we do not speak of trusting entities, yourself or others, of institutions, be they ever so grand, or the opinions of any, including us, be they ever so eloquent. If your heart and mind resound with an echo of recognition when we say that your Creator is love, then you shall see why we ask that the key word of trust offers much to one whose illusory or Earth life is being experienced as tragic, sorrowful, difficult or upsetting. Equally, we would say that of all who are successful in some way, for you see, the experiences of an incarnation are ever up and down, ever positive and negative. The clue is given in the lack of consistency of either state of mind within what is called the human condition. When one is content, one does not agonize over one's proper point of view, one's appropriate relation towards the Creator. It is the sorrows, the difficulties, the upsets, the tragedies which bring mind and heart to a state of attention, to a state of questioning, and we hope that this is persistent and determined, for there is a good outcome, that is to say, a satisfying and positive outcome to such a search.

The obvious and only reaction to love is love. When we speak of the love of the infinite Creator, we speak of the love that has created stars and all else, seen and unseen, within an infinite universe. We do not speak of personal love, for we find that among your peoples it is necessary to make this distinction. Neither do we speak of completely impersonal love. We are speaking of a love that is beyond any definition of love which words may offer. We ourselves know not how to convey what we have experienced. Words are paltry and often little more than useless. What we can say is that as we have studied more, we have found more and more evidence that those words which we share with you have some validity and usefulness to the seeker.

Now, if your consciousness partakes of love and your Creator is love itself, but love which reaches down to you in a personal manner, in an immediate manner, in a present tense manner, you may perhaps see that a relationship with this love shall be intimate and trusting. Portions of the Creator's love have expressed themselves to you before your incarnation as what you may call your higher self, your guardian angel, your teachers. We care not what the words be; we care that you know that you and these helping entities gazed at the harvest of your biases and your distortions, noted where there were lessons still to work on, lessons of love which you wished to learn, for this is the density of learning how to love and how to express love.

What you are experiencing now is the outworking of this plan. You have complete free will within this plan, although you were given nothing which you could not, with prayerful help, may we say, experience successfully. Yet still each entity has the complete right and privilege of altering whatever circumstance seems beyond bearing. This does not faze the higher self. It simply means that the same lesson which has been aborted shall be experienced again and another chance shall be had by the soul within you to reap the benefits of the harsh illusion which you experience at this time.

For nothing of what you see is what can by any means be called an accurate picture. You know, for instance, that you do not see light in its fullness, but only a small spectra within the great larger spectrum of light values and light vibrations. You know that you cannot hear, sense by touch, smell. Each of these senses is inadequate to convey to the self the completeness of the experience offered within your illusion.

Add to this the fact that it *is* an illusion, designed so that each experience would have impact far greater than it would have were you not within an illusion, and you have a challenging situation. It was intended to be a challenging situation. Each of you chose, with good spirits and much hope, to enter this land of forgetting that you call Earth, enter the strong illusory vibrations which yield to you the limitations of what you see and sense, give to you your seeming separateness from each other and from the truth. The basic goal within any illusion is to penetrate the illusion.

Which brings us back to the seeking soul, that Creator which is the original Thought of love and the relationship of that seeking soul with the infinite love of the one Creator. That relationship, my friends, is trust. Trust is not only for the good times. Trust is not only when the parking place opens up next to the store. Trust is an emotion which can be evoked only by implanting above the illusion of distance and difficulty another picture of what you are seeing, based upon your understanding of the Creator.

You see yourself as creator, attempting to learn how to be a creator; you see others equally befuddled, equally holy, and you come into various relationships with them and experience various situations. This is what is occurring—the Creator experiencing the Creator, whether the times are good or difficult. And the trust is that you shall not be given more than you can handle, that there is a plan and that all is indeed well.

This is, my friends, central. All is well right now, because your deeper reality is that you are love, and that all about there is love, so distorted sometimes it is an incredible challenge to perceive. Yet this deeper reality is an experience which is more and more substantial as the seeker persists in the journey undertaken by one who knows the way is long, infinitely long, and often rocky and lonely, for each must find answers for the self, and this means that in the end the soul is alone with itself to choose its manner of being.

We speak to those who already believe that there is a plane of absolute values. We speak to those who tentatively accept that God, as you call the Creator, is love, and that each is a portion of that Creator, a holograph of that Creator, and that the basic thrust of the life experience is to live it more and more lovingly and be of more and more service to the Creator and to each other, that love may abound and that this illusion may be penetrated.

We realize that those who are in mated relationships have special problems. This is due to their expectations of each other. Had you no expectations of another entity, it would be very easy to be polite. However, among your peoples the mated relationship is one in which two become intimately involved enough that each attempts to learn to treat the other as Creator, to trust each other. Yet each is a very distorted version of love, a very confused rendition of creation; therefore, trust is hard to come by between people.

We do not ask you, therefore, to trust each other first, but rather to step back from the mate, from the difficulties which intimacy brings and choose instead to live within the least distorted creation which you are aware of, to refrain from forcing changes, right or wrong, shall we say, in a situation, until you have moved your consciousness to a higher and therefore more real and less distorted plane of consciousness.

That plane of consciousness is that which one uses to meet with the Creator within. We speak here of meditation. What each of you truly is is an eternal spirit. Your natural state is so joyful that we can best compare it to your physical sensation of orgasm, held in a steady state. This is the consciousness of love which created all that there is, and in its distorted form as the sexual orgasm, created each; that is, not the spirit, but the physical shell or vehicle.

Let yourself be who you really are. Let yourself trust the Creator, yourself, the fact that you did plan on learning lessons and most of all the fact that you are never alone as you attempt to interpret and evaluate your experiences. Then you may with eyes of trust and an eye to seeing love look again at the difficulty. If it still makes no sense, it is well to return to the independent idea of the self in loving relationship with the Father and allow your deeper mind or intuition in cooperation with inner silence to open to you those realizations which will aid in seeing the lesson to be learned.

Often the lesson is one which you do not wish to learn consciously. Patience, restraint, caution, all these qualities have seemingly little to do with love and compassion, but many, many of the lessons of love concern the meticulous disciplining of the consciousness, so that no matter what the outer circumstances, the truer, higher self is expressed, that self which is love and which expresses in a loving manner those good works which you and the Creator have planned together for this day, this hour, this moment.

Once you trust in the process and trust in your ability to sustain the loving attempt to learn love, that which happens before the eyes may distress and scatter one to the winds, but not for long, for you always come to that place within yourself once again and close the door behind you and tabernacle once more with the Creator. We are with you, and we have ultimate, infinite trust that each of you is full of love and beautiful.

Our illusion is much less difficult to penetrate, our work is far more subtle, and we gaze with a mixture of fascination and remembered fearful distress [at] the violent emotions and reactions which are brought forth from one experiencing within your density. You chose, each of you, to work very hard in this lifetime, to learn much, to serve and manifest to others the love and the light of the one infinite Creator …

(Side one of tape ends.)

We are with the instrument. We are Latwii, and greet you once again in love and light. We continue.

Know that the difficulties that you have are perfectly designed to offer to you a gentle lesson, a way, another way, yet another way, of throwing up something which is semi-permeable; you can almost see through it but not quite with the physical eyes, and sometimes you cannot see through it at all. But if you gaze at it with your heart's eyes, trusting in the utter perfection of what is happening to you, and allowing nothing to sway that trust in the kindliness of the Father, you will see in the end the lesson to be learned. Perhaps nothing needs to change except the viewpoint, or perhaps once the lesson is learned, the situation may be left.

These decisions are up to you, indeed, all of your incarnation basically, in our opinion, has but one end: to allow you to make choices which will polarize you more and more towards being a manifestation of love to those about you, to yourself and to the one Creator. This is your reality, this is who you are, pieces, entireties, of the Creator, covered all up with illusion, seeking to find the Creator within. May you water your Creator-heart with silence, love and trust and allow no outer circumstance to sway you from love, trust and service. May you hold your head high and allow no one to demean you. May you be harmless, and above all, my brothers and sisters, may you love one another with an ever more compassionate love.

We have been told twice by this instrument that it is time for us to leave, and we, as always, are very sorry. It is such a joy to share thoughts with those who would seek them, and, indeed, as we desire to be of service greatly, you are our benefactors and we can but humbly thank you. We realize that there may be some questions, so before we conclude our discussion, we would transfer to the one known as Jim for that purpose. We would send greetings to the one known as S. Greetings and love, my sister. We are those of Latwii.

(Jim channeling)

I am Latwii, and greet each again in love and light through this instrument. At this time it is our privilege to ask if we might be of any further [help] by attempting to respond to queries which may remain upon the minds. Again we remind each that we offer that which is our opinion. May we attempt a query at this time?

A: I just want to extend love and thanks to you for caring for us and helping us.

I am Latwii, and we thank you, my sister. Is there a query at this time?

Carla: When you said we are not alone, did you have in mind invisible presences or did you have in mind friends, visible ones, other seekers?

I am Latwii. My sister, you are joined on your journey by those both seen and unseen, and even though there may be times on the journey that seem quite lonely, we assure you that many marching feet and loving hearts move with you.

May we speak further, my sister?

Carla: No, thank you.

I am Latwii, and we thank you, my sister. Is there another query?

A: Is there a way that we can get closer to our gods or our people that are in-between lives to help us?

I am Latwii, and each time that you move into the silence of your inner seeking, be it in meditation, contemplation, prayer or even that which you call the daydreaming, you move closer to those sources of inspiration, guidance and assistance that constantly surround you. It is the placement of the focus of the inner attention that allows you to touch more closely and clearly that reality which underlies all illusion.

May we speak further, my sister?

A: Yes.

I am Latwii, and we feel that we have failed in making our manner of speaking the clearest possible. We were asking if there might be a further portion of the query to which we could speak.

A: Not at this time.

I am Latwii. We thank you once again, my sister. Is there another query at this time?

Carla: So you're not saying if you have a difficulty then obviously the thing to do is stick with it; there are other ways of evaluating it. The reason I'm asking this—let me put it in a specific context so that you'll know what I'm saying. I have an acquaintance who is very rigid in her belief system, whom I wish to aid, and I have in the past found it completely impossible because we deal as Christians with each other and she wishes me to help her with a Christian pursuit. Unfortunately, she has discovered that I disagree with her on key points, like evangelism, which I don't believe in and she does. I am contemplating moving back into a relationship with her in order to serve not just her, but mostly the cause which she happens to have something to do with right now.

So you're not saying just because she's difficult I should go and get in relationship with her again, right? You're not saying that; you're saying to evaluate it and see the lesson and once you've seen the lesson, then you're more informed about what to do. Am I reading you right?

I am Latwii, and this is correct, my sister. When you have informed yourself to the greatest degree possible concerning the nature of the relationship and that which may be learned from it, then you may offer yourself as a more informed and aware entity that may contribute that which is yours to contribute in a clearer and more loving fashion because of that which you have found through your own seeking.

May we speak in any further fashion, my sister?

Carla: Merely a comment from me that it seems that though we're really destined to dance in the dark, because we can sort of come up with these feelings that we think we have, these realizations, but still there's no way to check them empirically. I guess you just have to go with the best that you know—which is what we knew in the beginning.

I am Latwii, and, indeed, that dance which you do is one which is filled with mystery, for within your illusion the knowing is not possible. Only the seeking is that which is important. That which is sought with the loving heart, the strong faith, and the persevering will is that which reveals itself to you as the truth of your experience and the fabric of love which enfolds all experience.

May we speak in any further fashion, my sister?

Carla: Along another line. I got the same feeling tonight, believe it or not, that I got last week on the same question, that is that you had a whole lot more that you wanted to put through. Is this correct?

I am Latwii, and it is a correct perception upon your part that there is an unending amount of information available, for as the one serving as instrument becomes more sensitive to the contact which it experiences, it begins to notice the avenues of connection between what may be seen as pools of information available upon a given topic and those which are related to this topic. We are able to transmit that which is most earnestly called for, shall we say, that which is of most importance or appropriateness at a particular time. The information which is transmitted, then, is a response to that which is sought, and the refinements of each point may continue in a parallel fashion when a certain grouping or level of information has been successfully transmitted. Thus, there is refinement and refinement further possible as well as the correlation between related subjects.

May we speak further, my sister?

Carla: I was evaluating whether I already knew the question. I guess I don't. So if we ask the same question next week with the same thing that we did this week, that we feel there is more, what you say is we get refinements, or what you're saying is we get a new body of information with endless refinements which is related organically to the original request? Is that what you're saying?

I am Latwii, and we are having some difficulty with this instrument, for it is attempting to analyze that which we give it at this time. We shall pause for a moment and allow the deepening of the meditative state.

I am Latwii, and we shall continue. There is information available upon any topic according to the degree of attraction that is generated by the group which seeks the information. As the instrument which is utilized in the transmission of the information is able to perceive the available information, the perception and transmission of this information then creates what may be seen as a metaphysical vacuum which draws into that vacuum further information that is related to the information originally asked about. There then is the connection seen between the information given and that which may be offered in response to further querying as further levels of the information are discovered and then transmitted. The one serving as instrument, if sensitive to the contact, will be able to perceive the connections between various portions of the information and then be able to transmit the further refinements and additions to the original information that was requested.

May we speak in any further fashion, my sister?

Carla: No, and my apologies to the instrument. I was persistent because I really wanted to know whether I should proceed next week with taking up the public meeting with this question, and I see if all are agreeable and each person in the circle would [find] that question interesting, that it would be satisfactory, so that's what I wanted to know. I thank you, and that's all for me.

I am Latwii, and we thank you, my sister. Is there a further query at this time?

A: Are there any accidental deaths?

I am Latwii. We speak of the general experience, and in this sense there are no accidents or mistakes, for the experience of each entity is carefully planned and considered before the incarnation, this including the experience of the death or the movement from the incarnation at its completion. There are, however, occasionally that which may be seen as surprises which the entity was not fully aware of. These, however, are not usual, and may be seen as somewhat [of] an anomaly.

May we speak in any further fashion, my sister?

A: No, that's all.

I am Latwii, and we thank you once again, my sister, for your query. Is there another query at this time?

Carla: Is the instrument fatigued?

I am Latwii, and we find that the instrument is not fatigued, but is somewhat concerned about its level of meditation and ability to transmit in a clear fashion.

Is there another query at this time?

A: I have a new grandson. How may I best help him?

I am Latwii. We cannot speak in any specific fashion upon this particular theory, or those which might allow for the infringement of free will, for we do not wish our words to direct another's choices, but may speak in general in suggesting that the new entity be greeted not only upon the physical level of interaction, but also upon the metaphysical or spiritual level of experience in the meditation that sees the new entity welcomed to its new environment with the love of the heart and the dedication of the life to walk upon the journey of seeking with this entity and to serve in whatever manner is most appropriate as each has already agreed upon and as each seeks to fulfill in manifestation those agreements made in spirit.

May we speak in any further fashion, my sister?

A: No, thank you.

I am Latwii, and again we thank you, my sister. Is there another query at this time?

(Pause)

I am Latwii, and as it appears that we have exhausted the queries, and perhaps the instrument as well, we shall again thank each for inviting our presence, reminding each that we wish to offer those concepts which may be of value in the seeking, and we look forward to each such opportunity in your future. We are known to you as those of Latwii. We shall take our leave of this instrument and this group at this time, leaving each in the love and in the light of the one infinite Creator. Adonai, my friends. Adonai.

L/L Research

L/L Research is a subsidiary of Rock Creek Research & Development Laboratories, Inc.

P.O. Box 5195
Louisville, KY 40255-0195

www.llresearch.org

Rock Creek is a non-profit corporation dedicated to discovering and sharing information which may aid in the spiritual evolution of humankind.

ABOUT THE CONTENTS OF THIS TRANSCRIPT: This telepathic channeling has been taken from transcriptions of the weekly study and meditation meetings of the Rock Creek Research & Development Laboratories and L/L Research. It is offered in the hope that it may be useful to you. As the Confederation entities always make a point of saying, please use your discrimination and judgment in assessing this material. If something rings true to you, fine. If something does not resonate, please leave it behind, for neither we nor those of the Confederation would wish to be a stumbling block for any.

CAVEAT: This transcript is being published by L/L Research in a not yet final form. It has, however, been edited and any obvious errors have been corrected. When it is in a final form, this caveat will be removed.

© 2009 L/L Research

Sunday Meditation
October 25, 1987

Group question: Reinvestigating the question of why it is so difficult for people to share the love and light good vibrations with those near and dear to family and friends, especially the mate.

(Carla channeling)

I am Latwii. We greet you in the love and in the light of the one infinite Creator. We are most grateful to be with you once again and bless each and offer our love. We wish also to express gratitude to the one known as Carla for her reliance upon feelings which many among your peoples move aside, assuming that intuition is imagination, for we indeed did wish to continue upon the subject of the difficulty each seeking soul encounters in expressing the love and the light of the infinite Creator in an intimate relationship over a sustained period of your time.

You shall recall that we spoke of joy, of a kind of joy which had to do with the inward realization of an immediate relationship with the Creator and Sustainer of all that there is. This concept requires more careful consideration, for in the context of the question there lies the implication that joy is the very thing which eludes discovery. Entities would be only too happy to manifest joy, compassion and understanding, could they only feel it within the heart, the mind, and the soul. Thus, let us consider how it may be that the seeker may accelerate the process whereby an expanded and strengthened inner realization will bear the sweet fruit of a joyful peace.

Because each of you has five senses and must operate within an illusion designed specifically to register upon these senses, that which is unseen is often not abandoned, but simply undiscovered. Yet, when the search begins for love, we would like to suggest that in our opinion that search first has what one may call a vertical axis, that is, at the base of this axis is the self; let us put that value at minus ten. At the height of this line is a plus ten. Neutral ground for the soul is the middle, the zero point. It is about this point that the individual which is reacting to the stimulus of the environment without spiritual consideration will hover, first perhaps a bit up towards the peak of the line, which is the Logos, the Creator, divine love, then move somewhat towards concentration upon the self, hovering around and round the zero point of neutrality.

We point out that neutrality, or a lack of bias, is the one thing which this illusion is designed to lessen or eliminate, for it is the purpose of this illusion to create the consciousness which contemplates spiritual choice: the choice to focus more upon the self or more upon the Creator.

By the self in this axis we intend to convey not the whole self but that self which obtains and values tangible possessions, useful friendships, and advantageous arrangements of social, economic and political influences. It is written in the holy work known as the Holy Bible that the master known as Jesus, when asked what it was important to do, that is, which commandments were the greatest within this master's tradition, the reply was, first to love the Creator with all the heart, the mind, and strength, and secondly to love the neighbor, the associate, the intimate, the stranger, the enemy as the self.

Those who attempt in all goodness of heart to achieve improved communication and a softening of heart, mutual expression, by going directly towards working upon the relationship have moved one step too soon and are very probably doomed to an unsatisfactory communication and an unchanged difficulty, for until one has achieved more and more consciousness centered upon the Creator, until one has lived in the immediacy of the very real love that lives between each consciousness in the universe and that great Consciousness of which each is a part, the results are bound to be disappointing.

Thus, we suggest that, as usual within an illusion, what apparently seems the difficulty is, shall we say a smoke screen to those who wish to meet problems seemingly head-on, for such problems are a by-product of a lack of closeness to love. The Creator is a mystery, yet like any unexplored land or person or idea, the mystery beckons, and through what you would call eons of time, many, many consciousnesses have come to what may be called the understanding that there are certain reportable aspects of divine consciousness which have been common to pilgrims upon the journey in planetary consciousness development time and time again. The reported manifestations emanating from love, when found within the relationship with the individual consciousness, are love, joy, peace and compassion.

Thus, the first mental, emotional and spiritual discipline of one's seeking to accelerate the pace of future tranquility's arrival is to dwell as much as possible upon that relationship with the Creator which may be honestly and sincerely felt within the self in times of meditation, contemplation, conversation with others, indeed, at any time whatsoever, although the quiet times are the best for invoking the discipline of seeking to feel at one with the Creator. This relationship is the most important and the most intimate within the seeker's experience, in or out of incarnation. And if this be not so, then it is that the seeker has work to do in consciousness, moving into quietness, moving into a trust that can only be grasped by blind faith that there is a Creator and that the reports that you have had of this Creator are correct.

Each entity whom you may become intimate with is a portion of that Creator, and you must know yourself to be the Creator's own son or daughter. You must grow up within the house of prayer and meditation, argue with the Creator, complain to the Creator, praise, thank, bless or curse the Creator; but accept for awhile the premise that you can have an intimate, lively, spontaneous, continuing and dynamic relationship with that great Self which is All That There Is. This Creator is not One which shall tamely do your bidding, nor are you one who shall tamely do the Creator's bidding unless much time has been spent, much realization gained concerning the dependability of the Creator's will. Therefore, there is work to do and much, much time to do it.

Now, you may see as upon the graph that you are attempting to move your point of contact with the Creator higher and higher along the vertical axis. Thus, if one were to draw a horizontal line through the zero point—also if minus ten being the self, plus ten being another consciousness—you start with indifference at the zero point. This is also a most important axis, one which is most sensitive to your good intentions, that is, great polarization towards love of others and service to others is possible whether the relationship bears fruit or not, for it is in the purity of intention and the wholeness of effort that the bias towards service to others is increased.

Now, if one were to put the most desirable of all possible mental, spiritual and emotional arrangements, one would, of course, gaze at the extreme right upper corner of this square graph. The one who is focusing upon the self rather than the Creator and manifesting love of self rather than love of others would find the point at the diagonal lower left corner of the graph. The goal, therefore, for those who wish to accelerate the process of spiritual growth is to find the meeting point of the seeking of the Creator and the seeking to do service in the right upper quadrant, moving more and more towards to the upper right hand corner.

It is in the intimate relationships that one is most prone to begin to expect from another a seemingly just or fair exchange of service for service, and this seemingly innocent and obvious assumption of fair play and justice is the mask behind which hides the difficulty, its root, its wellspring—that is, expectation from another consciousness rather than expectation from the Creator. The suffering spirit which is locked in weary combat with another consciousness is far less able to alter for the better or more positive the intimate relationship than to offer service to those from whom one expects nothing.

Therefore, we would commend to the consideration of the seeker the virtue and efficiency of turning, after the relationship with the Creator has been established, to those in need which come before your notice, those in whom you can seek to offer love, yet not seek be loved. It is comparatively easy to sit down with the prisoner, the orphan, the indigent, and the elderly in need, and share the fruit of that joy-filled time when the soul and its Creator were intimate together.

A further word concerning communication. The value, metaphysically speaking, of conversations from the heart is inestimable. It can be only on faith that these conversations may be had. Indeed, within the intimate, troubled relationship, there is often such a great burden of negative baggage, extraneous to the core of the difficulty, that communication may seem impossible, for at every turn there is blame upon both sides, and as each feels not only guilt but confusion, each becomes defensive and knows not the words or the ways to express or describe the pain, the need, the hope for peace.

We would therefore recommend that conversations be attempted only after the entity who wishes to improve the situation be grounded firmly within the primary relationship, that relationship with the Father, the Mother, the Sustainer which is often called God, but in reality is not separate, but rather All; for you are within the Father, the Mother, and the Father/Mother within you.

It is from the vantage of high upon the vertical graph, moving towards the Kingdom which is exemplified by ten, that one may look down upon a very small, very local, very foolish difficulty, where one may see the humor of two who love yet cannot speak, two who love but cannot help but contend. From the vantage point of love, creation is possible, and that includes the recreation of the self and the healing of relationships. From the higher vantage point, one may release the other self from all expectation.

The unthinking spirit naturally cries, "That is not fair, that is not just," yet we say to you that fairness and justice are not absolute concepts related to a dualistic illusion. It is well for fairness and justice to exist as concepts and to be used carefully of the regulation of social intercourse, yet it is not well to gaze upon them as what they are not, that is, absolute virtues, for that which is fair and just is always a relative choice, cases being able to be made for each side.

It is in the interest of the serious seeker to be view all relationships from the same stance, and that is the desire to love, to understand, to forgive, to give. It is the choice of priorities for most that the one whom the seeker wishes to serve the most is that intimate mate of the days and the nights, the months and the seasons of a lifetime. Yet the joy bubbles forth more and more freely as the entity is able to retain the memory of who that intimate soul to you truly is. That soul is, as you, a student seeking after truth, a soul searching for the source of love, a wanderer seeking a home. This consciousness, as yours, suffers, attempts to change, fails and succeeds, and moves through all the private seasons of anguish and pleasure. This soul has been given into your care, as are all whom you meet, not in an absolute sense—that is, not in the sense that one soul can be responsible for another, far from that—we mean that one soul's hope in contacting and blending with another's life stream is that he may be able to be of service.

Once the expectations are laid aside, that is, once the barnacles of barter and expectation are removed from the hull of that entity's spiritual vehicle, the waters betwixt your consciousness and theirs shall be far more peaceful. For if one calls another husband, one inadvertently within your culture thinks of a number of suppositions regarding the relationship. Yet when such a relationship is breaking down, it is well to go back to that which is in no way illusory, that is, the absolute principle that each entity whom you meet is a child of God, as yourself, to be loved as yourself, and to be served, if necessary, at the expense of the self if, in love's opinion within you, that service is appropriate. That is, we do not wish to advise needless sacrifice, for that is martyrdom for no cause. We advise only that that person with whom you hoped to spend a lifetime of love is worthy, as are you, of the greatest service.

How difficult it is, my friends, we know, to see past the hurtful lack of communication …

(Side one of tape ends.)

(Carla channeling)

… to move beyond the harsh and seemingly betraying acts of one's mate, how easy it is not to trust, not to nurture, not to stand firmly upon the two feet, knowing that one is completely and utterly safe and secure in a loving relationship with the Creator, and thus hold out the hand and say, "I love you. I accept you just as you are, I see and sympathize with your difficulties," or even for those whose hurtful behaviors include still others, "I accept your needs to be happy, and wish you well." These thoughts seem to be a way of subtracting the self from the relationship, removing the emotion from, and thus the intimacy from, the relationship. Yet, it is the best beginning of which we are aware for those who cannot read each other's thought, to move into a situation in which the relationship becomes more trustworthy. It often takes a great deal of an incarnation to rebuild trust betwixt two which have hurt each other in heart, mind or spirit. Yet it can be done in a moment if each turns first to the Creator, and then, knowing a new world within the self, turn to each other. Turn and turn and turn, becoming more and more graceful as each conversation and confrontation is experienced.

We may say in closing that many, many incarnations have been planned by entities incarnate at this time to include very serious challenges to faith and a life lived in love and service. Before the incarnation, each of you considered well that which you wished to accomplish. Now that you are experiencing the actual classes which you chose for yourself, you may feel, in this instrument's scholastic vocabulary, that you have taken too many hours, that you have enrolled in too many courses, and that you cannot possibly conclude and do well in this exercise of study and expression of the fruits of that study which is commonly called life upon your sphere.

When you become alive, as you shall after the gateway of death has been entered, you shall finally experience that which you think you experience now. Meanwhile, those of you who face a seemingly intractable intimate relationship, and yet have the feeling that there is something which has drawn you together, something which you must learn together, please know that it is possible, even probable, that you hoped for yourself that your mature reaction to seemingly negative circumstances shall be the recognition that as you are experiencing negative circumstances, so must your mind not be full yet of the Creator.

And so you must mount once again to the watchtower which gazes upon the kingdom of the Creator which dwells within that kingdom. It is something that you must do by yourself, yet that lover which you pursue, that divine love which you seek, sought persistently shall become to you real, intimate and very dynamic. And more and more as you seek consciously immediate experience of the love of the one infinite Creator, what you seek shall come to you. And as you seek that which is the highest of all things to seek, thus all else begins to fall into perspective.

And more and more, regardless of what happens in the intimate relationships, and in all areas of incarnation, your experience shall be that of joy, for the Creator has tucked joy into every atom of the infinite universe, has woven joy into sunlight and starshine, has plaited joy up in the leaves, branches and roots of your trees, the gurgling of the rivers, the busy hum of life. Each bee moves upon its way hearing the rhythm of the dance within. That great central sun which is the Creator in manifestation speaks as clearly to you and gives direction from within.

May you be blessed in your seeking. May you seek persistently the highest that you know, for that which you shall seek you shall find, and all else, once the highest begins to unfold, unfolds before you in reflection. Perhaps it shall be a sustained effort—as we said, some lessons are designed to be greatly challenging. Yet keep always the goal in mind, and seek not simply to serve others, but more to serve the Creator in others. And the reflections of life which come back to you shall more and more dance and sing with joy.

You in the watchtower, you who suffer, you who watch and weep and walk this day and night, you are not alone, for within you lies the greatest love, the only reality. Seek it in earnestness, experience in joy and laughter and lightness, and become the lamp set upon a hill. Not in and of yourself, but only as one in love, knowing the peace of the most intimate of all relationships—yourself and the Creator, your heart and love itself.

We would like to thank this instrument again for its insistence in following a quiet inner voice. We did have these thoughts to convey, and are most grateful for the opportunity to have the time to complete those thoughts which we felt might have some use to those who have asked this question. We encourage in this instrument close attention to such promptings, for through this means each answer may be given as we of the Confederation of Planets in the Service of the Infinite Creator may feel it is best, no longer limited by your time, for it takes much of your time to transmit these thoughts with words.

We would like to move to the one known as Jim, if this instrument would accept our contact. We are those of Latwii, and we shall transfer.

(Jim channeling)

I am Latwii, and greet each again in love and light. At this time it is our privilege to offer ourselves in the attempt to speak to any further queries which those present may offer to us. Is there a query at this time?

Carla: I received the impression that that was the end of the transmission on that subject. Can you confirm that?

I am Latwii, and this is correct, my sister. You have once again correctly perceived the nature of the inner response to our contact, and we again encourage this inner listening, for it shall be of assistance in many ways.

Is there a further query, my sister?

Carla: On a related issue. When I was challenging your contact—I do it the same way every time basically, and I always say, "Do you come in the name of Jesus the Christ, whom I serve with all my heart, all my soul, all my mind, and all my strength?" And you answered not what I'm used to hearing, which is something like "Yes, my child, I am pleased to come in the name of Jesus the Christ," or from Yadda, "Of course." You said, "We are with Jesus the Christ." Was there a reason for the change of language?

I am Latwii, and we have used this phrase this evening, for it best exemplifies that state of our being which we have activated in order to continue the transmission of concept which was begun previously. This has been our choice for this topic, for it is one which deals most wholeheartedly with the concept of love or compassion, and it was our feeling that our own tuning or placement of focus of being would be most helpful and informative with this level of understanding available. Thus, we called upon that manifested by the one known as Jesus the Christ within ourselves in order to be of service to those gathered this evening.

Is there a further query, my sister?

Carla: So from your perception, the phrase which the fundamentalists use, "Christ is Lord, Jesus is Lord"—what you're saying is that for you as well as for us, you see this Jesus consciousness as being the basic redeemer of human experience, the highest of compassion of love? Is that so? Or would you express your feeling about that phrase, "Jesus is Lord," in the context of challenging. I don't challenge that way. It doesn't seem necessary.

I am Latwii, and if we understand that which has been asked, we would say that that which is loved and accepted is that which has been redeemed. Thus, it is within the heart of love that redemption occurs.

May we speak in a further fashion upon this topic, my sister?

Carla: No. I was off on a wild goose chase when I first asked the question, because I just wondered if your social memory complex was the one that Jesus went to when he got through his incarnation two thousand years ago on Earth. I know he went to a fifth-density complex, and I thought perhaps it might be yours, since you said, "I am with Jesus the Christ."

I am Latwii, and our connection with the one known as Jesus the Christ is not as you have assumed, but is rather that which we may call upon and join with.

May we speak further, my sister?

Carla: No, thank you.

I am Latwii, and we thank you, my sister. Is there another query?

Carla: Well, just one more, then. Do you find as a fifth-density social memory complex, trying to do your work here with us, that it's better for us to ask questions and thereby give a focus, an overt focus, or to, as we call it, take pot luck, and receive whatever comes through? Which do you feel is more advantageous for fifth-density contact?

I am Latwii, and we seek to be of service. We do not know that which is most effective as a means by which we may serve in every case. We may in many instances assess the entities gathered in a circle of seeking and note great similarities in that which is sought, whether it be of a conscious or unspoken nature and thus speak upon that topic to seeming effectiveness. However, when we are offered a query which has been considered by the group, we then feel a greater confidence in that which we offer, for it has been called forth from us by those gathered in the seeking, and as a focus for the transfer of concepts is usually more efficient than the unspoken and undirected wishes of a circle of seeking.

May we speak further, my sister?

Carla: One last question that just occurred to me. I have no concept of being here, of time passing during that transmission. How close am I to being out of it? And is it safe and is it okay as long as Jim's holding my hand?

I am Latwii, and it is our estimation that your condition is that which is within the limits of safety as long as the hand is held, for it is not possible for the untrained entity to leave the physical vehicle while the tactile pressure is exerted by another entity upon the vehicle, thus infringing upon the auric field and requiring the spirit or enlivener to remain with its vehicle. We find your state of meditation to be quite effective as one through which information may pass with minimal distortion, and are honored that we are able to utilize your instrument in this manner at this time.

May we speak further, my sister?

Carla: I want to thank you for the compliment. It means a lot to me. I just wonder, is a cat on the lap good enough?

I am Latwii, and it is our understanding of the relative effect of the electrical bodies or auric fields of the second density feline that its interaction with your own would not, in most cases, be sufficient for the causing of the spirit enlivener to remain with its vehicle, for the spiritual component of the second density creature is most usually lacking, as it is at the level of development at which the mind begins to emerge in an individual fashion with the rudimentary functioning only, thus the infringement that it makes upon your own auric field is far less than that made by another third density entity which has the spiritual component developed to the minimal degree that the third-density experience allows.

May we speak further, my sister?

Carla: No, thank you. Thank you very much.

I am Latwii, and again we thank you, my sister. Is there another query at this time?

(Pause)

I am Latwii, and it is our observation that we have, for the evening, exhausted the queries, and we thank each for allowing our presence this evening. We have been most privileged to have been able to join this group of seeking. We are hopeful that we shall be able to continue the transfer of concepts to this group in its future gatherings when possible. We are aware that there are various factors which determine the most appropriate response, and indeed the most appropriate entities, to give response to the queries which this group offers to the Confederation of Planets in Service to the One Creator. It has been a great honor for us to join you this evening. At this time we shall take our leave of this group. We are known to you as those of Latwii, and we leave each in the love and in the light of the one infinite Creator. Adonai, my friends. Adonai vasu borragus. ♣

L/L Research

L/L Research is a subsidiary of Rock Creek Research & Development Laboratories, Inc.

P.O. Box 5195
Louisville, KY 40255-0195

www.llresearch.org

Rock Creek is a non-profit corporation dedicated to discovering and sharing information which may aid in the spiritual evolution of humankind.

ABOUT THE CONTENTS OF THIS TRANSCRIPT: This telepathic channeling has been taken from transcriptions of the weekly study and meditation meetings of the Rock Creek Research & Development Laboratories and L/L Research. It is offered in the hope that it may be useful to you. As the Confederation entities always make a point of saying, please use your discrimination and judgment in assessing this material. If something rings true to you, fine. If something does not resonate, please leave it behind, for neither we nor those of the Confederation would wish to be a stumbling block for any.

CAVEAT: This transcript is being published by L/L Research in a not yet final form. It has, however, been edited and any obvious errors have been corrected. When it is in a final form, this caveat will be removed.

© 2009 L/L Research

Intensive Meditation
October 30, 1987

(Carla channeling)

I am Latwii. I and my brothers and sisters of Latwii greet you, as do those of Laitos, in the love and in the light of the infinite Creator, the Creator who has made Him ourselves and has made ourselves Him, the Creator whose presence is timeless and whose time is the present moment. We send to you greetings and love and offer our thankfulness to be honored by the call to work with the new instrument at this time. What a joy it is to be of assistance. We of Latwii have nearly equal calls from this group at this time, and therefore the presence of both energies may be felt by those present. We do not wish to cause anxiety on the part of any who may sense more than one presence. The one known as Laitos is most interested in pursuing the adjustmental work so that the contact with the new instrument may become ever more fluid and stable.

We would like to offer an exercise this day by the telling of a story. For the purposes of this storytelling we shall keep our identifications to a minimum that the story itself may continue to fill the minds and hearts of those who wish to be a part of its telling. However, we do ask each instrument always to challenge as the contact comes to you in the name of the highest and best unshakable ideal in your particular universe. We shall begin.

There once was a young woman of Lustra named Penelope. Penelope was brown as a berry and ran among the thorns and berries, the rocks and crags of her neighborhood like a young, happy foal or kitten. She was a sweet and perfect child, untouched by tragedy, secure in her mother's and father's loving arms. One day a catastrophe caused Penelope to experience for the first time a seeming separation, a seeming abyss betwixt herself and all in which she put faith and trust.

We shall transfer.

(Jim channeling)

The catastrophe which Penelope suffered was one in which a member of her family, that being her father, was killed in a manner which seemed questionable, shall we say, in that the entity was engaged in taking from another that which belonged to the other, and in this act was killed. This was enough of a catastrophe in itself, that being the death of the father, that the additional burden of the nature of the death caused many to speak ill of Penelope's father, of her family, and, indeed, of herself. Her grief over the loss of father was increased by this ill speaking and feelings on the part of those in the surrounding environment. This situation caused Penelope to consider herself the taking of her own life, for she felt that without her father's love and the family's good name there was little for which to live, and for many days and indeed weeks, Penelope was distraught and on the edge of taking her own life.

After a period of time had elapsed and there had been some relief from the gossip of the neighborhood, Penelope encountered a young man who was traveling through the country and who needed assistance in the form of a place to rest and food to refuel the tired body. In the course of conversation with the young man, Penelope disclosed the difficult days which had passed and the source of the difficulty, sharing her entire story with the young man who listened quite patiently and compassionately to what Penelope related.

We shall transfer.

(Carla channeling)

I am Latwii, and interrupt this story to bring you a word from your sponsors. We realize that there is the block occurring in the new instrument's analytical mind, and we would say to the new instrument who has recently had experience in the handling of the motorcycle, that the practice of channeling requires an ability which is common with that needed by the cycles, that is, that the roads are not always straight, neither is intuition straight. The roads bend and curve and so do the ways of intuition. Upon the curving highways and byways the motorcycle must lean into and aggressively attack each corner, not knowing that which is around the bend, yet trusting in the balance of cycle and rider, trusting that the way is clear ahead, and trusting the instincts of hand and foot.

When the new channel moves down the road which intuition has fashioned, there appear many turns uphill and down, back and forth. And again the new channel must learn to trust the basic vehicle of thought, the self, which the new channel has created to deal with intuitively perceived invisible entities. The new channel must be able to trust the clearness of the road ahead so that the channel may lean into and aggressively take those turnings and bendings, thus smoothing the way for the long straight roads that lie between each turn and twist. We urge the new instrument to boldly attack with intuition, just as the road is attacked and best use made of it by the aggressive yet careful cyclist. Once the being is tuned and the declaration of self given so that challenging may be done, it is best to keep the proverbial metaphorical hand upon the throttle, for momentum is gained by attacking intuitive curves, and the benefits which rise from a more self-confident foray onto the road of intuition are too numerous to mention, opening to the new instrument as it does in ever-expanding vistas of beauty and challenge.

We shall continue the story through this instrument.

Penelope was most grateful for the understanding of the stranger and developed a great desire to be with this young palmist, for palmist he was, working with the hand and seeing within each line the clear sketch of natural beingness and potential development. Little by little Penelope and the palmist, Jonathan, became greater and greater friends. Penelope grew to be a young woman and Jonathan was always there to aid her when otherwise her father would have done so. When Penelope was sixteen, all in her family besides herself were struck with diphtheria and taken from her life in a matter of days. Penelope was on her own, quite penniless, with no dowry, no station in life other than mother's helper, and no prospects for the future. Again, Penelope in the darker recesses of her mind began to think more and more of suicide. Only Jonathan could comfort her, and comfort her he did.

We now transfer to the one known as D.

(D channeling)

Jonathan's love and kindness was as a balm to the wounds and albeit suffering, and drew her even more closely into the aura of his spiritual strength. With his nurturing through a period of many months, her despair departed and was replaced by hope and determination to make the best of the situation these events had created in her life. Having neither property or status, but through Jonathan's inspiration able to contact the spiritual strength deep within her, she determined to lay a constructive course in her life that would enable her to succeed without the benefits of inheritance or family support. She attained a position with a family whose head was a kind woman who had also succeeded in making her own way and entered into something of an apprenticeship. She also was able to acquire the experience of continuing a family life in the caring for the young children of her mistress. Through her own diligence and the infusing of the continuing strength and support of her friend Jonathan, she was accepted as a colleague and family member as well.

(Carla channeling)

We shall conclude through this instrument.

Penelope felt that she had every possible element for happiness, for although she had never married, yet she was nurturer to each child which played with those children which were in the care of those in the family of her friend.

But one day Jonathan came to offer what seemed to her another great piece of catastrophe. "It is time for me to leave," he said. "I have sensed it and I accept it. I do not know what the road ahead holds for me, yet I go on a faith, knowing that to do the will of the Creator is the sum of all that I ask of myself or this thing that we call consciousness or life."

To Penelope it seemed as though the nightmare days of her girlhood were again, for Jonathan had been her faithful friend. This she said to her friend, but Jonathan demurred.

"You have not lost me," he said, "simply because I am not present, nor have you ever lost all those who have died in your family." He took her hands and gazed at her palms. "I see much ahead for you," he said. "Many lines are developing which were not there before."

"Oh no," cried Penelope, "I cannot live on without you, for to whom would I speak? To whom would I turn in a time of need? I shall be all alone."

Jonathan looked carefully and deeply into her eyes. "Trust me," he said, "that through the experience to come, you shall learn to trust yourself." He went on. "I have seen your presence in the lives of many children as I gaze into their hands, for all have come to me, knowing that I am a palmist, in curiosity. I tell what I see, but not all of what I see, and one thing that I always see is that each hand has the mark of divinity drawn within the lines of the palm. You," he said, "shall be as I. The day will come when some young one turns to you, and then you shall be a faithful friend as I have tried to be to you."

Penelope cried, "Do you mean to say that you are not always sure, not always content, not always full of cheer and hope?"

Jonathan's hands tightened upon hers. "I tell you the truth," he said. "Each of us suffers, and in that suffering imagines we are alone. Yet within each, waiting for the asking, is the presence of the infinite, the unmeasured, the limitless Father and Mother of all."

Suddenly Penelope could see that which she had not glimpsed before, the panorama of a life of giving and receiving love. "Perhaps," she said, smiling for the first time in many days, "I shall be able to give until I have given all that I received and more."

Jonathan smiled in return. "Peace and farewell," he said, "I shall see you in the land where all giving and taking are one."

We ask each of you as you ponder this parable to examine the assumptions …

(Side one of tape ends.)

(Carla channeling)

… under which you labor. If the assumptions include the feelings of solitude within the spiritual search, then we say this is a true perception. But if one of these assumptions is that one is truly alone, then we suggest that this assumption is grossly in error. For each Penelope there is not only an outward Jonathan, but an inward and compelling Jonathan, a presence to comfort, to love, and to aid and counsel when requested. These inner seers, these Jonathans of the soul, are called by your peoples such things as the higher self, the inner guides, the guardian angels, and it is largely in catastrophe, in times of peril, and in danger that the soul first becomes truly aware of the strength and comfort available from within the self.

We wish to aid by these thoughts in the positioning of the mind and heart towards, shall we say, the spiritual east. We wish to express the sanctity of that comfort which lies within, which has so often been externalized within your holy work, the Bible, as the holy city, Jerusalem. Realize that your physical beings are as the cave within which dwells the fragile and infinite spirit. And look upwards through the chink in the roof of the cave and see the blinding shafts of light filling, nurturing, comforting and informing the spirit within. May each of you become independent of the outer world, so that addictions end, excesses may be laid aside with more and more ease.

We realize that this has been a difficult session for the one known as D, and ask this new instrument to take strong comfort, for each time that we work with this new instrument we are able to express more and more of those thought which we intend to express. We would at this time transfer to the one known as Jim. I am Latwii, and with me is the vibration of Laitos. We transfer now.

(Jim channeling)

I am Latwii, and at this time we are honored to have the opportunity of speaking to the queries which may remain upon the minds of those gathered, and we would offer ourselves freely in this capacity with the hope that we may offer inspiration and information without the dogma or the over-weighting of our offering by those present. Is there a query at this time to which we may speak?

Carla: It seems to me that the point of the story was pretty much that in the end Jonathan shared his feeling of inner inadequacy with Penelope and was trying to say that even though we're all very imperfect and scared and sometimes feel like not carrying on anymore, that we can still be of comfort to other people and to ourselves by seeking the guidance within. It was not the most hopeful message I ever heard, if I understand it, for it would imply that suffering is the universal theme in life. Can you comment on that?

I am Latwii, and we feel that you have given a quite substantial interpretation of that which we offered in the form of the story to this group. We do not mean to dampen those spirits which ever seek the hope-filled future and inspiration within the lives of others and the self, but wished by this rendition to illustrate the sustaining source of love and support which accompanies all travail and difficulty, for, indeed, within your illusion you shall find much that is difficult and hard to experience and accept, yet the seeker, and, indeed, all entities, is supported by a source of love greater than any outer difficulty.

And it is the seeker who avails the self most effectively of this love and support, for the conscious seeker is the one which looks beyond the outer way of experience in order to ponder the deeper truths and nature of experience, so that there may be gained from each experience, no matter how difficult, the seed or crystal of understanding that enriches the soul or inner nature of the being, much as the creature of your second density known as the oyster creates the pearl as the result of the constant irritation of the grain of sand.

May we speak further, my sister?

Carla: No, thank you.

I am Latwii, and we thank you, my sister. Is there another query?

D: I was wondering today, I was wishing I had some more direction about steps I could take on my own, given my own individual status with regard to learning the channeling. When such periods go by as have just gone by when I'm not able to be here, or even during the week between sessions here, are there suggestions for work I can do on my own? I think that Laitos advised against specifically trying to channel when alone, but are there other solitary exercises that would be suitable?

I am Latwii. Indeed, the new instrument often seeks the manner by which the facility in the channeling process may be aided, much as the athlete seeks to strengthen the muscle by the exercise in a disciplined fashion. We may make a suggestion which sounds at once too easy and too difficult to consider, but the life experience in each of its many portions is channeled by each entity on a day-to-day, and, indeed, a moment-to-moment basis. This is realized by each which seeks to place the attention within a certain attitude or ambiance of mind which looks upon the day and the moment as a dance in which one moves gracefully with any partner or experience that is placed before the notice.

As this attitude of acceptance and graceful movement with those entities and energies about one is cultivated, the primary requisite for serving as a vocal instrument is also strengthened, for the attitude of the mind which allows an entity to move freely and gracefully within its daily round of activities is the same attitude or quality which the vocal instrument exercises when it practices its art. Thus, as you seek in all manner of experience to balance your total being that it might move effortlessly and freely in harmony with those about one, you practice that which allows each entity to serve most effectively as an instrument for the one Creator to move within your being and for you to move within the being of the Creator.

May we speak in any further fashion, my brother?

D: That was very helpful. I don't think I have any further questions at this point.

I am Latwii, and we thank you, my brother, as well. Are there any further questions at this time?

Carla: No.

I am Latwii, and it has been our great honor to be with each during this session of working. Those of Laitos also send love and appreciation at being able to blend their vibrations with each and to assist in the practice of exercising the instruments present. We shall be with each in the meditations in your future. At this time we shall leave each in the love and in the light of the one infinite Creator. We are known to you as those of Latwii. Adonai, my friends. Adonai. ✣

L/L Research

Sunday Meditation
November 1, 1987

Group question: Concerns the higher self. When does an entity develop the higher self? Do second-density entities, for example, have a higher self? And after it is developed, how is it called upon and how is it used? What is the function that it performs?

(Carla channeling)

We are those of Q'uo. We greet you in the love and the light of the one infinite Creator, and are most grateful to be called to this circle of seeking. We wish to greet and express our love and blessing on each present and to be the deliverer of the message from those of Oxal to the one known as H that this entity joyously greets the instrument known as H and is happy to take time during this meditation period to touch into this instrument's energy web in love and greeting. We would like to correct the instrument who edited Oxal's desire. The desire of Oxal was the name J. This instrument chose to express the sound vibration with which she is most familiar.

You wish to know more about the higher self, and, indeed, it is good that you should, for the concept of a self that is larger and greater than that which is before the face in the mirror is a centrally powerful one. It is a concept without which humankind's understanding of the Creator would be severely crippled, for if one gazes in the mirror of mundane experience one quickly observes that the self is not overly saintly, as this instrument would say. It is the nature of the illusion which you now enjoy that the microscope of criticism is relentlessly placed before one's own and other's actions, thoughts and intentions, and in an illusion designed to confound the most noble sentiments, this is not surprising. Yet there is implicit and inherent and abiding in every third-density heart and mind an instinct as clear and true as the instinct for breath or food. That is the instinct to seek a higher purpose, a higher beingness, an enlarged point of view, and ultimately a movement decisively from the often uncomfortable illusion and its limitations which are meat and drink in third density.

Let us examine considerations concerning time. The higher self is a concept which is impossible to view in a sensible manner if the concept of linear time is clung to. The concept of one having the beginning and the end, either within one lifetime or within a creation of countless lifetimes, is a concept which creates unsolvable paradoxes with respect to considerations of the higher self. Your linear experience of time is a portion of your illusion, just as is space itself and all that you perceive with your senses. Within that illusion which we see as being the most sheer and least distorted of which we are aware, we see time as simultaneous; that is, the linear river of time perceived by the human self is deep within the self within, rounded into infinity, so that what you see as past, present and future are experienced at one time, that time being the present moment. At this precise moment as we speak, you contain all that you have experienced and will experience from the beginning of your consciousness until the sublime reentry of singular consciousness into the universal consciousness which is the Creator.

You contain memory of past and future, yet these memories are most deeply placed within what is known as the unconscious mind. They dwell within a zone to which the conscious mind is denied access. Without the concept of the higher self it is yet possible for an entity going on faith alone to open gradually the gates of perception and to become aware little by little of a larger beingness within the self, larger and larger that beingness, until it eventually encompasses all that there is, and for the first time you are aware of your true identity. Such determination and persistence is very rare. For most, not only ultimate discoveries of wisdom, love and power, but simpler understandings pertaining to specific mundane affairs, come hard. The way often seems unclear, the emotions frayed and worn, the spirit numbed with the repeated shocks of a callous and seemingly indifferent world. It is into this arena that what is known as the higher self appears. The character of the higher self may be perceived as glorious and majestic, or it may be perceived intimately as a boon companion and dear friend. The personality of the higher self is much amenable to that which is needed by the everyday waking self. Its identity, insofar as we are aware—and we wish to express that we are not infallible—is that of a future self, as you would call it, a self that is entirely yourself, yet a self which has experience, through that which you have experienced, to the present moment and onward events, far into lessons of love, wisdom and unity.

When your consciousness has reached that point where the lessons of unity are being well studied, this self turns and reaches back to the third-density self, to the self that is confused, puzzled and insecure. It is the most loving of presences, for by the middle of sixth density you shall have learned to love yourself, to embrace yourself, to protect yourself in light and love rather than with weapons of defense, words of anger and gestures of fear. This self is to you a great resource, dwelling within your consciousness, within those deep areas of consciousness where time is simultaneous and the great issues of love and service are always in incredible and lambent focus.

Thus, the avenue to the higher self is a road within the mind, a road which opens, seemingly impossibly, after one has left space and time behind in meditation. Perhaps what we are trying to express may be best approached by saying that the image of what we wish to express is that of one who, sitting in meditation, moves within the mind higher and higher until one has reached the very top of the watchtower of consciousness, and at that point when one is in a very small, protected environment, there is a harmless ordinary-looking door. Yet, through that door is the beginning of a highway that grows larger, wider, more capacious, more beautiful, more stately, until at last the inner vision opens and the self that is more you than you are now waits to greet you.

The consciousness which invites the higher self to help is one which in humility gazes at the world and says, "In and of myself I see only illusion. I must seek further." Seeking is the key to contact with this greater self, this larger edition of you. This higher self cannot choose for you that which you must or must not do. It is not an authoritarian presence. Each decision is your own to make within this illusion, and no responsibility can be given to any higher self, guide or teacher. Each is responsible for the self.

We would also encourage the seeker to open the self in meditation to those presences which are about each seeker, waiting to aid in deepening the meditative state in comfort and in succor. These guides, these presences, are also yours if you seek them. They are powerful helpers, yet it is always the turning from despair and sadness to hope and joy, the thought in confidence of sure help and the reaching out for it, that make these energies available to each who seeks.

(Pause)

We are sorry for the pause. The concept which we gave this instrument was unwieldy, and this instrument found herself in the position of being unable to express that which she could not grasp. We believe we have found a way to feed the concept to her a bit at a time.

The higher self ultimately is the Creator, just as you are the Creator already. There is what seems to be an impossibly long eon wherein the creation bursts forth into existence, flowers and moves back into the uncreated, that Highest Self. Each relationship which you enter into, if shared heart-to-heart and hand-to-hand, creates the higher self of the mated couple or the strongly bonded friendship. Each family has the group higher self, and insofar as that family may seek in unison, just so far shall its higher self be there in seeming intuition and interesting dream to convey messages concerning the most progressive and helpful service for the family to the family or for the family mated pair or friendship to the world which you experience about you.

Similarly, each group to which you may belong, if there is a common purpose which is idealistic and service oriented and sought in unity, develops a group higher self, one which can be enormously helpful, and so each nation, race and any group which bears a common identity can develop, and will ultimately develop, the higher self. Indeed, we, as social memory complexes, are an existing group mind. The higher self, then, is ever more clearly and intimately available. It is our dear wish and happy desire to join the ocean of the Uncreated, that Logos of undifferentiated love from which all is created and to which all shall return.

It is a blessing to have been able to speak with you. We would at this time transfer this contact. We are those known to you as Q'uo.

(Jim channeling)

I am Q'uo, and greet each again in love and in light. At this time it is our privilege to ask if we may speak to any further queries which those present may have to offer to us. We preface this service with what must now be well known to each, that we gladly offer opinion, and do not wish our words to be taken in any other fashion than opinion. Is there a query with which we may begin?

Questioner: Did I understand you correctly in saying that couples or families share a higher self?

I am Q'uo, and this is correct, my brother, for those who seek together in a dedicated and consistent relationship form that which is an energy of consciousness blended of the total being of each participating entity, thus the patterns of life experience become available as resources of learning and potential resources of service to each entity within the grouping that has joined itself of desire and experience.

May we speak further, my brother?

Questioner: No, thank you.

I am Q'uo, and we thank you, my brother. Is there another query?

Carla: When you were talking about others, guides and so forth, you were, I guess, intentionally vague. Is it because the distinctions between terms like angel, inner teacher, inner plane master, and personal guides are different ways of perceiving the same energies?

I am Q'uo, and in some cases this is true, my sister, for many within your illusion see but dimly those entities and forces which serve as resource for guidance and inspiration, and tend to name what is perceived in many fashions, each helpful to the namer, according to its ability to conceive of such possibility that there is a greater portion of the self and of the creation which lies beyond the physical senses and awaits the request for assistance.

In many cases there is the perceiving of a portion of what entities or sources of energy answer such calls, and this portion, then, is described in such and such a fashion. It is also true that those unseen resources upon which each third-density entity may call for assistance are various in ways unique to each entity. Thus, in some cases, the higher self will manifest a contact in a manner which utilizes intermediary means, shall we say, which may include those beings known as guides, those known as teachers in specific areas, and the coincidental events of an entity's life experience that, though seemingly small, prove to provide a point of turning for the entity in attitude or seeking or desire. Thus, there is an interweaving of unseen assistance from various levels of a seeker's greater self and the more unified portions of the creation itself.

May we speak in any further fashion, my sister?

Carla: Well, my brother, I just had one more question, a little bit of a different angle. You didn't say specifically when the higher self starts, but you did say that it was timeless, and from that I would intuit that from the very beginning of creation when our consciousnesses were moving through the elements and into time itself, and then into second density and so forth, from the beginning until the end, the higher self is there for us, and it's just a matter of learning more and more in each density to make it a conscious part of our experience. Is this, in general, the truth of it?

I am Q'uo, and this is a most rough approximation of that which is the condition of the higher self in relation to the individualized portion of the Creator which moves through the evolutionary cycle. We give this instrument the concept of the vague definition of energy and intelligence which is ever-present for the individual entity in its process of evolution, and which at some point is called by your peoples the higher self. This intelligent energy permeates each portion of what is the creation, as the first-density experience of simple awareness becomes drawn by the upward spiraling line of light towards the increased vibration of second-density movement and turning toward the light, the concept of what shall be known to you as the mind draws unto itself a vehicle for expression that will serve as what you call the body. And as this blending of energy complexes occurs in increasing frequencies of manifested expression, the mind and body complex of the second-density creature or entity becomes more and more individualized and partakes more of that which is the consciousness of self in contrast to that which it has experienced previously, which is the concept of the groupings …

(Side one of tape ends.)

(Jim channeling)

I am Q'uo, and am again with this instrument. To continue. The groupings known as the flock, the herd, the school, and so forth.

Thus, as the consciousness becomes aware of the self, the mind and body complexes then begin to draw unto themselves a concept that you would call the spirit, and through this concept are able to partake more intimately of the intelligent energy which shall continue to become available to this complex of mind, body and spirit as the higher self. Thus, the third-density entity is the self-conscious entity which is complete in that it contains the mind, the body and the spirit fully functioning and individualized according to the unique pattern of experience that has developed, is developing, and shall develop for the entity that moves within the creation toward the unity of All That Is.

May we speak further, my sister?

Carla: No, thank you, that was quite eloquent.

I am Q'uo, and we thank you, my sister. Is there another query?

(Pause)

I am Q'uo, and we feel that we have for this evening spoken to those queries which each has so graciously offered to us, and it has been our great honor to have offered our humble words in this joining of our paths of seeking this evening. We thank each for allowing our presence, and we shall be with each in your future gatherings. We shall at this time take our leave of this group. We are known to you as those of Q'uo. We leave each, as always, in the love and in the light of the one infinite Creator. Adonai, my friends. Adonai.

(Carla channeling)

I Yadda. I greet you in love and light of infinite One. We could not resist the opportunity to speak about the breath—you know, that a pretty good question. We feel there are points to be made and we will make them briefly.

The concept of life as breath and breath as life is natural for you, for you must breathe to live. However, the true breath is the breath of light—not the oxygen, but the prana which comes to all who recognize the tremendous power of that which move on the face of the water. You see, you as the body are like the planet. Your being, cell by cell, is water. Thus, as the physical breath moves upon the face of the water of your body, you have life. And as that which this instrument calls spirit move upon the face of consciousness, you have another kind of life, that which in your Christianity you call Holy Spirit. We do not wish to devalue the infinite goodness of heavenly food which is light, but we wish to have you respect yourselves, for what could this light enliven if it were not for the wonderful complex of vibrations which create the energy field which is yourself. You are the water of life. You are the material of the universe. You are the expression. Open, as you would open the lungs to breathe air. Open to that which move upon the face of the water. Think not about your condition, your foolishness, or your virtue, but only that you are material waiting for more abundant food. Such is the breath of the spirit.

We happy to speak with you, and we give this instrument trouble and more trouble, and we apologize. But she irritate us with this Jesus Christ, Jesus Christ, Jesus Christ. However, Christ is Christ, and we always are happy in the end, no matter how provincial we find an entity's expression of Christ, to come in the name of Christ, for that is the name of Love. And it is in that light and love—how you like our L's tonight? We doing better, eh? Heh, heh? It is in that love and light that we leave you now. Adonai. Adonai. We Yadda. Adonai. ☙

Intensive Meditation
November 12, 1987

(Carla channeling)

[I am Oxal. We greet you] in the love and the light of the one infinite Creator. We greatly appreciate this instrument's willingness to function, although in its own opinion it was marginal. We feel we have a good contact, and we thank this instrument for trusting the bond between us. We also thank this instrument for the extensive challenging which it did prior to our greeting you. It was indeed a well executed challenge and a needed one in terms of the service-to-others distortion. The opening in the group, and we say this for each instrument to hear, was that the instrument known as H in the beginning of the transmission was enough distracted by the experience, that the naming of the entity contacted by the instrument was not vibrated, nor was the source of all our desire and also its end phrase, "We come in the love and in the light of the one infinite Creator," and though we do not always speak these words at the beginning of each transmission, we did at that particular time, that is to say, the ones of Hatonn. We fear this instrument is going to sleep. We must pause.

(Pause)

I am Oxal. We wish to say at this time, for this call has come to us, that the love and light of the infinite Creator takes great measures of energy to probe into at any depth at all. The delicate balance between the positive and the negative move and turn, sway and twist within the distortions of each mind/body/spirit complex's universe, within each heart and each mind. For every excellent ideal and symbol, there lies upon just the other side of the coin, terror, need, ugliness and violence.

The drama of your third density is the drama of discovering duality and beginning the long trek toward balance. In this the student, the journeyer, the worshipper must choose one path to move, one face of the Creator to worship; one, and not the other. This is a most difficult choice. It is so difficult to make within your illusion that most do not begin to make that choice, but rather remain dancing about the bonfire of neutrality, tossing their garlands to and fro within the ethical and metaphysical universe, laughing, crying, hating and loving and moving neither towards the one great stage or the other, the glorious heavenly universe, or the equally glorious negative, each strong in its own way, each full of the Creator which is all things. Yet only by strong feeling, only by that feeling which this instrument would call worship, is either path traveled to the end.

We are those of the service-to-others path. We find that each within this circle has also advanced the cause of the great drama in the negative sense. Each has danced close and into the flaming fire of the glory and of the beauty of negative emotion and feeling. Each has in the mind and heart judged him or herself, each has been convicted and has lived within what your soul wishes to call hell, and each has for that very reason chosen. For when one path or the other begins to be intense, begins to move forward, then it is that the choice must be made, never in the happy middle of things, never around the bonfire.

Thus, as each travels along the path of service to others, let us say again what has been said often upon your planet. Let us respect and appreciate those circumstances of suffering, of judging the self, and of despair which have produced hearts and minds set with determination and persistence, but better yet with passion, the passion of experience and lessons learned and choices made. We ask each to respect that within the self which makes such a choice, to know that each will inevitably fail from time-to-time but that, the choice having been made, the life shall be, if such desire continues, a walk hand-in-hand with the Creator, for there is passion in the Creator for each of you, such a passion as you cannot imagine. We exalt in the joy of the love the Creator has for us, and we answered it with love and thanksgiving, and turn ever again to service to each other, and thereby to the Creator. And then in the end we turn to the Creator alone and see the Creator and know the One

We leave you at this time. We have been with you in sorrow, all those of us, those principles, entities, teachers and powers which move within the world of thought about your planet, within your metaphysical realms. We are losing transmission with this instrument. We are those of Oxal. We leave you in love and in light. Adonai. ✢

L/L Research

Sunday Meditation
November 15, 1987

Group question: Concerns wanderers, the difficulty that wanderers frequently encounter being within the third-density illusion, having to go through the forgetting process, and having some kind of a memory of previous existence and purpose for the current incarnation, yet running into, perhaps, problems in making that happen or manifesting it. And so forth.

(Carla channeling)

I am Q'uo. I greet you in the love and in the light of the one infinite Creator. It is a great privilege to be with you this evening, and we wish especially to greet those new to the group, new to the circle of this seeking, new to these particular vibrations. We bless and greet each. We would like to make a note at this point that we may have to pause in order to clear the breathing passages of this instrument. We hope you will be patient during these moments.

You have requested that we speak to you upon the subject of being wanderers. Perhaps we should begin by stating that the majority of your peoples did not arise from the planet, upon which you now enjoy existence, from second density, but have wandered in third density form to your planet, so that there is the archetypical or racial memory within quite the majority of those entities now incarnate upon your planet's surface who have come to finish their third-density experience from another place, another influence, another circumstance.

With this said, we wish to acknowledge first of all our compassion for the deep ache and loneliness of those who feel that they are strangers in a strange land. It is in no way a cowardly thing to feel the pangs of being where home is not. It is not an act of cowardice to wish for the climate and the friendly faces of a family half-remembered. Yet we speak to those who wish not merely to receive sympathy for their plight, but to learn more about how to celebrate that challenge and to rejoice in the time ahead.

Each of you has in your past either the experience or the sincere wish to experience the form of hands-on aid to needy people, which works such as your Peace Corps offers. In this organization, those who have much to teach aid those who have much to learn, both being equals in the experience, both learning, both teaching. Those who have had this experience most generally feel that the tasks, while arduous, have been most worthwhile. Such periods, however, are intense. To a wanderer, the entire incarnation is this type of experience. You will feel life more acutely moment by moment than others [who] are more comfortably lulled and distracted by the various gadgets and toys of your culture. Wanderers remain more of the time aware of the energies which riffle the waters of peaceful consciousness and break down ideals into ethics and ethics into situations.

But, my children, you came here, glad with the challenge of serving the Creator, and the key to moving gracefully through a sometimes distressing illusion is trust, trust in the greater self that is you, for before this incarnation, when you chose the manner of your being within this illusion, you created a place wherein you felt you could offer your love to the environment about you. Those people which you have met and will meet, those combinations of circumstance and people which trigger new beginnings, all of these things you laid up as treasures that during the incarnation you shall mine.

Further, you carry with you on the other side of the veil of conscious thought a level of consciousness which is tuned to a fuller love, because of your experiences before this incarnation. Your unconscious self, therefore, is uncommonly rich as a resource. It behooves wanderers, then, to pay especial attention to regular daily meditation, for the true self, which is your gift to a planet in need, lies waiting for you behind the door of conscious thought, within that unconscious part of your being wherefrom intuition and passion for love spring.

The conscious mind of any entity incarnate in third density is dealt the same approximate hand, as this instrument would say. Regardless of intelligence, each consciousness bears certain identifiable characteristics and can manipulate the tools of the culture. It is within your greater self, which is available to you largely through meditation and dreaming, that the harvest of your previous experience lies. And, as wanderers, each of you have excellent intuitions. However, without the trust in the self and the self's connection with the Creator, such resources forever lie a bit beyond the reach.

It is a difficult thing for one who is humble to perceive that each consciousness is a gift. Many are the times when one feels more like the before picture than the after picture, as this instrument would say, lacking in insight and seemingly powerless to aid a troubled planet. However, although we do not wish to interfere with your free will, we may say that as a general rule very few within your illusion are aware of just when they are working at their best in service to the one infinite Creator. You will find each time that you attempt to evaluate your service, that you have stopped the flow of that service. By this we mean not that it is not good to examine one's actions, but rather that it is an excellent idea to withhold judgment from the self.

Perhaps we may invoke the law of relativity upon the question of wanderers, wanderers such as the one which asked the question. Wanderers may have a greater treasure of experience on the unconscious level to bring to the drama of living the life within the illusion. Whatever the gifts that you have been born into incarnation with, it is this amount which you have to make prosper within this environment. Some of those who have arrived as wanderers have perhaps a relatively small amount of love and light compared to others. Those within third density who have not yet been able to deal with the strength of light necessary to move into higher density may have less. But in the currency of love, it matters not how much you have, but that your intention be to increase the flow of that infinite supply of love which is the result of your constant awareness of your contact with the infinite One.

As the instrument has previously stated on her own accord, we also state that the work of the wanderer is to exchange love in a completely open manner with those entities with which the wanderer comes in contact. All other activities are derivative of this service, for what is one who wanders except one who wishes to serve. The serving may be done in a very humble manner, yet if you serve one entity with purity of intention, it is as though you served the planet in its entirety. The difficulty within your conscious mind is that it does not seem as much a service to love another unconditionally as to form new social organizations or create some consciousness-raising project. We may say that those wanderers who choose these more public and dramatic life scenarios suffer in accordance with the magnitude of loneliness which renown brings. For the wanderer, it is a great blessing to be obscure.

Now let us move on to the greater realization that all who are conscious of self and conscious of the Creator are moving upon the same path, gazing at the same challenges. We ask you to think of yourselves as seeds. All that is is the Creator. You are the Creator. You are love. You speak and gesture and move in love, and you see love from all whom you meet. The distortions of love are many, so that love expresses itself often in negative forms, yet all are on the path, by the side of the path, sleeping by the side of the path, or somewhere in the vicinity of the path. It is impossible for that seed to be lost. You are very young expressions of the face of the Creator. Those who are wanderers will find it easier than those who have been moving through third density for the first time to make the choice of service to others. It will seem more obvious.

Thus, since you have made the choice, instinctively you are in the position of the older son. Now, those who are in the third density of this planet are in the position of the prodigal son. We refer to that parable in that holy work called the Bible, where the master known as Jesus described this prodigal son, this son who went away, taking his share of his father's wealth and disported himself in every desultory way, until he was penniless and humbled to the ground. The older son never left the father's side. Years later the older son gazes at the prodigal, limping home, hoping to be a slave in his father's house and happy for the chance. He has made the choice. He has come back to the positivity he left at birth. And the father blesses the prodigal with joy and laughter and feasting. But what about the older son? You wanderers, surely you can feel that plight. The older son says, "You never gave me a party, Father, you never made a fuss over me." And the father turns and says, "But everything I have is yours."

May we urge each wanderer to make the journey of the prodigal son in consciousness, not in action, to let the mind go blank, to start with a clean tablet and make that choice from the beginning, all the way through as a meditation, as a contemplation, as a prayer, and finally as a thanksgiving. For you shall not feel that you have come home to the kingdom of love until you have allowed yourself to experience the going away, the temptations, the failures, and the return as one who has had all assets of privilege stripped away. You see, it is fatal, spiritually, for a wanderer to put any particular emphasis upon this situation in terms of the expectation of increased closeness to the Creator or increased awareness of the Creator's will for you. Indeed, you must work harder, for you are only prodigal in your imagination, and it is very near to impossible for you to deny your link with the Creator.

Narrow your focus, my children, when these puzzlements come upon you and the discomfort of this illusion lies heavy upon your shoulders. You have come here to work. You have come here to carry the burden, a burden which is heavy, yet which is not more than you can bear. You have encased yourself in a very necessary and useful physical vehicle which effectively shields you from the awareness of your companions. For you are not alone. There are invisible forces which are with you, and those people whom you need to meet, you shall meet. Those thoughts of which you need to be aware shall come in front of you. Indeed, once trust is established between yourself and your whole self or higher self, you need but do that which is in front of you to do, moment by moment and day by day. And at the end of each day gaze back over the day and see where a smile, a word, a touch, or a sincere loyalty to an ideal has lightened the road for others.

How we wish we could take you within our vibratory web, that you might feel for a few moments that love without the baffling impediment of the physical vehicle, yet we cannot do this for you. You may, however, through meditation, find yourself upon holy ground and share heart-to-heart and hand-to-hand with the infinite Creator. My children, the Creator is a love that is astonishing in its intensity. The imagination reels at the infinity of creation. Yet this love is that which built, created, energized and enlivened all that there is with only a tiny portion of infinite energy. This is a love which is awakening within you, the love of the co-Creator for the Creator, the love of the child for the Father, the love of the beginning for the Source and the End. Center yourselves upon love and compassion. Attempt to intend well and to be harmless and above all to love each other. And when you consider yourself to have failed, grieve if you wish, but not overlong, for the intention is that which is recorded spiritually, the action within the illusion relatively incidental. We ask you to …

(Side one of tape ends.)

(Carla channeling)

We ask you to nurture the relationship betwixt yourself and the Creator, tuning, honing and intensifying the joy and love that you feel in communion with the One Who Is All, so that you may tap into the bubbling, joyous, free ecstasy which love is. This exercise of homing upon the Creator brings each entity, no matter what its vibratory level, to the highest level possible for that entity at that time. Each of us has still lessons to learn, and the source of the answer to the questions we have to ask, at whatever level they are, is the infinite Creator which is within each and every piece of consciousness. Trust yourself more and more deeply. Woo your own unconscious as does the lover the maiden, gently, lovingly and caressingly, and respect those things which you receive in dreams, visions and intuitions.

And above all, know that you are doing that which you came here to do. You cannot get far off track, for those forces within you which you devised before incarnation shall forever be giving you the proper vector toward the action that is appropriate. May your communion with infinite intelligence be ever more wonderful, and may your trust in each morning, each noontime, and each eventide be sufficient for you to do the will of your greater self, of that self which is closer to the Father and Mother of All That There Is. Each of you shall shine from within. May you also shine to yourselves. May you love and respect the Creator within you. Wanderer or native, these things are so, in our humble opinion.

This instrument is informing us that we have been talkative again, and we are sorry. It is a great joy to share thoughts with such a receptive group. Because you are so receptive, we wish especially to caution each to know that we are not infallible, but only your brothers and sisters somewhat more along a path than you, knowing the terrain, where the potholes are, where the rockslides might occur, and we come back to you, wanderers of our kind, in thought. We wish we could take every boulder out of your way and fill every treacherous piece of ground, so that you could walk straight and plain upon the path of seeking. Alas, we must watch you toil uphill and stumble down, become weary and find despair. Yet we and many others are right there with you in that despair, and if you request aid from the Comforter, such shall be offered to you immediately. You have only mentally to ask, and you will no longer be dealing with pain without help. Some call these entities guides, some call them the Holy Spirit. Whatever the name, the function is nurturing. For a wanderer this is sometimes vitally important.

Wanderer, in your agony, you shall comfort many; in your loneliness you shall share love, and every tear, every ache, every pain can be, if you respect these feelings, a crystallized bitter-sweet gift to the Creator, a memento of a dramatic play which seemed to have an unhappy ending. Trust that it is only play and that your true life-stream dances and rejoices. So in the end may wanderers reclaim within the illusion their deeper selves. Mourn first and then rejoice.

We would at this time transfer this contact to the one known as Jim, with thanks to this instrument. I am Q'uo.

(Jim channeling)

I am Q'uo, and greet each again in love and in light. At this time it is our privilege to offer ourselves in the attempt to answer those queries which may yet remain upon the minds, again reminding each that we offer that which is our opinion, offered joyfully, yet not infallibly. Is there a query with which we may begin?

D: Do we create the illusion by our own approach? Do we create the density that makes it hard for us to see the true light, or is it what we've come into?

I am Q'uo, and the answer to this query is one which is not easy to explain, yet it is that which you, as a greater portion of yourself—which is frequently called by many of your peoples the higher self—have created upon a cooperative basis in a specified and refined fashion, beginning with that which is given, shall we say, by the Logos, the creative intelligence of the one Creator. As you move into the incarnation within this illusion, you move into that which has been prepared for you by a greater portion of your self, and according to the way in which you have programmed your biases and attitudes for learning and service, you perceive and experience the creation in a certain fashion which is unique unto yourself. Thus, you are responsible both for the creation and the illusion within which you move and the manner by which you perceive it, in order that you might learn in such and such a fashion and also serve others thusly.

Is there another query, my brother?

D: Is it our job to untangle the illusion, or are we supposed to simply work within it?

I am Q'uo. That which is your responsibility within this illusion you have before the incarnation set for yourself. Thus, you shall move through the incarnation within the illusion in a manner which allows you to utilize each facet of the illusion in a manner which will aid those goals which you have set for yourself. A portion of each entity's incarnation is given to the learning and is oriented towards the growth of the consciousness of the self. Another portion, which increases in ratio as the consciousness of the self grows, is given to the service of others, so that that which is learned by the self might be shared as the fruit of the incarnation with other selves. Thus as you learn and as you serve, you become yourselves transformed by that which is your awareness, and as your awareness and as yourselves become transformed, the illusion about you is seen with new eyes and is itself transformed by your perception of it as yet a greater portion of the one Creator knowing Itself through each other portion of Itself.

Is there a further query, my brother?

D: No, that made very good sense. Thank you.

I am Q'uo, and we thank you, my brother. Is there another question?

Carla: *(Carla has been coughing.)* I know the physical reasons why it's difficult to keep infection down in hospitals, but most people in hospitals are not sick with contagious diseases. It's almost like comparing a hospital to a hotel, and people don't get sick in hotels, whereas it's quite common for patients to pick up a bug in a hospital. I was wondering if there was any metaphysical aspect to this, somewhat of psychic greeting going on when people's immune systems are down and stress levels are high? I don't believe that germs have any polarity, but can they be directed by unfriendly polarities?

I am Q'uo, and we feel that we might best respond to this query by suggesting that the ground for such infections is prepared by the mind which has fed certain concepts that then reflect within the body complex, often by means of reducing the immune defense system so that the condition of what you would call the disease of one form or another is able to find an opening and work in a fashion which corresponds to the pattern of thought expressed by the entity. Within the environment which you describe may be found many entities who have found the need to experience an imbalance of the mental complex to the degree which would then allow the physical vehicle to reflect this distortion in a manner which then would make it apparent to the conscious mind that certain distortions were in need of attention. Thus, the mind reflects to itself that upon which attention needs be given in order that greater balance and harmony within the mind/body/spirit complex might be achieved.

May we speak in any further fashion, my sister?

Carla: *(Inaudible)*.

I am Q'uo. Is there another query?

Carla: Not from me.

C: I'd like to have a better understanding of what happens inside the consciousness of those that our culture has labeled schizophrenic.

I am Q'uo. It is difficult to give the general description to a condition which is quite unique unto many of those who experience this splitting of the personality. However, a few comments may be given that will hopefully add some understanding to this condition.

The entity which faces the challenges within the incarnation which seem to overwhelm the ability to resolve them may, in some cases, choose to face these challenges with a smaller and smaller portion of the personality, with the larger portion choosing an alternate means of experiencing the nature of the illusion which the entity would find more able to cope with. In some cases the entity finds the necessity of dividing the personality yet again in order that various portions of the deeper self may be allowed expression without the need to interact with other portions of the same self which are in basic conflict, each with the other, upon a certain point.

This conflict, then, is that which the entity has found it unable to resolve in the normal, shall we say, fashion. Therefore, the compartmentalizing of different portions of the personality allows the entity to express basic features of the personality without the need to bring these features into harmonious balance with other facets of the personality which are more aware of the basic conflict. Yet, in each expression there will be the distortion of the characteristics expressed that is due to the primary conflict remaining unresolved. Thus, in each personality or portion thereof thusly expressed will be found a faint trace or trail that will lead to the conflict for the entity to travel eventually in order that the conflict might be harmoniously resolved.

Is there another query my sister?

C: What would be the most beneficial way to help this type of person in the healing process?

I am Q'uo. Again, our lot is the generality, for each case is unique. The offering of the self in unconditional love and acceptance of the other self provides the basic environment of healing in which the entity experiencing the splitting or separating of portions of its personality might find helpful. The acceptance of such an entity, given in an unqualified manner, will provide the support that is needed to encourage the revealing of the primary conflict by any portion of the personality which is most vulnerable or moved or sensitive to the giving of the love. Thus, the one experiencing the separation of personality may begin through some portion of its personality to move into an harmonious resolution with other portions of the personality.

May we speak in any further fashion my sister?

C: No, thank you.

I am Q'uo, and we thank you, my sister. Is there any further query at this time?

Questioner: Yes. Among the people whom I know there seem to be two theories, that is, that everything is going along fine as it should on the planet, and the other theory is that something's horribly wrong, evidenced by the fact of torment in so many people, children included, especially in the third world, the poisoning of the planet and the disruption of the planet's surface. Is something horribly wrong? And if so, are we supposed to do something about it?

I am Q'uo, and, my brother, we may suggest that the illusion, in which you find yourselves at this time, is one which seems most disharmonious and in need of great attention. We may suggest that the illusion has offered to many the opportunity to learn lessons great and small, intense in many ways, difficult, yet not without solution. By experiencing what seems to be the greatest separation of one entity from another, may each eventually find the bond between each that reveals the unity of all creation. It is for each within the illusion to take those opportunities for growth and service that will provide the further opportunities for expanding the realization of unity for each entity.

Thus, we look upon your illusion and those of your peoples which inhabit it as a child that is progressing through the lower grades of a school. There may be many disagreements among the pupils within the classroom and many, shall we say, bloody noses upon the playground, yet each shall learn much from the illusion and continue forward in the schooling, moving the boundaries further and further to include those about one, and eventually through the seeming separation of one from another, to begin to resolve those illusions of separations in order that each may look upon the face of the Creator, not only within the mirror, but across all boundaries which seem to separate nations and entities.

May we speak in any further fashion, my brother?

Questioner: Well, what about the specter of atomic war? Is it not possible for our world to be obliterated in that fashion?

I am Q'uo, and we shall speak briefly here, for we find that there is the need to bring the session to an ending.

There is the opportunity for the resolution of energies set into motion from times far distant in the past of many races upon your planetary influence. The seeds of these difficulties have once again found their flowering within your current illusion, and are being worked upon in their current manifestation by those entities which have been responsible for their sowing in times and places far distant.

There is room within the universe of the Creator for all possibilities. The use of the atomic energy which you have described is a portion of the creative energy of the one Creator which can be utilized in many fashions. The destructive capability of this energy has been released upon your planetary surface within your recent past and is that primary concern which now offers the nations of your world the path by which the resolution of difficulties might be achieved.

We beg your indulgence at this time. We find that there is the need to bring this meeting to an end, for there is the energy which is being drained at this time. We thank each for inviting our presence, and we leave each in the love and in the light of the one infinite Creator. We are known to you as those of Q'uo. ✣

L/L Research

L/L Research is a subsidiary of Rock Creek Research & Development Laboratories, Inc.

P.O. Box 5195
Louisville, KY 40255-0195

www.llresearch.org

Rock Creek is a non-profit corporation dedicated to discovering and sharing information which may aid in the spiritual evolution of humankind.

ABOUT THE CONTENTS OF THIS TRANSCRIPT: This telepathic channeling has been taken from transcriptions of the weekly study and meditation meetings of the Rock Creek Research & Development Laboratories and L/L Research. It is offered in the hope that it may be useful to you. As the Confederation entities always make a point of saying, please use your discrimination and judgment in assessing this material. If something rings true to you, fine. If something does not resonate, please leave it behind, for neither we nor those of the Confederation would wish to be a stumbling block for any.

CAVEAT: This transcript is being published by L/L Research in a not yet final form. It has, however, been edited and any obvious errors have been corrected. When it is in a final form, this caveat will be removed.

© 2009 L/L Research

Intensive Meditation
November 19, 1987

(Carla channeling)

I am Laitos. I greet you in the love and the light of the infinite Creator. We have had much difficulty getting the attention of the one known as D, as we find this instrument to be placed in a position wherein the promptings of the subconscious mind are rigidly enough controlled that subconscious thought is not being given free flow into the conscious mental apparatus used for making decisions. We would suggest that the instrument known as D, as well as each within the circle, realize and give value to the shyly hidden offerings of the subconscious mind, for deep concepts arise within the intuitive portion of the conscious mind only if there is a certain level of coordination betwixt the two minds, a certain mutual respect and conscious awareness each of the other.

We would like to speak this evening about love. We choose this subject not in spite of its familiarity or its centrality, but because of it. We have a desire to express enough consciously known principles as concepts to the new instrument that it will, by simple repetition of exercises, each concept being one exercise, regain the feeling of some small confidence within the one known as D.

That which each is is far other than the conscious mind can hope. These concepts which we channel due to your service are mere surface paint which glistens in the sun upon the surfaces beneath which lie the substantial metal of beingness. The process of channeling is a process of service to others. The entity which one brings to that service needs to be respected in its entirety. Both those things which are civilized, learned behaviors, and so forth, and those things which are archaic and seemingly vestigial, that is, instinct and the force deep within the mystery of the inner being, which is that very stuff which created all that there is within the infinite universes, sink down, then, within the conscious mind, becoming more and more [aware], more and more attuned to the slightest lifting of the veil between conscious and subconscious.

We would speak, as we said, of love. We would offer familiar words. We would speak of that love which goes beyond human expression, that love which men seek after without any proof of its existence. We speak of a Creator whose very nature is love. Each particle of consciousness has that seed of love at its center, known as the birthright of what this instrument would call divinity. Such words are not adequate, yet language is a difficult and limiting way to communicate. Before all else was, love is, and when the last sun flares into nova and shrinks into ultimate gravity, love still is, the Creator, endlessly brooding upon infinities, *(inaudible)*. And yet, this vast and mysterious love may be expressed within your illusion.

We will transfer to the one known as D at this time, asking as usual that the instrument accept thoughts as they arise, speak them, and be unafraid, refraining always from analysis during the exercise. I am Laitos. I transfer now.

(D channeling)

I am Laitos, and greet you again, our greeting in light and love being our way of answering your challenge. We wish to be channels of the infinite love that comes from one source, conduits by performing our humble service of love, brought from that source to the beings of third dimensions.

…

(The rest of D's channeling is not transcribed.)

(Carla channeling)

I am Laitos, and I am again with this instrument. We would like to thank the one known as D for his work and his willingness. We continue to feel that we are making good progress. The instrument will wish to know whether the variances in level of relaxation affect the channeling work, and perhaps the instrument need only remember the varying state of mind during this channeling exercise while gazing at or listening to the words to discover how very helpful it is to maintain a single point of focus during the channeling, for neither worrying nor considering—that is, neither worrying about what has been said nor considering what shall be said—and focusing only upon the immediacy, the breathing, the heartbeat, the slight but audible sound of the pressure of blood in the ear, the night sounds, all those things which go into being in the present and focused upon an inner listening.

We suggest as an exercise that the instrument work with imagery in meditation, holding shapes and colors within the mind for as long as possible. The instrument should not be discouraged at discovering the willfulness of the mind which wishes not to concentrate upon one image. A few seconds at first shall be a challenge to sustain. Yet this type of concentration is most helpful to the work of channeling, and where the conscious mind in its restless intelligence is used to roving in thought, there must needs be means of disciplining that very helpful thing, the intellect, and stilling its forward pace for the purpose of experiencing the present moment, as would one without the rational mind.

We do, however, continue to emphasize that the rational mind be tuned carefully before the control is given over to the intuitive self, and further we suggest that the powers of analysis are most helpful in revealing the experience of the intuitive mind and its fruit in collaboration with us who are of the principle of love. We feel that the encouragement which we offer the instrument is to an extent blocked by the instrument's dissatisfaction, and we ask that the instrument set aside that dissatisfaction or need to please the self, for in this matter the process of learning to serve as a vocal channel is greatly helped by a veritable lack of interest in the excellence of one's own work when one is not within the channeling mode of perception.

What we are saying is that this phenomenon is most natural and is in fact a portion of the birthright of the intuitive mind, that portion of the mind which is the largest, that being the frontal minds of your brain, yet being by far the least respected and the least used by your culture. Intuition vanishes upon attention and advances upon a relaxed peripheral view. Those who see intuitively see without focus and speak without hindrance, so many learn to channel themselves in spontaneity and joy and some few discipline that faculty for use as a medium through which impersonal principles may find [an] attuned gateway which resonates in energy with itself and which can thus be used to be of mutual service to those who may find value in words of love.

At this time we would transfer to the one known as Jim that this instrument may field queries and speak further. We transfer at this time. I am Laitos.

(Jim channeling)

I am Laitos, and greet each again through this instrument. We realize that we have exercised the one known as Carla and the one known as D to an extensive degree this evening, hopefully providing both exercise and information to each instrument. At this time we would offer ourselves in the attempt to speak upon any topic which those present may find the value in the asking. Is there a query to which we may speak?

D: Is what you were just saying about concern for the excellence of the material or for the excellence of the channeling meant to … I'm a little confused as far as my own efforts to get your feedback and make use of it, and whether that whole effort to do that through these questions is somehow misguided. I need a little clarification about that still. Does it show a wrong sort of concern of mine, for instance, in my questions in the past about the details of my own channeling?

I am Laitos, and, my brother, we would encourage your queries for as long as the information which is given in response to them has meaning to you. It is eventually hoped that each new instrument, through the exercise of its vocal channeling ability and through the resolution of difficulties and queries, both from our source and from those serving as teachers, might provide the necessary confidence that will allow a new instrument to proceed fearlessly and even foolishly in the chosen art. Thus, we are happy to speak to any query which you may find necessary in order to enhance your own understanding of the process that is now being actualized within your being, my brother.

Is there another query?

D: Well, I still don't quite understand what you were saying a short while ago about concern for the performance except during the performance. I've kind of lost my question, but I got the impression that the concerns that prompt me to ask about my performance were somehow misguided and … I'm sorry, I don't know how to ask this question. I do have another, however, and that is just very simply, if tonight I completed my channeling of you at the point at which you were ready to end it. I've felt in the past somewhat as if I stopped it because of my own fatigue and tonight I felt no fatigue, I just felt …

(Side one of tape ends.)

(Jim channeling)

I am Laitos, and am again with this instrument. We would speak to your first query, if we may, before addressing the second. We suggest the concern for the excellence of the effort be the focus of one's attention previous to and then following the exercise of the vocal channeling ability, and the giving over of any concerns for such excellence while one is serving as a vocal channel, for it is at that time that the analytical mind does not serve one well, for it is that analysis which is the greatest stumbling block for the new or old instrument. It is at that time that such analysis is given over to a surrender that will allow a clearing of the mind in order that impressions of those such as we are might be transmitted through the instrument.

In regards to your second query, we were quite happy to have been able to utilize your instrument for the greater portion of the time which we felt was appropriate for the exercise of a new instrument before either physical or mental fatigue tends to remove the one-pointed focus that is so critical in being able to transmit concepts as they occur and are perceived within the mind complex. Thus, we this evening were able to utilize your instrument to a greater degree than we have previously and are very pleased to be able to make this report.

May we speak further, my brother?

D: I appreciate that. I really was wondering if I responded to your ceasing to come through me, or if you would have gladly—if you were continuing to attempt to stimulate concepts that I had become just unable to respond to?

I am Laitos, and we were able to stimulate those concepts which we were utilizing both from our own source and those which we wished to choose from your experience and framework of conceptualization, shall we say, for we wish to use that which each instrument has to offer as an unique portion of its own seeking to enhance the message which is always and ever the same. Each seeker will refine the shared path of seeking in a manner which enriches that path when shared with another. Thus, this evening we were able to blend your offering with our own in a manner which we found of a balanced nature.

May we speak further, my brother?

Carla: I think what he's asking is, "Was the next that you were going to transmit that you were going to transfer?"

I am Laitos. We had some further information available that we could have transmitted had the instrument's focus been steadier at that point. However, it was beginning to falter and there was then seen the need for the transfer of the contact in order that the new instrument not become disheartened that it was not maintaining the validity that it had previously demonstrated.

May we speak further, my sister?

Carla: Not on my account. I spoke only for D. You need anything further, D?

D: I have another question. In weeks past you and—I'm sorry I don't remember whether it was Hatonn or who—made the analogy of channeling with catching a baseball and throwing it in order to free the hands in order to catch the ball again. In other words, to receive a word or a few words, speak them, in order to free the mind to receive more. And yet it's also been stressed that you work through stimulating concepts on the subconscious level through which we find the words. And I see these two ideas being somewhat in conflict with each other. Can you resolve that and help me to understand a little more deeply just what this process is?

I am Laitos. Whether the words which are perceived are words which we transmit in a word by word fashion or words which the instrument fashions in order to describe a concept which has been transmitted, the idea of throwing or speaking these words fearlessly is that which is helpful to the instrument, for the passing of the words is that which clears the way for further words, be they those which we have distinctly transmitted or those which the instrument has found to be the most nearly appropriate to describe the concept which we have transmitted as well. We utilize from time to time combinations of the concept and the word by word transmission as is most efficacious for each instrument. Most will find the concept means of transmission the easiest to utilize in the beginning of the service as a vocal instrument, with the addition of the word by word method of contact being that which is undertaken at a later or more advanced stage of serving as a vocal instrument.

May we speak further, my brother?

D: No, thank you very much.

I am Laitos. We thank you once again, my brother. Is there a further query at this time?

D: None from me.

Carla: Thank you, Laitos.

I am Laitos, and we also wish to thank each for the great offering of attention and service which we have experienced this evening. We appreciate the opportunity to speak our humble words through each instrument, and find a great joy in being able to transmit concepts through both the old, shall we say, and the new instruments in order that there might be some small enlightening of service and of the mental preparation for service in each instrument. We ourselves gain a great deal of experience as we work with each instrument, and feel that that which you offer to us is far greater than you can imagine, for we learn as we teach to be clearer channels for the love and light of the one Creator.

At this time we shall again thank each instrument, and, as always, leave each in the love and in the light of the one infinite Creator. We are known to you as those of Laitos. Adonai, my friends. Adonai. ☙

Sunday Meditation
November 29, 1987

Group question: On Breatharianism, the living on the air or sunlight, the prana, rather than on solid foods or liquids. What is it necessary for the third density human body to live upon in truth? Is it always necessary to live on the normal food and water, or at some point is it possible to live without these particular ingredients and to live upon a more pure substance that we would call air or prana?

(Carla channeling)

I am Q'uo, a member of the Confederation of Planets in the Service of the Infinite Creator. I and my brothers and sisters greet you in the love and in the light of the one infinite Creator. With joy we welcome each and express our love and blessing for each, especially the one known as C, whom we have not seen in this circle for some weeks. May we say how grateful we are to be called to your group and to be allowed to offer our humble opinions in regard to the questions which you may find it helpful to ask. Know that our journey into your dimension is for only one reason, and that is to be of service to you. Thus, should any of our words constitute a stumbling block or simply seem not to ring with truth for you, we sincerely ask that these words be disregarded, for all of us are citizens of consciousness, studying the Creator in ourselves, and ourselves in the Creator. As fellow travelers, we greet you in joy.

We find that the query this evening has to do with purifying the life experience, most especially focusing upon the body experience during physical incarnation, that it may reflect a higher spiritual reality. That which is called Breatharianism is not foolish, nevertheless the principles involved are misunderstood. Let us look at this question one layer at a time to attempt to unravel the seeming paradoxes of the concept that one may live upon air, not taking food or water, and yet survive within your physical illusion.

Firstly, given the state of consciousness normal to third-density entities, we feel that it is not desirable that entities set themselves the goal of attempting to live without the bread and water which is food for the body. A good deal of damage can be done by one who sees a symptom of a condition as having a life of its own, and those who indeed within your illusion do live upon air or that which is called prana, divinely filled air, do so through grace and not by design.

There are those who come into incarnation with memories of music, and before anyone could expect excellence from such entities, they are astounding concert audiences. Others have other talents equally astounding, each in its own way. There are those who come into this experience with certain key memories untouched, and because of these carry-overs from previous incarnations, these entities are able, by availing themselves of grace, to work with the connections between your physical body and your spiritual or electrical body, so that that which feeds the finer body then rains manna down upon the physical.

We wish to emphasize that such a talent is not that of which one can be proud, nor is it an attainment which can be earned. By grace each of you remembers certain experiences, certain skills, certain biases, and because of these particular memories the life pattern is shaped in such a way that the entity may manifest these gifts and add to the great store of beautiful, inspiring and impressive artifacts. When one speaks of the gifts of personality, one often speaks of artifacts that are as ephemeral as life within your illusion. And when those people who share non-physical gifts end the physical existence, only the memory of such grace-filled individuals remains. This is the first layer of gazing at the thought of living upon air.

The next layer of investigation of this is to gaze at the question of what physical use it might be to body consciousness as it too reaches for the Creator to attempt to be able finally to fast and fill the vehicle with only the most light-filled plenum of air.

Actually there are two decisions to be made in this regard. Firstly, it is very true that for the benefit of the physical vehicle, the selection of foods ingested is not only important to health, but also creates a certain atmosphere for doing spiritual work. We find that within your culture, as we believe that each is already aware, that excess food, excess protein, and excess carbohydrate intake create the form within which the spirit does not find gracefulness, liveness and movement. In other words, it is quite true that eating of heavily weighted foodstuffs such as high protein meats and greatly refined carbohydrate armors the physical being against the finer concepts which the mind and spirit yearn for. The food itself weighs the entity down physically. The anticipatory hunger and constant yearning for food hampers and befuddles the mind and spiritual complexes, and, thus distracted, the seeking entity finds the attitude towards food an attitude which is over against and unhelpful to a conscious acceleration of spiritual evolution.

It is indeed well to eat lightly, sparingly and naturally. These things are truisms, yet it is worth repeating from our point of view, so that one who wishes to become more pure in the eating need not be swayed by those who feel threatened by such a search for purity.

Secondly, it is well to know that the process of physical creation of a higher intention creates an improved atmosphere for doing emotional, mental and spiritual work of a similarly purifying nature. We alluded earlier to those who find certain gifts or skills quite easy to display. This is so also with those who seek the one infinite Creator. It is well not to gaze at another's journey or to compare one's footsteps with those of another. Perhaps another person has attained great compassion, and perhaps this entity is stocky and shapeless within the body. This is possible. It is also possible for an entity to eat and drink only those items which are most highly recommended for spiritually oriented entities to assist in the purification and simplicity of the life experience. Many of these people shall be healthy, slender and quite in the dark comparatively in the spiritual and emotional sense. It is a path to be picked up by those who feel its call, to place the physical body in purer and purer circumstances both inwardly and outwardly. It is not the only path. It is one valid tool which any seeker may use in order to sharpen and sensitize emotion, heart and spirit.

Let us now gaze at the concept of prana or breath. Your creation and mine is a plenum, a vast infinity completely full of that light which is life itself in first manifestation. To breathe this prana-filled plenum of air is to breathe in oneself the primal love of the Creator. To exhale is to exhale all that within which is to be eschewed, eliminated and cast away. Other organs do this for the solid food and drink which entities upon your planet enjoy. The careful, intentional breathing, on the other hand, deals with catching up the stress and stale thought, the tired emotion and keen sorrow of the day.

Thus, to breathe is to inhale life itself; to exhale is to deliver oneself of the past, so that always it is an helpful exercise to breathe intentionally, taking great draughts of life-filled prana into the lungs, into every cell of the body, and then with every hope bent towards the successful completion of this exercise, to breathe out all those dark and stale experiences of the day, with each breath gaining in light and being lifted up from the darkness created within one's own heart, emotions, mind, spirit.

It is especially helpful to have a safe and secure place within which to do this exercise, and it is recommended by us that those who wish to do this intentional breathing incorporate this exercise within the meditative period, perhaps at the beginning, as a kind of visualized mantra. For that which is done with the physical body, highly positive though that thing may be, is completely subject to the free will of yourself. You may breathe in all the air you wish and breath out again, but if the desire and visualization is not there and if there is no meditative state within which to anchor and ground this experience, the breathing will remain for you, as perhaps other things have, a kind of spiritual playtoy to take out and examine and then put away again.

Very, very few entities dwelling upon the surface of your planet at this time are able to live by breath alone. Those who do, do so by grace, that agency by which impossible things occur naturally, that agency which is one of the great primal distortions of a kindly Creator. We go now to the inner layers of the question of food for the spiritual self. The teacher known to you as Jesus the Christ fasted often, wishing to achieve not a pure life so much as an altered state of consciousness wherein the physical entity dropped away from consciousness and a union with the Father became possible. Often the Father came to the one known as Jesus in the form of what is known as the Devil or Satan. This is because any attempt to be of excellent spiritual devotion alerts the attention of those who do not wish that such pure light shine within the world which negatively oriented entities believe is already their own. To the one known as Jesus, fasting was simply a means of altering the consciousness and building more and more the tested and sure bond this entity found with the Father, whose Son he always felt that he was.

It is not in fasting precisely that our recommendations lie, but rather in a shift of focus, an alteration in our use of vocabulary, for the one known as Jesus the Christ stated during one confrontation with that portion of the Creator known as Satan, that man does not live by bread alone, but rather from every word which falls from the mouth of the Creator. This entity was expressing a principle, and the entity's use of the word "word," when saying that man lives by every word of the Father, was intended to be that which we would call the Logos or love.

There lives within each man and woman and child within creation the capacity for dwelling in realms of light, not only in those fragrant fields which await in larger life beyond the grave, but also and more importantly, at this time during this experience this involves a change of consciousness. Thus, we suggest that there is a food for which you hunger and for which you are starving. There is a drink which shall finally quench the thirst. This food and this drink is love, the Word, and you are seeking to become, as did the entity known as Jesus the Christ, the Son of Man, one who lives upon the Word of love.

The nature of physical existence is that of limitation and finite dimension. And those who seek that bread which no entity can have except by grace often become greedy and acquisitive, hoping to store up the love that made all of us, that Source to which we shall return. Yet this heavenly manna, this word, this love cannot be stored, but rather can only be gathered one day at a time. Thus, the one who wishes to live and think and feel more purely must turn not once but each and every one of your days to the seeking of that heavenly food and that paradisial drink, for love exists within the present moment. It is not a part of space/time in its fullest sense, but rather a part of time, that time being the time which is behind all illusion and which is infinitely and eternally the present moment.

We offer exercises in closing, simple breathing exercises which may aid in the deepening of meditation. Visualize these exercises as the taking in of the physical manifestation of love, and tune yourself by intending to exhale each and every negative thought and feeling, stress and worry. These exercises are two, and are known to your peoples. The first exercise is the quick breathing with the emphasis upon the outbreath. This breathing is done through the mouth and may be done very rapidly to build up a great sense of the fullness and beauty of creation. Yet in breath there is motion, and in motion there is a lack of attention.

The second exercise following directly upon the ending of the first is merely the completely indrawn breath, the closing of the throat by the swallowing, and then the listening to the self at rest, full of life and breath, yet not now in motion. A very helpful environment is created during those few seconds or minutes during which you do not breathe. The great amount of prana is distributed to each cell within the body, and the outbreath at the last may flush clean the entire system of those chemical and muscular distortions from comfort which may block spiritual seeking by mechanical means.

In closing, we wish to iterate that the process of spiritual evolvement may be aided by what one may call the teacher's aid such as the purification of diet or the disciplines of prayer. However, no amount of study can invoke the grace by which the spirit becomes able to allow the electrical body to receive that food and drink and thus hold the physical being in thrall. It is not a goal to be attempted in earnest, but rather a direction which may be suggested merely because those things which are important to one can be deduced by discovering the amount of time and energy associated with their procurement. Thus, a simple and natural eating, perhaps even a reduction in eating if such is deemed helpful, may be encouraged. All forms of purifying the physical body are helpful insofar as they engage the consciousness of the individual spirit.

That which is truly and inalterably helpful in every case is the turning of the trust of the spirit towards that manna which cannot be controlled, which cannot be grasped for or hoarded, but which is there in abundance for those who know and proclaim its abundance. The quality and the quantity of the manna which feeds the spirit is very much determined by the seeker itself, by the level of desire the seeker has to become a purer vessel for love and light, by the simplicity for innocence of the firm belief in that which is unseen. It is to the mind an insult to declare that something unseeable may be the food the spirit needs.

(Side one of tape ends.)

(Carla channeling)

Work with this in meditation, and joyfully rejoice in the manna of the present moment, knowing that in this way you are fed as is the prodigal son of your Bible. Not because you have earned it or because it belongs to you, although you certainly have earned it and it certainly belongs to you, but these are not spiritual thoughts.

The spiritual reason for a gradually improved resolution of third-density existence is grace, that word which suggests many things to many people, but which we mean to be understood as that bridge wherein the infinite generosity of life may be channeled into the energy web of your spiritual being. In seeking for the breath of life, for manna, you seek the Kingdom of Heaven which lies all about you, and that which you seek you shall most certainly find.

Whatever your level of seeking, whatever your pace of seeking, we wish you well, and would be with you always during your meditative periods should you request us to join you in your meditation. This instrument informs me that I have gone on speaking far too long, and we know that she is not scolding us, but we are apologetic. However, the information requested was requested with a very high level of seeking, and it was our desire to offer a small amount of that spiritual manna which can be uttered by the breath forming those symbolic representations called words, which are metaphors for consciousness. We would at this time transfer this contact to the one known as Jim. We leave this instrument with thanks and in love and light. We are Q'uo.

(Jim channeling)

I am Q'uo, and we greet each again in love and light. At this time we are hopeful that we might be of further service by attempting to respond to any queries which may be upon the minds of those gathered this evening. We are grateful to have this opportunity to refine our service in a manner which is more personally suited to those present. If there is a query with which we may begin, we would be honored to do so.

Carla: I have a food-related question. Number one, do people who eat a lot of meat have special problems when it comes to spiritualizing the consciousness? And number two, why is it necessary for channels like myself who get involved in especial contact like our contact with Ra, for the channel to eat lots of meat in order to avoid losing so much weight so as to become unhealthy?

I am Q'uo, and we shall begin with the first portion. The entity who seeks to provide the nourishment to the physical vehicle that the meat protein offers may find that there are some difficulties in the assimilation of this substance in direct proportion to the belief that the entity holds concerning those substances which are desirable for one who seeks in the spiritual realm and those which are not desirable. Thus, the belief of the entity is the primary concern which governs the ease of the physical vehicle's assimilation of this form of protein.

There is within the physical vehicle of third density the construction of the digestive tract which also mitigates against the over-indulgence, shall we say, in the meat products, for the digestive tract is one which is formed in a manner which is more prepared to digest the simpler proteins in the form of the grain and dairy products than it is to digest the meat protein. The intentions, the attitudes, and the desires of the entity in regards to the food substances ingested are of an overriding importance, for that which an entity is at heart is more a product of what the entity believes and the strength of that belief than it is what the entity ingests as a foodstuff.

In your own case, my sister, the partaking in the work of service to others through means of serving as an instrument for the contact with those known as Ra, which utilized the trance manner of communication, was one which required a somewhat harsh toll upon the physical vehicle, and due to the gross nature of this toll—that is, the loss of weight—the means by which this would most easily be alleviated was also gross in nature, that is, the suggested ingestion of the higher quality animal protein in order that your physical vehicle might be able to maintain its more normal weight configuration in a manner which would be the least taxing upon its digestive system, considering the alternatives available for the gaining and maintaining of the physical weight.

May we speak in any further fashion, my sister?

Carla: No, thank you.

I am Q'uo, and we thank you, my sister. Is there another query?

Carla: How long should one breathe like that before one holds one's breath, the way you described earlier?

I am Q'uo. The length of time is of less importance than the feeling of a subjective nature which one will experience that tells one that the vitality that [has] been accentuated by the breathing is at a peak point, shall we say. It is at this point that the breath then may be held in order that this vitality might then be observed and experienced.

May we speak further, my sister?

Carla: What about air pollution? Is it better spiritually to do this exercise in a place where the air is purer? Or does pollution have anything to do with prana?

I am Q'uo, and though there is no connection between the life force or prana within the air and its physical pollutants, as you call them, for the comfort of the one performing these exercises it might be suggested that the most harmonious environment be sought for the practice of such exercises, be that environment in your out-of-doors or within a certain room within the domicile.

May we speak further, my sister?

Carla: Only one more question of my insatiable curiosity, and I do apologize for keeping you, but you used Jesus as an example, forty days and forty nights out in the wilderness—he did that a couple of times in the Bible, and who knows what before or after—but what you suggested was that a significant part of his experience of fasting in order to purify the self and spend more time on holy ground, let us say, by the simple nature of things he would come in contact not once but several times with temptations to move in a self-aggrandizing or satanic, as in negative, spiritual way. Is this something that people going on a long fast need to realize ahead of time and sort of be prepared to deal with as one always deals with psychic greetings?

I am Q'uo, and in some degree, my sister, this is true for all who seek within the manner of fasting and of seeking to refine the purity of one's own seeking. It is often a common temptation for an entity who seeks the keys to purification through the fasting to look upon the self as one which is indeed advanced and perhaps more advanced or better than the other selves which surround it. Within this concept of pride may come the further temptations to act upon this feeling.

Thus, it is well for each who seeks the keys to purification to take with the self the humility to see the self within the great picture of the cosmos as one grain of sand upon the beach of time and space, in order that the pitfalls of pride and the accompanying difficulties which spring therefrom might be avoided.

May we speak further, my sister?

Carla: No, thank you, Q'uo.

I am Q'uo, and again we thank you, my sister. Is there another query?

(Pause)

I am Q'uo, and we find that we have, for this gathering, exhausted those queries which we thank each for offering to us, whether spoken or unspoken. We are grateful for the opportunity to share our humble experience with those who would seek to enhance their own journey of seeking by the sharing of our words and experience. We shall take our leave of this group at this time, leaving each, as always, in the love and in the light of the one infinite Creator. We are known to you as those of Q'uo. Adonai, my friends. Adonai. ✦

L/L Research

Message from Calenda
December 5, 1987

(Carla channeling)

(This was channeled from Calenda during the regular time for channeling from the Holy Spirit.)

I am Calenda. I greet you in the love and the light of the one infinite, perfect, omnipresent, omniscient, omnipotent Creator. We greet you as those who glow with the crystalline purity and who see those emanations from yourselves.

Woe, woe. You line the treasure boxes of your inward storage with the archives of mediocrity, with fashion and news.

I am Calenda. A voice who calls the true jewel to awaken within. I wish to be your walking stick upon the path. I wish to join my ceaseless prayer with the murmuring of all those within your race who pray incessantly, night and day, casting themselves upon that dark mystery of deity. Perhaps my voice has no use other than as an interesting friend who is new, is interesting. Yet, we burn within with the glory of compassion and with the joy of the yearning and adoration we feel for the marvelous tract, this heavenly pilgrimage, this journey within. We, too, are on that path.

We are sorry we have importuned this instrument, but the instrument [was] able to pick up our contact, something not often occurring, and we wished to share our love and our celebration of all that is.

We of Calenda leave you in the love and the light of the One. ✤

Intensive Meditation
December 9, 1987

(Carla channeling)

I am Hatonn. I greet each in the circle in the love and the light of the One and the Creator. May we say, as always, when we meet with yourselves what a great privilege it is to be allowed to share our opinions with you. And, indeed, we can not stress often enough, or severely enough, that these teachings are opinions. We have, in our way, developed a far greater and simpler technology. We have memory of each density and consequently we are most aware that the use of words is highly ambivalent within the channel, in regards to its contact. It is as though one were to clean a kitchen and scrub down each surface until it all was scoured clean. The surfaces may seem most fair, yet if the faucet runs with polluted water, of what excellence is the cleanliness of the room which now serves no function?

Each instrument with whom this teacher has been involved carries a certain level or complex of levels of illusion due primarily to the fact that within your culture, the science, the exactitude, the certainty, the proven, is all that is acceptable. If one may consider the fixtures in a sink or a toilet, one may see that if the water is poisonous by one means or another, there are many, many things which the person dealing with the water must accommodate in order to take from the offered water those particles of ill health.

Each entity who is a channel has complete choice over the entity to whom the contact will be allowed and given. There are, as there have always been, negatively-polarized entities who dwell amongst your peoples and sometimes rise to great levels of power and influence. The scrapping, scratching game, "King of the Mountain," has always been with us. These considerations are as the beautiful fixtures of commode and sink. Yet this builded structure of pipe and hardware does have a choice of the place, the time, the method, and the required tune to tap into many, many levels or principles of contact, each with its own general message to prevail. Thus, it is not possible when a contact speaks in the consciousness to determine solely from that word, that name, the identity of the contact. Therefore, the instrument must be prepared to tune for a matter of minutes after the original tuning of the group even though it seems obvious that to channel a being would be the same wherever one picked it up.

The conjecture is, in fact, erroneous. The light, which is the prana or life, of all the universe is offered equally to those upon the service-to-self path and those upon the service-to-others path who have obtained a certain degree of confidence in accepting and rejoicing in the light of love, of wisdom, and of courage. It may seem strange to wrap the mind around the concept that those who are of service to self are equally or perhaps more suffering than those which choose service to others, for the Law of Reflection requires that you shall be treated as you treat those about you, with the exception, of course, of those times when the balance betwixt two entities has lasted for several lifetimes. For souls who have been with each other repeatedly it is always the constant feeling of déja vu.

Yet, each of you is here this evening to attempt to learn better how to share that which some call philosophy and others call psychology with you. Let us speak for a moment about the concept of the "magical personality." This instrument would prefer to call it "spiritual personality," however, we feel that our nomenclature is more accurate. We have endeavored to offer to the new instrument a framework within which the instrument may learn to be more and more aware of the small voice that speaks in silence, as your Holy Bible puts it. In many cases it is a still, small voice and not that easily recognized. The first great challenge of the new instrument is its ability to challenge successfully and to be exercised by whatever speaking is required. The student who does not listen to the warnings can—we correct this instrument—concerning channeling by itself. There are grave difficulties at least in potential.

May we say that we are having some difficulty with this contact as this instrument has some internal difficulties due to the ingestion of the many pills that was needed at this time. We are sorry for those lapses whereby this instrument must need to remain silent and wait. This indeed is another lesson which we hoped to offer to the new instrument. That is, the waiting with calm.

Let us look for a moment at the life pattern which is the macrocosm of which the learning to channel is a fairly elegant analogy. The …

We must pause and return.

(Pause)

I am Hatonn. We shall continue, in love and life. Within the channeling framework, the entity must learn to deal with the heart of those entities that speak invisibly for the most part. In the life experience as a whole, this is also true. The waiting, watching, meditating, and praying may seem to be the throwing of good water into the field. It is not wasted, it is only changed. And this is what we hope when we work with new instruments. That is, that they may become those who recognize within themselves a balanced, hollow place wherein the self is safe, and from the position of unassailable faith and commitment may, indeed, deal with any entity, whether it be a man, beast, bird or thought form.

Sometimes, as in this evening, the contact comes and goes, just as in some days in the existence of the life pattern the general feeling at the end of such a day is that which is known to your baseball fans as, "I should have stayed in bed." See yourself as a person who believes passionately and as an advocate in the greatest highest principle which is possible at this time within your mind and heart. It may not be something so easily spoken as the challenge in the name of Jesus Christ. Yet, we suggest that those who find the face of God in nature or in any other way, position that self so that out of the center of that commitment and passion for life and love, the vibration most desired shall come. The contact shall come. And when all the challenges are done, the instrument's work is basically done, for the rest of the channeling of concepts is what one may call an intuitive rather than a rational process, whereby the instrument feels certain feelings and is able to express, in an acceptable way, the intense emotions of the spiritual search.

One cannot be inspired by one's own shoddy workmanship. If it is not important to any other in the world, as you quaintly put it, it is ultimately important to the channel. It is difficult to know how to help your peoples. It is difficult to see what one person can do, and part of what the new instrument is going through in determining that for which he would die and that for which he shall live. This is a difficult patch of road for one who has always felt himself to be an observer, an anthropologist gazing at the natives. We do not say that there is not some merit in this attitude in terms of accuracy of perception. But, rather, we suggest that one view all those who one may serve as equally worthy of service.

The straying from the challenging process almost always turns the group responsible for this contact gradually into a point from which they cannot recover, for it is the favorite tactic of negatively-oriented entities, within your sphere, to wait for times of despair and the dark feelings of defeat in one project or another, in order to lay claim to a portion of that mind and heart. Each time that there is the deviation from a basic desire to be of good will, to be of service …

We must pause. Please forgive us. I am Hatonn, and we find that this instrument is fatigued enough that we would transfer to the one known as D. I am Hatonn.

(D channeling)

I am Hatonn, and I am with this instrument. It is with some difficulty that the parameters of the challenging process are learned. When one views the challenge as a negative act, an act of repulsion of outside influence, it becomes hard to accept the benign influence until a great deal of experience has brought familiarity with subtleties of vibration of that influence or entity. We would recommend that the instrument begin to make note in a more or less objective fashion with perceptions that are encountered at the point of first contact, a cataloguing of these perceptions, the heightened ability to identify each identity upon its later contacts as well as providing a wider spectrum within which positively polarized energies can be perceived and identified, so that even strange, or should we say, unfamiliar contacts may be accomplished with confidence because of their fitting within previously established framework.

(Carla channeling)

I am Hatonn. I am again with this instrument briefly. To conclude. The flow of information is a part of love, of light, as you perceive it. Just as there are varying degrees of colors and so forth of illumination, so too there are those [who] use the same light. One, for service to others; the other, as service to self. As each, shall we say, soldier upon the plain of Armageddon is matched by the negative polarization of that warrior, so too is there what could be called a loyal opposition of service to self which is aware of and attempts to alter communications received. The conscious, awakened mind is not capable of discerning betwixt two voices, both of which who say, "I am Hatonn." Yet there cannot be two of Hatonn, for ours, like many others, is a social memory complex, and one could not defy the consensus without removing the entire population which we bring to this work for healing work before we come back at all.

We believe it to be true that service to others shall prevail, and we have seen in our teacher's eyes the certainty of that truth. Yet we know, also, that in a world where children are hungry, the positively-oriented and trained vocal channel may be of inestimable value. This service is very hard work. It is intense and concentrative, and while this particular instrument at this particular time is not becoming fatigued because of the contact, nevertheless, may we say that …

(Side one of tape ends.)

(Carla channeling)

… some altercation of personality in the direction of dilapidation inwardly frequently occurs. We very much hope that each new instrument that may see or may hear these words be aware that there is the cosmic battle, shall we say, of fourth-density beings which have not gotten into focus the face of the Creator within each of their brothers, thus they call them enemies.

We ask those present to consider carefully the desire to channel as a priestly avocation. We ask the instrument to consider carefully and, above all, to keep question of what concept or complex of concepts contains the limitless ideal for which you live and for which, if pressed, you would die. Within some entities the face of God resides upon the face of the child, the beloved. In a more spiritualized sense we hope that each will treat the child which is growing in knowledge of service to others with the same tender care that the one known as Jesus received, albeit difficult circumstances, in a cow barn, in the middle of a snow storm. This is, of course, recorded to your accounts within your Holy Bible.

May you be the best you can. Relax into the web of love which connects you to all in the universe, which is closer to you than your breath, and be careful of whom you seek, for though the Creator [is] all, yet the distortions are many. And although we are distorted, yet it is true to our best belief that we attempt to safeguard the vocal instruments of our message and are successful in the most part in doing so.

We would at this time transfer the contact to the one known as Jim. I thank this instrument for operating under somewhat adverse circumstances, and would wish to make one point in comment, that being that this instrument we now use might well consider carefully the process whereby the tension could be released from the system, whereby the worry can be released from the mind, whereby the heartache can be relieved. This said, we shall transfer to the one who is Jim. I am Hatonn.

(Jim channeling)

I am Hatonn. Greetings again in love and light. At this time we are privileged to have the opportunity to speak to those queries which may yet remain upon the minds present and we would seek to fulfill the opportunity to the best of our ability while reminding each that we do not operate *(inaudible)*, yet what we offer we offer in joy. Is there a query to which we may speak at this time?

D: I felt tonight that I was initially channeling at rather a low level and so much from my own thoughts that I really felt reluctant to trust, again, what I was saying as being accurate. Could you comment on that aspect of this night, at this point?

I am Hatonn. We have another opinion, my brother, and that is that the effort which you expended this evening was one which was focused on very carefully and which you carried out with a diligence that has exceeded that of your previous attempts. We are aware that you are yet quite uncomfortable with various portions of the process and are not yet come into your own ability to receive those thoughts which we send and to transmit them in a faithful manner. Yet, we may assure you that your diligence has provided a progress which it is a pleasure to note.

We suggest that the future attempts contain this same diligence and focus of attention along with the growing ability to set aside the mental concerns and attempts to analyze, for it is this characteristic of all new instruments to analyze the contact as it is ongoing which, in most cases, causes the eventual cessation or delusion of the contact due to the loss of concentration.

Thus, we again encourage you, my brother, to continue apace and be at peace in your own mind for the progress you have shown is commendable, and we expect this to grow into the art of serving as a vocal instrument will continue.

May we speak on any other subject?

D: Well, having spoken about the middle, I would like to address the beginning and the end, the point of contact itself and the challenging process and the difficulty of that. Can you speak to that process as it occurred without my being more specific about how it seemed to occur from my perspective?

I am Hatonn. As you become more decided, shall we say, and choose those qualities or that quality around which your life moves in harmony most profoundly, and adopt those qualities in a conscious fashion as that standard by which you ask or challenge each contact you meet, you will discover that the experience of initiating the contact and of being assured that that which you perceive is indeed that which awaits your perception; you will grow with the confidence that the process is beginning as it should. The ability to place the full force of the self in a chosen mode or focus according to that which is most important to your seeking will give you the firm ground upon which to stand as you offer the challenge, as you perceive the contact, and as you relay those concepts which are given to you.

May we speak in any other fashion, my brother?

D: I tried tonight, I think more successfully than usual, when I became physically tense, to relax, and as I did I felt an opening of the mind as well but towards the end of the contact after just those two or three sentences that I spoke. When I did this I had a feeling of great expansiveness and contact but without concept, without communication on a conceptual level. I was so confident of that feeling of contact that I was somewhat surprised when you began again to speak through Carla. Can you comment on this, on what I might have been in contact with or experiencing?

I am Hatonn. The state of mind that is achieved in the meditative practice is one which may be likened unto the carrier wave of one of your radio stations. Upon this wave may be placed information. When the instrument achieves this state for the first time in an obvious sense, as you have described, it is usually an all-engulfing experience. It is sometimes difficult for the continued transmission of thoughts especially for the new instrument which oftentimes will wander a bit within the parameters of the carrier wave and will need to be brought back, shall we say, by the transfer of the contact, if there is an instrument experienced enough to perceive this situation. The new instrument will then note that it has stepped into the river or the flow of information and will then be able to recognize this state and work with it in a more focused manner, shall we say, as the experience is gained.

May we speak further, my brother?

D: It was quite sometime before I felt this feeling dissolve. Is it something that—is it a state which to be in has a beneficial effect as far as governing building the ability to establish a strong contact or is it better to be more diligent and more controlled when that occurs and try speaking about this early stage of development and still try to focus?

I am Hatonn. There is great benefit to the conscious self when this state is contacted for the practice of meditation which allows the entity to enter this state. It is one which builds a bridge between the conscious self and a greater portion of the self which may be more or less informed by the higher self and the increasingly coherent and integral magical personality. Thus, the conscious self, during these times of meditation within this state of consciousness, is being nourished by the qualities of the greater being.

The attempt to be of service as a vocal instrument may be aided by the utilization of this state of consciousness to receive as the least distorted fashion as possible, information transmitted from sources outside the conscious mind. However, in the initial experiences of this state of consciousness, the ability to serve as a vocal instrument is determined by the experience that the new instrument has in focusing its attention within this state and perceiving those thoughts transmitted to it while refusing the temptation to analyze the thoughts, and at the same time refusing the temptation to, shall we say, float hither and yon within the most pleasant confines of this state of consciousness.

Thus, there is a balance as the new instrument seeks which attempts to move equally between the conscious mind and its activity and the subconscious mind and its inactivity. What the new instrument and any instrument seeks is the expression of energy or activity in a manner which is informed by the subconscious mind or sources acting through the subconscious mind in a manner which may be perceived and transmitted, then, in a more conscious sense.

May we speak further, my brother?

D: It sounds like you are, in a sense, suggesting that in meditation this state might be one in which you would—let me put it this way. In meditation it might be okay to somewhat dissolve into this state and go with it, whereas when attempting to channel, it's necessary to maintain a focus of *(inaudible)* communication. Is that what you are saying?

I am Hatonn, and this is basically correct, my brother, for the experience of this state is that which may be harnessed, shall we say, by the one who seeks to serve as a vocal instrument, rather than the simple enjoying of this state. It is utilized in a manner which is hopefully of service to others.

May we speak further, my brother?

D: Just a quick and rather pointed question. At the point of which this occurred this evening, were you aware of my state and what I was experiencing or do you become aware of it by my describing it and asking about it?

I am Hatonn. In most instances we are not aware of the details of the instrument's mental contents, shall we say. We are more aware of the balances that are being achieved by the effort of the instrument and our own effort as well. If we so desire and see the need to become informed as to the specific details of an instrument's mental workings that may be influencing its ability to serve as a vocal instrument we may do so if we are asked and if the response does not impinge upon a free will. However, for the most part we choose to ignore the detailed or specific reasons for certain mental qualities while a contact has been established and choose rather to focus upon the blending of energies which we are attempting with the instrument.

May we speak further, my brother?

D: No, thank you very much.

I am Hatonn, and we thank you, my brother. Is there another query at this time?

Carla: I have just one. I experienced a complete mental blockage several times during the transmission and actually had no idea what they were talking about, most of the time, because I kept going out and then coming back in. I wondered—there are various possibilities when that happens. The possibilities range from going to sleep or in trance, which I don't think I can do; just being a bad channeler; not keeping my mind on the game; what else? Anyway, are any assortment of things responsible for this fading out? Because I've had this happen *(inaudible)* before. It could be pills, too. I've taken some pills for the session. Could you comment on any of that? I'd like to know how to work around that. The way I did it was just to sit there in the darkness until I saw the next sentence, but it was an uncomfortable feeling because I didn't know what the rest of the message was. Could you comment?

I am Hatonn, and we may comment as follows, my sister. The medications that you have begun to ingest have an affect that is noticeable as you seek to enter those states of consciousness which are somewhat below the conscious mind level. These substances are used primarily for their effect upon the conscious mind and its quieting. However, their effect is somewhat pronounced upon other levels of your mind as well.

When the lower levels of the mind are in a state of suspension, shall we say, due to this effect, we recommend that you do as you have done and that is to wait the transmission of the next thought or series of thoughts when it is possible to do so, for the effect of the medications is one which is spotty and which will in time pass. Thus, we can only suggest your patience and we ask that you bear with us as well, for we, during those times, need to rework the balance of energies that are the fruit of the blending of our energies with yours.

May we speak further, my sister?

Carla: Let me think … Are we doing—Jim and I—doing appropriate cleansing to be good enough to be working on the Holy Spirit tapes? And do you have any suggestions?

I am Hatonn. We may not speak to the specifics of this query, my sister, for those preparations which you make as instruments for this service are those which are most necessarily made as free will choices. We would not seek to intrude upon this holy ground, for that effort is one which is most necessary to guard as a product of free will choice. We encourage, always, the persistence and the dedication to intention and the praising of the one Creator in all experience. These are simple requisites for any seeker and any instrument at any time.

May we speak further, my sister, upon any other topic?

Carla: No.

Is there another query?

D: Not for me, thank you.

I am Hatonn, and we are most grateful to each gathered this evening for inviting our presence. As always, we rejoice at the opportunity to lend our assistance to those who would learn more of service and share that which is learned. We also learned much in these workings and are most grateful for each opportunity to learn and to teach. At this time we shall take our leave of this group and this instrument, leaving each, always, in the love and in the light of the one infinite Creator. We are those of Hatonn. Adonai, my friends. Adonai. ☥

Sunday Meditation
December 20, 1987

Group question: What determines what entity is channeled through an instrument, and should everybody channel?

(Carla channeling)

I am Q'uo. I greet you, my friends, in the light of the one infinite Creator. I greet you upon a night which is most luminous. The candles of hope, thanksgiving and compassion are lit by so many who know not the good they do at this season which you are experiencing at this time.

You ask what people should and should not channel, and we say to you, first of all, that all of you are channels; all of you are instruments for good, for ill, or—most tragically—for nothing, neither good nor ill. As each of you engages his or her heart in communing with the great mystery which you call Christmas, so each of you channels that which cannot be found within the mind or the body in so much concentration except when the heart is awakened to a higher and purer caring for the situation of the self or the situation of those about you and for the great puzzle which all face—the precise situation which lies twixt self and Creator.

In this general sense there is no one who is not a channel; there is no life which is not primarily a channeled existence. By this we mean that each of you carries within the self deep and unconscious forces neither to the good nor to the evil as much as to the deepening of experience. The more times in which the student may recognize the depth of the present moment, just so shall that soul channel more and more in a biased fashion, in an engaged fashion, in an enabling fashion for service to all and for love of the infinite Creator.

For what is channeling, my friends? Many think of it, especially the vocal channeling, as a kind of letter left perhaps upon one of your telephone answering devices, telling interesting things which have happened in your past or your present or your future. Of oneself it is difficult to truly grapple with the questions of the heart, the heart being the closest connection to the spirit. Therefore, we affirm that all are and should be, in a general sense, channels for the one infinite Creator, for each of you is co-Creator, with that face of mystery which created your life as the open book with the blank pages. And as you are created in this image, the image of the open blank book, so by your living, your polarized thinking and your channeling, more and more you begin to fill the book of your life. Your penmanship matters not, the exquisite outcome of an hoped-for event matters not, for it is as has been mentioned earlier the task of the instrument only to attempt to channel a life lived in love and peaceableness. Sometimes these attempts are taken by the conscious self and made hard and brittle, so that in the name of good the self is broken as a piece of toast.

Thus, to each of you who is indeed the channel of his or her own living, we suggest a persistent, faithfully followed daily meditation, a meditation which does not have to be time-consuming, rather, a meditation which is just the perfect length for you for that day and for that moment. The purpose of meditation is to open up the heart portion of the mind, for the analytical portion of the mind carries you through most of your culture's activities, but the mind-heart has within it a deeper way, a more centered truth, a more balanced bias, and in the end a bias which moves more and more closely to that bias which you wish at the end of your incarnation to offer the Creator as your life gift.

A life is a solid, sometimes bulky, present to offer to the infinite One, yet each laugh, each smile, each encouragement to one who needed it, each hard truth to one who needed it, each and every effort that has been made is as the wrapping and the decorating and the wonderful ribbons about that solid, caring present to the Creator that is a channeled life.

Allow yourself to be conscious as much as possible that there is within you a channel to spirit, to the higher self, to the Self of all that there is. This contact shall never fade away, for as you desire you shall receive. Oftentimes you shall not receive that which you requested, for your higher self knows that which in the end will bring the understanding, the compassion, and the balance.

We began this way deliberately, somewhat off the main thrust of the query, because the question of channeling is so general due to the vocabulary lacks within your culture for an activity which is called channeling, as each channels the self each and every moment of the incarnation.

We turn now to the channeling which was intended to be queried about, and that query is, "Should everyone be a channel? How do channels and instruments contact each other? And is that in all cases a good idea?"

Let us look at the life of a poet or a musician. Many poets have written what this instrument would offer as, "Roses are red, violets are blue." These channeled thoughts are modest and pleasant, yet they shall not make the poet a man of renown. So it is with the music. What this instrument would call "Chopsticks" can be taught, and thus any entity can play the instrument of the piano. Yet is this, after all, a decisively important kind of channeling to be shared with others? It may well help the entity, but we submit to you that the equivalent of chopsticks on the piano, when placed in the context of spiritually-oriented channeling, it may suggest that not everyone, perhaps not even most, need to seriously consider a life lived as a [vocal] channel.

There is no entity so lost to desires of helpfulness that this cannot eventually learn to channel the love and the light of the infinite Creator. However, there is a certain temperament which finds its reward in being used as a vocal channel. A person with such a temperament is willing to undergo difficulties, misunderstandings, inconvenience and all the minor difficulties that a time-consuming activity causes. And this is where we begin to make the distinction between those who channel the equivalent of a simple tune upon the piano and those who wish to study the instrument of the self. The study required for being an instrument is a careful, persistent, dogged and light-hearted gaze at the life as it is lived from day to day, from week to week, from year to year.

As in any spiritually-oriented service, the honor of being a channel grows in direct proportion to the responsibility of living that which is channeled. The Creator is a fair and perhaps distant observer when an individual is making a dedication to a life of being able to channel. The vocal channel thus has not only the discipline, the ABC's, to learn about contact, how to govern contact and so forth, it also must gaze at the daily behavior which may be commented upon by that very entity's channeling of a higher and more informed source. This concept of a life lived in a certain way has in your culture been associated almost entirely with those who choose to wear clothing which is different from others which proclaims a religious status or importance. Those of you who speak with our thoughts mingling with yours are those who travel completely incognito. We do not wish to impress anyone with our reality. We do not wish to reveal the proof, the evidence, the material which would sway those who find the idea of vocal channeling either sacrilegious or unscientific.

Perhaps you can see by now that we are attempting to say that those who do not wish to take upon themselves the responsibility of attempting to live as they have learned are far better off attempting to be of service to the infinite Creator, which is within all beings, by any one of a number of ways of channeling cheerfulness and helpfulness to those who are needy. Many there are who need food, blankets, clothing and shelter, for upon your weary world there is the winter of the body, and the body becomes cold, and the most beautiful words shall not warm the bones of such a body, but rather the simpler channeling of hospitality and faith, warm places for saddened, wearied bodies.

We shall tell you how we came to speak to this instrument. We are those who listen to a certain vibration of request. We have found that vibration often within this group, and so we are most fortunate that we are called to this group by means of this group's desire to seek and know as much as possible about the true nature of beingness. We waited for this group to become one, to lose the self-consciousness, to join in a circle of light which by now, my friends, is visible for a large number of your kilometers, like a bubble, below the earth, above the earth, and all about you. This light you have created, and within that creation you have placed a call, and we who do not have telephone answering machines like this instrument does, we answer that call—and that right gladly.

For it is a great service to us that you ask the question that we may in our humble way attempt to answer. And may we say, as always, that we cannot state anything which is infallible. We are pilgrims along the same path as are you. We have stumbled over the stones which now confront you, and are stumbling now over different stones, and we in turn are helped by those beyond us. When all of us achieve the complete channeling which is the impersonal life, then it will be that this creation shall gather itself together in Oneness, in sleep, in timelessness, until once again the Creator bursts out with a new creation, and all the consciousnesses begin again upon a new level to learn new lessons, and to express to the Creator within each other the nature of holiness, compassion and love.

When a student presents itself to one who teaches the channeling, it is often very helpful that the one who wishes to channel has done significant amounts of thinking upon the true nature of the self. Even if you have passed the test of agreeing to amend your life to meet as best as you can the challenges of channeling, it is not always possible to so live. Yet those who wish to make vocal channeling their service have a certain frame of mind, a certain series of biases. This to us is not a problem. We welcome the difference between channel and channel. We welcome the diversity of ways in which the one great original Thought of creation is expressed, for ours is a most simple story, and we welcome each entity's ability to express our concepts in a slightly new and somewhat different way. For you, my friends, as channels are fishers of men, as your holy work describes it. You shine not only for the Creator, and not only for the Creator within the self, but primarily for those about you. You do not know how many lives you may reach, you do not know what smile or soft word shall lift up the heart of one who is very low. You do not know until it is over when a home truth must be told, so that baggage may be dropped that was no longer useful, leaving you free for your next experience.

It is our desire not [just] to make more vocal channels, but to make each aware of the channeling he or she is already doing. The conscious mind is so very small a part of your minds, dear children. When you feel you are thinking especially well, it is as if you were saying, "I am using two percent of my mental capacity," for, my friends, this is approximately the amount of your entire self which is used for logical thinking. The great and enormous depth, beauty, truth and a kind of terribleness which is the connection with deeply impersonal sources, all of these things are by far the greater extent of the mind which is yours at this moment within the incarnation, doing no other work, sitting at this circle and listening.

You are channels. You all should be channels. The call to be a vocal channel is a call to a religiously or spiritually-oriented life. There are things which one must turn one's back upon if one wishes to remain a positively-oriented channel, open for undistorted information giving. It is not well when all in a society decide to be priests, my children. Thus, if you find other ways of channeling [than vocal channeling] which are better [for you], then we urge you, by all means, to realize what kind of channel that you are, and be that wonderful, loving, compassionate self that this particular type channeling may bring

A weaver channels the beauty of the cloth. One who works with people channels a love and acceptance, a true listening ear for the entities around it. There are so many examples of the channeling which all may do—the cooking, the washing, the smiling at the sun, the enjoyment of water, all the excitement of daily life, all the little things which are like flowers in a bowl in unexpected corners of your daily life. You channel your daily life. We ask you to do it lovingly and honorably, honoring yourself and honoring that which this instrument would call the Christ consciousness in each and every face that you see.

Finally, with mixed emotion, which may indeed make this part of our message difficult, we urge that those who hear these words not assume by any means that vocal channeling is that which they are prepared to do. The entities which have begun as excellent vocal channels and have later disintegrated their contact are many, far too many. And although each entity shall be healed and disappointment shall cease, yet still, by following not the heart within, but the ambition without, they have condemned themselves to much disappointment. If you are to be a vocal channel, may we say that you shall not be able to resist that search, that practice, and the ponderings that intensive channeling meditations bring to one.

We urge each to listen to each channel with an open mind and gaze not at the mythology or story which surrounds the messages, but rather the messages themselves. We have purposely refrained from describing ourselves in any physical way because we would not wish to begin, in those whom we serve, some idealization of us as teachers, something that has a face and a name, something that will bear responsibility for them. My friends, each of you is upon your own stage in your own creation with your own audience, and no matter how many people there are in that theater, all of those entities are yourself.

There are few who are so oriented that they may gaze daily and lovingly at the many errors and peccadilloes of the human self. Therefore, in those who truly wish and are capable of being vocal channels, it is important that those entities judge not the temporary or ephemeral thoughts, feelings and conclusions, but rather with a good heart and a real sense of commitment move forward day by day, meditation by meditation, honing, refining and humbling the self that it may be a vocal instrument which is harmless but helpful.

Many contacts there are of entities which use light not for service to others, but for those messages which involve personal power over others and service to self. Thus, the first and greatest suggestion that we may make to all who channel the self in everyday life as well as all who seek a vocation as vocal channel, is that the self be regarded in some way so that as the days move forward, the more and more positive ways of reacting to difficult …

(Side one of tape ends.)

(Carla channeling)

… situations may become more smooth, more comfortable, less threatening, and more open.

The successful channel, whether vocal or otherwise, is one whose heart is happy, one whose wings are spread, yet one who is not impatient for the song to sing or the winds to take wing. It is up to each to decide in what way service lies. Many there are upon your planet who sit, shall we say, at the top of a great watchtower, gazing upon infinity and bearing the sadness and futility of apparent human existence, and with that open and terrible gaze, that pitiless eye, seeing the perfection, the beauty, and the harmony of that great plan wherein self shall meet self until all selves have met and merged and again we are One, the one Creator, the one original Thought which is love, not love as you and I know it in a personal sense, but the love that builds and explodes the very stars themselves.

This instrument informs us that we have once again spoken perhaps at too great a length, and we would like to apologize. As you know, we have great difficulty with the sense of passing time, as we are offering to this instrument a—we search for an adjective within this instrument's vocabulary—in perhaps, we shall say, a spontaneous way. It is time for us to leave this instrument that the questions which are on the minds of those here might be responded to. Please feel free to ask questions, for this, you see, is our service to you, and as we teach and supposedly you learn, my children, it is the other way around. You teach courage, curiosity, bravery and sweetness, and we learn time and time again that in your very difficult third-density illusion your spirit is there, joyful, uninhibited, strong and eternal. How we glow with the joy of our comradeship with you. How we admire your ability to gaze at a never-ending maze of shadow within shadow within shadow until the distortions are so deep that it is by faith alone that any perception of wholeness can be had. We thank you for these gifts and only hope that our words give you something about which to ponder. We would at this time transfer this contact to the one known as Jim. I am Q'uo.

(Jim channeling)

I am Q'uo, and greet each again in love and light through this instrument. It is our privilege at this time to offer ourselves in the attempt to speak to any queries which may yet remain upon the minds of those present. Again, we would remind each that we offer but that which is our opinion. We offer it joyfully, but not infallibly. We are your brothers and sisters who seek to serve. May we begin with a query?

Carla: I have always thought that people who wanted to learn to channel, if it was just curiosity it still was helpful to them as long as they didn't go beyond a certain point. And you didn't cover that, and I just wondered if that is a thought that you confirm?

I am Q'uo, and we are not averse to attempting the exercising and utilization of an instrument which has only the goal of satisfying personal curiosity, for in that way do we also serve in a manner which hopefully is instructive to the one with the curiosity. It is oftentimes a lesson well learned for one to practice an art long enough to discover that it is not the life's vocation.

May we speak further, my sister?

Carla: Not on that question, no thank you.

I am Q'uo, and we thank you, my sister. Is there another query?

Questioner: Q'uo, there are times when I am questioned about something, in class, that I really do not know the answer [to] in my mind. I don't know that I have ever touched upon the subject even. And yet it seems that my mouth will open and I will give an answer. The answer seems very acceptable and something that even I need to study, but I have wondered, I have felt that I was fraud, perhaps making it up or filling in, but there would be the answer. Am I to understand that this could be definitely channeling?

I am Q'uo, and, indeed, each conversation and activity which an entity partakes within is a channeling from some portion of the Creator, for are not all the Creator? Therefore, it is not surprising that each entity in the daily experience will utilize resources within the conscious and often within the subconscious mind as means by which an activity will be undertaken and a conversation will be initiated. There are many rooms to the mind of each entity. Many of these rooms contain information which will wait long before being utilized, yet there is a time and a season for the utilization of far more than is normally utilized by the conscious mind. As one seeks in a wholehearted fashion to be of service to others by the life and the various portions of interaction with others within a life experience, there is created within the entity a bridge, shall we say, or a channel which connects the conscious mind with other portions of the conscious and subconscious mind according to the nature of the information sought and the degree of desire which activates the seeking and searching within the self in order than another might be served.

Thus, each of you, my friends, cultivates this channel or pathway each day of your existence, and as you begin to ponder more and more the mystery of beingness, of the creation, of your purpose within it, of the direction in which you wish to travel, you begin to access the deeper rooms within the mind which contain information that shall be of use in this continuing journey and unfolding of the deeper levels of your being.

May we speak in any further fashion, my sister?

Questioner: Thank you. That answered very well.

I am Q'uo, and we thank you, my sister. Is there another query?

Carla: Well, I've got one. I was getting some contact from someone named Amira earlier. It passed the challenge three times, but in the past twenty years, I guess, I've seen at least four, maybe six different names that are supposed to be Jesus, and Amira is one of them. And I just wonder, if it is really Jesus, why does this entity have to use so many different aliases? Or is it Jesus at all?

I am Q'uo, and with this query we find that we must tread carefully in order that we not infringe upon the free will of some present, for the entity known to you as Jesus of Nazareth is one which is held in great esteem by many, and has in various ways been drawn to those who seek to serve in this entity's name, as are all entities of an unseen nature who seek to be of service to others. The one known as Jesus responds to a vibratory call which is congruent with its own.

However, in some cases those who call, even with this vibration, are not able to recognize a response that others may easily recognize. Thus, as in the case with any contact through the use of a vocal channel or instrument, a name or sound vibration is given which is acceptable and recognizable by the one serving as instrument and those within the supporting group, for the naming is a phenomenon which is not utilized to a great extent beyond the illusion which you now inhabit, for the naming is that which divides one thing from another and beyond your illusion much there is that no longer partakes in such division. For the eyeshot perspective is greater, and the identification of self with all about one within the creation is that which is pursued and recognized and experienced. Thus, the naming, for the most part, is in order that those within your illusion serving as instruments might more easily recognize the nature of the source of information transmitted through it.

However, along with the preceding, we must also state that there are always those entities both within your illusion and beyond it who would seek to misdirect the attention of many who would revere and cherish information from sources such as the one known as Jesus, and who in this desire to misdirect and confuse would utilize both this entity's name as known to your peoples and other forms or offices given to this entity. Thus, there is confusion, and each seeker of truth is advised to proceed carefully, using discrimination from within to determine the value of information from without.

May we speak in any further fashion, my sister?

Carla: No, thank you.

I am Q'uo, and we thank you once again, my sister. Is there another query?

(Pause)

I am Q'uo, and as it appears that we have for the moment exhausted the queries, we shall take this opportunity to thank each for inviting our presence and for having the patience to listen to our discourse, which is oftentimes somewhat lengthy in your terms. We appreciate greatly the opportunity to offer that which we have found of use in our own journey of seeking to you who travel that same journey. We look forward to each opportunity, and shall be with each in your meditations when requested in order that the meditation might be enhanced.

At this time we shall take our leave of the this group, again with gratitude to each, leaving each, as always, in the love and in the light of the one infinite Creator. We are known to you as those of Q'uo. Adonai, my friends. My friends, adonai.

(Carla channels a vocal melody.)

(Carla channeling)

I am Amira. I greet you in the love, the light, and the life of the Father. How plunged you are into the mystery of day and night, good and evil. How clear are the eyes of those who search out my face in every situation. Yet, we would not ask you to search out a physical face, for the physical face of the Son of Man is beside you, is looking at you from the mirror, is your stranger, your friend, your child. I and others have come to comfort you, to leave the comfort of love behind. May you release the discomfort of worldly doubt and turn and return to those glories of the Father which enter by eye or mouth or thought or death. You who come with me, you who share my steps, you shall share them all. May your journey be transfigured by the joy of your countenance, as with perfect faith you reach at last that place from which there are no more steps, no more false divisions, that place where you begin to feel yourself falling, falling and falling, more and more deeper and deeper into an unmeasured and eternal sea of creative, divine love. I reach out my wounded hands to bless and sanctify the wounds you bear, that they too may be marks of past courage, never scars of pain. I leave you in the full sun, the glorious light and infinite love of the Father. Farewell and peace.

(Melodic chanting.)

A-mi-ra. A-mi-ra. A-mi-ra. A-mi-ra. A-mi-ra. A-mi-ra. ☥

L/L Research

L/L Research is a subsidiary of Rock Creek Research & Development Laboratories, Inc.

P.O. Box 5195
Louisville, KY 40255-0195

www.llresearch.org

Rock Creek is a non-profit corporation dedicated to discovering and sharing information which may aid in the spiritual evolution of humankind.

ABOUT THE CONTENTS OF THIS TRANSCRIPT: This telepathic channeling has been taken from transcriptions of the weekly study and meditation meetings of the Rock Creek Research & Development Laboratories and L/L Research. It is offered in the hope that it may be useful to you. As the Confederation entities always make a point of saying, please use your discrimination and judgment in assessing this material. If something rings true to you, fine. If something does not resonate, please leave it behind, for neither we nor those of the Confederation would wish to be a stumbling block for any.

CAVEAT: This transcript is being published by L/L Research in a not yet final form. It has, however, been edited and any obvious errors have been corrected. When it is in a final form, this caveat will be removed.

© 2009 L/L RESEARCH

Sunday Meditation
December 27, 1987

Group question: We continue with the question from last week, should everyone channel, and what determines what type of a contact comes through an instrument?

The reason we're continuing is that, as with some previous times, Carla had a feeling that Q'uo had some more to say on the subject, after having spoken for fifty or sixty minutes last time. So we're going to go ahead again.

(Carla channeling)

I am Q'uo. I greet you in the love and in the light of the one infinite Creator. We communicate through this instrument to offer you our love, our peace, and our blessing, for this is more than any intellectual facet of our service, the very depth of the channeling process, the exchanging of a less exalted love or expression of love for a higher expression, a less distorted expression of that one great original Thought of love from which the creation has sprung and into Whose infinite inward parts all in time shall again coalesce into one being, one channel, one way, one life, one truth, and that distilled truth shall be the precise expression of the conglomerate level of the grasping of the one original Thought amongst all of those which dwell within your third-density illusion.

Indeed, there is, much like your stock market reports, an ongoing tally, shall we say, of the cumulative effect for good or for the negative of good in each expression of all towards all environments. By this we mean to suggest specifically that each channels each perception of environment and then in measured response offers some portion of the self in an effort to so order that which has been seen that the spiritual principles implicit in the event, situation or problem may be resonated and sung in lucid, clear tones, the truly channeled tones of clarified emotion.

Without asking all of humankind upon your planet's surface at this [time] to become priest or ministers or those in charge of other's spiritual activities, we mean specifically to state to each that each is an equal, considerable and infinite portion of the cumulate channeling of the one great original Thought of mankind. So often it is seen by those whose lives are full of toil that others, not themselves, are the only ones capable of responsibility of a moral or spiritual kind. The reverse is, in fact, far more true, for those who grapple with time-consuming and mind-numbing activities have reserved to themselves their own choice of interests, those faculties of mind, spirit and heart which may color the life experience, no matter what that life experience seems to deal in upon the surface of things.

We intend for each to see that each is an imponderably important portion of the channeled cumulative value of humankind at this time, and insofar as struggles have been rewarded with virtuous hope, as difficult dealings have been faced with honest courage, so moves the labyrinth of humankind, slowly yielding to the carefully penciled traces of the path we must retrace to that source of all channeling, of all being, the one infinite Creator. It is important to us that we express that it is not merely those whose sensibilities have been tuned and honed to be exquisitely fine upon whom the fate of humankind rests. Nay, far more is it the hard-won capacity of the busy, overworked, underappreciated man and woman of lesser circumstances whose response to these difficult environments generates the love and the light of the one infinite Creator for all of mankind.

We now switch in our focus from those areas in which all are channels to that area which is largely understood as being the environment wherein those who have chosen work in consciousness play out their little roles upon the large stage of the illusion you call life. We appreciate that this instrument was aware that there were things that we had to say which could not be generated within the time period set for such discussion, and for this we are sorry, for we see that were we to be terse, perhaps we could find more clarity in communication. However, the degree of wordiness which this instrument is comfortable with we find to be comfortable also to the ear of those who listen, and so we shall move on at this perhaps less than quick pace.

Let us look now at the channeling which has a special meaning apart from the channeling which all entities do throughout their life experiences. Some few there are in forest glade, in coldest mountain cave, in comfortable dwelling places and in the least comfortable of orientations, who have devoted the life which is theirs, until they pass from this experience, to the being of a channel in service to the one infinite Creator by accepting and repeating the humble opinions which we have. We have said already that all those who quickly learn the mechanics of the channeling process are not, because of this original learning, automatically ready for the life of discipline which follows a choice upon the part of the channel to be a channel for the one infinite Creator.

Our thesis is that some discipline in the living of a practical, modest and loving lifestyle is very helpful to a channel [and] may or may not suit the mood of those who wish to become channels. We shall say clearly at this point that it is not the desire of the Confederation of Planets in the Service of the One Infinite Creator to create channels through which we may comment upon physical disasters and other remarkable and unusual natural effects which have to do with the movement of your peoples and your planet itself from the end of third density to the merging with the beginning of fourth density as it shall occur more and more among you.

That which we look for, that in which we rejoice in a channel, is the clear statement of the channel's personality in a disciplined and unified way, for it is upon this level that channel meets channel, for make no mistake about it, channeling is a two-way conversation, and the channeling in light trance or heavy trance, during this exploration of a possible message for the day, is based very largely upon the level of commitment and serious intention which the channel offers at the time of challenge to the contact.

Let us look for a moment, then, at the work in consciousness which a channel may wish to consider accomplishing, for the channel is not the entertainer or the one with the job to do. The channel is rather a kind of person. Your closest word would perhaps be minister or priest. This human minister/priest gazes upon the face of the illusion and chooses to live in a loving, caring and openly spiritual way, bragging not one word, celebrating not one virtue, but instead learning the true humility of one who knows that what one wishes to be, one is only by will and faith, for it is the nature of humankind in third density that all seeming perfections shall be pierced with error. All glasses to a brilliant future are made murky by the inevitable, constant, dramatic game-playing of the illusion itself.

If the new instrument who decides to live a life of spirituality thinks at first that there is some ongoing trickster designed to test that channel, this instrument is not only accurate, but has foreseen the mere beginning of a long series, indeed, an endless series of challenges to see through, of seeming heartlessnesses to bring love to, of seeming dreadful inadequacies to enfold in consciousness until finally the one who seeks to serve as channel aches and cries with the agony of compassion in such a dark world, and yet at the same time trembles with the ecstasy of the limitless light and the glory of souls who gradually shed the used skins of ash and dust. New channels shall have an interesting transition at the time of your passing, for you have been intending to die to yourself for time out of mind, and when finally the poor ragged flags of personality flutter and lie limp in the breathlessness of death, the channel rises with lightsome step and with glorious enthusiasm for the light and companionship which lie ahead.

This topic has been to us an important one in two ways. In the first way, we wish to express to all the concept of the channeled life. We wish to confirm that all live a channeled life; none lives by rational thought alone, and that which is not rational is channeled through to the conscious and acted on as if it were fact, when it is, indeed, bias only. Each of you is a channel with biases, and each glad and sad activity within your experience upon this Earth plane is designed to teach you just how you wish to channel. This is not a vocation. This is a portion of the way a thinking entity regards the various forces of irritation and subconscious thought which creep into human discourse. If you know that you are indeed a channel, not to others but to the self, then you know that there are certain responsibilities. When you are offering the best you have in conversation, with perhaps unfortunate remarks made by others, may you find the patience, the light touch, the understanding and loving word in the face of the opposite which will make others rethink those conversations and wonder, perhaps for the first time, if they too could be responsible for such a wonderful thing as channeling a lighter, more joyful attitude.

To those who wish to be priests, ministers and light-givers, to those of you on the watchtower, mending fences, gazing into the heavens as sentinels of the lights of the cosmos, we urge you above all to find within the self that fundamental character which can offer the highest praise, the deepest felt purified emotion. If that means that you must function upon your own, then it is that you shall be lonely. It is unfortunate in the short run that experiences such as loneliness are considered to have great possibilities for learning among those who have chosen to live the life of the minister or the one upon the watchtower. Thusly, in the second place, it is your greatest hope to find those who are able to share the darkness, the misunderstandings, the despair and the doubt which accompanies a life lived in hope but executed with human error. May you find those who comfort you.

Lastly, to you whom we may call shepherds, there is sent a glorious company of those who surround you, love you and love the one original Thought that is slowly taking place and growing within each. Call upon those helpers which you know by names such as Holy Spirit, guardian angel, and inner guides. More than that, rest back into the recollection of the enormous web of caring, trusting, hoping and loving which your most mixed-up planet does indeed send out greatly.

We find that this is the end of that which we wished to discourse upon at this juncture. If there may be questions which arise from our humble opinions, we eagerly ask the opportunity to speak again upon this subject. Please know that those who wish to be channels are a mighty company, and beneath the claptrap and noise of normal human converse lie the sinews and tendons of a growing social memory, placing upon the skeleton of this planet's position in space each sublime thought, each remembered turning of channel to source. You, my friends, my children, my channels, make the first steps towards a new heaven and a new Earth, as we would quote this instrument's holy work, so that you are workers in the very beginning of the fourth density. May you be comforted by all your failures, for how could you succeed each time were there not a crying need for effort?

We rejoice in each effort of will, each movement in love, each word that has been prayed about and considered, each spontaneous expression that brings the Creator directly and engagingly into the surface, the center, the heart of a group. May each of you find your rejoicing in each other. May you love each other. May you see the Creator in each other. May your channeling become a channeled life.

We test the readiness of the one known as Jim to speak, and find that this instrument is somewhat less than enthusiastic, yet it is for us a great opportunity for us to exercise this instrument without the structure of the questioning …

(Side one of tape ends.)

(Carla channeling)

… Thus, we would at this time attempt to transfer to the one known as Jim that he may close this session, for which we gratefully thank those present. We shall leave this instrument now. I am Q'uo.

(Jim channeling)

I am Q'uo, and we continue through this instrument. It has been our great privilege to address this group upon this topic this evening, for without the focus of such intention and desire upon your parts, we have no place within your existence and may not serve in the manner in which we now serve. Thus, you do us a great honor by seeking in a focused manner information which will aid your evolution. For you see, my friends, though much of apparent intrigue and interest swirls and surrounds you daily within your illusion, your purpose for existence within such a fascinating illusion is to choose the steps carefully which shall carry you further along your chosen path of evolution of mind, body and spirit. All else is but the trappings and the setting of the stage that will [limn] the milieu in which you move and learn and serve.

To focus your desire to grow by means of the question, such as the one presented to us this evening, is to create an opening within the veil that shrouds that which is of essence from your inner and outer eye. Thus, we move through that opening and respond to that which is asked in manner which hopefully illumines a small portion of your journey. It is the desire, my friends, to learn and to serve which guides us all to that great welcoming home within the heart of all creation and the one Creator.

It has been our great honor to join you this evening, and again we thank you for inviting our presence. We shall at this time take our leave of this group, rejoicing, as always, in the love and the light of the one Creator. We are known to you as those of Q'uo. Adonai, my friends. Adonai vasu borragus.

Year 1988

January 3, 1988 to October 17, 1988

L/L Research

L/L Research is a subsidiary of Rock Creek Research & Development Laboratories, Inc.

P.O. Box 5195
Louisville, KY 40255-0195

www.llresearch.org

Rock Creek is a non-profit corporation dedicated to discovering and sharing information which may aid in the spiritual evolution of humankind.

ABOUT THE CONTENTS OF THIS TRANSCRIPT: This telepathic channeling has been taken from transcriptions of the weekly study and meditation meetings of the Rock Creek Research & Development Laboratories and L/L Research. It is offered in the hope that it may be useful to you. As the Confederation entities always make a point of saying, please use your discrimination and judgment in assessing this material. If something rings true to you, fine. If something does not resonate, please leave it behind, for neither we nor those of the Confederation would wish to be a stumbling block for any.

CAVEAT: This transcript is being published by L/L Research in a not yet final form. It has, however, been edited and any obvious errors have been corrected. When it is in a final form, this caveat will be removed.

© 2009 L/L Research

Sunday Meditation
January 3, 1988

Group question: Has to do with negative polarity, negative energy, and its direction towards us as seekers in various forms, whether it might be a magically powerful negative entity sending a greeting that has the purpose of disabling you in some way, or a person that just wishes you ill, all the way to the potential negative expression through the monetary system and the electronic funds transfer system where the controlling of the great majority of people is done by a few for their gain at the expense of the many, to what allows the energy to be sent and received in a certain fashion, or how does a seeker deal with these situations and the sendings, wishing one ill, attempting to control one or affecting one in a negative fashion. Are you getting that? Hopefully it's all there somewhere.

(Carla channeling)

I am Q'uo. I greet you in the love and in the light of the one infinite Creator whose presence is all that there is and whose distortions we are. It is a great blessing and privilege to be called to your group at this time, and we wish to touch and bless and love each, especially those whom we have not spoken to before or who have been long from this group.

Resting within the web of your vibrations is a joy, and the knowledge that you wish us to share our opinions with you is a deep joy, for in order for us to be of service as we must do to advance in our own studies, we must be asked to offer our opinions and teach what little we know. And we thank you for your curiosity and the integrity with which you seek the true nature and purpose of yourselves, of the Creator, and of all of creation.

We found this instrument to be very willing to move into a fairly deep state this evening. Indeed, we find this instrument quite bewildered by the various aspects of the question concerning dealing with negativity. But we would say to this instrument and to all that there is no ego or negativity; there are egos and negativities.

To assume that there is a good and an evil or a positive and a negative is to set up the parameters of a game, a game in which positivity and negativity could be measured two feet towards the negative goal, two feet towards the positive. There is no constant that has bias. The biases which each of you bring to the experiences which occur to you are those things with which you place values of good and negative on what you experience. Your own biases, your own thoughts, your own nature take an unbiased illusion which is far too great for that computer which is your mind to analyze and use, and your nature orders that computer to assess certain data. Therefore, you choose again and again what to think, how to react, and what to do. This does not change the unbiased state of the illusion as it is.

That which is within your mind and heart is that which determines your creation. We have said to you often that you are of the Creator and the Creator is of you. My children, each of you is co-Creator, as powerful as the deity whose mystery you seek to plumb. Your universe has been made small enough that you might put yourself to certain study. For this you have been given the intellectual mind, which we call your biocomputer, and the many resources of the deep mind. Our voice comes to you through this instrument's persistent use of faculties of the deep mind wherein outer and impersonal voices and principles may offer opinion from perhaps a slightly expanded viewpoint with somewhat more experience with illusion.

Thus, the first consideration when gazing at dealing with negativity is to examine the possibility, indeed, the probability that the biases which consciously or unconsciously create your choice of data, create your world, in other words, contain in them what you yourself would call negative elements. Perhaps there is something within your character which is useful in a way, but perhaps not greatly desirable. Because of the choices that must be made within the life illusion, these negative elements are tolerated because the positive use of them is sometimes extremely helpful in some way in providing supply, in manipulating those about you in a comfortable way or in changing that which, in your opinion, should perhaps be changed within your social group, your geographical location, or that which you call your nation. Were you to have no negative bias, each entity with whom you came in contact would appear as the entity actually is, a perfect unique prism of white light, child of the Creator, an inimitable perfect being. The name that you have for one who is supposedly of all positivity is "saint." You will find that saints do not feel threatened by outer circumstance, whether it be of things or of entities, if you are lucky enough to find one. My children, they are few among your peoples.

Now let us look outward. Each of you gazes upon a creation which is completely subjective. All of your instincts and your senses and your abilities greet the day, see the illusion, and feel the pulsing of the life within, the life that shall end and that life that shall not. And as you pass along your way, you find those things which cross and disturb one or another of the energy complexes of your being. Perhaps it is only inclement weather, and perhaps that red-ray, as this instrument would call it, desire for bodily health and strength curses the inclement weather and finds it negative. Perhaps there is a blockage in your orange ray, personal feelings ache and a glance out the window at this rainy weather seem to put a negative lid on a sad heart, one more reason to feel negative thoughts.

A great deal of the work of your people at this time is what this instrument would call orange-ray work. The orange-ray energy center deals, in our opinion, with personal relationships and difficulties of the person within the self. When that orange ray becomes blocked in relationship to another, the negative feelings can be very intense. We speak at first, of course, of those who know each other, those who have said they love each other, and now can find no positivity. Yet the orange-ray bias that is blocked is blocked within the individual self first. Therefore, when it is infringed upon by a stranger, it may well receive a very unwelcome mirrored picture of the negative blockage, and thus it is that the stranger is disliked upon sight.

The energy blockages of yellow ray, which is an expression this instrument uses to indicate what we would call those energies dealing with societal groups, is also an energy which is frequently rather blocked. Thus, the news all seems bad. Your games are lost too often, and all those energies put into group effort somehow seem to go awry. Fear not, we are not saying that the problems of the world are your fault; we are saying that your perception of the world is absolutely and completely your choice.

Now let us look at a different emphasis upon negative experiences which impinge upon you the individual. First let us take the mundane impingement of negativity upon the individual. Those who wish to control others because it is their job to do so are not intentionally being negative. Therefore, their negativity should not be taken personally. Thus, those who attempt to sell that which you do not need, those who wish you to worship as you do not care to, those whose enthusiasms you are invited all too heartily to share, are impersonal negative infringements which, because your own energies are unclear, cause some disturbance in those centers.

Now, the point of freeing the red, orange and yellow energy centers from blockage is that the entire and undisturbed fullness of the power of the one great original Thought of the one infinite Creator may rise to the level of the heart, which is sometimes called the green-ray energy center. The other type of negative entity is a specialized one and of interest largely to those who have at some time chosen to begin a journey, a journey to the source of their beingness. This journey takes the rest of the lifetime and, of course, continues infinitely, yet it is in this density and at this time that more and more entities are making that choice, the choice to serve the Creator by serving others, or the choice to serve the Creator by serving the self. We are of those who serve the one infinite Creator through service to others, and so are each in this seeking circle, and in this we rejoice.

In this circle, for instance, this evening there is a strong power and a strong light. Those who are negatively oriented by careful purpose, whether they be incarnate or discarnate, have an automatic battle with those spots of positivity which glow too brightly and stand too plainly upon the hills of personal experience, for you see, you as a positive entity work not for yourself in terms of what you may gather, but for others, for it is the normal and necessary experience of one who is on the journey of seeking through love in service to others that a very large percentage of the time that you experience there will be some elements of negative intrusion, so that the entity feels not at all positive, but sadly out of kilter, out of tune. These are the productive deserts of testing and temptation in which it is necessary only for the pilgrim of positivity to remain peaceful, loving, gentle, harmless and warrior-like.

Now, we say warrior-like in a very specific way. We ask that you consider what it is that you do in attempting to serve the one infinite Creator. Do you shamble along as a person and put together various collections of pretty things to share in happiness with other pretty people? Or do you wish to live a life in such a way that it is in the end a gift to the one infinite Creator, a gift you have made day by day, moment by moment? You have been given help, and we say from our standpoint, we have been given help. All those presences in the universe which are positive await your call. You are never alone. There is always a solid backing of love, courage, patience and the instinct for the proper time to walk away waiting for you if you can but disengage your computer. Your computer cannot evaluate the intuitions of positive and negative energy that are at the heart of your work in consciousness.

Thus it is that we say that the most effective way to deal with negative energies is constant, persistent, faithful daily meditation, which frees the computer [to] make connections deeper and deeper down into the intuitive and archetypical mind. All of your strength, all of your universe, all of your answers lie deeply within you, and that which you learn, you recognize, and that recognition is the mark of your knowledge. And until you have that recognition, you do not have the knowledge.

As a warrior of light you use no weapon but what may be called the armor of light, the sword of truth, and a wide open heart chakra, loving without stint, without expectation of return, and most of all with no judgment. It is not difficult to love negatively oriented individuals once you can connect into that portion of your deep mind which sees each person, whatever the vagaries of trouble and circumstance, as a holograph of the one infinite Creator. This entity becomes utterly essential to you, and you may pray with a full heart with this person and move from strength to strength, from learning to learning. All threat disappears, all separation vanishes.

We do not wish you to think that we have forgotten our third-density experience. We know that the biases of this very effective illusion make it very difficult to view negative individuals without some alarm. Yet there is no control that such an entity may have over you if you but know who you are, if you but know the choice that you have made.

A portion of the query which began this meditation spoke of an actual incarnate negatively oriented pilgrim which was attempting by means of the use of thought forms negatively to influence the lives and peace of mind of other incarnate entities. This negative entity has learned how to use the light of the infinite Creator. The negative path is very difficult, but it can be walked and light can be learned in its many uses, this as positively. Therefore, it behooves the student of positive polarity constantly to exercise the will to polarize further towards positivity, and when negativity is viewed, to stop and give that entity the honor of an unstinting love, of a generous prayer that it may [be] held upward, that it may be protected, that it may be cherished and loved as a child of the one infinite Creator.

We say to you that those who are armed with light and go forth with that breastplate shining offer their love to those who flee before the onslaught of that terrible powerful creative love. You cannot possess this love, you can only be a channel through which it may flow. If there is this love within you, even such negative societal plans as those monetary and banking schemes questioned about can only seem that which the world wags on about. True, in a society devoted to the orderliness of what you call your bureaucracy, positive individuals are constantly bombarded with those who wish to control you, usually with good humor, with the control seeming to be for your own good, but to the self the control seeming to be anything but good.

It is in these situations where one may see the hidden enemy as the self. It is your negativity that recognizes the paper-pushing negativity of bureaucracy. There is no actual reason that you cannot in such a situation constantly center your mind upon the best that you know, the love that you have experienced, the light that you have indwelt, the joy that has been yours, not because you wish artificially to change your circumstances and so be impregnable to evil, but rather so you may enjoy yourself and give a lighter, more joyful gift at the end of your incarnational experience to the one Creator.

For, my children, your job is to live a life. Positivity and negativity are passions. They are frames of mind which engage the heart totally. When the student begins the path that he has chosen, he cannot recognize all positive moments for what they are, he cannot know how …

(Side one of tape ends.)

(Carla channeling)

… he cannot make a positive experience out of a negative one. Yet he can ask to be shown where the center of love in this experience is. This is a function of hope and faith, and each of you dwells within this environment, not yet being saints, and we say again there are few incarnate ones. You have not mastered the ability to be constantly loving and giving and caring. You have inner mysteries to beguile you, you have many duties and honors within the world of illusion. All about you says a thing which you cannot believe, that there is only chaos, that there is only chance. Those who have made the choice have made as the basis of this choice the realization that there is indeed a Maker, a Creator, which created in such and such a way for a purpose. Thus, each of you seeks in partial ignorance and darkness, through hope and faith, to find more and more that center of the self which truly sees negative infringements as experiences in which a gift may be offered, a gift of love.

Perhaps one who has been threatened and is in a state of profound fear may find what we have to say unhelpful, and to such an entity we say that there are those materials available for those who wish to know certain symbolic actions to take. We can only add to this understanding our opinion that these physical acts are ways of focusing the deeper portions of the mind so that the mind may bring up that great material of channeled, creative, divine, immeasurable love.

You are not on your own, my children. There are always those who have made the same choice as you, who are your companions upon the road. We wish you the joy of your challenges and your victories. Most of all, we thank you for this query. This instrument requests us to note the clicking sound as a time to cease our discussion, and so we do. We would at this time like to transfer the contact to the one known as Jim, that any queries that you may have might be considered by our humble selves, always wishing each to be fully aware that we are only pilgrims upon the path, and know little more than do you, so we are far from being infallible and would not wish to become a stumbling block for any. Thus, take what is good, leave what does not speak to you and know that this is what we wish. We would leave this instrument at this time with thanks, and transfer. I am Q'uo.

(Jim's voice throughout the rest of the transcript was difficult to hear.)

(Jim channeling)

I am Q'uo, and I greet you in love and light through this instrument. At this time we would ask if there might be any further queries to which we may speak

B: I have no further query, but would like to express my thanks *(inaudible)*.

I am Q'uo, and we thank you as well, my brother, for without your queries we could not [serve you in this way]. Are there any further queries?

Carla: I guess I have one. I'm thinking of a specific instance in which some negatively very sophisticated magus discovered a friend of mine when she was living in Seattle, extremely positively polarized woman, B, and talked to her on the phone, never met her in person, but called her up and said that he had been sent to help her with her meditations, and the first thing that she was supposed to do was to make something to cover her eyes when she meditated so she could concentrate better. She went this far and then became quite hysterical and ended up leaving the city.

When specific people call specific people and start a trip like this on them, is it enough simply to express love over the telephone? This entity was very persistent and was able to follow her through two changed phone numbers. I'm not sure that what you have said would make this woman feel comfortable yet. Could you tune in to that a little bit? Or is there advice to give at this point?

I am Q'uo and am aware of your query my sister. As we spoke to this it is most important that one recognize the creative power and responsibility that is perfect in one's perception, and form that perception as best as one can with the foundation firmly rooted in the loving acceptance of what one sees as the Creator. With this foundation set, then, in love, one may construct any action that the conscious mind can form, and act upon this action as the means by which the heart of love may be made manifest. Therefore, if any ritual or image or procedure is engaged as a means by which protection for the self might be offered, it is our suggestion that love be the motivation, for in such fashion thus one may love and do as one will.

May we speak further, my sister?

Carla: No, thank you.

I am Q'uo, and we thank you, my sister. Is there another query?

E: I would like to ask if you have any advice for G and myself for this coming year as we start our new service?

I am Q'uo, and, my sister, we can offer no greater advice than to seek one's heart's desires as purely as one can and as you move with passion in that loving expression, for you see each of you have the ability to create the [world] of service and [love] from whatever illusion stands before you. Thus, we can only lend our blessings to those thoughts, feelings and actions which are well begun within your own life patterns.

Is there another query?

E: No, thank you.

I am Q'uo, and we thank you, my sister. Is there a further query?

Questioner: *(Inaudible).*

I am Q'uo, and we find that the measure of time which you have called your new year is a means by which one can take the opportunity to readjust the perceptions, that one might, in the new experiencing, open the eye chakra and point of view to include more of your illusion and your experience within it within the realm of the compassion and love which animates each portion of your creation. Indeed, each day and moment you spend within it in a day is an opportunity yet to find that among your peoples. This is the time which is taken to begin again a new cycle of experience which is shared each with the others, a time when all again seems new and unblemished. Each, my friends, is a new moment and a further opportunity to open the inner eye to greater love within all experience.

May we speak in any further fashion, my brother?

Questioner: *(Inaudible).*

I am Q'uo. Are there any further queries?

(Pause)

I am Q'uo, and it has been our great honor and joyful opportunity to speak to this group this evening. We thank you for inviting our presence. We hope that we have been able to speak in a fashion which has been helpful. Please remember that we speak from our own experience and opinion and do not wish to present the unhelpful thought. Please disregard any word which does not ring true. We shall take leave of this group at this time, leaving each, as always, in the love and in the light of the one infinite Creator. We are known to you as those of Q'uo. Adonai, my friends. Adonai. ✲

Sunday Meditation
January 10, 1988

Group question: About parenting and discipline in particular. Question asked by C. Focus upon the proper relationship of the parent to the child and how best to establish that relationship.

(Carla channeling)

I am Q'uo. I greet you in the love and in the light of the one infinite Creator. It is a great privilege for me and my brother Hatonn to be with you this evening. Hatonn has been called to strengthen the meditative vibrations of those present, while we have been called to share our thoughts with you upon the subject upon how best to come into relationship with those young selves which have been entrusted to your care. Indeed, it is far more appropriate to speak of not only the actions of the parents to the children, but those intentions the children have towards the parent. We shall explain this.

Those who become parents are entities like any other, and those who become children are entities like any other, yet each is unique as only a self-conscious, self-aware entity can be. Indeed, each of you has chosen those entities whom you wish to teach or be taught by, and indeed these roles move back and forth throughout the relationship of parent and child.

Firstly, we shall gaze at the cultural and physical situation in which the young self is unable by itself to support the self with food and shelter and to learn those things which its culture requires that it learn before it may become a productive, grown entity within that culture. Thus, it is a basic and necessary duty and honor which each parent feels in feeding and clothing those young selves with whom it has come into relationship by birth in teaching those things which are asked in fulfilling the curiosity that questions and questions, insofar as it is possible. This is the nurturing and domestic, shall we say, portion of the relationship betwixt the parent and the child, or to put it a more clear way, a somewhat more experienced soul within this illusion and the soul with small experience within this illusion.

It is to be realized that each soul which comes into manifestation within this illusion of Earth is already an old soul, having had many experiences in lives past, and having developed from those experiences certain biases, beliefs, characteristics and behaviors which are not taught within the present incarnation, but which are brought to the incarnation. These biases are those which it is desired by both the parent and the young soul to be those things which shall be worked upon and learned from within this life experience. Therefore, it is for both parent and child to realize that when situations become complex and disturbing, parent may help child and child may help parent by linking their wills together and taking the backward step to ask the question, "What do we wish from each other? How are we trying to teach each other?"

As the parent goes about your culture's rather complex business of creating the means whereby to purchase those things which are necessary within your culture for survival and comfort, the entity may perhaps become overly concerned with those things of the material world, for it is always seemingly difficult to, as you say, make the ends meet. By being concerned with these things, the parent is teaching the child the nature of the need for money, the need for power, the need for self-aggrandizement within the illusion. These lessons are helpful within the framework of the mundane world.

However, it is well that the parent also be concerned enough about itself and about its responsibility to that young self which has come into relationship with it to create and maintain a daily, loving, persistent and genuine search for that spiritual truth which cannot be found in the hustle and bustle of the busy world of the market place and your televisions. For children, as you call these souls with small experience, learn that which is offered to them, and will learn gladly from the television. We do not say there is anything inimical to a child's growth in this pursuit, we only suggest that if the child does not see the parents engaged in earnest and sincere and persistent spiritual seeking, the child shall be vulnerable to any charismatic entity teaching whatever distortion of the laws of love and service in whatever highly distorted manner.

In short, the key to the relationship of the more experienced soul and the less experienced soul within this illusion is a recognition of the fact that the lesser experienced soul shall learn from imitation, and though talk may aid to some extent, the actions are always the key to what the less experienced soul shall learn from the parent.

You ask about the best ways to discipline a child. This is a somewhat difficult subject upon which to speak, for we find in higher densities that the vibrations affecting and radiating from the self are such that the entity disciplines the self, no matter how young. If a young entity feels in a state of alienation and wishes to strike out, that individual will find itself in an environment which allows it to do just such things in an harmless manner and for as long as it wishes.

With higher density's more relaxed and capacious time dimensions, it is acceptable to allow a young soul to play and avoid learning what needs to be learned, for whatever time it may take for that entity to become curious, fascinated, hungry for knowledge. At that time the small entity moves to a teacher, asking to learn. The teacher teaches and would be considered a hard taskmaster. But because the pupil is ready now to learn by its own decision, this difficulty of study and learning is accepted by the student itself. Not all young entities desire to learn the same things. And thus the concept of the school to us is a concept of teachers which wait the desire of the young entity to learn. Each learning shall be different. Each entity is accepted as different.

And now we come to you, parents and children of third-density illusion. Your culture believes most thoroughly in the numbers. It assumes that all those that have been upon your planet for six trips about your sun are ready, willing and eager to learn that which is taught in first grade. And so forth, through each year, each grade, and often each mismatch of student and teacher. The regimentation of the schooling creates a great difficulty for the young soul, for the young soul knows that true knowledge is not boring, but exciting, and will learn fast and eagerly and with joy when subjects arise in which that young soul has an interest. Yet, with a sigh, the young soul must put that idea apart and away, for your culture's schooling is regimented. Thus, a large portion of the young soul's experience throughout what is known as childhood is a highly regimented scholastic situation in which all are required to learn bodies of information which may fascinate one and leave another completely indifferent.

Now let us look at the question of discipline. The keynote to discipline between parent and child or elder soul and younger soul is that the elder soul shall not take away the worth of the younger, but express only those corrections which may normalize, one might say, that younger soul's relationship to the culture in which it must live after it grows into a more elderly status. Often elder and younger souls of the same family are placed together to continue working upon the question of how to love, how truly to love, for this entire illusion is designed as an environment in which people go about that one learning activity from their earliest remembrances until, at long last in the fullness of age, that soul shuts its eyes and departs this small shadow of life.

Many of those things which the young soul may do which seem mischievous are those expressions which indicate the young soul's inability to express the pain through which it is going. And many of the punishments offered by those older souls called parents are ways of expressing the frustration and pain of knowing no way to aid the younger soul. Thusly, each soul is in distress and each has closed itself from communication, for it feels it cannot communicate.

One very positive way of communicating those behaviors which are acceptable in that which is called your society to a young soul is to behave as the older soul in the way in which the teaching would point that the parent is doing. Thusly, the young soul learns from imitation. There are many occasions when the young soul cannot at first see the wisdom of one or another behavior that has been chosen by the culture to be appropriate rather than another. These public behaviors are often appropriate simply to allow others which share that public space their own measure of quiet and relaxation. Thusly, within the social situation the discussion may be had prior to the public outing that certain behaviors are appropriate within the culture within which both souls live. This does not make behaviors right or wrong in any fundamental sense, but rather behavior of certain kind appropriate. The discipline for a younger soul which begins acting in an inappropriate manner for being within the public society would be to remove the self and the beloved younger soul from the public environment so that it is clear that there are some behaviors which cannot be acceptable within the public experience.

Similarly, there are those behaviors in dealing with others within the family which are appropriate in that they cause the family of souls which care for each other to become uncomfortable and strained, jarring and unhappy. The young soul, which at first is rebellious, may perhaps be allowed its point of view, spoken, listened to and understood by the elder entity. Yet then, if the parent considers that the young soul under his tutelage is acting in ways which are not appropriate for dealing with other selves, then it is that these behaviors must be changed by means of the explanation of inappropriateness or the simple removal of the young soul from the immediate environment of the distress which has been caused. It is to be realized that in any interaction of this kind, the discipline must needs be honest, sincere and compassionate, for though a child's soul is young in this illusion, it is the equal of any, and recognizes clearly any half truth or slanted or biased way of expressing thought.

As we gaze upon your culture and at the shifting, changing, turbulent relationships betwixt what you might call adult souls within your culture, we find it an expectable characteristic that those young souls which must come into this culture of uncertainty and materialistic eagerness to acquire things should be aggressive and disturbing in [their] behavior. Thus, after the process of living has been going on for the young soul for ten years, shall we say, we find that within your highly mobile …

(Side one of tape ends.)

(Carla channeling)

… culture the effect is that of, perhaps, twice that much of your time, nay perhaps more than that, in terms of the experience of a vicarious nature which the young soul has accumulated through the watching of information sources such as your television, the listening to your radio devices and your tape machines.

Perhaps to sum up our encouragement of the parent who wishes to know about discipline, we should suggest, number one, that they would live as they would suggest their children to live; number two, that they be honest in their dealings with those souls given into their care, meaning what they say and saying what they mean. And thirdly, when discipline is to be accomplished, allow that discipline to be such a one as may perhaps sting the pride of the young soul in a private way, but not in such a way that others might know that this soul is being disciplined, and that by this much loved parent.

Thus, we move the focus of discipline of children into two areas. Firstly, the arena of the parent, in which the parent is encouraged to think deeply about stressing the spiritual, the just, and the lovely, and second, the arena of the child, in which the child may learn to trust the honesty of the parent and may learn by imitation those things which are to be learned. We know that parents and children and all entities whatever shall fall and clamber up again many times. Mistakes are made upon top of mistakes, yet there is one deep and fathomless thing which binds parent to child, and that is love, for the parent cannot help but love the child, nor can the child help but love the parent. Let this love be communicated. Let this love be celebrated. Never let this love be taken for granted. Love each other, for you are both pilgrims upon the road, parent and child. The parent must do a good deal of guiding, suggesting and, yes, disciplining, for the best road to learn has its limits, its right side and its left side, and beyond that road lie desolate deserts of experience which are not helpful in the sense of learning of love.

My friends, we know that in an environment where alienation between all peoples is so common, we may sound impossibly idealistic, but we say to you that if a parent can trust a child, if a parent can keep its word to a child, both in good and in bad, if a parent may respect the young soul, the young soul shall reflect and imitate this behavior.

May you love each other. May you feel the harmony of the plans you have made together. May you trust even in hard times that this is part of the outworking of an harmonious plan, at the end of which you shall know more about how to love, the greatest lesson that this density has to teach.

At this time we would transfer this contact to the one known as Jim. I am Q'uo.

(Jim channeling)

I am Q'uo, and greet each again in love and light through this instrument. At this time it is our privilege to offer ourselves in the attempt to speak to any further queries which those present may have for us. Again we remind each that we give that which is our opinion, and we offer it joyfully and freely, asking that any words that do not ring true be left behind without a second thought. Is there a query to which we may speak?

C: Not a question, but a statement. The question that I did have has been well answered in your message tonight. It has shown me reinforcing things that I knew but did not implement, so I want to say thank you for your words.

I am Q'uo, and, my brother, we thank you, for without such queries we would have no means of being of service that would speak as directly to the heart of the needs. Is there a further query at this time?

Carla: I have been feeling uneasy about the possibility of channeling with only two people in the group, and I got a telephone call from a sister whom I believe to be on the watchtower, praying for me constantly. She felt that there was some negative influence that had become alerted to our presence for some reason. And I wondered if you could comment on the practice of two entities tuning, challenging and channeling with only two present?

I am Q'uo, and we feel that it is not a practice which is generally recommended, for there are, as you are aware, those who would wish to cause mischief in such a setting where the protective wall of light has not been added unto a sufficient manner. However, there are instances of entities who are so harmoniously prepared to work in tandem that this difficulty does not necessarily hold sway. We therefore can give only a limited recommendation to such efforts and can further suggest that if this be found to be necessary, that those presently partaking in such efforts redouble the desire to be of service through such vocal channeling and find the most clear and purified tuning together and within that is possible to achieve, in order that the desire to serve might be reflected not only in the protection, but in the inner preparation that allows such contact to occur. We are aware that those who presently partake in this activity are unable to fully grasp the means by which the protection is offered in any such gathering, and are therefore somewhat concerned that this means of carrying out such service be done in a manner which is stable and secured, and we commend the diligence that requires this question to be asked.

May we speak in any further fashion, my sister?

Carla: No, thank you.

I am Q'uo and we thank you, my sister. Is there another query?

(Pause)

I am Q'uo, and it appears that we have exhausted the queries for this evening. We would thank each for inviting our presence, and especially greet and thank the one known as A for allowing our presence and for being a part of this circle of seeking this evening. It has been our great privilege and honor to speak to each, and we shall be with you upon your mental requests in the future to aid your meditations and to speak when asked upon those topics that have meaning to you. We are known to you as those of Q'uo, and at this time we shall take our leave of this instrument and this group, leaving each, as always, in the love and in the light of the one infinite Creator. Adonai, my friends. Adonai. ☥

L/L Research

L/L Research is a subsidiary of Rock Creek Research & Development Laboratories, Inc.

P.O. Box 5195
Louisville, KY 40255-0195

www.llresearch.org

Rock Creek is a non-profit corporation dedicated to discovering and sharing information which may aid in the spiritual evolution of humankind.

ABOUT THE CONTENTS OF THIS TRANSCRIPT: This telepathic channeling has been taken from transcriptions of the weekly study and meditation meetings of the Rock Creek Research & Development Laboratories and L/L Research. It is offered in the hope that it may be useful to you. As the Confederation entities always make a point of saying, please use your discrimination and judgment in assessing this material. If something rings true to you, fine. If something does not resonate, please leave it behind, for neither we nor those of the Confederation would wish to be a stumbling block for any.

CAVEAT: This transcript is being published by L/L Research in a not yet final form. It has, however, been edited and any obvious errors have been corrected. When it is in a final form, this caveat will be removed.

© 2009 L/L Research

Sunday Meditation
January 17, 1988

Group question: Concerns reincarnation and the means by which the process of reincarnation enhances our overall growth as entities.

(Carla channeling)

I am Q'uo. I greet you in the love and the light of the one infinite Creator. It is a privilege and a blessing to be called to your group this evening, and we thank you for your hope, your desire to learn, and the beauty of your vibrations as you sit with ears that pray to hear and hearts that wish to understand. May we offer special love and greeting to the ones known as M and J, and welcome them to this circle of seeking. We ask, as always, that each entity understand that our opinions, which we give freely, are not infallible, therefore we ask that if any word which we say seems unwise in any listener's ear, that it be forgotten, for the truth is such that the seeker shall recognize it for itself, and we ask that each employ this discrimination.

That said, we shall turn to the question of reincarnation. We must begin with background information, for reincarnation takes place against the great stage of creation and is an integral part of a vast process which is at the heart most simple. We know that in your holy works you hear the words, "In the beginning," and yet we say to you that to the best of our understanding, the Creator exists infinitely, and that it is only this particular creation that has a beginning and shall have an end. It is our understanding that there shall be and there have been many creations, and that who each of you is is the Creator. Now, we shall certainly have to do some talking to explain such a bold statement.

Perhaps we could describe our concept of the Creator to you as a vast infinity which is also intelligent. The completeness of infinity is such that it cannot be held in the mind; it cannot be understood by that portion of the spirit which is within incarnation. It is beyond understanding. Yet it is our opinion that the Creator chose to create a universe, a vast, infinitely vast, universe, which would sustain the physical vehicles of entities which were as a holograph of the Creator, so that all that was in the Creator was in the conscious entity, and all conscious entities were the Creator.

A way of coming back to the Creator which had sent these entities forth was offered, a vast plan which has been unfolding for eons, and shall continue we know not how long. Each of what you call your planetary systems dwelt first in the consciousness that is the Creator, lived in a state of love, which is another name for the Creator, and in the fullness of time, planets were formed and that process you call evolution took place.

The first lessons were very simple. There was the lesson of existence itself, lessons that your rocks and your sea and your fire and your air still learn. Then came lessons of growth and a turning towards the light, and many plants flourished, and animals began that slow process of learning. And eventually within each portion of consciousness there came to be a turning not only towards the light, but towards the love that lies behind light, and thus an entity became ready in physical vehicle nature to receive infinity.

This is who you are. You dwell in a physical vehicle as any of your animals, and within you, through your many experiences before becoming what you would call human, and what this entity calls third density, you have made yourself ready to be self-aware. Many, many lifetimes ago you began this portion of a walk which seekers, having once begun, do not ever leave. You have begun the self-conscious awareness and seeking towards what? What has the Creator intended for those, who are self-aware and contain infinity, to pursue?

Now we shall move to a slightly different aspect of the same question. You have lived for many, many lifetimes already in this environment or density of experience, and by now you have observed over and over and over that much of the experience that you gather seems to be about love, love expressed in selfish ways and love expressed in service to others and to the Creator. The overall plan, which the Creator made available and which lasts not only through this density, but through many densities, indeed, those higher than are we, this process has to do with attempting to grasp the nature of the Creator. It is our opinion that the nature of this Creator is the nature of one singular thought, and that thought is the thought of love.

Now, the densities of experience and learning above your own are a process of refining that which you, within the density you now enjoy, have decided upon. This, your Earth world, is an exciting and difficult illusion, designed to create for you opportunities to make a simple choice, the choice to serve the Creator by serving others or to serve the Creator by serving yourself. Since the Creator's nature is that one great original Thought of love, service begins and ends in love. Since you are of the very nature and stuff of the Creator, you yourselves in your essence are perfect love. It is a matter of finding and recognizing that true nature and then of choosing to express and manifest that nature by loving and serving those about you.

To love and serve those to whom you are most close is very difficult. The environment of your illusion was intended to make such expression difficult. Thus, although you have had many experiences and have made many choices, some wise and perhaps some foolish, these things have been veiled from your memory. You come into this illusion through a veil of forgetting. The forgetting of past relationships, past biases, past opinions and experiences is intentional, for ever-new are the opportunities to make and remake the choice to serve and manifest the love of the one infinite Creator.

Thus, as you gaze back upon your many other lives, what is quintessential, and most profoundly so in your understanding of these past experiences, is kept within your feelings, within your deep mind and within your heart. They express themselves to you in promptings of emotion, in feelings of recognition, in the awareness of past experience and in frequent suppositions that perhaps a difficulty which cannot be explained by present circumstance may have been part of the outworking of energies which were not brought into balance in a previous life experience.

Thus, as we talk to you about reincarnation, we wish to not downplay the experiences of the past, but reassure each entity that when past experiences become a necessity, they will float into the conscious mind through dreams, or most especially through meditation. In general, we may say that it is not helpful in a deep way to know past life experiences, but rather it is helpful in terms of your desire to accelerate your process of spiritual evolution, to be more and more sensitive to the promptings of your intuition, your feelings, and your heart, thus becoming more and more sensitive to those energies that are passing between you and those about you. Thus, if you find yourself at odds with a co-worker, a friend, a companion, or a loved one, it is well to move into meditation, asking and releasing the question of where the balances of love and service have gone awry in this particular instance, and more than that, how you may bring love back into manifestation within the circumstance, how balance may be restored, how love may thrive.

What we are saying to you is perhaps too much in too short a time, yet this instrument reminds us that we wish not to be over-long in our message. But know that the greatest advantage that you may have within your experience is the advantage of daily meditation. It need not be for a great period of your time. It may be perhaps, as this instrument would say, a half hour or less. It may be the striking of a clock that may cause you to stop and find the silence within. Any attempt whatsoever at clearing the mind and asking for deeper understandings to come into one's ken are to be encouraged, and most of all to be encouraged is the dailyness of this activity. You will find that meditation itself begins a process of change, and it is well that those who are mated together begin and continue the process together, for that which you seek you shall find. This is indeed a spiritual truth.

We are speaking to those who have already made the choice to serve others as a means of learning to know the Creator, as a means of experiencing relationship with the Creator. Therefore, we may freely and joyfully urge each to know the self as one who may be a channel of light, a channel of love, not by your own Earthly energies, for they fail, but by becoming through meditation aware of that which comes through one from the infinite creation, that which is infinite love. Thus, more and more you may become a light to those about you, not so much by what you do as by the smile in your eye, the peace of your expression, the gentleness of the reply to a hard rebuke, the kindness to a stranger. And each time that you attempt to serve, you run the risk of failure, and when you feel that you have failed, it is a temptation to think poorly of oneself. We ask you never to feel such sad feelings, but simply to pick oneself up and continue, for you are an harmonious part of an infinite plan whereby the Creator in its infinity learns more and more about Itself, for each of us who are companions upon the path back to the Source in our relationships with each other express the Creator's thoughts to the Creator, for each of you is a spark, an infinite part of an infinite Father.

Many of those whom you meet within your incarnational experience shall be familiar to you one way or another. See each as the Creator. Serve each in love, for loving each other is the greatest service that consciousness is capable of. Eventually, as the process of refinement goes on, you may learn as we believe we have learned, that all consciousness is one, and that we are all one great being, a portion, infinitely precious, of the Creation itself.

Your third-density experience upon this planet grows short. Soon there shall be new lessons, a new illusion and an exciting new beginning. Yet the nature of that experience is shaped by your decision to serve the cause of love during these final life experiences. May you see and bless the many, many lives you have learned in your deep-felt biases and opinions, in your love of the good, the beautiful, and the true, and your distaste for that which is dark and negative. May you believe in your strength as those who have been choosing and learning for many thousands of your years, and may you always have the light touch in your studies, laughing together in times of joy, and finding the light side in times of sadness, that your life may become more and more a balancing of all those energies with all those with whom you are in relationship.

You have heard of the word, karma. The end of karma is forgiveness. If you find a certain entity particularly difficult, seek the seeds of forgiveness in the infinite love which lies within you, for as you forgive the other entity and yourself, so you have balanced in love that which before blocked energy and stopped the process of spiritual growth.

At this time we would transfer this contact to the one known as Jim that he may answer any further questions that this group may have at this time. We have been most joyful to have been able to speak with you, and we thank you once again. I am Q'uo.

(Jim channeling)

I am Q'uo, and greet each again in love and light through this instrument. At this time it is our privilege to attempt to speak to any further queries which any of this group may offer to us. Again we remind each that we offer our opinions freely but hope that any word that does not ring true will be forgotten immediately, for we do not wish to present a stumbling block in your journey of seeking. Is there a question at this time?

Carla: Yeah, I've got one. How about contemplatives, that don't see anybody or interact with anybody, and just keep silent and sit in mountain caves and contemplate? How are they serving each other?

I am Q'uo. There are many among your peoples who move in the daily stream of activity, partaking of all that your illusion and your experience has to offer and distilling [from] this experience that which they themselves have determined before the incarnation would be the point, the goal of the incarnation. These lessons have to do with some aspect of learning that quality that you might call unconditional love or compassion. Each learns in an unique fashion according to what has been learned in previous incarnations and according to that which remains to be learned. Those that find the solitary experience of most use in the life pattern learn the same kind of lesson but in a fashion which is more inwardly directed, rather than utilizing the outer stimulus of other entities and the relationships that are formed in the normal, shall we say, means of living and experiencing the incarnation. Those who learn in a solitary fashion enhance their own understanding of the purpose of their incarnations and express that love which they have learned in a manner which is likened unto the radio station which broadcasts a certain frequency of information. These then, as all who have learned any portion of the lesson of love, become likened unto beacons for this love that is felt by all fellow entities upon the subconscious levels, as you would call them, and provide a kind of nourishment for the species, much as the gardener provides the fertilizer for the plants within its garden. Thus does the great creative power of love move through all its creations, whether they be found in the fertile valleys or the high mountain caves.

(Side one of tape ends.)

(Jim channeling)

I am Q'uo, and am again with this instrument. May we speak in any further fashion, my sister?

Carla: No, thank you, Q'uo.

I am Q'uo. Is there a further query?

(Pause)

I am Q'uo, and we find that for this evening we have exhausted those queries which it has been our honor to entertain and to speak to. We thank each for the invitation to join this group and for the great offering of love that we feel from each. We return love in kind. We look forward to the future opportunities to join this circle of seeking, and at this time shall take our leave of this group, leaving each, as always, in the love and in the light of the one infinite Creator. We are known to you as those of Q'uo. Adonai, my friends. Adonai.

Intensive Meditation
February 3, 1988

(Carla channeling)

I am Hatonn. I greet each of you this evening in the love and in the light of the infinite Creator. We had been intending to continue attempting to make contact with the one known as D, until that instrument spontaneously initiated a contact. However, we find that the one known as D has the divided mind due to the desire to hear our opinions on subjects which interest him at this time. This is considerably dislocating the readiness to channel, and we understand that perhaps it is better for us to speak to the subject requested and then to exercise the instrument. May we say, however, that in our opinion, it is a most helpful skill to be learned by a new instrument to initiate a contact, for in sessions to come, where there is not a more experienced channel, this ability will be necessary, and, indeed, is not a difficult lesson to learn once that leap of faith has been taken, the preparation done well, and the releasing of all eventualities made so that once the channel begins to speak the words heard within, the channel is no longer any part of the message in an initiatory sense, but is only expressing that which has come through to the conscious mind. This skill shall come to the one known as D, and we do not wish to make it seem harder than it is. However, we recognize the difficulty of doing it for the first few times.

And so let us turn to some thoughts we may share which you may find some value in. As always, these are our opinions only, and not to be taken as a kind of gospel.

We dwell at this moment with three entities who wish to heal the planetary energies and the energies of the people who live upon that planet which you call Earth. Healers come in different disguises. Some are doctors and nurses, some parents, some friends, some ministers, and some those who use the techniques of probing through into the deeper mind in order to bring up material which may be of help in assisting the conscious mind to sort out the pattern of an incarnational experience. Thus, it is well for each in this circle to think of itself first as a healer, and only secondly as a teacher or channel or hypnotherapist.

There are certain requirements if one is to heal, that is, if one is to heal in a spiritually balanced manner, healing with the self rather than with chemicals or with mechanical devices such as surgery. The one great requirement of a healer is that the healer be one with the desire to live a balanced life. The balance of a life is unique to each entity, yet the key to that balance is that within the hurry-scurry of the daily round, the healer has hollowed out a place within heart, mind and spirit wherein the light exists and is acknowledged, so that at all times the healer is capable of being and functioning as a living crystal.

It is this balance which enables a healer to use a tool such as channeling, teaching or hypnotherapy as a focus for those intuitions and deep promptings which may see far more deeply into the one who presents itself to be healed than could one whose eyes were those not filled with crystal light, but rather with human error. The process of healing is a process whereby the healer acts as a catalyst, arranging the sensing, thinking and feeling apparati of the one to be healed in such a way that, for a short time, a new vision of a new balance may be brought before the attention of the one to be healed. It is then the matter of free choice for the one to be healed. It may choose to accept the new balance made possible by this catalyst, or it may choose, in time, to disregard it and remain unbalanced. Thus, even the most powerful of healers is not itself expected to use its will upon another entity, but rather simply to act as a living crystal which may correct unbalanced light vibrations within the energy web of the one to be healed.

We say these things because, as the one known as D and as anyone gazes at an opportunity for service, we feel it is important that the gaze first be turned inward, to ask if the entity may pay the price for this service, for to begin enthusiastically and to lose so much energy that the service must be ended is perhaps a wrong use of will, and clearer listening needs to be done as to what sort of service is appropriate. If the healer is prepared to pay the price of living a certain kind of life, and we feel that each in this group intends to be so, then it is necessary only to choose the manner of service and maintain, with the greatest of enthusiasm and ardent love, the manner of life, living, thinking and being which nourishes and feeds that crystal soul within.

Now we would say a word about the efficacy of gazing into the past. The ability of the mind has never been appropriately estimated. Within each entity's mind lies the personal and racial record of biases, learning, wisdoms, teachings and experiences. There is no loss within the Creation. There is a burning away of matter, yet the flame of energy remains, and that is called memory. The power of a teacher to tap into another's far memory is variable, and it is well that this practice be handled in a most delicate and forthright fashion. Delicate in the sense of moving slowly and considering with the client each question to be asked carefully. Forthright in that each dealing, each suggestion, each new understanding be made available to the student just as the teacher is available for discussion concerning the material uncovered.

There is within some entities naturally given to the lifting of the veil greatly enhanced opportunity to go far deeper into the mind than is usual. For the most part we would guide warningly against taking advantage of these opportunities. It is possible to carry out this kind of research upon oneself, working deeper into the racial memory through working with the dreams and working with autohypnosis. In this way, the student of the hypnotherapy may gain information without disturbing the integrated personality of another being. Thus, we caution one who approaches a subject to guard against taking the opportunities with another entity. Unless this entity becomes a staunch co-worker and associate, such work is too risky for the subject to be considered an acceptable practice.

Gazing at the obverse side of a warning, we do find it so that when a student comes to a healer to ask for that which the healer does, the student has therefore done a great deal of preparatory work to engage in its own healing. Thus, the healer who is a hypnotherapist or a teacher or a channel is offered an opportunity to be of service, and this is cause for rejoicing for those whose wish is to serve the Father and to love each brother and sister with a spiritual embrace that magnifies the opportunity to gain in spiritual learning.

Now, there may be many questions upon your mind at this time, but before we work with questions, we would like to exercise the instrument known as D, and so would speak about related subjects. We would, as always, encourage the instrument and speak our thoughts as they come to him. We have had a very good contact now for several sessions, and are pleased with this instrument's growing awareness of us. We thank the instrument for its tuning, and encourage it in its channeling to challenge before the channeling. This is sometimes disruptive, yet if the patience is kept the challenging may be done so that the words may begin.

We transfer now to the one known as D. I am Hatonn.

(D channeling)

I am Hatonn, and I greet you again through this instrument in love and light. We would speak briefly on the subject of this instrument's challenging, which we find to be effective in its mode of initiating contact and exercising the required degree of control over that contact, but we would encourage further work and attention to clarifying the process in the instrument's own mind, so as to make it more comfortable and less cause for confusion, anxiety or doubt.

We would continue our discussion on the subject of healing, especially *(inaudible)* the mental phenomenon of trance or hypnosis.

(Long pause.)

We do find a basis of *(inaudible)* and preconception in the mind which arouses the critical mind as we attempt to address this subject. For physical relaxation and the mental relaxation and flexibility …

(Long pause.)

We are seeking to offer this instrument experience of inner process which may be instructive and give insight into the experience of hypnotic trance. An inner conflict, struggle which the mind is capable of creating within itself, can indeed give rise to fragmentation of the mind and *(inaudible)* up, so to speak, of the mind's conflict when both of the conflicting inner voices are allowed to express themselves, if this conflict is not attended to and resolved in some measure.

We are attempting [to answer questions] the instrument itself posed. Our lesson is that the answers to these questions are available through the process of inner questioning. This gives rise, of course, to the question of why are so many sincere seekers apparently led astray when they listen to the voice within them, the answers that arise from their own deeper minds in response to questions posed to it. The answer, of course, is that truth is not absolute. The process of posing questions and going within to find answers leads to a course of action which brings the light of truth into the experience of the seeker and creates in his life the circumstances for the spiritual unfoldment of both that seeker and those who share in his experience, while another, posing the same question in his own sincere meditations may find a completely opposing answer being given, but one which creates in his life the same truth in the form of a course of action leading to lessons which contribute to the highest good [of] those involved in that action.

We will have some comments about the effects of the critical mind on the channeling process which shall be given through the instrument known as Carla. We will now transfer to that instrument. I am Hatonn.

(Carla channeling)

I am Hatonn, and am again with this instrument, greeting you once again in love and in light. We ask this instrument's permission and receive it to move back some few seconds in your time and verbalize the actual challenging procedure which this instrument used during the regaining of this contact. You will note the use of the critical mind, balanced by the use of intuition. This instrument first repeated several times, "Lord, make me an instrument of Thy peace." We shall proceed from there without expressing who said what to whom, as it should be obvious.

"Who comes in the name of Jesus the Christ, whom I serve with all my heart, all my mind, all my soul, all my strength?"

"I am Hatonn."

"I challenge you in the name of Jesus the Christ."

"I am of that principle."

"Begone if you are not of Jesus the Christ. Begone. Begone. Begone."

"Very good. We are of Jesus the Christ, for we are all Christ."

"I ask in the name of Jesus the Christ."

"Yes, my child. Jesus the Christ. We answer that challenge."

"Are you ready for me to begin?"

"No, my child. Tune again."

"Lord, make me an instrument of Thy peace. Lord, make me an instrument of Thy peace. Lord, may every word I speak be Your Truth and none other. Am I ready?"

"You are ready?"

"Very well."

This is the process in a somewhat shortened form of the challenging which this instrument is attempting to teach. The form is shortened because it is not the first tuning and challenging of the session. Note that the critical mind is an all-important factor in the listening and evaluating both of the condition of the self as channel and the words which answer the challenge. The fact that these are heard mentally rather than audibly means, however, that the faculty of intuition be, in a balanced fashion, brought to bear upon the process. Indeed, at one point within this session, the instrument through whom we speak at this time was able to detect the gradual moving of the state of mind of the one known as D into that neutral area which is untuned and therefore far more easily sullied with negatively-oriented channeling.

This instrument has been given an ability to believe its own visualizations, which is helpful. In other words, the use of the critical mind in attempting to detect places where light may be leaking from the circle is not advised. Intuition and visualization are to be advised. This is, of course, important in the context of the one known as D being responsible for its own cleansed atmosphere before any spiritual working and during the working itself. This instrument, through a series of visualizations, peeled away that which was perceived as a glowing scaly shell which was blocking positive thought. And when it, at last, peeled away, it was the top of the head which peeled away the last, thus symbolically indicating that the source of the detuning was indeed within the critical mind.

The rule is simple: one applies every discrimination and uses the critical mind with the utmost of care, for the critical mind, the conscious mind, the thoughtful self, is a tool, a wonderful, smoothly working, highly complex, efficient tool for accumulating data and making decisions. Like any other tool, it can become the master of the user of that tool. We do not suggest to any of an intellectual bent the speaking ill of the activity of the mind, for if the mind is critical and discriminatory, then this tool was meant to be, and meant to be used.

But an entity is not a mind any more than an entity is a stomach, a foot, a hand or a heart. Instinctively, entities within your illusion recognize your physical body as a series of excellent tools, and by using hands and mind and senses and sensibilities, humankind has created a great many, many artifacts, thought a great many thoughts worth preserving and passing on, and accomplished far-sweeping histories of war and crime and sadness, as well as peace and honor and joy.

And when the scales have tipped toward the negative, you may be sure that there is a band of entities whose conscious minds have made harsh judgments, and who then require their will and their faith to stand in support of those ideologies, be they philosophical, religious or simply dominating. We urge balance upon each, for working with intuition only, without the use of the intellect, produces an entity lost in a sea of experience, sensation and wonder, an entity who is without the tools to express what is occurring, to refine an understanding of it, and to seek ways of manifesting that beauty which has been received in some service to those about it.

Do not see the mind that is critical and the mind that intuits as two sides of a coin or two separate things. See rather, to use our favorite image, that portion of the tree which is above the ground, which blossoms and rocks in the breeze of summer, and stands naked and proud against the winter cold as the conscious mind, in intimate contact with the illusion, able to flower, blossom and expand, and able also to hunch the back, stiffen the self, and be protective against difficult influences. See the intuitive mind as a great underground system of the roots of this same living tree. In winter and in summer alike, they are in contact with the Creator, drinking in nourishment from earth and water, storing, nurturing and keeping watch over the life of that visible tree which nods above the ground. There are far more roots to the mind than there are visible trunks and branches, and the ends of the roots lies in the center of the Sun. Thus, the deeper mind has the opportunity to contact intelligent infinity itself, eternity and everness.

How precious is the entire being, the entire consciousness that you call the mind and that is truly yourself. May you see it in a loving and holistic way. May you glory in your branches, in your thoughts, in your ramifications, in your distinctions, and in your conclusions as you go onward from conclusion to conclusion. But may your faith be in the system of roots that links you to eternity, and may your will be more and more to place the tree above ground in the service of that greater consciousness which lies within the nurturing darkness of earth and water and, finally, fire.

We thank each that we have been able to speak this evening, and shall forego the question period, as the energy of the circle begins to wane due to the length of time during which you have been focused upon this contact. We thank you for calling us to you this evening, and especially we thank the channel which is becoming less new, and more and more able. We hope to speak with you again, and for now we will leave you in the love and in the light of the one infinite Creator. Adonai. ✻

Sunday Meditation
February 7, 1988

Group question: C has a question about a friend of his who is suffering what has been diagnosed as narcolepsy. He's able to contact his wife, for example, and to have what seems to be out-of-body experiences during the seeming sleep. We're wondering how out-of-body experiences in general, and in this case as well, could be used to advance one's spiritual growth?

(Carla channeling)

I am Q'uo. I greet you in the love and in the light of the one infinite Creator. What a blessing it is, my friends, to greet each of you, to bless you and to express our love to you and our thanks for that you have called us to offer our unworthy opinions upon the subjects that are close to your heart at this time. We are most happy to serve in this capacity, and wish only to say, as always, that we do not claim to be infallible, for we are not. We are your brothers and sisters, and we may share with you what we have gleaned from our walk along the pilgrim's path, that and no more. We are learning and we hope we may give you a hand up in your studies. May we join you in praise to the one infinite Creator and in the joy of fellowship, as vibrations of gentleness and peace and joy move in ever more purified strength about the circle that you have made within this domicile at this time.

You have asked a question concerning spontaneous movements from the body and their use. We may speak to some extent in a more general way before we move back to this particular phenomenon, for there is a basis or a principle which applies to many seemingly unrelated events.

It is our understanding that each of you in that timeless time, before you began your incarnation upon your world, chose carefully the manner by which you would prefer to learn each lesson which you put yourself to study. In that way you are like the student in the school, knowing that your ultimate examination shall take place when the schoolroom is no more and the physical body that carried the brilliance within is also no more. Thus, no matter what circumstance appears before you, whether it be seemingly usual or seemingly unusual, there is in that circumstance, in the relationships about you, and in your days whatever they may be, every bit of catalyst that you need to bring to your attention the conflicts about which you need to make the choice between finding love and offering compassion and using control and effecting separation.

As this classroom of yours is attempting to study love, many lessons are concerned with the right use of compassion and love. There is the same energy generated by a mother who watches her children at play as by what you would call the most advanced and illumined being who was watching the doors of eternity, for no matter what the object of that love, that emotion has within it the strength to create and the terrible strength to destroy. It is an energy which your atomic bombs and your hydrogen bombs barely begin to express. And this energy which created you now flows through you. You may either block that energy or use that energy in order to accelerate the rate at which you learn about your environment, yourself, your Creator, and, as this instrument is so fond of saying, the relationship betwixt those two.

What are you to your deity? What is your Creator to you? We raise more questions than you asked, yet it is important that we lay this foundation, for we find that those who may move out of the physical shell, just as those who have other extra-sensory gifts, have been put in a special position. The scheme which is moving in order to influence the student, the pilgrim, to think about certain things, to come to certain conclusions and define certain areas of service, all of these things are to be considered, no matter what the circumstance. Thusly, if an entity has the controllable ability to leave the physical body, then perhaps there is some lesson of service, compassion and love to be learned within the use of this practice, just as those who [are] given other spiritual gifts are given them not only in order that they may grow, but that they may take their responsibility for that growth and become channels each in his own way, using the gift which has been given him in order to serve those about him.

A note about the practice of moving out of the body at will. Most entities which do so are not highly polarized, and are therefore not in particular danger by confrontation with those entities which do not like the light when it is used for compassion, and wish instead to use that light in a controlling and service-to-self manner. Thus, it is well in this instance when a gift has been given, to ask in meditation, not anxiously, but eagerly and with sincerity, "What may I do to serve the Creator with this gift?" Or, indeed, if this seeming gift in reality affects the entity as a limitation, the question should be, "What may I give as a result of those things which I learn from this condition?"

The space into which your Earth is moving at this time is more and more altered from the space/time you have enjoyed upon your planet for many thousands of your years. It is a space/time which contains a more generous fullness of the Creator's light. Sensitive entities are more and more able to use paranormal gifts. We make a plea to each who experiences these gifts and the interest which these gifts generate to seek not just the comparison of one gift with the gift of others, but also to begin through meditation, contemplation, the use of dreams, the reading, the talking with friends, to begin the process of knowing the true self, and once you have found that ground within you which is not your heartbeat or your thinking processes, but is your consciousness itself, once you have met yourself face-to-face for what you are, with your gifts and your limitations, then the time has come for you to make this an offering in humbleness and sincerity to the Creator, offering your talents, your gifts and your limitations with thanksgiving and praise.

If what you have seems to be very, very little, know that this is an illusion and what you are working on by this dedication is the lessening, little by little, of the power of this illusion you call life over you. Each entity brings much into the experience of incarnation. Rejoice in the richness of your deep mind. Rejoice in exactly who you are and seek to place that honest, naked, uncovered soul in the light and love of the one infinite Creator, knowing that that Creator is within you and you the Creator. Then can you stand on your two feet and be proud to offer whatever it is you have in a spirit of love and in the hope of sharing that love.

What can be the outcome of an ability to move in thought from the body? One may consider teaching. One may consider being taught. One may consider working consciously in such a state with that which is called in the Western tradition white ritual magic, strengthening the essential person which is that person which is removed from the physical vehicle so that it becomes a person of ability and power, able to meet other entities who have similarly slipped their fetters and may be bewildered and off course and in need of comfort. When you ask how you may offer your gifts, listen for the answer, but do not anticipate it. It may come in a moment or there may be a period of sustained disciplined meditation, a daily and sometimes difficult discipline. And eventually, because you have asked, you shall be answered.

In the meantime, the appropriate emotional and mental outlook and attitude is confusion, a state which is uncomfortable but very productive of new thought, new systems of thought, and the transformation from the lower to the higher entity of that of which you are capable. Remember always when you gaze upon the so-called occult gifts, that they are gifts, just as the gifts of supply which are given to some and not to others, the gift of intellectual intelligence given to some and in lesser degree to others. All the gifts which one may name, just as all the limitations, are created not because they are your true and eternal personality—for personality is very much a thing of your illusion—these things are those tools with which you have to work. The more realistically you identify your gifts, the more clearly you assess your limitations, and the more readily you accept the discipline which allows more and more knowledge of how to use that self in compassion towards the rest of the Creator—that is, your brothers and sisters—the more quickly you shall indeed accelerate your rate of spiritual growth.

Sometimes this period of confusion may last an entire incarnation. Never think of yourself as failing because you have not yet been given the answer intellectually to why, for instance, the out of body experience is spontaneous. It is not important intellectually that you understand your gifts or your limitations. What is necessary is that you go through enough processes of acceptance and forgiveness that you come into full acceptance of the self, a full love of the self as a part of the Creator, and a full and single-hearted commitment of the self as an outreaching portion of the Creator through whom compassion and love may shine.

We would like to greet each to the group, and rejoice to see new faces. We bless and offer our love to each. At this time we would transfer this contact to the instrument known as Jim. I am Q'uo.

(Jim channeling)

I am Q'uo, and greet each again in love and light through this instrument. At this time it is our privilege to offer ourselves in the attempt to speak to any further queries which those present may offer to us. We again would remind each that we offer that which is our opinion. We offer it joyfully, but do not wish any to trip over any word which does not seem appropriate. Take that which has value to you and leave that which does not. Is there a question at this time?

Questioner: Yes. This question has to do with my personal life. There is a female minister who I've just come to realize I'm very much in love with and she is in love with me. She has moved to another state. After being hurt many times, I feel doubt, it's hard for me to accept the fact that she loves me. The question is, what do I use as a rule and guide to judge whether or not she is sincere, or should I just go ahead and accept what she has told me?

I am Q'uo, and am aware of your query, my brother. We look upon your desire to tread upon the ground which is firm and which is safe, and we must suggest that for each who seeks the truth within your illusion, there is the mystery and the difficulty of knowing for sure that which is right, shall we say, or appropriate in each instance, for the illusion which you inhabit is one which contains the Creator of all in many disguises. We cannot guide your steps infallibly, for each step that you take in your own journey is most sacred, and each step in your journey as you take it will provide you the strength to move yet further upon your path. Yet you must be aware that there is the chance that you will move in areas in which you have not planned, and yet in those areas of seeking you will learn that which is most appropriate for you, for each step upon your path contains the opportunity to teach in ways which will seat your lessons most firmly.

As you consider your current possibilities of movement in your own life pattern, we can only suggest that you look within your own heart in your deepest meditative state and observe that which is your heart's desire. To know the direction of one's life pattern is to place before one the guiding star. Look then to the other with whom you consider joining and consider as carefully the guiding star towards which this entity moves, and consider you carefully if together you can move as one, pulling together that each may aid the other in the journey, for there shall be those situations which are difficult for each. Yet if one has the common bond and goal shared with another, the journey can be made smooth in those places that may be rough. Look then to your heart and look to the heart of the other and observe if there is the harmony between the two, that you share a love for that which is greater than each.

Is there a further query my brother?

Questioner: Yes. It seems like there is. My mind is completely made up as to going to and being with and marrying this lady who is a minister. But there seems to be guilt trips being put on me by members of my immediate family, my children. I have—you know they seem to see that … I don't know whether it's jealousy that they don't want to turn me loose, don't want to let me go, and I'm having a hard time dealing with them. I've tried everything. I've tried telling them it's twenty hours by bus, two hours by plane up here if I'm needed. It's hard for them to understand. I'm having a hard time dealing with this.

I am Q'uo, and we consider the words which you have spoken and may again suggest that as you consider the concerns of each about you, that you take those considerations into your meditation as often as is necessary in order to move your steps through the maze of seeming difficulty in the manner which is true to that guiding star which is yours to follow, for the journey is not often without difficulty. By facing those obstacles which present themselves in your path and resolving each with the greatest amount of love and compassion that you have within your being, you gain the strength of love and the sureness of your desire to move in harmony with the pattern which is appropriate for your growth as an entity and your service to others as one who has reaped a harvest of growth.

My brother, your steps may not be easy, but there is much of inner strength that can be gained in times of difficulty and we recommend the meditation for as long as is necessary to discover where the heart of love moves you most forcefully and surely at this time, for within your heart of hearts the plan for your life's pattern which you proposed before this incarnation lies complete, and by intensely seeking this heart of hearts it shall be revealed to you in the way that is most appropriate at this time.

Is there a further question, my brother?

Questioner: Yes. First, I would like to thank you very much for your most welcome advice. Second, I would like to ask how I could invite someone like yourself, Q'uo, to be with me and to guide me—an entity as yourself with the intellect as you have.

I am Q'uo, and we would suggest that, indeed, there are those about you and about each seeker who desires to know more of the mystery of the life pattern, that waits for each query that you may ask from your heart and which offers guidance in many ways to each seeker. There are those about you who place before you the appropriate book or person or situation or insight which will point the direction. Many times these guidances pass unnoticed, yet for each who seeks with a whole heart in the silence of the self, is the direction pointed, in a manner which is noticeable and clear to the seeker. We of Q'uo are happy to aid our brothers and sisters gathered here this evening in their meditations at any time that we are requested. Our assistance is in the form of aiding the deepening of the meditative state in order that each may become more aware of that silence within through which the still, small voice may speak to the heart.

May we speak in any further fashion, my brother?

Questioner: One other question. Can you tell me, I have felt the presence of an entity on several occasions. Can you tell me if this is a true feeling, and if so, what the entity is?

I am Q'uo, and we cannot speak to this specific query, for this experience of which you speak is one which is most fruitfully pursued by your own means of seeking. Were we to speak specifically, we would take from you the opportunity to learn of this experience in the manner which is appropriate for you at this time.

Is there a further query my brother?

Questioner: No, that's all. I would like to take this opportunity to thank you very much and it has been a pleasure, and your advice has been very, very well taken and well informed, and it has removed quite a bit of doubt I have had in my mind in listening and sitting here meditating about the love that this woman who I am contemplating on marrying has for me. It has brought me around to realize that people can love me without me doubting, and again I would like to thank you very much, and it has been a very enlightening, warm, well accepted advice. Thank you very much.

I am Q'uo, and we thank you, my brother, for without your queries we could not serve.

We find that we must pause briefly in order to allow this instrument to attend to the recording devices. We shall pause briefly. I am Q'uo.

(Side one of tape ends.)

(Jim channeling)

I am Q'uo, and am again with this instrument. Is there another query?

S: I have a question about the nature of service. It's easy to conceive of how we can serve others in terms of their physical lives or contributing to their mental well being, enriching their mental lives. I wonder if you could give some enlightenment about the range of ways in which we can consciously contribute to the spiritual well being or evolution of others?

I am Q'uo, and am aware of your query, my brother. We would begin by suggesting that there is nothing one can do that is not service. We understand your query, to seek those means by which service might be enhanced. We would suggest that for one who wishes to serve in a conscious fashion those entities about one, that the daily practice of meditation is most helpful as a means of returning periodically to the source of one's being, and in that experience of unity, again with the Creator and the creation about one, one may remind the conscious self of those patterns of learning which are most appropriate in the life pattern. By undertaking the opportunities that are presented one in one's daily round of activities, no matter how seemingly insignificant or immense, one then processes the catalyst into that experience which is likened unto the fruit of the tree. This fruit, then, is available for service to others in a means which may take any form which one may choose.

Indeed, it is not necessary in many cases to choose a form for service if one allows the life pattern to become imbued with the quality that you may call compassion and concern for those about one. The opportunities to offer this compassion and concern will present themselves as a normal part of the daily round of activities. The interaction with other selves is the most frequent opportunity that any seeker may be presented to offer what is asked in a manner which speaks to the highest principles one is aware of and with the compassion that is enhanced by the desire to serve those within one's life pattern. Thus, we do not offer so much the particular means by which one may serve as we offer the suggestion that no matter what one does, the doing may be enhanced by the quality of compassion that becomes the essence of the action of the thought of the service.

May we speak in any further fashion, my brother?

S: I can understand how the exercise of compassion would help one's own spiritual unfoldment. Are you saying that apart from simply contributing to the creation of a life situation which may be the situation that another person requires, may offer the experience he requires for growth at a certain period, that that compassion itself has a spiritual or more, could I say, eternal rather than transitory, offering to make to another person?

I am Q'uo, and this is correct, my brother, for the force or quality which moves one to serve, if it be of compassion, has far more effect upon another life pattern than the most carefully wrought mental form of service that lacks the compassion. The conscious mind left to itself attains to that which one may call wisdom, and is useful in many ways to discern that which is most appropriate for the moment and the future moments, however, without the quality of compassion even the most carefully considered service may not find the fertile ground for the seed of thought to be planted within. It is the quality of compassion which makes possible the condition for any seed of thought to be nourished into growth.

May we speak in any further fashion, my brother?

S: No, thank you.

I am Q'uo, and we thank you, my brother. Is there another query?

Questioner: I have one other. This deals with the entity that I sometimes feel. How can I know or identify this entity? The point is, up until six months ago, I could not … I always had a desire to sing, then all of a sudden I start singing with the voice of Elvis Presley, which I'm very, very good at. I cannot carry a tune. I find myself periodically, just out of a clear blue sky not attempting to sing like him, not even trying, but just naturally a voice flew forth. Could you explain this to me?

I am Q'uo, and am aware of your query, my brother. Again we find ourselves in the situation of wishing to be of the greatest service and finding that that service is to allow your own free will to remain intact in this particular area, for the process which you describe is a portion of the means by which you currently seek to know a greater portion of your own self. Were we to lay out plainly the answer to this query, we would work for you a puzzle, the solving of which would aid your own growth most if it were accomplished by your own free will and seeking.

Again, we may recommend that in meditation or prayer that you determine for yourself that which is your guiding star, that quality, be it love or the

Christ consciousness or the one known as Jesus the Christ or compassion or wisdom or truth or whatever quality has for you the greatest meaning and vibrancy. And in that name ask this entity to come to you and identify itself, but ask that entity if it comes in the name of that which is your guiding star, that it might assist you in that journey upon which you now find yourself traveling.

We wish to serve each seeker by providing those principles which may allow it to more clearly apprehend the nature of its own being and of the creation in which it finds itself. For us to speak in a specific fashion and describe each step in a personal manner for a seeker is to infringe upon the sacredness of the free will, and in the long run pattern, shall we say, of the seeker's life, this is not of benefit.

May we speak in any further fashion, my brother?

Questioner: Yes, one other question. There are quiet times that I usually find myself going into the Cave Hill cemetery. This may sound strange, but a lot of times I just feel compelled to go in there. Could you explain this compulsion?

I am Q'uo. For each seeker there are those places and times and people which aid in the inner journey. Each seeker is drawn to those in a fashion which may be of a subconscious nature in order that the conscious mind may be rested and informed by other sources of information, be they those entities known as guides or simply deeper portions of one's own subconscious mind. It is not unusual that one would be drawn to an area such as that of which you speak, for within your cultures the area in which the physical vehicle is placed upon its cessation of vitality is one which is considered sacred.

May we speak in any further fashion, my brother?

Questioner: No, that's all, and again I would like to extend to you my heartfelt thanks.

I am Q'uo, and we thank you once again, my brother. Is there another query at this time?

Questioner: One other question. Could one ask you for guidance?

I am Q'uo, and it is our impression that this has been done this evening, and we have responded in the manner which we felt most appropriate. We would not suggest that such guidance be sought outside of this circle of seeking, for we wish to safeguard each seeker, and the circle of seeking is one means by which each present may feel secure in the knowledge that the entity sought is indeed who it presents itself to be, for there have been specific means used in this circle this evening to provide the protection for each that is necessary. There are many entities who would be available to any with the sensitivities that we are aware are possessed by many of your peoples at this time who would not in every case offer the most helpful of information, thus we would request that each ask for our assistance within this circle of seeking.

May we speak in any further fashion, my brother?

Questioner: I was just, you know, unlearned and new, and I was not aware of this. And again I would like to thank you very much for your most helpful information.

I am Q'uo, and again I thank you, my brother. Is there another query?

Carla: How's the energy of the instrument?

I am Q'uo, and we find that there is sufficient energy for another query or two of normal length. Is there another query at this time?

(Pause)

I am Q'uo, and as we observe the silence, we feel that we have spoken to the limit of the queries, and we thank each for offering the queries to us, for without your desire to seek as you seek, we would have no beingness within your life patterns. It has been our great joy and privilege to join you this evening, and we look forward, as you would say, to those opportunities of doing such again. At this time we shall take our leave of this group and this instrument, leaving each, as always, in the love and in the light of the one infinite Creator. We are known to you as those of Q'uo. Adonai, my friends. Adonai.

(Carla channeling)

I Yadda. I greet you in name of love and light. I am happy to be with you. It is your call to me, you say to universe, "Ah, I have a winter heart!" You say, "Look at the landscape." How you like my new, better English? Ha ha, I good. You do not know what is going on in winter energy if you think that all is gray and desolate. You do not see the joy of the seed, the patient gathering of food in the roots of being of your second-density trees. You cannot feel the explosive joy that the forms of your water find themselves taking when by the gift of cold they may make visible their crystalline nature and show their magic to the world.

We wish you to warm your winter heart and to be silly and playful in the cold of winter, for your heart does not need to wear the winter underwear and your throat is not stilled because birds sing not so often in your outer ear. Come with me in knowledge that warmth is yours within and that the fire of spring is only possible because of the joy, the dancing joy of the collection of food and drink for growth. Every season happy. No season sad, for all work together. Be merry.

We leave you in joy, in peace, in love, and in light, and even because this instrument insists in name of Christ. We have stopped holding out for Buddha. Zoroaster is not acceptable. We know we have said this before, but we wish this instrument would think about what we say. Adonai, my friends. You know all is one. Somebody tell this instrument. Adonai. Adonai. ❧

L/L Research

Intensive Meditation
February 10, 1988

Group question: If our lives are unfolding in an appropriate manner and all is well and there are no mistakes, how do we operate within this environment to enhance our service to others?

(Carla channeling)

I am Hatonn, and I greet you in the love and in the light of our infinite Creator. It is a most great privilege to be called to your group this evening, and we wish to send love and blessing to each, and to thank each for the privilege of sharing this time with you.

We would like to confirm to the one known as D that we were at the point of speaking through him, we thought. Indeed, we had almost felt that there was an initial message that would be allowed. However, we understand this instrument's reluctance to take the chance and take the leap, and assure this instrument that it is progressing well, and that this initiating of contact is merely one small hurdle upon a long and increasingly faith-filled path of service.

And so we shall speak through this instrument for the nonce, not forgetting our responsibilities to the one known as D. We shall be exercising this instrument, also.

Your general query to us this evening has to do with how, since all things are as they should be and there are no mistakes, can anyone who hopes to heal actually be a portion of healing, how can anyone who wishes to enter a situation and change it be spiritually correct. The answer to that lies within that feeling that is a portion of your deepest self, and that is that all who are upon your planet are your brothers and your sisters. It is an impeccable question to ask, since there are no mistakes, if alterations should be attempted, and we say to you that it is for the purpose of aiding each other that each of you incarnated and is enjoying quite a busy schedule of learning at this time. Indeed, in the way of teaching, even we who are not of your world may speak through instruments such as this one, leaving always so many doubts as to our reality that no one could possibly feel that we were to be obeyed without question. We are very careful about this, for we come among your peoples in thought in order to offer information that might be requested.

Now, this is what you entities may do for each other. In one way or another, a healer acts as a catalyst for the one to be healed. When crystals are used, the healer's ability functions with the crystal in order to create the catalyst, the space and the time wherein the entity to be healed may pick up the heart and the will and claim the healing that the catalyst is offering. If this is not claimed, it does not happen. Therefore, free will is not abused. Yet, catalysts do appear as solutions to difficulties, and this, too, is a portion of that which was planned. It was not planned before an incarnation that a certain condition or limitation be applicable for an entire lifetime. Thus, even if one chooses a certain path, it is not known to the entity within a lifetime at what point that path should change. Indeed, as always, living, learning and loving are daily matters, those that cannot be pulled over the scorched ground of yesterday or shot like Roman candles into the mist of tomorrow. Help between brother and brother lies in the present moment.

A healer is a special kind of minister. Some use your tarot cards, some use your tea leaves, some use your radionic devices, some use your herbs, some use your ability to think, some use chemicals, and some use the knives and the stitches. Yet all of these things shall not heal the emotions, the mind, the spirit, or even the body if, cell by cell, thought by thought, and with the firm thrust of will, the entity does not accept the catalyst of healing. It is almost impossible for an entity born upon your planet to so interfere with the free will of another.

There is one distinct disadvantage to certain types of healing, and we would state that these offer a concern to the instrument who happens to feel strongly upon this point. However, we assure this instrument that we are using the instrument as a channel, and not allowing the soapbox. We find that it is possible for service-to-others oriented healers such as the one known as D, or any understanding, caring and sensitive healer, it is possible to make a patient derive not a leap forward in free will and the use of it, but rather [have] a dependence develop between patient and catalytic healer. This cannot be avoided entirely, for there are certain of your people who, while seeking very diligently, have become somewhat disassociated in thought and emotion, and are, therefore, confused and feel that they need someone upon whom to depend for the correct answers to those difficulties and conditions which seem to face them.

It is well, therefore, for the healer always to call upon the will, the hope, and the power within the individual itself, and not to express the self as anything but a catalyst through which healing may take place. We hope that this ethical consideration is understandable.

There is more we wish to say upon this matter, and although the entity known as D may not wish to take the contact at this time, we shall offer it to him that this entity, we feel, is ready to pick up thoughts it has not already conceived before in just the same way. As always, relax, hear the thought, and speak the thought with no more care than this instrument has shown. It is by far the better way, the quicker way, and the more accurate way to express such information as we have to share. I now transfer. I am Hatonn.

(D channeling)

I am Hatonn, and I greet you again in love and light through this instrument. We appreciate the time and effort of presenting the challenge, but would state again our wish that the instrument diligently work to clarify the process in its own mind. It is often advisable and efficacious in serving as a vocal instrument to allow spontaneity and creativity to be prominent in the mind, but, during the process of challenging a contact, it is … it serves the purpose of the instrument—that is to say, efficient and safe establishment of a clear contact which can be maintained with confidence on your side and our own—if the instrument has a well established stance or posture which it can present to us and to any other entity which may attempt to infringe on the contact, the posture or routine which the instrument can have confidence as to its effectiveness and efficiency. If such an effort to create such a posture is made from week to week, we can perhaps assist in fine-tuning the finer points, the details of the challenge. The instrument will find that as this process is repeated and becomes routine, he will sense our interaction initially, our approach to the mind, as it were, more easily from week to week.

We would attempt now to return to our original topic, despite the trepidation of the instrument, and urge again the most complete relaxation possible.

The healer …

(Pause)

(Carla channeling)

We realize our contact is still good, and we would, were the instrument's energy levels higher, continue this work, for we and the one known as D are very close to finding our voice, finding the end of fear, and finding new eloquence for our very simple thoughts with this entity. However, it is well not to push an entity beyond its ability, for there is a kind of tiredness which is spiritual, that is not a state we would prefer to produce, it being that which dims the day. And so to conserve this instrument's energy and enthusiasm we choose to move to another instrument at this time, with our apologies and explanation.

The healer, then, uses a variety of tools. These tools are, in the end, not necessary. They are a means of focusing the mind and occupying it while opening up the connections between deeper mind and conscious mind. Thus, the use of that which is called hypnotism is in actuality the use of that which is magnetic within the human heart, which finds itself willing to achieve a certain state which it is normally unable to achieve. The healer here is using words and images, working as a catalyst, querying as the seeker would have him query. And in the end, when there has been enough work done, the healer inevitably becomes aware that it is not the tool that has truly been the catalyst for healing, but rather it is the healer as it is, and the degree of crystallization of the energy centers and of the desire to serve which the healer has undertaken.

All things are indeed as they should be. This in no way inhibits the action of free will. You came to this place you call Earth hungering for the opportunity to feel, to sense, to see, and to wonder at the sensations of a physical vehicle. You came knowing that these sensations, these feelings, these feelings of memory which lead to battle and to the bone-weariness of the old were the gateway through which you would learn, in a more and more and regularized fashion, the omnipresence of love, the unity of all of the creatures of the Creator, and the joy of choosing to serve others, each in its own special way. Never mistake the tools of the trade for the wisdom, the compassion, and the intuition of the trade.

Seek further in your book learning, you who seek to heal, and apprentice yourself to teachers you deem worthy, but remember always that the true work of the healer lies within, in the healing of the self, in the regularizing of the fire of love, the heat of compassion, in the willingness to be open to those things which are not possible, to the compassion that stands unmoved before life and death and wishes only that the highest will and the most harmonious plan be fulfilled.

These things the healer must learn, and we wish the one known as D the joy of that learning, even as we sympathize with occasional feelings of dislocation which this may cause.

We would transfer now to the one known as Jim in order that we may field any queries that there may be at this time. I am known to you as Hatonn.

(Jim channeling)

I am Hatonn, and greet each again in love and light through this instrument. At this time we would offer ourselves in the attempt to speak to any further queries. We would hope that our humble words might provide some insight and inspiration to those who seek with us more of the clarification of the mystery of the Creator and the Creation. Are there any further queries at this time?

D: This seems like sort of a niggling sort of question, insignificant in a sense, but at the close [of] what I was able to speak tonight, I said the words "The healer," and felt at that point that I was only making an effort in my own mind to return to the subject of healing, and try to reestablish that pattern and align my mind, so to speak, on that topic, to make communication again, to move it along. But I could get nothing else beyond that. And then when you began through Carla with those words, I wondered if actually I picked those words up from you, was I successful in doing that at the end, or did you choose those words to begin with because I had chosen them? I just wonder what the process was at that time as far as those choices of words were concerned.

I am Hatonn. We spent a good deal of your time exercising your instrument with the subject of the nature of the contact itself, for we not only wished to make this information available to you as well, but were aware that this topic was one which was more comfortable as a topic and would therefore allow an easier transmission of thought, especially preceding a topic which, though of great interest and concern and focus in your present situation, would allow us to move into this more challenging area of the healer and the healing.

Therefore, when we felt that your contact was as firm as we could hope for under the present conditions of the desire and the fatigue due to the headache pain, we embarked upon the continuation of the healing topic begun through the instrument known as Carla. However, the challenge of this topic and the continuing weight of the pain was enough to block the further transmission, which you correctly perceived. Therefore, we found it most helpful at that time to your own instrument to transfer the contact in order that the information be transmitted through the one known as Carla. We again wish …

(Side one of tape ends.)

(Jim channeling)

I am Hatonn, and am again with this instrument. Is there another query, my brother?

D: Both tonight and two weeks ago, when I was not able to establish any effective contact at all, really, I had had some caffeine before the sessions. Can you detect that influence, whether it's detrimental, or whether it was a contributing factor either tonight or at that time?

I am Hatonn, and we do not feel that the addition of the caffeine to the bodily system is detrimental in any way to the ability to receive telepathic contact. Indeed, there does seem to be some indication that for a significant portion of those that practice the art of vocal channeling that this ingredient is somewhat of an aid in that it serves to sensitize certain neuronal receptors within the brain and facilitate the reception of thought from the deeper portions of the mind complex. The movement of intuition, shall we say, seems in some entities to be enhanced by this ingredient.

May we speak in any further fashion, my brother?

D: Not on that topic. I wonder if you would have anything to add at this point to what was said about challenging. Of course I tend somewhat to—not necessarily to feel that I perceived your concepts one hundred percent accurately. It's a topic that I would like to be sure I understand one hundred percent accurately of what you would have to say about the topic. Would you care to modify or correct anything that I received earlier about that topic?

I am Hatonn, and we are pleased with the information regarding the challenging process that we were able to transmit through your instrument, and we would at this time add only one additional concern, and that is that each instrument be reminded that the process of tuning and the challenge is an ongoing process that will change as the entity grows in the ability to function as a vocal instrument, for the process of spiritual growth is a process by which the seeker continues to move closer and closer to the heart of truth and the essence of the self which harbors this truth, shall we say. And as the entity becomes more aware of who it is and that guiding principle towards which it moves and for which it stands, by which it is inspired, the entity will have an additional intensity or richness to call upon and to offer as the heart of the challenge, that any contacted discarnate being might become more aware of who you are and how it is you wish to serve. Thus, the continued refining and enhancing of the tuning of the instrument and the offering of the heart of self in challenge is recommended.

May we speak in any further fashion, my brother?

D: Are you present throughout the tuning process in our minds, and in my mind in particular, and, if so, would you have anything to observe about that process as I go through it now, although I might call it an invocation, with any comments about how that has evolved over the last few weeks?

I am Hatonn, and, indeed, we deem it an honor to be present as each instrument continues with the inner tuning in preparation for contact with us and with any that should be contacted in a session such as this. We commend you for your continued refining of the tuning process, and can only suggest to each instrument, whether new or experienced, that this tuning be accomplished with as great a degree of fastidiousness as one is capable of providing, for this tuning is the factor which allows for the construction of the actual channel, the receiving antenna, shall we say. Its polishing, its tightening, its sensitivity, enhancing that will allow for the greatest degree of both freedom of transmission and accuracy of transmission. Thus, to ask again if one is tuned and ready to serve as an instrument is well.

Is there another query, my brother?

D: If I can have a moment to formulate it, I think there is something I would like to ask.

This is sort of a corollary to the initial, primary question tonight. I see the potential for a lot of good, as I would define it from this perspective, to come [from] work with using hypnosis to facilitate the communication between the conscious mind and deeper levels of the mind, or the higher mind, or the guides, or other entities not necessarily personal spiritual advisors. And yet this is a faculty that we have chosen not to have as we come into this Earth experience.

So again I would ask, although I have [heard] what you said earlier about the changing of the path in the course of the life in mind, I would still question whether it is ever advisable to use hypnosis in this way, or does it risk speeding things along too quickly, does it risk contradicting or making an effort to contradict a higher purpose?

I am Hatonn, and though there is no general answer to this query that can hope to be accurate, we would suggest that the intentions of the one seeking the hypnotic experience are the salient point to be considered, for the degree of desire to know more of the self, in order that a further step might be taken up the evolutionary path, is the necessary ingredient for the balanced approach to any means of seeking to enhance this evolutionary process.

There are many other reasons why some entities engage in different means of seeking, and one must be able to speak in a clear fashion to all who would seek the services of the self as hypnotist, as to what one wishes to offer and in what manner the tool will be offered to others. The focusing of the conscious mind—of the attention more specifically—through the hypnotic practice and induction allows for a penetration to some degree of the veil which separates the conscious and unconscious minds, and for that time allows for the movement into the unconscious mind, to some depth and degree, in order that information and experience might be achieved that will add illumination to the process of evolution which is constantly ongoing in each seeker.

The higher self, as it has been called, is aware of the desires of each seeker, and will, with the appropriate intentions on the part of the seeker, work in a fashion that brings forth the appropriate experience and information, no matter what avenue is chosen to pursue and obtain these experiences and this information. Thus, the one serving as the hypnotist or teacher in any fashion must establish the clear and honest dialogue with any seeking its services, in order that it be clearly understood what is desired in the service and how this goal shall be sought, the steps which shall be taken.

I am Hatonn. We have been instructed by this instrument that it is well to bring this session to a close at this time. We look forward to joining this group in your future gatherings, and we thank each for inviting our presence this evening. We leave each, as always, in the love and in the light of the one infinite Creator. Adonai, my friends. Adonai. ☥

Intensive Meditation
February 13, 1988

Question from S: What was the reason that compelled me to infringe that feeling of bliss to come here?

(Carla channeling)

I am Latwii. I greet you with joy in the love and in the light of the one infinite Creator. It is a rich blessing indeed to share this meditation with the one known as S, whom we greet through this instrument for the first time in much of your time. We have been working with the instrument in order to utilize the instrument without overworking this instrument's energy web, and we are pleased with the contact now.

You have asked for us to talk about why an entity who is in bliss would leave that bliss willingly to go into hardship. We find that we ourselves still ask ourselves this question with much less reason, for there is always in the entity incarnate some catalyst that there is not when the entity is at home and at rest, and that catalyst fills the mind and the heart, and as the nerve fails, we too wonder why we have willingly left a paradise in order to suffer in one way or another.

We could say to you that this decision has to do with the great opportunities of your local time as you experience it, yet this would not perhaps be the clearest answer. It is true that this time of yours in third density is a peerless illusion against which to set the drama of polarization. For each of us casts itself into the waters of illusion for the purpose of using that illusion, of using that time, of experiencing certain outward and inward biases, and thus suffering, and in the fullness of time revising or eliminating bias.

This is the mechanical answer to the question of, "Why leave a blissful situation?" The answer in brief is: in order to make use of the enhanced learning capacities of the density in which you have incarnated.

There is, however, as we have said, a clearer way to get at the heart of the reason for this seemingly masochistic choice, and that is a consideration of the word "joy." When the veils are lifted and the form maker Creator, your most subtle and most true body, is in union with the Creator, there is bliss. When an entity is engaged in contemplation, there may be bliss. However, into the bliss there comes, as if by the restless pull of the moon or magnetization of the self by some unseen current, the beginnings of the sadness that comes to those in bliss who have a desire built within them to go forth and act.

There is then the feeling of an honor and a duty, of a desire for right action, and eventually the need to act in service to others in an active way expresses itself. This is a part of almost every entity's journey, if that entity has chosen the path of unity. So the situation of those who have chosen to enter the current incarnation upon your planet have chosen to move into that which will make them sorrowful, in order that the wellspring of joy and bliss which is brimming and overflowing within may be liberated from the inner expression and manifested within the illusion in service to others.

The long years of service which does not seem service and which seems sorrowful, in which the one who serves is upheld only by a blind faith, will eventually, as faith becomes stronger and stronger, take the sorrowful experience and allow the balance of bliss without illusion to come, that is, as one was sorrowful within bliss, now one may be blissful within sorrow. This is the balance that is sought by those who venture forth to experience consciously, and consciously to serve the one Creator.

We are aware there are many questions upon your minds concerning right vocation, right service, and right action, yet we say to you that that which is directly before the face, that which comes with each day's coming, is the work at hand. And whether that work is simple or complex, little or dramatic, menial or grand, within that work, within that companionship, within that which is before the face lie the seeds of joy and the opportunity for service.

With this understood, the pressure may be taken off of the entity who no longer needs to search for vocation, action or any manifestation. It is indeed true, a seeking entity cannot help but be doing the work it has come to do, for the creation is an harmonious whole and the plans of learning the lessons of love set by each soul before incarnation are part of the very electrical magnetic field of the entity and will attract that work which needs attention along the lines intended by the higher self and the seeking spirit.

We may say that we have found that there are states of mind which may be pursued and sought as desirable within an incarnation, the entity realizing that all is illusion and that the face is, though invisible, the most real component of the seeking entity's self. To live in joy, [and] joyfully apprehend the present moment, is the result of accepting in full that which is laid before one to do and to be. The feelings of acceptance of all situations and the elimination of the seeking for bliss return one most quickly to greater and greater opportunities for joy within the illusion.

For if it is understood by faith that faith is the journey, and that the deepest faith is that all that is with one and being experienced by one is that which is correct, then one may simply turn the attention to being, for each entity is a story within the mind of the Creator, and each incarnation a small gift, a bouquet, a scent upon the wind which informs and blesses the Creator as that infinite entity learns ever more about Itself.

Thus, the deepest goal of one who leaves bliss in order to suffer is to find the joy within the suffering, to find the light within the darkness, to accept and thus solve the riddle of opposites. For if the life is a gift, a holy one, one set apart, then to live, to love, to feel, to be, is the true vocation, and all actions stem then not from the necessities of the employment or the personal situation, but from the inner agenda which is to experiment continuously with the being, seeking always to polarize more and more towards a conscious inner realization of the wholeness and perfection that lie within the illusion that make of the life a beauty and a gift. It is difficult sometimes for one who is suffering to see the beauty within the self, to realize that the self by itself without action is the true gift to the Creator and the true reason for this experience you call living.

One who expresses joy from within is doing the greatest work in consciousness which it is possible to do within your illusion, and the more passionately and ardently and eagerly one turns to each moment, whether it be a challenging moment or a relatively peaceful one, the more you shall rejoice as you gaze back upon the incarnation, for the jewel that each entity is is polished by that entity, and the polishing is very efficient within your density.

It is easy to remember the bliss and forget that desire to be more full of positivity and service when one is within the illusion. Entities remember selected things and forget others. If they are healthy, their deep memories are blissful. And so you seem strangers in a strange land, yet we urge you to nurture yourselves within your sorrow, nursing the faith within the heart that even if joy cannot be seen through long seasons of living, yet still the light within moves forward, experiences and learns what it can and moves ever closer to supernal joy.

We wish each that joy, that perception, that realization which may transform each and every experience. May we extend our love to you and our sorrow that we cannot speak longer, for it is sweet to converse with this group. However, for this little moment, we shall leave you, wishing for better ways to express the central understanding which we have gained, which is that all is love, and that one casts oneself into illusion to find experience and manifest that love within the illusion and forever in and out of illusion, in and out of bias.

We are those of Latwii. With joy we take our leave of you in the love and in the light of the one infinite Creator. I am Latwii. Adonai, my friends. Adonai. ✺

L/L Research

Sunday Meditation
February 14, 1988

Group question: (From R.) Concerns the breakdown of the bicameral or use of the two-lobed brain/mind and the development of consciousness as a result of that breakdown, so that the entity is no longer experiencing a direction from inner resources or the voices of the gods, shall we say, but is acting on his own as a conscious being, and in doing that seems to cut himself off from those sources so that he is on his own in his evolution, but once he is able to find his way back, shall we say, to the Creator and penetrate the veil, we're wondering how this is related to the dropping of the veil between the conscious and the unconscious mind, if that is manifested in any way in the brain, and if the penetration of the veil, the contact with intelligent infinity, is something that occurs in a moment and the veil is shattered, or if it is something that occurs as a process that is ongoing, and the veil is slowly rent so the entity, in whatever the case is, returns again to the unity of the Creator, this time as a conscious being, having worked his way back there.

(Carla channeling)

I am Q'uo. I greet you in the love and in the light of the one infinite Creator. It is a great blessing to be with each of you, and we especially greet those to whom we speak through this instrument who have traveled so far to dwell in meditation and seek our opinions. To immerse ourselves in your life-stream is a great pleasure and privilege, and we are most thankful.

We would like, as always, to remind each that we are brothers and sisters along the same way that you tread, having gone, as you would put it, farther down the path and then turning back to offer a hand to those who seek aid in their own journeys. We are not without fallibility. Our opinions cannot and should not be taken as gospel, and therefore we ask that each of our thoughts be considered and discarded if not useful, for we wish only to be of service, not to present a stumbling block in anyone's search for that ineffable greatness which is the mystery of the Creator.

We turn now to your question, which has to do with the consideration of the bicameral mind of your physical vehicle and its possible association with the veiling process which shrouds the third-density conscious self from knowledge of its own deeper mind.

Firstly, we would say that these two concepts are not congruent, nor is it possible in a simple way to find major comparisons which are not riven by contrast and detail. Consequently, we shall speak to the subject, moving from various points of view in our attempt to put the material into perspective, shall we say.

That which this instrument calls the mind/body/spirit complex takes a fragile dwelling place when it enters your illusion, and within this physical vehicle, this frail canoe which you must paddle along your time's river, your mind complex activity is considered as seated within the physical brain. This is indeed the portion of the chemical body within which the activities of consciousness manifest themselves within the physical vehicle. It is, however, shall we say, a leased rather than a purchased dwelling place. This is the cause of there being relatively little direct comparison betwixt the bicameral mind and the veiling process. Therefore, let us look first at the veiling process.

That which we and others of the Confederation of Planets in the Service of the Infinite Creator have called the veiling process is a precondition of third-density consciousness. This is due not to any petty attempt of the Creator to frame a challenge which must be overcome. It is rather an integral part of the learning process during which it is hoped by the discarnate entity preparing for incarnation that the self within the incarnation will feel deeply certain catalyst, will consider those feelings and that catalyst, and through the course of the incarnational experience come little by little in subtle and dramatic ways to alter the system of biases which is the essence of the innate consciousness which each entity is. These biases then form a kind of field of a weak electrical nature in physical manifestation, yet of a strong and binding manifestation in the more subtle or metaphysical bodies.

Thus, the goal of the seeker is not specifically to remove the veil, but rather through a series of experiences to form a carefully protected shuttle, shall we say, through that veil which may be used by faith and will in order that the deeper self may speak in language clearer than dreams usually are. For, indeed, the veil is without any effort on the seeker's part made somewhat transparent through the dreaming process. It is a diaphanous rather than a completely opaque veil. This veil then is to be seen as an ally, as the seeker either with joy or without it moves through the lessons, and as this instrument would say, the recesses and the vacations of an incarnational experience.

There are occasions in which this veil is shattered briefly either through the use of your so-called mind-altering substances or by means of regimens as the extended fasting or the shamanic dancing which move the consciousness to a state in which that shutoff lies open and inner light pours forth into a sometimes startled and sometimes grateful waking consciousness.

We encourage meditation for the specific purpose of strengthening the link and opening the shuttle between the conscious mind and the deeper mind in order that what the one known as R has called …

We must pause. We are those of Q'uo.

(Pause)

(Carla channeling)

We are those of Q'uo, and greet you again in love and light. This instrument was moving dangerously close to trance, and we felt it necessary that we waken the instrument and position the body contact betwixt this instrument and the one known as Jim in a more satisfactory manner. We shall continue exercising the instrument for a few seconds while the trance state recedes somewhat.

It is most helpful to meditate upon a daily basis in order that the voices, as the one known as R has called them, which speak from an enlarged point of view may be a portion of the consideration of the conscious mind. However, that which lies [behind] the threshold of the conscious mind is so vast and so varied that not all of that which is deep within consciousness is helpful to the seeker. Thus, if one, especially through artificial means, manages to create a constant hole within the veil, the situation for that entity is random and potentially harmful to that particular incarnational experience in the sense that there are portions within the deep mind which deal with those archetypes which, when brought through to the conscious mind without analysis, create strongly negative thought patterns and emotions. For you see, you contain literally the universe, and all that may be essential to consciousness is within the deep mind in careful regularized structure.

The meditation, upon the other hand, moves into the deep mind as does the lover to the beloved, the intention being to woo and win the beloved with these positive feelings and thought which accompany the desire to meditate. An atmosphere of love for the Creator and for that deeper portion of the self in which the essence of the Creator does lie is strengthened, and that which then is touched within the deeper mind is that which strikes the most plangent tone, offers the most needed medicament to the seeker.

Thus, we say it is well to work towards the growing transparency of this veiling, this forgetting, and, indeed, if it is desired, it is well to attempt to move more quickly. However, those who move more quickly move at risk, and may, rather than becoming possessed of new insight, simply become possessed by the more strident and seemingly negative portions of the creation which dwells within. As our desire is to aid each seeker in accelerating the rate of spiritual growth, we constantly urge daily meditation as being that tool which is most carefully designed to aid with a minimum of accompanying hindrance.

To sum up our feelings about this veil which you experience in third density, may we say from our standpoint that it is most advantageous, for when the forgetting has occurred, the emotional, mental and physical experiences of an entity are sharpened to a degree beyond your imagination.

Compared to creations and densities above your own, your third density is seen as a marvelous and exciting place and time in which experiences are vividly beautiful and exponentially more powerful than in later experiences which focus far more upon refining that which has already been decided. Without the veiling process, the decision making which is the testing portion of the lessons of love would be attenuated and the power of the decisions lost. Yours is a valley of decision. You live many lives, but only as many as it takes to formulate in a final way your particular system of biases in such a way that a harvestable amount of light may be accepted by the seeker. Thus, you dwell in the darkness of unknowing, and in honest unknowing, depending upon your biases, your thoughts, your dreams, and whatever shuttle you have been able to make through to the deep mind. You the seeker spend third-density time deciding how to love. What a great decision, my friends. What a pivotal one, and for it the veil is necessary.

We move now to some thoughts on the bicameral mind. We would not take issue with any entity, and are aware that our views are different than those discussed previous to this meeting, and therefore we especially wish to iterate our caveat that we are not infallible. These are our thoughts and we gladly share them with you as we hope to serve you. But we could be wrong, and we wish you to be aware of this.

We are not the experts upon the mind/body/spirit complex's connections with the physical body that perhaps you may expect. We can use an entity's mind if that entity has tuned itself to us. We cannot if the entity's receiver, shall we say, is turned off. However, within the channeling process the right brain or the brain which feels and creates by intuition is used for the grounding and the groundwork, the earthing of the contact. It is in the so-called right brain that we are able first to make the contact with an entity. Now, in mechanical or physiological terms, we are actually touching into that which is called the frontal lobes, both left brain and right brain. However, in the sense which this question was asked, the voice which we are, and many other comforting voices which may be helpful to you, are grounded in the right brain.

This instrument uses, as do all instruments, both the intuitive and the analytical portions of the brain in doing this service because the entity is channeling on a free will basis in a lighter trance which the instrument could break at any time it so chose. It is rare that utter right brain activity, as it may be called, offers a manifestation for the benefit of others rather in the artistic or creative temperament. The right brain and left brain, as these are called, are used in tandem. The more successful the artist, seeker or mystic is in creating an intelligible manifestation, the more smoothly the two faculties have learned to work together, the ideal being that neither intuition nor rational thought be the more highly regarded but rather that that portion of the mind complex which dwells without the need for any physical vehicle be able to guide both analytical and ratiocinative abilities and processes.

The advent of the yellow-ray activity which is fundamental to third density has more and more within the history of your peoples reduced right brain activity in favor of intellectual analysis. The reasons for this are simply time and civilization. Within a small community whose way of life is bound to natural rhythms, the intuition forms the greater part of the mental activity of entities dwelling therein. In time the population of these entities grows, and because of the number of entities, that which is called civilization begins to occur. Again, although fraught with strife, war and every seeming degradation, the advent of civilization is an integral and important portion of the catalyst presented for humankind at this time upon your planet.

(Side one of tape ends.)

(Carla channeling)

The advent of civilization, then, is to be seen as the arena against which the analytical mind, the beginnings of wisdom, is begun its course of teaching. For as intuition shall become compassion, so shall intellectual thought become wisdom once the decision has been made to serve, by both intuition and intelligence, the Creator and others or the Creator within the self.

The denser the number of entities within an area, the less possible it is for intuitively directed activity to remain harmonious, as intuition requires information in order to be accurate, and, sources of information being so many, become muddied and therefore unavailable. Thus, although it shall not be for another creation, another density, another experience that wisdom is truly the order of the day to be worked upon, yet still within third density that which is called the intellect or the rational mind is offered as that which may be master or slave, just as intuition may be master or slave of that which is essentially the entity, that which lies beyond, within and all around all powers of mind, both intuitive and intellectual.

As we speak to you, your peoples have become most fascinated with the intellect and the fruit of intellectual thought and we are often called to those who are starving for the fruits of intuition which have been obliterated by overuse of the intellect, for the intellect can be slave or master and it is well that the intellect be a disciplined servant of the self and not a master. Yet, it is well also that the intuitional self be a disciplined servant and not the master. The master is indeed that which is your own self, and you are mystery as great as the Creator.

If entities wish to encourage the use of their own intuition, to encourage its findings, its acceptance, and its use also, then it is recommended naturally that the entity seek a more solitary portion of your planetary surface where the conditions of the more primitive peoples who do indeed hear many spirits speak are available. It is not necessary to attempt to revert to the level of savagery within which the epitome of intellectual achievement is a certain shrewdness, for as each is at this moment, so is the proper beingness.

Each of you has an highly developed intellect. We would like to point out that each within this group and most who seek have also a more and more highly activated intuition. Beyond recommending that the intuition and the intellect be brought into balance, we would not recommend the use of one faculty of the mind without the other. In other words, what we are saying is that the voices which the questioner spoke of are not drawn solely from the right brain, but are drawn rather from a deep self which has only a suitcase unpacked in the motel of the human brain. Its home is eternity, and you are a dweller in eternity.

What we hope to turn both minds to is the face of the Creator. We care not how this face is addressed; we care not which function a seeker may deem appropriate through which to seek to know more of the truth of that which is unknown about creation. We care only for that which is called desire and hope to evoke in each that strong faculty of will and faith which lies beyond any discussion of right and left brain. For wherever each seeker is, it is from that stance that we hope that the seeker with a happy heart and a singleness of purpose turns itself to that which is at hand, gazing upon it to find that which can barely be discerned.

You see, because your experience is so vivid, entities who seek often feel that it is in a dramatic burst of light that so-called illumination shall occur. However, we believe that that which you are seeking is not within phenomena, not within feeling, and not within thought, but is rather that which one of your holy works has called the still, small voice, the silence that speaks within. To ponder out the parts and parcels of that which you see, measure, test and study is an hopeless task. Illumination will come, sometimes, indeed, with great light and radiance, sometimes with a turn of the heart that changes its bias forever in one way or another, sometimes in a very gradual process, unseen by the self, which creates the same change in bias.

Each entity's path is unique, just as each entity is unique. If you think in terms of crystals, each one of you is, indeed, a priceless gem in an uncut form, and as you seek, the facets begin to appear and the jewel begins to show an outward and manifested beauty rather than keeping the beauty hidden beneath roughness and dullness.

Within this illusion, we encourage you above all things to seek the face of the Creator without analysis and without intuition, but with hope and faith of passion. Trust that this process is harmonious and efficacious, and that by your meditations you are able in the focusing of your desire and the calling of that to you which is the mystery, that you may more and more offer all unknowing and without conscious thought the light upon the hill that shines that all may see the Creator within.

As an afterthought we would add that it is more difficult by far for that entity ruled with intellect alone to enter into a conscious seeking in smoothness and grace than it is for one who is highly intuitive, yet all paths are valid and each path shall in time lead to the face of mystery. We have gazed into that face as have you in timelessness and in time, in darkness and in light, in nothingness and in space, and we say to you that the mystery recedes before you as the waves do move out at low tide, always coming in again to immerse the seeker in power, love, beauty and joy, but always then moving again out to sea so that the path leads ever onward, the mystery beckons always. And as the path unfolds, it becomes clearer and clearer that that mystery which we so seek to know is the only concern which we may carry with us through eternity. We know not the Creator. We know only the intimations and reflections, the currents and the winds of a beautiful mystery which we have learned to call Love Itself.

In all your deliberations, my friends, we urge you to return always to that which this instrument calls the watchtower, to call to the self, that most nearby Creator, that its love and light may fill and transform the self and the self's service. May you love one another, may you know, as we feel that we know, that we are most beloved by the Creator who is love. May you find joy in your seeking.

We would have the question and answer period at this time, and would thank this instrument for allowing us to work with it. At this time we would transfer to the instrument known as Jim. We are those of Q'uo.

(Jim channeling)

I am Q'uo, and greet each again in love and light through this instrument. At this time it is our privilege to ask if there are any further queries to which we may speak and offer our opinions. Is there a query at this time?

Carla: I thought it was impossible to go into trance when I was holding hands. What happened to me?

I am Q'uo. We found when we were utilizing your instrument that your fatigue was enhancing the depth of your meditation to the point where the tactile pressure was being [released] and needed [reinforcing]. It would be difficult for the trance state to be achieved with the auric infringement of the holding of the hand, however, the fatigue and subsequent lack of conscious impingement to remain within the physical vehicle was presenting risk enough that we felt it worth the effort to rectify.

Is there another query, my sister?

Carla: No. Thank you for your help.

I am Q'uo, and we thank you, my sister. Is there another query?

R: *(Nearly inaudible.)* Are the two processes used for establishing this similar in nature to the work which would be efficacious for establishing a healing?

I am Q'uo, and this is correct, my brother, for the point of the consideration or purpose of this meeting is to focus the intention and the desire in such a way that [a] channel or focus is created through which energy in one form or another may move relatively unhindered to those locations or entities which had requested the energy, be it of healing or inspiration.

Is there another query, my brother?

R: During the channeling of healing, is it recommended to have a similar group as you have here, or is it harmful in any way for a person to attempt to single-handedly *(inaudible)*?

I am Q'uo. It is often an aid in the amplification of the energy direction [finder], shall we say, for other entities to be present with some form of healing, especially those utilizing visualization or the production of sound vibration. However, in those types of healings which require the one serving as healer to make a contact with intelligent infinity in some form, it is not necessary that others be present, and indeed it may not be efficacious for the actual transmission of the healing energy. It is not a service which endangers, shall we say, either the one to be healed or the one serving as healer, as long as the one serving as healer has developed the necessary preparation of the self and observed those practices which have formed its art, that the careful building of the crystallized personality and the careful use of this personality are within the domain of the one serving as healer and when used in a responsible manner, shall we say, do not cause risk to either the healer or the one to be healed.

Is there another query, my brother?

R: Can the use of [symbol] or pattern, patterns of quartz crystals be efficacious in enhancing or amplifying the energy necessary to make a strong, viable contact for healing?

I am Q'uo. The use of crystal amplification is helpful in the healing process, however, the purity of the crystal is a point of concern, for the attempt to amplify the healing energy is one which requires the finer crystals, shall we say, those that are without flaw and which may be counted upon to *(inaudible)* the healing love/light in a faithful and undistorted fashion. Thus, it is also a point of greater consideration that the one serving as healer also have the crystallized personality in as regularized fashion as is possible for that entity and for that entity to have prepared itself for that moment in which it shall offer itself as healer.

Is there another query, my brother?

Carla: Well, let me jump in and follow up something he asked. In that case, would water, purified water, perhaps be the best crystal of all, with possibly the addition of pure salt to form a house to house the disease that wishes to be taken away? It would certainly be cheaper than perfect gems.

I am Q'uo. It is true that the water is a crystal of potential in the healing process, as is that which you call the salt. The salt, however works in an [adsorptive] fashion, whereas the crystal, be it the gem or the water, works in a fashion which amplifies the healing love/light. The use of the water as an aid in the healing process is somewhat more difficult to construct, for the purity and quantity and relative motionlessness of the water would necessitate considerable effort upon the healer's part within your third-density illusion. This effort is greatly *(inaudible)* by the use of the *(inaudible)*, however it is well known by many that the simple immersion of the physical vehicle within the heated water and indeed in the swirling waters is of aid when general relaxation and removal of muscular tension is desired.

May we speak in any further fashion?

Carla: No, I was just attempting to link back into my Christian tradition which uses sanctified water, that is, salted water which is blessed, in baptism and in blessing holy places and in the Catholic church in holy water which is used for healing. I thought perhaps that was why that was chosen by some inspired entity, the water, because it was indeed crystalline, but it was also inexpensive and [when] magnetized by the healer/priest, efficacious. Thanks.

I am Q'uo, and we thank you, my sister. Is there another query at this time?

R: Just wish to thank you for the *(inaudible)*.

I am Q'uo, and we thank you as well, my brother, for your queries are those opportunities to serve which we treasure. Is there a final query before we close this session?

(Pause)

I am Q'uo and again we wish to thank each for inviting our presence. It has been a great honor to join with each in this circle of seeking, for we are brothers and sisters upon the same path of movement, from the One to the One. ✷

Sunday Meditation
February 28, 1988

Group question: (From R.) Are we sometimes influenced by the negative polarization of thought forms which have been created perhaps unknowingly through the mental activity of social groups? Do these thought forms tend to congregate in generalized areas, and if so, how may they be disbanded or neutralized?

(Carla channeling)

I am Q'uo, and I greet you in the love and in the light of the one infinite Creator, whose blessing and ours be upon you as we greet each and thank each for allowing us to share. We are most grateful to be given this opportunity of sharing with you in that sweet communion which is called meditation, for as we join you in meditation we slip into a sea, an archipelago dotted with so many small islands of light of all who sit in prayer and meditation, and as we come into your presence so share we and you also in that great undergirding strength of the many, many entities seeking truth and generating light just as you are.

There is much beauty in the increase in lights and the increase in hope, and as we speak to you and meditate with you, we rest in the joy of the shared quest, the brotherly journey, and the great work of service to all the sons and daughters of light. We are but here as your humble brothers and sisters. You must know that we carry no gospel, give no testament but only our opinion, a testament of its own, for it is true to our perception of our experience. We are hounded, however, by the relentless subjectivism of our identity, and though that which we know has brought us this far and gives us hope for further learning and joy, yet also must we say that we cannot see the other side of mystery, nor should any answer to any question which we or any give be considered substitutes for that unblinking focus which the pilgrim has upon the love within which lies all truth, that beacons always around the next bend of the path of the pilgrim. Move forward, and that beaconing presence casts its shadow one more ridge further along the way, or so it would seem.

We are speaking of our attitudes toward the Creator, of the great humility we feel as we attempt to communicate with you, pilgrims along the same path, in a tone of general awe, for we feel that especially in regard to the question which has been asked it be understood that beyond all powers of good or evil lies the mystery of the necessary existence, for why should we perhaps not be? Yet we are. And in astonishment that seems to go on forever, we gaze upon the tempting dark forest of mystery whose heavenly trees forever cloud the vision of ultimate truth. The central and persistent regard for this mystery, the coming into relationship with this mystery, is central. Any teaching which we may give you which speaks of polarities needs to begin with a forthright stance of worship, not of facts, not of techniques of service or seeking, but always the mystery itself.

The question which you have asked concerns the possibility that those within your planet's influence, especially those who are in physical incarnation upon its surface, may generate populations of random negative thought forms, and if so, what may be done, without abridging free will, to remove these agents of discomfort?

Most of those upon your surface are seldom capable of creating the strength—or shall we say polarity—of negativity in a trustworthy enough manner that thought forms of independent existence might emerge into being upon the levels of what you would call the lower astral plane.

However, a significant amount of suffering or any extreme emotion along certain lines, either positively or negatively polarized, can and does create an aura or nimbus of like weak thoughtforms which together seek then to become the psychic vampire, taking the energy needed for independent survival, if they are negatively polarized, from the fear of others; if they are positively polarized, from the awe, love and compassion of others.

Perhaps the greatest single life-threatening instance of the negative thought form is that found within your hospitals, for those who are there are often experiencing extreme physical catalyst in the distortion towards pain, and thus are immensely radiant of vibration along physical lines which often entrain, depress and nearly madden the emotional circuitry of the same entity. This rich harvest of pain and suffering, fear and despair is well enjoyed, and thus those who are already ill experience even more unease of mind, body and spirit as they must remain free from those emotional expressions manifesting from the catalyst of pain which attract negative thought forms.

Indeed, this relentless positivity of thought, that is, the sheer reluctance to view or experience negativity, is most powerful as a weapon, a shield and buckler, against which armor negative thoughtforms have little sway, for the mind that is stayed already upon those truths within dwells in unity and peace. There is no entrance for surrounding negative auras into the experience of one who, by the habit of positive thought, does not express itself in terms of negative emotions which may then provide food for those vampiric entities called negative thoughtforms.

We may gaze upon many, many sources of negativity, many clouds of negative thought-forms. The difficulties which lie behind, beneath and around the waking experience of those upon your planet at this time have caused those entities younger in your years to experience a speeding effect mentally and emotionally, and sometimes physically also, so that there are those who have experienced your culture's more painful problems of stress and importance put upon relatively unimportant things. Even those who are young in years have become no stranger to despair, no stranger to pain, and thus no stranger at all to those thought-forms which dwell upon depression, anxiety and fear, so that depression itself becomes food and the thoughtforms become stronger, and other vulnerable entities are then, shall we say, infected and encouraged by such vampiric entities.

We would mention one other source of negative thought-forms beyond those which are obvious from the sufferings of hunger, poverty and other wretchedness, and that is the thought-forms which may be termed the husband and the wife. These conditions of being and manifesting have, as do so many experiences which have become mixed in their blessings, both negative and positive [aspects]. An immense and centuries-old thoughtform of dissatisfaction has over many of your hundred years, centuries, produced a situation in which it takes conscious effort upon the part of any entity which is mated, for there are the energies wherein one is mirrored to another where disharmony shall take place, and this disharmony, then, attracts the great intensifier of that which feeds upon emotion.

In conclusion, we may say that to any whose feet are set upon the path towards the true and the beautiful in service to others and in the love and the light of the one infinite Creator each occasion for negative emotion shall also be an occasion in which it is possible to accept the relationship of food given to those who would feed from the negativity expressed, and as in all cases where negative thought-forms are encountered, the solution is—this instrument has just informed me, "Much too simple"—the conscious turning of the mind and heart to positive thought, to the generation and the remembrance of service offered and love given as the one only weapon of mind and heart which may starve away those thought-forms which can so intensify and make meretriciously enjoyable the experience of negative emotion.

Please remember that in all your behavior you are but manifesting that which you are, and that which you are dwells so deeply within you that it is the journey of a million lifetimes to discover. And, ah, how we too seek our true identity, and when we [find] it we shall be no more at last, if we are successful. Yet we shall be all that there is.

Turn to the Source. Turn then to the end of all seeking, and know that from one to the other is a perfect circle. Love each other, my brothers and sisters, in spite of all, love. And then those thoughtforms which are positive shall radiate and your light power shall grow. And thoughtforms which are positivity shall with angel wings come upon you and take food from you and give back to you the desire for more positivity, more joy, more compassion and peace.

Sate your desire, my friends, and moment by moment when you find yourself discouraged or in any more severe negative emotion, know in your heart that you have a choice, for though the universe is populated with many energies, they must not all come to you. It is your choice. We are who come to those who seek in positive ways. You will find more and more the virtue of such a turning. And if you feel a wrench and a pull and a tearing loose when the turn is made inside the mind and heart, know that you have broken the bands of those who have placed you neatly for consumption and have had to go away quite hungry.

And know, finally, that if it is a time for your being to experience a negative-seeming manifestation, gaze steadily into your brother difficulty. Know and accept that this too is a portion of the self, nor does it need to give rise to the negativity of thoughtform, for peace may be found in sorrow, yet sometimes the sorrow may be long in order that the spirit survive and heal. In those cases the sorrow is well if the spirit have faith in the positivity that surrounds that which is needed to burnish the tapestry which one incarnation creates, for suffering done in nobility of mind, dignity of spirit, and greatness of heart creates a somber, bright beauty that flames amongst the other stitches of the tapestry, giving to it a character and richness it would otherwise not have. Never mistake difficult challenges and others' negativity to you for that which must be put into your tapestry, those stitches made by your heart and your mind. You are a sovereign being, an image of the Father. My friends, we are young gods. Let us search together for the face of our true identity

We would close through the one known as Jim. We thank this instrument for working with us, as it was somewhat fatigued, and would now transfer. I am Q'uo.

(Jim channeling)

I am Q'uo, and greet each again in love and light through this instrument. It is our privilege at this time to ask if there might be further queries to which we may reply before taking our leave of this group. Is there a further query at this time?

R: Would you care at this time to complete the answer to the question of whether or not Jesus the Christ was the true son or the only son, as begun in the September session of last year?

I am Q'uo, and we feel that this topic would be one which would be most appropriate as the focus of another meditation, for there is sufficient information yet remaining that if it were given at this time the length of this session would be quite long and, we are afraid, somewhat draining to those in attendance.

Is there another query at this time to which we may speak?

Carla: If negative thought forms are from the lower astral, are positive thought forms from the upper astral?

I am Q'uo. There are, as you are aware, within the astral planes of your planetary vibration those middle and upper levels which are home to the more positive vibrations of entities which would form in accordance with the generation of the appropriate vibration within a sufficient number of your population. The higher frequencies of vibration of the thoughts of the population of your planet find, as do grades of a liquid, a more appropriate home within those upper reaches of what you have called the astral plane.

May we speak in any further fashion, my sister?

Carla: I've long been fascinated by the seeming congruity of the functions of UFO entities, such as yourselves, and angels, and I remember getting from

Latwii a veiled answer which suggested that the angelic hosts and the Confederation of Planets in the Service of the Infinite Creator were two fronts, shall we say, for the same organization. Could you comment on the accuracy of this perception?

I am Q'uo, and as we all seek to speak and act and give witness to the one Creator, we are all indeed a portion of the same front, as you have said. However, there is a distinction which many have made which does have some merit in that those entities whose native planetary influence is your own planet and who have moved there seeking in ways harmonious to the positive vibration are those which are often referred to as the angelic host. Yet these who have called your Earth home are as we who find our home planet in another location, for each seeks to serve and express the principles of the radiance of the light of the one Creator.

May we speak in any further fashion, my sister?

Carla: Well, it has puzzled me that if angels and the Confederation are like-minded, the angels, since we have only made it to third density on this planet, perforce have to have come from the Logos and dwell in the Logos, because we haven't produced fourth, fifth and sixth and so forth density people here very much, just a few in the fourth. And yet you are all people who, rather than coming from the Logos, and not going through incarnations, have come from the Logos then and started this long series of incarnations in physical vehicles. Is this an actual distinction, or is it only an intellectual one? I'm puzzled about it.

I am Q'uo, and we must admit our difficulty in perceiving the thrust of your query, my sister, for it is our perception that we, as those of your planetary influence, have moved through a series of traveling the densities of creation and learning within each those lessons.

Carla: Did you say you were a product of incarnation on Earth, Q'uo?

I am Q'uo, and we do not mean to suggest that we are of your planetary influence, my sister, but are of an influence other than your planetary influence which has also moved through the same previous experiences. Before asking for another …

(Side one of tape ends.)

(Jim channeling)

I am Q'uo, and am again with this instrument. May we speak in any further fashion, my sister?

Carla: Let me clarify. You've probably said something already that I just missed, but the distinction I was making was, the angels from our planet seem to have come from the Logos, like little portions of sun, little portions of light, because logically speaking they couldn't have come up through the densities, not on this planet. The members of the Confederation have all come up through the densities. That seems to be the distinction between the angelic hosts and the Confederation of Planets. Is this correct?

I am Q'uo, and though there are many instances of this kind of path, shall we say, it is our understanding that there are many of those beings which are referred to as the angelic hosts which have indeed moved through the incarnative patterns and densities that have preceded the experience that you now enjoy upon your planetary surface.

Carla: In this octave of creation, or in a previous one?

I am Q'uo, and it is our understanding that these entities are those which have experienced this planetary influence in its progression through the densities and who have by their placement of vibration chosen to remain in those time/space realms for the purpose of serving those within your physical incarnation.

Carla: So what they have from the Logos is what we all remember between incarnations?

I am Q'uo, and this is correct, my sister.

Carla: Which would be similar to any density higher than our own, which is why you and the angels can be said to have so many congruities. I see. Thank you.

I am Q'uo, and we thank you, my sister. Is there another query at this time?

R: Did you suggest earlier when you were talking about the institution of marriage that by associating oneself with the institution of marriage, that you somehow fall heir to a mass or an agglomeration of negatively polarized thought-forms that have been built up over the centuries? Is that what you were communicating?

I am Q'uo, and this is correct, my brother, for there have been in many cultures of your planetary history the construction of the means of mating which is at its heart somewhat adversary in nature. This is a portion of your experience which is the outgrowth of the natural attraction of those entities who share the nature of their catalyst or means by which they shall learn and serve.

This experience of growth within your illusion is one which partakes in large degree of those experiences which are of a traumatic nature when viewed only from the perspective of the illusion, which does not give the full breadth and depth and purpose of the difficulties that one might encounter within an incarnation in conjunction with another that serves to mirror and intensify and provide the opportunity to balance these distortions.

Thus, the means of mating that in your culture is termed the marriage has as part of its official structure the segregating of rights and responsibilities, the agreeing upon a contractual basis to the fulfilling of various duties within this marriage process, so that there is seen to be by those parties who engage within this process the necessity to give and receive in a measured manner so that there is the fulfilling of the duties. The process of culturally constructing this type of relationship is one which enhances the, shall we say, more difficult nature of the mating and provides additional catalyst to many who find the working through the preincarnatively programmed catalyst difficult enough.

This is a complex topic and we do not feel that we can do it justice in a short response, but shall ask if there is a further query at this time?

R: Thank you for your response, and I do have other questions, but I'll reserve them for communications at perhaps other sessions.

I am Q'uo, and we thank you, my brother, for the opportunity to speak and to serve as we may. Is there a final query at this time?

(Pause)

I am Q'uo, and again we wish to express our profound gratitude at the opportunity to join this circle of seeking and to speak our humble words with the hope that there might be some enriching of your own journeys of seeking, as ours are enriched by your presence and your seeking. We look forward to each opportunity and remind each that we walk with you upon your journey and share with you the joy and the agony of incarnation, for the experience of the seeker is one which moves from mountaintop to valley to mountaintop, and there is much experience between. We shall at this take our leave of this group, rejoicing, as always, in the love and in the light of the one infinite Creator. We are known to you as those of Q'uo. Adonai, my friends. Adonai. ✣

Intensive Meditation
March 9, 1988

(Carla channeling)

I am Hatonn. I greet you again through this instrument in the love and the light of the Father.

We are pleased with the homework done so well by the new instrument, by the shifting of priorities and attitudes that have been so difficult a challenge for the new instrument. We are pleased and delighted, and welcome to that group of light workers which seeks to offer the self in this service of vocal channeling. We have said before that the service of channeling and the learning of its practice is of much practical help in learning how to live within the illusion and we shall say it knowing that it shall strike the new instrument with a special force at this time as this instrument has, more than ever before, trusted in the foolishness of the word not heard, where so much of the surface mental processes concerning the surface perceptions of happenstance among your peoples is sheer illusion. And not only unhandy but [such] a stumbling block to discernment that it is a valuable goal, in our humble opinion, to attempt to channel the life as a whole, not in the same sense, precisely, as the one known as D channels the one known as Hatonn, but in the sense that there is a lack of concern about all else save that process which the player in the game understands to be that portion of the game which is his responsibility.

There is much distress amongst your peoples about such terms as livelihood and service, and the more ardent one is towards the quest for truth the more liable the mind is to attempt, upon its own, without recourse to the vast aid available, to use mentation only in determining what course to take to be of service or to attain right livelihood. In actuality, as long as the balls, shall we say, keep coming into the life, it is a neutral, emotional matter to catch the ball and dispose of it according to the rules of the game. There are societal rules which may or may not be accepted but as the student prospers in his studies, he discerns, more and more, the backbone of his own nature, the skeleton of ethics and compassion and caring, that which is unique to that seeker alone.

It is into that system of biases that events occur, are born, flourish, and are dealt with. When the hope of outcome is eliminated by the player—who is the seeker—and concentration lies only upon the accuracy of the catch—that is, the accuracy of the perception of the circumstance—then the knowledge of the self, which by instinct then moves that ball within the game to its rightful place, is made plain. Love itself prospers in such an atmosphere, for the entity which you are contains infinite love in a form which is, almost always, unavailable to the conscious mind. It must be touched within that inner silence by that infinity of the love of the infinite Creator which then channels through the seeking student joining with the infinity of love within and thus enabling the channeling of infinite love to occur.

In life, as you know it, in the experiences of love, there are many times that the balls—the thoughts, the perceptions—are dropped, misplaced, thought about past the point of ethical consideration, pulled and puzzled and torn, and so the flow stops, just as in the channeling process. So then the experienced student chooses that moment of gazing at the dropped balls and without blame of self or rancor of any kind, delivers himself over to the ministrations of patience, for there are those times within the illusion when the channeling stops, the channel being blocked. Then it is that the instrument of life, of love, or of service may sit patiently upon the mound, still in the ball game, but, shall we say, between innings, doing work which is just as difficult and just as important as active channeling, that is, waiting, and in the waiting, knowing that success is inevitable, that this ball game of love, of life, and of service, shall always go on. It is those who walk away from the game, disappointed in themselves or in others, who may find it difficult, then, to remain balanced and centered in faith.

We commend the one known as D for that patience which has been so dearly bought and for his growing abilities as a channel. Each entity has an unique voice, and we wish to assure the one known as D that this voice too shall be a gift …

(Side one of tape ends.)

(Carla channeling)

For as we have said, ours is a very simple message. We speak of the one great original Thought, which is love, if that which creates all that there is can be called in one word. Language is a poor thing indeed when it comes to superlatives.

We would at this time transfer to the one known as Jim, that he too may speak in some wise or another of love and love's many, many faces, for no matter what the subject, love is the source and the answer. And each entity's web of experience, learning and thought create one more way to express the inexpressible, to bring to illusion that brightest reality that shines already within, in each beacon heart. I am Hatonn.

(Transcript ends.)

L/L Research

L/L Research is a subsidiary of Rock Creek Research & Development Laboratories, Inc.

P.O. Box 5195
Louisville, KY 40255-0195

www.llresearch.org

Rock Creek is a non-profit corporation dedicated to discovering and sharing information which may aid in the spiritual evolution of humankind.

ABOUT THE CONTENTS OF THIS TRANSCRIPT: This telepathic channeling has been taken from transcriptions of the weekly study and meditation meetings of the Rock Creek Research & Development Laboratories and L/L Research. It is offered in the hope that it may be useful to you. As the Confederation entities always make a point of saying, please use your discrimination and judgment in assessing this material. If something rings true to you, fine. If something does not resonate, please leave it behind, for neither we nor those of the Confederation would wish to be a stumbling block for any.

CAVEAT: This transcript is being published by L/L Research in a not yet final form. It has, however, been edited and any obvious errors have been corrected. When it is in a final form, this caveat will be removed.

© 2009 L/L Research

Sunday Meditation
March 13, 1988

Group question: There are various kinds of unseen energy or life-forms within the universe that various people see from time to time, all the way from UFOs to spirits associated with the plant and mineral kingdoms, and other forms of life and energy that we are unaware of usually. How can we make contact with them? How can we become friends with them? How can we use what they have to teach us in order to serve other people?

(Carla channeling)

I am Q'uo. I greet you in the love and in the light of the one infinite Creator, and I greet each of you. We are most grateful to be called to your meeting this evening, and to share our thoughts with yours. It is an especial pleasure to meet those who are with us for the first time, and we extend to you our greetings and the love of the Father, which flows through us, though it may seem from our words to come [from] us.

Before we begin speaking about the question asked this evening, we would like to be sure that each understands that we, like you, are pilgrims upon a path. We have not yet reached that end which is the source of all things, for still, though we have advanced and learned different lessons from you, yet there are many things we do not know. Yet you call to us, and we turn back to you as brothers and sisters, sharing our opinions with you, we who have perhaps experienced more. You do us a great service by asking for us to share within your beautiful meditation, and to become a portion of your unified circle of seeking, for were you not to call us, we would be unable to serve you. And it is by serving you that we ourselves may learn and grow and refine our own knowledge and love of the one infinite Creator.

We turn to the question of phenomena and love, for you ask us how, if one has seen those beings generally unseen, can one tap into the wisdom and knowledge of those entities, learn what they have to offer, and improve one's service within your life experience within this illusion which some have called the shadow of death. And so we begin, asking always that this caveat be remembered, take what seems correct to you and leave all else behind, for we would not be a stumbling block to any.

Many there are who have incarnated upon this sphere in these days by choice, in order to aid the planetary consciousness at a time when your planet as a whole is making its final choice, as one could hope, a unified being. Failing that, the time inexorably draws near when each entity must make that choice for itself, the choice betwixt the path of lightness and that path of darkness, the path of unity and the path of separation, the path of service to others and the path of service to self.

Thus, much of your incarnation you will find yourself in the process of making choices, and as you begin to seek in a conscious fashion those spiritual lessons which you believe are there for you to learn, you begin little by little to include in those considerations for choice thoughts and biases which you have developed in the process of your seeking, thus transforming what may seem to others to be a mundane and unspiritual choice as a truly spiritual means of making some manifestation of love and service for others overt, enlightening the consciousness, not only of the self and those others about you which may be affected, but also upon another level, the consciousness of the planet itself.

For there lies within the peoples of this sphere a growing and nearly critical mass of those who in one guise or another seek peace and light and joy. And as each seeker seeks and fails, and picks itself up and seeks again, and takes one step back and two steps forward, as we all do in our stumbling way, as each persists, so the light grows, the web of light about the planet becomes stronger, and planetary consciousness is being transformed. There is a concept among your peoples called critical mass, and it is towards this point that the planetary consciousness is moving.

A significant harvest of souls shall be moving on to a different reality, a different illusion, more refined lessons and a gentler emotional, mental and physical experience, which, upon the other hand, is far, far greater in what you would call the length of time, for now within this life experience you gaze upon what you see, whatever it may be, and you make your choice: service to others or service to self.

With this fundamental information in place, we would then speak of phenomena [such as] the seeing of many lights, the seeing of visions that are clear, the hearing of messages and answers to prayers, and [other] phenomena which are experienced by those whose consciousnesses are awakening from the sleep of what you would call life and turning the eyes upon the infinite creation, seeking to know the deeper truths which lie behind that which your own scientists tell you is truly an illusion of energy fields, interacting and appearing quite solid and real.

Yet each of you is, in truth, light formed by divine consciousness, containing a gem that is that portion of you which was, as your holy work the Bible says, "before the world began," that part of yourself which sees with eternal eyes, and loves and gives with infinite supply. In the prison of your Earthly body, you have perhaps not been able to offer infinitely those things which you would wish to offer. Perhaps you have felt you do indeed need wisdom from those phenomena which signal to you the presence of a greater self, a fuller light, a larger reality.

We would ask you to see, as you gaze upon phenomena of however beautiful or persuasive a nature, that it is nothing but dust and ashes, holding no meaning whatsoever, unless it strike within the heart of the perceiver the chord of recognition, for in truth, as you are truly a portion of the Creator and have that divine spark within you, you have the ultimate resource given by grace. And you shall not learn, but remember and recognize those truths which are yours and which are needed by you in order for the consciousness which you are attempting to polarize toward service to others to have the best atmosphere in which to do so.

In the case of wanderers especially, that is, those who have come here from elsewhere in the infinite creation of the Father to be of service to those who attempt harvest in this and following generations, there are often come delegations of those who would wish that visiting soul well, and as in some higher densities, these forms are those of light, so in some cases the phenomena is nothing more than a visit from friends, not intended for information, but only for support and greeting. In other cases there are those whose souls cry out, while consciously they may yet be only half-aware of the reason for their discomfort with life as they know it. In some cases, those invisible entities which dwell helpfully about each child of the Creator will sometimes manifest briefly as a signpost indicating the mystery of creation.

Many lights within your skies are there to advertise the mystery, to suggest and remind those who may have not thought deeply about the subject that humankind knows nothing, that science itself as you call it, is based upon that which has been observed, not that which has been understood, that the fundamental values which scientists use are values of an unknown origin and nature. A sense of mystery is a very, very strong motivation for many of those who visit your sphere at this time in light to do the work of the Father and to awaken those who yet are asleep within their bodies of clay, not recognizing their prison, but rejoicing in their cell. Each entity has its time to emerge from that prison, to look through the bars and then to find the key that unlocks the door of finiteness, of beginning and ending as a human being upon your planet, for eternal you are, and you share an exciting, rich, challenging, fascinating and joyful pilgrimage, a pilgrimage in which we are those who walk with you.

There is another category of light phenomena and your so-called UFO phenomena which expresses and manifests in ways which generate negative emotion, terror, control, fear and so forth. These experiences are those offered by entities which are upon the negative path, who have chosen within your density of learning to follow the path of service to self. These entities have a philosophy to offer, and to those who are willing to carry this message, the message is given. These entities also appear in vehicles of light or in shapes of light. This is due to the fact that those who worship the Creator can only serve. Whether they serve other or the self, all are one, and consequently, if their service is pure enough in a negative sense, they too may use the Creator's light which falls upon all in a fearless blessing of free will, for the Creator wishes those who come to Him in the end, to come in an irresistible love by total free choice and with every faculty ablaze with the spirit.

We have not yet addressed the true, or shall we say, the more efficient method, of obtaining aid from those sources which you have identified with manifestations and phenomenon. The tool that is the most efficient in this way may be called meditation, prayer or contemplation. It involves not only expressing oneself inwardly and asking those petitions you would for the self and for others with needs that you know of, but also of listening quietly, persistently and in a daily manner to that which the holy work known as the Bible has called the still, small voice, the voice of silence, and the true voice of enlightenment. For the knowledge which you would wish to know is not knowledge, but an inner knowing which cannot be expressed, a way, shall we say, of being wired, that you may glow the brighter as an entity in mute witness to the beauty of love.

Within meditation the work is done. Within the listening, within the silence, within the daily persistent seeking heart, that which is of true wisdom and compassion is an environment which is more and more dwelt within with a steady and unremitting faith, built by constant turning within to the Creator within. The entity more and more becomes a kind of being and is or exists or expresses in a certain way.

The entity may not notice, but those to whom the entity is manifesting do indeed notice, and are blessed by the light which shines through them, blessed indeed by the focus which sees into the heart of each, to see the consciousness and the perfection of Christ and Christ consciousness. For this [is] your intended and true nature, a nature which gives and receives love freely, wisely, gently and unstintingly. To love, to exist in love, to begin discovering the selfhood of the self in love, is the basic work of those who wish to lighten the planetary consciousness. It may seem most undramatic—and it is. It may seem most unlikely to produce the riches of the world—and it is. To work for planetary lightening is a service-to-others act. To do it daily is a blessing to your beloved and fragile home in space and time.

We would turn now to the question of how best to manifest and express the joy, the peace, and the love of consciousness which is held within what you would call the Kingdom of Heaven. How can one best share with others? How can one find what this instrument has called right livelihood? We wish that we could move within the experiential nexus of your culture and find some persuasive way to express the extreme biases and distortions among your peoples concerning those ways of living which are of most service.

Perhaps the key to what we would say concerning service and livelihood that is what you may call righteous is this. The consciousness of the Creator, unique parts of which manifest as yourselves in a highly distorted form, is completely unified. You may love one and serve one, and give as clearly and beautifully and fully as the entity who shares that same light and love and passion for light and love with ten million. The service is the same, for the service is in the preparation of consciousness that it may do the work before it in such a way that that work becomes positively polarized, serving in gladness, so that those about one who is serving in any capacity whatsoever may witness the light, the joy, and the peace which cannot come from one within an illusion in which so much is distressing. That which you call human faculties fail. The love of the one infinite Creator is infinite.

We do not wish to discourage an entity which finds a desire to use those visions which it has received from so using them. We wish to make each aware that it is well to express the desire that only those entities which wish to aid in service to others be accepted, and after that determination of consciousness has been repeated frequently enough that it has pierced the veil of the subconscious mind and moved therein, that then that level at which these entities enter the conceptual web of a being upon your planet may be stopped at the gateway of your subconsciousness if they are of a negative orientation. It is most practical to place the guardianship of love in service to others as deeply in the mind complex as it may be sent, and to keep the self within this place of choice, that those things which might come into the consciousness from an impersonal source be those things which shall redound to the beauty of the Creator and the kindly love and blessed light which that Creator offers to each and through each each day in every conceivable way.

We find that this instrument informs us we have overstepped our speaking period, and once again we apologize for our prolixity, but this is a subject of much interest to us, as we speak to you from that which this instrument would call the wisdom density, which may be perhaps more easily understood as a kind of experience in light which perhaps equals in our experience the imagination of those which think of the kingdom of heaven. We do not put ourselves forward, but only describe the environment which we enjoy.

We admire each of you and all of humankind. Our decisions are easy, for we have no veil. Our subconscious mind, our archetypical mind, our impersonal or Creator mind, all these levels of awareness are open to us, and we share our thoughts with all those within our society. Our eyes our open, our hearts are open, yet still we find work to do, my children. Yet you have eyes clouded with the grossest of illusions, ears and all senses inundated with a sea of experience. And because you cannot see the thoughts of those about you, communication fails most often and pain is inflicted that could never be inflicted in the time to which all of you are looking, that next step in the evolution of very, very young sparks of divinity and heirs of a birthright of divinity, as it makes its blessed way to a larger and larger realization of the true nature of the self.

We see that we have begun again and we must stop, so that if there are queries which you have decided to ask at this time, you may. We do apologize for wordiness, but we are most pleased to be asked such an interesting and central question, and hope that in each right livelihood that each may choose, that each may feel that presence of divinity which is more truly the self …

(Side one of tape ends.)

(Carla channeling)

It is not that we wish to discourage any from following their talents and their abilities, but we find most often that those among your peoples who ask about right livelihood have every opportunity for love, giving and receiving of love, in that which lies just before the eyes, in that task which is just to be done. There is no gift, no thought, no action which may not be sanctified by its dedication to the will of love, to the will of the Creator. We would transfer at this time. We are those of Q'uo.

(Jim channeling)

I am Q'uo, and greet each again in love and light through this instrument. At this time it is our privilege to offer ourselves in an attempt to speak to any further queries which those present may offer to us. Again we remind each that if we speak a word that does not ring true, that you should disregard all such words immediately, taking only those which have meaning. Is there a query to which we may speak at this time?

Carla: I noticed that you said something about Christ, and then called it Christ consciousness also. Do you see those two terms as interchangeable?

For the most fastidious of considerations, there could be seen to be a difference between one who holds an office and the office itself. And yet the nature of [this] office is such that any which moves into the unity with the Father that this office signifies becomes then that office. Thus, for the consideration of those who find this entity and its station or office holy, we would not make a differentiation.

May we speak further, my sister?

Carla: Yeah. Thank you for that. I have thought to myself, why, why did one man have to go through all that he went through, knowing that he was going to have a horrible death, and even though he didn't even believe the way his Pharisitic friends did in the Jewish law, going through a sacrificial procedure which was totally Jewish, you know, pouring one's blood out upon the altar and so on. Was it because he had to create a framework within which his story would persevere, would catch in the mind over a long period of time while Christians, shall we say, those who were following him up until now, could work on their own path with his help?

He says at one point, "These things and more ye shall do," indicating that he thought we were fellow heirs in Christ or Christhood, and he always called himself the Son of Man, and yet none of us has had to go and be nailed up on a cross. Obviously, there was only one time that it needed to be done. And it just puzzles me. I'm guess I'm just a doubter or something, but why just the one time? Why just that one unique suffering, and then all of us finding our sufferings to begin to have meaning as we study Jesus' sufferings? Was it necessary that this story be done in this way?

I am Q'uo, and am aware of your query, my sister. The one known as Jesus the Christ wished to offer to all of humankind the symbol of the path which all must travel in some fashion in order to become the love of the Father and to express that love to others. The nature of the sacrifice of the life and the mundane world was exemplified as this entity sacrificed all that one may have—the life—knowing that it lived not of this world, but of a greater world. And by making this sacrifice in such a dramatic and fulfilling manner, there was instilled then within those whose hearts are turned toward the truth of love, the path boldly and brilliantly blazed so that there could be no doubt as to the nature of the journey and the value of the sacrifice.

May we speak further, my sister?

Carla: It's still a great mystery, but I'll think about it, I'll read it after. Thank you.

I am Q'uo, and we thank you, my sister. Is there another query?

Questioner: I have one. In the scripture, Jesus says that he is the way, the truth and the life, and that all men must come to the Father through him. Is that an absolute truth? And what about the people who follow other examples, like Buddha and Hinduism and such like that?

I am Q'uo, and am aware of your query, my sister. That which Jesus was and is was far more than a being that moved among your peoples and lived a life in a certain fashion. All the teachings of this entity were in the form of that which you call the parable, so that those who had ears and hearts and eyes inclined in a fashion to perceive greater truths could look beyond the surface of the teaching and dig far more deeply for those treasures which awaited the hungry heart, hungry for truth and love.

That which the one known as Jesus the Christ exemplified was above all else unconditional love, a love so great that it was willing to lay down the Earthly life that others might live eternally. Thus, the pattern was given in a manner which each will approach from a unique point of beginning. Many will find the journey seems to lead in lands far distant from that spoken of by the one known as Jesus the Christ, and yet as each through experience and time moves closer and closer in its seeking towards greater and more refined expressions of that which you call truth, each will find that it moves closer to the heart of that which the one known as Jesus the Christ exemplified, the unconditional love and compassion that is the gateway through which each shall pass at some point within the evolutionary process.

Thus, though many shall travel roads that seem other than this path, there is a meeting point at which time and place all become as one.

May we speak in any further fashion, my sister?

Questioner: I'm not very familiar with your manner of speaking, and so I find that I'm still a little bit confused about your reply.

Carla: Are you saying that unconditional love is the I AM? Like the "I Am That I Am" of God's name in the Old Testament? And that I AM is another way of saying unconditional love, is that what you're saying? Like unconditional love is the way, the truth and the light?

I am Q'uo, and this is basically correct, my sister, for within your illusion there is the choice which each has to make in order to progress yet further. The choice is how to love, to love others without condition as has been demonstrated by the one known as Jesus the Christ, or to love in a lesser fashion. All your great religions and philosophies teach at the heart of their dogma the need to love without condition. Jesus the Christ was a perfect example of this means of loving, and thus learning that lesson which is the great lesson of your third-density illusion.

May we speak further, my sister?

Questioner: I think I have a better understanding, and I thank you for that.

I am Q'uo, and we thank you as well, my sister. Is there another query at this time?

Carla: Is this why Jesus said at one point that unless you are as little children you cannot enter the Kingdom of Heaven, because little children have not yet learned distrust and they love unconditionally?

I am Q'uo, and this is correct, my sister.

Carla: Okay, thank you. No more from me.

Questioner: I have another one. Is it good for people to see miracles and fantastic things to convince them of God's ability and existence, so that they may decide to develop their life to God?

I am Q'uo, and we find, my brother, that it is more the reverse of this case, that is, those who through their own experience make the dedication more and more firmly to know the truth of that which you call God or life, or the purpose of the life, are those whose eyes shall begin to open and shall see those experiences which are not seen by other eyes.

It is the free will choice that is made in the direction of love and service which then begins to open the eye to another reality and the heart to another reality and the ears to a greater reality which speaks in ways not understood in the mundane world.

May we speak in any further fashion, my brother?

Questioner: *(Inaudible).*

I am Q'uo. Is there another query at this time?

Questioner: So, another form of what I'm asking is beyond the person that's asleep, that is, not spiritually aware, can't he be awakened in any kind of way? Unless he decides to do so by faith?

I am Q'uo, and this is a roughly correct statement, my brother, for the power and value of such a centrally crucial choice comes from the choice having been made by the entity itself to move in a certain direction. If an entity were given undeniable or miraculous demonstrations of the reality or truth of a certain belief, then this entity's work would have been done for it, much as the child's schoolwork would be done by the parents. And though the entity would know the correct answers, [it] would not be able to reproduce this experience within its life pattern. Thus, slowly for many, and more quickly for others, does the desire to know the truth build, until there is born within the entity the faith that there is a greater reality which upholds the life and its purpose.

Is there a further query, my brother?

Questioner: No, thank you.

I am Q'uo, and we thank you, my brother. Is there another query?

(Pause)

I am Q'uo, and as we have observed that we have exhausted the queries for the evening, we would take this opportunity to thank each for offering those queries to us, for they are the means by which we may further our service to each and to the one Creator. We feel a great honor at having been asked to join your meditation this evening, and shall be with you in your future gatherings upon your request. At this time we would take our leave of this group, again thanking each and leaving each in the love and in the light of the one infinite Creator. We are known to you as those of Q'uo. Adonai, my friends. Adonai. ☙

Intensive Meditation
March 16, 1988

(D channeling)

I greet you again through this instrument in the love and light of the one infinite Creator.

(Pause)

This instrument has *(inaudible)* tonight refer to as the power of our insistence but we know *(inaudible)* to impose our will on that of any individual though there was reluctance because of fatigue and poor tuning to speak. We wish only that our so-called insistence might be perceived rather as encouragement and a demonstration of the aura of confidence and patience in which this instrument is able to experience its unfolding as a vocal channel. Since there was reluctance to speak we shall like to remind the one known as D of that which he is already aware, which is to say his purpose in being here so faithfully.

(Pause)

(Carla channeling)

I am Hatonn. I great you once again in the love and in the light of the one infinite Creator. We have moved from engagement with the instrument known as D due to our determination that the limit of this instrument's ability to learn at this working session had been reached in terms of the technical or mechanical rituals prior to and during the act of channeling.

We were of the impression that we would be of the most service by persistently contacting the one known as D in order that the deeper service might be recollected in the midst of most disquieting circumstances. This simple lesson may seem to be an allegory of the life that is lived so narrowly in the midst of such abundant glory. There must come that time when it is seen that the channel, as imperfect as it is, and remiss, nevertheless is becoming more and more able to perceive the contact. For the confidence of the instrument to continue to rise, the ability to contact, we felt, needed to be affirmed to the instrument and by the instrument at this time. We do apologize for seeming perhaps too persistent. However, there is no study at which a task master is not sometimes an aid. Incorporate then into each practice of meditation, centering, tuning and challenging that fine honed singleness of purpose which is yours in depth so that you, being your own task master, move harmoniously with your own requests and are to the maximum ready to serve as a vocal channel. For do not all those who wish to serve the Father wish to do so at their highest and at their best?

The other side of this high-sounding coin is the cheerful laughter of imperfection guaranteed by the illusion in which you dance. The channel is as the color sparkling off the facets of a diamond which gleams so whitely. Each glint is unique in its spectrum in the rainbow of itself and so are each of you distortions of that white light. We have our own distortions in the concepts which we give to you and to our distortions are then added two things. Firstly, the combined strength and desire of seeking and areas of seeking of all those present in the circle and secondly, that gem which is the channel. Thus may we speak of the infinite Creator infinitely as through even one channel the infinite moods, experiences and thoughts of each day make each unique being a little different. It is an exciting way of being of service to us for we learn much as we see the poetry, passion and strength which instruments such as yourselves create from the solid prose of our one statement and that is that there is one thing—that one great original Thought which created all that there is which is all that there is and which is you. And you It.

How very stolid that message seems. How very tame, staid—we correct this instrument—beside the many beautiful creations which have been channeled through so many positively oriented channels. We have most certainly a great debt of gratitude to each and every one.

And to those who are new, such as the one known as D, we encourage that second side of the coin, that laughter and that self-forgiveness. There is always the falling down. There is always that portion of the experience which deals with the things of the earth. And it is well that the self be reminded again and again to look upward to eternity and to ask for the truth, not the answer. For that which your peoples call the answer is never the truth, for that which is true is infinite and your peoples measure and balance and weigh finity.

May you be all that you wish to be as a channel, my brother D. If we may aid you in any way we are most humbly grateful for the chance to do so.

At this time we would transfer this contact to the one known as Jim. I am known to you as Hatonn.

(Jim channeling)

I am Hatonn, and greet each again in love and light through this instrument. At this time we would ask if there might be any queries to which we may replay with our thoughts and opinions. Is there a query at this time?

D: I'd like to just say first of all that you take my doubts and my impatience with myself and my anger with myself and perceive it in a much more elevated way than I am able to and it's a great help to me when you raise my perspective up to yours by reinterpreting, insofar as you can, by reinterpreting those feeling that I have in times like this, that I am very grateful for that. I really don't feel like I have any specific questions at this point. I'm a little bit disturbed by the course of this session but as you say it's permissible, I suppose, to stumble on the path. *(Inaudible)*. I have no questions. Thank you.

I am Hatonn, and, my brother, we are most grateful to serve in any manner which may be helpful to you as a new instrument and we speak as we have spoken concerning your efforts this evening for it is our perception that each new instrument will find those times when the facility with the speaking of concepts is less than others, and even very difficult for each new instrument as the life within the mundane world draws from it the vital energy which is most helpful in contacts such as this contact. And there are many concerns which draw this energy and make it difficult for the new instrument to find the peaceful center of its being where it may perceive with clarity and transmit with equal clarity those concepts which are given it.

We commend you, my brother, for persevering under the conditions of fatigue and for continuing the training which shall provide you with another means of serving the one Creator. We hope that the efforts which fall short do not disconcert you overly much as we equally hope those efforts which are easy and free flowing give you confidence but do not make you overconfident, for there is much to learn from that which you call failure and much to learn from that which you call success.

Are there any further queries at this time?

Carla: I had a very irrelevant and very unimportant question. Before the contact began through D I was sniffing around and wanting to know who you were and you identified yourself and just the way you answered my challenge and especially about the third time through you started giggling … and then I was going … I was really worried about D. I was going, "Why don't you want to come to me now?" And you were going, "Have patience, child." It just … you just seem very feminine and I wondered if you were … if we had contact with a woman from Hatonn today?

I am Hatonn, and we are those which at this time in this particular contact are of a feminine nature. We are an individualized portion of a larger group and yet we speak of ourselves as we, for though you speak with an individualized portion of a social memory complex we do not feel that we exist apart from those of our brothers and sisters in a manner which bears a descriptive term.

Carla: I understand.

(Inaudible) less than we and we are happy that you have enjoyed our vibrations. We are pleased to assist old instruments as well in renewing the ability to be patient and also to giggle.

Carla: *(Giggles)* Thank you.

Are there any further queries at this time?

Carla: Not from me.

I am Hatonn, and we thank you, my brothers and sister, for once again inviting our presence and allowing us to be of service in that way which is a treasure to us. We cannot thank each enough for this honor and look forward to each such gathering. At this time we shall take our leave of this group, leaving each in the love and the light of the one infinite Creator. We are known to you as those of Hatonn. Adonai, my friends. Adonai.

Intensive Meditation
March 23, 1988

(Carla channeling)

I am Hatonn. We greet each in the love and the light of the one infinite Creator and do apologize for beginning before your recording devices were engaged. However, we surprised this instrument, for we had been expressing to this instrument the request for the instrument to remain patient until the instant we changed our minds. This instrument chose to request again the status and we simply began to speak through her as she was tuned, had challenged well, and was ready to begin.

We find that there is a reluctance in the one known as D to channel at this point because there are deep portions of this entity's being which at this time desire greatly to receive whatever thoughts we might have to offer in the way of guidance. The instrument known as D must be aware by now that we attempt carefully to keep to the right side of the boundary of free will. However, there are reflections we may make which are of a general nature which we shall make at this time through this instrument before we exercise the one known as D, for we feel that [with] this dual method of working first with the more deeply requested service and secondly with the second most deeply requested service that we shall, shall we say, be of a more satisfactory quantity of service.

This instrument and all those in the circle were engaged in a fairly realistic conversation about change, we thought, just prior this session. However, there are changes which have to do with circumstance and there are changes which fall within the category one may call genetic. Sometimes these two kinds of changes occur within your illusion at the same time. Consequently, that which is a physical manifestation of change due to happenstance becomes overlaid with a deeper and [more] organic change and the two kinds of change become linked within the mind so that that which is a less than important consideration is perceived as that which has a great deal of emotional weight.

It is well to sort out these two avenues of expression and experience to determine the level of change which one wishes to deal with at one time, for the changes of the body, which over a period of time reach, shall we say, a critical mass and create a necessary adjustment of programming of the bio-computer, are those changes which contain the, shall we say, inside track for the most available use in accelerating the process of spiritual growth. It is well to disassociate this feeling of fundamental shift in attitude from the circumstances which are occurring at the moment, and to view the circumstances which are occurring at any given moment as that which they are—a drama, an illusion, a lovely play, or perhaps a not so lovely play, depending upon the circumstances, put there not for your—the audience's—total enjoyment but also, the author hopes, for clues, hints, inspirations and nuances which may function as parables or allegories for those more theoretical and general thoughts which concern the process of bodily change which contains the great emotional content.

Now, this great emotional content, when isolated, is quite neutral, having little to do with happenstance or illusion of any kind. And if it may be perceived in such a clear way, it may also be used as clear energy, thus functioning as a continuing catapult for a speeding up of the evolutionary spiritual process. The difficulty with linking the process of genetic change, shall we say, and the various vagaries of circumstance is that undue emphasis may be placed and inevitable bias formed by the nature of the illusion at the time it has had to carry the weight of such emotional load. Thus, the lessons are muddied and confused and the progress is slower, though, of course, it continues.

As we have so often recommended, once again we urge the practice in, and the trust of, the process of daily, spiritually directed, inner silence, the listening ear, if you will, that is tuned to those words which cannot be heard, those words which are not words at all but concepts far deeper than any clothing of vocabulary. This source of peace, in the short run, becomes the facilitator of strife in the long run, in that one who meditates is facilitating the process of genetic change, for indeed, your physical entity is finely tuned to respond to the needs of the integrated spiritual entity which, as a total being, each is.

We trust that this has been thought provoking in some small way and invite queries at a later time. However, we have instructed this instrument that this instrument is to spend some conscious time teaching. Indeed, had this instrument been more quickly aware of our request, we would have already been working with the one known as D. However, again, we do feel that in the end this has been the better pattern for this evening's work. We would therefore leave this instrument and pause while this instrument recovers full consciousness and may do the work it has been encouraged to do with the one known as D. I am Hatonn.

(Conversation between Carla and D.)

(Carla channeling)

I am Hatonn. I greet you once again in the love and the light of the one infinite Creator.

We have moved from engagement with the instrument known as D due to our determination that the limit of this instrument's ability to learn at this working session had been reached in terms of the technical or mechanical rituals prior to and during the act of channeling.

We were of the impression that we would be of the most service by persistently contacting the one known as D in order that the deeper service might be recollected in the midst of most disquieting circumstances. This simple lesson may be seen to be an allegory of the life that is lived so narrowly in the midst of such abundant glory. There must come that time when it is seen that the channel, as imperfect as it is and as remiss, nevertheless is becoming more and more able to perceive contact. For the confidence of the instrument to continue to rise, the ability to contact, we felt, needed to be affirmed to the instrument and by the instrument at this time. We do apologize for seeming, perhaps, too persistent.

However, there is no study at which a taskmaster is not sometimes an aid. Incorporate, then, into each practice of meditation—centering, tuning and challenging—that fine-honed singleness of purpose, which is yours in depth, so that you—being your own task master—will move harmoniously with your own request and are to the maximum ready to serve as a vocal channel. For do not all those who wish to serve the Father wish to do so at their highest and at their best?

The other side of this high-sounding coin is the cheerful laughter of imperfection guaranteed by the illusion in which you dance. The channel is as the color sparkling off the facets of a diamond which gleams so quietly. Each glint is unique in its spectrum in the rainbow of itself So are each of you distortions of that white light. We have our own distortions in the concepts which we give to you. And to our distortions are then added two things: firstly, the combined strength and desire of seeking and areas of seeking of all those present in the circle; and secondly, that gem which is the channel. Thus may we speak of the infinite Creator, infinitely, as through even one channel the infinite moods, experiences and thoughts of each day make each unique being a little different. It is an exciting way of being of service for us, for we learn much as we see the poetry, passion and strength which instruments such as yourselves create from the song and prayers of our one statement, and that is that there is one thing: that one great original Thought which created all that there is, which is all that there is, and which is you, and you, it.

How very stolid that message seems, how very tame beside the many beautiful creations which have been channeled through so many positively oriented channels. We have most certainly a great debt of gratitude to each and every one, and to those who are new, such as the one known as D, we encourage that second side of the coin, that laughter and that self-forgiveness. There is always the falling down; there is always that portion of the experience which deals with the things of the Earth, and it is well that the self be reminded again and again to look upward to eternity and to ask for the truth, not the answer, for that which your peoples call the answer is never the truth, for that which is truth is infinite and your peoples measure and balance and weigh finity.

May you be all that you wish to be as a channel, my brother D. If we may aid you in any way, we are most humbly grateful to do so.

At this time we would transfer this contact to the one known as Jim. I am known to you as Hatonn.

(Transcript ends.)

L/L Research

L/L Research is a subsidiary of Rock Creek Research & Development Laboratories, Inc.

P.O. Box 5195
Louisville, KY 40255-0195

www.llresearch.org

Rock Creek is a non-profit corporation dedicated to discovering and sharing information which may aid in the spiritual evolution of humankind.

ABOUT THE CONTENTS OF THIS TRANSCRIPT: This telepathic channeling has been taken from transcriptions of the weekly study and meditation meetings of the Rock Creek Research & Development Laboratories and L/L Research. It is offered in the hope that it may be useful to you. As the Confederation entities always make a point of saying, please use your discrimination and judgment in assessing this material. If something rings true to you, fine. If something does not resonate, please leave it behind, for neither we nor those of the Confederation would wish to be a stumbling block for any.

CAVEAT: This transcript is being published by L/L Research in a not yet final form. It has, however, been edited and any obvious errors have been corrected. When it is in a final form, this caveat will be removed.

© 2009 L/L Research

Sunday Meditation
March 27, 1988

Group question: "Q'uo: You have wished to know what we may think about the right use of will."

(Carla channeling)

I am Q'uo. I greet you in the love and in the light of the infinite Creator. It is indeed a privilege and an honor to rest as part of your circle of seeking this joyful evening. Your blends of energy are beautiful, and we are most grateful that we have been called to offer what thoughts we might have to share with you. Please know that each and every word that we say is guaranteed not to be the truth, but to be our honest approximation and opinion of the way things are from our point of view. We are anything but infallible, and we ask most humbly that as you consider each idea which we may offer, you do so with the understanding that any which does not seem appropriate be dismissed, for we would not be a stumbling block in front of any, but rather one more light upon the hill, one more means of sharing in communion with the one infinite Creator.

For no matter what our capacities, our states of advancement and our several opinions of ourselves, yet this one thing remains true of all equally who seek the face of that great mystery which is the uncreated: all of us are pilgrims, equal. All of us are one: one in seeking, one in feeling we are missing the point, one in willful misunderstandings, and one in rueful new beginnings. Yet do we all keep on, step by step, along an infinite road, paved with hope and love.

You have wished to know what we may think about the right use of will. We would speak to you of one of your teachers, whose vibrations are with the Earth plane at this time, due to the intense focusing of many upon that which you call Easter. We would look at an entity who you call Jesus the Christ. This was an entity of enormous and generous will, a quiet, pure and undiluted belief that that which was claimed could then be manifested. Although the theoretic understanding of this principle is available to those within your illusion, it is a rare entity whose level of remembrance is such that such a truth may be manifested. And it certainly was [the] faculty of will, harnessed in twin to faith itself over and over in this entity's incarnation.

With the season's roll come many stories, and for many centuries the story of the one known as Jesus the Christ and his journey from carpenter to cross is much focused upon. At this point in the story, my friends, the one known as Jesus is experiencing the hosannas and the palms thrown before for the humble beast to trod upon. The entity's will has been tested and shall be tested again. The story is an old one, and the answer to the question of what happened next is not long in forthcoming. Late in the night watch, the one known as Jesus begged for the release from death upon the cross, and at that time the concluding prayer was, "Yet not my will, but thine." In worldly terms, this entity made a wrong decision in accepting the will of the Father. This decision led directly to the entity's death. In metaphysical terms, however, the turning of the will towards the Father is the means whereby will and faith become one, and the entity a crystallized being.

Think back, each of you, over those things in which you have faith. Think carefully. You must have faith in something. Is it the social order? Much has been said about the instability of that order. Shall you put your faith in that? Shall you put your faith in your science and technology, seeing the usefulness and efficiency and marvelous doings possible. Where are the ultimate answers? Few rigorous thinkers put their trust in that which cannot explain the grounds of its field of study.

Let us look, then, shall we believe in anything, have faith in anything? We turn the mind at once to that which you have implicit faith in, and that is something called love. There is no entity in incarnation in third density who has not experienced both love and the loss of love, joy and sorrow. It is more tangible than anything which may be touched, more acutely real than anything which can be measured. It is the stuff of sentiment and emotion in many ways, for your peoples call by one name a thousand different emotions and feelings. Yet we speak of that love which all consider as that which is to be believed in, and that is unconditional love, for such is the nature of that love which has created all that there is, that one Logos, that one great original Thought which is all things.

Thus, we suggest that that which one has faith in is by its nature love, for any lesser faith shall fail. And when the seeking entity wishes to become one whose use of will is most pure, one may call upon love itself to teach the spirit that will and faith may be united, that the being may be polarized further, crystallized further and take one more dusty step along the long road.

It is difficult for us to express to you, who feel so keenly where your energy fields end and others begin, our concept of the right use of will, for we find that we think of our will as that which is indeed imperfectly known until we have included that portion of ourselves which fits in no energy field, but rather is a part of the one infinite Creator. Applying the will, then, without matching it, yoking it with and to love itself is to minimize and fail to fully explore the nature of the self and of the will.

It would seem perhaps that in many cases love need not be sought and its wisdom listened to, for many things seem cut and dried, as this instrument would say. Yet let there always be that thought in the mind, "Not my will, but thine," knowing that that love to which you pray is your own self in a greater manifestation. It may have crossed your minds that you are all gods. We acknowledge with joy the truth of this statement, but only caution that we are all very young gods, and God's will is sometimes hidden from the surface portions of young god's minds.

We urge each to trust and follow the urgings of the self, to express the self by whatever means needed in order to feel whole. We certainly do not wish to encourage blind obedience, but as you meditate, as you become more and more thirsty for and comfortable in the presence of the one infinite Creator, you will find less and less that there is a paradox betwixt the will of self and will of the one infinite Creator. May you be patient with yourselves in the learning of this and every lesson. May you meet whatever disappointments you feel you have with the sure knowledge that you have been making a good effort. This is all that is necessary—to intend, to desire, and to want to be a not-so-very-young manifestation of love. May you have joy in your quest and its fruit.

We would at this time transfer the contact to the entity known as Jim, expressing through this instrument once again our happiness at being called to your group. May each of you be most blessed. We would leave this instrument at this time. I am Q'uo.

(Jim channeling)

I am Q'uo, and greet each again in love and in light through this instrument. At this time it is our honor to ask if there might be further queries to which we may speak and offer our opinions, fallible though they are. Is there a further query at this time?

Questioner: I have a question, Q'uo. I have two questions. One's personal and having to do with myself, and then the second part is the area that I'm living in. First of all, about a year and a half ago I had an out-of-body experience. Since that experience, I've had a "pulling" sensation in my third eye, and I haven't really come across anything on that sensation, that pulling sensation in my third eye. What does that mean for me, is the first part of the question. The second part is the area that I live in had a, what we call, a UFO flap in 1987, which is very much UFO activity around Belleville, Wisconsin and around [Mosinee], Wisconsin, many daylight sightings, and the ships were hovering for hours at a time over certain areas in the country out there, and I'm kind of wondering where those particular vessels were, from what planet did they originate, and what was their mission in our area?

I am Q'uo, and am aware of your queries, my brother. The experience of which you speak, that of leaving the physical vehicle and moving in the lighter body, is a portion of your own process of awakening, which has served to get your attention, shall we say. The experience of leaving that which has been one's home for all of the known incarnation and experiencing the freedom and lightsome feeling outside of that home serves to point a direction which is at this time continuing in its progress that will focus the attention upon the breaking of boundaries and the traveling into the mystery of the unknown. One might see this experience as a kind of training aid that continues to motivate the seeking further along the path.

The feeling of the pulsing vibration at the third eye location is an indication that the indigo ray energy center, as this instrument would call it, is being activated and balanced for further explorations, not necessarily of the same kind as the first. We can speak in this manner, for we feel that your understanding already includes this basic information. Were this not the case, we would feel responsible to speak in more general terms.

To turn to the second query. In this instance we find the necessity of speaking in somewhat more general terms, for there are many other entities involved in the experience of the sighting of craft which appear to be from elsewhere and to be quite unusual within your illusion. It is not the practice of the positively-oriented entities of this nature to appear in this manner, for there are many considerations which the more positively-oriented beings from other planetary influences would naturally consider before offering themselves to the physical sight of your planet's population. The more positively-oriented of these entities choose, rather, to appear in more isolated instances, whether they be the dream state, the meditative state, or the isolated physical sighting which is not available to the general population of the one which is the focus of this sighting.

The large scale sightings of these craft, which have come to be called the UFO, is a phenomenon which is most frequently utilized by those entities which wish to enter the emotion of fear and the quality of manipulation into the experience of those Earth entities which have the physical sighting in great numbers. The great numbers and continued presence of such mysterious craft tend in general to the great majority of your population to suggest forces beyond the control of your Earth population, and therefore are seen consciously and unconsciously as a kind of threat. This then acts as a force which can be used to divide portions of the population from themselves.

May we speak in any further fashion, my brother?

Questioner: One last thing. Would it be possible for me to have a sighting sometime? A possible sighting? I've never personally seen a UFO.

I am Q'uo. The experience of the sighting of such a craft is one which is understandably unique enough to attract the desires of many such as yourself which seek the keys to the mystery of being and the process of evolution. Yet we might suggest to each such ardent seeker that it is not necessary to experience that which is considered greatly unusual and other dimensional, shall we say, for within each life pattern there moves a rhythm and giving and receiving of that quality called love which is appropriate for each entity.

The desire to accelerate this process is also understandable, and to this desire we would speak by suggesting that to each seeker of truth will be attracted those experiences which are the most appropriate for the proper unfolding of that life's journey. For many this includes such experiences such as the one of which you speak. To each is attracted that which will most efficaciously promote the learning of those lessons set before the incarnation by the self for the self, and the offering of those services which are the fruits of that learning. If such an experience would be helpful in any seeker's path, then such will be a portion of that journey.

Is there a further query, my brother?

Questioner: No, thank you very much.

Sunday Meditation, March 27, 1988

I am Q'uo, and we thank you, my brother. Is there another query?

Questioner: Yes, I have one please. I had an experience last August, late July or August, with energy, and I have what I think is an understanding of it, but I would like to see if I correctly understanding it. There may be others who have had similar experiences, so this may be a question of some general applicability.

I was having a session in which a friend of mine was using some hypnosis with me to do some past life clearing; I was in hypnosis, and he was the hypnotist at the time. After I had worked on clearing on the past life material, I began to experience an inrushing, from head to toe, of a tremendous amount of energies. There was a sensation like a cool wind from this energy, and with my eyes closed, I could see clairvoyantly, I could see it as a tremendous light, very brilliant light. It went on for about a half hour, and I had various experiences while it was going on. I even had some muscle spasm, not painful, but my hands were sort of paralyzed and twisting, there was such an inrush of energy. And I had the unusual experience of seeing something as if pieces of my finer bodies were breaking apart and flying away from me under the pressure of this energy. It was like black outlines of the shape of my body were flying in pieces away from me. And it was as if the light was so brilliant that they were dark against the light, the way a person who stands against a bright light, their face will be in shadow, there'll be a silhouette. Is it possible to comment on what that experience was?

I am Q'uo, and we may speak in a general fashion, my sister. The source of all distortions is the limitation of the point of view, as has been stated by those known to this group as Ra. Each belief which an entity contains and forms and by which it lives serves to offer certain opportunities for experience to that entity. When that belief or group of beliefs has been fully utilized, then there is the need to move beyond that belief and to enlarge the point of view, or the field of vision.

When this enlarging of the point of view meets some resistance, perhaps due to the comfortable nature of an old belief which has perhaps become likened unto a friend, the entity then may begin to experience a limitation within this area which may be expressed in any of a number of ways which will be perceived by the entity as a difficulty or perhaps even a mental or physical disease of one kind or another. This may in fact occur from incarnation to incarnation, so that those patterns previously experienced in a fruitful manner in an earlier portion of the incarnation or in another incarnation may then become sources for the agitation or irritation within the total being of the entity.

When such a limiting belief or knot or tangle of thought is released by whatever means, there is a release of the energy which was used to form and hold that belief in place in order that it might be of service. This energy then is free to be utilized in forming yet another field or scope or reach of possibility which will then further allow the entity to experience more of that which is its food for growth, the catalyst which becomes experience.

May we speak in any further fashion, my sister?

Questioner: That is helpful. Thank you.

I am Q'uo. We thank you, my sister.

Questioner: Yes, I have a couple of questions. One question has to do with dreams, and I've had several very unusual dreams, but I'll speak to one in particular, and I'm going to ask is this a dream state, or did it really happen? It was that …

(Side one of tape ends.)

Questioner: … was the first part of my question, having to do with my dreams, having to do with two crystals being implanted. Can you tell me, is that coming from my higher self, or is that something that actually happened to me in dream state? *(Pause)* Have I been among extraterrestrials?

I am Q'uo, and apologize for the delay, as we were rejoining this instrument after its resetting of the recording device. The experience of which you speak is one which we find has an important significance as a symbol within your consciousness at this time. Because of its current importance and semi-veiled nature, we wish to give only that information which will not infringe upon your own free will, for it is the exercise of that free will and its application to the resolving of such experiences that is the heart of the process of seeking that which you call the truth. The image of the crystal is quite significant to you at this time, for each seeks to become that which might be called the crystallized and seeks in this process to regularize those patterns of energy expenditure which will allow one to move further along the path of evolution and to experience that quality of love which is the prime mover and creator of all that is.

We see the experience of which you speak as one which occurred within that state that you call the dreaming, and yet many experiences occur within this state which are as significant or important or what you would call real as those experiences which occur within your waking reality. Thus, the fact that this experience occurred within the dreaming state may be seen as the necessary conditions that would allow the image of a new thought formation to be seeded within you. The new thought or direction in thinking is that which has begun to make itself apparent to your conscious mind through the unconscious mind as a possibility which may prove fruitful in your own personal journey. Thus, this experience begins to point a direction which you have already considered and this experience serves to reinforce that consideration.

Is there another query, my sister?

Questioner: The other part of that question had to do with another dream in which there appeared to be a vision, and I'd like to understand what that is. I don't feel that I was asleep, I feel that there was a vision. Can you tell me? Can you give me information on what the vision was? This occurred about close to two years ago.

I am Q'uo, and we scan your recent memory and find that this query is one which is most important in your own journey at this time, and one which continues to hold a significant degree of mystery. It is that which we feel most comfortable in allowing to remain as a mystery, for we do not wish to infringe in this case upon your own discernment. The experience of such visions is one which is as the momentary opening of a door into a room which is as yet unexplored, but one which holds a great deal of interest and potential for the expansion of one's own abilities and desire to seek and to serve. Thus, the momentary opening of the door serves as that which becomes the riddle, and the constant pondering of this particular riddle is that which was desired by that portion of yourself which brought unto you this experience. Thus does that portion draw your smaller self onward in a manner which insures that the free will to move in this fashion remains intact.

Is there another query, my sister?

Questioner: Thank you, no.

I am Q'uo, and we thank you once again, my sister. Is there another query at this time?

Questioner: I have a question, Q'uo. I wish to ask you a question that has been in my mind most recently as being significant, never really before. I've never had the feeling that I was a part of this planet, except for one recurring dream, and basically, to make a long story short for you, I wish to be of service to myself first in order to discover where my past lives and how its significance can be cleared towards service to both myself and other selves. And I'm in the dark on the best means for myself to find this out. Any help would be appreciated.

I am Q'uo, and am aware of your query, my brother. There are many within the Earth planes at this time that are, indeed, not indigenous to this planetary influence and which have come in order to be of service to the population of this planet which calls for the service that these entities have to offer. However, each, as it has become a portion of this planetary influence, has taken on the complete array of characteristics of a third-density being, which is to say that much of the nature of the creation in general and the nature of one's own being and movement through the creation remains a mystery.

To those such as yourself which seek to remove some of that mystery and to illumine the path that lies before them, we would suggest that first of all the desire that motivates this seeking be cherished and enhanced in order that to the heart of one's being one may seek to understand more and more clearly that power which moves each of us within the one creation of the one Creator, for the desire to know, the desire to serve by that which is known, is that which within this illusion of mystery is most important for the removing of any portion of those veils which stand between seeker and truth. For one may accomplish great things in worldly terms, and yet if that entity does not desire to understand the nature of the life which moves through the physical vehicle and which pulses all about one, those great accomplishments have served little purpose.

This desire, then, is that which shall attract to each seeker those experiences which provide the opportunity to learn and to serve. The desire is likened unto the magnet which attracts the iron filings. This desire may be enhanced within the meditative state or the state of contemplation or that of prayer, where the desire is offered unto all those sources and forces of light within and without which are a part of one's being, and is offered as that which is one's only gift to the Creator and to the purpose of the life.

It is not, in our opinion, as important what one does or how one does it as it is that each thing one does and thought one thinks be motivated by the desire to know the heart of truth and to offer that which is found as the heart of truth to others who seek also this truth.

Thus, my brother, we do not have specific suggestions as to a path to take. We offer only the suggestion that one hone the desire to the greatest degree possible and allow that offering of the desire and the will to know and to be of service freely in order that that which is most appropriate be attracted to you through that desire.

May we speak in any further fashion, my brother?

Questioner: That feels very good. I have one more query which may have something to do with the first question or it may not. You may have already answered my question. But I have recently felt a calling to the northwestern section of this country, or perhaps of Canada, I know not which yet. I know no one there, I know not why, and I know not where to look. My desire is inhibited not only by the fact of the unknown, but as to whether or not this is meaningful as a portion of my service.

I am Q'uo, and am aware of your query, my brother. In this particular instance we feel the weight of the law of free will that would prohibit a specific recommendation, for the taking of such a step is most important in a seeker's journey. To offer the principle which might be utilized, then, by such a seeker is our proper role in our opinion. To give a direct suggestion that this or that step be taken is beyond the bounds of that which we feel is appropriate in our relationship with seekers such as yourself.

We may, however, suggest that when one feels the drawing to a certain place or thought or thing that there is indeed a purpose for that feeling, and the consideration of the practical nature of that feeling versus the symbolic or abstract nature of that feeling may be considered carefully, for in some cases there is only the need to travel in thought, whereas in others there is also the need to travel in space and in time. Thus, our suggestion to you, my brother, is that within your own meditative state the query may be more fruitfully asked and the answer found.

Is there another query, my brother?

Questioner: No, thank you very much. I appreciate it.

I am Q'uo, and we thank you, my brother. Is there another query?

Questioner: Yes, I have a question, please. I have recently started doing art, and at times I feel a great intense energy when I'm doing this art. And I'm interested in who this entity might be, and also how I can further open myself to receive the art that's coming through and be a better channel for it?

I am Q'uo. We do not mean to be repetitious, but again we would suggest that this query is one which may be most fruitfully presented to the self within the meditative or even within the sleep and dreaming state, for the nature of experiences that are of a mysterious origin within one's being is likened unto the tip of the iceberg which moves within the water, greatly hidden, yet giving an indication of its nature by that which is shown above the water's surface. Within your meditative or dream states, it is possible that through your desire to know the nature of this experience and the entity or entities connected to it, that more shall be revealed at a pace and at a time which is most appropriate for encouraging clear understanding of how this service may be utilized by you to enhance your learning and that which you may offer others.

The subconscious mind is greatly underutilized by most entities, for there lie within this portion of the tree of mind great mysteries and all that which is unknown to the conscious mind. However, the unconscious mind responds to the desire which the conscious mind generates to know or experience this or that thought or concept if, through the conscious desire to know more of that which the unconscious mind may funnel through to the conscious mind, the entity may utilize those states of consciousness which bypass the conscious mind in order to receive a clearer indication of, in this particular case, the nature of that ability which is now finding flower within your being.

As you build a focus or channel, shall we say, consciously with your desire to know, and build it so that it connects to the unconscious mind, then there is the greater probability that you will experience further illuminations of this experience which you have described. We recommend the contemplation, the meditation and the prayerful attitude in approaching such mysteries in order that their full scope of potential be availed to each seeker in the appropriate time.

We at this time would thank each for offering the queries through which we may perform our humble service. We have utilized both this instrument and the one known as Carla in order to be of that service which is ours to offer. We would again thank each for offering the opportunity to us to blend our vibrations with yours and to serve in this manner.

Again we remind each to take only those words and thoughts that ring of truth for one's own use, and to leave behind those that do not, without a second thought. At this time we shall take our leave of this instrument and this group, leaving each in the love and in the light of the one infinite Creator. We are known to you as those of Q'uo. Adonai, my friends. Adonai vasu borragus.

Sunday Meditation
April 3, 1988

Easter

Group question: Has to do with suffering. What causes suffering? Is it something to do with the general lack of a person's feeling and knowing of the unity of all of creation? Is it something that can be generally stated? What can be done to alleviate the suffering that a person goes through? Is the suffering that people go through an individual kind of thing? How do individuals deal with their suffering? How can we use the suffering for growth and learn from it?

(Carla channeling)

I am Q'uo. I greet you in the love and in the light of the one infinite Creator. It is a great privilege to be called to your group to answer your query about suffering. As we revel in your company and the loveliness of your meditation, we revel also in the extreme beauty which surrounds and permeates your domicile at this time, for we are able in consciousness to share with those within the domicile their impressions of the burgeoning blooming of the countryside, the singing of your birds and all the beautiful colorations of sky and land and water that create such ineffable beauty, that great manifestation of the bounty and the ever-living quality of life which, though in winter it may seem gone, resurrects from the winter earth each springtide into new freedom to seek the light in the humble way of plant, animal and element.

You wish to know what the cause of suffering may be, whether it may be due to a lack of perception of oneness, what its cause is, and what its cure.

We are minded to discuss a suffering life that all within your culture are aware exists, that of a teacher, master and Christ known to you as Jesus of Nazareth. When we examine the life pattern of this individual we see an entity thrown apart, even within childhood, suffering the loneliness and lack of companionship which accompanies the unusual and serious student in the small child's body, for by the age of what you call your teens, the one known as Jesus was very learned, speaking as a rabbi would, knowledgeably of much literature, much memorization, much insight. This lonely entity walked in his curiosity into many places, always the stranger, seeking information, seeking guidance, seeking understanding, and suffering always the loneliness of the stranger.

When the time had come to make the final dedication of the life's work the one known as Jesus was aware of this great and momentous necessity. There had been clear communication within this entity with that which this entity called "I AM." The ministry, the one known as Jesus knew in advance, would be difficult and would end in the physical death of his body.

Why did this instrument of the one infinite Creator accept this suffering with no strife or struggle, no contentional argument? This is what we would explore.

There is much of what is called truth which is indeed not truth, but a multiplicity of ever-shifting truths which function in what you may call a social way, in order to slide one through the incarnation with the least possible friction. There is another truth, an absolute and unchanging truth, a mysterious, puzzling, ever-calling truth which any within your illusion cannot see but only know through the experience of love.

Love is the great one original Thought. It cannot be bought; it cannot be manipulated; and it cannot be killed. It may become obvious that we are not speaking of romantic love, which is prey to all these difficulties. We are not speaking of the love of friendship or any other definition of love which may be put into words. Indeed, could we find an unique word which would express the beautiful, terrible love which created all that there is, we would use it. Yet this concept lies so far within the area of the deep mind its reality can only be reached through the non-words which may be called "faith." This love is single, and within it are all things, all entities, thoughts, artifacts, seeming objects and each and every energy within the infinity of creation. Each of you is love. This is your reality, your absoluteness, your unchangeable nature, your truth.

Suffering lies not upon this level but upon the level, for the most part, of half-seen truths, truths that are relative to the situations and conditions of your society and culture. We realize that there are those who experience suffering in physical ways: pain, hunger, sickness and death, that process which is so feared among your peoples. By far, however, the greatest amount of suffering among your peoples is due to the ingestion and acceptance of cultural and social truths—and in this we include theology of all kinds—as standards against which to measure the self.

This instrument, for example, experiences continual pain to one degree or another. The instrument's suffering, however, is far more emotional than physical, for this entity suffers in wonderment that she cannot fulfill her own expectations of what her service, her energy, and her life should contain.

Are you then suffering emotionally, each to whom we speak? We assert that this suffering is paramount.

Let us gaze at the panoply of emotional suffering. Within most of your culture, to have a skin color at variance with the fleshtone which you call, to our puzzlement, white, is to suffer from the narrow-mindedness and the prejudice of those not of your race. And whether each race knows it or not, each suffers from prejudice, and this prejudice becomes a suffering. Each who is born homosexual within your culture is denied the consolation of your cultural institution's regularizing relationships. Further, there are many, many cultural obsessions which form a rejecting net of discrimination, and so in the name of truth suffering is perpetrated. There are those who in their mated relationships, experiencing in the mate much love, find that in the passage of time, the mate has turned to other energies, other entities, other positions in time and space. The separation creates suffering, not because the separation is real, but because there is a loss of love perceived

My children, we could weep at the suffering caused in the name of truth. And as we go back within your planet's history, we see and ask you to see with us, how each time and age and culture created its own bigotry, narrow-mindedness and distortion of harmony and unity, marking each person out in some way as unacceptable. And because all of the culture expresses much the same bias, the entity experiencing incarnation at any cultural moment will find that it is suffering because it cannot be that which the culture and the society have declared appropriate.

May we say that those whose spiritual orientation is rigid, by their judging of others in a harsh and overt manner, create much suffering in the name of the very teacher, the one known as Jesus, who moved into this vibration to call those who suffered, those who were mocked and despised. This entity was not interested in the righteous, those who knew the truth of the culture, and we specifically in this term, culture, include organized religion, as this instrument calls it, for these judgments carry an enormous, though specious weight among your peoples. Ah, we weep for you. Yours is a planet of sorrow, even upon the joyous day of Easter.

We move now to the contemplation of unity. We move out of the realm of the relative to the absolute, and we ask you to follow us. We ask you to release the opinions of the world, to release the dictates of what is expected, and especially in those suffering spiritually from teachings that do not show them the face of I AM, to release those harsh theological strictures which, though most helpful for some, have not been helpful for you, but have instead caused tremendous guilt and suffering. We ask you to turn from opinion, all opinion, and most especially your own, because this is Easter, because the energy of this planet at this moment is most light and full of life. We would ask you to experience directly the promise of which Easter is the symbol, the promise of the infinity of I AM.

When one moves away from, "I want, I feel, I think, I like, I dislike," and so forth, one is left empty, and may perhaps feel that the comfortable structure that houses one's ethics and principles have been left behind also. It is a naked feeling. It is a difficult feeling to achieve, for one who has not carefully examined the huge weight of opinion and accepted authority in one's life has no idea of the percentage of the active portion of the conscious mind which is involved in processing catalyst using these distortions rather than experiencing catalyst with an open heart, an open mind, and a knowledge of the self's true identity.

My children, it is difficult, we know, to deal with the intricate and wonderfully made illusion which begins with your very body and its electrical field, and continues with that which the organs of the body may perceive, all those things about one, all those thoughts spoken to one and by one, all the infinite details of a daily life. How much of the time is spent in the consciousness of I AM?

Thus, before we speak upon the purpose of suffering, we wish with steady hand and firm heart to present to you the concept that the truths which are relative and cultural must needs be examined carefully and analyzed closely, so that one may see to the best of one's ability what one's own selfhood truly feels and thinks about that which the culture demands of one. This includes everything from the choice of career to the intricacies of relationships. So much of your communication is distorted by each entity's attempt, conscious or unconscious, to manipulate one's environment in such a way that one is positioned in a satisfactory angle to one's culture, one's acquaintances, and oneself.

Cultures change. The self changes. These truths are relative. Those rules regarding behavior, for the most part, need constant reexamination, for that which has been true for you at one time, will of necessity change and transform as you change and transform. We do not wish to suggest that it is necessary to change any thought or action. We only ask those who are suffering because they are homosexual, divorced, addicted or any other calamity need not think of themselves lost to Oneness, for all of these things are taking place within an illusion which is designed for a certain purpose. This certain purpose is absolute, and within the absolute purpose of spiritual evolution towards love, suffering is an absolute necessity.

Now, not all those within the creation find the necessity to experience suffering. Many are the entities which have been created never to leave the Logos, never to leave love, never to leave the absolute, but always to experience and be the I AM which is love. Each bloom which breaks forth its tender shoots through the softening winter earth is expressing absolute ecstasy, absolute joy, and this joy is fragrant and beautiful, and may be perceived by all.

The one known as Jesus the Christ noted that his kingdom was not of this world. Think you then that he meant the kingdom of the world of flowers and birds, spirits and beauty? May we hasten to give our opinion, fallible though it may be, that this was never this entity's intent. This entity had been courted as the hoped-for and earthly king of a specific people in a specific region. These people had a truth which was theological, and therefore relative, made of opinion. This opinion was that this entity could lead a revolution, topple a government, and reign as the kings of Judah and Israel of old, a Jewish king for a Jewish nation. This entity wished none of the limitations of relativity. He wished to be limited in no way, for this entity focused always upon the absolute, and in his converse, he turned as much to his Father, Abba[1], as he did to any friend or student.

"My kingdom is not of this world," he said. Not, we say, the world of experience, the world of opinion,

---

[1] An Aramaic word which translates as the equivalent of a familiar name for a male parent, such as "Papa" or "Daddy."

the world of cultural demands, the world of theological limitations. When this instrument of the Father came at last to face that man which could spare the entity, the one known as Jesus made no defense. His judge was puzzled, for he saw the suffering which had occurred and the suffering which was to come which was prepared for the one known as Jesus, and could not understand why this humble teacher would not defend himself. Finally, in desperation, this entity simply asked, "Are you king of the Jews?"

Jesus the Christ, eyes calm, spoke clearly. "You say that I am so," said he. "Yet for one purpose came I unto this world, to bear witness to the truth."

His judge was immediately fascinated. "What is truth?" he asked. Jesus the Christ only gazed into Pontius Pilate's eyes, and Pontius Pilate saw the I AM of Love.

What is truth, my children? In seeking for this answer, the greatest spiritual suffering may be experienced, for as we have said, truth is most often sought in the culture and in religious theology. And in this we include, to some extent, our own work with this instrument, not excepting ourselves from the world of opinion, but consciously accepting that we who use words can never be, but only express, thus offering a manifestation which is but the shadow of our being, our I AM. Truths and Truth, the relative and the absolute. There is a Truth, there is an absolute, and thus there is an end to suffering. That Truth lies in the kingdom which the one known as Jesus the Christ stated was not of this world, not of this world of opinion.

We ask you to gaze within. We ask …

(Side one of tape ends.)

… [you to gaze] upon that which lies behind that which we are saying, our consciousness. All of you are suffering within the confines of a prison. It is the prison of your limitations. Your fingers stop and the air begins, your feet stop and the ground begins. There are separations of space between you and all other beings. There is the curtain behind the eyes of those with whom you wish to communicate which limits harmony. You are, to this extent, dead in a very real sense, and we want you to enter into the consciousness of life.

We want you to experience I AM. As you rest, speak that word, "I AM," and find something come to life deep within. I AM. This is the kingdom of which Jesus the Christ spoke. For the essence of being, the essence, I AM is that which we have called divine love. It is not only that which loves all that there is; it is all that there is. It is not that through any agency you may become an associate of Christhood; it is that all of you shall eventually perceive the self as Christ. Or to put it another way, that one day, if we may use inaccurate terms, you shall be all Christ, all absolute, pure being. Rest in this consciousness for a moment, and experience life.

Where is truth? Truth is in the absolutes that shine through the relative. Truth is in the smile, the laughter and joy, the moments of kinship, the body's intimate ecstasy in the making of physical love, the spontaneous reaction of deep compassion. And in the end, truth in an absolute sense may, to the disciplined mind and heart, become the companion that walks beside you, through whose eyes you may see anew the whole and unified life lived in love. That which is suffering is that against which the entity seeking to know love for the Creator, love for the self, and service to others may push against, may use, not as the stumbling block, but as the starting block. For each difficulty which causes suffering is that which has been arranged that some distortion concerning the essence of love within your understanding may be examined, thought about further, and perhaps revised somewhat.

Without the challenges, the suffering, the problems, there would be a heedless, naive and unschooled joy, the second-density joy of those small creatures you call animals, which frolic and play, hunt and kill with no sense of anything but wholeness. This is a wonderful experience, yet for those within your density, it is not an altogether instructive experience, not an experience designed in the end to move one along in the spiritual evolution.

Each challenge gives one the chance to turn to I AM, to Beingness, and ask that infinite intelligence which is love, "What is the absolute principle which illuminates this situation?" Absolute love may be hidden for long periods of time, and the questing process, the experience of pain and separation, may go on for a seemingly infinite period of time. Your peoples attempt to avoid, cover over, and patch up these situations to alleviate discomfort, without seeing the spiritual opportunity for new understanding in the light of that which is absolute.

We ask each to remember the experience of true living consciousness, and then in faith to turn to the self and bless each wound, each limitation, each pain, and each circumstance that causes suffering, for suffering is the sacrament, the food of spiritual evolution. May you rejoice in your troubles even as you suffer. May you roll the stone away from the tomb of your limited acceptance of damaging thoughts. May each look you take be fresh, and may you live in love, and so love each other with a passion and a zeal that blesses each with whom you come in contact. You need say nothing. The I AM in you, that Kingdom of Heaven, of which Jesus the Christ spoke, lies deep within you, for you are all that there is. It is simply the illusion which keeps you from that ultimate knowledge. By faith, in the love you have observed in whatever limited form, may you enter into that life which is love.

We will be with you in meditation if you so desire company, and we shall share that unlimited, absolute love as we are given it to channel from the kingdom within ourselves, which is the kingdom within you, the kingdom of love.

We would leave this instrument at this time with many, many thanks for this question and for your call to us. We humbly accept the limitations and distortions that language causes, and ask that each be aware that anything which is spoken is not the truth, but must be subject to your own discrimination, for we speak to the limited mind. It is each seeker's occupation to bring that which speaks deep into that kingdom, that from that kingdom there may issue the hallelujahs of angels, the shouts of infinite joy which herald the incredible, energetic, peaceful feeling of infinite love which may carry you into and through each suffering moment and sanctify and bless each experience.

We hope that you do not accept suffering as something which must be done so that in the next incarnation, stage of experience, or density you shall be rewarded. Instead, in all humility, know that your heaven lies waiting within you, just as your hell waits to embrace you. Your life experience is a matter of choices. Shall you follow truths, or shall you more and more attempt to experience your own true being, your own inner I AM, and thus prepare the meeting ground, the holy ground whereon you may see the face of your God, your Christ, your Love, your peace, your light, your life?

We would now transfer this contact to the instrument known as Jim. I am known to you as Q'uo.

(Jim channeling)

I am Q'uo, and greet each again in love and light through this instrument. At this time we would offer ourselves in the attempt to speak to any further queries which may yet remain upon the minds. May we speak to a query at this time?

Questioner: I have no query, but I am thankful for the information that I received tonight.

I am Q'uo, and, my brother, we are most thankful for your query, and honor the sincere desire that has prompted this query. Is there another query at this time?

Carla: I have one. It's been on my mind all week because last week something happened to me that happens frequently.

My suffering is largely at this point physical, I just have pain. And you're absolutely right—I think you said that the suffering doesn't come from just the pain as much as what you think about the pain. I've had this trip laid on me by myself and by numerous people through the years, and every time I bring it up again, it hurts the same, and that is that people tell me that I am creating and responsible for my own illness. This I accept, but further, that illness is a kind of blockage or imbalance due to things that I am holding in myself, which if I would let them go, I would automatically be healed.

I suppose like a lot of people who have been disabled, I would like to think that there is something more to it than that, that there is some higher purpose for my suffering. Or I suppose most of all, that if I don't get well there isn't cause for guilt, which I feel a lot of every time I go through this process. And I know this all lies within the realm of human opinion, but I must admit I do believe I am responsible for my illness. I just don't feel the necessity of focusing my entire life upon getting rid of the illness because I find so much value in the life that the illness has caused me. Could you speak to my feelings about where I have put the emphasis in my life, that I have taken off the responsibility for making myself well, and put it on other things, and I feel guilty about that? Could you speak to that?

I am Q'uo, and am aware of your query, my sister. It is true that each entity is responsible for that which occurs within the life pattern, for each entity has taken the primary role in designing that pattern of life experience which shall serve as the lessons teaching further aspects of love and service. Yet most of the responsibility has been taken by a portion of the self which is far more informed than is that smaller self which experiences the incarnation. Thus, that smaller self often feels isolated and abandoned or too powerless to be able to affect forces within its life pattern which have control and impact upon that life pattern.

Before incarnation this greater portion of the self looks with careful eye to see what within the entire being contains that which is yet to be fulfilled, that which yet remains to be exercised as an avenue for offering the self to the Creator and for allowing the Creator to know through that offering greater portions of its own being. Thus, before each incarnation does this greater self look most carefully to see where there might be an increase in the learning and offering of the lessons of love, of wisdom, and of unity to all those which might come in contact with this self.

As these determinations are made, they [are] set into motion in what you might see as a program that unfolds step after step, with each succeeding step building upon that which has been firmly laid in the experience of the entity. Thus, the completion of one level of understanding and the offering of this understanding as a service to others will spark the next level of experience. These programs of experience are often, most often indeed, hidden within the symbolic framework of the life pattern and are largely unrecognized by each entity as the life pattern unfolds. Thus, it seems to [an] entity within the incarnation that the experiences happen to it and are beyond its control, when indeed the experiences have been chosen by it for specific purposes.

There are, for many entities, lessons and opportunities to serve which are of such a primarily profound nature that what will be seen within the incarnation as extraordinary means are then employed to allow this extraordinary offering and lesson to occur as desired.

In some cases that condition which is known as disease, illness, tragedy and suffering of one kind or another is seen as the most effective tool for generating within the depths of the being those responses which are desired, much as the grain of sand, within that creature which you call the oyster, creates the irritation that is the source of that pearl which eventually forms within this creature. So does the suffering and disease then offer to such an entity with this intense desire the pearl of great price, shall we say, which may teach those lessons which would not be available without such an extraordinary effort being made. Thus, many experience the suffering and limitation of disease which does not yield to healer of any kind, though many should offer their services in heartfelt sympathy and compassion and desire to alleviate the suffering and remove the limitation.

However, those healers and, indeed, entities of any nature which are more familiar with the wider scope of the life pattern and purpose will see in such an instance that purpose for the disease or limitation which lies beyond that normally associated to such. Such an entity or healer will begin to look into those areas which examine the opportunities offered by such a disease or limitation and will, instead of continuing the fruitless effort to remove the disease or limitation, begin to counsel the entity with this disease or limitation in the ways of seeing where doors are opened rather than shut by such a pattern of experience. For within your illusion, all that is central to the accomplishing of the preincarnatively chosen purposes for the incarnation is hidden from the sight of the outer eye, and must be sought in the careful and prayerful attitude of one which looks beneath the surface of things and beyond the scope of the outward seeing eye.

Thus, my sister, in your particular case it is well known to your conscious mind that you have chosen the limitations which you experience for a specific purpose. Indeed, there are more than one purpose for these limitations, and it has come to your attention frequently and in the distance of your past that you have been able to focus upon your inward journey far more effectively because your outward journeying has been limited in many ways. Thus, by this limiting, you have been able to penetrate the outer shell of the life pattern and tap more easily into those deeper truths which nourish the soul and inspire through such nourishment the efforts of others.

That you experience a kind of guilt for having this condition and having it be unresponsive to the healing efforts of any is understandable when seen within the limits of the illusion and the sincere good intentions of those who offer their services as healers.

Yet each entity in any life experience must at some time begin to look beyond the general principles which it finds are helpful to view the life experience through, and then must begin to make individual application of the deeper principles which apply to each situation, for though are all indeed a portion of one great Thought of love, each portion and entity which expresses that love in the life pattern does so in a manner which is unique to that entity. And those general principles which may give a surface description of many entities at one time, yet do each entity an injustice if there is no further examination of the individual life pattern and expression that is manifested in each life pattern.

Thus, my sister, we would counsel you more in the area of removing your own feelings of guilt, rather than in redoubling your efforts to find healing release from these limitations which have served your purposes well.

May we speak in any further fashion, my sister?

Carla: No, I think that's really complete. Thank you very much. That's all the questions I have.

I am Q'uo, and we thank you, my sister. And if there are no further queries this evening, we will at this time …

Carla: I do have a request. Is that permissible?

I am Q'uo. Yes, my sister.

Carla: The request is that you be with us, and all helpful entities be alerted to be with us, as we speak to the people who may ask us questions on the radio program that we're about to do, that we will be aided in the thoughts which come into our minds and the way in which we answer questions, for we wish to speak of eternal truths, not human opinion.

I am Q'uo, and it is our honor, as always, to join you there and to lend our light in whatever manner is possible.

Carla: Thank you.

At this time we shall again thank each for enlightening our presence and for offering us the gifts of your desire to know more of that which each of us seeks, the way of the great truth of love and unity which binds and moves all through the great creation of the one Creator. At this time we shall take our leave of this instrument and this group, leaving each in the love and in the light of the one infinite Creator. We are known to you as those of Q'uo. Adonai, my friends. Adonai.

(Carla channeling)

I am Nona. I greet you, as this instrument requests, in the name of Jesus the Christ, this instrument's expression of the one infinite Creator. We greet each in the mystery. Healing has been asked for, and to that entity, though not present, we through this instrument would express healing. We finish speaking with thanksgiving, in love, in light, in unity.

(Healing melodic tones channeled by Carla.)

L/L Research

Sunday Meditation
April 10, 1988

Group question: (From H1.) Has to do with nuclear warfare, and the cause of the tensions that build toward the feeling of separation and anger that are strong enough to lead to warfare, and to—since we have the nuclear bombs at our disposal—the chances of using them. What kinds of energies are necessary for us to understand in order to back away from the kind of confrontation that might bring about the use of nuclear weapons? What type of growth would signify the understanding that we would rather preserve our environment and illusion than destroy it?

(Carla channeling)

I am Q'uo, my brothers and sisters, and I greet you in the love and in the light of the one infinite Creator. It is both a privilege and a blessing to be called to your meditation, and our hearts rejoice in this sharing of blessing and energy.

You have called us with a question about your living conditions upon your planet at this time, wishing to know what energies were in motion concerning nuclear war and whether humankind is capable at this present moment you experience of avoiding the destructive action of nuclear war.

First let us say that our basic message springs from one Thought, and that is that love is all that there is, that creative and divine love is the one original Thought, that this thought is the closest representation in words which we know to the unseen and ever-mysterious infinite Creator, and that each of you is a portion of that Creator and the infinity of that Creator a portion of yourself.

Thusly, when we speak of the energies involved in experiencing an illusion we are speaking of that which is apparent, but not real, that which is experienced in an illusory pattern in order that work in consciousness may be done by those infinite selves that you are. With this basic nature of humankind understood as being all in the Creator and the Creator in all, we can then speak in a more relative manner concerning certain appearances and behaviors which you are experiencing at this time upon your planet's surface.

The energies concerning nuclear war that are in motion, indeed, all energies concerning the use of nuclear power, have their origin in the origins of many of those which walk upon your planet at this time and have for thousands of your years. Many of those spirits, which are now within the Earth's many dimensions of experience, have experience in third density during which the patterns of nuclear warfare and similar global catastrophe were carried out by humankind upon humankind. The mass of group thought concerning this error within the racial past has never been completely healed, to the point at which we are speaking, and these energies shall continue to be in need of healing until each entity involved in a planetary catastrophe in the past, as you would call it, has had an opportunity to balance this misaction by self-forgiveness and forgiveness of others.

The pattern is at a more hopeful state as we speak with you than has been the case since we began our observation of your nuclear activity, indeed, since it first became a tool used by your scientists and armed entities. There is much of hope in the growing improvement within many entities' balancing process. As more and more of those who have been involved karmically in this matter are able to attain a balanced state of self-forgiveness, the crisis may well pass. We encourage all efforts which may be made by any within the area of self-forgiveness and balancing, the conscious balancing within the mind of passion and wisdom.

We would bring this thought before you before we close this discussion, and that is this. The arena in which you move is indeed an illusion, yet it is indeed excellent that you should be active within that illusion, not overcoming it or ignoring it, but engaging the self with each and every aspect in which you as a self feel that you have strength, something to offer, some way to be of service. This illusion, including any catastrophe, is designed not to destroy nor to build according to the infinite whims of humankind, but to offer opportunities for learning and growth. It is the unsettled times, the traumatic times, the confrontative times that are so often productive of the most rapid inner growth towards that maturity of spirit which all who are on a path of seeking hope endlessly for.

"This is not," said the teacher known as Jesus, "the kingdom of God," this little planet and its wars and rumors of wars. The kingdom, the absolute, the truth lie within, within each, whole and perfect and very dimly perceived. Through crisis and contemplation each seeker processes through an infinite series of realizations which give a richer point of view, a deeper point of view, and hopefully a more and more balanced point of view. Each increases in inner peace, and as that inner peace blossoms in the heart, the entity becomes one who is doing his very utmost to avert nuclear catastrophe.

Peace on planet Earth is possible. It is possible because humankind wishes to progress. We do not know whether or not the possibility shall become reality, and we would not prophesy. We only wish to encourage each entity to know that his or her own inner peace is the road which must be traveled by each and every person. And when that inner peace meets other inner peace, boundaries drop, hostilities end, and a realization of oneness occurs. When you are truly self-forgiven and at peace within, you are doing planetary healing work—you are averting war. You are being a reflection of that beloved and ever unknown Creator. May each of you hold peace within the mind. Take it into meditation and open the self to allowing self-forgiveness.

We thank this instrument and would move on at this time. We transfer. I am Q'uo.

(Jim channeling)

I am Q'uo, and I greet each again in love and light through this instrument. At this time it is our honor to ask if there might be any further queries to which we may offer our humble opinions in the attempt of being of service. Again we remind each that that which we have to offer is that which we have found in our own journeys to be helpful, yet we would not suggest to any that we are infallible. We would request that each take that which rings as truth and use it as one wills, leaving behind that which does not ring of truth to the self. Is there a query at this time?

Carla: I have a very quick query. Were you, or was a Confederation member working with H2? Right at the end of my contact I became aware of it and I was just checking my accuracy.

I am Q'uo, and we were offering the conditioning vibration to the one known as H2 as a link between the one known as H2 and those of Oxal, which were pleased to make a renewed contact with this instrument.

Is there another query?

Carla: I guess I do have one question, and that's just this. H1 and I had been talking all afternoon, off and on, and the question of relative ethics versus absolute idealistic ethics came up and we were sort of tossing it back and forth, and from what you say, you depict the Earth scene as one in which no absolute is possible, that it is an illusion, and thus by its very nature relative. Is that an accurate perception, or is it true that even in an illusion things work in a mathematically metaphysical manner?

I am Q'uo, and am aware of your query, my sister. Within your illusion, the range of sight is limited by the great veil of forgetting, which effectively separates the conscious and unconscious mind, so that when one looks upon one's experiences and daily round of activities, one sees with the accumulated experience of this life only, and though there may be those ideals which such a mind may hold and see as absolute in their purity and may indeed attempt to move in harmony through each daily experience with such ideals, yet within the limits of your illusion, each ideal is colored with the limitations of the perception, the limitations of the incarnation, for by so limiting the self, the attention may be drawn ever more closely and more carefully to certain balances, distortions, lessons and directions that, worked upon successfully, aid an entity in its overall evolutionary process by making the experience specific and intensively experienced, so that it is set or driven within the personality. This is the great benefit of the limitation of the viewpoint.

Yet on the other hand, as you would say, the difficulty that such limitation presents is removing from the consideration of such an entity the wider point of view that is more informed, shall we say, and which partakes more purely of those qualities that are the ideal of thought and action.

Thus, each thought and action within your illusion is achieved in intensity and purity by the limitation of the viewpoint, and at the expense of the wider point of view. Yet, there are those times between the incarnation when the wider point of view is brought to bear in order that that which has been learned in previous experience might be the foundation for that which awaits the learning in future incarnational experience. Thus, each seeker of truth within your illusion is as the one upon the long journey through darkness with but a small candle to light the way, seeing only what is within the light given off by the candle of hope and faith. And within such a circumstance can those fine adjustments of perception be made that aid the seeker to take each small step upon this great journey.

May we speak in any further fashion, my sister?

Carla: Certainly not any more inspirationally. Does the end ever justify the means, or is this question in itself one which belongs in the area of worldly ethic?

I am Q'uo, and we view this query as one which does not have great application to those entities which move within your illusion, for in order for any goal or end of action and thought to justify the means by which the goal, action or thought was attained, one would need the wider view in which all elements and ingredients which are part of such thought and action might be clearly seen and much—most, in fact—of that which is an integral part of your experience within this illusion is hidden from your sight. Thus it is that we have often said that it is the intention, the motivation for thought and action which is that of most importance, for within your illusion there is not the ability to see wisely and to act according to clear seeing. Thus, the pure intention is that which is of most importance for you within your illusion at this time.

May we speak in any further fashion, my sister?

Carla: No thank you, Q'uo. Thank you very much.

I am Q'uo, and we thank you, my sister. Is there another query?

Questioner: I have a question. I would like to know what part fear plays in my life. I mean I know that fear is there and it certainly drives me. I'd like you to speak about fear a little bit.

I am Q'uo, and we find that we have been asked to move into an area which is quite large in scope, but will attempt to be brief in its discussion.

The concept of fear is a concept which has its root in a more basic concept, and that is the separation of the self from a significant part of the creation. When an entity finds that its point of view operates from this basis, then there is the possibility of viewing another portion of the creation as not only being other than self, but of being in some way threatening to the self and in some way hindering the movement and choices and potential of the self. When such a root perception has taken hold, or been taken hold of, shall we say, by an entity, this quality of fear then may become a secondary source of motivation for thought and action. Secondary, we say, because though it may indeed motivate an entity to move in a pattern which in the overall sense may aid the entity in many ways in its own growth and serving of others, yet is a distortion of the greater means of motivation which is available to each entity in the form of the feeling of an harmonious balance and flow of energy between the entity and each portion of its environment and the natural desire to move into that harmonious environment that comes from the feeling of harmony with it.

Thus, when an entity finds that there is any kind of fear within its pattern of experience, the entity may find not only a source of motivation to thought and action that may serve it well for a time, but the entity shall also find upon further investigation of that which is feared that there is a greater opportunity to explore the nature of the fear to the point that the feeling of separation is identified at the point within the incarnation in which it was first experienced. And through such discovery the entity may then seek to balance that fearful experience with one which views that previously feared in a more accepting and compassionate light, for the outer environment is a mirror in which each seeker may view a portion of its own self and respond to that outer environmental segment or experience, as it is a portion of the self.

Thus, each sees its world, shall we say, through eyes that see inwardly and project outwardly and respond to that which is seen in a manner which allows the learning of certain lessons that have been programmed previous to the incarnation. Thus, many entities may look upon one situation within your illusion and see as many interpretations for that situation as there are entities viewing it.

Thus, the experience of fear is that which needs be approached with the same loving acceptance and looking forward with eager opportunity as any gift that one may present to the self or another, for each portion of your experience is a portion of yourself which exists in order to reveal itself to you.

May we speak in any further fashion, my sister?

Questioner: I feel like you've answered my question very well. Thank you.

I am Q'uo, and we thank you, my sister. Is there another query?

(Pause)

I am Q'uo, and we would thank each for inviting our presence this evening. And thank each as well for those queries offered to us, for they are as gifts which allow us to perform our humble service and to walk a distance with you upon your journey of seeking, and for this great honor we are most humbled and privileged. At this time we shall take our leave of this group, leaving each, as always, in the love and in the light of the one infinite Creator. We are known to you as those of Q'uo. Adonai, my friends. Adonai. ☙

Intensive Meditation
June 22, 1988

(Unknown channeling)

I am Hatonn. I greet you in the love and the light of the infinite Creator. It is a great privilege once again to be with this group and to focus with you upon the development of the ability known as channeling. The one known as Laitos is also with each of you and will be working to aid in deepening the level at which each of the instruments is working, relaxing, focusing and allowing the energetic thought forms, which become words when put into the conscious mind, to form. To be at once energized and focused and relaxed and dreamy seems a great paradox and yet, as with all spiritual paradoxes, the dynamic tension betwixt these two simultaneous states of mind create a consciousness that is capable of receiving and sending information of a sort much desired among your people at this time. Information which inspires, information which offers a way to seek ever more steadily and with ever more passion that great and unimaginable Creator Whose Thought we view in each density, for each of you is a thought and each of your creations, your own creation and none other.

We would like to speak about love and we shall be transferring frequently. Because of this use of technique, we shall be identifying ourselves to each of you mentally and we shall be expecting your challenge. However, it is not necessary to begin and end each portion with the spoken signature as we work at this time now not upon accuracy of perception, but upon adjusting the feeling tone of each channel to the highest, the best, and the most comfortable that it may stably be. It is the allowing of fluency which we are encouraging each channel to allow during this training session. We shall begin.

"My love is like a red, red rose." We gave this thought to this channel, aware that the instrument would question it. And well she may. Yet during the channeling process, once contact has been established, it is unwise to question. It is unwise to interrupt. Let us look at the love and its symbol. That which is created is pure beauty. Yet its attainment is often met. We direct this instrument is often accompanied by the sore fingers one gets from the thorns which accompany each rose. So is love a beauty, but not an easy beauty. Rather a beauty which may create both infinite joy and temporal pain. Such is the nature of love expressions within your density. Each of you is a hunter in search of its prey, that being love. The trail towards that true and whole love, which is the Creator, begins with the word as it is used among your people and the most shallow of images, which the sentimentalization of that word has produced.

We shall transfer now.

(Unknown channeling)

Be love, that most of your people's experience in a lifetime is that which [coaxes] that which we call love, for within your vision there is no other possibility other than the distortion of that which you call love, as each attempts in his own way to approach a clearer experience and understanding of what it means to love and to be loved. The experience of romantic love, as it is called, is that which is new in a relative sense for most people of your culture and is that which is a further refinement upon the kind of love that builds its base upon devotion and commitment. The idea that the emotions might add their portion to the concepts of love is both a refinement of that which has been known as love among your people and a distortion of that which we see as the [giving] of self without condition to all who seek in service or interaction *(inaudible)*. And is an experience which from our point of view enhances the generation of catalyst among your people, for the concept of romantic love is that attraction which brings together those which might learn each from the other. However, we find that much disappointment follows many who do not find this quality or portion of love remaining in a strong and steady fashion in its manifestation in any relationship.

Yet, by involving the emotional aspects of each entity, the catalyst that each has to share with the other is made more vivid, more pure and is therefore driven more deeply into the conscious mind that one might consider more pointedly that which is to be shared and how it shall be done.

We shall transfer at this time.

(Unknown channeling)

(Singing)

(Ellipses throughout the rest of the transcript represent inaudible channeling.)

In the love is … aspects in … each of these times in your modern language … you tend to use a single term of love that … consciously experiences … in your consciousness of … attracting, imagining of Creator … your experiences of emotion is a gift which also point in … is to say that your experiences involve … expands your consciousness … enable you to contact … which makes us … the source … the opportunities in your eyes are … emotions that you call …

To live along the ladder of realization is about love. It is helpful to view what love is for that which we call love is all things seen and unseen, all things everywhere, all consciousness, and all knowing. Love lies not only in the sentimental, not only in the romantic, and indeed not only in those sufferings of love which cause the pricked finger from the touch of the rose's thorn, but, rather, love is to be seen in every possible substance within the universe, no matter what it is, no matter what its connotation to a particle of consciousness such as yourselves.

Not only are the fresh vegetables and fruits that you eat divine love, but also that which is excreted after that which your physical body needs has been removed. In fact, one may see your illusion as a swirling mass of love constantly rearranging itself into various patterns in a coherent and intelligent manner. How then does one come to see the love, which is in each moment, in each challenge, in each difficulty as well as in each happiness? How can one see that love is equally at work in peace and in war, in richness and in poverty, in saintliness and in the blackest soul?

We transfer at this time.

(Unknown channeling)

There is in love the power to create. This is the very essence of that which we call love. Within this creative power is the necessity of what one may see as the mover and that which is moved. There is the further refinement into those qualities you see as that which is good and that which is evil. That which is radiant and that which is black. That which is male and that which is female. By these polarities, or should we say by this polarity, and its many expressions is all of what you know as creation set into motion and through this creative motion does the Creator experience that which is Itself creating and creating, recreating ever more varied and pure forms, portions of Itself that allow It to experiment and to know what it is to be. In just such a way is each conscious entity within the creation able to know this very same thing: what it is to be, to move, to be moved, to love, and to be loved, to experience, to grow from experience and to create the self ever new. All creation moves through this polarity.

Thus does each portion of the creation then find avenues for knowing the self, the creation and Creator. All of this is accomplished by the power of love, which moves every particle of your existence and in whose field of force and flow one is always moving in harmony, whether one is consciously aware of this movement or of the harmony or not.

Yours is the dance to experience the self-conscious aspect of love and to refine this aspect into a selfless kind of love that learns to move beyond the boundaries of that which you identify as your own self and your sphere of influence, shall we say.

We shall transfer.

(Unknown channeling)

Every action that you take is an expression from the Creator's … for are you not … Creator? Love in itself is perhaps more properly said that Creator is love … the expression of consciousness … some simplistic explanation … is that … many of the people on your planet, even those who express love … to others fail to accept the example of the Creator's … each to love himself or herself … love is like a flower that blossoms and … heals the self and … acceptance of the self …

We *(inaudible)* men see the beauty of the full-blown rose. They may well feel that love is to be sought in higher and higher realms that are further and further away from the imperfections of the self and many are the seeking souls who ask the Father to show them love as though it were something that was brought in from outside to be beheld as on a screen so that one may know the truth. And yet we say to you, that if the whole of love is infinite, then each of its parts is also infinite. We say to you that you are not only the beholder of the rose but also the rose, the mysterious rose, the rosa mystica, the rosy cross. This is your inner nature; this is your seed.

To encourage a seed one offers it the manna of sunshine and water. The seeds of love will grow in you as you pay attention to the most mundane and everyday duties and responsibilities, pleasures and pains. The suffering you may see as the dead portion of plant or animal matter that has been sloughed off, excreted, removed from its roots and left to move back into the larger infinity of the impersonal love. The attitude informs the eye rather than the eye, the attitude. Thusly …

(Side one of tape ends.)

(Unknown channeling)

Thusly, it is in working with the tools and resources of meditation, contemplation, the listening ear, and the eager mind that love may begin to bubble within and call to the love without so that infinity may begin to hollow a channel through the soul of each seeker. If the love within is unmoved, the reception of love from without shall be hollow, not finding the answer within which produces joy under any circumstances. May we encourage each of you to practice love. Some have called this the prayer without ceasing. We call it observation. More and more use those tools which feed you on a daily basis, which instruct you to move the mind to its center, to its peace, its joy, and its understanding that when the eyes see that they may perceive in a certain way, a way which renews and transforms that upon which the eye has fallen. The eye which sees through the illusion of each perfect petal and each sharp thorn of the rosa mystica, which is the valley of the shadow of death.

Gaze at the incarnation before you. Gaze quietly and realistically. All of the dance of this illusion is a dance rejoicing in life and rejoicing in death for each of you in incarnation have come from infinity and shall move again into infinity at the end of the time allotted for your lessons here. May you find the bubbling spring of love within, the God-self, if you will, that calls and desires with purity to infinite love that there may be a renewing of passion, a caring, about each moment of life. Such enthusiasm is infectious. Love may be transmitted from person to person and as one person and then another joins the host of those who seek to move in harmony with universal love more and more may the face of the earth be renewed. And the Creator ever more gladdened.

We are most pleased with the new instrument's progress. The earnest attempt to tune and to be sure by challenging that the spirit contacted indeed comes in the name of the in-service-to-others polarity. We are pleased and honored and would now transfer to the one known as Jim in order that any questions that may occur may be answered to the best of our humble ability.

I am Hatonn. I now transfer.

(Jim channeling)

At this time it is our privilege to ask if we might serve further by attempting to answer queries that may remain upon your minds.

Intensive Meditation, June 22, 1988

Carla: I have one that is kind of a burning question to me right now. I expect you to answer, if at all, in a general fashion, but my experience is specific. I am experiencing an enormous desire to spend a great deal of money on clothing. I have experienced this for some months, actually since I realized that we simply did not have the money to spend on clothing that we used to. I have been unable to determine that there is any worth to this desire and am yet reluctant to call it entirely error because I do respect myself. This situation where I am covetous of money for the purpose of such petty purposes as buying clothing is concerning me about my spiritual path and I wonder if you have any comments to make on this kind of situation.

I am Hatonn, and our only comment, my sister, is the comments that we would give to any expression that seems to find its roots outside the self. In this particular case you seem to your own discernment be seeking the adornment that will enhance your appearance in a visual fashion. We would suggest to each seeker that would experience such a yearning, that the yearning be seen to be a symbol, a riddle, if you will, a trail, which may be examined and a deeper meaning uncovered. This may be done either by the simple mental process enhanced by meditation and prayer, contemplation, or by the addition of the actual pursuing of this desire in addition to the foregoing methods. The desire is that which offers an insight into the self in each such case.

Is there another query, my sister?

Carla: On another subject, yes, and I thank you for that answer. It is not an easy one, but certainly offers a pattern of working with it. The other question is similarly specific and I similarly expect you to generalize. I have experienced sexual infatuation many times and what I considered at the time to be an experience of being in love, once when I was 17, 18 and 19. When that experience was ended for me, I assumed that that was the love of innocence, which I would no longer feel and for over 20 years this was, indeed, so. My love for people was steady and strong and for those with whom I was intimate, most loyal and sturdy. And above comfortable in the sense that I did not feel helpless in the face of emotion. In the middle of my forties, I find myself once again experiencing that which is either sexual infatuation or being in love. However, unlike my younger days, I experience this not as a steady state, but as an extremely unsteady state, which resembles at times an emotional roller coastal. This has caused me to doubt my perceptions somewhat and to question the nature of what we call romantic love. Is it an illusion within an illusion? Is it indeed sexual infatuation carried over a longer period of time? Or is it something that occurs as a natural form of universal love?

I am Hatonn. And you ask me clearly [that] which is most thoughtful and considered and offered for our consideration as well. We may suggest at this time that the emotional aspect of the experience of love which you now are in the process of examining is in a close manner connected to your overall experience of love and its application to your personal identity. We apologize but we are having some difficulty transmitting these thoughts to this instrument. The symbolic nature of all experience must be kept in the corners of the mind when attempting to evaluate the value of any particular experience upon your life pattern. And again, we would turn your gaze inward, not wishing to negate that which you feel for another, but wishing your focus to include the self and its need for and deserved nature of love.

We hope that we have not spoken too specifically in this case for we do not wish to influence your free will in too great a manner and will simply ask if we might speak in any further fashion?

Carla: Using my intuition, and thinking upon that answer, I would simply ask you to confirm the following possibility. I believe that I came here to give, not to receive, and I believe that in the environment and relationship with which I am experiencing these feelings, this extremely deep level of love may well be the one thing which I may give to my other self which is a truly selfless gift. And, therefore, a gift which balances the extreme amount of love offered to me. Perhaps balance is the wrong word. But I will let it rest and ask for a confirmation of that, if it is indeed on the right track of what this emotion is doing in my life at this time. In other words, that it is not for me, but for the person to whom it is given freely.

I am Hatonn. And we would suggest that the track of thinking is that which may be pursued in your continued deliberation and may provide further insight if the further ramifications with connection to the self are explored.

May we speak in any further fashion, my sister?

Carla: Meaning love for myself as well as love for another?

I am Hatonn. And this is the correct message.

Carla: You have been very helpful to me. Thank you very much. I have no more questions.

I am Hatonn. And we thank you, my sister. Are there any further queries at this time?

Carla: God bless, Hatonn. God bless, Laitos. Thank you.

I am Hatonn, and we thank each as well for the opportunity of working with each and of sharing our journey at this time within this circle of seeking. We have been with each and shall continue to join each upon request within the meditative state. At this time, we shall take our leave of this instrument and this group, meeting each, as always, in love and light of the one Creator. We are those of Hatonn. Adonai, my friends. Adonai. ☥

Intensive Meditation
June 29, 1988

(Carla channeling)

I am Hatonn. I greet you in the love and the light of the infinite Creator. It is, as always, a great blessing and privilege to meditate with you and to engage with each channel in the study of being and the craftsmanship of listening and speaking with minimum distortion that which is heard.

As we gauge the energy level in this circle this evening, we find a malaise … a lack of passion. Do not think that we say these things to criticize you, but merely to hold up the mirror to the face. We know that each of you is deeply passionate, deeply caring, deeply wishing to serve. And so this evening we would speak with you about what this instrument would call passion, and what we would call the fusion of free will and purified emotion.

We shall transfer this channel to the one known as D. I am Hatonn.

(Pause)

(Carla channeling)

I am Hatonn. I am again with this instrument. We find that the instrument known as D has much concern within the mind which is creating difficulties for the channeling, and in this way becoming what this instrument would call a self-fulfilling prophesy. Therefore, we will use this instrument to speak for awhile about this all-important subject.

Most often we discuss the love and light of the infinite Creator. In fact, in every discussion which we are privileged to share with those who seek to hear our voice, we speak of that which is all that there is, love and light. Yet these, like any other words, are cold and damp. It is passion, imagination, creativity, hope and daring which invest love and light and life with the energy needed to accomplish.

Let us examine passion. As we have said, it is the enclosure of two very powerful forces, purified emotion and that free will within the entity which chooses to stand behind that purified emotion. The most basic passion and perhaps the one most clear in the mind of each here, is sexual, physical passion. Because the body cannot speak, it is most often true within your illusion that true passion is felt in this way rather than in an intellectual or spiritual manner. This is as it should be, for it is the cornerstone of your carefully contrived illusion that physical passion shall bring people together.

Now, each of you knows those who are passionate about certain activities, and each of you knows within the self that each is passionately devoted to pursuing the mysterious face of a beloved but invisible Creator. In third density, that which you enjoy now, you are learning to experience using time. In time, there is the capacity to either intensify what one thinks or to disperse what one thinks, to intensify a feeling or to disperse a feeling. In time there is the making of choices, the finding of one's own passion, one's own heart, one's own true ground of reality. It's not an easy task, for emotions must be purified to a certain extent and the will brought to bear upon the desired object. Those who wish to be channels for love and light, regardless of what their service to others is, need to feed the intensity of their love for the Creator, need to allow time to feel the intensity of the Creator's love for each of Its creations.

The passionate affair that you experience with your Creator is an eternal passion, a holy and divine love, yet it is the free choice of any, no matter how well learned or seemingly advanced, to choose to intensify the life passion or to choose to relax and rest and let passion drift away upon a sea of detail and mundane activity.

There are exercises which hone the will and purify emotion. These exercises may vary from entity to entity. The most simply efficacious of them, of course, as we always suggest, is meditation. The will that drives one to a daily meditation is a free choice intensifying the emotion of love from the Creator, that a seeker pursues in the silence of meditation, in reading words of inspiration and contemplating them, or in prayer. Remember the saying of the master known as Jesus, "Let your yea be yea and your nay be nay," and find within yourself in a daily and dedicated fashion to recommit yourself as if it were your first choice to living and expressing as much of the Creator as you can. Vocal channeling is one way. There are an infinitude of other ways to serve your fellow man, but without passion to stoke the fire within, the energies which are locked in eternity find great difficulty moving through the blocked channels of the electrical and physical body.

Thus, we would suggest to the new instrument, and to all who wish to live what this instrument would call a Godly and righteous life, to embrace the self and the nature of the self, to embrace the risk of attempting to be of service, to embrace that courage that causes the coward to speak up for that which it believes. Passion may come to you; however, if the instrument is not tuned, that is, if it does not grasp that food which it needs to be who it is, that passion will be distorted and will become petty.

Thusly, we wish to encourage each by saying, in your meditations focus upon the love that you feel and the love that you are receiving in the eternal and infinite process which is real life. We realize that this may not seem at first blush to hold the key to someone who is making a decision about how to be of service to others. However, once the self has worked for some time upon developing an inner intensity, a fiery and creative love, and an awareness of the infinity of love and power and wisdom which come from the Creator, the person who feels these things will find the *(inaudible)* of self-doubt and feelings of unworthiness fall away.

There is no voice which is incapable of serving as inspiration for others through vocal channeling. We realize that some bring into this illusion memories which have been gift-given, by the self, to the self, for use in incarnation. We realize it may be discouraging to those who have not been born with such a gift to attempt by sheer practice and persistence to duplicate even one tithe of such inspirational beauty. Yet we say to you that there are many, many entities upon your sphere who wish to grasp their nature, who wish to know their Creator and the nature of their Creator, and who wish to understand to some small extent the nature of the relationships betwixt humankind and Deity.

Thus, one who is most modest, one who is facing a block, one who doubts the self, may certainly do so. It is not relevant to the choice, what is more relevant is the turning within to find the passion. Where does the passion within lie? In the answer to that question, the enormous power of the will is finally grasped and able to be directed as a magic wand, and the emotions purified through suffering and contemplation, through meditation and worship, are purified and whatever the central service is for each, the passion will tell the instrument its own nature.

It is, of course, a trick when you are encased in a physical vehicle which must needs be maintained in so many ways, to spend the time necessary in meditation. However, we find that where there is the will, the meditation follows. Not only during meditative periods, but again and again throughout the day and perhaps even the night watches, depending upon incarnational patterns at any particular time.

Do not accept yourself as a person caught in boredom or indifference. Do not accept yourself as less than a passionate, vital and creative being, a child of the Creator, with an infinite birthright. We would leave in this discussion an image with you concerning passion and service to others. If one group stands and hold hands together facing each other, each looks into another's eyes, the energy moves from left hand to right hand around the circle, in negative polarity service-to-self [direction].

What service to others is all about is taking that same group which, indeed, needs to be of service to itself, and encouraging its own members in their services to others, and turning each person outwards so that when the hands are again held and the energy [again] is moving from the left to right hand, the energy then moves clockwise, the service-to-others direction[2]. Realize that whatever your service is to be, it has to do with facing outwards and offering without any expectation what it is you feel you can do and may do to be of spiritual service to another. Never stop holding hands with those companions you have been blessed with along the way, and gazing into each others' eyes and enjoying the sharing of the group energy that feeds you, but always remember that those who truly wish to serve shall be turning vulnerably outward and offering the gift of self, with the Creator shining through, that light may be seen in a dark world.

What is each person's passion? Let each ask and then let each pursue that passion deeply, persistently, daily. If upon occasion one can find no passion within, do not be discouraged. It is simply time for the comedy, the laughter, the lightness, and the bubbling over which is the easy side of passion, the free side of free will. When you laugh, you are the Creator. When you serve others, you are the Creator, His face to another who knows the Creator not, but who knows you.

We would once again transfer to the one known as D. Realizing that the entity is apprehensive, I can only encourage this entity to feel free and easy and to allow that freedom to loosen the lips and engage the imagination, for we can only give concept; it is the channel's part …

(Carla channeling)

I am Hatonn, and am aware of the instrument's decision which we accept with grateful thanks for the opportunity to do the work we have done in adjusting to the instrument. We leave you with your choices, and we assure you too of an unfailing love and a source of creative inspiration in that if you ask us to be with you, so shall we be.

None of what we have said was meant to indicate that any should not channel. It is a point to encourage the process of knowing the self, so that which one does is done from inner conviction, from inner passion and not accepted upon authority from without, from us, or from any teacher whatsoever. We ask the one known as D especially to let the laughter come, to relax the tension, to feel the stress, like little electrical impulses, move down from the head, down into the shoulders, down into the arms, down to the fingers through the body, the torso, the hips, the legs off the toes. Relax and by all means avoid self-criticism.

We ask you clearly, each of you, to remember what you know already, that the statements you make about yourself to yourself determine your incarnational experience. Many new channels are caught in a trap which has been waiting for them since that time early in the incarnation when there began to be doubts about the self or stress placed upon the self that was seemingly more than could be borne. These occasions occur throughout the incarnational experience, but none affect the incarnate spirit like those experiences occurring in the early years of the incarnation.

Virtually each entity with whom we have worked—and we have worked with quite a few by now—has been blocked in what this instrument would call orange ray, that is, the relationship of the self to the self and the relationship of the self to another self. It is a feeling of relative unworthiness, relatively low advancement, a feeling that is persistent and pervasive, but untrue. That is, it is a distorted reflection offered to you by those about you which were very distorted. Now, at this moment, each is a free being and each has free choice.

---

[2] Carla: I had to do this physically to recreate the image fully in my mind. If one turns outward and holds hands around the circle, the energy is still moving from the giving hand to the taking hand, which the Ra is assuming is from the giver's right hand to the taker's left hand, or in terms of direction, from left to right, which becomes counter-clockwise. When the 180-degree turn is made and hands are again held, the energy still is moving from the giver's right hand to the taker's left hand, but the direction of flow around the circle has been changed from counter-clockwise to clockwise. Clockwise is traditionally the "deosil" or service-to-others direction.

As long as each realizes this fact and as long as each attempts to carry that realization into the present moment, the process of work for your planet and for the raising of the consciousness of the people of the planet will go on. Encourage yourself and speak well of yourself to yourself. If there are wounds to be healed and errors to be forgiven in relationships, pray unceasingly, speak and communicate persistently, until there is a feeling of peace, a feeling of righteousness, a feeling of freedom. Let that energy become unblocked. That energy is needed for the challenges of being in service to others. That energy that is blocked is the deepest part of your passion.

May you find that passion, may you rediscover that passion each day, may you become more and more purified and intense until you have moved into that kingdom where the life experience is created by the self, not by reaction to outside influence from the illusion. The key, of course, is meditation, but we are equally desirous of expressing our beliefs that for each serious thought, each deep philosophical utterance, an entity must needs observe and laugh at the absurdities of the illusion, the dear eccentricity of humankind, the ultimate, bleak, black, but funny happenstance of life lived in the shadow of death. This is your legacy of a being incarnate in third density. Each of you knows you are eternal and it is for this reason you wish to serve. Find the passion in that and hone it as if it were a weapon, a weapon to pierce most sweetly the hearts of those ready to receive love and light and life and joy.

At this time we would transfer to the one known as Jim.

(Jim channeling)

I am Hatonn. I am Hatonn and greet each again through this instrument. At this time, it is our privilege to offer ourselves in the attempt to speak to any queries which might remain with those present. Is there a query at this time?

D: I'd like to ask you to speak a little more on meditation block. *(Inaudible)* returning good will *(inaudible)* meditation as welfare *(inaudible)*. A question first of all *(inaudible)* different purposes give meditations different, different [perfect] purposes *(inaudible)*. You say that meditation is a key and, of course, my purpose now is coming a better vocal instrument, more in tune with energies beyond my own *(inaudible)* energies *(inaudible)* becoming a less distorted channel. The meditation that I do at present is only about five minutes, and I wonder if that's enough time to be. A benefit of it, of course, is that I'm more likely to put in those five minutes a day than a much longer period. Can something effective be accomplished in that short of *(inaudible)* of time or would you more specifically name *(inaudible)* specifically my present goal, recommend my approach.

I am Hatonn, and we are happy to speak upon this topic, my brother, for it is one which is great in depth and breadth. To meditate, the will, as [you] have put it, is the primary factor which allows one to achieve whatever goal one has for the meditation. Thus, the time which one has to offer in this attempt is of less and even little importance, for if the desire be strong and the discipline be regular, then the foundation has been laid for the effort to construct the building as desired. Thus, we would encourage you to continue with your discipline and to complete it upon a regular basis in order that the desire continue to be exercised and to be strengthened through its use and continual expression.

The meditative state itself is one which is quite elusive to those who truly look within their own experience for the peace that passeth understanding, for within your illusion the daily round of activities repeating one upon another is so powerful upon the conscious mind, to the extent that one may truly feel at home, at peace, and within the center of one's own being. Being at the persistent practice of this art, may we say, is that quality which will allow one to continue to refine the meditative practice in order that the goal of the perfect peaceful practice [will be] obtained in whatever manner is desired by the practitioner.

Meditation, as you are aware, may be used for a number of purposes. Many there are [who] utilize that peaceful moment for the solving of a persistent problem. Others for the visualizing of healing or loving energy being given to those in need of such. Yet others will find the goal of their meditation to simply [be] the obtaining of a blank and quiet mind to listen, shall we say, to the infinite silence within oneself. Others, as you are being more well aware, utilize the meditative state for the purpose of receiving information of one nature or another, in one manner or another, in visual images, in feeling tones such as we have accomplished here this evening.

There are as many uses for the meditative state as there are entities wishing to find within this state, for the meditative state is one which might be seen as clear seeing or clear being, in contrast to the normal conscious mind activity which may be seen as the diffuse seeing or being, where the waters of the mind are much stirred by concern and activities that surround the entity as weather upon the sea moves the ship upon the waves.

Thus, within the meditative state one is able to calm the waters and direct the will and the mind in a much more efficient manner in order that whatever goal be deemed important by the entity within the life pattern, this goal, then, might be more clearly seen, visualized and examined in whatever means have the ability to present to the entity the experience or the product of the experience that it desires.

Thus, in your own practice of meditation, we would encourage you, as we have said before, to continue as you have with the regularity and to be not be overly concerned with the length of time during which this practice is accomplished but to remember always that the desire which you bring to the meditative state is that quality which will enhance your experience whatever your goal might be. In a grateful *(inaudible)*, we know we have little to offer in the way of refining or changing your practice other than to suggest the very basic rule, shall we say, of attempting to maintain the erect spine, and the location of the meditation in a disciplined fashion, that is to say, a particular place within your domicile or exterior wherever you find the atmosphere most conducive to that which you wish to accomplish. That you make of this place a place dedicated to that which you wish to accomplish during meditation and allow that place to be used only for that purpose, in order that the vibratory pattern which you set up in that location might be builded upon, shall we say, and become a resource that you may call upon each time that you enter therein to practice the art of meditation. You will at once be calling upon it and adding to it as you continue in this way upon a regular basis. Thus, you will have consecrated a portion of time and a place within your life pattern for a special purpose, the purpose of your own design.

We feel at this time that the suggestion will suffice for the comment upon your own practice and the description of the uses of meditation in general. May we speak in any further fashion, my brother?

D: Thanks, brother.

I am Hatonn, and we thank you, my brother. Is there another query at this time?

Carla: I have an experience that I would like to share with you and any comment you could make on it would be appreciated. There was a terrific amount of energy in the room when meditation began, and I got a name even before the music was half over and I was just calming down, I wasn't really in a good state yet, but I got this name and it was, sounded like "Kumi" or "Coo-me" or something like that. I challenged it and it wavered, so I challenged it again, with by that time a better state of focus and concentration, and it broke down into some pretty good looking snakes, and I've seen that before and just let 'em go away.

But this time I thought, no, perhaps I can do something better, so in my mind, I gathered all these snakes up and took them to me to accept the fact that the snakes were part of me and when I hugged them to my breast, they turned into Monarch butterflies and flew away and suddenly it was a sunlit, summer's day, with a breeze blowing and I was standing in a field. This lasted for the couple seconds it took for me to register the impression, and then I sort of walked the boundary of the room again in my mind and it was clear and the energy was calm again. Do you have any comment on this experience?

I am Hatonn, and our only comments this time would be to suggest that this experience is a good example of the ability of any entity to transform that which seems difficult or negative into that which is a thing of beauty, for within the entire creation there is no being other than the one Creator. Though in many disguises does the one Creator move, the attitude of taking the snakes within your own being in the welcoming embrace of love and compassion is the attitude which will serve each seeker best, in our opinion, when dealing with any difficulty, for the seeming difficulty and negative experience with which many seekers of truth encounter upon their journey are not encountered in order that the seeker be required to prove itself in any particular fashion or to make of the seeker any kind of victim, but these experiences are encountered in order that the seeker might be provided yet another opportunity to see within the face of another self and to welcome each experience as though the Creator stood before one and offered to one the fruit of experience.

May we speak in any further fashion, my sister?

Carla: No. Thank you very much, that was inspiring.

I am Hatonn, and we thank you, my sister. Is there another query at this time?

Questioner: No, thank you.

I am Hatonn, and we have greatly enjoyed ourselves this evening, my friends, for we feel that there has been a great deal of progress made by each instrument present. Though the program may be somewhat of a mystery to the one known as D *(inaudible)* that there has indeed been progress made, for as we just spoke in answer to the query of the one known as Carla, the seeming difficult situation is one which is also heavily laden with fruit for the entity that continues to look beyond the exterior of a difficulty and is able to use each experience which it encounters upon its journey in order to learn and to grow, and in this fashion enhances its ability to serve.

At this time, humbly and gratefully and joyfully, we shall leave each in the love and in the light of the one infinite Creator. We are known to you as those of Hatonn. Adonai, my friends. Adonai.

Intensive Meditation
August 1, 1988

(Carla channeling)

I am Laitos, and I greet you in the love and the light of the infinite Creator. We are going to make this instrument's voice louder, so that we may be heard. We will attempt to remember to influence this instrument to speak louder than usual. May we ask at this time if all are able to hear? Very well.

What a privilege and blessing it is to us to be with you, my friends. We waited a few extra moments, for each was adjusting to the novelty of meditating in brightest noonday, for such seems the light within this room due to the television equipment. However, it did not take very much extra time for each to settle into a circle of seeking; a circle that rises highly to the sky and beyond the ethers; a circle of light that seeks and calls; that call we see and that call we answer. We are always pleased to work with new channels, and we greet each of you as colleagues and partners in the great work of enabling the spiritual growth of humankind. As this instrument has said, there is only one message, there is only one truth, but there are an infinite number of ways to express that truth. Thus, each new channel to us is an infinite treasure, an unique collection and organic system of biases, experiences, notions, thoughts and ideas which we may move through in a fashion no one else could possibly perceive. We, who speak to this instrument, will be the same which speaks to each instrument. Yet, each instrument will add its own flavor, its own consciousness to the contact during the time each entity is channeling. So let us begin.

We would at this time begin very simply. We would simply make ourselves known to each of you. We shall do this first in a silent manner, and you may expect feelings of adjustment, either psychic or physical, as we find the ways to fit into each instrument's unique vibratory pattern. We do come through the energy at the top of the head, at some angle. Each of us comes in at, shall we say, a different metaphysical angle, but you may wish to view this specifically as it is a concept easier to grasp in a specific manner than in a metaphysical one.

Thus, we shall simply be adjusting to each of you during this pause. We ask that you do not fear us, but simply remain passive and allow us to attempt to adjust within so that when we do work with you in the vocal channeling, you will feel the least discomfort possible, even the first time. We do not wish to cause any discomfort. At the end of that time, we shall again move around the room, offering each new channel an opportunity to hear and respond to the announcement of our name and that in which we come, that is, the love and the light of the infinite Creator. This is our statement of who we are, and we do our own challenging of those contacts among your Earth people that we do use. So you see it is a true partnership; one in which perhaps we supply all the concepts but certainly one in which the conscious channel makes a substantial contribution of vocabulary and thought. For this great effort, for this desire to serve, we thank you. And now we shall pause for this period of adjustment. I am Laitos.

(Pause)

I am Laitos, and am again with this instrument. We would like to observe that in two cases, the entity Hatonn, as well as those of our community, were working with the new channel that is the case of the one known as R and the one known as M. The one known as Hatonn as well as ourselves were doing adjustment work, as there are some cases in which one vibration will seem to be somewhat easier to accept than another. This might have caused a bit of confusion, if so, we apologize. We shall be moving about the room again at this time, and we ask each, when each hears the phrase, "I am Laitos," to put all thought aside and repeat that which has been perceived. We ask that there be no exploration, examination, or analysis of that which has been put into the conscious mind in the present moment, within the context of the channeling, for once there has been the tuning and the challenging, it is time to surrender to the greater self in each of us, that together we might serve the Creator. I am Laitos.

(Pause)

I am Laitos, and I am again with this instrument. We see that perhaps we are lacking in offering the confidence of the naming. Thus, we shall name that entity to which our energy is directed. We move first to the one known as Jim. I am Laitos.

(Jim channeling)

I am Laitos.

(Carla channeling)

I am Laitos, and would move at this time to the one known as J.

(Pause)

I am Laitos. We shall continue working with the one known as J, and meanwhile move to the one known as R.

(Pause)

I am Laitos. We shall move on again at this time while continuing to work with the one known as R. And would at this time contact the one known as E. I am Laitos.

(E channeling)

I am Laitos. *(Inaudible)* to you.

(Carla channeling)

I am Laitos, and we thank the one known as E for being lionhearted. We would move now to the one known as M. I am Laitos.

(Pause)

I am Laitos and I am once again with this instrument. May we say to the one known as M, that there were two times when the instrument came very close to apprehending the process excellently. And we encourage the instrument, for there is progress from the first adjustment. We would now move to the one known as K. I am Laitos.

(K channeling)

I am Laitos, and I greet you once again …

(Carla channeling)

I am Laitos, and am once again with this instrument. We shall move about this circle once more, attempting further to adjust our contact with those who have not perceived our signal clearly enough to speak forth. May we say to each, that there is no shortage of doubt within the context of any endeavor undertaken in the area we are mutually interested in. Although there are no doubts from our side to yours as to the reality of this service and this process, yet there are doubts as to our fundamental service, for the subtleties of service to others is great. Yet, we urge each to be confident, to refrain from analysis and to grasp our signal enough to repeat that name which we are known to you by. We would once again attempt to make first contact with the entity known as J. I am Laitos.

(J channeling)

I …

(Carla channeling)

I am Laitos, and we would apologize to the one known as J. We find we have blown her circuits. We shall attempt to step down our signal but caution this instrument that each time the energy is felt, there will to a lesser and lesser degree be a feeling which this instrument would call a rush. This energy is the energy of a somewhat mismatched connection, and we shall be attempting to correct for comfort each time that we contact this new instrument. We thank the one known as J and again apologize for discomfort.

We would at this time transfer the contact to the one known as R. I am Laitos.

(Pause)

I am Laitos, and we thank the one known as R. We would say briefly to this instrument that all is not as it seems. It seems that the production of this verbalization may be self-willed. We ask this instrument to allow this ambiguity to continue without concern. The beginning of the process is not the end of the process. The first contact is not the ultimate contact. There is a settling period with each new channel, there is the growing of confidence. May we say to this instrument, that which occurred was a real contact and we are well pleased, and though respectful of each opinion, we may say from our point of view we are quite real and the contact with the new instrument was most satisfactory.

We would move to the one known as M at this time. I am Laitos

(M channeling)

Laitos …

I am Laitos, and perhaps you are getting tired of hearing my name by now, but perhaps there are questions you would like to ask. We are extremely pleased to have begun our work together. No matter who else is with you during this process, we offer ourselves at all times to you as strengtheners of meditative states and as comforters, for we are those of love and it is our dearest pleasure to offer support and service to those who call. We would at this time transfer to the one known as Jim, that those questions which you may have may have the opportunity for the answering. We thank each, we are pleased with each, and we look forward to more work together in the service of the infinite Creator. We now transfer.

(Jim channeling)

I am Laitos, and greet each again in love and light through this instrument. At this time we would offer ourselves in the attempt to speak to any further queries which those present may offer to us. May we speak to a query at this time?

Questioner: Can you explain in some detail what was happening when my heart rate speeded up when you were trying to contact me?

I am Laitos. As we approached your aura, or auric field, you were aware that contact was potentially possible at that time. The combination of your anticipation and our misjudgment of your finer sensitivity caused the resulting blend of our vibrations, and yours, to manifest itself in the physiological racing, shall we say, of your heart. This, for you, at this time is a means by which you are able to alert yourself that you are about to engage in a service which you desire to offer as a service to others. However, we hope in the future that we are able to blend our vibrations in a manner which will minimize any possible discomfort. We do apologize for any discomfort which we have inadvertently caused.

May we speak further in any fashion, my brother?

Questioner: I'm trying to remember the way that two or three phrases that I saw flash in my mind arrived [at the scene]. It seems as though they spell the, "I am Laitos," and "Laitos is here," of the first contact. I wondered about [that] several times because [there's] nothing spoken and there was no visual picture, so to speak, with more like a written sentence. Does that make some sense to you?

I am Laitos. Each instrument, whether new or experienced, will perceive the initial contact in a manner which is acceptable to the conscious mind as our contact is filtered through, or should we say, transmitted through, the subconscious mind. We were desirous of speaking our simple identification through each new instrument, and when we have the opportunity of working with your instrument we were perceived in the manner in which you have described. As a function of your subconscious tendency towards trusting the written word within the self, shall we say, that you could read that which was about to be transmitted was the further means that you were able to utilize to verify to yourself that a contact from without yourself was being made. Each instrument shall find a manner of perceiving any such contacts such as ours that will make sense, shall we say, to that instrument according to its own nature.

Is there another query, my brother?

Questioner: *(Inaudible).*

Questioner: I have a query. I … this period of meditation before, I had it very dramatically this evening, where my head is pulled back so that my eyes are looking straight up, [if] they were open, they'd be straight up. It's not a comfortable position. I ultimately had to pull my head back, and then it would fall down to my chest. I'm wondering what is the reason for this *(inaudible)*, and can you suggest if something needs to be done and how I can make it more comfortable?

I am Laitos. We would suggest in each session of working during which you wish to exercise your instrument that you request to us, or to any entity working with you, that your positioning of your head be that which is comfortable to you. We would further suggest that this request be given not only to any entity wishing to utilize you as an instrument but that this request also be given to your own subconscious mind which has found some necessity for preparing for the anticipated contact by bracing the physical vehicle in the manner in which you described. As any entity such as ourselves works with each new instrument, that entity will assess both the conscious and subconscious desires of the entity, whether the desires might be logical or irrational, in order that our vibrations might blend in a manner which is most suitable and comfortable to the new instrument.

However, in the case of many new instruments, the novelty of the experience of serving as a vocal instrument will call from the subconscious levels of mind complex a certain configuration or anticipation that will serve to ready or prepare the new instrument in a certain fashion. If the resulting blend of our vibrations with the instrument's vibrations causes discomfort in any way, then we suggest the request on the part of the new instrument, both to the contact and to its own subconscious mind, that a more comfortable configuration of the blending of vibrations be attempted.

May we speak in any further fashion, my sister?

Questioner: Thank you very much.

I am Laitos, and we thank you, my sister. Is there another query?

Questioner: Could you, tell my why I think that [I stutter]?

I am Laitos. And we notice the repetitive nature that you call stuttering is somewhat apparent as you seek to assure yourself that the contact is actually occurring, and seek to do this by repeating it one layer upon another, in an almost simultaneous fashion. We would suggest that as you continue to exercise your instrument that the ability to relax and to speak without analysis and to gain in the confidence will allow the more normal speaking of those thoughts and concepts which are being transmitted through you.

May we speak in any further fashion, my sister?

Questioner: Thank you.

I am Laitos, and we thank you. Is there another query?

Questioner: I would like to press that on just a little bit further, because I felt that there was an uneven energy flow, and that—that was, I mean, I felt an uneven energy flow at that time. And, is that another way of saying what you said?

I am Laitos, and this is correct, my sister.

Questioner: OK.

Is there another query at this time?

Questioner: Laitos, for me, I saw the words clearly, "I am," and did not see the name Laitos. Also I felt energy flush more like thermal, more like a heat flush, [and a] racing of the heart, or any other physical manifestation. I also found it interesting that twice, the first time around, twice, I perceived something and your *(inaudible)* suppose was apprehensive but it was twice and it seems to me, it's going to take me a while for this. Will it become clearer?

I am Laitos. Yes, my brother, as you continue to practice the art of offering the self as a vocal instrument you will find that the apprehensions begin to dissolve and the validity of the contact increases. However, each new instrument will find a varying amount of practice and experience is necessary in order to gain the level of confidence that will allow the concepts to be perceived and transmitted through your instrument in the fashion which is most comfortable to you. There are those times in any instrument's service when the doubts and apprehensions again appear in order that the lessons of learning to surrender the self in the faith that there is a service of a positive nature to be rendered, to be accomplished, may proceed in a more firmly established manner. Thus is each foundation stone placed and set within the being of each entity desiring to serve as an instrument. The realignment of each foundation stone is the work of the continual practice that each instrument is able to achieve through a period of time.

May we speak in any further fashion, my brother?

Questioner: I found that the spelling of the word, the words, "I am," mechanically were in a—"I" was upper case, rather, capital letters, and "am" was a lower case letter. Am I dissecting properly how it works for me individually?

I am Laitos. It appears that you are doing that which you surmise as a result of the cultural teachings that you have been exposed to in which this is the proper form for a sentence.

(Pause)

(Jim channeling)

I am Laitos, and I am again with this instrument. Is there a further query at this time?

Questioner: … [puts on] in the adjustments to M and myself, who in the initial phases of contact?

I am Laitos. To each instrument is drawn those entities which are most able to offer the services which each new instrument requests either in a mental sense or by the general nature of the beingness that is the new instrument. Those of Hatonn found that your instrument, and the one known as M's instrument, were able to be aided in the deepening of the meditative state by those known as Hatonn. From time to time, we of Laitos shall be joined by those of Hatonn as well as other entities within the Confederation of Planets in the Service of the Infinite Creator in order that the instruction in the vocal channeling might proceed as smoothly as is possible for each new instrument.

May we speak in any further fashion, my brother?

Questioner: During that test, I had sensation in the lower part of my legs, very briefly, but very abruptly, and in the left rear portion of my head. Does that reflect some of the adjustments that you were making and can you be specific about how? They didn't repeat.

I am Laitos. The physical sensations that you have described are what we might call a side effect of the blending of the vibrations of those of Hatonn with your own. The blending of the vibrations of any contact with a new instrument, or any instrument, is a blending which occurs primarily within one of your energy centers or chakras. However, as the blending has the purpose of aiding and the deepening of the meditative state, there may be a residual or sideeffect of that deepening of the meditative state through one or more of the energy centers. The areas which you have described are merely likened unto the waves that lap upon the shore after the boat has passed.

May we speak in any further fashion, my brother?

Questioner: Thank you.

I am Laitos, and we thank you, my brother. Is there another query at this time?

J: Laitos *(inaudible)* I would like to ask a question about what you meant by my circuits were blown?

I am Laitos. This is a phrase which we find that is popular among your peoples to describe a situation in which the contact with another energy source has momentarily disabled the entity perceiving the energy. It was our perception that our blending of vibrations with your own had momentarily disoriented your perception of our vibrations.

May we speak in any further fashion, my sister?

J: Is there anything I can do to aid you, that this doesn't happen again?

I am Laitos. Again, we would simply recommend that the request be given to us by you that we seek to blend our vibrations in a manner which is more comfortable. We are as inexperienced in blending our vibrations with the instrument as a new instrument is in perceiving and speaking those concepts which we transmit. We are able to ascertain a general vibrational frequency with the necessary anomalies in each instrument, but in many cases are unable to specifically adjust our vibrations to each unique facet of a new instrument, and therefore request that each new instrument give us a feedback, shall we say, and request adjustment in such and such a fashion, in order that we may blend our vibrations in a manner which is mote comfortable to the new instrument.

May we speak in any further fashion, my sister?

J: I also experienced some cluttering of my *(inaudible)* or vibrating, it was [not] uncomfortable. I was wondering if this was the same kind of effect as my head tilted back or if this was some kind of a signal of contact?

I am Laitos. Each instrument will feel a certain set of physiological, mental, emotional or spiritual sensations that will be a combination of the blending of our vibrations with yours and the new instrument's eager and perhaps somewhat anxious anticipation of that blending. There is the usual increase of flow of that substance we find you call the adrenaline that any performer, shall we say, will experience before taking the stage. This is natural and is of little concern unless there is discomfort associated with this anticipation.

May we speak further, my sister?

Questioner: Ah, no thank you, it's been very helpful.

I am Laitos, and again we thank you, my sister. Is there another query?

Questioner: I felt [at] the beginning [of] the session that was as a *(inaudible)* contacting me. Can you tell me about what was going on, and, if not, what was?

I am Laitos. And we find that those of *(inaudible)* have had contact with your instrument not only this evening, but in previous evenings of your private meditations in order that you might become acquainted with these entities who await your desire to serve as a vocal instrument for their thoughts as well. You have exercised your instrument sufficiently in your training that you have now become able to perceive additional vibratory frequencies, and the way is now open for you to serve as an instrument for these entities as well, according to your own desire.

May we speak further, my sister?

Questioner: No. Thank you very much.

I am Laitos, and we thank you, my sister. Is there another query?

Questioner: I have one that breaks from the intensity somewhat, and it may be a two part question and *(inaudible)* answer it first. Is Laitos a social memory complex, an individual entity, a portion of the social memory complex?

I am Laitos, and when you speak to those of Laitos, you speak to a social memory complex, or grouping of entities that are as one in the seeking of the love and light of the one Creator. However, for the purpose of the working with this circle of seeking or with any such circle of seeking, we speak with an individualized or as an individual portion of that social memory complex. However, we are complete in our nature so that when you speak to any portion of those of Laitos, you speak as if *(inaudible)* all portions.

May we speak further, my brother?

Questioner: OK then, it precipitates what I have to ask in the second question. As a hurricane is pre-named by our weather services here in the—on Earth, I'm kinda curious to know if the human race will eventually become a social memory complex at some point in time or whatever complex we're working with. Is—has the human race been given a name to contact its, its entities that it will eventually serve? In other words, will … has the cosmos sort of named that social memory complex as it will eventually come through an instrument?

I am Laitos. And we apologize for our pause and the pause of those within our *(inaudible)*. We shall continue.

We appreciate the fondness that your peoples have for the naming, but may suggest that the naming is accomplished by those which have the need for it. For instance, in our case we have chosen the name "Laitos" to use when we contact this group, as it is the blending both of our nature, or vibratory frequency, and the limitations of your language system. You will find as your peoples do indeed progress into the next density of beingness that the naming is, as you know it, unnecessary, for all thoughts and beings are transparent, and are composed of a great variety of qualities which sum into what you may [call] a vibratory frequency, or tone, or note. This quality then may be translated when necessary into what you call the name.

The naming, however, is not utilized unless it is necessary, and should that grouping of entities which shall become your social memory complex find the opportunity to be of service to those such as yourselves are now, and find that the naming is helpful in that contact, then the name shall be chosen accordingly to the vibratory frequency which best represents the totality of the social memory complex and the language system of the entities' contact.

May we speak in any further fashion, my brother?

Questioner: That pretty much answers that.

I am Laitos. Is there another query at this time?

Questioner: I'd like to ask as to the instrument's energy level?

I am Laitos, and we find that this instrument is able to serve as an instrument for another two or three of your queries this evening.

Questioner: Very well.

Is there another query at this time?

Questioner: *(Inaudible)* one. Could you talk about what does tire an instrument, and why some people seem to tire more than others who are at different times, and not just a tiring on the short-term things, that drainage of energy on a long term basis or affecting physiological functions, and how that is a part of the process of channeling?

I am Laitos, and though this is a large subject upon which to speak, we shall attempt to be brief at this time. In the short run, shall we say, of the channeling session itself, the facts which serve to cause an instrument to lose vitality are the overall physical strength of the vehicle, the position chosen to hold in the meditative state, and the degree of concentration necessary in order to transmit the concepts in a word by word fashion.

The longer term factors, shall we say, that affect the ability of an entity to serve as a vocal channel, have to do with the overall blend of energy of mind, body and spirit, which together sum into a quality which we would call the vital energy or *elan vitale* of the entity. These are in turn affected greatly by the entity's efficiency and determination to utilize the catalyst which is a daily portion of the experience of the entity and which when processed efficiently causes the increase of the energy of mind, body or spirit, or a combination of these, so that the overall vital energy of the entity is enhanced.

The difficulty, especially when prolonged, in processing any catalyst which presents itself to the entity is a draining factor to the vital energy of the entity, for with the difficulty in utilizing the opportunity for growth and remaining within the configuration which continues to present the catalyst which continues to be less than efficiently utilized, [it] then focuses and requires greater vital energy in that area until the catalyst is efficiently utilized and the next opportunity for utilizing catalyst is presented to the entity.

Is there another query, my sister?

Questioner: No. Thank you.

I am Laitos, and we thank you once again, my sister. Is there a final query for this evening?

Questioner: Can you suggest anything between now and [the] next session tomorrow night that we might do that would be especially helpful in improving our ability to blend with the contact that you offer?

I am Laitos, and for each new instrument we would simply suggest the careful examination of the desire to serve as a vocal channel for any contact of a positive nature and to find within the self the primary reason for this desire, and if this reason is found to be sound and of a nature that the new instrument can heartily endorse, then that this new instrument take this purpose for serving as a vocal channel and begin to build upon it the qualities of self and inner being, which will become the signpost or primary character for which the instrument shall move in service to others as a vocal channel.

This building upon the desire to serve and the realizing of the purpose of the service and the nature of one's inner being that one brings to this service, will allow each new instrument to define for the self, and that which is the heart of the self, and that which shall be offered as the successful challenge to all spirits that would seek to utilize the entity as an instrument. This is a process which shall in most cases be ongoing and shall take a period of your time and your reflection in careful consideration to arrive at. We can suggest that this is a process which each shall find useful, whether the vocal channeling is pursued as a vocation or whether there is another direction in which the new instrument would choose to offer itself in service to others.

At this time, we shall take our leave of this instrument and of this group, thanking each for offering us the great opportunity and privilege of working with each. We are full of the joy of your desire to be of service to others by inviting our presence in the beginning exercising of your instruments. We leave each, as always, in the love and in the light of the one infinite Creator. We are known to you as those of Laitos. Adonai, my friends. Adonai.

L/L RESEARCH

L/L Research is a subsidiary of Rock Creek Research & Development Laboratories, Inc.

P.O. Box 5195
Louisville, KY 40255-0195

www.llresearch.org

Rock Creek is a non-profit corporation dedicated to discovering and sharing information which may aid in the spiritual evolution of humankind.

ABOUT THE CONTENTS OF THIS TRANSCRIPT: This telepathic channeling has been taken from transcriptions of the weekly study and meditation meetings of the Rock Creek Research & Development Laboratories and L/L Research. It is offered in the hope that it may be useful to you. As the Confederation entities always make a point of saying, please use your discrimination and judgment in assessing this material. If something rings true to you, fine. If something does not resonate, please leave it behind, for neither we nor those of the Confederation would wish to be a stumbling block for any.

CAVEAT: This transcript is being published by L/L Research in a not yet final form. It has, however, been edited and any obvious errors have been corrected. When it is in a final form, this caveat will be removed.

© 2009 L/L RESEARCH

SPECIAL MEDITATION
AUGUST 2, 1988

Group question: The value of channeling and such information considering the difficulties that any group can run into with the temptations offered by negative entities to deviate from the original purpose of the channeling, and the general value of channeled information for any seeker of truth, considering all the other sources of information that are available, what is the value of channeling, how should one weigh it in one's total gathering of information?[3]

(Carla channeling)

I am Q'uo. I greet you in the love and in the light of the one infinite Creator. It is a great privilege and a blessing to us to be able to share our thoughts with you, to experience the beauty of your vibrations and to share in your meditation. Because we find we speak not only to this group but to a larger audience, we would also bless and send our love to each who may see or hear these words, for we come in service not to one, nor to a special group, but to those who call for aid in seeking the truth.

We ourselves seek the truth. This is our journey, a journey we have found to be full of joy, love, companionship and power. We may also say we have found the past to be one of many ordeals, one of long discomfort, from time to time, as you would say, challenge and difficulty. Such is the nature of the illusion that you call life, whether or not the choice to seek accelerated spiritual growth is taken. However, with the accelerated spiritual growth that comes through a daily practice of meditation and an honest attempt at service to others, comes growth and change. And there is no change that is not painful to those within material forms.

And so we speak from a standpoint of joy, gazing at an illusion in which such suffering must take place in order that the lessons of love might be learned, for love is another way of saying the Creator, not a weak love or a romantic love, a family love, a national love, or a world love, but a love that is so creative it has often been described in terms of fire and passion, a divine passion to conceive a world that would speak to the Creator of Itself. And so each of you dwells within this illusion of life upon your planet, experiencing each other while the Creator experiences all. Each of you, then, is infinitely precious to the Creator who loved enough to create you and all that there is.

This loving Creator has given to all within each density of existence that which is called free will, and

---

[3] Carla: For this meeting, video recording equipment was used to make a video record of a session of channeling. The equipment did not work well with available light, and had sound difficulties, so nothing was ever done with these videotapes. Fortunately, our usual audio taping system worked, and we were able to make a transcript of the session.

therefore one may choose to sleep and enjoy the illusion, thinking not of what is beyond, but enjoying the beautiful planet, the companionship of friends and family. This is quite acceptable, for progress will still take place spiritually—it merely is at a slower pace than some would prefer. We speak to those who would prefer to accelerate the pace of their spiritual growth.

Your question at this meeting concerned channeling. There are many difficulties involved in learning. It is time-consuming, and much experience is often needed in order that one may become a clear channel, a channel which may choose carefully its contact, a channel which may find apt expression and do justice to the concepts arising from the combination of that which we are and that which the channel is. And we would speak first in general of the very nature of the illusion which you now enjoy.

You may have noticed, those of you who seek to serve others, how very difficult it is to serve others, for to serve others truly is to know that which they would desire or require and to give them that which they desire or require without question. This is difficult service to perform. Nevertheless, the instinct for service to others is a sign of wholeness within each who feels it, a sign that a choice has been made, the basic choice that this entire illusion was designed for each seeker to have the opportunity to make. Shall you choose to serve yourself, be *numero uno* and follow those false images of the self which your culture would give you to wear as masks? Very well. We are with you in love and light and honor you as perfect beings. Do you choose instead to surrender that small self, that self of ambition, greed and hunger, to empty the self of petty things, that instead a greater self may assist your consciousness in more rapid growth and service to others? Very well. That is why we are here, that is why many are here—to help those who do wish to progress.

It is in this context, the knowledge of suffering in general, the knowledge of the difficulty of service to others, that we address the matter of channeling. Channeling is one of many, many ways of service to others. It is a way of engaging the highest and best within the channel in a collaboration with a deeply impersonal source of love, which we are, that has what we may call the larger point of view. We, as contact, and this instrument are equal partners, respecting each other, experiencing a growing friendship with each other and a respect for each other that cannot be underestimated. This channel is most careful to challenge all spirits, and we are most thrilled that this channel is so inclined, for our service is that which could easily be missed, for there are always those who do not come in service to others, who would wish to take the new channel and move that channel away from the highest and best tuning that is in that channel, the goal being to dim the light of channeling, seeking and the group sociability that adds so very such to the light network upon planet Earth.

How difficult it is to be of service, my friends. How difficult it is to share without pushing your opinions upon someone else, without moving from inspiration to doctrine. Yet, this is the hallmark of channeled material. This is our service to you, to attempt to provide information and inspiration, not that of which is wise, but that of which is compassionate, loving and serving. We speak of the one original Thought to those who would wish to hear of that great Logos called love, that one original Thought that made in unity all that there is so that you are members, one of another, and all of the Creator.

Why would any who wishes to be of service to others choose a sacrificial way of giving? In the beginning many things seem like sacrifice. When a mated pair has a child, the father sacrifices his freedom. He must provide now for a small and fragile entity, a stranger, so he thinks. And what of the mother? Ah, what freedom she loses, what sacrifices she makes, yet the joy of knowing, loving and sending forth into the world a small being is so far from describable that it would make most parents laugh, for the joy they have received is inestimable.

So it is, in a different sense, with the channeling. There is in the beginning the sacrifice, and always the need for continued faithfulness and persistence, the need to move in meditation enough to gain that infinite point of view, that infinite source of supply that enables the giver to give without tiring.

Can channeling help people? My friends, we believe that the answer is yes, or we would not be here. We believe that each who wishes to learn to channel is an unique being, has an unique vocabulary, experiences, and way of thinking. We have one very simple message to offer—the message of unity, of perfect compassion and love which brooks no judgment, of the reality of peace and joy that is intertwined within the illusion and transcends the illusion also. We urge people in our channeling first to move into meditation and experience peace, quiet and love until, through meditation, the seeker has become ready to feel well about the self and move on into service to others. There is the beginning turning inward, and we who channel attempt to support that and encourage the daily meditation, the contemplation, the talking with those of like mind, the rejoicing in companions upon the path.

When much work has been done to ready the self, when the work is over and all feels easy, then it shall come naturally to each to do some service, or perhaps a cluster of services. The service may be the raising of children, and to the mother, the muse of Mary speaks. There are some who are called to the musical instruments or to the dance or to some other artifact of your culture which creates beauty and myth and wonder for those who see it, and they sing or dance or move to their muse. There are some few who will feel the call to the special kind of muse, an odd, rather philosophical kind of muse, not one given a name among your peoples. Shall we call it the philosopher muse? At any rate, some are called to learn to share in a collaboration that is intended both to inspire and to inform. And so the choice is made, a teacher is chosen, and a program is undertaken.

Since the program of learning to channel includes much work in consciousness, clearing lower energies, working with the identity of the authentic and deep self, this process is helpful for those who wish to channel healing or other energies, not merely the vocal channeling. It is always to be remembered, however, that once the training is done, and the vocal channel moves out into the world, there will always be those to whom the material appeals and those to whom it does not. As we have said, service to others is difficult, and it is well to leave any attachment to that work which the channel is doing behind. It has no place in service.

However, there are two great aids that you as a channel may offer. Firstly there is that aid which any which seeks the aid of the infinite Creator may offer and that is that in the becoming a more and more consciously directed authentic human, each seeker becomes a light that glows brighter and brighter. Those who move into a group about a channel form this kind of light in an exponential manner, the strength of the light being far more than a linear addition of the people in the group could hope to create. Thus, by the simple attempt to channel, the planet has become lighter, the consciousness of the planet has been raised and the great work is being done.

Secondly, to the instrument itself this service satisfies that desire to be of aid, to be worthwhile, and to be active and caring in the world of spirit. It is an invisible world, and there are many, as we have said, who care not at all for it. Yet for those who do care for the inner world, the outer world is gazed upon with some dismay, and there is the desire to help. For those whose desire is to help by aiding the environment, for those whose desire to help is expressed in political or other social manners we say, "Know yourself and know your muse, whether it be justice, honor, beauty or fairness," and then ask yourself what relation this muse bears to truth.

Truth is what we are here to discuss, to discover, to rejoice at, and to dwell in. Not a truth that can be expressed in words or with the mind, but a feeling tone of truth, a validity of things that begins to be created within each person. Truth is not without you. Without you is a relativistic illusion. Truth lies within you. We who channel to instruments such as this hope to put these thoughts within the mind in order that each may attempt to grow, and at the same time, each may see that all so-called failures and errors are part of the path and are those things to be hugged to the self, accepted, forgiven, and from which it [is] time to move on.

Do you wish to be of service by channeling? By teaching? By offering the self in the deepest way that is important to you, that is the essence of yourself? We encourage you to the ordeal, for no matter what you give to others—and you cannot judge that—you shall daily be working upon that self which in its being is love itself. It may seem selfish to continue working upon self-realization, to continue working until the self feels entirely self-worthy, self-forgiven and self-esteemed. Yet, must you not love yourself to love your neighbor enough to give all that you have sacrificially, that that neighbor, that perfect stranger, that face of the Creator which is another part of yourself—to give to this entity is surely a wonder and a blessing. And yet that entity shall give back to you more than you give away, so the end of the suffering is always joy.

Now, we know there have been many who have had the psychic greeting of what this instrument would call the loyal opposition, those who serve in love and light to the infinite Creator, but on a negative path, those who wish to dim and remove the light upon this planet. We encourage each to love and offer up the incense of your prayers for your brethren upon the negative path, feeling no fear, but asking them clearly and firmly to be gone, or if they are stubborn, working within the self to open the self to the realization that each self is all that there is, and that that negativity without is merely a part of the negativity within.

In such a way does love indeed conquer all, yet it must be true love, true service and a true feeling of unity. We do not underestimate any of the negative parts of being of service to others through vocal channeling, yet it is our humble opinion that to attempt to teach the laws, shall we say, of love is an attempt eternally blessed, eternally gratefully received by a world hungry for inspiration, and certainly one excellent way of sharing all those experiences which have combined to make you the gem-like faceted, crystallized soul that you are, for in channeling the instrument shares deeply of the self in a way not usually available within your culture.

We do not urge all to take up channeling. We urge entities who seek to serve to take that desire into meditation and await an answer, a leading, a synchronistic coincidence, something that subjectively tells or calls to the seeker. If that call is to vocal channeling, we most gratefully accept you. If that call is to another service, yet still as we love all upon your planet, we love and support you in your service, whatever it may be. We may indeed acknowledge that there are many muses which do not have the psychic greeting component as part of the long term aspect of doing this particular work, however, we believe you will find that all who are of genuine service to others make great sacrifices of the personal self, and we urge each when that ordeal comes upon them to embrace change, to allow the little self to die as it will, knowing and trusting that the greater self that fills that hollow is a blessing, a wonder, a joy and in itself a service to others, for as the conscious entity opens its eyes, the love of God shines through. As the conscious entity holds out the hand, the Creator touches man to man, person to person, in intimate caring that the Father cannot effect in and of Itself.

Yours is the manifestation, yours the experience now. Now is your time to choose. Choose first whether to serve yourself or others. Move into the period of meditation, urge your mate to move into it with you, that you may change and grow together, and in a month, a year, ten years, in the time of your heart, in the time of the Creator, the need to serve will come upon you and it will be joy as well as work, and your work will become your joy and your joy your work.

We bless each, we welcome each who come to us as vocal channels. We bless all who do not but who seek to serve the infinite Creator, all of you in your own unique ways. May you be faithful and persistent in your seeking, single-hearted in your desire to know the mystery of the infinite Creator, and above all may you love each other and attempt to serve each other, for as you do so, you shall enter what this instrument would call the Kingdom of Heaven.

Yes, my friends, the Kingdom of Heaven lies within you. Offer yourself sacrificially when your time has come, and you will not feel the pain, but only the joy, a joy without end, for you dwell in eternity when you seek to serve. May you always be merry, my friends, for the seekers upon the path must laugh, must make the jokes, must have the light touch. Do not be solemn in your seeking, or flail yourself with the sackcloth and ashes, but keep yourself self-forgiven and open yourself to the utter redemptive perfection of the infinite Creator's love.

It has truly been a blessing to speak with you. We cannot express our thanks enough that you would call us to you. May we allow you to know that we shall always hear each call, not that we would speak to each, but that we would act as a carrier wave in the deepening of the meditation. You have only mentally to request that service, and those of the Confederation of Planets in the Service of the Infinite Creator shall hear each entity receiving the Comforter within its vibratory pattern.

We thank this instrument, and would at this time transfer to close the meeting through the one known as Jim. I am Q'uo.

(Jim channeling)

I am Q'uo, and greet each again in love and light through this instrument. It is our privilege at this time to offer ourselves in the attempt to speak to any queries which may remain upon the minds of those present. We would wish each to know that that which we offer is our opinion, that which is the fruit of our seeking. Please take those words which we speak that ring of truth to you and use them as you will, leaving behind those that do not ring of that truth, leaving them behind without a second glance. Is there a query at this time to which we may speak?

Carla: Could you talk to me about devas, nature spirits?

I am Q'uo, and am aware of your query, my sister. This, as you know, is quite a large field of inquiry, and we would not be able to do it justice if we were to attempt in such a short gathering as this to speak extensively. But we may suggest that the entities which you describe as the nature spirits, devas, are those which inhabit your plant and animal kingdom as thickly as your plants and animals themselves, for there are many such spirits which work in conjunction with the natural world about you and serve as a kind of caretaker and communicator between the various forms of second density life and the third-density creatures such as your population of entities upon the surface of your planet at this time.

There are beings in each realm of existence which are responsible for enhancing, shall we say, the communion of the plants and the animals with each other and with the Earth itself. They are such as you would see guides and teachers of your inner planes in their function and relationship to third-density creatures. They inform the various plant and animal life-forms according to these life-forms' desire to gain a self-conscious awareness which is the hallmark of your third-density population, for all of life moves toward the light and love of the one Creation, and all of life has those helpers or guides which assist in this movement, the assistance being necessary for those who are less aware of that towards which they move, and which, by their desire to move in that direction, call for the assistance of those who answer. In the case of the plant and animal life-forms, those who answer in many cases are those who you would call the nature spirits and the devas.

Is there another query?

Carla: I just wondered as to their nature. Are they second-density graduates that have chosen to turn back and help their brothers and sisters until they can all graduate into our density of humanity? Or do they come from elsewhere? Are they third-density graduates who have decided to turn back and help second density?

I am Q'uo, and am aware of your query, my sister. The origin of these entities is one which is somewhat difficult to describe in your terms, but we feel that the concept of …

(Side one of tape ends.)

Carla: I appreciate that information, Q'uo, because I'm working with someone for the first time who wants to work with nature spirits, and I'd like to feel more familiar with their nature so that I may help her further. Thank you.

I am Q'uo, and am again with this instrument. And we thank you, my sister. Is there another query?

J: Q'uo, I have a question I'm trying to formulate in my mind so that it makes sense to you. The question I have is regarding that comment on muses, and do I understand you correctly that in our channeling or in our quest for self-knowledge we respond to your call of the muse?

I am Q'uo, and in regards to your query, my sister, we would suggest that our use of the term, muse, in relation to the seeker of truth and the means by which the seeking is carried out, refers to that quality or perhaps cluster of qualities within the seeker which speaks with a special power and glory, shall we say, for each seeker will discover within the self as the journey of seeking progresses that there are certain avenues of inquiry that hold a special interest, and others which hold that interest not so long or so intensely.

Thus, as this is discovered by each seeker, the seeker may be said to hearken to the voice of the inner muse. The poet hearkens to the use of words to express greater concepts than words themselves contain. The artist looks upon the canvas and the palette as the grounds upon which it shall express the song of the inner muse. The muse for each seeker is that voice which speaks most clearly of truth, and each seeker then, as this is discovered, may follow that voice and hearken to its speaking in order that more of the truth of its existence, purpose, and means of expression might be made known to it.

Is there another query, my sister?

J: Yes. Thank you. That really explains what I wanted to know. Further, you had made mention that some areas of interest are more prone to drawing those who wish to dim the light, and others are not. Is my understanding of that correct?

I am Q'uo. This is basically correct, my sister, for as any seeker or group of seekers becomes more efficient, shall we say, at seeking and radiating the light of the one Creator, this light is seen as a power on the metaphysical or time/space levels of existence, and it is within these levels of existence that other beings of thought [and] power move and are attracted to the light. The negative entities are attracted to such light because it is a spiritual kind of power that they wish to utilize for their own purposes in service to self. Thus, their means of utilizing that light for their own uses is seen by those radiating and seeking that light in an efficient manner as the dimming of the light, for it is removed, shall we say, from whence it sprung.

May we speak further, my sister?

J: Yes, I do have another question, and again, I need to have a few seconds to formulate it.

Carla: I'll take that time just to say that isn't what you meant more or less that like that if you were a plumber, you might be following a muse of copper or something, but you're not going to be attracting negatives, because you're not polarizing positive, you're just putting in pipe. Isn't that what you meant, Q'uo?

I am Q'uo. This is correct, my sister, for the endeavor of the seeker of truth is that which increases the polarity or the ability of that entity to welcome and enjoy the love and the light which is a power of the one Creator. Just as your battery within your automobile is able to function because of the potential difference between the positive and the negative charge, so is the seeker of truth able to do work in consciousness according to its ability to polarize itself in the positive, or service-to-others fashion, in an effective manner.

When this has been accomplished to a significant enough degree, that polarization is as a light and a source of energy or power which might be utilized by that seeker for further service to others and further journeying upon the path of service to others itself. Or the light may be used by those of negative polarity if they are successful in infringing upon this power through means not of their own design, but of openings or invitations, shall we say, on the part of the positive seeker of truth which has perhaps for a moment unwittingly or unthinkingly moved itself away from the truth it knows and entered into a disharmony which is as the opening an invitation for the negative entity to intensify to the degree that it will perhaps be able to dim the light for a time and use that power for itself, as it has removed the light from the service of others.

Is there another query, my sister?

Carla: I turn it back to J. Thank you.

J: Okay. Given that there is increased popularity, if you will, of channeling, unless this activity is carefully taught, it seems like the potential for negative energy to see the light, to be attracted to it, and to divert it, to dim it, it seems like that probability is increased. How would you suggest that we prevent that kind of thing happening?

I as Q'uo and am aware of your query, my sister. To each entity which engages in the process of offering its service to others in any fashion which is successful, there shall be the temptations offered which serve as a balancing mechanism in order that the entity which has manifested the desire to be of service to others might be offered an equal temptation to move from that service and to join the negative path in some fashion within the life pattern for some period of time. This may be seen also as an opportunity for that same entity to strengthen its desire to serve others and to move ever more faithfully upon that path as the temptations to glorify the self or to gain a power and recognition for the self are recognized and refused.

As the one known as Jesus the Christ experienced the temptations of the one known as Satan, as the one known as Jesus spent the forty days and nights in the desert, demanded that the one known as Satan get behind him, each seeker of truth will find that as progress along the path is made, that there are those opportunities to test the progress that it be true, and if there be a weakness in that seeker's pattern of expression of service to others, those weaknesses or lesser areas of strength shall be made known to it through the difficulties, shall we say, that are a natural portion of this path, and through recognizing those areas which lack strength, the seeker of truth then may repair these areas and gratefully acknowledge their presence to any entity which has aided in pointing them out.

Thus, we do not offer the information concerning negative entities and their offering of temptations to positive entities as that which is to be feared, but that which is a normal part of the evolutionary progress within your illusion, in order that the progress of each path, both positive and negative, might through their interaction strengthen the other, in order that the one Creator might through these experiences know Itself more fully and each entity within the creation, through these experiences, might know itself more fully and the one Creator more fully and more intensely.

May we speak in any further fashion, my sister?

J: I have no further questions, but so I can understand this—as being an opportunity to strengthen faith, is that correct? That's a question—I said I wasn't going to ask a question, but I lied.

I am Q'uo, and this is quite correct, my sister. Is there another query?

J: No. Thank you very much.

I am Q'uo, and we thank you, my sister. Is there another query?

Carla: Just to follow up on that. From previous channeled information, isn't it also true that the negative path eventually ends, and must turn to a positive path, so that in the end, there is only one path, it's just that there is a split for a while during this illusion and perhaps the next?

I am Q'uo, and this is correct, my sister, for just as the creation itself and every portion of it shall eventually return to the complete unity of the one Creator, bringing all the experiences that have been gathered during the great octave of being as seeds for the next great octave of being, so those entities of negative polarity shall at some point within their evolutionary progress find the necessity of releasing the negative polarity and adopting that which is the positive polarity, for it is the positive polarity which, though it partakes of illusion and separation in some degree, seeks to affirm the unity of all creation and the divinity of all beings, and seeks to serve all beings as the Creator, whereas the negative polarity is based upon that which is not, that being the separation of one being from another, which lays the groundwork, shall we say, for the potential ruling of one being over another and over others.

As the negative entities continue to pursue this path of separation and control, at some point in order to continue in the process of evolution and to know more of the Creator and to exercise the power of the Creator, it becomes necessary to see other selves as the Creator and as the self. This is not difficult for the positive polarity, but is difficult for the negative polarity that the negative polarity must be abandoned and the power that has been gained from it be used to reverse, shall we say, the polarity in order that continued evolution be possible.

Is there another query, my sister?

Carla: No, thank you very much.

I am Q'uo, and again we thank you, my sister. Is there another query at this time?

Questioner: Oh, that's a necessary function of this creation, obviously, and an exercise of polarity by those entities of the negative. They perform a function for the positive polarity by being in service to self. They also become in service to others and we of the positive polarity are witness to that and thereby experience both biases. I'm not sure what my question is. I guess what I'm trying to find out is, that's an integral part of what's going on here, and it sometimes is hard to feel the separation from those negative entities, knowing that they are part of the creation, part of what we all are, knowing that we all fall within that creation.

I as Q'uo, and we would comment upon your comment by suggesting that indeed all entities, whether of positive or negative or of no polarity, are a portion of the same creation and the same Creator, and that the most effective means for a positively oriented entity to deal with negative polarity is to generate within the heart the overwhelming love for such an entity, and to send that love to that entity in the meditative state if possible, and to bathe that entity in the love and the light of the one Creator as you perceive it.

For all beings are truly a portion of the Creator and of the self, and as the seeker of truth looks within to find that of truth within itself, any experience or entity that it comes upon in its journey of seeking will reflect some portion of inner truth to it, and as the seeker is able to draw unto itself all expressions of the Creator and to see them as the Creator, as the self, and as love, then so they become that which they are, and no longer are that which they seem.

The persona, the mask, is removed and for that seeker of truth, that seeker stands before the mirror which looks into its own soul and the heart of the Creator.

Is there a final query at this time?

J: I do have a question, and this is regarding the scenario where the negative polarity eventually makes a shift to positive polarity—I don't know if I'm saying that correctly. It's what Carla was talking about to you in her previous question, where the negative eventually seeks the positive. My question is, is this a scenario that we're witnessing on the Earth at this time, where there seems to be an accumulation of negative polarity, and that negative polarity wishes to make a shift? Has that occurred on the Earth, and has there been a call for light coming from the Earth? Or has it come from somewhere else? Is the positive polarity reaching out to the Earth? I guess I'm trying to find where the initial recognition was made, of the need for light. Was it from those who are of the light? Or from those who have negative polarity?

I am Q'uo, and am aware of your query, my sister. The call for light has long emanated from those within this planetary influence who have chosen for themselves the service-to-others polarity. This choice and the following of this choice is likened unto a call for assistance in journeying upon this path, as any student which seeks to learn any art will learn more efficiently from a teacher. Many are the ways in which the student of positive polarity is taught. Most means are unseen and go unrecognized in the life of the seeker of truth in the positive sense: the many coincidences and pleasant surprises, shall we say, which occur in the life pattern, the dreams of a prophetic or informative nature, the meeting of an entity that changes the life, the experience that appears seemingly out of the blue, and forever marks the life pattern with a note of joy. These are the means by which the call for assistance is answered—and there are many more.

The expression of the mass consciousness upon your planetary sphere, moving in a more positive direction, is far more a function of those upon your planet who have chosen ever more faithfully and steadfastly to continue their seeking for light and service to others rather than any shift in negative entities' desires, for the desire of those [of] negative polarity exists far past the evolutionary progress which your planet has thus far achieved.

The negative polarity is one which exists with great strength into the fourth density of love, and into the fifth density, the density of wisdom. It is beyond that expression of wisdom and light into the sixth density, where love and wisdom are joined and blended into one, where the negative polarity must needs abandon the service-to-self polarity and shift its focus to that which is the service to others in order to continue the progress of seeking union with the one Creator.

At this time we shall again take the opportunity to thank each present which has invited our presence in joining your group and in sharing that which has been the fruit of our seeking. It is a source of great joy for us to sing with each seeker the song of seeking, the song of love, the song of the one Creator, experiencing the great mysteries, adventures and joys of the creation all about. We are known to you as those of Q'uo, and at this time we shall leave each, as always, in the love and in the light of the one infinite Creator. Adonai, my friends. Adonai.

(Carla channeling)

I Yadda. I with this instrument, greet you in love and light of infinite Creator. We like this instrument. She challenge in name of Jesus Christ. We say, "How about Buddha?" We not fully grasp this instrument's fanaticism, but even she be provincial, we say, "Okay," because she passionate, she care, and she real. And so are we. We come in love and light of infinite One, One Who is All, and we come only because we wish to underscore need for laughter, need for merriment, and need for intensity of life. Not the outer life. You must forget all those clothings you put on your body and on your mind and on your head. All those hats you wear—mother, father, employer, employee, all those things—take them off, throw them away. You want a reputation? Do not go into spiritual seeking. No reputation to be had there. No, sir. You must think carefully before you become one interested more in the inner journey than in the outer journey. You know you gonna die. But you know why you alive?

Did you like that? I got "L"—I said "a-Live." I did that! I'm getting better! We urge you to see that many things drop away, so you may find the true intensity of your being. May you do so with jollity.

Ah, jollity! I am almost speaking this instrument's language now!

We so glad to speak to you. We thank you for calling us here. We bless each, and we go, for we not talk long. We yours in love and light of infinite Creator. On behalf of this passionate Christian, this provincial one, who yet knows the universe, and to all of you provincial people, whatever you believe, believe passionately, believe wholly, believe without the thinking and without the judging and without the reputation and the respectability, but find the jolly times. Adonai. Adonai. Adonai, my friends. I Yadda.

Intensive Meditation
August 4, 1988

(Carla channeling)

(The quality of the original recording is poor.)

I am Q'uo, and greet you, my friends, through this instrument in the love and in the light of the infinite Creator, whom we all seek to serve with all of our being. It is, as always, a great privilege and honor to be called to this group for the purpose of exercising those who have chosen to be of service as vocal channels, and also to be of service in offering ourselves to you in whatever capacity you may find to be useful. As always, we urge you to take to yourself that which rings of truth for you, and to discard without a second thought that which you do not find to be helpful to you at this time, for we offer only our humble opinion, our brothers and sisters, of the fruits of our own path of seeking to be of service. There are many upon your planet at this time who are seeking to know the truth of the infinite Creator. Each will find that truth which resonates with clarity and harmony according to the vibrations of each.

The truth is very simple, my friends. It is the message that we and our brothers and sisters of the Confederation of Planets in the Service of the Infinite Creator bring to you. The truth is very simple and always the same, and yet there are as many ways to attempt to explain and demonstrate the truth as there are entities seeking for the truth.

Thus, each shall find what is of value to each, and shall proceed upon the path chosen by each until that time when all who seek the truth shall surely find it, for they shall be one *(inaudible)* each other and the Creator.

You are aware, my friends, that this is the indeed the true nature of reality at this time, despite the seeming separations that exist within your illusion. You are also aware that all of creation continues to merge itself together more and more closely to the One Original Thought. In this shall all not only find the truth, but become the truth, for in your seeking now you see only portions of that great truth which encompasses all that there is. You see only portions, my friend, because in your heavy illusion much is veiled from you at this time. Thus, you may seem to find many perhaps somewhat different truths at different times, as you penetrate more and more the dense layers of the veil of the illusion.

We ask again that you not be disheartened in your quest for truth, for though the way is long, and the ultimate truth ever receding just beyond the grasp, yet there is a signpost of those seekers of the bright gleam of truth, moving together along the path, stumbling at times, falling at times, then resuming the journey once again and encouraging each other as we journey. You are all a part of this great mass of truth seekers, as are we also, for this journey in the quest of the truth continues from density to density.

We urge you to treasure those pearls and truths and wisdom which you find that resonate with great clarity and purity with your deepest *(inaudible)*.

Hold the truth inside yourself, my friends. Keep its flame burning brightly, for it will serve also as a beacon to those around you which seek the desire to seek, but do not see so clearly the way. Thus, we are all pilgrims, and as we journey upon the path together, may we each hold our own particular beacon *(inaudible)*, the light of truth which burns brightly within your spirits. We join with the light of all others who seek the truth, and thus seek to enlighten and brighten the planet upon which you sit at this time.

It is our desire to help you in this search for *(inaudible)*, to aid you with brightening of the beacon and devote *(inaudible)* for you and *(inaudible)* in this day. At these times, my friends, you have only to mentally request our being, and we will be glad to offer whatever assistance we may.

At this time we will leave this instrument and this group in the love and the brightly shining light of the one infinite Creator. We are known to you as those of Q'uo. Adonai.

(Carla channeling)

I Yadda. I come in love and light of infinite Creator. We come with thanksgiving too. What would the one known as Yadda—we ask this instrument perhaps to become with this one erect … that work better, the lying down, not working. I Yadda. I now attempt to transfer to the one known as *(inaudible)*. I Yadda.

(Pause)

(Carla channeling)

I Yadda. I again with this instrument. We say, "Hah, we almost got it, we wish he be patient." We now transfer to one known as R. I Yadda.

(R channeling)

(Shouted) I Yadda. I am with this instrument. This is very interesting. We want to do this really much. Oh, I forgive myself. I come light and love of infinite Creator, and then finally in *(inaudible)* of Christ. Yadda! Very good! This instrument exercise *(inaudible)*. Hhmm. Long time, long time ago, Yadda walk this Earth. Yadda wish to thank this instrument for patience, for Yadda very anxious *(inaudible)* waiting, WAITING, WAITING, WAITING! For such a long time. He's waiting. Sometimes, you know, it gets very hard. Anyway. Ah, we begin.

Maybe I tell you a story, but I don't quite know how to get into it. This instrument, he … Tell you what, we going to rest this instrument, cause we got GOOD THING HERE. And we be VERY CAREFUL with this one. He good. You know why? Why why? I was waiting why? He like it.

Carla: Your "L's" are better, Yadda.

You know what? Your "L's" stink. *(Laughter from group.)* There really nothing wrong with Yadda "L!" You're letting "L" just plain, when Yadda got right *(inaudible)*. *(Laughter.)* This instrument listen. He happy too, but sometime he want to get in and play a little. Have to find a way to put his somewhere. You know what? He say it okay. He did. I not kidding. He say, "Can I say this?"

Yes. HE SAY, *(unclear, though very loud, sounds like "transplay!")*. She never say this, NEVER! She's afraid. That's the reason, but this one not afraid. Yadda protect *(sound too loud and too inarticulate to be understood)*. Yadda almost use words not nice. I don't know—maybe I do it anyway. Well … It came easy, this one, because he like to swear. But you know why I STOP? Because this one GIVE ME WORD! HAH! I taking no word from this one, I ought as *(inaudible)* not as prompter. Hah, hah, hah, hah. This very happy business. I like this a lot. You may get very tired of Yadda. Hhmmm.

Please, please understand. This *(inaudible)* Yadda tell you secret. Yadda come differently to this one than to that one. That one over there, WHOM I LOVE BECAUSE she lets me speak in spite of fear. She knows I'm good, rather just rough. RUFF RUFF RUFF. RUFF. I need a voice like this one because, I tell you something. She right. Yadda … Not this. Cause I tell you, I use it anyway. You being kind. I carry baggage. I don't wish to say baggage. I carry BAGGAGE. I carry murder, because for LONG TIME, YADDA HATE! HATE, HATE, HATE, HATE, HATE! Now Yadda love. Much to learn in this, I think. I didn't tell you what I hate, I hated the Chinese. The Chinese KILL AND KILL AND KILL AND KILL. Yadda learn how to kill, oh, Yadda very good at this. If you can say good—but it's not bad, either. Is INSTRUCTIONAL!

Don't worry—I give it up. I don't need to do this anymore. And I don't need to hate the Chinese either. *(Very softly.)* Love the Chinese. I tell you why I love the Chinese. May I do this? I love the Chinese because Chinese make Yadda hate. And when Yadda hate, Yadda find out what love is. This instrument think that Yadda like Ramtha. Yadda not like Ramtha. Ramtha there. Ramtha think hot stuff! Yadda think think this instrument hot stuff. Because now Yadda can talk, and talk out loud and talk in terms you want to know. Because you speak in this group, Yadda speak. You all speak in this group of the negative … Yadda like. You speak of the negative side, the one who make you hate. Okay, I speak of this, because the side that make you hate, you made service to look like that. YOU MUST LOVE 'EM! *(Shouted phrase not understandable.)* Must have hate. I get carried away because it was long and hard.

Ohhhh. Think how it feels. Buddha cares. This one challenge not in Buddha's name, don't worry, little one, he CHALLENGE SMART CHALLENGE. HE CHALLENGE WITH … He say, I came in fellowship of the eternal truth of the Christ. Christ everywhere. I no problem with Christ! Only with Jee-sus. But I tell you, this one does not know Buddha, so he say, if I challenge with Buddha, I don't know what *(inaudible)* I don't use that word. I give you new word. He *(inaudible)* this one, because he don't like making up stuff he never heard before.

(Sounds like) SHUT UP! You know what?

(This is very difficult to transcribe, and it goes on at some length. The delivery is alternatively violently loud and fading completely away into inaudibility, then back to absolute ROARING. This is an unclear recording with lots of background noise on tape. With this, in addition to bombastic and emotional nature of delivery, and the significant loss of sibilant and other consonant sounds, it is just too difficult to transcribe. It has to be listened to to be believed, anyway.)

(Group retunes after Yadda's explosive closing.)

(Carla channeling)

I am Hatonn, and I greet each through this instrument in the love and the light in the name of the One Who is All, and the All Which is One. We are first concerned to ensure that the process by which the one known as Yadda has exercised the instrument known as R [be] completely released, and in order to avoid the overeager and somewhat *(inaudible)* source of inspiration our brothers and sisters *(inaudible)*, coming back too quickly to this instrument, we would ask that the instrument known as R [move on] to the [the back] in which posture Yadda cannot use his instrument.

There is in this young contact the *(inaudible)* for speaking, yet Yadda itself wishes only to offer spiritual principles, and has the considerable work in wisdom plumbing the self to patience, using an instrument in strength and in power in a stable manner. We would suggest to the instrument known as R that he request the highest and best contact that he may carry in a stable manner, to avoid certain effects upon his *(inaudible)* of the physical vehicle becoming somewhat distressed. As the one known as Yadda has need to use the ability of the physical vehicle to move forward and backward in the *(inaudible)* in order to fully breathe as it used to breathing within a physical.

We thank this instrument for its cooperation. We have been at its side during the communication which this instrument is aware has been an adventure in which the instrument has had a portion. We ask this instrument not to be concerned overly as to the amount of content it itself has provided, for this is the normal beginning of a new contact. The percentage of that which the ones known as Yadda may wish to say shall of its own accord become greater with the experience gained and the feeling of adventure and the joy of finding a proper voice honed to the steadying task of humble greeting, inspirational, and truthful information to the best of the one known as Yadda's ability.

The one known as Yadda is a representative [of many]. Perhaps the awareness that you may have of this entity's speaking of that which is called the Chinese seems unuseful, yet it is so, for the Chinese are an ancient race, both upon this planet and *(inaudible)*. Also those within it are of, on this planet, the Oriental race. It is a rare instrument which one such as Yadda may find within the culture of your peoples, and the one known as Yadda is strongly intending to refine, subdue, discipline and make ever more pure and refined the *(inaudible)*. We express for Yadda through this instrument the heartful and warm joy.

We would [move] on now, and we would say to the one known as E that this instrument should imagine the feet bare upon the earth, feet in the luxurious soft grasses, smell of the flowers about, the buzzing of the bees. Before her stands the great oak, behind her the great maple. On her right hand the yew, upon the left [sequoia]. We ground this instrument and suggest that this instrument prepare for contact while tuning by grounding the self and feeling the protection and the infinite energy of the Earth, for it is the Earth that this instrument wishes to serve, therefore the Earth which is full of love loves this instrument infinitely.

With that grounding complete, we shall pause so one known as *(inaudible)* may work with the one known as E at this time. I am Hatonn.

(Long pause, then lengthy but inaudible channeling by E.)

(Carla channeling)

I am Hatonn, and we thank the one known as E for availing herself of this most beloved contact which has been waiting her and which she is now learning. We ask that the protection be [applied] in addition to any protection the instrument may feel that it needs, for it is the nature, shall we say, of nature to need the signs of protection, a symbol that peace is truly reigning, and that the Logos rules in all the clarity of that which this instrument would call [nature]. *(Inaudible).*

(The rest of Carla's channeling is inaudible.)

Questioner: I felt you with me, Latwii, very early on, and then when Yadda came and left, and I was wondering, why did that occur?

I am Latwii, and as aware of your query, my sister. We of Latwii, as the channeling process was being initiated in the one known as R, sought to be of assistance to the one known as R, as did others of the Confederation of Planets in the Service of the Infinite Creator at that time, for this entity was experiencing a contact which was unique in nature and which was in need of, shall we say, all the assistance that it could get, thus we, shall we say, stood guard and gave what assistance we could, returning to your instrument as it was possible.

Is there another query, my sister?

Questioner: No. Thank you very much. I thought you were scared.

I am Latwii, and we do not scare so easily, my sister, but did enjoy the humorous aspects of the one known as Yadda. This entity has much to *(inaudible)* but we feel that it is quite capable of learning to utilize an instrument without such wear and tear.

Is there another query at this time?

(Tape ends.) ☘

L/L Research

L/L Research is a subsidiary of Rock Creek Research & Development Laboratories, Inc.

P.O. Box 5195
Louisville, KY 40255-0195

www.llresearch.org

Rock Creek is a non-profit corporation dedicated to discovering and sharing information which may aid in the spiritual evolution of humankind.

ABOUT THE CONTENTS OF THIS TRANSCRIPT: This telepathic channeling has been taken from transcriptions of the weekly study and meditation meetings of the Rock Creek Research & Development Laboratories and L/L Research. It is offered in the hope that it may be useful to you. As the Confederation entities always make a point of saying, please use your discrimination and judgment in assessing this material. If something rings true to you, fine. If something does not resonate, please leave it behind, for neither we nor those of the Confederation would wish to be a stumbling block for any.

CAVEAT: This transcript is being published by L/L Research in a not yet final form. It has, however, been edited and any obvious errors have been corrected. When it is in a final form, this caveat will be removed.

© 2009 L/L Research

Sunday Meditation
August 14, 1988

Group question: Concerns the changes on the Earth in relation to the greenhouse effect. There's been a lot of talking recently with our hot, hazy and humid weather as the cause, and we're wondering what kind of shape the Earth is in? Has the greenhouse effect been responsible for the changes that we've seen in the weather patterns? And just in general, what kind of shape is the Earth in?

(Carla channeling)

I am Q'uo, and I greet each in the love and the light of the one infinite Creator, whose power, glory and majesty you see about you in earth and sea and sky, in grassland and woods and desert plain. I greet you in the love that created all things and in the light of which all things are made. Above all I greet you in the polarity of service to others, for that question which you have asked this evening revolves quite directly around the question of service to others.

You wish to know basically the temperature, shall we say, or the readout of your native island home's situation as regards its viability at this particular point or nexus in time. You want to know [what] you can do and what can be done, you want to know if it is reversible or irreversible. May we thank the one who asked this question, while noting that there is a most basic misconception within the question itself, about which our message will deal perhaps more nearly primarily than the original question, for of the precise state of this planet, we cannot tell you, nor would we, could we; however, we cannot.

We can tell you that stasis is not a natural state, but rather change and evolution, and this includes the second density and the first as well as all the others. It is inevitable, therefore, that the planet which you call Earth shall undergo not just one, but many calamities in the course of its existence. You must remember that its lifetime and its children are more numerous than one can imagine from your perspective. Entire portions of your planet have been unviable in the past, and they shall again be in the future. This is the nature of the living process. That which comes into being has a various state of wellness, and in the end will dissolve into the dust from which it was formed. This is true of your planet, as it is true of each of you in a physical, or, shall we say, chemical yellow-ray body sense. Each building constructed shall one day be ruined, charred and piles of stone. Each smiling child and newborn babe shall one day have the wrinkled cheek of old age and cease the breathing in this little life you call life.

There is a great difference betwixt your planet which is of second-density awareness and yourselves which are of third-density or self-conscious awareness. The Earth itself lies within the power of the Logos, and does not fear change, even if the change be major and what those to whom we speak would call catastrophic. If there is to be the glacier or the greenhouse effect or the planetary shift or the great earthquake or the great conspiracy—one of several, we may add, that this instrument has heard—yet still the Earth itself shall not be afraid. Perhaps it shall feel sorrow, but it is still with the Logos; it is still imbued with love, wishing only to give and to receive that love.

For this simple reason, we would conclude this portion of our speaking by encouraging each of you to refrain from fear with the same faith of those who do not have self-consciousness, but know only the love and the light of the infinite Creator. This is a service-to-others planet, and one may see in the example of the helpful environment, the trees that breathe that which entities such as yourselves expire, and expire that which those of your kind breathe. This is one example, a rather obvious one, of the loving, serving, giving nature of second density. It moves to the light. Whatever happens to it, it shall survive in its own way, unless it be blasted to pieces, in which case it would simply die.

The planet can do a limited amount to aid a limited amount of people who are aware of places of energy which for them may be helpful. However, this aid is limited to those concepts and feelings which cannot be put into words. Thus, those whose church is the green cathedral of the forest, the mountains, and nature itself will find themselves as tongue-tied as the trees and flowers in attempting to describe or put into some meaningful context the experience of worship within the setting of nature, although it is perfectly acceptable to the Creator that the face of the Creator be seen in this density so filled with the Logos and Its consciousness.

Before we go on, we would note at this time that your yellow[-ray] physical bodies are also second-density creatures. We would now move on to the more important complex of ideas concerning what one may do to aid the planet.

As the planet and all the creatures upon it that grow and flower and turn to the light have consciousness, that consciousness is inspired and made to rejoice and flow in harmony and rhythm with any whose attention to it is loving and sweet. This is why the song sung in love aids the flower, and the soft voice helps the vegetables grow. This is why there are things other than your fertilizer and your—this instrument uses the word—pesticide that can truly aid the planet on a far more basic level for you. If you correct the soil or plant the correct crops in order to grow according to that soil, you are indeed aiding the planet by aiding its productivity, but if you have not love for the seed and love for the soil, then the second-density creatures which are the object of your dutious tending do not become self-aware, or aware of their own beauty or their own usefulness or their own sacrifice.

Beauty, function and sacrifice are three great principles of self-consciousness. They, that is those creatures which dwell in second density, are attempting to become self-conscious enough, that is, invested with enough personal consciousness of self to become fully human and begin to interact and move about the planet to learn the lessons of love once again, those very lessons which they surrender at second-density graduation in order to move into third density, study, think, experience, feel and integrate the catalyst therein and make the choice between fourth-density positive or service to others aspects of love and service to self aspects of that same love.

Thus, what one may do to aid the planet begins with the being which walks upon the grass, aware of and thanking the Earth for its energy. It is the entity which forms relationships with those second-density creatures about it, speaking with them or silently caring for them, that invest in love those creatures turning to the light to the point where they not only turn to the light, but know that they are turning to the light. It is your density's confusion as to how to use that light, for, oh, how easy it is to choose to use that light, that power, that glory of being independent, to make free choices that do not polarize one in service to others or in some way to not aid the survival of the entity. Indeed, there are many actively self-destructive souls who polarize neither towards the positive nor the negative, but in a self-destructive manner sabotage the good with the bad, the bad with the good, remaining forever in the well of indifference which lies between the two polarities.

To aid the planet, we urge each to walk upon it and bless it, to admire the accidents of the day, the blooms that have been freely given, whether there is an eye to see or no. We urge each to be aware of the beauty, the truth, the sanctity of that green cathedral that lies without the shuttered windows of human habitation upon your planet. Were we not aware of the fragility of your physical vehicles, we would urge each to sleep upon the ground; we would urge each to make the connection, for there is a vitality to the Logos which the second-density physical body has, but which the mind complex of third-density entities most usually disables because of cultural conditioning to the contrary.

The Earth wishes to aid. It loves its human entities. It is aware that much negative energy is being stored within the Earth's crust at this time, yet it is not resentful, but merely rueful that it may be forced to inflict damage upon creatures of third density at some time. This is the natural attitude of one which is nurturing by nature. There is no negative feeling within your planet. That which is negative within your planet are those vibrations which have been placed within it by the thought forms of those which have dwelt upon it. In order to serve those life forms, it would gladly die. May we say that the effect upon the life forms which blew it up would be burdensome in terms of your sense of time.

We would like to end this discourse on an encouraging note, and we may, we are happy to say. The planet has hit, as far as we can tell, a critical mass for raising planetary consciousness. It has done so through the help of numerous—may we use the word "wanderer"—wanderers, many of whom have chosen the arts, especially the music, to express their views, so that what this instrument would call "USA for Africa" and other such planetary events, days such as your day of forgiveness and your day of peace being planetary events also, these have aided in an exponential fashion the light quality within the planet which you love.

Therefore, the deepest and most profound change that you may make within the planet is that change which you make within yourself, for you may feel that only your feet touch the planet, yet it is your heart which touches the heart of the planet, and the heart of the planet and the heart of the self touch the heart of the great Self, the one Creator, which unifies and is both planet and entities. Thus, if you have the mind full of light, you answer in perfect unison with the planet which is already filled with light, and already, before you have even brought together a group of light-givers to the planet, you have a majority, shall we say, of two: all those upon the planet which may feel your light and yourself.

Thus, to be concerned about weather, catastrophes and other things upon the planet, is to be concerned in a macrocosmic way with that which you should be concerned in a microcosmic way—that is, the death of the self. And what you would do to aid the planet is precisely what you may do to aid the cells of your second-density body. Indeed, there is no density which is not moved by the honest declaration of love, faith and unqualified support. We do not ask you to do this as a duty. We do ask you perhaps to find affirmations in which you believe, and to repeat them often, or simply to tell that earth, tree, bush, flower, plant about you mentally or out loud, "I love you." Enjoy the sun; enjoy the rain: "You give me pleasure." Thus do you, in second-density terms, polarize the entity towards personhood.

May each of you place his feet upon the earth and know it to be holy ground. May your heart move in rhythmic consciousness with all that is. May you feel and allow yourselves to be part of an infinite creation which is all one thing. May you seek that All-Consciousness daily in silent meditation, for there in the silence shall be not only the response to this question that is most true for you, but the recognition of all that is truth for you. We ask you to use that discrimination when listening to any words, most of all our own, for we have our opinions, but we are not infallible.

We thank you for calling us to your group, and we thank the one known as H for offering this question, which is an interesting one, and one which allows us perhaps to reverse some of the panic which entities upon your planet feel as they see seemingly irreversible destruction. Fear not. Short of mankind blowing up this particular sphere, this sphere itself shall do whatever is necessary, including major surgery, shall we say, to adjust to new vibrations and to thrive and grow in consciousness, in love and in personhood. May you invest all of nature that you can with its own knowledge of itself. May you love it as it loves you. May you love each other. May you love your bodies.

We find that there is more upon this subject. However, we do also find that this instrument feels that the cosmic sermonette, as she calls it, has proceeded long enough for one night, and we are beginning to respect this instrument's sense of the local time more than our own, as we have been wrong constantly in gauging the amount of your time our apparently lengthy discourses do take. Please forgive us. At this time we would pause to allow the one known as Jim to retune and when this instrument is in a state in which he feels comfortable, we would invite him to ask for our contact. We will pause until that moment. We are those of Q'uo.

(Pause)

(Jim channeling)

I am Q'uo, and greet each again in love and light through this instrument. At this time it is our privilege to offer ourselves in the attempt to speak to any further query which may remain upon the minds of those present. Again we remind each that we offer that which is our opinion. We offer it joyfully, that you may use it as you will, leaving behind those portions which do not ring of truth for you. Is there a query at this time?

Carla: Well, I have one. You stopped by saying, "love your body." You just stopped, and then it's like there was more, but … Was that what there was more of? I mean, was it at that point? Should we ask, "What can we do to love our bodies?" Or is it a question that it's okay to ask now?

I am Q'uo. As we gave that thought to your instrument, we thought ourselves of the admonition in regards to time, and thus, at another working such as this, if additional information concerning your Earth home is requested, we would be most happy to speak upon the topic of your Earth and of your bodies, of their relationships, and of the care that may be shown to each and which may, when applied to the body of the Earth, aid in its healing, as the healing of your physical body is accomplished by repair.

Carla: We'll definitely wait on that one, then. Thank you.

I am Q'uo, and we thank you, my sister. Is there another query?

Carla: Well, what about the people from Maldek that blew their planet up, and the people from Mars? Those two civilizations both. Look at Lemuria—it's a continuing pattern here of people basically wiping out their habitat. Is it inevitable for third-density people to do that? No, don't answer that question. You really already did. It just seems so strange that it's happened again and again and again.

I am Q'uo, and we would comment only to suggest that within your solar system there has been a great variety of experience, from the most disharmonious to the most harmonious, and it is within this range of experience that much has been learned. Not all progress is achieved in an harmonious fashion. Much there is of love that is learned by experiencing its polar opposite.

Is there another query at this time?

J: I have a query, but as usual, I'm thinking it through before I throw it out. My question is in regards to our concern with survival in the context of the coming planetary adjustment. Would you comment, please, regarding if our concerns are focused on personal survival, can that be construed as service to self? Are we overly concerned with personal? And is that a distraction from what we should be doing, which is service to others?

I am Q'uo, and am aware of your query, my sister The concern which many of your peoples feel at this time for their physical survival is not pursued by these entities in most cases in a manner which could be construed to be of a negative nature, for the negative path of service to self is a rigorous path which requires that one traveling this path utilize all the energies of the self and the concerns of the self to master the environment and those about one in order that the self may be served by these entities. Most upon your planet which are concerned at this time with the potential for destruction and the hope for survival are utilizing the situation that has developed as a result of the increasing technological abilities of your various nation states, as you call them, and the continuing tendency towards the disharmonious events and feelings that tend to divide one group from another and cause the potential for further disharmony to increase.

The focus upon this situation can be utilized by an entity in any number of ways which may or may not increase the polarity, and thus the harvestability, of that entity. One may look upon the situation and see an opportunity to give selflessly of the energies and abilities that one has accumulated within the life experience, and to share the knowledge of how to resolve the difficulties, how to give that which is needed to those which need. Another may look upon the same situation and find reason for frustration, confusion and hopelessness to ensue with the life pattern, and thus begin to color the catalyst that belongs to this entity with the fear, the doom, the dread, and the withdrawing of the self from those about one. Yet another entity may look upon the situation and see that which is improbable and, if probable, too great for one's concern and thus ignore the entire situation, retiring into the concerns of the self and the family.

There are many, many ways in which entities upon your planet may look upon any situation. The situation that is focused upon is not that which determines the polarity of the entity, but rather, how the entity looks upon the situation and how the entity responds to it. This in turn is greatly influenced by the, what we would call, preincarnative programming or the framework [of] reference, the perception that one has as the foundation of one's personality and the opportunity for learning that is presented thereby.

Thus, all catalyst that is presented to an entity within an incarnational pattern will be filtered through the unconscious biases of that entity before entering the conscious mind of that entity and will thereupon be deflected or diffracted in such a way that the entity will be able to utilize this catalyst, whatever its nature, in a way which is unique to that entity and which matches that entity's preincarnatively set lessons and potentials for service.

May we speak in any further fashion, my sister?

J: I do have a question, but I haven't formulated it, so if anyone would like to ask a question, go on ahead. Thank you for your response.

I am Q'uo, and we thank you, my sister. Is there another query at this time?

Carla: I guess I'll have to read that answer. Let me ask the question another way. Is it of service to others simply to move to the country simply because you enjoy it, but of service to self to keep people from enjoying it with you in a time of crisis? Is that basically what you were saying?

I am Q'uo, and am aware of your query, my sister. We find that this is a new area of investigation, one that is more specific to the query than the previous query covered. Again, the action of moving to your rural environment can be utilized by an entity in any manner, that of polarizing toward the service to self or the service to others, or in most cases, remaining betwixt the two. It is the motivation or intention of an entity, whatever the action taken, that tends to bias the action in one manner or another. There is the potential for either polarity or neither polarity to result from any action. The polarity is determined by the intention that motivates the action. This is the principle which we were attempting to share in our previous response.

May we speak in any further fashion, my sister?

Carla: To just further nail it down. So if we decide that some elite can be with us, but some who are not elite cannot, then we've probably moved over into service to self. Is that correct?

(Side one of tape ends.)

(Jim channeling)

I am Q'uo, and am again with this instrument. Is there another query at this time?

Carla: Well, I hate to hog the show, but I do have a query, and please feel free to advise me that this is an infringement. I will not go through all that occurred with the one known as R, but will simply ask for any comment that you might have, either on the situation, what could be done to aid the teach/learner in spotting and ameliorating and avoiding such a situation in the future for everybody, any comments you have about the teach/learning of the channeling process and of the magical personality. I know it's a wide question, but I have a feeling that the comments are not so wide. So. You'll probably tell me that I've got to think it through myself, right?

I am Q'uo, and am aware of your query, my sister. We find in this instance that there is a great deal of information which is desired in order that a more harmonious experience in future teaching sessions might be achieved, for there has been the difficulty with the one known as R which has caused concern for each entity. And we would add our blessings to the concerns which each feels, for there is the need to learn from that which has been experienced. However, we find in this instance that there is yet much work which may be accomplished upon the personal level in regards to this experience, and would recommend that the line of querying or consideration which has been undertaken since this experience be continued, for we find that there has been much of a fruitful nature that has resulted from this intensive investigation into the nature of the self, the nature of the teach/learner and the nature of the channeling experience itself. We feel that each has been able to profit, shall we say, from this experience in regards to reaffirming to the self the level of care that is necessary upon each entity's part when attempting to teach and to learn the vocal channeling process.

We find that we have exhausted that which we may share without infringement at this time and apologize for seeming to be so shy of words or advice.

Carla: I understand, because my concern is whether I should be teaching channeling or not, and you can't tell me that, can you?

I am Q'uo. We choose, my sister, not to infringe, for we do not see that as a service, as you are aware.

Carla: I understand. I'm just very soft-hearted, and I don't like to hurt people or put them in a position where energies might cause them to fall apart. I guess I have a lot of thinking to do. Thank you. It never happened to me before, so …

I am Q'uo, and we share with you great compassion, my sister, for we recognize the desire to serve burns very, very brightly within your being. And it is the method by which such sharing shall proceed that you are now considering, and we add our blessings to your considerations.

Carla: Thank you.

Is there another query at this time?

J: I would like to speak to the same question as Carla, and again I realize you may not wish to answer it, and that's okay. But having been part of the "R experience," if we can call it that, I have to say that I was a bit spooked, and being a new channel student, it was probably an experience that if I had to have it, I wish I would have had it down the road as opposed to during the first week. I have to admit that it has me in a major state of confusion, and understand that you cannot address that personal problem, and I will continue to try to work it out for myself.

But if there is some way that you can comment on the experience, maybe suggest a viewpoint that those of us who were there might take to turn it to a positive experience so that we will continue to channel. Basically I guess I feel that I'm not very trusting of the protections that I thought were there. Or that I don't understand them. I haven't asked you a clear question yet—I'm trying to do that. I guess what I'm asking for is some kind of understanding that will give me confidence to try it again at some form, and if you could comment on that.

I am Q'uo, and am aware of your query and its ramifications to you, my sister. First of all, we might suggest that the experience which you witnessed and which you have called the "R experience" is one which is quite unusual and is not one which many students, whether new students or old students of the vocal channeling process, would encounter within their learning of this means of service. It is one which required very unusual circumstances—the gift for visualization and deep meditation upon the part of the one known as R, the extremely enhanced energy vortex which was created by the entire group of positively-oriented entities during the time of sharing, and the disregarding of techniques of protection by the one known as R at a critical time within his own personal process of growth. These are circumstances which each taken separately would not be remarkable, but when combined, did indeed provide the experience which has been remarkable.

We might encourage each new instrument which seeks to learn the vocal channeling process by suggesting that the process itself is quite simple. The protection, as well, is quite simple. However, the clear understanding within the heart and mind of each student that partakes in this process is necessary in order that these simple procedures be accomplished in a pure fashion. The desire and the motivations of each student must be examined by each student in a most careful fashion in order that the channel within the being is open in as clear and simple a fashion as possible. When these protections and motivations are thus accomplished, the process may be expected to proceed with little risk or danger to the student.

May we speak to any further query, my sister?

J: Not at this time, thank you.

Carla: I'd like to ask a shorty. Could you confirm that the protection that I give the circle itself is adequate, or even more than adequate? That people can be confident of it, unless the entity is part of the personality of the new channel, in which case I would have no jurisdiction over it, and that is why I could do no more than talk to Yadda and make sure that Yadda was attempting to control the situation.

This is what I believe happened. I just wondered if you could confirm it.

I am Q'uo, and your assumption is basically correct, my sister. The protection that you as teach/learner provide for the circle of new instruments, and the protection that each within the circle provides each other in the seeking is a function again of the clear and simple motivation, the desire and the practice upon the part of each which partakes within the circle. Thus, the circle is, as we find your saying speaks, as strong as the weakest link. However, even the weakest link may be enhanced by the combined efforts of each within the circle. Thus, each adds unto the wall of light, shall we say, that forms about such a circle of seeking, as this circle of seeking has provided its own wall of light.

Is there another query, my sister?

Carla: I'm just arbitrarily going to stop, because I don't want to wear the instrument out. Thank you very much. I'll ask another time.

I am Q'uo, and we thank you, my sister. Is there another query?

J: I have one. Again, I realize you may not be able to answer this question, but with the "R incident," I realized it was not really … it was our incident, it was not what we call the "R incident," but I'm doing it because I don't have another name for it. But I just want to clarify, let them all realize that we were all key players in that situation.

What I'm confused about is when the situation did occur, how much R was channeling himself, and how much he was channeling something outside of himself. The reason I'm concerned is because of something he said in reference to me which has *(inaudible)*. Let me try to put this question in a way that you might be able to answer it.

Okay. If you can give me percentages, say, how much R was channeling something inside himself, how much of Confederation membership he was channeling, and how much was psychic greeting?

I am Q'uo, and we find that there is a difficulty in answering with precise percentages in regards to the efforts of the one known as R to serve as a vocal instrument in the one case, and the efforts of the one known as R to deal with a difficult personal situation in another case. We may suggest that all new instruments—and this includes the one known as R—begin the channeling process with a fairly significant portion of the channeled message being of their own origination. This is in order that the new instrument might begin the process, and we of the Confederation of Planets in the Service of the One Creator find it helpful to spark those personal memories and experiences within the new instrument which are congruent with our understanding of the Law of Love and the Law of Understanding and Unity in order that a beginning might be made.

As the new instrument becomes more experienced, this percentage of personally originated material shrinks until it is approximately thirty percent, and thus our portion would be the greater, that is, seventy percent. Thus you may see, the new instrument begins with a fairly significant, even a majority of the information channeled having its origin within the self of the instrument. We may suggest, therefore, that you not be overly concerned with any information which was transmitted during the experience of the one known as R which each present within that circle did indeed have a part to share, however small. We would not suggest that the information channeled through the one known as R therefore be given very great weight.

May we speak to any further query, my sister?

J: No, thank you. I really appreciate your answering the question, but I like your answer.

Carla: I can't stand that—I've got to ask a related one. From what I could tell, by the time R was on the floor, he was channeling a mixture of a negative entity, which called itself anything it wanted to, and wanted to control, and a portion of his own personality which had the same basic motives, thereby forming a rather efficient service-to-others channel out of a very sensitive, positive instrument. Can you confirm this? That there was not Confederation content in that message on the floor?

I am Q'uo, and we may make this basic confirmation with additional notation that there was a slight misperception in your query concerning the nature of the service offered.

Carla: Does that have to do with my Christian background? That distortion?

I am Q'uo. We simply meant to speak to what we feel was a misstatement on your part in using the term "service to others" rather [than] "service to self."

Carla: Oh, thank you very much. Yes. I meant service to self. Yeah.

I am Q'uo. Is there another query at this time?

Carla: Is that why he wouldn't [let] me touch him, and he wouldn't let me in the circle? Because I was too much of a polarized towards service-to-others nature?

I am Q'uo, and we find that we again approach that line of infringement across which we do not wish to step at this time.

Carla: May I ask if there is more than one motive for not allowing the touching? Or if there is only one? That would help me in my thinking.

I am Q'uo, and am aware of your query, my sister. We do not wish to either confuse your thinking or to clarify it at this time, for to do either, we feel, would be an infringement. Thus, we choose not to speak to this query.

Carla: You would recommend simple analysis then?

I am Q'uo. We would recommend your powers of analysis be applied, your powers of prayer and meditation be added, and that the clarification of time passing might also be an aid in this case.

Carla: Well, I sure do thank you a lot for answering. I've been pestering you. I'm sorry. I'll stop.

I am Q'uo. We thank you. Not only for your queries, my sister, but for your deep desire to serve, as well. Is there another query at this time?

Questioner: I do have a question, and what sparks it is that in our circle tonight we have a young gentleman, and given what we were talking about earlier, about Earth adjustments—which is my favorite phrase—how can we best prepare children, or how can we talk to children about this kind of thing, and how can we make them understand their role? Kids at this age—and I'm talking about children probably eighteen and under—are not especially aware of their personal power. They haven't had a lot of experience with personal power, so they may not understand that they really do have a significant role to play. How would you recommend that that could be described to them? Does that question make sense?

I am Q'uo, and we feel that there is quite sufficient sense within the query in order that we might speak. The universe is the classroom for each student, whether the student be young or old in experience and in years. Each has within the life pattern a portion of the universe; each may look within any portion of the life pattern and see a reflection of that which is within and that which is without. Your own solar system is much likened unto the molecule within any portion of your creation. Each molecule is much likened unto a universe itself, with atoms moving with incredible speed and fluidity. Each person may be seen to be composed of many smaller parts of organs, of veins, of arteries, of cells, of tissue, and each plays a part within the scope and health of the entire organism.

Each person within a family, within a community, within a classroom has a part to play that influences the whole. The whole of the classroom, of the family, of the community has an influence upon each individual. The touch and presence and mark made by each entity is felt not only within the family, the classroom, and the community, but is felt within the planetary being and indeed throughout the one creation, for there is a connection between all portions of creation. As a note played upon a musical instrument is heard by any ear within its range of sound, thus are feelings and thoughts and actions recorded within the self, within the family, within the Earth itself and indeed each is heard as a note throughout the one creation.

Thus, each student of life may learn of that which is great by looking at that which is small, may learn of that which is without by looking at that which is within, may also learn in the reverse order, as correlations can be made from small to large, from within to without. Those connecting fibers and pathways which bind each to the other and each to the planet and each planet to the creation are those pathways which lead from understanding of one kind to understanding of another. Thus may each discover that which one sees within the realm of one's own being.

May we speak in any further fashion, my sister?

Questioner: No, thank you.

I am Q'uo, and we thank you again, my sister. At this time we shall take our leave of this instrument and this group, for we find that we have brought each to the point of information gathering which begins to move beyond the ability to process at this time. As always, we are most humbly grateful to have been invited to join your circle this evening, and we hope that we have been able to serve in the manner which has been asked of us. We look forward with joy to each future, as you call it, gathering, and shall be with you upon your request. We are known to you as those of Q'uo, and we leave each at this time in the love and in the light of the one infinite Creator. Adonai, my friends. Adonai.

Sunday Meditation
August 31, 1988

Group question: Has to do with lying. How does the concept of lying, deliberately and willfully misrepresenting a position or information, get introduced into our creation? From the beginning of the creation when that which is created is created out of that which is uncreated.

(Carla channeling)

I am Q'uo.

(There are no other contents in the file.)

L/L Research

Sunday Meditation
September 4, 1988

Group question: How does the seeker balance the various polar opposites such as passion in the seeking and yet discrimination in the seeking? Love and giving and wisdom and how to do this? The unconscious and the conscious mind? The female nature being receptive and the male nature being active? All of these polar opposites are part of following the path. How does the seeker balance them?

(Carla channeling)

I am Q'uo. We greet you in the love and in the light of the one infinite Creator, and we thank you for calling us to your group to share our thoughts on the paradoxes of the spiritual journey and how to balance them. We thank you for the great privilege of sharing in your vibrations, and we shall attempt, as this instrument has mentally requested, to be extremely brief, for us, that there may be ample time for the soul-satisfying inner journey of silence.

Since it is accepted by those present that in the beginning all things were one, it is difficult to comprehend the nature of paradox, or opposites—not precisely the same thing. And as the student attempts more and more to accelerate its spiritual growth, it finds itself faced squarely again and again with paradox: service to others makes one feel good, therefore, it is service to self.

Waiting, the reaching, the female archetypal personality becomes a passive power that paradoxically holds the riches for which the male active principle must most carefully reach and most sensitively find. And when it comes to speaking of passion, we come to a paradox that is different for each seeking entity, the paradox between passion and skepticism.

Let us look at the nature of each of you. Each of you has a heart, a center of being, and in that center of being, beneath all the dust and rubble of sadness and sorrow, pain and suffering, and the petty details of mundane life, lie the fiery jewels of passion, that creative force that sleeps within from the beginning of creation as you know it. For that of you which is of God is passion in its most manifest expression, thus passion is not something for which one strives as much as it is something for which one looks within the self.

The easiest passion to understand is the passion of the sexes—man for woman and woman for man. But has there ever been a man so passionate, or a woman, that there was not the skepticism also, certainly when it was deserved, and often when it was not. This is due to each entity's having biases that cause a lack of trust, and cut the flow of power at some lower energy center, depending upon the difficulty, thus effectively removing the self from the experience of passion. And anyone to whom we speak within third density who has not had the experience of the infinitely divine act of love being spoiled by a lack of trust, we commend that person, for it is almost inevitable that in interpersonal relationships, sexual energy shall from time to time be strangled by the skepticism of one partner for another, the doubt one has in another's trust and loyalty.

Thus, you see, you yourselves contain paradox. It is not something that has been thrust upon you. What has been thrust upon you by a serious program of meditation and seeking are new ways of perceiving blockages of power, imbalances in interpersonal energies, and any similar lack of complete communication.

It is no good to seek to encourage oneself to feel passion for a casually selected object. This is true of the generative chakra or of red ray. This is true in the higher elements of interpersonal relationships, for mental and spiritual passion may unite and strengthen and teach each, yet where also much hurt, inevitably, [much] will be shared. This is true in the passions one may have towards society, for as much as one wishes that in your illusion all may be fair and all may be just in all states, men and women may be honorable, and all plans tending towards peace, yet it is impossible to become active and work within your social systems and not develop a healthy and accurate skepticism. The illusion lacks paradox only to those who have not thought about the illusion.

The more one thinks about the illusion and about one's relationship with the Creator, the more one is plunged into a series of paradoxes. Life as we know it—and we must remind you that we are students, such as yourselves—is a spiral, the best symbol of which we may find in this instrument's mind being the double helix of that which this instrument calls DNA, that which has within it the intelligence, microscopic though it may be, to create an entire physical body, ready for a soul to use.

Thus, in one incarnation, the balance between passion and skepticism may be reflecting imbalances towards passion in previous incarnations, or an imbalance toward wisdom or a skepticism in earlier incarnations. Perhaps our best advice upon the subject is ceaselessly to seek your passion, whether it be an established path toward the face of mystery, or whether you make it up as you go along. That which is your truth, that which is your passion, will develop, resonate and become passion. It does not normally spring full-blown, although as one has heard of love at first sight, meaning instant red ray infatuation, which may well deepen into love, so may the spiritual student lay aside skepticism in the excitement of a system of thought which later is found to be wanting, and skepticism again takes over.

It is well to expect the movement back and forth betwixt the two horns of any paradox within your illusion, for upon the one horn is eternity, upon the other infinity; upon the one hand, yourself as a portion of the Creator, upon the other hand, yourself as you perceive yourself, experiencing that which you perceive that you experience.

Needless to say, we urge skepticism whenever there is the slightest doubt that the path that one is on is the correct one for that person. And we urge those who have faith and passion and care deeply about their paths already, ceaselessly to examine with the powers of skepticism and the rational mind what the mind feels about that passion. Now, the mind is not a passionate being; it is in essence what this instrument would call a biocomputer. Therefore the mind will tend to analyze the experience of worship, faith, joy, unity, consolation, forgiveness and love. And in that we say, please proceed and think and ponder, because the mind has a part in the evolution of the spirit.

But to grasp with the mind that which is occurring in spiritual worship experience, or in passion of any level, is to ask the impossible of the linear mind, therefore there must be a bridge betwixt the two. That bridge is, of course, meditation. We could choose any other seeming opposite. For the sake of simplicity, we again turn to the male and female antitheses of being. Again, in some instances, it is well for a male to behave as a male has been taught to behave in one's culture, no matter what the sacrifice. On the other hand, if one cannot with joy and in some sense of peace perform such duties, they become only duties and never honors. Therefore, one must take time for oneself and in the same life experience take sacrificial time with those who may require, need or be grateful for the listing[4] ear, the understanding heart, and the patient tongue.

---

[4] The Oxford English Dictionary gives "listing" as a synonym of "listening" and dates it as a 17th century usage.

There are other times when neither patience nor introspection may suffice, when that which must be said honestly is said to the temporary sorrow of each. Remember, however, that if the seeker remains day by day by day focused upon the treasure of life itself, the treasure of consciousness, and the goal and desire of progressing in consciousness, one may become ever more sensitive to the needs of the self for the balancing that exists at that spiral at that moment, for you do not go around in small circles, not in your job, not in your home life, not in any part of your experience. Each day there is the seeing of new things, and if this be not so, it is time to look for paradox, for you are spiritual beings, and there is more than gusto to grab, my friends.

We would at this time pause for silent meditation, hoping that that which we have said, which is an outline only, may be in some degree helpful. Further questions will be welcomed at the end of the meeting. In thanksgiving and praise to the one Creator, we leave this instrument. We wish to say to the one known as T, that if this entity is experiencing the energy of Hatonn, that is as it should be, as this entity wishes to aid the one known as T in deepening the meditative state in a stable and comfortable manner without the fatigue of the day, shall we say, catching up with him. For now, we leave this instrument in love and light. I am Q'uo.

(Transcript ends.)

L/L Research

L/L Research is a subsidiary of Rock Creek Research & Development Laboratories, Inc.

P.O. Box 5195
Louisville, KY 40255-0195

www.llresearch.org

Rock Creek is a non-profit corporation dedicated to discovering and sharing information which may aid in the spiritual evolution of humankind.

ABOUT THE CONTENTS OF THIS TRANSCRIPT: This telepathic channeling has been taken from transcriptions of the weekly study and meditation meetings of the Rock Creek Research & Development Laboratories and L/L Research. It is offered in the hope that it may be useful to you. As the Confederation entities always make a point of saying, please use your discrimination and judgment in assessing this material. If something rings true to you, fine. If something does not resonate, please leave it behind, for neither we nor those of the Confederation would wish to be a stumbling block for any.

CAVEAT: This transcript is being published by L/L Research in a not yet final form. It has, however, been edited and any obvious errors have been corrected. When it is in a final form, this caveat will be removed.

© 2009 L/L Research

Sunday Meditation
September 18, 1988

Group question: Asking for general information on the subject of selfishness.

(Carla channeling)

I am Q'uo. I greet you in the love and in the light of the one infinite Creator. It is a joy to meditate with this circle, and we thank this group for calling us to you to share our humble opinion upon the subject of selfishness. Indeed, it is most selfish that we are here, for by our choice of serving you, we find the possibilities of accelerating our own spiritual growth much improved. Thus, we are being selfish as well as unselfish, when we speak in groups such as your own. Indeed, the question of selfishness has its root in the question of self. Some concepts are known to you all: that there is one Self, and that that one Self is love, and that therefore, one is always serving the self.

With that said, we may say that in your illusion each unique portion of the greater Self or love moves into incarnation in your lifetime now with a predetermined character and biased way of hearing and perceiving stimulus. That is, each person sees things quite differently. Some have little capacity to register or perceive the difficulties of others besides themselves, and this is perceived as very selfish behavior. It is in fact not a selfish behavior, but a constitutional or preincarnative way of being. There are others whose selflessness or lack of interest in the self and the things pertaining to the aggrandizement of the self is so marked that these entities are often known as saints, especially those who have died, especially those who have died for that in which they believed, that for which they lived, that for which they received persecution.

Between lie the vast majority of souls which inhabit your physical Earth sphere at this time. These are entities whose personalities are constitutionally capable either of self-involvement or involvement with others. It then becomes, for the vast majority of entities, a matter of choice as to whether to serve the self by controlling and manipulating others, or to serve the self by serving others.

When one serves the self by manipulating others, one is often known as selfish. Another way of gazing at this trait in an entity is to see the entity choosing a path of polarization that would be called the left-handed path or the negative path in which the self is seen as the equivalent of or substitute for the Creator, and the constellation of those beings which move about the self are seen as those entities which may or not be of use in some way to the God-self which lies within the self. Such entities are not known for their spiritual humility or their lack of confidence in what they feel to be right.

All of these hard edges that we described, these overassurances, pomposities, rash assumptions and manipulations, create catalyst for those about them, catalysts in which they may experience the infringement upon the free will in one way or another, and they then make their own choices as to how to react. There are, in fact, two perfectly acceptable ways to react, one being service to self, one being service to others. Due to the nature of your illusion, it is far easier to react in service to self than it is in service to others. It is not easy to love those who are discriminating against you, causing you difficulty, or creating pain by catalyst in your existence. Consequently, many people there are who inadvertently do polarize by becoming enangered by the selfish reactions of another person. It is well to remember that each entity creates its own universe by its reaction to the catalyst it receives. You may choose to create a positive, though challenging, universe, faced with just such a relationship. This, however, is certainly a challenge, as it always a challenge to love those, as it says in the holy work, your Bible, who despitefully use you.

There is the service-to-others way to react to the entities about one. One may choose to attempt to be of service. This may seem very selfless and generous. It is interesting to note how very difficult it is truly to be of service to another. Yes, one may please another, but pleasing and serving other selves are two separate processes. In the first place, that which you may think is helpful to another may not be welcomed by that entity. In the second place, that which that entity wishes, you may not be able to perform. In both cases, service to others then seems to be a null option.

This logic, as all logic when applied to spiritual reasoning, is fundamentally incorrect, for one's basic service to others and sense of self are the same thing. The way that entities are, that is, the sum total of vibratory patterns generated by the thoughts, actions and feelings of an entity at a given moment are the gifts one gives to the Creator and to the world about him. The beingness is the first act of selfishness or unselfishness, of radiance or absorption. When your beingness touches in with the tabernacle of the most high and a portion of your consciousness remains in that holy place, then all places are holy; all entities are of the Christ consciousness, and the eyes with which you look at those entities are eyes infinite in their ability to channel the one original Thought of the infinite Creator—love.

Let us look at one more aspect of selfishness before we leave this instrument. It often concerns those who are highly oriented toward service to others that they continually must spend a large amount of time working upon themselves. This is not selfish, my friends, and do not for a minute think that it is selfish to work upon a relationship with yourself, with the creation about you, and with the Creator who made you. If you are to prepare and discipline your personality so that you may be of the maximum amount of service, a hollowing out process takes place, in which the concept of self as you know it now begins to undergo a change.

Those things which are of the material world may seem most desirable, those things which are of the invisible world, most distant. Yet may we say that your material world is an illusion, known so to your scientists, who describe everything as whirling masses of energy, not masses of things, so that dependence upon the reality of anything upon the outside world plane is a jest, although a very convincing one.

To move into the true nature is gradually to move away from consensus reality as it is known by your culture and your society, and to move into an individual and idiosyncratic way of thinking, feeling and acting, a way in which you interpret your relationship with eternity in the light of your temporary involvement with your own body as well as the bodies and inextinguishable spirits of other souls, other portions of the Creator with whom you may come in contact. Never begrudge the time it takes to keep yourself as clear as possible of those things which block the energy from the heart, those fears and possessions, being possessed, being trapped, being lost. All the inadequacies and fears that you may have, we ask you gradually to clear those from the conscious mind, to allow them to drift away upon the wind.

Needless to say, we urge you to do this through meditation, through affirmation, and through any other process which functions well for you, for you are different and special, and not like anyone else, and those things that are true for another may not be so for you. Therefore, the work continues in a lonely and individualized way. Yes, there are companions along the way. Yes, there may be teachers when you need them. But always it is each seeking soul's choice to follow the self to the higher self, and thus empty out the little self and become as nearly selfless and impersonal as possible when dealing with others with true compassion. Or fill in the self more and more with the little self until the material world becomes quite solid and eternity recedes and is hidden behind a screen of forgetting.

We feel that the true selfishness is to choose the path of service to others, and we are not playing with words here. We have found it to be the quicker path, the easier path, and by far the more joyful path. We find the increasing lack of competition to be most satisfying, and the ability ultimately to merge together as one creative, collaborative being infinitely gratifying. We do not grasp the reasons for the choice of service-to-self entities, and so we simply say to you, there is that choice, yet it is not what we teach, nor is it what you *(inaudible)*.

Therefore, we ask that each self free the self from self-accusations of selfishness. We ask each who feels that another is selfish to forgive and cease from judging, for who knows where the selfishness may lie and who must be forgiven in final accounting. How interesting shall it be, my friends, for each of you to gaze back over the pages of this incarnational experience and find how accurate you were in the many, many times you took your spiritual temperature. We assure you, you are too hard upon yourselves. We assure you, your sense of humor will come *(inaudible)* you.

Thank you again for calling us to you, and we would now transfer, that we may answer any questions that you may have at this time. We would at this time transfer. I thank this instrument, and am known to you as Q'uo.

(Jim channeling)

I am Q'uo, and greet each again in love and light through this instrument. At this time it is our honor to ask if there might be any queries which we may speak to. Is there a query at this time?

T: Yes, I have a question. It regards affirmations and changing your thought processes using affirmations. I've been doing this for the last couple of months pretty regularly. My question to you is, to change a thought process, you affirm what you want to change to, and you affirm that you no longer have a need for whatever blocking or limiting beliefs keep you in what you're thinking now, your limiting patterns now.

My question is, when you use affirmations, is the most important thing just faithfulness and repetition, or is it necessary to develop an intensity or kind of a fervor when you do affirmations, to make them more effective? Or is it just a combination of both?

I am Q'uo, and am aware of your query, my brother. The field of which you speak is one which is large in scope, when applied to personal belief in the behavior and the roots from which they spring. The attempt to change beliefs and the behavior which is associated with such beliefs through the process of reaffirming or reforming that belief in an alternate manner will find success according to a number of factors, including those which you have mentioned.

The attempt to change belief that is an integral portion of one's being, having been chosen previous to the incarnation for a specific purpose, will be somewhat less successful than attempting to reform a belief which has been created during the incarnational pattern of existence. Many are the roots of each entity's system of belief, some reaching as far back as the preincarnative choice, others taking root in the early years of the incarnation, according to the experiences and the teachings that the entity is exposed to at that time, yet others taking root at a much later portion within the incarnation, having been consciously accepted as a portion of one's system of thought and resulting behavior.

In general, we might suggest that the attempt to reconfigure the belief patterns through affirmation and the fervent and repetitive type of affirmation will be more successful the more recent the belief is which is being reformed. There are within the incarnational pattern various suppositions or beliefs which have to do with the heart or focus, the purpose of the incarnation. These are not so easily reformed, for the power and fervor which formed them in their beginning was not only of the conscious mind, but of the subconscious mind as well. These will yield not so easily to conscious affirmations, but if they yield at all, will need to be worked upon from the level of the subconscious mind, the level at which they were formed.

May we speak in any further fashion, my brother?

T: Well, is there any easy way to tell which is which? I realize through meditation, if you meditate long enough, you'll probably start to know what is what, and maybe I'm answering my own question, but if you could comment on that?

I am Q'uo. The means by which one might ascertain the strength and source of current belief patterns are also various. There are entities who have studied the nature of their own self for a long enough span of your time that they are aware of the parallel patterns that have appeared with the incarnation and are able to pinpoint the beliefs which have formed about these repeating patterns. There is the means of determination which you have mentioned, that being contemplation, prayer or meditation, during which there is the opening of the conscious mind to deeper portions of the conscious and of the subconscious minds in order that information may be obtained in some form, whether it be verbal, mental, imagery or feeling tones, as you may call them.

One may also utilize what this instrument would call the blunt instrument and become aware of increasing difficulty in changing beliefs by affirmation and make the assumption after a number of attempts have failed that the belief is one which moves from a deeper portion of the being, in which case further attempts may be structured about the use of other tools such as the dreaming process or the hypnosis in which the entity will attempt to create a door through which it will move into the subconscious mind, and through this movement attempt to discover more of the nature of the belief and the means by which it is affecting the incarnational pattern and the means by which it may be altered during the incarnation.

May we speak further, my brother?

T: No, that's fine, thank you.

I am Q'uo, and we thank you, my brother. Is there another query?

Carla: I have a question sort of along the same lines. I've had trouble with my mind ever since 1984 when Don Elkins died. It brings up thoughts that I don't like to have there, and using my mind to try to control my mind is a joke, because the mind isn't working right in the first place, or I wouldn't be making myself miserable with these images and so forth. And I find myself doing it even to this day. The images have changed somewhat, you know. At this point I probably have as much frustration because I can't do as much as I used to be able to do, because I didn't do everything I wish I could have done for Don. But, the basic principle is the same. I don't seem to be able to have control of certain emotional states that hit me, and I wonder, this is obviously subconscious stuff that is coming up through the conscious and that is creating a situation in which affirmations are not going to work and prayer is not going to work and … What works? Is there anything that works? Or is just time the only thing that works?

I am Q'uo, and am aware of your query, my sister. Though time is the great healer of all distortion, there are instances in which the seeker, for reasons of its own welfare and comfort, must look to other means by which healing may be achieved. In your experience, we find that there is a great deal of complexity within the patterns which have formed to create the current condition which you experience as the whirlwind of the mind which brings the pattern of weather across your field of experience seemingly unbidden, working its way as it will, leaving as it will.

As we see that the use of hypnosis and trance is not indicated due to previous experience which has potentiated possibilities which are undesirable, we may suggest that the utilization of your dreams be that means by which you may be able to find the release in a controlled fashion of the great whirling energy which moves within your mind complex at this time. The attempts to work with one's subconscious mind via the medium of the dream and the conscious analysis of the dreams, as they are experienced and recorded, is a technique which offers the subconscious mind a safe place in which to release portions of experience in a symbolic form that one might then decipher …

(Tape ends.)

L/L Research

L/L Research is a subsidiary of Rock Creek Research & Development Laboratories, Inc.

P.O. Box 5195
Louisville, KY 40255-0195

www.llresearch.org

Rock Creek is a non-profit corporation dedicated to discovering and sharing information which may aid in the spiritual evolution of humankind.

ABOUT THE CONTENTS OF THIS TRANSCRIPT: This telepathic channeling has been taken from transcriptions of the weekly study and meditation meetings of the Rock Creek Research & Development Laboratories and L/L Research. It is offered in the hope that it may be useful to you. As the Confederation entities always make a point of saying, please use your discrimination and judgment in assessing this material. If something rings true to you, fine. If something does not resonate, please leave it behind, for neither we nor those of the Confederation would wish to be a stumbling block for any.

CAVEAT: This transcript is being published by L/L Research in a not yet final form. It has, however, been edited and any obvious errors have been corrected. When it is in a final form, this caveat will be removed.

© 2009 L/L Research

Sunday Meditation
October 9, 1988

Group question: "Q'uo: We have been asked to speak to you this evening about hatred."

(Carla channeling)

I am Q'uo. We apologize for the slow transmission, but we are working at deeper levels of the conscious but trance-like state, as this instrument has requested information which makes this state appropriate, due to this instrument's own synchronistic queries. Before we begin, we would like to answer a question we find heavy upon this instrument's mind. This instrument has been wondering, ever since the last time the beloved entity known as Aaron was part of a circle of seeking, why we were able to offer material of a high intellectual content. Firstly, the one known as Aaron is most intelligent, and will pick those truths of which he has the need, in a simplistic way. There is much of what you call your time for subtleties. Secondly, this entity is an humble entity, one which is grateful to sit in a circle of beloved entities and enjoy their company. Therefore, this entity is a very strong battery within the circle, and does not expect to understand each word, but is very pleased to be with each. This unconditional love offers the highest of vibration within your group at this time. Never estimate an entity's worth by age or accomplishment, but by the ability it has for unconditional love.

We have been asked to speak to you this evening about hatred. Because this channel had also wished to ask a related question, we find this deeper state necessary, and will continually be attempting to preserve the depth of this contact. Please pardon any pauses.

That which is hatred and that which is anger, and all of those emotions which may be called negative, are distortions of love. They manifest through the distorted individual by blocking energy and trapping this energy in the center involved in the changing, confusing difficulty which is catalyst for distorted love. This catalyst may be extreme. However, may we say that that which the questioner considers hatred it does not know in full intensity, for it is incapable of achieving the purity of negative emotion which would be necessary for those which wish to polarize negatively. Nevertheless, we in no way disregard or lessen any of those emotions which are beyond the control of the entity at this time.

When an entity is extremely positive, as each within this circle is, that which may be seen by others to be unimportant or non-catalytic, upon the contrary sensitive entities which seek will certainly use this catalyst and experience painfully negative emotions. Thus, hatred is love which has been hurt badly. Anger is that which comes of hatred. Beneath the hatred is what this instrument would call the orange-ray blockage. This is especially painful when the entity who is in pain has some difficulty in experiencing self-worth and self-acceptance, self-forgiveness and self-love.

The one which loves the self has the most undistorted energy available to manifest in love in an undistorted form of intimate others which offer negative catalyst, shall we say for the sake of brevity, though this is not the exact description. Beneath both of these concepts is the concept of separation. The illusion in general, made up of many seemingly other selves separate from the self, is most powerful. Thusly, it is possible to see each entity as unique. However, the veil has dropped betwixt the waking vision and the evidence that each is also the Creator, each perfect and all one, one with each other and one with the original Thought of love which is the Creator.

We are aware that each has chosen the path of unity, peace, the love of neighbor, the hope for peace within all nations, all hearts and all peoples, and above all the seeking of the one infinite Creator. To those who wish to ameliorate the negative emotions they feel, action is necessary. The first action one may take is to outlast the length of time one is capable of feeling the same catalyst. This is, as this instrument would say, an easy way out, in that no effort must be expended, but merely existence prolonged. However, we are aware that each wishes to move as quickly as possible along the pilgrim's path towards the mysterious face of truth. Thusly, we would give you harder ways to work upon the distortions of love which are the result of blockages which keep energy from moving through the lower energies into the heart energy of unconditional love, which the one known as Aaron has such a great deal of.

Each of you has, buried within, an unconditional love. In each case, this unconditional love withstood many trials, but ultimately the illusion made its mark, and each of you has separated the self from the other self to the extent that the unity of all is not reflected in the relationship which is under consideration in each case. In each case, the difficulty which is, shall we say, the proximate cause of separation is that which paradoxically seems to unite, that is, the rite of marriage. To those which find that they need change nothing of their relationship in order to live in a married fashion, the catalyst which is negative will be minimal. To those whose expectations are raised by marriage or who have in some way separated themselves from their true selves during marriage, [they] will find that that unifying ceremony has instead placed great pressure upon the entity which creates the illusion of separation.

We would now say a word about marriage. This instrument has been reading the work of your author, Joseph Campbell, and we find within the instrument's mind the concept which is consistent with his theory that myth explains the truer nature of humankind. The phrase is, "Marriage is an ordeal." It is through the great sacrifice of both entities that a marriage becomes a spiritual reality. The gestation of this primal and cornerstone unity is that consideration which you may call deep love or deep friendship or deep commitment. The unmarried who have these feelings do not have as many raised expectations of change as do those who choose the married state. There is indeed much sacrifice in creating the first social memory complex. To be together is the nature of the density which you enjoy. The lessons are only partially those of aloneness and solitude. Much necessary catalyst awaits the seeker within the illusions of relationship.

Thus, we would say to those present, especially the instrument itself, which is at this time married, to ever lower the expectations of another self, to remember the desire for the truth, and to remember also the desire to be a positively-oriented being. Now this is to say that without minimizing the effects of negative catalyst, the self-forgiven and self-loving self will stand upon its own two feet and consider not judgment of any other, but the most helpful way to respond. If there is no blockage within the feelings and thoughts, expectations and hopes within the entity, the energy shall flow through to the heart chakra, and the negative catalyst will fade, slowly or quickly.

The effort this takes is the utmost an entity can make, and when that utmost is not enough, when the entity which seeks fails to love without distortion, the entity must immediately begin to forgive the other, the self, the situation, and the illusion. The illusion is designed as an ordeal, indeed, a series of ordeals, within which, again and again, each soul chooses the positive path of unity, peace, joy, love and light, or the negative path of discord, despair, hatred and darkness. When the periods of darkness strike without warning, they are needed, for each entity has all of the varieties of humanity within the self. The most positive entity can be negative. The most negative can be positive. This illusion fools each as it ought and as it must.

In the end, we must move towards meditation as our primary suggestion for acquainting the self more and more with an undistorted love, a light which does not fail. In short, we recommend the daily meditation, the reading of thought provoking or inspirational material, the contemplation upon that material, and the attendant praise and thanksgiving for the moment of consciousness. All of these are but the frosting upon the cake of silence, for as one dwells within the green cathedral of the forest or mountaintop's bleak aspect, or the splendorous church, waiting in what feels to be a holy silence for the service of group worship to begin, one is entering the silence within as well as sharing the silence without. Within there lie infinite spaces, for within lies all that there is.

Each of you has two basic parts. One part is that of the Creator, that of undistorted love, and to the body, to each cell, is given this awareness. In moving and knowing the body, an avenue into an excellently unblocked state of consciousness is encouraged. Therefore, if the entity is not able to meditate, it may walk about within the creation of the Father, for as this entity sings in its head, "I walk in the garden alone, when the dew is still on the roses," this image was given to you by the teacher and Christ known to you as Jesus. Think of your inner space as the garden, and realize that it is your deepest desire not to be loved, not to be understood, but as this instrument's favorite prayer gives, "To understand and to love," for each of you is a radiant being. Each of you has strayed from the concept of unity, due to perfectly understandable catalyst. It is time to forgive. Remember always that the negative emotion is that which is as real as the positive emotion in that it creates the electrical atmosphere of certain of your higher bodies, and therefore affects your health and your experience within the illusion.

Those upon the pilgrim's way need these obstacles not, and we are aware that each has sincerely tried to remove them. We may suggest only what this instrument would call prayer and silence. Each moves in change at all times. Change is painful. Those which have not together pulled to form that which can be termed an "us" must eventually separate in mind, if not in the physical or chemical form.

We have no discouragement for each. It is not right or wrong to act to think or to feel. It is, in addition, well to express the self honestly. The key to unity with others remains a responsibility [of] unity within the self, so that the self is a true manifestation of what the self has faith in and lives for. If that which is done in relationships manifests the love and the light of the infinite One, there can be no more beautiful gift to the relationship, to the other self, and to the Creator. When one loves the self, one loves the Creator. When one loves the self through one's own perceptions of self-failure, or regains the love of self and moves once again in quiet confidence, this one will find the heart chakra unblocked, and the positive energy able to be manifested.

When there is an excess of sensitivity and feeling in a seeking entity, it is then that the difficulties of the illusion are most poignant. We can only urge your thoughts, insofar as you are able, towards either a higher and better cause or towards innocent distraction, which enables the self to regroup. If the negative emotion is called by the other self in a persistent way, we suggest for the sake of the seeking entity that it express the self insofar as it is deemed necessary for survival.

Beyond this, the responsibility lies from self to self. In enlarging and purifying the point of view, each other self is the Creator. Each other person is truly a mirror of yourself. Those hatreds, those distortions of love which the seeking soul feels for another are only reflections of the feeling for the self. Thus, it is the self which must be turned to in forgiveness and total compassion. "That which is beautiful," it says within your holy works, "that which is good, that which excellent, that which is of virtue, love, enjoy, do." These are words of simplistic advice. Yet we say to you that your thoughts are those things which people, populate, indeed, your consciousness, and in fact move your destiny. Attempt, therefore, to seek the Creator, to feel the oneness of love and light and to carry that flame within you which has been lit into each and every relationship and situation you may possibly achieve in this way. You are of maximum service to the self as a creature or child of the Creator, to the other self as the Creator, and finally turning at last from the illusion, the choice having been made, to the Creator Itself, to the great mystery which draws us all ever forward in love and light.

There is time enough, as this instrument would put it, in further densities to refine the lessons which follow the choice of the positive path. Each of you is a wanderer, each couple which has been asked about is already aware that it is of a different level of density than the mate. This creates certain problems of communication. The thinking is quite different from density to density, as the lessons change.

Tolerance of irremediable differences is learned only through the Creator within the self, not from the self which moves through the illusion in a wounded fashion, one way or another. May you each choose to love and to understand. This giving, without expectation, shall place a call within the universe for its balance, and to one who loves much, shall much love be given.

We ask each to live each day as if it were the last, to be as impeccable warriors of peace—of inner and outer peace—as possible, to pick the self up if it may fall, and to tabernacle with the one infinite Creator by going into the silence within. These are your tools. Remember the breastplate of righteousness within your Bible, and all the other armor of love. My friends, it is true—love is its own armor. Those about whom you have distorted emotions are …

(Side one of tape ends.)

(Carla channeling)

… light and love of the Creator at what this instrument would call the lower energy centers.

Let not these things be a stumbling block before your search for unconditional love any longer than necessary. The first order of business is forgiveness of self. Do not attempt forgiveness beyond the self at first, but only work upon the self. We find that each expresses its positive aspect, so we need not encourage this aspect of behavior. We do not encourage false behavior. We find each to be by nature friendly towards other entities and compassionate. Exercise your nature in this regard whenever you can, giving each passing stranger, into whose eyes you smile, a smile a bit longer, a bit wider, and from the heart. You will never know how many lives you touch by the gentle word, the kindly gesture, the gentle smile.

This aspect of the approach to living in a positive or service-to-others-oriented way is the completion of what we have to offer through this instrument, and so with many thanks to you for calling us to your group, and as usual with our warning that we are not authorities but pilgrims which have walked perhaps further along the path than you, we would transfer to the one known as Jim for the closing of this session. I am Q'uo.

(Jim channeling)

I am Q'uo, and greet each again in love and light through this instrument. At this time we would ask if there might be any further queries to which we may respond?

Carla: That pretty well did it for me. I don't think I have any intellectual quibbles with anything. I'm satisfied.

L: Aaron must be too.

Carla: Well, that does prompt a question. When somebody like Aaron goes to sleep, does it drag down the energy like it does if an adult goes to sleep, Q'uo?

I am Q'uo. It is indeed well if each within the circle of seeking remains in the conscious meditative state, for in this manner the vital energy which each provides to the circle may be provided as a function of the waking conscious will which is somewhat blunted or blocked when the entity moves into those deeper levels of meditation and then into that sleeping state. The provision of the vital energy from such sleeping states is only of a residual nature, then, and as there is some necessity for the circle to provide a vitality to the one now sleeping, thus is the circle in that degree depleted.

Is there another query?

Carla: So, it weakens the contact, but it doesn't kill it? Does it detune it?

I am Q'uo, and though the contact is somewhat weakened in either intensity or duration, the contact is able to proceed without stopping or without being detuned, as you have used this term.

Carla: Thank you, Q'uo.

I am Q'uo, and we thank you, my sister. Is there a further query?

Carla: No, thank you.

I am Q'uo, and we are most grateful to each within this circle of seeking for inviting our presence. We rejoice with each desire to further refine the expression of the one Creator which moves through each and which is unique to each, and which is tested within each life pattern in order that it might be made pure and fine and strong and ever-present as a manifestation and glorification of that one Creator. We are known to you as those of Q'uo, and at this time we shall take our leave of this instrument and this group, leaving each, as always, in the love and in the light of the one infinite Creator. Adonai, my friends. Adonai. ☥

L/L Research

L/L Research is a subsidiary of Rock Creek Research & Development Laboratories, Inc.

P.O. Box 5195
Louisville, KY 40255-0195

www.llresearch.org

Rock Creek is a non-profit corporation dedicated to discovering and sharing information which may aid in the spiritual evolution of humankind.

ABOUT THE CONTENTS OF THIS TRANSCRIPT: This telepathic channeling has been taken from transcriptions of the weekly study and meditation meetings of the Rock Creek Research & Development Laboratories and L/L Research. It is offered in the hope that it may be useful to you. As the Confederation entities always make a point of saying, please use your discrimination and judgment in assessing this material. If something rings true to you, fine. If something does not resonate, please leave it behind, for neither we nor those of the Confederation would wish to be a stumbling block for any.

CAVEAT: This transcript is being published by L/L Research in a not yet final form. It has, however, been edited and any obvious errors have been corrected. When it is in a final form, this caveat will be removed.

© 2009 L/L Research

Sunday Meditation
October 17, 1988

Group question: Who are the entities that speak through our instruments that allows them to come in the name of Jesus the Christ? What is the nature of their makeup that allows them to do this?

(Carla channeling)

I am Q'uo. We greet you in the love and in the light of the one infinite Creator. It is a rare privilege for us to be called to a group so finely tuned as yours is this evening. We are delighted at the opportunity to share our thoughts with you, insofar as your language can be used to compass the concepts which we would offer concerning our identity. We continue to work in adjusting this instrument to a deeper level of meditation, so that, while conscious, the instrument may be more purely aware of the nuances of each concept which we offer. We find this to be in the case of this instrument, very nearly as satisfactory as the trance sleeping state, in that the instrument's mind and vocabulary are capacious.

We have been waiting for this opportunity to speak upon our identity for some time, as this instrument would say. We even gave our group a name which compassed the query which to this instrument is crucial, that is, that as this instrument has noted with its intellectual mind previously, our name in the language you call Latin would mean literally, "Who?"

You wish to know why we of the Confederation of Planets in the Service of the Infinite Creator can pass the challenge of the Christ and can say to you, "Jesus is Lord." You wish to know what relationship we have to Christ. That which we have to say is both that which is desired and that which is not. Yet our nature is such that it is bound to disappoint each, that is, the intellectual and the faithful.

We shall begin with our identity as manifestations. We are citizens of various planetary groups which have attained thought communication and are therefore able to communicate without the language barrier. This ability to share concepts is fundamental to the Confederation. In the terms of your illusion, we live, have our various physical vehicles, and remain at this stage of our growth, individualized, but aware and harmonized with those within the group especially, and by careful extension, all those of the Confederation.

Each of us has our own areas of specialization. Some wish to speak to introductory students, some the intermediate, some the advanced, and some, those of any level in a certain area of inquiry, such as healing. We are those which seek out the more experienced or pure … We must pause.

(Pause)

I am Q'uo, and greet you again in love and light. We must return this instrument to its former depth of contact. If you will be patient, we shall pause again.

(Pause)

I am Q'uo, and greet you again in love and in light. We are those which seek the purer or more experienced channel with the aim of producing philosophically based inspirational material. The contact with this group has been rewarding for us, and we rejoice in the love of the one infinite Creator, which binds each to the Creator and to one another. This is our manifestation. It is, like all manifestations, a mask and an illusion, real, in a manner of speaking, but of a limited duration. Such is the nature of manifestation. By its very nature it calls to infinity.

Upon another level, we address the query concerning our relationship to Christ. Our faith differs somewhat from this instrument's, which is not surprising, considering that our experience is somewhat better realized within our manifestation. Nevertheless, when any seeking entity discovers compassion, that is to say, unconditional love, that entity has discovered and defined Christ.

We come from a race which worships the Christ in a somewhat different way, having, however, the understanding, if we may use that term, that the agent of redemption, be it the Christ principle or such an one as Jesus the Christ, is indeed Lord and one with the Father and Creator, Mother and Nurturer of all that that there is. We do not mean to demean this instrument's religion, but to say that a Christ is a Christ, that is to say, that "Jesus is Lord," is to say the obvious, for within the universe of this instrument, we are identical to that which is termed the Holy Spirit. This conjures up images of angels' harps and clouds. These scenes occur only within your thought worlds, and are created by your thoughts, not those of the one infinite Creator.

We are those who worship the Creator, and seek to serve the Creator, thus we move as close to infinity in our purity as we are able, and offer to those who wish to hear the one simple message of love. Again and again, we suggest that the nature of the creation is love, unmanifest and manifest, and that by moving more and more in harmony with the original Thought of love, a seeker of the mystery of the Creator may accelerate his pace upon the journey.

We are then the Holy Spirit or Comforter, in this instrument's terms. We have appeared as many, many things, including angels. We appear in thought alone at this time, and find that the mass of those who would seek our information prefer the, as this instrument would say, mythology, of the spacecraft and the visitors from elsewhere to the equally valid manifestation in thought of the angels or the vision. Were we to appear as ourselves, those of the Confederation would look most variously, and we feel our impact upon your people is more proof against abuse of free will by our speaking through instruments such as this one and using the most desired metaphors and images concerning our inner nature and function in order that we may aid the most entities.

It matters not who entities think we are. We attempt to satisfy the need for otherness, mystery and solemnity, and to indicate our polarity in a clear way. After that, our dependence is upon the relationship we may forge with a carefully tuned instrument, and in that way, by collaboration, we offer what humble gifts we have.

There is a third nature which shall disturb this instrument, although it has been intellectually considering this possibility for some time and has discussed it. Yet it will be sorry to hear from this contact that in our opinion we are completely within the instrument's mind, that is, we are allowed to speak because the instrument has made a pathway deeply enough into its own subconscious levels of thought that it is able to contact principles which lie deep within the mind and are influenced by the various energies of gravity in a spiritual sense which flow rhythmically through the metaphysical portion of each individual as well as the physiological portion. The study of the latter is called astrology; the study of the former could be called metaphysical astrology, and would reveal an inner universe of which the outer infinity of galaxies is but an hologram which moves in a predictable fashion, allowing at various times the various life-giving, gem-like energies of the archetypal subconscious to flash through to the surface and produce each day differently, each moment slightly variously, the message of love and light.

This instrument, therefore, may identify us with itself in the deepest reality of which we are aware. The infinity and reality lie not outside, but inside the non-thing which is each entity's consciousness.

All studies concerning an entity are studies in a mirror, the true self, the inner self, being invisible. One learns of the inner self by looking very carefully in the mirror.

We are those principles within the infinity of the Creator which speak the words of Jesus the Christ to the world at this day. For those of other belief systems whose journeys have led them to a purity of a certain level, we identify ourselves equally with that entity's deity and come into relationship as those who may confess faith in this deity. If this entity were not dwelling with an heart full of faith, we could not come in the name of the Deity. It is our understanding—and again you must forgive our use of that word, for we feel our grasp is limited—that the Deity, the Creator is one, and each distortion which moves entities into a life of faith is acceptable to us.

It is the faith, the peace, the inner surrender to the will of the infinite Creator which marks the one which has decided to become a servant of the Creator, or, to put it another way, one who has decided to lose oneself in praise and worship of the one infinite Creator, for worship always produces the manifestation, not the manifestation the worship.

We very much thank this instrument for being courageous enough to be willing to risk what this instrument considers to be wonderful work lost. This risk the instrument chose to take by requesting our true nature. We do not think that this instrument will need to separate its faith from its work with us, yet it is the free will of the instrument which thinks and considers ethical questions deeply. We can only suggest to any whose religious beliefs attempt to strangle information that that information which is not truthful for an entity will not be retained by the entity. Were our energy fields not completely consistent with this entity's careful tuning and challenging, we could not speak.

Therefore, without wishing to infringe upon free will, we are nevertheless sanguine that we shall indeed be acceptable to this instrument at the end of each deliberation, as we are indeed of the principle of love, and that is the Christ, and the one known as Jesus was a complete Christ, Son of Man, and servant of …

(Side one of tape ends.)

(Carla channeling)

I am Q'uo, and greet you once again in love and light. To repeat that which was lost. We are servant of All and lord of All, as the one known as Jesus was both the servant and lord, because we are those disciplined to the principle of love, to the refinement which allows us to live comfortably and therefore to comfort. There is that position which is attained at many times throughout the infinity which seems to stretch before one such as yourselves, to be many, many things. We have refined and refined our natures to become one with the principle of Christ, the principle of love, that which moves the consciousness to the consciousness which is the Creator.

Thus, in this instrument's Christian terms, we are those of the Holy Spirit, of Jesus the Christ. We leave to careful imagination our means of speaking to those who worship in a different way. The message is always the same, the philosophy unified, the hope of manifestation, inner peace, outer joy and the productivity of the good vine as each contributes in spiritual lightening of the consciousness of your planet.

We are those of Q'uo. We find that this instrument has only some confusion, but no queries, consequently we shall close at this time, thanking each who is somewhat fatigued for the privilege of speaking and attempting to serve. We would share our love and blessing and thank each for persistent faithfulness. We are most privileged to work with this group and to share in your quiet meditation. We are known to you as those of Q'uo. We leave you in the love and the light of one infinite Creator. Adonai vasu borragus. ☥

L/L Research

Sunday Meditation
October 30, 1988

Group question: Is there any value to the seeker in studying, in reading, in trying to apply everything that's been learned consciously day-to-day in the daily life, or can you get just as far in spiritual illusion by being a "nice guy" and living an ordinary life?

(Carla channeling)

I am Q'uo. We greet you in the love and in the light of the one infinite Creator. The one known as Latwii also lends their vibrations to our own as we join your meditation. However, we are happy to answer your call for information on the subject of the acceleration of spiritual growth by various means within incarnational experience. We shall attempt at this particular meeting to restrain ourselves from our usual length of speaking and to function in a more conservatively informational manner while expressing ourselves carefully and to the best of our opinion. As always, we wish to express that this is a fallible opinion, and not to be taken as an opinion which carries the authority of one who knows, rather than one who seeks, and hopes to grasp.

The difficulties of accelerating the spiritual growth are numerous, and it is possible without conscious acceleration of spiritual growth for some entities among your peoples successfully to complete the course offered, to complete the lessons learned, and to complete that which is needed for that particular entity to polarize sufficiently, in service to others or service to self, that it need not form any relationship with *(inaudible)* various tools and resources of the meditator.

(Pause)

I am Q'uo, and greet you again in love and light. We apologize for the delay, but this instrument had lost her, what she calls, microphone, and was adjusting it.

Within these entities, the maturity of many incarnations is compellingly enough remembered that there are no resources necessary to encourage the entity to be true to the self, to always seek and express the true nature of the self to the best of its own ability and to treat each other person with honor, dignity and compassion, even at the expense of a sacrifice to oneself. These entities are necessarily rare among your peoples, that is to say, "necessarily" because yours is a third-density planet, and when one has learned all the lessons which may be learned within your density and therefore has no more need of catalyst, the question then becomes, "What purpose has that entity's incarnation?" "Why did that person choose to come into incarnation?" and "What polarity does that entity expect to gain or what goal achieve within its higher self aspect during the incarnation?" This is another subject, and we leave it, for the main query is, "Must one go through ritual, reading, contemplation, meditation and prayer, and all the exercises, resources and tools of a spiritual student in order to accelerate the spiritual growth?"

Let us observe one who has a worldly ambition. This entity perhaps begins with saving the funds from a salaried position to open the store, begin the business, buy the real estate, or in some way begin to attempt the building up of treasure, power and what may be called a mundane kingdom. This entity who is ambitious for worldly goods and power must exercise much discipline in order to achieve its goals. It must do this over a period of time, and after a period of time, if the effort has been well made, it is rewarded by worldly goods and worldly power. There are those among your peoples with just such ambition, just such goals and these entities realize not that they are as much a practicing spiritual or religious seeker as one who approaches the infinite Creator from another level, for that which an entity considers its ambitions bent toward is that which is that entity's true spirituality or religion. We would look for less emotionally-laden words, but do not find such words in this instrument's vocabulary.

Similarly, the piano player which wishes to play extremely well and perform for the concert audience must spend many years in doing apparently meaningless exercises which give the pupil of the piano a deep subconscious knowledge of the instrument, which allows the entity to express and manifest through this instrument far more harmony and euphony than can be expressed by one which has the lesser hours of practice, the lesser ambition, the lesser devotion to the muse of music.

One may consider such worldly ambitions as this to be a kind of idol or icon, that which is worshipped, but that which does not bring one to eternity, unless the personality of the entity is such that happiness and exaltation of spirit, when all goes well within the ambition, gives one a feeling of worship and offers one the opportunity to offer daily thanks and praise to the Creator which has made each entity. This obeisance to the Creator, however, is not often found among those which are worshippers of the money, the science, or the muse of one kind or another. That which artists and mystics have in common—and we wish at this point to give credit to this instrument's own reading, for we are using this instrument's reading as a good example of what we mean …

We must pause. I am Q'uo.

(Pause)

I am Q'uo. We greet you in love and light, and shall continue.

That which the artist and the spiritual seeker have in common is the lack of an icon held in space and time. Rather, the true artist and the true spiritual seeker or mystic is fascinated by the mystery of the present moment, and seeks in that moment, in each and every moment, the face of that mystery, the face that shall not be known, the ineffable face of the one Creator, the face of love. Because this entire concept of what we might call Creatorship or Godhood is completely beyond the resources of any of your languages, we can only speak in ways which may be poetically satisfactory in inspiration concerning the one great original Thought of love and the importance to the spiritual seeker of using those resources which seem helpful to the seeker, that is, not all seekers need the same rituals, aids, resources and tools. For one entity, the silent meditation may be that which is truly needed. For another entity, a long period of reading and study and intellectual growth may be needed, for that entity may well be all faith and no awareness of the environment.

In order to communicate about eternity to those living temporal lives, it is well to place the self within eternity, within the tabernacle of the Father—to use a phrase from your holy works—as often as is physically possible, and certainly upon a daily basis. Others will need the inspirational reading and the discussion with the self or with others of the contents of that reading. Contemplation of a reading, which we may suggest might be read aloud, is also very helpful. There are also objects which may be taken into the mind for a visual meditation when the mind is having difficulty in quieting. The word "love," or any other single word or phrase which moves one's attention to the center of one's being, sometimes called a mantra, is indeed helpful, as is any visual symbol, such as the rose or the cross, to one whose spiritual resources include those symbols.

The entity which has a good deal of maturity coming into the incarnation may indeed choose or never be aware of the choice of serving others or serving the self. However, instinctively, such naturals, may we call them, those who remember, do not need that which is to move them to an harvestable level. If they are at this incarnational moment prepared to walk the steps of light and move into the fourth density, then they have only to enjoy the pain and joy of this illusion you call third-density life. The probable future of such entities is the graduation and the moving onward to create the fourth-density social memory complex of what you call Earth, or Terra.

None of those to whom we speak is able at this time to reflect that he or she is free of the need to accelerate the spiritual growth at this time. When those of the road or the way who seek to express eternity within the prism of the earthly vessel make that conscious decision, the corollary to that decision is an action, for that which remains within the mind alone has no meaning unless it is followed up with the well-intentioned attempt to manifest that which is understood.

It is often the temptation of those who seek their very most deepest desire to pull back from the … We must pause, for this instrument knows not this word … maelstrom which shall ensue. Once the accelerated pace of meditation, contemplation, reading and analysis has taken place, changes then begin to take place which seem to the seeking entity to be brought about specifically by the desire to lead the more simple, the more peaceful, and the more joyous life.

Yet, indeed, it is a false assumption that those who progress more quickly along the spiritual path shall find "the crooked places made straight," to use this instrument's knowledge of your holy work called the Bible, and "the rough places plain." Instead, the mountains are higher, scaling them is more difficult, and the plunges into that which is the opposite of the mountaintop experience are all too frequent.

When one accelerates one's process of learning, one is also accelerating one's process of changing. One begins to die, losing this and that part of the self which is no longer true about the self, but merely that which has been kept and not thrown away. Much like old clothes stowed in boxes in the attic, gathering dust, there is not use to them, but the room that they take up in the memory, the biases and subconscious reasons for peculiar actions which the conscious self does not approve of are due to this extra baggage.

The more time one spends in the presence of the Creator, any minute, three minutes, or five minutes during the day, and especially one concentrated time of at least fifteen or twenty minutes in silent meditation, listening for the Creator's will and the will of your higher self, for you is inestimable aid, an armor of light, shall we say, that moves about that body which is the inexhaustible spirit in a protective way, so that though the body and the mind and the emotions may ache from the metaphysical muscle sprains of increased metaphysical activity, yet there is no lasting injury. It is merely a matter of reducing a necessary discipline to that which is pleasant, manageable and able to be done on a daily basis.

Each entity has a different need for ritual and worship. Therefore, we do not recommend the same experience for each entity, but recommend that each entity seek without stopping, until each entity has found that in which the entity feels unity with the Creator, a worship of the Creator, an adoration and oneness with the Creator, and above all, complete and utter union with the Creator.

For this instrument, the Christian bias creates joy and manifests in much fruit. This is not a path which appeals to all. For others, the search is the same, however, as it was for this instrument, the search for caring, for something in which one has faith. It is an article of faith not to give up this search until a path has been forged by the self or found by the self which may be expressed in a daily manner and which contains the discipline necessary to hollow out those free will portions of the self which have removed themselves from the mind, body and spirit of the self and have become willful without a reason.

It is the moving from willfulness to willingness to surrender, from the taking and controlling to the use of the will to control the self, that one may in some small way assist one's own fullness of effort along one's chosen path. Whatever the way the path and the seeking lies for an entity, the entity must indeed undertake the sorrow and the sacrifice of discipline, a disciplining of the self to worship, to contemplate, and to listen to the wisdom of those who have written in the past.

Yes, one is responsible for these things, and one is responsible to them, for what one knows and has learned in the head must then be grounded in the heart. For this reason, the reading and the contemplation and the discussion need to be followed by the listening, that one may hear that voice which speaks within.

That principle of love which stands ready for the seeker to open the door, the key to that door, behind which wisdom and compassion lie, is meditation. If no book is read, if no symbol is imaged, if there is nothing in the worship but the most devout silence, yet still this vehicle alone may be all that is needed for the entity to have that larger point of view which enables the entity to see each situation in terms of compassion and love, rather than feeling in any way personally unworthy or in any other way inadequate.

The beginning of spiritual maturity is the acceptance at last that one is forgiven. Those who follow various of the well-known religious sets of belief use various symbols for the principle of redemption or forgiveness. The one known as Jesus is perhaps the best example. However, as each self is made up of that which is the Christ consciousness and that which is the free will consciousness, there is only to be needed a simple recollection by a very complex entity within the illusion. So many, many illusions must be stripped away before one can see clearly one's true nature and begin to wish to become the consciousness of love and not the consciousness of variousness or free will. Both characteristics are part and parcel of each entity, yet those which attempt to be of service to self, which are not aware of their doing so, but instead are happily ignorant of any decision that needs to be made between service to self and service to others, shall not be troubled until it is their time to be troubled with such simple choices as face each who has awakened to his path.

As you awaken, so you find more and more that without the constant centering, the accelerated changes, the accelerated sensitivity, the accelerated gentleness of spirit, the accelerated compassion and vulnerability, will be such that there will be a considerable degree of pain, emotional for the most part, upon the part of any seeker. The more the seeker seeks, the more the seeker may expect to suffer.

And why, may you ask, should one then try to polarize, to seek to serve others, and to seek to love the self and the one infinite Creator? We suggest that in the same way that those may observe that the tide will come in and will go out, you may consider that you have crawled as metaphysical animals from the sea of deeper consciousness, and lie parched with spiritual thirst upon the shore of an inexhaustible ocean, fertile with archetypical images and a larger point of view. And so, movement by movement, you attempt to move at last back into the water of nourishing, fulfilling, deeper consciousness. As you do so, you shall become more polarized in service towards others, you shall begin to feel the true worthiness of that which is you, the true perfection which you wish to arrive at in your conscious knowledge of yourself, and above all, your goal is to forgive the self of each and every iniquity, as this instrument would call it.

That which is called the karma is not inevitable, but rather that which may be stopped by self-forgiveness. In this state of self-forgiveness, one may see all others as forgiven, regardless of their behavior or appearance at any particular moment.

In short, yes, it is necessary for almost all to work in a conscious manner upon the spiritual life in order that that which is so obvious and in front of the face, that which is the illusion of time and space, may be made transparent and the veil metaphysically lifted, so that faith becomes more important than words, and eternity more important than the mundane days and nights of an incarnational experience.

We ask you to take yourselves seriously in your seeking, and yet at the same time to retain that light touch which is part of the essence of self-forgiveness. All entities are programmed to go through difficulties and challenges. Meditation may help each more and more to respond in creative and loving ways to situations, rather than reacting in a blind and uncontrolled way. The straitjacket of emotional programming is difficult to unravel, and there may need to be the help of one to which one may speak which can give the true reflection, the clear image, that which the personal eye is too close to see. But we must tell you that you truly do need to work at the meditation and at the living of a certain kind of life, a life that is not what this instrument would call "goody goody," but rather a life of deep caring, lasting compassion, and a love that comes not from the heart, but through the heart, from the Creator.

We would at this time like to transfer this contact to the one known as Jim. I am Q'uo.

(Jim channeling)

I am Q'uo, and greet each again in love and light through this instrument. At this time it is our honor to offer ourselves in the attempt to speak to any further queries which those present may have for us.

If there is a further query, may we take it at this time?

Carla: Yeah, I have a doozy. It's something that I prefer not to channel, and the question is, and you can refuse it if you like, please understand. I have had many people ask me how to teach, if I could teach them how to work with their guides alone. Now, I have some idea of how to introduce them to their guides. I know about the protection by swirling the red and violet together and then the white light together, but there is something within me that says that I need to learn more before I let even this much loose upon people that I will not be teaching further. Could you comment? Is it possible, and if so, how, to teach this?

I am Q'uo. We shall do our best to respond through this instrument. It is our opinion, my sister, and please remember that it is opinion, that those who serve as guides for those upon your planetary sphere, and any within your third-density illusion, will make themselves known to such entities as the opportunities present themselves and as the time is appropriate. Many of your …

(Side one of tape ends.)

(Jim channeling)

I am Q'uo, and greet each again in love and light. The means of communication through each entity which is in need of such communication varies according to the situation. This instrument, for example, has had its own means of communication that was quite obvious as the spoken word at one point within its evolutionary process. This was the only time in which this entity was communicated with in this manner by those that may call themselves or be called guides. Other means of communication, perhaps the book appearing upon the shelf at the appropriate time, or the person with the needed information making a similar appearance at the appropriate time, or the inspirational dream or thought which seems to appear quite vividly or dramatically within the life pattern, are means by which those you would call guides have done and do their work within your illusion.

To attempt to form or shape or control that contact is oftentimes an effort in confusion for the seeker, for it at once declares that there is at this time no contact with a messenger's existence which is ongoing, and declares that the seeker will fashion of its own will and effort the means by which this contact shall be established. These assumptions, in our opinion, my sister, are erroneous, and will simply cause additional confusion within the seeker, for there is at all times the nurturing assistance for all seekers from those called guides, and this assistance is given in the manner which is the most appropriate, given the seeker and the opportunity.

Thus, to attempt to aid those which would desire to seek an understandable contact with their guides, understandable in their own terms, is an effort which has significant attendant difficulties. Thus, it is not an effort which we can wholeheartedly recommend, for it is one which makes presumptuous assumptions, shall we say.

Is there another query?

Carla: Not presumptuous assumptions—what you're trying to say is that the assumption would be that there's no problem, and that that person should just go ahead, and that that's sufficient protection, and that sometimes that's not true. That's basically what you're saying, yes?

I am Q'uo, and these are correct observations, my sister. In addition to others.

Carla: Okay. Now, as to the nature of the guides and also all that stuff, I have long thought that, like you and every other thing that comes through positive service-to-others type channels, this is some part of the principle of love, which as a Christian, I would term the Holy Spirit or the Comforter, and I figure that the guides and so forth are a more personal vibration of that same Comforter. Are these assumptions correct? I believe them to be so from questions I've asked you before, but I just want to make sure.

I am Q'uo, and though the difficulty in describing the nature of the guides is significant, it may be stated with a reasonable degree of accuracy that those who offer themselves in the service of a guide or teacher offer themselves from the point of view of that quality which you have called love, and are able to stand somewhat closer, shall we say, in their own life pattern to this quality, or we may even describe it as an office or level of vibratory beingness, and, standing closer to this quality, may then share some of its essence in one manner or another with those who they have placed themselves in custodianship over, shall we say.

Is there another query, my sister?

Carla: I'll have to read that answer. I don't exactly understand that one. Yeah, I had a half-baked one, but when I didn't understand that last thing, it kind of flew out of my mind. I really feel that there ought to be some way that is harmless of sharing with people the experience of not feeling alone inside, because all too often the person who needs the most to feel at peace is, for some reason at least, psychologically isolated to some extent in some way. And it seems to weigh heavy on the seeker who is alone. Is there any way other than introducing the person to their guides that I as a teacher of channeling can safely teach entities that experience in a way that they can do it by themselves?

(Pause)

I am Q'uo. We waited for some time in order that this instrument might reach a more comfortable depth of concentration. In our opinion, there is no way in which the seeker may experience a connection with those entities that you have called guides that is able to satisfy the mundane mind with the proper degree of safety, shall we say …

Carla: So the best thing I can do, then, is to channel and collaborate in some sort of inspirational talk?

We will attempt to complete the previous response. The transmission is somewhat slow at this time. The feeling of isolation that is so significantly a part of each seeker's journey is oftentimes an invitation, or shall we say, an initiation for the inner strengthening that is necessary in order that the seeker be able to welcome and enjoy a greater portion of the light energy and be able to reflect it in a responsible manner in the life pattern.

There is oftentimes the need for what you have called the desert experience, in order that the finest qualities of the being be enhanced and refined by the trials of the isolation and the testing of the resolve to exercise the will and the faith that are the rod and staff of the seeker. The conscious mind, in such instances, which asks for the assurance in an understandable manner that the self is not alone or that the experience has such and such a purpose, are oftentimes the crying in the wilderness which must be accepted, but if the initiation and the testing is to be successfully completed, must be endured rather than catered to, shall we say.

The process of the evolution of mind, body and spirit within your illusion, your illusion having such great mystery, is one which is, as the progress is accelerated, oftentimes difficult in nature. But, as we are aware that those in this group have heard it said, the happiness and the contentment are not the goals. The enhancing of the quality of compassion and the offering of its fruits are more to the heart of the purpose, from our point of view. Thus, there is much of difficulty that must simply be endured, and must be allowed to work its unseen function over a period of what you would call time, in order that the deeper qualities of the being which will survive such storms and tempests might be reinforced, and, indeed, brought to the fore in order that the evolutionary progress of the seeker will find its greatest expression within the life pattern.

Is there another query at this time, my sister?

Carla: No. I think I can say that about the best thing I can do with a big group like that is to lead some kind of an inspiring meditation and just lead them that far. Thanks a lot. It's what I needed to know.

I am Q'uo, and we thank you, my sister. Is there another query at this time?

Carla: Not from me, thank you. Thanks so much.

T: No, thank you.

And we thank each for inviting our presence, and we hope that we have been able to utilize each instrument well enough that the heart of our message has found its mark within your hearts, as well. Let that which does not strike to the heart of your concerns fall away. We shall at this time take our leave of this group, leaving each, as always, in the love and in the light of the one infinite Creator. We are known to you as those of Q'uo. Adonai, my friends. Adonai.

www.ingramcontent.com/pod-product-compliance
Lightning Source LLC
Chambersburg PA
CBHW080421230426
43662CB00015B/2168